**If you think you've heard it all,
you probably haven't heard this . . .**

SMELLIEST FLOWER: Also known as the corpse flower, the *Amorphophallus titanum* is the smelliest flower on Earth. When it blooms, it releases an extremely foul odor—comparable to that of rotten flesh—that can be smelled half a mile away. This plant is native to the Sumatran rainforests and very few have flowered in Europe or the USA since first discovered in 1878.

LARGEST PUBLISHED BOOK: The world's largest published book, entitled *Bhutan,* weighs 133 lbs, contains 114 full-color pages, and measures 5 ft high and 7 ft wide when opened. It was devised by teams from MIT, Acme Bookbinding, and the Friendly Planet, and unveiled on December 15, 2003, in New York, USA.

QUIETEST PLACE ON EARTH: Ultrasensitive tests carried out on January 21, 2004 at the Anechoic Test Chamber, Orfield Laboratories, Minneapolis, Minnesota, USA, gave a background noise reading of -9.4 decibels A-weighted (dBA).

Accreditation

Guinness World Records Limited has a very thorough accreditation system for records verification. However, whilst every effort is made to ensure accuracy, Guinness World Records Limited cannot be held responsible for any errors contained in this work. Feedback from our readers on any point of accuracy is always welcomed.

Abbreviations & measurements

GUINNESS WORLD RECORDS LIMITED uses both metric and American measurements (metric in parentheses). The only exception is for some scientific data, where metric measurements only are universally accepted, and for some sports data. Where a specific date is given the exchange rate is calculated according to the currency values that were in operation at the time. Where only a year date is given the exchange rate is calculated from December of that year. "One billion" is taken to mean one thousand million.

"GDR" (the German Democratic Republic) refers to the East German state which unified with West Germany in 1990. The abbreviation is used for sports records broken before 1990.

The Union of Soviet Socialist Republics split into a number of parts in 1991, the largest of these being Russia. The Commonwealth of Independent States replaced it and the abbreviation "CIS" is used mainly for sporting records broken at the 1992 Olympic Games.

Guinness World Records Limited does not claim to own any right, title or interest in the trademarks of others reproduced in this book.

General Warning

Attempting to break records or set new records can be dangerous. Appropriate advice should be taken first and all record attempts are undertaken entirely at the participant's risk. In no circumstances will Guinness World Records Limited have any liability for death or injury suffered in any record attempts. Guinness World Records Limited has complete discretion over whether or not to include any particular records in the book.

GUINNESS WORLD RECORDS™ 2005

BANTAM BOOKS
NEW YORK • TORONTO • LONDON • SYDNEY • AUCKLAND

Dedicated to Norris McWhirter MBE 1925–2004

GUINNESS WORLD RECORDS

RECORDS

MANAGING EDITOR
Claire Folkard

CONTENTS

INTRODUCTION

This year marks the 50th anniversary of the first edition of what is now known as *Guinness World Records*.

In 2003, the 100-millionth copy of the book was published—a staggering achievement in publishing history, making *Guinness World Records* the biggest selling copyrighted book ever. From its relatively humble beginnings, today the book is sold in 100 countries around the world and translated into 23 languages.

The origins of the book date back to a shooting party in County Wexford, Ireland, in 1951, when Sir Hugh Beaver (right), Managing Director of Guinness Brewery, was involved in a dispute as to whether or not the golden plover was Europe's fastest game bird. To his frustration, he was unable to find a book that could give him an accurate answer.

It occurred to Sir Hugh that disputes such as this must happen often, especially in social gatherings, and so a book that could provide all the answers would be in great demand. At the time, the record-breaking athlete Chris

Chataway was working as an underbrewer at Guinness's Park Royal Brewery in London and he recommended Norris and Ross McWhirter (both left), whom he had met at athletic events, to Sir Hugh as the ideal people to compile such a book. At the time, the McWhirters were running a fact-finding agency and publishing company in London, specializing in athletics records. Indeed, when Roger Bannister (page x) broke the four-minute-mile barrier on May 6, 1954, with a time of 3 min 59.4 sec, it was Norris McWhirter who announced the record-breaking time at that historic event. This was one of the "new" athletics records to make it into the first edition. Sir Hugh liked the idea of a book of superlatives and commissioned the twins to create what was to become the first edition of *The Guinness Book of Records*.

After a busy year of research into the fastest and the slowest, the biggest and the smallest, the heaviest and the lightest, and the longest and the shortest of everything, the first copy was printed and bound on August 27, 1955. An instant success, the book was quickly recognized as the authoritative source of records in Britain and around the world.

Although the death of Norris McWhirter (pictured at right with the first edition of *The Guinness Book of Records*) in April 2004 in some ways marked the end of an era, the legacy of the iconic book he and his brother Ross created all those years ago lives on. Over the years, Norris inspired generations of children, delighting them with his encyclopedic knowledge and remarkable ability to recall records in a moment as regularly demonstrated on the long-running BBC TV children's program, *Record Breakers*.

As well as his famous television partnership with the late Roy Castle he also worked with Sir David Frost (below) on Sir David's American Guinness specials from 1973 to 1988. Sir David remembers Norris as "a man with passion for facts and the accuracy of them, but also a man who had a heart-warming appreciation of man's ingenuity and determination to succeed. He loved to recount anecdotes about the remarkable individuals he had met over the years, whether they were Olympic record holders or people who had established records in fields that nobody else might have ever wished to attempt—like Mark Gottlieb, the underwater violinist, or Frank Freer, the man who peeled the world's longest unbroken apple peel. In their different ways, in Norris's eyes they were all superlatives.

Today around 3.5 million copies

of *Guinness World Records* are sold annually, demonstrating that humankind's desire for knowledge combined with a passion to be a Guinness World Record holder is undiminished. Now a household name around the world, no other enterprise collects, confirms, accredits and presents world record data with the same investment in comprehensiveness and authenticity.

Although no longer part of or associated with Guinness Brewery, *Guinness World Records* remains the global authority on world records. This year's edition offers some unique features: we tell the story behind some of the most famous world records, and also hear from a selection of record breakers themselves in a number of fascinating and exclusive interviews.

As ever, remember that you don't have to be a movie star or world-class athlete to have a Guinness World Record. You just need to have the determination and dedication to succeed!

If you want to approach us with an idea for a record, turn to the back page to find out how.

FIFTY YEARS OF CHANGE

The world's population has more than doubled since the first edition of *Guinness World Records* (formerly *The Guinness Book of Records*) went on sale in 1955. Here we chart some other key changes that have taken place over the past 50 years.

1955: the first edition The *Guinness Book of Records* was launched in the same year that a truck driver from Mississippi named Elvis Presley (USA) signed for RCA Victor. Fast-food entrepreneur Ray Kroc (USA, with sign) opened his first McDonald's restaurant in April of that year, and Walt Disney (USA) opened a theme park in Anaheim, California, USA.

Other firsts Competing with Guinness for bookshelf space in 1955 were JRR Tolkien's (UK) *The Lord of the Rings: The Return of the King* and Ian Fleming's (UK) third James Bond novel *Moonraker*. Playing on the jukebox was Bill Haley and His Comets (USA, pictured on page xv) "Rock Around the Clock" (which is still the biggest selling single by a band), and the rights to the design of the "Pluto Platter"—the toy that would be better known as the "Frisbee"—were sold by the inventor Walter Morrison (USA) to the Wham-O toy company.

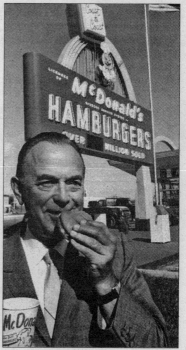

Births and deaths In 1955, three giants of modern communications were born: Bill Gates (USA), Tim Berners-Lee (UK)—the inventor of the World Wide Web—and Apple Macintosh co-founder Stephen Jobs (USA). The year also saw the deaths of Sir Alexander Fleming (UK)—the bacteriologist who discovered the effects of penicillin—and the physicist Albert Einstein (USA, b. Germany, pictured on p. xiv).

The world today is a very different place, of course. Over the past five decades we've seen the advent of space travel and satellite communication, the creation of a global marketplace, the seemingly limitless expansion of the Internet coupled with an equally astonishing miniaturization of technology, and a worldwide population explosion (about 1,000 more people will be born in the time it takes you to read this page).

CHARTING THE CHANGE

Here's a selection of Guinness World Records—past and present—that illustrate some important changes that have taken place over the last 50 years. Figures from 1955 are taken from the first edition of *The Guinness Book of Records* and are quoted verbatim.

World population (2005): 6.31 billion

World population (1955): 2.56 billion

Remotest known body (2005): Using the Hubble Space Telescope and the Keck Observatory, astronomers from the California Institute of Technology (USA) have discovered a small and compact system of stars about 2,000 light years across, with a redshift of 7.0. This corresponds to a distance of around 13 billion light-years away.

Remotest known body (1955) *The first record published in the first edition of GWR!* The universe is the entirety of space and matter. The re-

motest known heavenly bodies are extra-galactic nebulae at a distance of some 1,000 million light-years or 6,000,000,000, 000,000,000,000 miles. There is reason to believe that even remoter nebulae exist but, since it is possible that they are receding faster than the speed of light (670,455,000 mph) [1,078,992,730 km/h], they would be beyond man's "observable horizon."

Highest soccer transfer fee The highest club-to-club payment quoted for a player is a reported 13 billion Spanish pesetas ($66 million) for Zinedine Zidane (France) from Juventus to Real Madrid on July 9, 2001.

Highest football transfer fee The world record transfer fee is the 105,000,000 lire (£60,375) ($167,000) paid in May 1952 by Napol to Genoese Atlanta for the former Swedish International Hans Jeppson, 27.

Most expensive bottle of wine The most expensive commercially available bottle of wine is the Chateau d'Yquem Sauternes (1787), priced between $56,000 and $64,000 depending on the retailer.

Most expensive bottle of wine The most expensive bottle of wine obtainable would be a bottle of Feinste Trockenbeeran Auslese of 1949 or any other good vintage. This is a white wine made in the Rhine Valley in very small quantities from specially selected grapes and retails at £8 [$22] or more.

Highest paid TV performer The world's highest paid TV actor per episode is Ray Romano (USA), who earned $1.8 million per episode of *Everybody Loves Raymond* (CBS, USA) for the eighth series in 2004/05.

Highest paid TV performer The biggest contract ever signed for television appearances was between Jackie Gleason, the American comedian, and the Columbia Broadcasting System on behalf of the Buick Division of General Motors, in December 1954. Under this contract, Jackie Gleason will receive £2.5 million [$7 million] over the next two years for a once-weekly half-hour programme.

Largest passenger liner The Cunard Line's *Queen Mary 2*, which made its maiden voyage in January 2004, is 1,132 ft (345 m) long and has a beam (width) of 135 ft (41 m). At approximately 150,000 gross registered tons (grt), *Queen Mary 2* is nearly three times larger than *Titanic* (46,000 grt), and has space for 2,620 passengers and 1,253 crew.

Largest passenger liner The *Queen Elizabeth,* of the Cunard fleet, is the largest passenger vessel in the world and also has the largest displacement of any ship in the world, with a gross tonnage of 83,673. She has an overall length of 1,031 feet [314.2 m], and is 118 feet 7 inches [387.17 m] in breadth. She is powered by steam turbines which develop about 200,000 hp [149,140 kw].

DID YOU KNOW . . . NOT ALL THE RECORDS HAVE BEEN BROKEN?

Here are some records that haven't been broken in 50 years!

Tallest man The tallest man in medical history for whom there is irrefutable evidence is Robert Pershing Wadlow (USA), who when last measured on June 27, 1940 was 8 ft 11.1 in (2.72 m) tall.

Longest solar eclipse A total eclipse of the Sun that took place on June 20, 1955 west of the Philippines lasted for 7 min 8 sec. The maximum possible duration of an eclipse of the Sun is 7 min 31 sec.

Longest reign as world heavyweight boxing champion Joe Louis (USA) was champion for 11 years 252 days, from June 22, 1937—when he knocked out James Joseph Braddock (USA) in the eighth round in Chicago, Illinois, USA—until announcing his retirement on March 1, 1949. During his reign, Louis made a record 25 defenses of his title.

Largest concrete dam The Grand Coulee dam on the Columbia River, Washington, USA, has a concrete volume of 8,092,000 m³ (285,766,282 ft³) to a weight of 19,595,000 tons (43,199,528,900 lb). It was completed in 1942 at a cost of $56 million. It has a crest length of 1,272 m (4,173 ft) and is 550 ft (168 m) high.

Best selling record In 1955, Irving Berlin's (USA) "White Christmas" had sold 18 million copies. By 2005, sales exceeded 100 million copies.

Bing Crosby's (USA) recording of this song accounts for more than 50 million copies.

Largest office building The Pentagon, in Arlington, Virginia, USA, built to house the US Defense Department's offices and completed in January 1943, is the world's largest office building. Each of the outermost sides is 281 m (921 ft) long and the perimeter of the building measures about 1,405 m (4,610 ft). Its five stories enclose a floor area of 604,000 m^2 (149.2 acres), the corridors total 28 km (17.5 miles) in length, and there are 7,754 windows to be cleaned. There are over 26,000 military and civilian employees working in the building.

Largest stadium The Maracanã Municipal Stadium (pictured) in Rio de Janeiro, Brazil, has a standard capacity of 205,000 spectators, 155,000 of whom can be seated. It was built for the 1950 soccer World Cup and housed a crowd of 199,854 for the final match of the tournament, Brazil v. Uruguay, on July 16, 1950—the greatest ever attendance for a sporting event.

GWR ON TV

From BBC TV's *Record Breakers* to FOX's *Guinness World Records: Primetime,* Guinness World Records on television has always been loved for the programs' celebration of amazing achievements. Today Guinness World Records appears on TV in around 85 countries!

GWR comes to TV Guinness World Records' most famous television past is, of course, BBC TV's *Record Breakers,* which appeared on UK TV screens for over 30 years. Fronted by the energetic and enthusiastic Roy Castle (shown here on the right, with Norris McWhirter and a model of Robert Wadlow), the show featured a weekly array of record attempts, along with the chance to put Norris McWhirter "on the spot" and test his

encyclopedic record knowledge—a test that he famously only failed once!

In the 1980s, Sir David Frost fronted *The Spectacular World of Guinness Records*—a show featuring many more weird and wonderful human achievements—which ran successfully for six years.

Guinness World Records: Primetime
The end of the 1990s saw the arrival of a spectacular new show launched in the USA on the FOX network. *Guinness World Records: Primetime* was a dramatic, exciting show that has since gone on to be shown around the world in over 75 countries, including Canada, Brazil, the Seychelles, the Philippines and the Czech Republic.

Oliver Welke, host of *Guinness World Records: Die Grössten Weltrekorde*

L'Été de Tous les Records After a hugely successful initial run in 2003, 2004 saw the return of *L'Été de Tous les Records*—a fun summertime road-show that travelled each week to a different location in France. An enter-taining mixture of record attempts by local people combined with some impressive feats by established record holders, the show was a huge hit. Fronted by well-known TV sports presenter Pierre Sled, the show also fea-tured Barry White as the Guinness World Records official judge, who, with

Shridhar Chillal (India), owner of the world's longest nails on a single hand, on *Guinness World Records: Primetime*.

Georges Christen (Luxembourg), holder of the record for most telephone directories torn in two minutes, on *L'Été de Tous les Records*

his catchphrase "Are you ready?," proved immensely popular.

Guinness World Records: Die Grössten Weltrekorde

An exciting new show launched in Germany in 2004—a two-hour special presented by Oliver Welke, with celebrated professional boxer Henry Maske as the Guinness World Records judge. Four new records were set on the show, including Wim Hof's famous ice endurance record (bottom)—he managed to stay in the ice box for an incredible 1 hr 7 min. Broadcast live from the studio, the show was a huge success, and is to be followed by a second one in autumn 2004.

The 2003 *L'été de Tous les Records* team

Guinness World Records: Fifty Years, Fifty Records

In celebration of the 50th anniversary, this year sees the long-awaited return of Guinness World Records to the UK TV screens in the form of a two-hour live extravaganza broadcast from a massive sound stage in London on September 11—almost 50 years to the day since the historic first meeting between Sir Hugh Beaver and the McWhirter twins. Over the duration of the show an attempt will be made to break 50 records—an impressive record in itself!

Wim Hof (Netherlands) on *Guinness World Records: Die Grössten Weltrekord*

HUMAN BEINGS

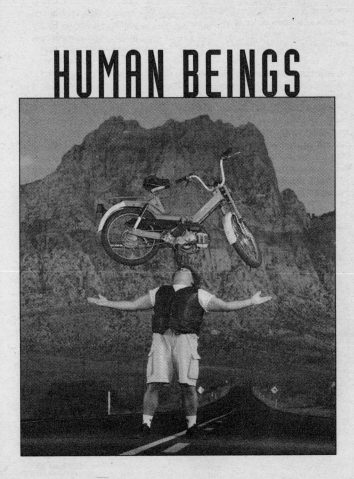

EXTREME BODIES

Tallest living man After seven measurements taken over the course of April 22–23, 1999 in Tunis, Tunisia, Radhouane Charbib's (Tunisia) height was confirmed as 7 ft. 8.9 in. (2.35 m).

Tallest woman Zeng Jinlian (China) measured 8 ft. 1.75 in. (2.48 m) when she died on February 13, 1982.

Tallest living woman When last measured, Sandy Allen (U.S.A.) was 7 ft. 7.25 in. (2.31 m) tall. Her birth weight was a normal 6 lb. 7 oz. (2.95 kg) but her abnormal growth began almost immediately. She stood 6 ft. 3 in. (1.9 m) by the age of 10 and was 7 ft. 1 in. (2.16 m) at the age of 16.

Shortest woman Pauline Musters (Netherlands, b. February 26, 1876), measured 12 in. (30 cm) at birth, and at nine years of age she was 21.5 in. (55 cm) tall and weighed 3 lb. 5 oz. (1.5 kg). When she died of pneumonia with meningitis on March 1, 1895 in New York City, U.S.A., aged 19, a postmortem examination showed her to be exactly 24 in. (61 cm). Her "vital statistics" were 18.5–19–17 in. (47–48–43 cm).

Shortest living woman Madge Bester (South Africa) is only 25.5 in. (65 cm) tall. She suffers from osteogenesis imperfecta (characterized by brittle bones and other deformities of the skeleton) and is confined to a wheelchair.

Heaviest man The heaviest person in medical history was Jon Brower Minnoch (U.S.A.), who had suffered from obesity since childhood. He was 6 ft. 1 in. (1.85 m) tall and weighed 392 lb. (178 kg) in 1963, 698 lb. (317 kg) in 1966 and 974 lb. (442 kg) in September 1976. In March 1978, Minnoch was admitted to University Hospital, Seattle, U.S.A., where consultant endocrinologist Dr. Robert Schwartz calcu-

SHORTEST MAN The shortest mature human of whom there is independent evidence was Gul Mohammed (India). On July 19, 1990, he was examined at Ram Manohar Hospital, New Delhi, India, and found to measure a height of 22.5 in. (57 cm).

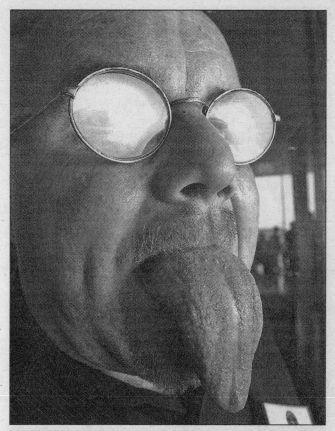

LONGEST TONGUE Stephen Taylor's (UK) tongue measures 3.7 in. (9.4 cm) from the tip to the center of his closed top lip. It was measured at Westwood Medical Centre, Coventry, Warwickshire, UK, on May 29, 2002.

lated that Minnoch must have weighed more than 1,399 lb. (635 kg), much of which was water accumulation due to his congestive heart failure.

Heaviest woman Rosalie Bradford (U.S.A.) is claimed to have registered a peak weight of 1,199 lb. (544 kg) in January 1987.

Living person with the largest hands Hussain Bisad (Somalia), who resides in the UK, has hands measuring 10.59 in. (26.9 cm) from the wrist to the tip of his middle finger.

HEAVIEST TWINS Twins Billy Leon (1946–79) and Benny Lloyd (1946–2001) McCrary, alias McGuire (both U.S.A.), were normal in size until the age of six. By November 1978, Billy and Benny weighed 742 lb. (337 kg) and 723 lb. (328 kg) respectively, and each had a waist measuring 84 in. (2.13 m). Both died from heart failure.

Longest ear hair Radhakant Bajpai (India) has hair sprouting from the center of his outer ears (middle of the pinna) that measures 5.19 in. (13.2 cm) at its longest point.

Longest hair The longest documented hair belonged to Hoo Sateow (Thailand), a tribal medicine man from Muang Nga, Chang Mai, Thailand. On November 21, 1997, his hair was unraveled and officially measured at 16 ft. 11 in. (5.15 m) long. He stopped cutting his hair in 1929 at the age of 18.

Longest fingernails on a single hand The aggregate measurement of the five nails on the left hand of Shridhar Chillal (India) was 23 ft. 1.5 in. (7.05 m) on February 4, 2004. His thumbnail measured 62.2 in. (158 cm), his index fingernail 51.5 in. (131 cm), his middle fingernail 54.3 in. (138 cm), his ring fingernail 140 cm (55.1 in.), and his little fingernail 138 cm (54.3 in.). Chillal last cut his nails in 1952.

Largest chest measurement Robert Earl Hughes (U.S.A.) had a chest measurement of 124 in. (315 cm).

GWR TALKS TO Lee Redmond

Lee Redmond (U.S.A., pictured) holds the record for the longest fingernails. She hasn't cut her nails since 1979, and has grown and manicured them to a total length of 24 ft. 7.8 in. (7.51 m).

Why did you grow your nails? I didn't want to—they were really healthy and I decided to grow them to see how long they'd get before they twisted out of shape. But they never did twist so I just grew them!

Would you ever cut them? I trim them back once in a while, but cut them clear off? No way! Psychologists have said my nails were a shield I'd put up to stop men getting near me. And you know what? All my fans are male!

Have you ever bitten your nails? Oh, I just couldn't imagine it! People chew their nails because they're lacking a certain mineral in their body. They tell me that if a bomb was to go off, I could go into a shelter and live off my fingernails!

Is it true that some people want to buy your nails? Yeah—I turned down $10,000 when they were just nine inches (22.8 cm)! It was for a TV show—I was asked along with the lady with the longest hair. I didn't accept, but she had over 7 feet (2.13 m) of hair cut off! My nails are priceless!

What kind of reaction do your nails usually get? It used to be negative. Now, so many people have seen me in the *Guinness World Records* books and on TV shows, they're more amazed by them. People see the difference between my nails and those on the man from India (Shridhar Chillal, see p. xix), they want to know how I keep my nails looking so much better than he does.

So, what's your secret? You are what you eat, for one thing—the nail is nothing but protein—so I eat high protein. But they get dry and brittle so I soak them in warm olive oil.

Do you worry about damaging them in your sleep? No—they just hang off the side of the bed! I don't even think about it.

How do you get dressed? My nails are like an extension of my fingers, so I just slide them down the sleeves as usual. Now that gravity has pulled my nails straighter they're much easier to slip through. I just can't put on anything that goes over my head because I can't coordinate putting my hands up and feeding the nails through, so everything has to come up over my bottom!

How does it feel to be in the book? It's an honor. I get asked to sign a lot of books! I use them to teach self-esteem classes. I really think it helps kids: meeting me and seeing me in the books gets their minds going, knowing they can do anything.

One more question! How do you go to the bathroom? That's usually the first question people ask! I usually say, "Very carefully . . . and I don't have hemorrhoids!"

TALLEST MAN

The record for the tallest man ever was held by Robert Pershing Wadlow (U.S.A., pictured), who stood at 8 ft. 11.1 in. (2.72 m). His record is one of the most popular Guinness World Records and is recognized as a true classic.

Early days Robert Pershing Wadlow (U.S.A.) was born at 6:30 a.m. in Alton, Illinois, U.S.A., on February 22, 1918 to Addie and Harold Wadlow (both U.S.A.). Robert was the eldest of five children. He had two sisters and two brothers, all of whom were of normal height and weight. His birth weight of 8 lb. 8 oz. (3.85 kg) gave no indication of the amazing growth that was to come. In fact, Robert grew at a normal rate until the age of two, when he underwent a double hernia operation. From then on, he grew at an astonishing speed, so that by the age of five he stood 5 ft. 4 in. (1.63 m) tall and weighed 105 lb. (48 kg). By the age of nine, he was able to carry his 5-ft. 11-in. (1.8-m), 169-lb. (77-kg) father up the stairs of the family home. With a peak daily food consumption of 8,000 calories, his greatest recorded weight was 491 lb. (223 kg) on his 21st birthday.

Robert's Guinness World Records As well as being the tallest man in medical history for whom there is irrefutable evidence, he also holds Guinness World Records for the largest hands and feet. His hands measured 12.75 in. (32.3 cm) from the wrist to the top of his middle finger, and his feet were 18.5 in. (47 cm) long—his shoes were size 37AA. When he was 12 years old, doctors found that he had an overactive pituitary gland, the source of the human growth hormone somatotropin. Corrective surgery was dangerous and not guaranteed to work, so his parents let nature take its course.

Robert's everyday life Robert tried to lead as normal a life as possible. He enjoyed photography and collecting stamps, and at 13 years old he became the world's tallest Boy Scout when he measured 7 ft. 4 in. (2.23 m). By the time he reached 18, he was 8 ft. 3.5 in. (2.53 m) tall—his clothing required three times as much cloth as normal-sized clothes and his massive size 37 shoes cost $100 a pair. Robert's younger brother Harold once recalled on *Guinness World Records: Primetime* how his brother went about his day-to-day living: "He had to duck to go through all doorways. No room on a bus, no room on a train, no seats, no airplane—everything was made for a person six feet tall or under. He probably wished that he wasn't as tall as he was and wanted a normal life, which he couldn't possibly live."

Incredible feet! Robert had his shoes custom made by the International Shoe Company, and when he was aged 20 he was invited to become a goodwill ambassador for the firm. Robert and his father made an extensive tour around the western U.S.A., promoting the company who made his shoes free of charge. His brother Harold commented:

"He couldn't go anywhere without being stared at and drawing a crowd. Some people would bother him, you know, because of his height. They might come up behind him and pinch his leg or something else, you know, or even maybe try to kick him in the shins, make sure he wasn't on stilts."

When did he break the record? Robert gained a place in the history books when he exceeded 8 ft. 3.5 in. (2.53 m) in 1936, beating the record

Robert Wadlow pictured with his family (from left to right): brother Eugene, mother Addie with brother Harold Jr., sister Betty, father Harold, and sister Helen.

held by Irishman Patrick Cotter O'Brien who measured 8 ft. 1 in. (2.46 m) before he died in 1806.

Why did he die so young? Apart from the difficulties associated with his abnormal height, Robert was very healthy, but for many years he was troubled by medical problems with his huge feet. He had poor circulation in his long legs as well as limited sensation in his feet and did not feel any rubbing or chafing until blisters had formed.

In July 1940, when aged 22, Robert was provided with a brace designed to strengthen his ankles. However, the brace was poorly fitted and a septic blister formed on his right ankle. His poor circulation and lack of sensation meant that the blister went unnoticed for some days and by the time he arrived in Manistee, Michigan, a week later to make a guest appearance, a fatal infection had set in.

Robert passed away in his sleep at 1:30 a.m. on July 15, 1940. He was buried in Oakwood Cemetery in his hometown of Alton, Illinois. The 10-ft. 9-in.-long (3.28-m) coffin was carried by 12 men. Out of respect, the town of Alton closed for the day and over 40,000 people signed the register at his funeral. After Robert's death, his family destroyed most of his belongings as they did not want collectors to put his personal items on display.

★ ROBERT WADLOW HEIGHT CHART ★

AGE	HEIGHT	WEIGHT
5	5 ft. 4 in. (1.63 m)	105 lb. (48 kg)
8	6 ft. (1.83 m)	169 lb. (77 kg)
9	6 ft. 2.25 in. (1.89 m)	180 lb. (82 kg)
10	6 ft. 5 in. (1.99 m)	210 lb. (95.6 kg)
11	6 ft. 7 in. (2.00 m)	—
12	6 ft. 10.5 in. (2.10 m)	—
14	7 ft. 5 in. (2.26 m)	301 lb. (137 kg)
15	7 ft. 8 in. (2.34 m)	355 lb. (161 kg)
16	7 ft. 10.24 in. (2.40 m)	374 lb. (170 kg)
17	8 ft. 0.38 in. (2.45 m)	315 lb. (143 kg)
18	8 ft. 3.5 in. (2.53 m)	—
19	8 ft. 5.5 in. (2.58 m)	480 lb. (218 kg)
20	8 ft. 6.75 in. (2.61 m)	—
21	8 ft. 8.25 in. (2.65 m)	491 lb. (223 kg)
22.4	8 ft. 11.1 in. (2.72 m)	439 lb. (199 kg)

Robert Wadlow is remembered by his family as a "quiet young man who overcame a unique handicap, and who was an inspiration to all of those that knew him." His record remains one of the most popular and memorable in the 50-year history of *Guinness World Records*.

AMAZING ANATOMY

Largest muscle Muscles normally account for 40% of human body weight in men and 35% in women. The bulkiest of the 639 named muscles in the human body is usually the gluteus maximus or buttock muscle, which extends the thigh. However, in pregnancy the uterus or womb can increase from about 1 oz. (30 g) to over 2 lb. 3 oz. (1 kg) in weight.

Smallest muscle The smallest muscle in the human body is the stapedius, which controls the stapes in the ear. The muscle is less than 0.05 in. (0.127 cm) long.

Most active muscle It has been estimated that the eye muscles move more than 100,000 times a day. It is believed that many of these rapid eye movements take place during the dreaming phase of sleep.

Longest muscle The longest muscle in the human body is the sartorius, which is a narrow, ribbonlike muscle running from the pelvis and across the

LARGEST SESAMOID BONE The patella or kneecap is the largest sesamoid bone in the human body. Sesamoids are ovoid like the seeds of the sesame plant and most are only a few millimeters in diameter. They are usually embedded tendons close to joints or where the tendons angle sharply around bone. Their function is to take compression when a tendon is going around a joint, as when a person is kneeling.

front of the thigh to the top of the tibia below the knee. Its action is to draw the lower limb into the cross-legged position.

Longest bone Excluding a variable number of sesamoids (small, rounded bones), there are 206 bones in the adult human body, compared with about 300 for children (as they grow, some bones fuse together). The thighbone, or femur, is the longest. It constitutes 27.5% of a person's stature normally, and may be expected to be 19.75 in. (50 cm) long in a man measuring 6 ft. (1.8 m) tall. The longest recorded bone was a femur measuring 29.9 in. (76 cm), which belonged to Constantine, a German giant.

Largest internal organ The largest organ in the human body, the adult liver can weigh between 2 lb. 10 oz. and 3 lb. 4 oz. (1.2 and 1.5 kg)—about one thirty-sixth of the total body weight. Located behind the lower ribs and below the diaphragm, it performs over 100 separate bodily functions and can measure up to 8.6 in. (22 cm) long and 3.9 in. (10 cm) wide.

Largest gallbladder On March 15, 1989, at the National Naval Medical Center in Bethesda, Maryland, U.S.A., Prof. Bimal C. Ghosh (U.S.A.) removed a gallbladder weighing 23 lb. (10.4 kg) from a 69-year-old woman.

Largest gallstone The largest gallstone reported in medical literature was one of 13 lb. 14 oz. (6.29 kg) removed from an 80-year-old woman by Dr. Humphrey Arthure (UK) at Charing Cross Hospital, London, UK, on December 29, 1952.

Largest bladder stone Dr. Kadri Al-Ban removed from one of his patients, Mohammed Ali A. Al-Muleiki (both Yemen), a vesical (bladder) stone weighing 9.17 oz. (260 g) and with a diameter of about 2.75 in. (7 cm) at the Al-Kadri Clinic, Ibb, Yemen, on October 25, 1998.

Rarest blood group A type of Bombay blood (subtype h-h) has so far been found only in a Czechoslovak nurse in 1961 and in a brother (Rhesus positive) and sister (Rhesus negative) named Jalbert in Massachusetts, U.S.A., reported in February 1968. Using the ABO system, one of 14 systems, group AB occurs in less than 3% of persons in the UK and 1% in the U.S.A.

Most common blood group On a world basis, group O is the most common blood group (46%), but in some countries, for example Norway, Group A predominates.

Largest artery The aorta is 1.18 in. (3 cm) in diameter where it leaves the heart and by the time it ends at the level of the fourth lumbar vertebra, it is about 0.68 in. (1.75 cm) in diameter.

Largest vein The inferior vena cava, which returns the

SMALLEST JOINT The smallest joint is in the ear, between the smallest bone, the stapes or stirrup bone (bottom), and the incus or anvil bone (middle). The stapes measures a mere 0.1–0.13 in. (2.6–3.4 mm) in length and weighs 0.03–0.066 grains (2–4.3 mg).

LONGEST LIFE OF A CELL Brain cells last for life. By way of comparison, bone cells may live for only 10–30 years.

blood from the lower half of the body to the heart and is slightly larger than the aorta, is the largest vein in the body.

Largest cell The megakaryocyte, a blood cell, measures 0.007 in. (0.2 mm). It is found in the bone marrow and produces the "stickiest" particles in the body—the platelets—which play an important role in blood clotting.

Smallest cell The brain cells in the cerebellum measure about 0.0001968 in. (0.005 mm) or 5 microns.

Longest cell Motor neurons are some 4 ft. 3.12 in. (1.3 m) long; they have cell bodies (gray matter) in the lower spinal cord with axons (white matter) that carry nerve impulses from the spinal cord down to the big toe. The cell systems that carry certain sensations (vibration and positional sense) back from the big toe to the brain are even longer. Their uninterrupted length, from the toe and up the posterior part of the spinal cord to the medulla of the brain, is about equal to the height of the body.

Most abundant cell The body contains in the region of 30 billion red blood cells (erythrocytes), approximately 8.75×10^{12} in every pint of blood (5×10^{12} in every liter). The function of these cells is to carry oxygen around the body.

Longest-lived human cells The cells of Henrietta Lacks (U.S.A.) are still alive and being grown in laboratories worldwide decades after her death from cancer on October 4, 1951 when she was 31. A single cell was removed and was subsequently found to lack chromosome 11, which is now known as the "tumor suppressor." As a result of this biological error, the cell is immortal and is one of the most helpful tools in biomedical research.

Fastest turnover of body cells The body cells with the shortest life are in the lining of the alimentary tract, where the cells are shed every three to four days.

Longest memory of a cell A lymphocyte is a type of white blood cell that is part of the body's immune defense system. As successive generations of lymphocytes are produced during one's life, they never forget an enemy.

Heaviest brain In December 1992, Dr. George T. Mandybur (U.S.A.), at the University of Cincinnati, Ohio, U.S.A., reported the weight of a 30-year-old male's brain as being 5 lb. 1.1 oz. (2.3 kg).

Lightest brain The lightest "normal" or non-atrophied brain on record was one weighing 1 lb. 8 oz. (680 g). It belonged to Daniel Lyon (Ireland), who died aged 46 in New York, U.S.A., in 1907. He was just over 5 ft. (1.5 m) in height and weighed 145 lb. (66 kg). A normal adult brain weighs in the region of 3 lb. (1.4 kg).

Highest hyperacuity The human eye is capable of judging relative position with remarkable accuracy, reaching limits of from 3 to 5 seconds of arc. In April 1984, Dr. Dennis M. Levi (U.S.A.) of the College of Optometry, University of Houston, Texas, U.S.A., repeatedly identified the relative position of a thin, bright green line within 0.85 seconds of arc. This is equivalent to a displacement of some 0.25 in. (6 mm) at a distance of 1 mile (1.6 km).

Strongest joint The hip joint is the strongest and one of the most stable joints as the head of the femur fits almost perfectly into the socket of the pelvis.

Most mobile joint The shoulder joint is the most mobile and as a result is the joint that is easiest to dislocate.

MEDICAL PHENOMENA

Earliest successful artificial eye On January 17, 2000, it was announced that Jeremiah Teehan (U.S.A.), who lost his sight after a blow to his head 36 years before, could see again thanks to an artificial eye developed by William Dobelle (U.S.A.). Jeremiah became the second person to receive surgery of this kind, and the first to have had successful results.

Largest plate inserted in human skull Tom Thompson (U.S.A.) had a titanium plate measuring 5.9 × 4.33 in. (15 × 11 cm) inserted into the left side of his head by neurosurgeons at DeKalb General Hospital, Decatur, Georgia, U.S.A., on April 30, 1971. The surgery took place after he had been struck by a car and was pronounced dead on arrival at the local hospital.

Strangest diet Michel Lotito (France), known as Monsieur Henri Mangetout, has been eating metal and glass since 1959. Gastroenterologists have X-rayed his stomach and have described his ability to consume 2 lb. (900 g) of metal per day as unique.

Heaviest object removed from stomach The heaviest object extracted from a human stomach was a ball of hair weighing 5 lb. 3 oz. (2.53 kg) from a 20-year-old female compulsive swallower in the South Devon and East Cornwall Hospital, UK, on March 30, 1895.

Oldest patient to undergo surgery The greatest recorded age at which anyone has undergone an operation is 111 years 105 days for a hip operation on James Henry Brett, Jr. (U.S.A.) on November 7, 1960.

FARTHEST EYEBALL POPPER Kim Goodman (U.S.A.) can pop her eyeballs to a distance of 0.43 in. (11 mm) beyond her eye sockets. Her eyes were measured on the set of the television show *Guinness World Records: Primetime* in Los Angeles, California, U.S.A., on June 13, 1998. Kim first discovered her unique and somewhat startling talent when she was accidentally hit on the head with a hockey mask and one of her eyeballs popped out much further than normal. Ever since that day, Kim's eyes would protrude out of her head every time she yawned, and she has now taught herself to pop her eyes out on cue.

Farthest distance traveled by a human voice The normal intelligible outdoor range of the male human voice in still air is 590 ft. (180 m). Silbo, the whistled language of the Spanish-speaking inhabitants of the Canary Island of La Gomera, is intelligible under ideal conditions at 5 miles (8 km).

There is a recorded case, under optimal acoustic conditions, of a Silbo speaker being heard at a distance of 10.5 miles (17 km) across still water at night.

Highest g-force endured nonvoluntarily Racing driver David Purley (UK) survived a deceleration from 108 mph (173 km/h) to zero in 26 in. (66 cm) in a crash at Silverstone, Northamptonshire, UK, on July 13, 1977. He endured 179.8 G and suffered 29 fractures, three dislocations, and six heart stoppages.

Highest blood sugar level Two-year-old Alexa Painter (U.S.A.) survived a blood sugar level 20.7 times above average at 2,495 mg/dekaliter (139 mmol/liter) when she was admitted to the Community Hospital of Roanoke, Virginia, U.S.A., to be treated for severe diabetic ketoacidosis on December 30, 1991. The normal blood sugar range is between 80 and 120 mg/dekaliter (4.4–6.6 mmol/liter).

Longest medical operation The most protracted operation reported lasted for 96 hours and was performed in Chicago, Illinois, U.S.A., on February 4–8, 1951 when an ovarian cyst was removed from Gertrude Levandowski (U.S.A.). During the operation her weight fell 616 lb. (280 kg) to 308 lb. (140 kg).

Earliest heart transplant patient The first heart transplant was performed on Louis Washkansky (South Africa), aged 55, at the Groote Schuur Hospital, Cape Town, South Africa, between 1 a.m. and 6 a.m. on December 3, 1967, by a team of 30 headed by Prof. Christiaan Barnard (South

FIRST HAND TRANSPLANT During a 14-hour operation in Lyon, France, in 1998, an international team of eight surgeons attached the hand of a dead man to the wrist of 48-year-old Clint Hallam (Australia).

FURTHEST TRACED DESCENDANT BY DNA Adrian Targett (UK) has been linked through some 300 generations and shown to be a direct descendant, on his mother's side, of Cheddar Man, a 9,000-year-old skeleton, one of the oldest complete skeletons, found in Great Britain in 1903.

Africa). The donor was Denise Ann Darvall (South Africa), aged 25. Washkansky lived for 18 days.

Longest heart transplant survival Sammy Katy King (U.S.A.) survived 24 years 142 days after having received a 24-year-old male's heart at Stanford University, Palo Alto, California, U.S.A., on April 4, 1975.

Earliest recipient of an artificial heart On December 1–2, 1982, at the Utah Medical Center, Salt Lake City, Utah, U.S.A., 61-year-old Barney Clark (U.S.A.) became the first recipient of an artificial heart, a Jarvik 7. The patient died on March 23, 1983, 112 days later.

Longest artificial heart transplant survival After his heart transplant on November 25, 1984, William J. Schroeder (U.S.A.) survived 620 days.

Longest cardiac arrest The longest cardiac arrest is four hours in the case of fisherman Jan Egil Refsdahl (Norway), who fell overboard into the icy waters off Bergen, Norway, on December 7, 1987. He was rushed to nearby Haukeland Hospital after his body temperature fell to 75°F (24°C) and his heart stopped beating. He made a full recovery once he was connected to a heart-lung machine.

Earliest successful kidney transplant The first successful kidney transplant in a human was performed by R. H. Lawler (U.S.A.) at Little Company of Mary Hospital, Chicago, Illinois, U.S.A., on June 17, 1950.

Most fluid removed after hydronephrosis A 35-year-old Egyptian patient suffering from hydronephrosis—an enlargement of the kidney caused by a blockage of normal urine flow—had 46.49 pints (22 liters) of urine removed from his kidney on June 16, 1999, at the Bugshan Hospital, Jeddah, Saudi Arabia. (The kidney's normal urine capacity is 0.105–0.175 fl. oz. or 3–5 ml.) The kidney was eventually removed on July 6, 1999, measuring 19.6 × 15.7 × 9.8 in. (50 × 40 × 25 cm) and weighing 24.6 oz. (700 g).

Most sets of teeth Cases of the growth of a third set of teeth in late life have been recorded several times. A reference to a case in France of a fourth dentition, known as Lison's case, was published in 1896.

Most lightning strikes survived The only man in the world to be struck by lightning seven times was ex-park ranger Roy C. Sullivan (U.S.A.), the "human lightning conductor" of Virginia, U.S.A. A single lightning strike is made up of several 100 million volts (with peak current in the order of 20,000 amps).

Longest survivor of a porcine aortic valve replacement Harry Driver (UK) received a porcine (pig's) aortic valve replacement on April 12, 1978 under surgeon Dr. John Keats (UK). It functioned for 25 years 238 days until it was replaced by another on March 16, 2004 by Dr. Philip Kay (UK).

Fastest sneeze The highest speed at which expelled particles from a sneeze have been measured to travel is 103.6 mph (167 km/h).

BIRTH & LIFE

Lightest birth A premature baby girl weighing 9.87 oz. (280 g) was reported to have been born on June 27, 1989 at the Loyola University Medical Center, Illinois, U.S.A.. The lowest birth weight recorded for a surviving infant, of which there is definite evidence, is 10 oz. (283 g) in the case of Marian Taggart (UK), who was born six weeks premature in 1938 in South Shields, Tyne & Wear, UK.

Heaviest birth Anna Bates (Canada), who measured 7 ft. 5.5 in. (2.27 m), gave birth to a boy weighing 23 lb. 12.8 oz. (10.8 kg) and who measured 30 in. (76 cm) in length at her home in Seville, Ohio, U.S.A., on January 19, 1879, but the baby died 11 hours later.

Most premature baby James Elgin Gill was born to Brenda Gill (Canada) on May 20, 1987 in Ottawa, Ontario, Canada, 128 days (18 weeks) premature and weighing 1 lb. 6 oz. (624 g). The normal human gestation period is 280 days (40 weeks).

First "Siamese" twins The term "Siamese" was first applied to congenitally united twins in connection with the celebrated Chang and Eng Bunker, born at Meklong, Siam (now Thailand), on May 11, 1811. They were joined by a cartilaginous band at the chest. In April 1843, the twins married sisters Sarah and Adelaide Yates (U.S.A.) and fathered 10 and 12 children respec-

MOST CHILDREN DELIVERED AT A SINGLE BIRTH TO SURVIVE Bobbie McCaughey (U.S.A.) gave birth to a set of septuplets on November 19, 1997 at the University Hospital, Iowa, U.S.A.. Conceived by in-vitro fertilization, the four boys and three girls were delivered after 31 weeks by cesarean section, and weighed between 2 lb. 5 oz. and 3 lb. 4 oz. (1,048 g and 1,474.3 g). Another set of surviving septuplets was born eight weeks prematurely on January 14, 1998 to Hasna Mohammed Humair (Saudi Arabia). The four boys and three girls were born at the Abha Obstetric Hospital, Aseer, Saudi Arabia.

tively. The twins died within three hours of each other on January 17, 1874 aged 62 years 251 days.

Oldest mother It was reported that Rosanna dalla Corte (Italy, b. February 1931) gave birth to a baby boy on July 18, 1994 when she was 63 years old.

RAREST FORM OF SIAMESE TWINS The most extreme form of Siamese twins is known as *dicephales tetrabrachius dipus* (two heads, four arms, and two legs). The only fully reported example of this is Masha and Dasha Krivoshlyapovy (USSR), who were born on January 3, 1950 and died within 17 hours of each other on April 17, 2003, aged 53 years 104 days.

OLDEST WOMAN EVER The greatest fully authenticated age to which any human has ever lived is 122 years 164 days by Jeanne Louise Calment (France). Born on February 21, 1875, she died at a nursing home in Arles, southern France, on August 4, 1997.

Most albino siblings Of the eight children born to George and Minnie Sesler (both U.S.A.), four of their five sons were born with the rare genetic condition albinism. John, George, Kermit, and Kenneth were born with translucent skin, pinkish blue eyes, and white hair.

Most generations born on leap day The only verified example of a family producing three consecutive generations born on February 29 is that of the Keoghs. Peter Anthony (Ireland, b. 1940), his son Peter Eric (UK, b. 1964), and his granddaughter Bethany Wealth (UK, b. 1996) all celebrate their birthdays every four years.

Most generations born on the same day Four families hold this record. Ralph Betram Williams (U.S.A.) was born on July 4, 1982 in Wilmington, North Carolina, U.S.A.. His father, grandfather, and, in 1876, his great-grandfather were also born on July 4.

Veera Tuulia Tuijantyär Kivistö (Finland), born in 1997, shares her birthday of March 21 with her mother (b. 1967), her grandfather (b. 1940), and great-grandfather (b. 1903).

Maureen Werner (U.S.A.) was born on October 13, 1998 and shares her birthday with her mother (b. 1970), her grandfather (b. 1938), and great-grandmother (b. 1912).

Jacob Camren Hildebrandt (U.S.A.) was born in 2001 and shares his birthday of August 23 with his father (b. 1966), his grandmother (b. 1944), and great-grandmother (b. 1919).

Most children delivered at a single birth The highest recorded number of children born at a single birth is nine to Geraldine Brodrick (Australia) at the Royal Hospital for Women, Sydney, Australia, on June 13, 1971. None of the children (five boys and four girls) lived for more than six days.

Most consecutive generations of twins Three consecutive generations of the Roy family (Canada) have given birth to twins: Joyce Roy, a twin born May 22, 1951, gave birth to Diane and Carole on January 17, 1973. Diane gave birth to twin boys Derek and Ricky (b. December 16, 1999) and Carole had twin girls Kelly and Ashley (b. May 12, 2001).

> Centenarians surviving beyond their 113th year are extremely rare: the present absolute proven limit of human longevity is just over 122 years. Data on centenarians has shown that only one 115-year life can be expected in 2.1 billion lives.

Oldest living woman Hendrikje Van Andel-Schipper (Netherlands, b. June 29, 1890) took the title of the world's oldest living woman at the age of 113 years 335 days on May 29, 2004.

Oldest living man American Fred Hale (b. December 1, 1890) became the world's oldest living man on March 5, 2004 at the age of 113 years 95 days.

Oldest man ever Born on June 29, 1865, the oldest man ever recorded was Shigechiyo Izumi (Japan), who was listed as a six-year-old in Japan's first census of 1871. He died on February 21, 1986 aged 120 years 237 days.

★ OLDEST LIVING PEOPLE SINCE 1955 ★

NAME	COUNTRY BORN	BORN	DIED	COUNTRY DIED	AGE
1. Betsy Baker	UK	August 20, 1842	October 24, 1955	U.S.A.	113 years 65 days
2. Martha Graham	U.S.A.	December 1844	June 25, 1959	U.S.A.	114 years ca. 180 days
3. James Henry Brett, Jr.	U.S.A.	July 25, 1849	February 10, 1961	U.S.A.	111 years 200 days
4. James Hult	UK	April 23, 1852	September 9, 1961	Australia	109 years 139 days
5. Lovisa Svensson	Sweden	November 20, 1853	February 17, 1963	Sweden	109 years 89 days
6. Kiet Portier-Tan	Netherlands	May 13, 1855	April 21, 1963	Netherlands	107 years 343 days
7. John Mosely Turner	UK	June 15, 1856	March 21, 1968	UK	111 years 280 days
8. Johanna Booyston	South Africa	January 17, 1857	June 16, 1968	South Africa	111 years 151 days
9. Marie Bernatkova	Czech Republic	October 22, 1857	alive October 1968		111 years + days
10. Ada Roe	UK	February 6, 1858	January 11, 1970	UK	111 years 339 days
11. Josefa Salas Mateo	Spain	July 14, 1860	February 27, 1973	Spain	112 years 228 days
12. Alice Stevenson	UK	July 10, 1861	August 18, 1973	UK	112 years 39 days
13. Elizabeth Watkins	UK	March 10, 1863	October 31, 1973	UK	110 years 235 days

14. Mito Umeta	Japan	March 27, 1863	May 31, 1975	Japan	112 years 65 days
15. Niwa Kawamoto	Japan	August 5, 1863	November 16, 1976	Japan	113 years 103 days
16. Shigechiyo Izumi	Japan	June 29, 1865	February 21, 1986	Japan	120 years 237 days
17. Mamie Eva Keith	U.S.A.	March 22, 1873	September 20, 1986	U.S.A.	113 years 182 days
18. Mary McKinney	U.S.A.	May 30, 1873	February 2, 1987	U.S.A.	113 years 248 days
19. Anna Williams	UK	June 2, 1873	December 27, 1987	UK	114 years 208 days
20. Florence Knapp	U.S.A.	October 10, 1873	January 11, 1988	U.S.A.	114 years 93 days
21. Carrie White[1]	U.S.A.	November 18, 1874	February 14,1991	U.S.A.	116 years 88 days
22. Jeanne Calment	France	February 21, 1875	August 4, 1997	France	122 years 164 days
23. Marie-Louise Meilleur	Canada	August 29, 1880	April 16, 1998	Canada	117 years 230 days
24. Sarah Knauss	U.S.A.	September 24, 1880	December 30, 1999	U.S.A.	119 years 97 days
25. Eva Morris	UK	November 8, 1885	November 2, 2000	UK	114 years 360 days
26. Marie Bremont	France	April 25, 1886	June 6, 2001	France	115 years 42 days
27. Maud Farris Luse	U.S.A.	January 21, 1887	March 18, 2002	U.S.A.	115 years 56 days
28. Kamato Hongo	Japan	September 16, 1887	October 31, 2003	Japan	116 years 45 days
29. Mitoyo Kawate	Japan	May 15, 1889	November 13, 2003	Japan	114 years 182 days
30. Ramona Trinidad Iglesias-Jordan[2]	Puerto Rico	August 31, 1889	May 29, 2004	Puerto Rico	114 years 272 days
31. Hendrikje Van Andel-Schipper	The Netherlands	June 29, 1890			113 years 335 days*

[1]Authentication called into question by census data   *still living as of May 29, 2004
[2]Title given to Charlotte Benkner (U.S.A. b. November 16, 1889, d. May 14, 2004, aged 114 years 181 days) on November 13, 2003 aged 113 years 362 days and withdrawn on March 29, 2004 following receipt of documentation supporting Ramona Trinidad Iglesias-Jordan's claim.

YOUNG TALENT

Youngest physician Balamurali Ambati (U.S.A., b. July 29, 1977) became the world's youngest doctor when he graduated from the Mount Sinai School of Medicine in New York City, U.S.A., on May 19, 1995 at the age of 17.

Youngest actor to receive star billing Leroy Overacker (U.S.A., b. May 12, 1932), known on screen as "Baby Leroy," was chosen at the age of six months to play opposite Maurice Chevalier in *A Bedtime Story* (U.S.A., 1933).

Youngest consultant On April 15, 2000, supermarket chain Tesco announced that it had procured the services of seven-year-old Laurie Sleator

MOST SPOONS BALANCED ON THE FACE Jonathan Friedman (U.S.A.)
was able to balance 13 stainless-steel spoons on his face (one on each
ear, two on each cheek, two on his chin, one on his lips, one on his
nose, and three on his forehead). He balanced them for 2 minutes at
Lake Oswego, Oregon, U.S.A., on March 30, 2004, aged 12.

  Guinness World Records photographed Jonathan in November 2003
balancing nine spoons.

(UK) to advise senior executives on the Pokémon craze that was sweeping the globe. His advice contributed to Tesco selling over £1 million ($1.55 million) worth of Pokémon goods over the Easter weekend. Laurie was remunerated in the form of Pokémon products.

Youngest billionaire The world's youngest billionaire is His Serene Highness 12th Prince Albert von Thurn und Taxis (Germany, b. June 24, 1983) with an estimated net worth of $2.1 billion according to the *Forbes* Rich List 2004. On his 18th birthday, he became the sole heir of a royal family fortune that includes extensive landholdings, real estate, castles, works of art, and businesses.

Youngest person to visit both poles The youngest person to have visited both geographical poles is Jonathan Silverman (U.S.A., b. June 13, 1990), who reached the North Pole on July 25, 1999 and the South Pole on January 10, 2002, aged 11 years 211 days.

Youngest person to visit the North Pole Alicia Hempleman-Adams (UK, b. November 8, 1989) stood at the geographic North Pole at the age of 8 years 173 days on May 1, 1998, the youngest person ever to have done so. She flew to the pole to meet her father, the well-known adventurer David Hempleman-Adams (UK), at the end of his successful trek to the pole.

YOUNGEST SOLO CIRCUMNAVIGATION The youngest person to sail solo around the world is David Griffiths Dicks (Australia), who was 18 years 41 days old when he completed his circumnavigation back to Freemantle, Western Australia, in a time of 264 days 16 hr. 49 min. on November 16, 1996.

Youngest person to walk to the South Pole Andrew Cooney (UK, b. April 9, 1979) became the youngest person to walk from the edge of the Antarctic continent to the South Pole, when he arrived there at the age of 23 years 268 days on January 2, 2003, 54 days after setting out.

Youngest person to travel to all seven continents The youngest person to have traveled to all seven continents is Tanya Daniella Donkin (South Africa), who visited her seventh continent on November 16, 2000 at the age of 3 years 319 days. All her travels were with her parents, Dave and Irene Donkin (both South Africa). Tanya was born in South Africa (Africa) on January 2, 1997; landed in Zurich, Switzerland (Europe) on February 20, 1997; in Buenos Aires, Argentina (South America) on December 14, 1997; on Deception Island (Antarctica) on December 28, 1997; in Miami, U.S.A. (North America) on December 17, 1998; in Sydney, Australia (Australasia) on December 17, 1999; and in Dubai, United Arab Emirates (Asia) on November 16, 2000.

Youngest published male author At the age of six, Dennis Vollmer (U.S.A., b. July 21, 1980) wrote and illustrated *Joshua Disobeys* and had it commercially published by Landmark Editions, Inc., of Kansas City, Missouri, U.S.A., after his story won a national student writing contest in 1987.

Youngest published female author The youngest commercially published female author is Dorothy Straight (U.S.A., b. May 25, 1958), who wrote *How the World Began* in 1962, aged only four. It was published by Pantheon Books in August 1964.

Youngest figure skating world champion The youngest female win-

YOUNGEST RADIO HOST On January 16, 1999, Cody Morton (Canada, b. June 12, 1988) hosted a show on CHOO FM in Tofino, British Columbia, Canada, aged 10 years 218 days.

ner of a world title is Tara Lipinski (U.S.A., b. June 10, 1982), who won the individual title on March 22, 1997 aged just 14 years 286 days.

Youngest Wimbledon competitor The youngest Wimbledon competitor was Mita Klima (Austria) who was just 13 years old in the 1907 singles competition.

Youngest person to win a match at Wimbledon The youngest person to win a match at Wimbledon is Jennifer Capriati (U.S.A., b. March 29, 1976), who was aged 14 years 89 days when she competed in her first Wimbledon tennis match on June 26, 1990.

Youngest soccer World Cup player The youngest player to play in soccer's premier tournament is Souleymane Mamam (Togo) who played for Togo against Zambia aged 13 years 310 days in a preliminary qualifying game on May 6, 2001.

Youngest professional artist Dante Lamb (U.S.A., b. November 16, 1999) is the youngest artist to have his work purchased and displayed. Dante's abstract paintings hang in the Monkey Love Dessert Bar & Gallery, St. Simons Island, Georgia, U.S.A., and his first piece sold on October 6, 2003 for $85 when he was only three years old.

Most consecutive pea shooting world championships The most consecutive pea shooting world championships won is three by Mike Fordham (UK) in 1983–85 and David Hollis (UK) in 1999–2001. Hollis was also the youngest world champion, aged just 13 when he scooped the title in 1999. The championships are held every year in Witcham, Cambridgeshire, UK.

Youngest international gymnast Pasakevi Voula Kouna (Greece, b. December 6, 1971) was aged 9 years 299 days at the start of the Balkan Games in Serres, Greece, on October 1, 1981, when she represented Greece.

Youngest world line dance champion Siobhan Dunn (UK, b. June 30, 1991) won the Junior World Line Dance Championship in Nashville, Tennessee, U.S.A., on January 10, 1998 aged just 6 years 194 days.

Youngest TV host The world's youngest host of a regular television program is Sheridan Jobbins (Australia) who, at the age of nine, began hosting *Cooking With Sheri* (Channel 7, Australia) in April 1969. The five-minute weekly (and then daily) show continued to air nationally for three consecutive years, ending when she was 11 years old. In total, 26 episodes were filmed.

Youngest solo rap artist Jordy Lemoine (France, b. January 14, 1988) was at No. 1 in the French charts with techno/house rap "Dur dur d'être Bébé" ("It's Hard to Be a Baby") at the age of four and a half in September 1993. The song later entered the U.S. *Billboard* chart.

Youngest DJ Llewellyn Owen aka "DJ Welly" (UK, b. February 21, 1992) headlined at London's Warp Club on May 1, 2000 aged 8 years 70 days. Welly was paid the standard rate for headlining DJs, $190 an hour. Since his professional debut, he has headlined at famous clubs such as Ministry of Sound (UK).

Youngest film director-writer-producer *Lex the Wonderdog* (Netherlands, 1973), a thriller of canine detection, was written, produced, and directed by Sydney Ling (Netherlands, b. November 20, 1959) when he was 13 years old. He was the youngest ever director of a professionally made feature-length film.

UNUSUAL SKILLS

Most body skips in a minute Ved Prakash Sharma (India) was able to "skip" with his arms while handcuffed, by stepping through his arms and bringing them up and over his head, a total of 27 times in a minute at Bhim Stadium, Bhiwani, India, on August 15, 2003.

MOST BALLOON SCULPTURES CREATED IN ONE HOUR John Cassidy (U.S.A.) made 529 balloon sculptures in one hour in New York City, U.S.A., on October 14, 2003. He made one sculpture every 6.8 seconds.

Furthest basketball slam dunk from a trampoline Jonathon Thibout (France) managed to slam-dunk a basketball from a trampoline placed 19 ft. (5.8 m) from the backboard of the net on the set of *L'Été de Tous les Records,* Port Leucate, France, on August 29, 2003.

Greatest distance zorbing The greatest distance traveled by a zorb ball in a single roll is 1,059 ft. 8.5 in. (323 m) by Rich Eley (UK) near Glynde, East Sussex, UK, on May 10, 1999. During the attempt, the zorb reached a record speed of 31 mph (49.8 km/h). The zorb originated in New Zealand and is a large, round, bouncy ball that can accommodate one person. As it rolls, the person strapped inside rolls too. A zorb ball weighs approximately 198 lb. (89 kg), and keeps the "zorbonaut" in an air cushion about 2 ft. (60 cm) off the ground.

Most divisions of a human hair Alfred West (UK) succeeded in splitting a human hair 17 times into 18 parts on eight occasions. All the divisions were made from the same point.

Tallest coin column The tallest single column of coins ever stacked on the edge of a coin was built by Dipak Syal (India) on May 3, 1991 and was made up of 253 Indian one-rupee pieces on top of a vertical five-rupee coin.

Greatest number of skips on a tightrope Walfer Guerrero (Colombia) achieved 1,250 consecutive turns skipping with a rope on a high wire at the Wereldcircus Carré, Haarlem, The Netherlands, on June 1, 1995. The tightrope was 31 ft. 5 in. (9.6 m) high.

Most "ducks and drakes" The record for the most consecutive skips of a stone on water is 40, held by Kurt Steiner (U.S.A.). The cast was achieved at the Pennsylvania Qualifying Stone Skipping Tournament held at Riverfront Park, Franklin, Pennsylvania, U.S.A., on September 14, 2002.

Most tennis balls held in the hand Francisco Peinado Toledo (Spain) placed 18 tennis balls in his left hand and held them for 10 seconds at Valencia, Spain, on September 18, 2003.

Furthest toss of a cowpat The record distances in the country sport of throwing dried cowpats, or "chips," depend on whether or not the projectile may be "molded into a spherical shape." The greatest distance achieved under the "non-sphericalization and 100 per cent organic" rule (established in 1970) is 266 ft. (81.1 m), by Steve Urner (U.S.A.) at the Mountain Festival, Tehachapi, California, U.S.A., on August 14, 1981.

Most teacups caught on the head while unicycling In 1952, unicyclist Rudy Horn (Germany) became the first person to throw six cups and saucers with his feet and balance them on his head, while mounted on a unicycle. He rounded off this feat by adding a teaspoon and a lump of sugar. At the time, he was performing with the Bertram Mills Circus at Olympia, London, UK.

MOST BASKETBALLS SPUN SIMULTANEOUSLY Michael Kettman (U.S.A.) spun 28 basketballs simultaneously on May 25, 1999 at Guinness World Records, London, UK. He is pictured setting his previous record of 25 in 1998.

MOST RATTLESNAKES HELD IN THE MOUTH Jackie Bibby (U.S.A.) held eight live rattlesnakes in his mouth by their tails for 12.5 seconds without any assistance at the Guinness World Records Experience, Orlando, Florida, U.S.A., on May 19, 2001.

Most powerful lungs The inflation of a standard 35-oz. (1,000-g) meteorological balloon to a diameter of 8 ft. (2.44 m) against set times was achieved by Manjit Singh (UK) in 42 minutes at Rushley Pavilion Centre, Leicester, UK, on September 16, 1998.

GWR TALKS TO Ashrita Furman

Ashrita Furman (U.S.A., pictured on following page) holds an amazing total of 19 Guinness World Records, including the fastest mile traveled on a pogostick—12 min. 16 sec.—set at Iffley Field, Oxford, UK, on July 24, 2001. His latest record successes include balancing 23 milk crates with a total weight of 88.01 lb. (39.92 kg) on his chin for 11.23 seconds on June 17, 2002 in Jamaica, New York, U.S.A., and the record for the running a mile while balancing a full milk bottle on his head, which he achieved in a record time of 8 min. 27 sec. at the TSV 1880 Sports Association Track, Starnberg, Germany, on November 9, 2003.

You set your first record in 1979. Why did you choose the jumping jacks record? Well, I know how to do it! At first I tried juggling—100,000 throws and it took all night—but there was no category! So I trained for the jumping jacks record.

How do you get the inspiration for your records? I take inspiration from all sorts of different places. Most records are already in the book, but I'm more open-minded now; anything is possible. I like the idea of people competing for the same record. It just comes down to "Can I do better?" It's fun to create your own category but it's also a challenge to break an existing record—you have a certain standard to reach.

What do you think about your versatility record? I'm really chuffed. A lot of it is just down to having an active imagination. The fastest milk bottle mile, the hula-hooping record—they were just off the top of my head.

What's the attraction of breaking records all over the world? I travel a lot anyway, so while I'm away I try to break records. I really wanted to go to Antarctica because I wanted to have set records on all seven continents. Someone I know in the Argentinian Navy got me a flight over the Antarctic where I was able to set my "fastest mile on a pogostick" record.

How do you train for pogosticking in Antarctica? It's difficult! It was certainly not the best place to set a pogo-stick record but it was a fantastic adventure! I almost got blown off the pogo by a helicopter leaving the base and at about the 0.75-mile point the spring of the pogostick got more and more sluggish until it froze and I fell off! Fortunately we had a spare.

What's your next record attempt going to be? I'll try skipping again, then glass balancing, then something in China. Maybe a somersault record. My current record is 8,341 forward rolls in 10 hr. 30 min. over 12 miles (19.67 km). I set it in 1986, but now I think I'm fitter.

What do you do to keep fit? I go to the gym and I run a couple of times a week. Skipping keeps you in great shape. And I juggle shotputs!

What would you say to young people wanting to break records? I became interested in breaking records as a kid and I still feel like a big kid! My dream was to get in the book and I didn't think I could, and now I have 19 records. Everyone has a special talent. I really believe there is something that everyone can do that will get you into *Guinness World Records*.

LIFELONG ACHIEVEMENTS

Longest working career as a barber Peter J. Vita (U.S.A., b. April 30, 1910) has been cutting hair professionally since 1922. Mr. Vita started his career in his father's barbershop when he was 12 years old. He opened his own barbershop in 1930 where he worked until 1988, before moving his business to Port Chester, New York, U.S.A., where he continues today.

Longest working career in the merchant navy From May 2, 1953 until June 23, 1969, Robert Morris (UK, b. September 16, 1928) served as cook on a total of 50 ships.

Longest working career as a bartender Angelo Cammarata (U.S.A.) started his career as a bartender on April 7, 1933 when Prohibition was repealed. He served beer at his family's grocery store on the stroke of midnight and was still working in his own bar *Cammarata Days* in July 1998—69 years later.

Longest working career as a radio DJ Ray Cordeiro, aka "Uncle Ray," (UK, b. December 12, 1924) has been a regular disc jockey since 1949, first working for the station Rediffusion Ltd. (Hong Kong) and then moving to (the now) Radio Television Hong Kong on September 15, 1960. He still hosts a regular four-hour nightly show called *All the Way with Ray* transmitted 10 p.m. until 2 a.m. Monday to Friday.

Oldest working mime artist American mime artist Arnold Jones (U.S.A., b. January 13, 1914) is still working six hours a day, five days a

OLDEST BAREFOOT WATERSKIER George Blair, aka Banana George, (U.S.A., b. January 22, 1915) successfully waterskied barefoot on Lake Florence, Winter Haven, Florida, U.S.A., at the age of 87 years 18 days on February 10, 2002.

week entertaining crowds in Hollywood, California, U.S.A. He has been a professional mime artist for over 70 years, starting at the age of 14 as "The Mechanical Man" at fairs across America's Midwest.

Longest working career as a circus bandmaster Merle Evans (U.S.A.) was bandmaster with Ringling Brothers-Barnum & Bailey Circus for 50 years. From 1919 to 1969 he led the band for about 30,000 performances, never missing a show.

Longest career as a radio actor in the same role Norman Painting (UK) took part in the first broadcast of BBC Radio 4's *The Archers* on January 1, 1951 and is still in the series as Philip Archer.

Oldest chorus line member The oldest "showgirl" who is still regularly performing in a chorus line is Beverly Allen (U.S.A., b. November 4, 1917). A member of The Fabulous Palm Springs Follies, her jitterbug routine—in which her partner lifts her over his head to spin her "head-over-heels"—has become an audience favorite.

Longest working career as a stadium announcer Walter Miceli (Brazil) has been the stadium announcer at the Estádio de São Januário, Rio de Janeiro, Brazil, home of Club de Regatas Vasco da Gama, since February 12, 1947.

Oldest BASE jumper James Talbot Guyer (U.S.A., b. June 16, 1928) parachuted off the 486-ft.-high (148-m) Perrine Bridge, Idaho, U.S.A., on August 2, 2002 aged 74 years 47 days.

Longest distance covered over a working career Stanley E. Rychlicki (U.S.A.) walked for 37 years of his 40-year career as a "pipeline inspector" and covered a distance of 136,880 miles (220,288 km), sometimes walking in excess of 20 miles (32 km) daily in Pennsylvania and New York, U.S.A.

Oldest dance instructor Gisel Weser (Germany, b. February 1, 1921) is the oldest dancing teacher, having worked at Triebel-Hölzer (founded 1883) in Lutherstadt Eisleben, Saxony-Anhalt, Germany, since 1949. She became head of the school in 1968 and continues to teach.

Oldest bell ringer Reginald Bray (UK, b. October 28, 1902) is an active member of the bell-ringing team of St. Cyr and St. Julitta, Newton St. Cyres, Devon, UK. He rang bells on October 30, 2003, two days after his 101st birthday, and continues bell-ringing today.

Oldest authors The oldest male author is Constantine Kallias (Greece, b. June 26, 1901), who published a 169-page paperback entitled *A Glance of My Life* in February 2003 at the age of 101.

Sisters and coauthors A. Elizabeth Delany and Sarah Louise Delany (both U.S.A.) published *The Delany Sisters' Book of Everyday Wisdom* in October 1994, when Sarah Louise was 105 years old and Elizabeth was 103.

Oldest competitive billiards player Jim Turton (UK, b. January 2, 1909) has been playing competitive billiards since 1924.

Oldest competitive pool player Wesley Walker (U.S.A., b. April 24, 1916) plays for Southern Vending in the Valley National 8-Ball Association league in Oklahoma, U.S.A.

Longest working career as a builder Edward William Beard (UK, 1878–1982) retired in October 1981 after 85 years with the firm he founded in 1896.

Oldest drivers Two male drivers were issued

FASTEST TIME TO TYPE ONE TO ONE MILLION Les Stewart (Australia) has typed the numbers one to one million manually in words on 19,990 quarto sheets. Starting in 1982, his target to become a "millionaire" became a reality on December 7, 1998.

LONGEST WORKING CAREER AS A SALSA ARTIST Celia Cruz (Cuba) was a leading salsa artist for 50 years and recorded over 50 albums. She began her career singing with Cuba's then-leading band Sonora Matancera in 1950, before leaving Cuba permanently to pursue a career in the U.S.A. in 1960. She recorded some 20 gold LPs and received more than 100 awards.

with new driver's licenses at the advanced age of 104: Fred Hale, Sr. (U.S.A., b. December 1, 1890—currently the oldest living man) was issued with his license in February 1995, and drove until it expired on his 108th birthday in 1998. Layne Hall (U.S.A.), whose date of birth is uncertain (b. December 24/25, 1884 or March 15, 1880), was issued with a license on June 15, 1989 when he was either 104 (according to his death certificate) or 109 (according to his driver's license). It was valid until his birthday in 1993, but he died on November 20, 1990.

The oldest female driver was Maude Tull (U.S.A.), who took to driving aged 91 after her husband died. She was issued a renewal on February 5, 1976 when aged 104.

Oldest competing aerobatic pilot Ian Metcher (Australia) was 85 years old when he won the basic aerobatics section of the Western Australia Light Aircraft Championships at Jandakot Airport near Fremantle, Australia, on February 24, 2001.

Oldest person to rappel Mary Maughan (UK, b. October 3, 1908) rappelled down a 124-ft. (38-m) cliff in Parrock Quarry, Ambleside, Cumbria, UK, on June 30, 2000 when aged 91 years 8 months and 27 days.

Oldest person to "loop the loop" On May 21, 1998, 95-year-old Adeline Ablitt (UK, b. 1903) flew in a glider as it performed a loop over the Soaring Centre, Leicestershire, UK.

Most blood donated Maurice Creswick (South Africa) has donated blood for a record 59 consecutive years since 1944, giving his record 336th unit of blood on July 9, 2003. Having given blood since turning 18, he has donated a total of 50 gal. (188.9 liters).

Oldest working general practitioner Dr. Kauromal M. Chandiramani (India, b. May 9, 1899) practiced as a general practitioner in Mumbai (Bombay), India, for 75 years 198 days from September 22, 1923 to May 9, 1999—his 100th birthday.

MASS PARTICIPATION

Largest human chain On August 23, 1989 up to 2 million people joined hands to form a human chain 370 miles (595 km) long across Estonia, Latvia, and Lithuania, commemorating the 50th anniversary of the non-aggression treaty between the USSR and Nazi Germany.

Largest human rainbow The world's largest human rainbow was made up of 11,273 staff, students, alumni, and families from Hong Kong Polytechnic University, and was formed at Hong Kong Stadium, Hong Kong, China, on October 6, 2002.

Largest human national flag A total of 10,371 spectators at the Scotland v. Germany soccer match on September 10, 2003 in Westfalenstadion, Dortmund, Germany, formed the shape and colors of the German flag in the south grandstand. Participants wore colored T-shirts and caps to form the black, red, and gold flag.

Largest walking bus On October 8, 2003, the Royal Borough of Kingston-upon-Thames and Transport for London (both UK) organized a "walking bus" of 1,109 people to the schools of Fern Hill Primary, St. Agatha's Catholic Primary, and Latchmere Infants and Junior Schools (all UK).

Largest human logo On July 24, 1999, 34,309 people organized by Realizar Eventos Especias gathered at the national stadium of Jamor, Lisbon, Portugal, to create the Portuguese logo for Euro2004, as part of the successful Portuguese bid to UEFA to hold the European Football Championships in 2004.

Longest human conveyor belt A conveyor belt consisting of 1,000 students from the University of Guelph, Canada, was formed on September 7, 1998. A surfboard was transported along its length.

Largest group hug A total of 5,117 students, staff, and friends from St. Matthew's Secondary School in Orleans, Ontario, Canada, hugged each other for 10 seconds on April 23, 2004 in support of The Force, a local cancer charity.

Largest circle dance The greatest number of participants in a circle formation dance were the 6,748 people who performed the hokey pokey at Bangor, County Down, UK, as part of the VE Day anniversary celebrations on May 6, 1995.

Largest locomotion dance A total of 669 people danced the locomotion for seven minutes in the grounds of Haydon Bridge High School, Hexham, Northumberland, UK, on October 19, 2001.

Largest game of musical chairs On August 5, 1989, the largest game of musical chairs began with 8,238 participants at the Anglo-Chinese School in Singapore. Three and a half hours later, the game ended with the lucky 15-year-old winner Xu Chong Wei on the last chair.

Largest simultaneous yodel The world's largest simultaneous yodel involved 937 people all yodeling the popular Swiss song "Von Luzern uf Wäggis zue" for more than one minute. The event was staged at the Ravensburger Spieleland, Meckenbeuren, Germany, on October 5, 2002.

Most people on unicycles On May 18, 2003, 100 students from the circus school Circus Jopie traveled on unicycles for a distance of 1,150 ft. (350 m) at Utrecht, The Netherlands. Their first attempt was in a single line wearing a 1,475-ft.-long (450-m) dragon costume. Unfortunately, the costume separated into two halves during the journey.

LONGEST HUMAN DOMINO LINE On September 30, 2000, 9,234 students aged 18–21 from NYAA Poly Connects formed a human domino chain stretching 2.6 miles (4.2 km) across Siloso Beach, Sentosa Island, Singapore.

LARGEST YOGA CLASS Manoj Gupota (India) led a yoga class of 6,315 people at Pandit Ravishankar Shukla (Wright Town) Stadium, Jabalpur, India, on February 13, 2003.

Most people sitting on one chair On September 20, 2002, 407 pupils from Otto-Hahn-Gymnasium (high school) in Springe, Germany, sat on one chair at the same time. The unbroken line of pupils, each seated on the knees of the person behind, measured 199 ft. 1.2 in. (60.7 m) long.

Largest unsupported circle The largest number of people in an unsupported circle (where you sit on the lap of the person behind you) is 10,323, achieved by employees of the Nissan Motor Company at Komazawa Stadium, Tokyo, Japan, on October 23, 1982.

Most people skipping rope simultaneously On April 2, 2003, a total of 1,356 schoolchildren skipped ropes simultaneously at Bishopston School, Swansea, UK.

Largest snowball fight The world's largest snowball fight involved 2,473 participants (1,162 against 1,311) and took place at Triel in the ski resort of Obersaxen-Mundaun in Graubunden, Switzerland, on January 18, 2003.

Largest dog walk A total of 4,372 dogs took part in the Catherine Cookson Great North Dog Walk, organized by Anthony Carlisle (UK). The walk was held on June 22, 2003 and started from Gypsies Green Stadium, South Shields, UK.

Largest simultaneous "dog stay" Dogs for the Disabled and Pets at Home organized a "dog stay" involving a record 514 dogs on August 16, 2003 at The Wag and Bone Show, Ascot, Berkshire, UK.

Largest cookery lesson Princess Household Appliances BV (Netherlands) organized a cookery lesson involving 357 students who were taught how to make paella by Cas Spijkers (Netherlands) on June 15, 2003 at Estepona, Marbella, Spain.

Largest water balloon fight On September 13, 2003, the University at Buffalo, New York City, U.S.A., played host to a water balloon fight involving 422 students throwing 5,214 water balloons.

Largest simultaneous whoopee cushion sit The UK's CBBC *Xchange* TV show organized a simultaneous whoopee cushion sit involving 1,504 participants at Tottenham Hotspur Football Club's stadium, White Hart Lane, London, UK, on January 13, 2004.

Most people simultaneously slimed On October 27, 2003, during Nickelodeon's *Slimetime Live* show at Universal Studios in Orlando, Florida, U.S.A., 762 people were simultaneously slimed by around 150 gal. (568 liters) of green slime.

Most people to pop balloons simultaneously On January 22, 2004, 1,603 basketball fans popped balloons simultaneously during halftime of the Metro State against Fort Hays State University men's basketball game at Gross Memorial Coliseum at Hays, Kansas, U.S.A.

Most couples kissing simultaneously A total of 5,327 couples kissed simultaneously for 10 seconds on February 14, 2004 as part of the Close-up Lovapalooza festival in Manila, Philippines.

Largest sleepover/pajama party On February 1, 2003, McLean Bible Church and Dulles Town Center, Virginia, U.S.A., hosted a sleepover party

MOST PEOPLE BRUSHING THEIR TEETH IN THE SAME VENUE A total of 10,240 students brushed their teeth simultaneously for at least 60 seconds at Ai Guo Road, Luohu District, Shenshen City, China, on September 20, 2003. The event was organized by the Health Bureau of Luohu District, the Education Bureau of Luohu District, and the Chamber of Commerce of Luohu District and sponsored by Colgate-Palmolive (Guangzhou) Co. Ltd.

for 1,045 students. All participants wore pajamas and slept on the floor in sleeping bags.

TEAM EFFORTS

Fastest men's mobile garbage-bin race On February 21, 1999, at Westfield Devils Junior Soccer Club, Launceston, Tasmania, Australia, Shaun Viney and Aaron Viney (both Australia) completed a 360-ft. 9.6-in. (110-m) mobile garbage-bin race in 31.1 seconds.

Fastest women's woolsack race The "Mega Movers" team of four ladies completed the woolsack World Championships in Tetbury, Gloucestershire, UK, in 3 min. 52.01 sec. on May 25, 1989. The event involves competitors racing up and down a steep hill while carrying a 60-lb. (27.21-kg) bag of wool on their shoulders.

Fastest 31-legged race over 50 m Students from the Sugikami Elementary school in the Kumamoto Prefecture, Japan, ran a 31-legged race covering a total of 164 ft. (50 m) in 8.94 seconds at Yokohama Arena, Japan, on November 23, 2002.

Farthest distance covered in a lawn mower race Ian Dobson, Robert Jones, and Steve Williams (all UK) of the team "Extreme Headless Chickens" covered 313.6 miles (504.7 km) in the annual 12-hour lawn mower race at Wisborough Green, UK, on August 29–30, 1998, organized by the British Lawn Mower Racing Association.

Longest supermarket cart push A team of 801 staff from Woolworths, BCC, and Jack-the-Slasher supermarkets took turns to push a supermarket shopping cart from Cairns to Brisbane, Queensland, Australia, covering 1,098 miles (1,767 km) in 36 days, from June 20 to July 26, 1987.

Farthest distance to push a bed A team of nine employees from Bruntsfield Bedding Centre, Edinburgh, UK, pushed a wheeled hospital bed 3,233.65 miles (5,204 km) from June 21 to July 26, 1979.

Fastest time to dismantle a car A team from Espoon Ammattioppilaitos technical school (Finland) consisting of Tapio Heino, Panu Natunen, Aaro-Pekka Nousiainen, Sami Rissanen, Sampo Vuolteenaho, Ahmed Abdirizag, Mikael Gorski, Janne Spanow, and Juha Määttä (all Finland) dismantled a five-door sedan in 35 minutes on November 28, 2001. All parts were removed except for the bodywork, chassis, and axles.

Fastest time to swap an engine A team of four mechanics—Stefan Klotz, Markus Jung, Ralf Kaelche, and Stefan Worner (all Germany)—took

FASTEST 4-x-100-M SACK RELAY RACE The 4-x-100-m sack relay race, held on June 17, 2003 at Ivanhoe Grammar School, Mernda, Victoria, Australia, was won in 2 min. 29.09 sec. The members of the winning team were Patrick Holcolmbe (second from left), James Osbourne (fifth from left), Luke MacFarlane (sixth from left), and Andrew Rodaughan (second from right, all Australia).

the engine from one Volkswagen Beetle and installed it in another, then drove the car 16 ft. 5 in. (5 m) in a time of 1 min. 37 sec. on the set of *Guinness—Die Show der Rekorde,* Munich, Germany, on January 17, 1999.

Most people on a motorcycle wheelie On June 12, 1998, a total of nine people, led by Todd Colbert (U.S.A.), did a motorcycle wheelie in Lake Whales, Florida, U.S.A.

Most people crammed into a Smart car A total of 13 girls from Team IGA-Optic (Germany) crammed into a Smart car on the set of *Guinness—Die Show der Rekorde,* Munich, Germany, on April 2, 1999.

Most plaster casts applied in an hour by a team A team of 10 people applied forearm plaster casts (one per person) to 825 volunteers in an hour at the main square of Herentals, Belgium, on July 5, 2003. The event was organized to celebrate the 750th year of Herentals Hospital.

Most faces painted in an hour by a team At an attempt organized by Face2Face International (UK), a team of five people consisting of Susan Howard, Rosemary Jones, Emma Edworthy, Ann Ardern, and Andrew Griffiths (all UK) painted a total of 239 faces in an hour, using a minimum of three colors per face at Crealy Park, Exeter, Devon, UK, on August 1, 2003.

Longest daisy chain The longest daisy chain measured 1.31 miles (2.12 km) and was made in seven hours by a team of 16 villagers from Good Easter, Chelmsford, Essex, UK, on May 27, 1985.

Fastest loaf from field to oven On August 21, 1999, a team led by baker John Haynes and farmer Peter Rix (both UK) at Alpheton, Suffolk, UK, took 18 min. 11.4 sec. to produce 13 loaves from growing wheat.

Most trees planted in an hour A team of 96 people, including schoolchildren from St. Therese's School and other volunteers (all UK) from Neath Port Talbot, planted 4,100 trees in one hour on April 8, 2003. The event was organized by Neath Port Talbot County Borough Council (UK) and was held at Margam Country Park, West Glamorgan, UK.

Largest human mobile The largest human mobile was made up of 24 people from the Height Rescue Fire Department Team, at Fire station 33, Veddel, Hamburg, Germany, on June 14, 2003. Suspended from a crane, the lowest point of the mobile was 164 ft. (50 m) off the ground.

Most heads shaved in an hour by a team A team of 10 hairdressers shaved a total of 56 heads in one hour at the Victoria Oval, Dubbo, New South Wales, Australia, in aid of the Cancer Council's Relay for Life on September 28, 2002.

FARTHEST WHEELCHAIR PUSH OVER 24 HOURS A team of 75 volunteers pushed a wheelchair a distance of 240 miles (386.2 km) in 24 hours at Copeland Stadium, Whitehaven, Cumbria, UK, on September 8–9, 2000. The event was organized by the Maryport branch of the Cumbria Cerebral Palsy Society.

Fastest time to pop 1,000 balloons A team of 37 participants (all UK) popped 1,000 balloons in 1 min. 44 sec. on the set of *Blue Peter* at BBC Television Centre, London, UK, on November 7, 2003.

Largest can pyramid built in 30 minutes On September 23, 2000, the Malaysia can team, consisting of students from the INTI College Subang Jaya, built a pyramid created from 9,455 empty aluminum drink cans in 24 minutes at the Midvalley Mega Mall in Kuala Lumpur, Malaysia. It had a square base of 30 × 30 cans, measuring 6 ft. 6 in. × 6 ft. 6 in. (1.98 × 1.98 m).

Farthest distance traveled by a team on a water slide in 24 hours Harald Bachmann, Markus Ullmann, Jörg Hofmann, Robert Bachmann, Franz Walter, Werner Müller, Aaron Pfeffer, Dominik Radler, and Stefan Wolf (all Germany) slid a total distance of 420.652 miles (676.974 km) together on a 334-ft. (102-m) water slide in 24 hours in Kempten, Germany, on July 12 and 13, 2002.

Longest reading-aloud marathon by a team Phillipp Haag, Eduard Maier, Martina Holdermann, Sabrina Holzäpfel, Simone Jordan, and Franziska Sobe (all Germany) from Calmbach Secondary School, Bad Wildbad, Germany, read aloud for a record 75 hours from July 16 to 19, 2003.

FASTEST BOEING 737 100-M PULL BY A TEAM On January 27, 2001, a team of 10 Royal Marine reserves (UK) pulled a Boeing 737–300, weighing 81,500 lb. (37 tons), over a distance of 328 ft. (100 m) in 43.2 seconds at Manchester Airport, UK.

STRENGTH

Heaviest aircraft pull by wheelchairs A team of eight members of the Suffolk Braves Wheelchair Basketball Club (UK) pulled a Cessna 421 Eagle executive aircraft weighing 8,818 lb. (4 tons) a distance of 1,640 ft. (500 m) in 16 min. 20 sec. on December 9, 1998 at Marshall Airport, Cambridge, UK.

Longest duration aircraft restraint Using ropes looped around his arms, Ilkka Nummisto (Finland) prevented the takeoff of two Cessna airplanes pulling in opposite directions for 54 seconds at Räyskälä Airport, Finland, on August 1, 2001.

Fastest 50-m trailer pull Juan Antonio Valdecantos Mayor (Spain) pulled a trailer weighing 1,554 lb. (705 kg) a distance of 164 ft. (50 m) in a time of 17.95 seconds at the studios of *El Show de los Récords,* Madrid, Spain, on November 22, 2001.

Heaviest vehicle pulled by hair The heaviest vehicle to have been pulled by the hair alone over a distance of 98 ft. (30 m) is a double-decker bus weighing 17,359 lb. (7,874 kg), by Letchemanah Ramasamy (Malaysia) at Bruntingthorpe Proving Ground, Leicestershire, UK, on May 1, 1999.

Heaviest vehicle pulled by teeth Walter Arfeuille (Belgium) used his teeth to pull eight railway passenger coaches with a total weight of 493,570 lb. (223.8 tons) over a distance of 10 ft. 5 in. (3.2 m) along rails at Diksmuide, Belgium, on June 9, 1996.

Heaviest train pulled by beard Ismael Rivas Falcon (Spain) pulled a train weighing 6,069 lb. (2,753.1 kg) over a distance of 32 ft. 9.6 in. (10 m) using only his beard at the studios of *El Show de los Récords,* Madrid, Spain, on November 15, 2001.

Heaviest vehicle pulled over 100 ft. Kevin Fast (Canada) pulled a truck weighing 55,512 lb. (25,180 kg) over a distance of 100 ft. (30.48 m) along Queen Street, Cobourg, Ontario, Canada, on June 7, 2003.

Heaviest ship pulled by teeth Omar Hanapiev (Russia) pulled the 1,269,861-lb. (576-ton) tanker *Gunib* a distance of 49 ft. 2.4 in. (15 m) using a rope connected only to his teeth, on November 9, 2001 at Makhachkala, Russia.

Heaviest boat pulled David Huxley (Australia) pulled the *Delphin,* weighing in at 2,217,847 lb. (1,006 tons), with a cargo of 175 cars plus passengers over a distance of 23 ft. (7 m) on 19 November 1998 in Rostock, Germany.

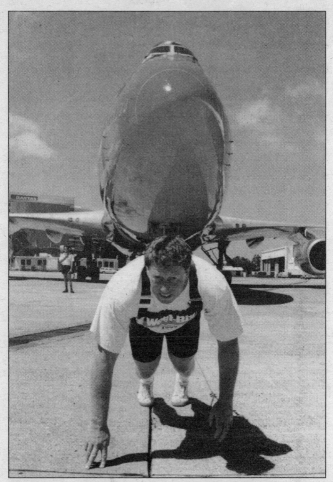

HEAVIEST AIRCRAFT PULLED BY AN INDIVIDUAL David Huxley (Australia) pulled a Boeing 747–400 weighing 412,264 lb. (187 tons) a distance of 298 ft. 6 in. (91 m) in 1 min. 27.7 sec. on October 15, 1997 in Sydney, Australia.

Heaviest truck pulled by arm The heaviest truck pulled with an arm-wrestling move weighed 7,185 lb. 7 oz. (3,259.3 kg). Oscar Olaria Paris and Mariano Macor Stopello (both Spain) set the record on *El Show de los Récords* in Madrid, Spain, on October 4, 2001.

Human Beings

Heaviest human pyramid Tahar Douis (Morocco) supported 12 members of the Hassani Troupe (three levels in height) with a total weight of 1,700 lb. (771 kg) at the BBC television studios, Birmingham, UK, on December 7, 1979.

Heaviest dead lift with the little finger The heaviest dead lift with the little finger is 197 lb. 8 oz. (89.6 kg) by Barry Anderson (UK) on October 14, 2000 at the Bass Museum, Burton-upon-Trent, Staffordshire, UK.

Greatest weight lifted by nipples Sage Werbock (U.S.A.) lifted a total weight of 48 lb. 4.2 oz. (21.9 kg) suspended from his pierced nipples for five seconds at the Tritone Bar in Philadelphia, Pennsylvania, U.S.A., on May 20, 2003.

Greatest weight lifted by teeth Walter Arfeuille (Belgium) lifted weights totaling 620 lb. 10 oz. (281.5 kg) a distance of 6.75 in. (17 cm) off the ground using only his teeth in Paris, France, on March 31, 1990.

Greatest weight balanced on the head The greatest weight ever balanced on the head and held for 10 seconds is 416 lb. (188.7 kg), by John Evans (UK) who lifted 101 bricks at BBC Television Centre, London, UK, on December 24, 1997.

BED OF NAILS CONCRETE BLOCK BREAK Chad Netherland (U.S.A.) had 21 concrete blocks weighing a total of 692 lb. 10.8 oz. (314.21 kg) placed on his chest and then broken with a 16-lb. (7.25-kg) sledgehammer while he lay on a bed of nails at The Great Lakes Aquarium, Duluth, Minnesota, U.S.A., on November 9, 2003.

Most boat lifts Sami Heinonen and Juha Räsänen (both Sweden) continuously lifted a boat and 10 crew with a combined weight of 1,440 lb. (653.2 kg) 4 in. (10 cm) off the ground a total of 24 times on October 9, 2000 on the set of *Guinness World Records,* at Studio Werne, Helsinki, Finland.

Greatest weight of bricks lifted Fred Burton (UK) lifted a horizontal row of 20 bricks, weighing a total of 226 lb. 7 oz. (102.73 kg), and held them at chest height for two seconds on June 5, 1998 at Cheadle, Staffordshire, UK.

Most weight sustained on the body Eduardo Armallo Lasaga (Spain) lay beneath 3,086 lb. (1,399.8 kg) of concrete blocks on the set of *El Show de los Récords,* Madrid, Spain, on October 18, 2001.

Greatest weight lifted by beard The heaviest weight lifted with a human beard is 135 lb. (61.3 kg) when Antanas Kontrimas lifted Ruta Cekyte (both Lithuania) off the ground for 15 seconds on August 18, 2001 at the VIII International Country Festival 2001, Visaginas, Lithuania.

Longest four-finger hang Daniel Dulac (France) was hoisted up to a bar housing two fingerholds (as used in artificial climbing walls). Using just

GREATEST WEIGHT BALANCED ON TEETH Frank Simon (Hungary) lifted a 136-lb. (61.8-kg) motorcycle above his head and balanced it on his teeth for 10 seconds on the set of *El Show de los Récords* in Madrid, Spain, on October 4, 2001. He is pictured here demonstrating his skills with another bike at Red Rock Canyon, Nevada, U.S.A.

Human Beings

two fingers of each hand, he was suspended for 2 min. 18.1 sec. on the set of *L'Émission des Records,* Paris, France, on May 14, 2002.

Fastest time to bend an iron bar and fit it into a suitcase Firas Kichi (Spain) bent an iron bar 19 ft. 7.2 in. (6 m) long and with a diameter of 0.47 in. (12 mm) a total of 16 times to fit it into a suitcase measuring 19.6 × 27.5 × 7.87 in. (50 × 70 × 20 cm), all within 38.61 seconds on the set of *El Show de los Récords,* Madrid, Spain, on December 14, 2001.

Most telephone directories torn in three minutes Mike West (U.S.A.) ripped 30 telephone books, each containing 1,052 pages, from top to bottom, at Eclectics Training Center, New Albany, Indiana, U.S.A., on December 14, 2002.

Longest duration lance lifting Raymond Janin (France) held a lance measuring 9 ft. 2.16 in. (2.8 m) long and weighing 6 lb. 8.53 oz. (3 kg) horizontally at shoulder height for 26 seconds on the set of *L'Été de Tous les Records,* Sete, France, on August 21, 2003.

Most flips of a 25-kg weight in a minute Johnny Lindström (Sweden) flipped over a 55-lb. 1.54-oz. (25-kg) weight with one hand a total of 24 times in a minute on the set of *Guinness World Rekords,* Stockholm, Sweden, on November 24, 2001.

STAYING POWER

Longest banjo marathon Doug Young (U.S.A.) played a banjo for 24 hr. 57 sec. at the Good/Bad Art Collective, Brooklyn, New York City, U.S.A., on May 12–13, 2001.

Longest church organ marathon On June 20–21, 2003, Roelof Hamberg (Netherlands) played a church organ for 32 hours at the Joris Church, St. Jorissant, Venlo, The Netherlands.

Longest drumming marathon Allister Brown (UK) played the drums for 58 hr. 17 min. on September 8–10, 2003 at the Lisburn School of Music, Lisburn, County Antrim, Northern Ireland.

Longest percussion marathon Hermes Arango Saenz (Colombia) played nine different percussion instruments for 40 hours in Medellín, Colombia. The instruments played were: drum kit, kettledrums, congas, bongos, guiro, dominican guiro, cumbiemberan maracas, salsa maracas, and bell. The marathon started at 6 a.m. on August 2, 2001 and finished at 10 p.m. on August 3, 2001.

LONGEST GUITAR MARATHON BY AN INDIVIDUAL Sanjeev Babu
(India, center) played a guitar for 24 hr. 30 min. from August 14 to 15,
2003 at the YMCA Ground, Trivandrum, Kerala, India.

Longest tuba marathon The longest tuba marathon by an individual
lasted for 24 hr. 8 min. and was achieved by Rodney Kenny (UK), on August
16–17, 2002 at The Salvation Army, Gosport, Hampshire, UK.

Longest karaoke marathon featuring multiple participants Organized by Mark Pearson (UK), the karaoke marathon at the Keighley Festival, Keighley, West Yorkshire, UK, featured 85 different acts and continued
for 80 hours from June 14 to 18, 2003.

Longest singing marathon by an individual A.C.E. Anderson
(U.S.A.) sang continuously for 49 hr. 30 min. at Washington County Regional Park, Hurricane, Utah, U.S.A., on June 27–29, 2003.

Longest club DJ marathon Club DJ Martin Boss (U.S.A.) performed a
mixing session that lasted 74 hours at Vinyl Frontier in Orlando, Florida,
U.S.A., from February 1 to 4, 2002.

Longest radio DJ marathon DJ Christoph Stöckli's (Switzerland)
broadcast on Radio Extra Bern, Bern, Switzerland, lasted for 105 hours. He
began his marathon attempt at 6 a.m. on July 24 and finally closed his program at 3 p.m. on July 28, 2002.

Longest joke-telling marathon Working on the basis that a joke must
have a beginning, a middle, and an end, Mike Hessman (U.S.A.) told 12,682
jokes in 24 hours on November 16–17, 1992.

Longest dance party The "Heart Health Hop," a dance party marathon organized by St. Joseph® Aspirin, held at the Rock and Roll Hall of Fame and Museum, Cleveland, Ohio, U.S.A., began on July 29, 2003 with 42 dancers, 41 of whom completed the marathon after 52 hr. 3 min. on July 31, 2003.

Longest ironing marathon Eufemia Stadler (Switzerland) ironed continuously for 40 hours while standing at an ironing board on September 16–18, 1999. She ironed a total of 228 shirts.

Longest rocking chair marathon Garry Hamilton (UK) rocked on a rocking chair continuously from August 24 to 26, 1999 for 21 hours at the Hilton Hotel, Glasgow, UK.

Longest card-playing marathon Gareth Birdsall, Simon MacBeth, Finn Clark, Gad Chadha, Sonia Zakrezewski, Tim West-Meads, Sebastian Kristensen, and David Gold played bridge for 72 hr. 9 min. at St. John's Wood Bridge Club, London, UK, from October 31 to November 3, 2003.

Longest time spent on a bed of nails by a woman Geraldine Williams (UK, aka Miranda, Queen of the Fakirs) lay on a bed of sharp nails 6 in. (15.2 cm) tall and 2 in. (5 cm) apart for 30 hours on May 18–19, 1977.

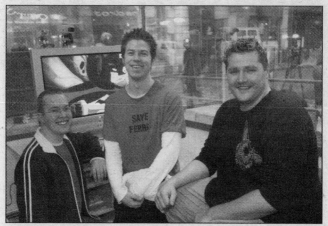

LONGEST TV-WATCHING MARATHON Nick Tungatt, Adam King, Steven Hayes (all UK, pictured from left to right), and Sam Beatson (UK) continually watched television screens for 47 hr. 16 sec. from December 4 to 6, 2002, in an event sponsored by CNX at Covent Garden, London, and at The Printworks, Manchester, UK.

Longest lecture marathon Errol E. T. Muzawazi (Zimbabwe) talked on the subject of democracy for 62 hr. 30 min. from December 12 to 15, 2003 at a student residence at Politechnika Wroclawska, Wroclaw, Poland.

Longest quizmaster marathon Quizmaster Gavin Dare (UK) asked a total of 3,668 questions continuously in 32 hr. 15 min. at The Goff's Oak Public House, Hertfordshire, UK, from October 25 to 26, 2003.

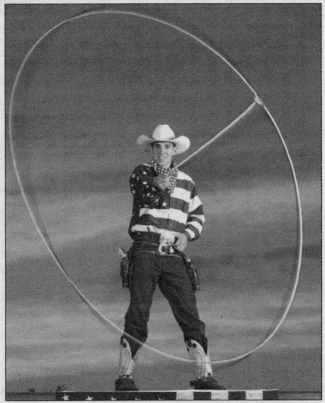

MOST CONSECUTIVE TEXAS SKIPS Andrew Rotz (U.S.A.) achieved 11,123 consecutive Texas skips at the National Convention of the Wild West Arts Club in Las Vegas, Nevada, U.S.A., on March 11, 2003, smashing the previous record set at 4,011. The attempt took 3 hr. 10 min. to complete. A Texas skip is a vertical loop that is repeatedly pulled from one side of the body to the other. With each pass, the roper jumps through the center of the loop.

Farthest pool-rescue marathon The farthest pool-rescue distance is 63,320 ft. (19,300 m) and was completed by the Wong Tai Sin District Life Saving Society at Morse Park Swimming Pool, Kowloon, Hong Kong, China, on August 31, 2002. A total of 386 trained lifesavers towed a mannequin for a distance of 164 ft. (50 m) each for 8 hr. 27 min.

Fastest backward-run marathon Timothy Bud Badyna (U.S.A.) ran a marathon backward in 3 hr. 53 min. 17 sec. in Toledo, Ohio, U.S.A., on April 24, 1994.

Longest parasailing marathon Berne Persoon (Sweden) parasailed for 24 hr. 10 min. on Lake Graningesjön, Sweden, on July 19–20, 2002.

Longest sustained ball control by a female Cláudia Martini (Brazil) juggled a regulation soccer ball for 7 hr. 5 min. 25 sec. nonstop using her feet, legs, and head without the ball ever touching the ground in Caxias do Sul, Brazil, on July 12, 1996.

Longest skiing marathon Christian Flühr (Germany) skied nonstop for 168 hours at Tyrol, Westendorf, Austria, on March 8–15, 2003. During that time he skied a combined distance of 4,101.06 miles (6,600.03 km) and a combined altitude of 2,972,559 ft. (906,036 m).

Longest duration for underwater kissing Antonio de la Rosa Suarez (Spain) was able to stay underwater at the bottom of a water-filled tank for 6 min. 13.49 sec. by being given air through kisses from Nerea Martinez Urruzola and Vanesa de la Rosa Suarez (both Spain), who took it in turns to swim down to him. The attempt was made at the studios of *El Show de los Récords*, Madrid, Spain, on November 22, 2001.

Longest spinning marathon The record for the longest spinning (static bicycling) marathon belongs to Jennifer Johnston (U.S.A.) who bicycled for 73 hr. 13 min. continuously at the National Fitness and Racquet Club, Klamath Falls, Oregon, U.S.A., from November 8 to 11, 2003.

PUSHING THE LIMITS

Highest dry-air temperature endured During U.S. Air Force experiments held in 1960, the highest dry-air temperature endured by heavily clothed volunteers was measured at 500°F (260°C).

During the same tests, the highest dry-air temperature endured by naked volunteers was measured at 400°F (205°C).

Temperatures of 284°F (140°C) in saunas have been found quite bearable.

Longest time to remain standing motionless Om Prakash Singh (India) stood motionless, except for involuntary blinking, for 20 hr. 10 min. 6 sec. on August 13–14, 1997. Om Prakash Singh started his attempt on the

GREATEST ALTITUDE REACHED BY HELIUM-FILLED TOY BALLOONS
Ian Ashpole (UK) achieved the highest flight powered by toy helium balloons, reaching 11,000 ft. (3,350 m) on October 28, 2001 over Chatteris, Cambridgeshire, UK. Owing to the low air pressure at this altitude, some of the 600 balloons (each with a diameter of 3 ft. or 90 cm) burst, forcing him to parachute to safety. Ian is shown here during a non-record-related stunt: he lies in a hammock suspended between hot-air balloons, then free-falls out of the hammock and parachutes to the ground.

HIGHEST BUNGEE JUMP FROM A BUILDING A.J. Hackett (New Zealand) leaped off the Sky Tower Casino, the highest building in Auckland, New Zealand, plunging 590 ft. 10 in. (180.1 m) on October 5, 1998. His fall ended just 40 ft. (12 m) above the concrete sidewalk before he rebounded.

eve of the golden jubilee of India's independence as an homage to unknown martyrs.

Longest time spent balancing on one foot Arulanantham Suresh Joachim (Sri Lanka) balanced on one foot for 76 hr. 40 min. at Uihara Maha Devi Park Open Air Stadium, Sri Lanka, from May 22 to 25, 1997.

Longest time spent balancing on a tightrope Jorge Ojeda-Guzman (U.S.A.) spent 205 days, from January 1 to July 25, 1993, on a wire 36 ft. (11 m) long and 35 ft. (10.7 m) above ground.

During his time on the tightrope, he entertained crowds by walking, dancing, and balancing on a chair.

Farthest distance walked backward The greatest exponent of reverse pedestrianism was Plennie L. Wingo (U.S.A.), who completed his 8,000-mile (12,875-km) transcontinental walk from Santa Monica, California, U.S.A., to Istanbul, Turkey, from April 15, 1931 to October 24, 1932.

Longest fire walk Gérard Moccetti (Switzerland) walked 165 ft. 8 in. (50.5 m) over embers with an average temperature of 1,230°F (665°C) at Scairedo, Barbengo, Ticino, Switzerland, on January 19, 2003.

Longest time to endure full-body ice contact Wearing only a pair of swimming trunks, Wim Hof (Netherlands) was able to stand in a tube filled with ice cubes for 1 hr. 7 min., beating his previous record by 56 seconds at the studios of *Guinness World Records: Die Grössten Weltrekorde* on January 23, 2004.

Longest time spent in a balloon The Fédération Aéronautique Internationale (FAI) endurance record for a gas and hot-air balloon is 19 days 21 hr. 47 min. It was set by Brian Jones (UK) and Bertrand Piccard (Switzerland) from March 1 to 21, 1999, when they flew from Chateau d'Oex, Switzerland, and landed 300 miles (500 km) from Cairo, Egypt.

Greatest height to jump onto an air bag On August 7, 1997, Stig Günther (Denmark) jumped from a height of 342 ft. (104.5 m) off a crane on to an air bag measuring 39 × 49 × 15 ft. (12 × 15 × 4.5 m). His impact speed was about 90 mph (145 km/h).

Longest full-body burn (without oxygen) Stig Günther (Denmark) endured a full-body burn without oxygen supplies for 2 min. 6 sec. in Copenhagen, Denmark, on March 13, 1999.

Highest bungee jump by altitude Curtis Rivers (UK) performed a bungee jump from a hot-air balloon at 15,000 ft. (4,632 m) over Puerto-llano, Spain, on May 5, 2002.

Highest bungee jump from a structure Chris Allum (New Zealand) jumped 823 ft. 6 in. (251 m) from the New River Gorge Bridge, West Virginia, U.S.A., in 1992.

Deepest freshwater cave scuba dive On August 23, 1996, Nuno Gomes (South Africa) scuba-dived to a depth of 927 ft. 2 in. (282.6 m) at the

BLINDFOLD MOTORCYCLE SPEED RECORD Billy Baxter (UK, left) reached a speed of 164.87 mph (265.33 km/h) while riding a 1200-cc Kawasaki Ninja motorcycle blindfolded at RAF Boscombe Down, Wiltshire, UK, on August 2, 2003.

Boesmansgat Cave in the Northern Cape province of South Africa. Essentially a very deep sinkhole, the cave at the surface resembles a small lake with vertical sides.

Deepest seawater scuba dive The deepest scuba dive was one of 1,010 ft. (307.8 m) made by John Bennett (UK) on November 6, 2001 off Escarcia Point, Puerto Galera, The Philippines. The descent, aided by a weighted sled, took just over 12 minutes, while the ascent took 9 hr. 36 min. to allow for decompression.

Highest shallow dive Danny Higginbottom (U.S.A.) dived from 29 ft. 2 in. (8.9 m) into 12 in. (30 cm) of water at the studios of *Guinness World Records: Die Grössten Weltrekorde* on January 23, 2004.

Longest scuba dive in open freshwater Jerry Hall (U.S.A.) spent 71 hr. 39 min. 40 sec. underwater in South Holston Lake, Bristol, Tennessee, U.S.A., using scuba gear from 6 to 9, August 2002.

Longest scuba submergence using one air tank Mick Brown (UK) remained underwater for 7 hr. 15 min. 44 sec., breathing off a single standard 12-liter scuba tank, in a swimming pool at Walton-on-the-Naze, Essex, UK, on 1 February 2003.

Blindfold car speed record Mike Newman (UK) reached 144.755 mph (232.960 km/h) in a Jaguar XJR at Elvington Airfield, North Yorkshire, UK, on August 13, 2003.

Highest speed on a quad bike (ATV) Graham "G-Force" Hicks, a deaf-blind daredevil from Peterborough, Cambridgeshire, UK, reached 104.02 mph (167.4 km/h) on a quad bike, or ATV (all-terrain vehicle), at Bruntingthorpe Proving Ground, Leicestershire, UK, on June 22, 2002. He received instructions from his passenger Rob Hall, who told him where to steer via a system of touch-based commands.

Longest time spent on "Wall of Death" Martin Blume (Germany) spent 7 hr. 13 sec. on a "Wall of Death" in Berlin, Germany, on April 16, 1983. He rode a Yamaha XS 400 over 12,000 laps on a wall with a diameter of 33 ft. (10 m), averaging 30 mph (48 km/h) over 181.5 miles (292 km).

Longest time to keep an aircraft airborne Robert Timm and John Cooke (both U.S.A.) kept their Cessna 172 Hacienda aloft for 64 days 22 hr. 19 min. 5 sec., from December 4, 1958 to February 7, 1959. They took off from McCarran Airfield, Las Vegas, Nevada, U.S.A., and landed at the same place after covering a distance equivalent to six times around the world, with refueling taking place in the air.

Greatest distance flown in a wing suit Sky diver Adrian Nicholas (UK) flew 10 miles (16 km) in a wing suit over Yolo County, California,

U.S.A., on March 12, 1999. He exited the plane at 33,850 ft. (10,317 m) and reached speeds of approximately 150 mph (241 km/h). He "flew" for 4 min. 55 sec. and only opened his parachute 500 ft. (152 m) from the ground.

AGAINST THE ODDS

Lowest body temperature survived The lowest authenticated body temperature is 57.5°F (14.2°C), the rectal temperature for Karlee Kosolofski (Canada), then aged two, on February 23, 1994. She had accidentally been locked outside her home for six hours in a temperature of -8°F (-22°C). Despite severe frostbite, which meant the amputation of her left leg above the knee, she made a full recovery.

MOST DEATHS ON MOUNT EVEREST IN ONE DAY On May 10, 1996, a blizzard with winds of up to 90 mph (145 km/h) and temperatures of -40°F (-40°C) claimed the lives of eight climbers on Mount Everest—the most in one day. Dr. Seaborn "Beck" Weathers (U.S.A.) was trapped on the South Col of Mount Everest for 16 hours. He lost his right hand, part of his left hand, and his nose owing to frostbite.

Most operations endured From July 22, 1954 to the end of 1994, Charles Jensen (U.S.A.) had 970 operations to remove tumors associated with basal cell nevus syndrome.

Longest underwater submergence survival In 1986, two-year-old Michelle Funk (U.S.A.) made a full recovery after spending 66 minutes underwater in a swollen creek.

Deepest underwater escape with no equipment The greatest depth from which an underwater escape has been made without any equipment is 225 ft. (68.6 m) by Richard A. Slater from the rammed submersible *Nekton Beta* off Catalina Island, California, U.S.A., on September 28, 1970.

Longest time trapped in an elevator At the age of 76, Kively Papajohn (Cyprus) was trapped in her apartment block elevator for six days from December 28, 1987 to January 2, 1988. She survived the cold and beat dehydration by rationing out some fruit, vegetables, and bread that she had in her shopping bag.

Longest fall survived in an elevator Betty Lou Oliver (U.S.A.) survived a plunge of 75 stories (over 1,000 ft. or 300 m) in an elevator in the Empire State Building in New York City, U.S.A., on July 28, 1945, after an American B-25 bomber crashed into the building in thick fog, severing all the elevator's cables.

Highest fall survived down an elevator shaft Stuart Jones (New Zealand) fell 23 stories (229 ft. 7 in. or 70 m) down an elevator shaft while carrying out structural work on the roof of a temporary elevator compartment at the Midland Park Building, Wellington, New Zealand, in May 1998. He suffered multiple injuries, including a broken hip, broken left kneecap, open fracture in his left lower leg, and broken rib.

Longest time adrift at sea The longest known time that anyone has survived adrift at sea is approximately 484 days, by the Japanese Captain Oguri Jukichi and one of his sailors, Otokichi. Their ship was damaged in a storm off the Japanese coast in October 1813 and they drifted in the Pacific before being rescued by an American ship off California, U.S.A., on March 24, 1815.

Longest time adrift at sea alone The longest recorded survival alone on a raft is 133 days by Second Steward Poon Lim (Hong Kong) of the UK Merchant Navy, whose ship, the SS *Ben Lomond,* was torpedoed in the Atlantic 565 miles (910 km) west of St. Paul's Rocks at 11:45 am on November 23, 1942.

He was finally picked up by a Brazilian fishing boat off Salinópolis, Brazil, on April 5, 1943 and was able to walk ashore.

Longest survival without food and water The longest recorded case of survival without food and water is 18 days by Andreas Mihavecz (Austria), then aged 18. He was put into a holding cell on April 1, 1979 in a local government building in Höchst, Austria, but totally forgotten by the police. On April 18, 1979, he was discovered close to death.

Longest survival with heart outside body Christopher Wall (U.S.A., b. August 19, 1975) is the longest known survivor of the condition ectopia cordis, in which the heart lies outside the body at birth. The mortality rate is high, with most patients not living beyond 48 hours, but Wall still lives with the condition.

Longest time survived without a pulse The longest time a human has survived without a pulse in their vascular system is three days. Julie Mills (UK) was at the point of death from severe heart failure and viral myocarditis when, on August 14, 1998, cardiac surgeons at the John Radcliffe Hospital, Oxford, UK, used a nonpulsatile blood pump (AB180) to support her for one week. Her heart recovered in this time and the pump was removed.

Greatest ever lifesaving operation at sea The greatest ever rescue at sea was that of 2,735 people from the American aircraft carrier *CV-2* USS *Lexington* on May 8, 1942 after it had been sunk between Australia and New Caledonia in the Battle of the Coral Sea.

Greatest rescue at sea without loss of life All 2,689 people on board the American vessel *Susan B. Anthony* survived when it was sunk off Normandy, France, on June 7, 1944.

HIGHEST FALL SURVIVED WITHOUT A PARACHUTE Vesna Vulovic (Yugoslavia) was 23 and working as a Jugoslavenski Aerotransport hostess when the DC-9 she was working aboard blew up on January 26, 1972. Vulovic survived a fall inside a section of tail unit from 33,333 ft. (10,160 m) over Srbsk, Kamenice, Czechoslovakia (now Czech Republic), despite breaking many bones. She was in a coma for 27 days and remained in the hospital for 16 months. On the left is one of her rescuers, Zdenko Kubik.

LONGEST POST-EARTHQUAKE SURVIVAL BY A CAT On September 21, 1999, an earthquake struck Taiwan, killing an estimated 2,400 people. Eighty days later in December 1999, a cat was discovered alive in Taichung after being trapped by a message board that had fallen during the quake, pinning it to the ground in the rubble of a collapsed building. The cat, dehydrated and barely breathing, weighed less than half the weight of a healthy cat of its size. It was rushed to a veterinary hospital where it made a full recovery.

Largest object removed from human skull The largest object removed from a human skull is an 8-in. (20-cm) survival knife with a serrated blade, which was plunged into the head of 41-year-old Michael Hill (U.S.A.) on April 25, 1998. Michael survived the operation and the next day astonished doctors by being able to speak and function normally, although the years to come proved that the knife had permanently damaged his memory and paralyzed his left hand.

Most hangings survived There is a tie for this record. The survivor of the most legal hanging attempts is Joseph Samuel (Australia), a 22-year-old who was sentenced to death for murder in Sydney, Australia. On September 26, 1803, the first attempt at execution failed when the rope broke. The second attempt failed when the rope stretched so much that the victim's feet touched the ground. At the third attempt, the second replacement rope broke, after which Samuel was reprieved.

In Exeter, Devon, UK, in 1885, John Lee (UK) also survived three attempted hangings. On each occasion that his hanging was due to take place, the trapdoor failed to open.

Longest surviving headless chicken On September 10, 1945, a Wyandotte chicken named Mike had its head chopped off but went on to survive for 18 months. Mike's owner, Lloyd Olsen (U.S.A.), fed and watered the headless chicken directly into his gullet with an eyedropper. Mike eventually choked to death on a corn kernel in an Arizona motel.

Longest survival of a sheep in a snowdrift On March 24, 1978, Alex Maclennan (UK) found one ewe still alive after he had dug out 16 dead sheep buried in a snowdrift for 50 days near the River Skinsdale on Mrs. Tyser's Gordonbush Estate in Sutherland, Highland, UK, after the great January blizzard in that year. The sheep's hot breath had created airholes in the snow, and the animal had gnawed its own wool for protein.

EPIC JOURNEYS

GWR TALKS TO Sir Ranulph Fiennes

Explorer Sir Ranulph Fiennes (UK, pictured) currently holds four Guinness World Records: the first pole-to-pole circumnavigation, the longest self-supporting trek (1,350 miles or 2,170 km during a 94-day trek with fellow Briton Michael Stroud), which was also the longest unsupported Antarctic trek, and the fastest Antarctic crossing. The last record comprised the 2,600-mile (4,185-km) transantarctic leg of the 1980–82 Trans-Globe Expedition from Sanae to Scott Base, and was achieved in 55 days, from October 28, 1980 to January 11, 1981. The expedition reached the South Pole on December 15, 1980. For this record-breaking attempt, Sir Ranulph was accompanied by Oliver Shepard and Charles Burton (both UK).

How did you come to be an explorer? I spent eight years in the army and led a number of adventure training journeys. When I left the army in 1970 I extended these activities to make a career out of expedition organizing and leading: the expeditions became a way of life.

What drives you to take on these great challenges? To keep at "the top of the tree" internationally in expedition work it was, through the 70s, 80s, and 90s, necessary to attempt the biggest available geographical challenges and succeed, where possible, before my rivals.

What do you consider to be your greatest achievement to date? If pressed to name which of the expeditions over a 32-year period I am most proud of, I would find it very difficult to be specific. I'd say it was the discovery of the lost city of Ubar. It took me a period of 26 years on and off, and some seven separate expeditions between 1968 and 1991, before I finally discovered the site in the oasis of Shis'r in Dhofar, Oman.

What other challenges do you wish to take on in the future? There are various challenges in the pipeline but the rule of our expedition group is to discuss them as little as possible to avoid others getting there first.

How do you prepare for some of these expeditions/challenges? Our group has usually prepared for expeditions with meticulous care and by choosing the best available team, equipment, and advisors. This includes physical fitness and nutrition experts. Fitness regimes and special diets alter according to the nature of each challenge.

What does it mean to you to have a Guinness World Record? Many sponsors, without whom our projects would be impossible, respect the internationally accepted judgment of Guinness World Records as to what does or does not constitute a world record. Also the ability to cite Guinness World Records we've previously achieved always helps when requesting sponsorship.

What advice would you offer anyone seeking a similar career? I usually recommend joining the Royal Geographical Society and taking advantage of its unique Expedition Advisory Centre, the nerve center of 90% of all ongoing UK expedition work.

Who inspired you as a child? As a child in South Africa, I was inspired by stories about my father (killed in World War II, four months before I was born) and about his father, both of whom led adventurous lives in often remote regions. Later on I was inspired by the desert travels of Wilfred Thesiger and the polar travels of Wally Herbert.

Longest lifeboat journey When his ship, the *Endurance,* became trapped in Antarctic sea-ice, Sir Ernest Shackleton (UK) and his 28-strong crew had to abandon her. Their three lifeboats set course for Elephant Island, 100 miles (161 km) to the north. Once there, and knowing that rescue was unlikely, Shackleton selected five of his best men to sail the largest lifeboat, the 22-ft. 6-in.-long (6.85-m) *James Caird,* towards a whaling station in South Georgia, 800 miles (1,287 km) away. In a journey that is still regarded as one of the greatest rescue journeys of all time, Sir Ernest and his men reached the island after 17 days, on May 19, 1916.

Longest nonstop ocean voyage by raft During the Raft Transpacific Expedition, the raft *Nord,* captained by Andrew Urbanczyk (U.S.A.), sailed from Half Moon Bay, California, U.S.A., to the U.S.-owned Pacific island of

LONGEST MOTORCYCLE RIDE BY A TEAM Chris and Erin Ratay (both U.S.A.) covered 101,322 miles (163,061 km) on separate motorcycles on a journey that covered 50 countries on six continents. They departed from Morocco on May 21, 1999 and returned home to New York City, U.S.A., on August 6, 2003.

Guam, a straight-line distance of 5,110 nautical miles (5,880 miles or 9,463 km), in 136 days from August 26, 2002 to January 28, 2003.

Fastest circumnavigation by a crewed sailing vessel Millionaire adventurer Steve Fossett (U.S.A.) and a crew of 13 sailed around the world nonstop in 58 days 9 hr. 32 min. aboard the 125-ft. (38-m) catamaran *Cheyenne,* from February 7 to April 5, 2004. The voyage started and finished at Le Stiff Lighthouse, Ushant, France.

Longest motorcycle ride Emilio Scotto (Argentina) covered over 457,000 miles (735,000 km) through 214 countries and territories on a motorcycle from January 17, 1985 to April 2, 1995.

Fastest solo unsupported trek to the South Pole Fiona Thornewill (UK) walked and skied her way to the South Pole from Hercules Inlet at the edge of the Antarctic continent in 42 days from November 30, 2003 to January 10, 2004. She was pulling a 285-lb. (130-kg) sled containing all her supplies and equipment, yet still managed to cover up to 22 miles (35 km) per day.

Most sovereign countries visited in six months John Bougen and James Irving (both New Zealand) visited 191 of the world's 193 sovereign countries in 167 days 15 hr. 39 min. from August 28, 2002 to February 12, 2003. Their journey, called the All Nations Quest, was in support of the Save the Children charity.

FASTEST CIRCUMNAVIGATION BY MALE SAILING SOLO Francis Joyon (France) carried out a solo nonstop circumnavigation in the 88-ft. 6-in. (27-m) trimaran *IDEC* in a time of 72 days 22 hr. 54 min. 22 sec., from November 22, 2003 to February 3, 2004.

Fastest time to travel the Pan-American Highway by bicycle
Giampietro Marion (Italy) bicycled the Pan-American Highway, from Prudhoe Bay, Alaska, to Ushuaia, Argentina, in 140 days 6 hr., from June 28, 2000 to November 15, 2000.

FASTEST TIME TO VISIT ALL NFL STADIUMS Peter Baroody (U.S.A.) watched a complete National Football League (NFL) game at all 31 NFL stadiums in the U.S.A. in just 107 days, from September 5 to December 22, 2002. He began in New York City and finished in Kansas City.

Fastest circumnavigation by car The record for the fastest circumnavigation by car (under the rules applicable in 1989 and 1991) embracing more than an equator's length of driving (24,901 road miles or 40,750 km) was by Mohammed and Neena Choudhury (India). The journey took 69 days 19 hr. 5 min. from September 9 to November 17, 1989.

Greatest distance covered in 24 hours by wheelchair Rafael Emilio de León Lebrón (Dominican Republic) wheeled himself over 112.5 miles (181.147 km) in 24 hours on December 13–14, 2001 at the Juan Pablo Duarte Centro Olímpico, Santo Domingo de Guzmán, Dominican Republic.

Longest journey by wheelchair Rick Hansen, paralyzed from the waist down in 1973 as a result of a motor accident, wheeled his wheelchair 24,901.55 miles (40,075.16 km) through four continents and 34 countries. He started his journey from Vancouver, British Columbia, Canada, on March 21, 1985 and arrived back there on May 22, 1987.

NATURAL WORLD

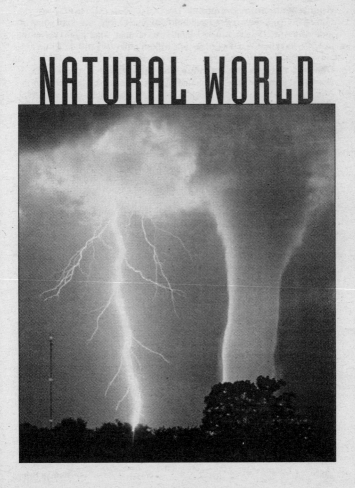

THE UNIVERSE

Brightest nebula The Orion Nebula (M42 or Messier 42—i.e. number 42 in Charles Messier's 1781 catalog of nebulous objects) is the brightest nebula in the sky with an apparent magnitude of 4. Located in the "sword" of the constellation Orion, only the brightest central part of this vast, diffuse cloud of gas and dust is easily visible to the naked eye.

Brightest supernova remnant The Crab Nebula (M1) in the constellation of Taurus is the brightest supernova remnant in the sky, with a magnitude of 8.4. It is around 6,300 light-years distant. One light-year is the distance light travels in a year, about 6 trillion miles (9.5 trillion km).

Deepest note in the universe The deepest note in the universe is caused by acoustic waves generated by a supermassive black hole in the center of the Perseus cluster of galaxies, 250 million light-years away. The sound, which propagates through the extremely thin gas surrounding the black hole, is a B-flat, 57 octaves below middle C. This is more than a million billion times lower than a human ear can detect. The sound waves are

NEAREST EXTRASOLAR PLANET On August 7, 2000, a team led by Dr. William Cochran (U.S.A.) of the University of Texas McDonald Observatory announced its discovery of the nearest planet outside the Solar System. The planet, which is probably slightly larger than Jupiter, orbits the star Epsilon Eridani (an artist's impression of the planet is shown here). This star, only 10.5 light-years away, is one of the closest stars to the Sun.

estimated to have been consistently produced by the black hole for around 2.5 billion years. They were discovered using observations by the Chandra X-Ray Observatory, by astronomers led by Professor Andrew Fabian, Cambridge University, Cambridge, UK.

Biggest globular cluster in the Milky Way Omega Centauri, in the constellation of Centaurus, is the most massive of the roughly 140 globular clusters surrounding our galaxy. Consisting of several million stars whose combined mass equates to five million Suns, it is just visible to the naked eye. It is about 10 times more massive than the other large globular clusters and some astronomers have suggested that it is the remnants of the nucleus of another galaxy which merged with ours billions of years ago.

Coldest place in the Milky Way The Boomerang Nebula, a cloud of dust and gases 5,000 light-years from Earth, has a temperature of -457.6°F (-272°C). It is formed by the rapid expansion of gas and dust flowing from its central star.

Nearest globular cluster The nearest globular cluster to the Earth is M4. It is located in the constellation of Scorpius at a distance of around 5,600 light-years and is visible through binoculars and small telescopes as a fuzzy smudge.

Most distant object in the universe Astronomers from Caltech (U.S.A.), using the Hubble Space Telescope and the Keck Observatory, have discovered a small and compact system of stars about 2,000 light-years across, with a redshift of 7. This corresponds to a distance of about 13 billion light-years away. These results were announced in February 2004.

Most distant planet with an atmosphere On November 27, 2001, astronomers using the Hubble Space Telescope announced the discovery of an atmosphere on a planet orbiting another star. This unnamed planet orbits the star HD209458, 150 light-years away. It was discovered in 1999 thanks to the wobble its gravity inflicts upon HD209458 as it orbits it.

Most massive extrasolar planet Announced in January 2001, the discovery of the planet HD168443 orbiting a star 123 light-years away challenges conventional definitions of planets. Jupiter, the largest planet in our Solar System, weighs more than all the other planets and moons combined. But HD168443 is 17 times more massive even than Jupiter.

Most massive star visible to the naked eye Eta Carinae is a rare supergiant some 9,000 light-years from Earth. With a mass estimated at between 100 and 200 times that of the Sun, it is one of the most massive stars in the galaxy. It is just visible to the naked eye with a magnitude of 6.21.

Oldest planet in the Milky Way The oldest planet discovered so far in our galaxy is an extrasolar planet in the globular cluster M4, some 5,600 light-years from Earth. With an estimated age of at least 10 billion years, this distant planet is more than twice as old as our Solar System. Its discovery was announced in July 2003.

Oldest star in the Milky Way The oldest star identified to date in the Milky Way galaxy is HE0107–5240, a giant star around 36,000 light-years from Earth. Its age is measured by its composition: when the universe formed, it consisted of hydrogen with some helium. As it evolved, the rest of the chemical elements appeared, formed by nuclear synthesis in stars. HE0107–5240 has almost no metal content in it, meaning it must have formed from clouds of gas consisting of almost pure hydrogen and helium when the universe was young. It could date back to the very beginning of the universe.

Most luminous star in the galaxy The latest observations of LBV1806–20, a star 45,000 light-years from Earth, indicate it is between five and 40 million times more luminous than the Sun. It has a mass of at least 150 times that of the Sun and has a diameter at least 200 times greater.

Farthest object visible to the naked eye The most remote heavenly body visible to the naked eye is the Andromeda Galaxy in the constellation of Andromeda (M31, magnitude 3.47), a spiral galaxy 2.2 million light-

FLATTEST STAR The least spherical star in our galaxy studied to date is the southern star Achenar (Alpha Eridani). Observations made from September 11 to November 12, 2002 using the Very Large Telescope (VLT) Interferometer at the European Southern Observatory's Paranal Observatory, in Atacama, Chile, have revealed that Achenar is spinning so rapidly that its equatorial diameter is more than 50% greater than its polar diameter. The results were released on June 11, 2003.

GREATEST EXPLOSION EVER Most astronomers now believe that the universe began around 13.7 billion years ago in a cataclysmic explosion called the Big Bang (shown here in an artist's impression). All the matter and energy in the universe had its origins in this event, along with time itself. One second after the Big Bang, the temperature was around ten billion degrees, or about six hundred times hotter than the interior of the Sun.

years away. Under good observation conditions the spiral galaxy in Triangulum (M33, magnitude 5.79) can be seen by the naked eye at a distance of 2.53 million light-years.

Largest galaxy The central galaxy of the Abell 2029 galaxy cluster, 1.070 billion light-years distant in Virgo, has a major diameter of 5.6 million light-years—80 times the diameter of our own Milky Way galaxy—and a light output equivalent to two trillion (2×10^{12}) Suns.

Closest planet to a star A Jupiter-sized gas giant orbits the star OGLE-TR-3. This "hot Jupiter" orbits just 2.1 million miles (3.5 million km) from its parent star and has an orbital period of just 28 hr. 33 min. OGLE-TR-3 is a G-type star (similar to the Sun) some 4,900 light-years away. The planet was discovered using the Optical Gravitational Lensing Experiment, and announced in April 2003.

THE SOLAR SYSTEM

Fastest winds in the Solar System The planet Neptune has the fastest winds anywhere in the Solar System. Measured by NASA's *Voyager 2* probe in 1989, they blow at around 1,500 mph (2,400 km/h).

Most distant object in the Solar System The minor planet 1999DG8 was discovered by a team of astronomers led by Brett Gladman (Canada) from the Canadian Institute of Theoretical Physics, using the 11.81-ft. (3.6-m) Canada-France-Hawaii Telescope (U.S.A.) in February 1999. With a diameter of around 62 miles (100 km), this icy body was around 5.6 billion miles (9 billion km) from the Sun when it was observed on two different nights. Because its orbit has yet to be properly calculated, 1999DG8 could follow a path which takes it closer to or further from the Sun.

Hottest place in the Solar System Although never visited by man, the very center of the Sun is the hottest place in the Solar System. The latest estimates of the temperature are 15.6 billion°C (60 billion°F). The pressure in the core is also immense, around 250 billion times the pressure at sea level on Earth. It is here that around 600 million tons of hydrogen are fused into helium every second. This ongoing nuclear reaction is what makes the Sun shine.

LARGEST CYCLONE IN THE SOLAR SYSTEM The Great Red Spot on the planet Jupiter is the largest cyclone in the Solar System. It varies in size but can be up to 24,800 miles (40,000 km) long and 8,700 miles (14,000 km) wide.

LARGEST RECORDED SOLAR FLARE On November 4, 2003, the Sun
unleashed a solar flare rated as an X28 event by the Space Environment
Center of the National Oceanic and Atmospheric Administration (NOAA)
in Boulder, Colorado, U.S.A. Considered a major event, X-class flares
are the most powerful and can cause planet-wide radio disruption.
Images of solar flares (shown) and other phenomena are captured daily
by the Extreme ultraviolet Imaging Telescope (EIT) on board the SOHO
spacecraft.

HIGHEST MOUNTAIN IN THE SOLAR SYSTEM The peak of Olympus Mons (shown) on Mars rises 15 miles (25 km) above its base—nearly three times the height of Mt. Everest. Despite its great height, Olympus Mons has a very gentle slope and is therefore designated a shield volcano: it is over 20 times wider than it is high.

Closest moon to a planet Of all the moons in the Solar System, the one that orbits closest to its planet is the tiny Martian satellite Phobos. Phobos is 5,827 miles (9,378 km) from the center of Mars, which is 3,716 miles (5,981 km) above the Martian surface. Using the surface-to-surface measurement, Phobos is roughly 60 times closer to Mars than the Moon is to Earth.

Largest corona Coronae (roughly circular features surrounded by multiple concentric ridges) are so far unique to the planet Venus. They were discovered by the U.S. *Magellan* spacecraft, which orbited the planet for just over four years from August 10, 1990 to October 11, 1994. The largest is Artemis Corona, which has a diameter of 1,300 miles (2,100 km). Planetary scientists are in disagreement as to the origin of coronae, but it seems likely that they are the result of hot magma welling up from the Venusian mantle.

Largest canyon in the Solar System The Valles Marineris canyon on the planet Mars has an overall length of around 4,500 km (2,800 miles). At its widest it is 600 km (370 miles) across and is also up to 7 km (4.3 miles) deep. It is named after the *Mariner 9* spacecraft, which discovered it in 1971.

Satellite with the thickest atmosphere Saturn's large moon Titan has the thickest atmosphere of any moon in the Solar System, and exerts a surface pressure of 1.44 bar. Consisting mainly of nitrogen gas, Titan's atmosphere is the most similar to our own in the Solar System.

Largest observed coma The coma (the cloud around the nucleus in the head of a comet) on a comet seen in 1811 was thought to be around 1.2 million miles (2 million km) in diameter.

Highest volcanic eruption On August 6, 2001, NASA's *Galileo* spacecraft performed a close flyby of Jupiter's volcanically active satellite, Io. Over the following months, as the data was transmitted back to Earth, scientists realised that the spacecraft had passed through the top of a 310-mile (500-km) high volcanic plume. This is the highest volcanic eruption plume ever witnessed in the Solar System.

Most distant moon from a planet Announced by the International Astronomical Union on September 3, 2003, S/2003 N1 orbits Neptune at an average distance of approximately 31 million miles (49.5 million km). It has an orbital period of approximately 26 years and measures around 24 miles (38 km) across.

MOST VOLCANICALLY ACTIVE BODY Photographs of Jupiter's moon Io (pictured), taken from the *Galileo* spacecraft, revealed enormous volcanic eruption plumes reaching hundreds of miles into space. Io's activity is driven by tidal energy—the result of gravitational interactions between Jupiter, Io, and one of the other moons, Europa. Io is so active that it has turned itself inside out during its lifetime.

Fastest planet Mercury, which orbits the Sun at an average distance of 35.9 million miles (57.9 million km), has an orbital period of 87.9686 days, thus giving the highest average speed in orbit of 107,030 mph (172,248 km/h). This is almost twice as fast as the Earth.

Largest planet Jupiter has an equatorial diameter of 89,405 miles (143,884 km) and a polar diameter of 83,082 miles (133,708 km). It has a mass 317.828 times—and a volume 1,323.3 times—that of the Earth.

Smallest planet The discovery of Pluto by Clyde William Tombaugh (U.S.A.) of the Lowell Observatory, Flagstaff, Arizona, U.S.A., was announced on March 13, 1930. The planet has a diameter of 1,444 miles (2,324 km) and a mass 0.0022 that of the Earth.

Largest moon compared to its planet Charon, the only known satellite of Pluto, has a diameter of 790 miles (1,270 km). Pluto itself is only 1,444 miles (2,324 km) across. The Pluto-Charon System is regarded by some as a "double planet."

Hottest planet Venus has an average temperature of around 896°F (480°C). This scorching heat is hot enough to melt lead and, coupled with the atrocious atmosphere, makes exploration of the surface by probes very difficult. If you were to step onto the surface of Venus you would be simultaneously crushed by the pressure, incinerated by the heat, dissolved by the sulfuric acid, and suffocated by the carbon dioxide.

Planet with the longest day While the Earth takes 23 hr. 56 min. 4 sec. to complete one rotation, Venus takes 243.16 "Earth days" to spin once through 360°. As Venus is closer to the Sun, its year is shorter than Earth's, lasting only 224.7 days, so a day on Venus is actually longer than its year. Another Venusian curiosity is that it rotates backwards compared with all of the other major planets (apart from Uranus, which spins on its side).

Planet with the shortest day Jupiter spins around on its axis once every 9 hr. 55 min. 29.69 sec.

Most powerful aurorae in the Solar System The aurorae on Jupiter are around 1,000 times more powerful than the aurorae seen on Earth. Jupiter's aurorae are caused by energetic particles from the Sun being channeled onto the planet's poles by Jupiter's magnetic field and causing atoms in its upper atmosphere to glow like the gas in a neon tube. This process produces around a million megawatts of energy, enough to power 100 major cities on Earth.

CLIMATE & WEATHER

GWR TALKS TO Professor Joshua Wurman

Professor Joshua Wurman (U.S.A.), a professional "storm chaser," runs the Center for Severe Weather Research in Boulder, Colorado, U.S.A. He operated the University of Oklahoma's "Doppler on Wheels" mobile weather observatory when it measured the highest winds ever, during the Bridgecreek/Moore/Oklahoma City tornado that caused F5 damage and nearly 40 deaths. The wind speed on this occasion was between 281 and 321 mph (452–516 km/h).

How long have you been a storm chaser? Professionally, since 1995; for recreation, since 1992.

What was it that inspired you to do this as a career? Interest in nature combined with the excitement of a young science that had big questions to be answered.

How close do you get to tornadoes? We have been hit by weak tornadoes, but we usually stay 1–3 miles (1.6–4.4 km) away from the centers.

What is your favorite part of the job? Discovering new things. Observational scientists like myself are the inheritors of the tradition of exploration. In

MOST POWERFUL SHORT-TERM NATURAL CLIMATE CHANGE The El Niño Southern Oscillation occurs as a result of cyclic warming of the eastern and central Pacific Ocean. Apart from the seasonal effects of the Earth moving around the Sun, it is the most powerful short-term natural climate change on Earth. The entire cycle of El Niño and La Niña (its cooler counterpart and opposite) lasts between three and seven years. It causes unusual weather conditions all around the world, particularly notable in the 1982/83 and 1997/98 events.

the future we may explore space further. But for now, the reachable unknowns are inside tornadoes and hurricanes, and in deep sea trenches, et cetera.

What has been the scariest moment in your career? It sounds boring, but we actually are very, very safe. We are constantly tracking the course of the tornado and plotting escape routes if necessary.

What does it mean to you to have a Guinness World Record? Since I was a very small child, I read the Guinness book every year and memorized a lot of it. As an adult, to finally have a record in the book is great.

What advice would you give to anyone following in your footsteps? Stay curious . . . and be very determined.

Greatest depth of snow In March 1911, the snow on the ground at Tamarac, California, U.S.A., was recorded as 37 ft. 7 in. (11.46 m) deep.

Most destructive geomagnetic storm The most destructive geomagnetic storm ever recorded was the "Great Geomagnetic Storm" of March 13, 1989, which was classified G5 (the most severe) on the space weather scale. The result of an abnormally strong solar wind, it caused major disruption to the power grid all over North America and changed the orbit of a satellite. The solar wind is a stream of particles radiating from the Sun into the Solar System, and it is this phenomenon that is responsible for the northern and southern lights (aurora borealis, aurora australis).

Lowest temperature in an inhabited area The coldest permanently inhabited place in the world is the Siberian village of Oymyakon (pop. 4,000), 63°16′N, 143°15′E (2,300 ft.), in Russia, where the temperature reached -68°C (-90°F) in 1933. An unofficial -72°C (-98°F) has been published more recently.

Lowest temperature on Earth A low of -128.6°F (-89.2°C) was registered at Vostok, Antarctica (altitude 11,220 ft.), on July 21, 1983.

Clouds with the greatest vertical range The cloud form with the greatest vertical range is cumulonimbus, which has been observed to reach a height of nearly 65,600 ft. (20,000 m) in the tropics—that's nearly three times the height of Mt. Everest.

GREATEST SNOWFALL IN 12 MONTHS Over a 12-month period from February 19, 1971, to February 18, 1972, 102 ft. 0.5 in. (31,102 mm) of snow fell at Paradise, Mt. Rainier, Washington, U.S.A.

Longest lightning flash At any time, around 100 lightning bolts per second hit the Earth. Typically, the actual length of these bolts can be around 5.5 miles (9 km). In 1956 meteorologist Myron Ligda (U.S.A.) observed and recorded a lightning flash, using radar, that covered a horizontal distance of 93 miles (149 km) inside clouds.

Greatest pressure drop measured in a tornado The greatest pressure drop ever measured inside a tornado was 100 millibars. It was recorded by severe storms researcher Tim Samaras (U.S.A.), who was able to successfully place an instrument probe in the path of an F4 tornado, near Manchester, South Dakota, U.S.A., on June 24, 2003.

Driest place For the period between 1964 and 2001, the average annual rainfall for the meteorological station in Quillagua, located in the Atacama Desert, Chile, was just 0.02 in. (0.5 mm). This fascinating discovery was made during the making of the documentary series *Going to Extremes,* by Keo Films in 2001.

Largest hole in the ozone layer Scientists at NASA's Goddard Space Flight Center, Maryland, U.S.A., detected the largest hole so far seen in the ozone layer in September 2000. With an area of around 11 million miles^2

MOST TORNADOES IN 24 HOURS The record number of tornadoes in a 24-hour period is 148. They swept through the southern and midwestern states of the U.S.A. on April 3–4, 1974. This region of America is often referred to as "Tornado Alley."

(28.3 million km²), this hole above Antarctica is roughly three times the area of the U.S.A. The ozone layer in the stratosphere (about 7–28 miles above the ground) shields the Earth's surface from the Sun's damaging ultraviolet (UV-B) rays.

Greatest display of solar halos On January 11, 1999, at least 24 types of solar halos were witnessed by scientists at the geographic South Pole. Solar halos are formed by sunlight being reflected and refracted by ice crystals in the atmosphere, causing rings around the Sun. Atmospheric conditions at the South Pole are conducive to this type of phenomenon.

Oldest fossilized raindrops On December 15, 2001, Indian geologist Chirananda De announced his discovery of the fossilized imprints of raindrops in ancient rocks in the lower Vindhya Range, Madhya Pradesh, India. These fossils prove that rain fell on Earth at least 1.6 billion years ago.

Greatest annual rainfall By average annual rainfall, the world's wettest place is Mawsynram, Meghalaya, India, with 4,678 in. (11,873 mm) of rain per annum.

THE EARTH

Coolest erupting lava The natrocarbonatite lava of the volcano Oldoinyo Lengai, Tanzania, erupts at temperatures of 930–1,110°F (500–600°C). Common basaltic lavas erupt at temperatures between 2,010 and 2,190°F (1,100 and 1,200°C).

Tallest sea stack Ball's Pyramid near Lord Howe Island (Australia) in the Pacific-Ocean is 1,843 ft. (561 m) high but has a base axis of only 660 ft. (200 m).

Largest active volcano Mauna Loa, Hawaii, U.S.A., is the largest active volcano. It has the shape of a broad gentle dome 75 miles (120 km) long and 31 miles (50 km) wide (above sea level), with lava flows that occupy more than 1,980 miles² (5,125 km²) of the island. It has a total volume of 10,200 miles³ (42,500 km³), of which 84.2% is below sea level.

HIGHEST NATURAL ARCH The red sandstone Rainbow Bridge on Lake Powell National Monument, Utah, U.S.A., is the highest natural arch in the world. It is only 270 ft. (82.3 m) long, but is a massive feature, rising to a height of 290 ft. (88.4 m). The Rainbow Bridge was formed when an ancient stream eroded away some of the weaker sedimentary rock in the area, leaving the natural bridge behind.

Largest geode A geode is a rock cavity filled with minerals—most are small enough to fit in the palm of a human hand. The largest geode discovered to date is near Almería, Spain. It forms a mineral-lined cave 26 ft. (8 m) long, 6 ft. (2 m) wide and 6 ft. (2 m) high, and is around six million years old.

Deepest valley The Yarlung Zangbo valley, in Tibet, has an average depth of 16,400 ft. (5,000 m). In 1994 explorers discovered that its deepest point was 17,657 ft. (5,382 m). The peaks either side of the valley—Namche Barwa (25,436 ft.) and Jala Peri (23,891 ft.)—are just 13 miles (21 km) apart with the Yarlung Zangbo river flowing between them at an elevation of 8,000 ft. (2,440 m).

Deepest canyon The Vikos Gorge in the Pindus mountains of northwest Greece is 2,950 ft. (900 m) deep with only 3,600 ft. (1,100 m) between its rims. Gorges in many countries have a higher depth/width ratio, but none are as deep.

Oldest confirmed impact on Earth On August 23, 2002, a team of U.S. scientists led by Gary Byerly and Donald Lowe (both U.S.A.) announced their discovery of a 3.47-billion-year-old asteroid impact on Earth.

LARGEST LAND GORGE The largest land gorge in the world is the Grand Canyon on the Colorado River in north-central Arizona, U.S.A. It extends from Marble Gorge to the Grand Wash Cliffs, over a distance of 277 miles (446 km). It averages 10 miles (16 km) in width and 1 mile (1.6 km) in depth.

They had studied ancient rock samples from Australia and South Africa and analyzed the spherules contained within. These tiny particles are a common by-product of meteoritic strikes and, along with local zircon crystals, were used to date the impact. The spherule beds in the rock indicate that the impacting body had a rough diameter of around 12 miles (20 km). No crater has been found, as the Earth's geological processes have erased it.

Highest continent Excluding its ice shelves, Antarctica has an average elevation of 7,198 ft. (2,194 m) above the OSU91A Geoid (similar to, but more accurate than, sea level).

Largest geological feature discovered from space The Richat Structure in the Sahara Desert of Mauritania is an almost circular, multi-ringed sedimentary basin with a diameter of around 30 miles (50 km). Originally thought to be an impact crater, it is now believed to be the eroded remains of an uplifted sedimentary dome. The distinctive "bull's-eye" shape was discovered from orbit by U.S. astronauts Jim McDivitt and Ed White during the *Gemini IV* mission in June 1965.

Largest liquid body on Earth The largest liquid body on Earth is its outer core. The inner core is solid iron/nickel and measures around 758 miles (1,221 km) across. This is surrounded by the liquid outer core, with a thickness of 1,403 miles (2,259 km). The outer core has a total volume of around 1.719×10^{20} m³. It represents around 29.3% of Earth's mass and 16% of Earth's volume, or 100 times the volume of water in Earth's oceans.

Largest doline Xio Zhai Tien ("The Great Doline"), situated in the Sichuan region of central southern China, measures 1,600 ft. (500 m) across and 2,100 ft. (660 m) deep. Dolines are basins formed when limestone caves subside.

Largest sandstone monolith Uluru, also known as Ayers Rock, is a huge exposed sandstone monolith that rises 1,143 ft. (348 m) above the surrounding desert plain in Northern Territory, Australia. It is 1.5 miles (2.5 km) long and 1 mile (1.6 km) wide.

Fastest land mass on Earth Owing to convection currents in the Earth's mantle, all the continental plates slowly move relative to each other. The greatest movement occurs at the Tonga microplate, near Samoa, which is moving further into the Pacific at a rate of 9.4 in. (24 cm) per year.

Deepest permafrost Permafrost more than 4,500 ft. (1,370 m) deep was reported from the upper reaches of the Viluy River, Siberia, Russia, in February 1982.

Largest steam rings The active volcano Mount Etna in Sicily, Italy, is the tallest and most active volcano in Europe. A complex physical process is causing it to emit huge steam rings, similar to more familiar smoke rings.

LARGEST MODERN-DAY LANDSLIDE The landslide on Mt. St. Helens, Washington, U.S.A., was the largest ever observed by a survivor. On May 18, 1980, about 96,000 million ft.³ (2,800 million m³) of rock slipped off the mountain immediately prior to the volcanic eruption. This is equivalent to a block of earth nearly 0.8 miles (1.2 km) high, wide, and long.

Etna's steam rings are around 650 ft. (200 m) across and can last for around 10 minutes, as they slowly drift upward to a height of about 3,300 ft. (1,000 m) above the volcanic vent.

Weakest region in the Earth's magnetic field The Southern Magnetic Anomaly, found off the coast of Brazil, is a region in the Earth's magnetic field that is some 30% weaker than the average for the whole planet. This "dip" is due to eccentricities in the Earth's core, and causes increased doses of radiation in satellites passing over this region.

Longest day on Earth The tidal bulges in the Earth's oceans caused by the gravitational effect of the Moon are gradually transferring momentum from the Earth's rotation to the Moon's orbit. As a result, the Earth's rotation is slowing at a rate of around 0.02 seconds per century, and each day is a little longer than the day before. Therefore, the longest day is always today.

Oldest volcanic rocks on Earth Volcanic rocks dated at 3.825 billion years have been discovered in the Inukjuak area in the northern reaches of the province of Québec, Canada. The precise dating of the rocks was performed by the University of Québec, Montréal, and the Simon Fraser University in British Columbia (both Canada).

HIGHEST MOUNTAIN

The highest mountain in the world is Mount Everest. Its peak rises to 29,028 ft. 9 in. (8,848 m)—the highest point in the world.

Mount Everest is situated in the eastern Himalayas—its summit ridge separates Nepal and Tibet. It was discovered to be the world's highest mountain in 1856 by the Survey Department of the Government of India. Measurements from theodolite readings taken in 1849 and 1850 gave the first accurate measurement and revealed the peak to be the world's highest.

Naming Everest The mountain was named after Col. Sir George Everest (UK), who was Surveyor-General of India from 1830 to 1843, and who, in fact, pronounced his name "Eve-rest" as opposed to "Ever-est." Mount Everest is also known by the Tibetan name Chomolungma (Goddess Mother of the World) and by the Nepali name Sagarmatha (Forehead in the Sky).

Climbing Everest Many human triumphs and tragedies have been played out on Everest's slopes. George Mallory (UK) was one of the first to lead an expedition to climb the peak, in 1921. He perished not far from the summit on his 1924 expedition and his body was discovered in 1999. The challenge to climb the highest mountain has not waned since the peak was first conquered in 1953 by Sherpa Tenzing Norgay (Nepal) and Sir Edmund Hillary (New Zealand).

A record-breaking mountain Mount Everest has been the inspiration for many Guinness World Records: from the simple fact of being the world's highest peak, to being the site for the world's highest-altitude concert. Many of the records achieved on Everest are broken regularly—and some of the current record holders are featured on these pages. As the world's highest peak, Everest will always attract adventurous climbers and records will continue to be broken on its slopes.

Fastest ascent of Everest Lakpa Gelu Sherpa (Nepal) **(A)** made a successful ascent of Mount Everest in 10 hr. 56 min. 46 sec. on May 26, 2003, the fastest ever climb from Base Camp to the summit.

Longest stay on the summit Babu Chhiri Sherpa (Nepal) **(B)** stayed at the summit of Mount Everest for 21 hours without using bottled oxygen in May 1999. Most climbers stay less than an hour. He climbed Mount Everest again just weeks later, becoming the first person to climb the mountain twice in the same season.

Most conquests Apa Sherpa (Nepal) **(C)** completed his 13th successful climb of Mount Everest when he reached the summit on May 26, 2003. The dates of his climbs are: 1990, 1991, 1992 (spring and fall), 1993, 1994, 1995, 1997, 1998, 1999, 2000, 2002, and 2003.

Oldest man to reach the summit Yuichiro Miura (Japan) **(D)** reached Mount Everest's summit aged 70 years 222 days on May 22, 2003, becoming the oldest person ever to have done so. Miura, a professional skier, formerly achieved fame by skiing down Everest from 26,246 ft. (8,000 m) in 1970.

Oldest woman to reach the summit Tamae Watanabe (Japan) **(E)** reached the summit of Mount Everest at the age of 63 years 177 days at 9:55 a.m. on May 16, 2002, becoming the oldest woman ever to do so. More than 50 people reached the summit on the same day.

Earliest solo summit Reinhold Messner (Italy) **(F)** was the first to successfully climb Mount Everest solo, reaching the summit on August 20, 1980. It took him three days to make the ascent from his base camp at 21,325 ft. (6,500 m), and the climb was made all the more difficult by the fact that he did not use bottled oxygen.

GWR TALKS TO Sir Edmund Hillary

Mount Everest was first conquered at 11:30 a.m. on May 29, 1953, when the summit was reached by Edmund Percival Hillary (New Zealand, left) and Sherpa Tenzing Norgay (Nepal, right). The successful expedition was led by Col. (later Hon. Brigadier) Henry Cecil John Hunt (UK).

How did you become involved in mountaineering? When I was 16 years old I traveled with a school party 200 miles (320 km) south to the Tongariro National Park, and that was the first time I saw snow, really heavy winter snow, and for ten days I skied and scrambled around the snowy mountainside. I was by now pretty big and strong, and I reveled in this new experience. There was no doubt that it changed my life. I'd found something that I could enjoy and do well and it became an important part of my existence.

How did you come to be involved in the 1953 Everest Expedition? I did a great deal of mountaineering in New Zealand and Europe, so I'd become a pretty competent climber. Then four of us decided to go to the Himalayas and we climbed a number of peaks well over 20,000 ft. (6,090 m).

Eric Shipton—the famous explorer/mountaineer—invited two of us to join him. He'd just got permission to approach Everest from the south side, which nobody had done before. So I sort of got swept in.

During the ascent did you experience doubts that you'd reach the summit? I was never completely confident at any stage that I was going to get to the top. My whole attitude was that I would tackle any problems that I happened to meet, hopefully overcome them, and then if all went well I'd get up to the south summit and finally to the top. And that's the way it worked out. I've always felt that if there's a big challenge ahead of you, and you're absolutely confident that you can do it, why bother starting—it's not worth the effort to give it a crack. But that wasn't the case with Everest—I didn't really know whether or not I would be successful, so I was determined to give it everything I had.

What was for you the single biggest challenge? Probably the most demanding bit was on the summit ridge, this rock step around 40 ft. (12 m) high, which nowadays they call the Hillary Step. I had to find a way up this so I wiggled and jammed between the rock and the ice cornice, never knowing if the ice would break off, but I did it. That was the first time I was confident that I was going to be successful.

What are your thoughts on how Everest is tackled today? I don't like the increasing commercialization of Himalayan mountaineering. If you have $60,000 you can more or less buy your way into an expedition and be conducted up the mountain. We were in Kathmandu recently and there were 15 expeditions located at Base Camp on the south side of Everest, and another 15 on the north side—literally hundreds of people trying to climb the mountain, many with little or no experience, being conducted by more experienced leaders. I strongly believe that the number of expeditions on the mountain at any one time should be reasonably limited. To have 30 expeditions on the mountain at any one time is absolutely ridiculous. There's no challenge to it, and that's the whole point.

Why was climbing Everest an important thing to have done? It was the biggest and the best, so it was the major challenge. And of course I'd read so much about George Mallory and Andrew Irvine and the enthusiastic climbers in the 1920s and 1930s, which had built up a feeling that it would be great to have a chance to have a crack at the mountain, to see if we could get up it too.

Could you tell us a bit about your work with the Sherpas? As I got older I became more interested in the welfare of the Sherpa people and have worked with charitable institutions for 40 years building schools, hospitals, and many other projects for the Sherpas. We've also helped train their teachers. We love doing it—it's no sacrifice as far as we're concerned. We're very fond of our Sherpa friends and they work hard on these projects too, so it's been a very satisfying experience.

Is there somebody that you particularly admire? To me Ernest Shackleton epitomized the great explorer, the man who could deal with great problems when they arose, the man who kept his team alive, kept their spirit up.

Do you have any unfulfilled ambitions? Well I'm pretty ancient, you know, I'm fast approaching 85, but I'm still very energetic about raising funds for Sherpa projects and I'm still very enthusiastic on environmental matters as well, and with the reestablishing of the forests in the Mount Everest area. So, the environment and the welfare of the mountain people, I would say, are now my main motivations in life.

LAKES, RIVERS, & OCEANS

Deepest point in the ocean The deepest part of the ocean is "Challenger Deep," which lies at a depth of 35,797 ft. (10,911 m) in the Marianas Trench in the Pacific Ocean. Named after HM Survey Ship *Challenger II* (UK), which discovered it in 1951, it was first reached in 1960 by the manned U.S. Navy bathyscaphe *Trieste*. The record depth—almost 7 miles (11 km)—was confirmed in March 1995 by the unmanned Japanese probe *Kaiko*.

Largest continuous ocean current system The Thermohaline Conveyor is a vast global system of ocean circulation driven by differences in sea water density and salinity. It transports cold and salty deep water from the North Atlantic down to the Southern Ocean where it then travels east and north to the Indian and Pacific oceans. Here it rises and becomes warm, traveling back westward where it sinks again in the North Atlantic. The entire cycle can last for a thousand years.

LARGEST ICEBERG The largest tabular iceberg measured over 12,000 miles^2 (31,000 km^2). The flat-topped, blocky iceberg was 208 miles (335 km) long and 60 miles (97 km) wide—that's larger than Belgium—and was sighted 150 miles (240 km) west of Scott Island in the Southern Ocean, Antarctica, by the USS *Glacier* on November 12, 1956.

Greatest submarine mountain range The submarine Mid-Ocean Ridge extends 40,000 miles (65,000 km) from the Arctic Ocean to the Atlantic Ocean, around Africa, Asia, and Australia, and under the Pacific Ocean to the West Coast of North America. Its greatest height is 13,800 ft. (4,200 m) above the base ocean depth.

Fastest ocean current During the monsoon, the Somali current in the northern Indian Ocean flows at 9 mph (12.8 km/h).

Highest ocean temperature The highest temperature recorded in the ocean is 759°F (404°C) for a hydrothermal vent measured by an American research submarine some 300 miles (480 km) off the American West Coast in 1985.

Largest ocean Excluding adjacent seas, the Pacific Ocean represents 45.9% of the world's oceans and covers 64,186,000 miles^2 (166,241,700 km^2) in area. The average depth is 12,925 ft. (3,940 m).

Largest area of calm water An area known as the Sargasso Sea in the north Atlantic Ocean covers about 2.4 million miles^2 (6.2 million km^2) of relatively still water. Its surface is largely covered by sargassum seaweed.

LARGEST LAGOON Lagoa dos Patos ("Lagoon of Ducks"), located near the seashore in Rio Grande do Sul, southernmost Brazil, is 174 miles (280 km) long and extends over 3,803 miles^2 (9,850 km^2). It has a maximum width of 44 miles (70 km), and is separated from the Atlantic Ocean by long sand strips.

HIGHEST WATERFALL The Salto Angel on a branch of the Carrao River, Venezuela, is the highest waterfall (as opposed to vaporized "Bridal Veil") in the world. It has a total drop of 3,212 ft. (979 m)—the longest single drop being 2,648 ft. (807 m). The Angel Falls were named after the American pilot Jimmie Angel, who recorded them in his logbook on November 16, 1933. The falls, known by the native Venezuelans as Churun-Meru, had been reported by the Spanish explorer Ernesto Sánchez la Cruz in 1910.

Longest river From its farthest stream in Burundi, the Nile extends 4,160 miles (6,695 km) in length. Credited as the longest river, the Nile's main source is Lake Victoria in East Africa.

Greatest river flow The Amazon discharges an average of 7.1 million ft.³/sec. (200,000 m³/sec.) into the Atlantic Ocean, increasing to more than 12 million ft.³/sec. (340,000 m³/sec.) in full flood. The lower 900 miles (1,450 km) average 55 ft. (17 m) in depth, but the river has a maximum depth of 407 ft. (124 m). The flow of the Amazon is 60 times greater than that of the Nile.

Largest basin The vast Amazon river basin covers around 2,720,000 miles^2 (7,045,000 km^2). It has countless tributaries, including the Madeira, which at 2,100 miles (3,380 km) is the longest tributary in the world, being surpassed in length by only 17 rivers.

Deepest brine pool The Orca Basin in the Gulf of Mexico lies 7,200 ft. (2,200 m) below sea level. This 4 × 13-mile (7 × 21-km) depression is filled with water that has a salt content of around 48 oz./gal. (300 g/liter)—around eight times saltier than the Gulf itself. Effectively a hypersaline lake at the bottom of the sea, the salinity is caused by salt leaching out of the salt deposits under the sediment on the sea floor.

Largest inland island The largest inland island (i.e. land surrounded by rivers) is Ilha do Bananal, Brazil, at 7,700 miles^2 (20,000 km^2).

Largest freshwater island The largest island surrounded mostly by freshwater is the Ilha de Maraj in the mouth of the Amazon River, Brazil, which measures 18,500 miles^2 (48,000 km^2).

Largest lake island The largest island in a lake is Manitoulin Island, which covers an area of 1,068 miles^2 (2,766 km^2) in the Canadian section of Lake Huron.

Saltiest lake Don Juan Pond in Wright Valley, Antarctica, is so salty that it remains liquid even at temperatures as low as -63.4°F (-53°C). The percentage of salt by weight is 40.2%, compared with 23.1% and 3.38% for the Dead Sea and the world's oceans respectively.

Greatest waterfall annual flow On the basis of the average annual flow, the greatest waterfall in the world is the Boyoma Falls in the Congo (former Zaïre), with a flow of 600,000 ft.^{3}/sec. (17,000 m^3/sec.). The flow of the Guaíra (Cascade of the Seven Waterfalls) on the Paraná River between Brazil and Paraguay attained a rate of 1,750,000 ft.^{3}/sec. (50,000 m^3/sec.), although the closing of the Itaipú Dam gates in 1982 ended this claim to fame. However, it now holds the record for the greatest waterfall submerged by a reservoir.

Highest tides The greatest tides occur in the Bay of Fundy, which divides the peninsula of Nova Scotia, Canada, from the U.S.A.'s Northeasternmost state of Maine and the Canadian province of New Brunswick. Burncoat Head in the Minas Basin, Nova Scotia, Canada, has the greatest mean spring range, with 47 ft. 6 in. (14.5 m). A tide range of 54 ft. 6 in. (16.6 m) was recorded at springs in Leaf Basin in Ungava Bay, Québec, Canada, in 1953.

Largest polynya The largest area of open sea surrounded by sea ice ever recorded, measured around 106,000 miles^2 (275,000 km^2). It occurred in the

Weddell Sea, off Antarctica, during the winter months of 1974, 1975, and 1976. This spectacularly large polynya was discovered using satellite imagery.

Largest atoll The slender 176-mile (283-km) coral reef of Kwajalein, in the Marshall Islands in the central Pacific Ocean, encloses a lagoon of 1,100 miles^2 (2,850 km^2).

Largest atoll land area Christmas Atoll in the Line Islands in the central Pacific Ocean has an area of 251 miles^2 (649 km^2), of which 124 miles^2 (321 km^2) is land.

Most southerly ocean The most southerly part of any ocean is located at 87°S, 151°W, at the snout of the Scott Glacier, 200 miles (320 km) from the South Pole.

PREHISTORIC LIFE

Largest dinosaur skull *Torosaurus* ("piercing lizard"), a ceratopsid, had the largest skull of all known land animals. A herbivore, *Torosaurus* measured around 25 ft. (7.6 m) in length and weighed up to 17,600 lb. (8 tons). Its skull measured up to 9 ft. 10 in. (3 m) in length and weighed up to 4,400 lb. (2 tons).

The largest single dinosaur skull ever found measures 10 ft. 6 in. (3.2 m) in height and belonged to a *Pentaceratops* ("five-horn lizard") skeleton.

Dinosaur with the longest tail The diplodocid *Diplodocus* ("double beamed") was a long-necked sauropod dinosaur from the late Jurassic period (145 to 155 million years ago). It had a tail length of up to 43–45 ft. (13–14 m).

Oldest fossilized animal food store In November 2003, a team of scientists from the University of Bonn (Germany) announced their discovery of a 17-million-year-old fossilized rodent burrow—probably for a hamster or a squirrel—containing more than 1,200 fossilized nuts.

Oldest known marsupial The *Deltatheridium* ("little delta [tooth] beast") found in Mongolia's Gobi Desert in November 1988 has been estimated by scientists to be 80 million years old. This means it lived among dinosaurs and that marsupials possibly originated here.

Oldest fossilized embryos Around 100 embryos of *Markuelia hunanensis*—an extinct species of worm—were discovered in Hunan, southern China, by a team from Bristol University (UK) and Beijing University (China). They date back around 500 million years. The discovery was announced in January 2004.

LARGEST CROCODILE EVER *Sarchosuchus imperator* was a prehistoric crocodile species that lived around 110 million years ago. Fossilized remains found in the Sahara Desert suggest that this creature took around 50–60 years to grow to its full length of 37–40 ft. (11–12 m).

Largest carnivore ever A skeleton of *Giganotosaurus carolinii,* the largest predatory dinosaur, was discovered in Neuquen, Patagonia, Argentina, in 1995. It was 41 ft. (12.5 m) long, and weighed 17,600 lb. (8 tons). The bones suggest that it is taller than *Tyrannosaurus rex.* It lived about 110 million years ago—30 million years before *T. rex.*

Longest prehistoric tusks The average length for the tusks of the straight-tusked elephant *Hesperoloxodon antiques germanicus,* which lived about two million years ago in what is now Germany, was 16 ft. 4.75 in. (5 m).

Largest duck-billed dinosaur The duck-billed *Lambeosaurus* ("Lambes lizard") grew to 30–50 ft. (9–15 m) long and weighed roughly 12,000 lb. (5.6 tons). A herbivore that lived during the Cretaceous period, it roamed the Earth in herds 65–83 million years ago.

Longest dinosaur The longest vertebrate on record was a diplodocid excavated in 1980 from New Mexico, U.S.A. It was named *Seismosaurus halli* ("earth-shaking lizard") and estimated to be 128–170 ft. (39–52 m) long based on comparisons of individual bones. In 1999, the bones were reconstructed at the Wyoming Dinosaur Center and measured 134 ft. (41 m).

Largest herbivorous dinosaur Sauropod dinosaurs, a group of long-necked, long-tailed, four-legged plant-eaters, lumbered around most of the world during the Jurassic and Cretaceous periods 65–208 million years ago. The largest measured 131 ft. (40 m) and weighed up to 220,000 lb. (100 tons).

Oldest spider in amber A spider trapped in amber has been dated at 125–135 million years old. From the family Linyphiidae, it was found in Lebanon and analyzed by David Penney and Paul Selden (both UK) and announced on December 26, 2002.

Oldest spider silk The oldest spider silk in the world dates from the early Cretaceous period, more than 120 million years ago, and was described in the journal *Nature* by Swiss researcher Dr. Samuel Zschokke from the University of Basel. The strand is 0.1 in. (4 mm) long and has tiny glue droplets which, in modern-day spiders, are used to catch insects. The specimen was

LARGEST AND MOST COMPLETE *TYRANNOSAURUS REX* SKELETON
The largest, best preserved, and most complete skeleton of a *Tyrannosaurus rex* that has ever been found is "Sue" (pictured). It measures 13 ft. (4 m) tall and 41 ft. (12.5 m) long, and is approximately 90% complete. It was found in South Dakota, U.S.A., on August 12, 1990 by explorer Sue Hendrickson (U.S.A.), after whom the dinosaur has been named. The skeleton is currently displayed at The Field Museum, Chicago, Illinois, U.S.A.

recovered in 1969 from amber beds located near Jezzine, Lebanon, but it was only in 2003 that its importance was recognized.

Largest prehistoric mammal The largest prehistoric mammal was *Indricotherium* (also *Baluchitherium* or *Paraceratherium)* of the family Hyrachyidae, a long-necked, hornless rhinocerotid that roamed across western Asia and Europe roughly 35 million years ago. It was first known from bones discovered in the Bugti Hills of Baluchistan, Pakistan, in 1907–8. A restoration in the American Museum of Natural History, New York City, U.S.A., measures 17 ft. 9 in. (5.4 m) to the top of the shoulder hump and 37 ft. (11.2 m) in total length.

Earliest prehistoric salamanders The earliest salamanders date back 165 million years and thousands of fossilized remains have been discovered in volcanic ash beds in China and Mongolia. These animals are related to the salamanders that now inhabit North America and Asia.

Longest prehistoric snake The longest prehistoric snake was the python-like *Gigantophis garstini,* which inhabited what is now Egypt around 38 million years ago. Parts of a spinal column and a small piece of jaw discovered at Fayum in the Western Desert indicate a length of roughly 36 ft. (11 m). This is 3 ft. 3 in. (1 m) longer than the present-day longest snake.

Most dinosaur footprints discovered in one place About ten different dinosaurs are thought to have made the 100 or more impressions in China's northwest Gansu Province. The prints date from around the junction of the late Jurassic and early Cretaceous periods, 140 million years ago. One of the footprints was approximately 5 ft. (1.5 m) long and 4 ft. (1.2 m) wide.

Largest prehistoric insect The dragonfly *Meganeura monyi* lived around 280 million years ago. Fossil remains (i.e. impressions of wings) discovered at Commentry, France, indicate a wing expanse of up to 27.5 in. (70 cm). This compares with the largest dragonfly living today *(Megaloprepus caeruleata)* from Central and South America, which has been measured up to 4.72 in. (120 mm) in length with a wingspan of up to 7.52 in. (191 mm).

Largest prehistoric bird The largest prehistoric bird was the flightless *Dromornis stirtoni,* a huge emu-like creature that lived in central Australia between 25 thousand and 15 million years ago. Fossil leg bones found near Alice Springs, Northern Territory, Australia, in 1974 indicate that the bird must have stood around 10 ft. (3 m) tall and weighed about 1,100 lb. (500 kg).

Largest armored dinosaur *Ankylosaurus* ("armored lizard"), a herbivore protected with thick plates covering the skin, also had a double row of spikes running down from the back of its head to its club tail. Measuring 24 ft. 7 in.–35 ft. (7.5–10.7 m) long, 6 ft. (1.8 m) wide, and 4 ft. (1.2 m) tall, it had plates to protect its eyes and only its belly was left unprotected. The last, and at 8,800 lb. (4 tons), by far the largest of all the ankylosaurids, it lived in the late Cretaceous period, about 65–70 million years ago.

MAMMALS

Largest land mammal The adult male African elephant (*Loxodonta africana*) stands 9 ft. 10 in.–12 ft. 1 in. (3–3.7 m) at the shoulder and weighs 8,800–15,400 lb. (4–7 tons). The largest specimen ever recorded measured 13 ft. 7 in. (4.16 m) in a projected line from the highest point of the shoulder to the base of the forefoot, indicating a standing height of about 12 ft. 11 in. (3.96 m).

Smallest elephant species The world's smallest elephant is the Borneo pygmy, which is 30% smaller than the Asian elephant (*Elephas maximus*).

LARGEST EYES ON A MAMMAL The Philippine tarsier (*Tarsius syrichta*, pictured) is one of the world's smallest primates. They have a tail measuring 5.3–10.8 in. (135–275 mm), a head and body length of 3.3–6.3 in. (85–160 mm), and their large forward-pointing eyes have a diameter of 0.6 in. (16 mm). Their eyes are so enormous that they would be equivalent to grapefruit-sized eyes in a human being. They are the only primates, along with animals from the Galago genus, able to turn their heads through 180° in each direction. Tarsiers live in the forests of Borneo, Sumatra, and the Philippines.

Mammals 97

Adult males are 5 ft. 6 in.–8 ft. 6 in. (1.7–2.6 m) tall, whereas female are slightly smaller at 4 ft. 11 in.–7 ft. 2 in. (1.5–2.2 m). The average estimated weight is 5,500 lb. (2,500 kg). The current population is under 2,000, all living in Borneo, Malaysia, where they were confirmed as being a separate subspecies in September 2003, following DNA research funded by the World Wildlife Fund.

Longest gestation period for a mammal The Asian elephant (*Elephas maximus*) has an average gestation period of 650 days (over 21 months) and a maximum of 760 days (over two years)—more than twice that of humans.

The shortest mammalian gestation period is 12–13 days and is common in a number of species, including the Virginia opossum (*Didelphis virginiana*) of North America, and the rare water opossum or yapok (*Chironectes minimus*) of central and northern South America.

Fastest mammal on land over short distances Repeated modern scientific studies have shown that over a short distance on level ground, the cheetah (*Acinonyx jubatus*) can maintain a steady maximum speed of approximately 62 mph (100 km/h). However, research completed by Professor Craig Sharp (UK) of Brunel University, London, UK, back in 1965 recorded accurate speeds of 64.3 mph (104.4 km/h) for a 77-lb. (35-kg) adult female

LARGEST MAMMAL TO BUILD A NEST The largest mammal to construct a nest is the gorilla (*Gorilla gorilla,* shown) of Africa, where adult males measure 5 ft. 6 in.–5 ft. 9 in. (1.7–1.8 m) tall and weigh 300–500 lb. (136–227 kg). Every day, the gorillas each create a new ground nest from the surrounding vegetation. The nests are circular and typically measure 3 ft. 3 in. (1 m) in diameter.

TALLEST MAMMAL
The giraffe (*Giraffa camelopardalis,* shown), found in the dry savannah and open woodland areas of sub-Saharan Africa, is the tallest mammal. An adult male giraffe typically measures 15–18 ft. (4.6–5.5 m) tall.

over a distance of 660 ft. (201.2 m).

Fastest mammal on land over long distances The pronghorn (*Antilocapra americana*) is the fastest land animal when measured steadily over a long distance. These antelope have been observed to travel continuously at 35 mph (56 km/h) for as far as 4 miles (6 km). The pronghorn is found in western U.S.A., southwestern Canada, and parts of northern Mexico.

Largest litter for a wild mammal The greatest number of young born to a wild mammal at a single birth is 31 (30 of which survived) in the case of a tailless tenrec (*Tenrec ecaudatus*), a hedgehog-like insectivore found in Madagascar.

Largest mouth for a land animal The hippopotamus (*Hippopotamus amphibious*) of Africa can open its jaws to almost 180°. In a fully grown male hippo, this equates to an average gape of 4 ft. (1.2 m). Although they are herbivores, hippos have canine teeth that typically measure 28 in. (71 cm) and which continually grow. The largest canine recorded for a hippo is 48 in. (122 cm).

Fastest heartbeat in a mammal The shrew (family Soricidae) has the fastest heartbeat of any mammal, with a rate of 1,200 beats per minute, which is similar to that of a hummingbird when hovering. Shrews are roughly the size of a thumb and weigh a tiny 0.15 oz. (4.5 g).

Largest structure built by a land animal Beavers (*Candor canadensis*) of North America use mud, wood, vegetation, and stones to dam up water and form a pond, then build a lodge for winter refuge. The largest lodge ever recorded was 40 ft. (12.1 m) across and 16 ft. (4.8 m) high, and the longest beaver dam measured 0.9 miles (1.5 km) long.

Mammal with the most names In the English language alone, the puma *(Puma concolor)* has over 40 names, including cougar, mountain lion, red tiger, and Florida panther.

Highest living mammal The large-eared pika (*Ochotona macrotis*) has been recorded at a height of 20,100 ft. (6,130 m) in Asian mountain ranges.

The yak (*Bos mutus*) found in Tibet and China climbs to an altitude of 20,000 ft. (6,100 m) when foraging.

Largest colony of mammals The black-tailed prairie dog (*Cynomys ludovicianus*), a rodent of the family Sciuridae found in the western U.S.A. and in northern Mexico, builds large colonies. One single "town" discovered in 1901 contained about 400 million individuals and was estimated to cover 23,706 miles^2 (61,400 km^2)—the size of the Republic of Ireland.

GWR TALKS TO Sir David Attenborough

Sir David Attenborough (UK) has had the longest working career as a writer and presenter of TV nature programs. His first series, *Zoo Quest* (BBC, UK), was broadcast in 1954 and his most recent, the BBC's *Life of Mammals,* was broadcast in the UK in 2002.

What has been the most enjoyable TV series to put together? *Life on Earth.* At the time it was the most ambitious series ever produced by the BBC Natural History Unit. It was seen by an estimated 500 million viewers and people still comment on the impact that the series had.

Have you ever been attacked by any animals? No, never. Usually the only scary moments are when human beings are involved. But having said

that, I was once filming in Kenya with Iain Douglas Hamilton, the elephant expert, and we were on the receiving end of a nasty rhino charge which wrecked our Land Rover.

Is there any particular creature that fascinates you over and above all others? I have a private passion about birds of paradise which are found only in New Guinea and its offshore islands. Their courtship displays are simply ravishing and many have never been filmed. Once when we were trying to film Wilson's Bird of Paradise, we'd been waiting in the bird hide since before dawn and the sound recordist waiting some distance away told me that he knew when the bird arrived as he heard my heartbeat double!

If you could bring back any extinct species of plant or animal what would it be? A giant plant-eating dinosaur.

Do you intend to keep on making television wildlife programs? I'm doing what I want to do and as long as people want me to go on doing it, I'll continue. I don't know what I'd do otherwise!

What advice would you give any budding naturalist? Learn all you can about animals.

What does it mean to you to have a Guinness World Record? It's something with which to surprise my friends!

BIRDS

Largest bird The largest living bird is the North African ostrich (*Struthio camelus camelus*). Male examples of this ratite (flightless) subspecies have been recorded up to 9 ft. (2.75 m) tall and weighing 345 lb. (156.5 kg).

Smallest bird The smallest bird is the bee hummingbird (*Mellisuga helenae*) of Cuba and the Isle of Youth. Males measure 2.25 in. (57 mm) in total length, half of which is taken up by the bill and tail, and weigh only 0.05 oz. (1.6 g). Females are slightly larger. This is believed to be the lowest weight limit for any warm-blooded animal.

Most abundant bird The red-billed quelea (*Quelea quelea*), a seed-eating weaver of the drier parts of sub-Saharan Africa, has an estimated adult breeding population of 1.5 billion. At least 200 million of these "feathered locusts" are slaughtered annually without reducing this overall number.

Highest g-force experienced by a bird American experiments have shown that the beak of the red-headed woodpecker (*Melanerpes erythrocephalus*) hits the bark of a tree with an impact velocity of 13 mph (20.9 km/h), subjecting the brain to a deceleration of about 10 G when the head snaps back.

Longest feathers The longest feathers grown by any bird were recorded in 1972 on a phoenix fowl or Yokohama chicken (a strain of red jungle fowl, *Gallus gallus*) whose tail covert measured 34 ft. 9.5 in. (10.6 m). It was owned by Masasha Kubota (Japan). The longest feathers on a bird found in the wild (i.e. not bred for ornamental purposes) are those of the male crested

LONGEST BILLS The longest bill belongs to the Australian pelican (*Pelecanus conspicillatus,* pictured), and measures 13–18.5 in. (34–47 cm) long.

The longest beak in relation to overall body length is that of the sword-billed hummingbird (*Ensifera ensifera*) found in the Andes from Venezuela to Bolivia. The beak measures 4 in. (10.2 cm) making it longer than the bird's actual body (excluding the tail).

Argus pheasant (*Rheinhartia ocellata*), whose feathers reach 5 ft. 8 in. (1.73 m).

Fastest bird swimmer The gentoo penguin (*Pygoscelis papua*) has a maximum speed of about 17 mph (27 km/h).

Shortest bills The shortest bills in relation to body length belong to the smaller swifts (the Apodidae family), and in particular to the glossy swiftlet (*Collocalia esculenta*), whose bill is almost nonexistent.

Fastest wing beat of a bird During courtship, the ruby-throated hummingbird (*Archilochus colubris*) can produce a wing beat rate of 200 beats/sec. as opposed to the normal 90 beats/sec. of all other hummingbirds.

Highest flying birds The highest altitude recorded for a bird is 37,000 ft. (11,300 m) for a Ruppell's vulture (*Gyps rueppellii*) that collided with an airplane over Abidjan, Ivory Coast, on November 29, 1973. The impact damaged one of the aircraft's engines, but the plane landed safely.

Largest bird's nest A pair of bald eagles (*Haliaeetus leucocephalus*), and possibly their successors, built a nest near St. Petersburg, Florida, U.S.A., that measured an incredible 9 ft. 6 in. (2.9 m) wide and 20 ft. (6 m) deep. When it was examined in 1963 it was estimated to weigh more than 4,400 lb. (2 tons).

Smallest bird's nest Hummingbirds build the smallest nests. That of the vervain hummingbird (*Mellisuga minima*) is about half the size of a walnut shell, while the deeper but narrower nest of the bee hummingbird (*M. helenae*) is thimble-sized.

Smallest bird egg The smallest egg laid by any bird is that of the vervain hummingbird (*Mellisuga minima*) of Jamaica and two nearby islets. Two specimens measuring less than 0.39 in. (10 mm) in length weighed a minute 0.0128 oz. (0.365 g) and 0.0132 oz. (0.375 g).

Most airborne land bird The common swift (*Apus apus*) remains airborne for two to four years, during which time it sleeps, drinks, eats, and even mates on the wing. It has been calculated that a young swift completes a nonstop flight of 310,000 miles (500,000 km) between fledging and its first landing at a potential nesting site some two years later.

Most airborne bird The most airborne of all birds is the sooty tern (*Sterna fuscata*) which, after leaving the nesting grounds as a youngster, remains aloft for three to 10 years while maturing, settling on water occasionally, before returning to land to breed as an adult.

Fastest land bird The world's fastest bird on land is the ostrich

HIGHEST DENSITY OF FEATHERS The penguin has the highest density of feathers. In his book, *The General Biology and Thermal Balance of Penguins* (1967), Dr. Bernard Stonehouse (UK) counted 70 feathers per in.^{2} (11–12 per cm^2) in emperor, Adélie, yellow-eyed, and little (blue) penguins. Each feather has its own small muscles associated with it to allow control. On land the feathers stay erect to trap air, insulating them; in the water they flatten to form a watertight barrier.

(*Struthio camelus*), which can reach speeds of up to 30 mph (50 km/h) when running. Unlike most birds, the ostrich cannot fly, and therefore uses its powerful legs to sprint at such speeds. The ostrich has one of the largest strides of any animal—it can exceed 23 ft. (7 m) at full pace.

Fastest bird in level flight The fastest fliers in level flight are found among the ducks and geese (Anatidae). Some powerful species such as the red-breasted merganser (*Mergus serrator*), the eider (*Somateria mollissima*), the canvasback (*Aythya valisineria*), and the spur-winged goose (*Plectropterus gambensis*) can sometimes reach 56–62 mph (90–100 km/h).

Slowest-flying bird The slowest-flying birds are the American woodcock (*Scolopax minor*) and the Eurasian woodcock (*S. rusticola*), which have been timed during courtship displays at only 5 mph (8 km/h) without stalling.

Largest penguin colony The largest penguin colony is on Zavodovski Island in the South Sandwich Islands. Approximately two million chinstrap penguins (*Pygoscelis antarctica*) breed on the slopes of the island, which is an active volcano. Chinstraps get their name from a thin line of black feath-

KEENEST VISION OF ALL BIRDS Large birds of prey have the keenest vision as they can detect a target object at a distance three or more times greater than that achieved by humans. A peregrine falcon (*Falco peregrinus,* shown) can spot a pigeon at a range of over 5 miles (8 km) under ideal conditions.

ers that runs under their chin. They are also considered the most common penguins in the world with a population of around 12 million, mainly found in the Antarctic.

Smallest bird of prey The smallest bird of prey in the world is a title held jointly by the black-legged falconet (*Microhierax fringillarius*) of Southeast Asia and the white-fronted or Bornean falconet (*Microhierax latifrons*) of northwestern Borneo. Both species have an average length of 5.5–6 in. (14–15 cm), including a 2-in. (5-cm) tail, and a weight of about 1.25 oz. (35 g).

Longest migration by a bird The Arctic tern (*Sterna parasidaea*) migrates the greatest distance of any bird species. It breeds north of the Arctic Circle and then flies south to the Antarctic for the northern winter and then back again, a round-trip of about 21,750 miles (35,000 km).

Longest incubation An egg of the mallee fowl (*Leipoa ocellata*) of Australia, took 90 days to hatch, compared with its normal 62 days.

Lowest temperature endured by a bird The lowest temperature endured by any bird is an average of -4°F (-20°C) by the breeding emperor penguin (*Aptenodytes forsteri*) on the Antarctic sea ice where wind speeds can vary between 16 and 47 mph (25 and 75 km/h).

Largest wingspan of any living species of bird A male wandering albatross (*Diomedea exulans*) of the southern oceans holds the record with a wingspan of 11 ft. 11 in. (3.63 m). The bird was caught by members of the Antarctic research ship USNS *Eltanin* in the Tasman Sea on September 18, 1965.

WATER LIFE

Smallest whale There are two contenders for the smallest cetacean: Hector's dolphin (*Cephalorhynchus hectori*) and vaquita (*Phocoena sinus*), which grow to only 3 ft. 11 in. (1.2 m) long.

Largest animal brain The brain of the sperm whale or cachalot (*Physeter macrocephalus*) weighs approximately 19 lb. 13 oz. (9 kg). In comparison the weight of a bull African elephant's brain reaches 11 lb. 14 oz. (5.4 kg) and a human brain is, on average, 3 lb. (1.4 kg). Sperm whales are found in all waters except the polar regions. Their name comes from the waxy oil, which is produced by the spermaceti organ on their heads.

Largest offspring In the two months before it is born, a blue whale (*Balaenoptera musculus*) increases in weight by as much as 4,400 lb.

(2 tons)—it grows about 1,000 times faster than a human baby in the womb. The newborn calf is 19–26 ft. (6–8 m) long and weighs 4,400–6,600 lb. (2–3 tons). Everyday, the baby drinks about 350 pints (200 liters) of its mother's milk and gains as much as 198 lb. (90 kg) in weight—the same as the weight of an adult human being. By the time it is weaned at seven months old it has roughly doubled in length and weighs an amazing 44,000 lb. (20 tons). The blue whale is the world's largest mammal.

Greatest weight loss During her seven-month lactation period, a 264,000-lb. (120-ton) female blue whale (*Balaenoptera musculus*) can lose up to 25% of her body weight nursing her calf.

Slowest heartbeat in a mammal The mammal that is presumed to have the slowest heartbeat of any warm-blooded animal is the blue whale (*Balaenoptera musculus*), with between four and eight beats per minute—dependent upon whether or not the whale is diving. By comparison, the average adult human heart beats at 70 beats per minute. Blue whales also have the largest heart of any animal and their heartbeat can be heard up to 20 miles (32 km) away underwater.

Largest jaw for a mammal The largest jaw ever recorded on a mammal measured 5 m (16 ft. 5 in.) and belonged to a male sperm whale (*Physeter*

FASTEST MARINE MAMMAL On October 12, 1958, a bull killer whale *(Orcinus orca,* pictured) an estimated 20–25 ft. (6.1–7.6 m) long, was timed at 34.5 mph (55.5 km/h) in the northeastern Pacific. Similar speeds have also been reported for Dall's porpoise *(Phocoenoides dalli)* in short bursts.

HIGHEST JUMP BY A DOLPHIN Some bottlenose dolphins *(Tursiops truncatus,* pictured) have been trained to jump as high as 26 ft. (7.92 m) from the surface of the water.

macrocephalus) nearly 25.6 m (84 ft.) in length. The massive lower jaw is now exhibited in the Museum of Natural History, London, UK. Sperm whales are also the largest-toothed whales.

Densest fur The sea otter (*Enhydra lutris*) has over 650,000 hairs per in.^{2} (100,000 per cm^2) that insulate its skin. Most of the world's sea otters are found off the coast of Alaska, U.S.A.

Oldest pinniped A pinniped is a carnivorous aquatic mammal with flipper-like limbs (such as a seal). The greatest proven age for a pinniped was estimated by the Limnological Institute in Irkutsk, former USSR, to be 56 years for the female Baikal seal (*Phoca sibirica*) and 52 years for the male.

Smallest pinniped The smallest pinniped, by a small margin, is the Galapagos fur seal (*Arctocephalus galapagoensis*). Adult females average 3 ft. 11 in. (1.2 m) in length and weigh over 60 lb. (27 kg). Males are usually considerably larger, averaging 4 ft. 11 in. (1.5 m) in length and weighing around 141 lb. (64 kg).

Rarest seal With fewer than 400 remaining, the rarest seal species is the Mediterranean monk seal (*Monachus monachus*), found in remote and undisturbed areas of the Mediterranean Sea and northwest African coast. Its closest relative, the Caribbean monk seal (*M. tropicalis*), is already extinct.

Largest gray seal colony Over 100,000 gray seals (*Halichoerus grypus*) arrive at Sable Island off Nova Scotia, Canada, every winter to breed.

After 18 days the resulting pups are then left to fend for themselves. The gray seal's name *Halichoerus grypus* comes from the Greek, meaning "hook-nosed sea pig."

Largest amphibian The largest of the amphibians are the giant salamanders (family Cryptobranchidae) of which there are three species. The record holder is the Chinese giant salamander (*Andrias davidianus*), which lives in mountain streams in north-eastern, central, and southern China. One record-breaking specimen collected in Hunan Province measured 5 ft. 11 in. (1.8 m) in length and weighed a massive 143 lb. (65 kg).

Smallest newt The smallest newt or salamander is the Mexican lungless salamander (*Bolitoglossa mexicana*), which only grows to about 1 in. (2.54 cm), including the tail.

Largest frog A specimen of the African goliath frog (*Conraua goliath*) captured in April 1889 on the Sanaga River, Cameroon, by Andy Koffman (U.S.A.) had a snout-to-vent length of 14.5 in. (36.8 cm) and an overall length of 34.5 in. (87.6 cm) with its legs extended.

Smallest toad The smallest toad is the subspecies *Bufo taitanus beiranus* of Africa, the largest specimen of which measured only 0.94 in. (24 mm) long.

LARGEST PINNIPED The largest of the 34 known species of pinniped is the southern elephant seal (*Mirounga leonina*, pictured) of the sub-Antarctic islands. Bulls average 16 ft. 6 in. (5 m) in length from the tip of the inflated snout to the tips of the outstretched tail flippers, have a maximum girth of 12 ft. (3.7 m), and weigh about 4,400–7,720 lb. (2,000–3,500 kg). The largest accurately measured specimen of the elephant seal was a bull, killed at Possession Bay, South Georgia, on February 28, 1913, that weighed at least 8,800 lb. (4 tons) and measured 21 ft. 4 in. (6.5 m) after flensing (stripping of the blubber or skin).

Most paternal amphibian The West European midwife toad (*Alytes obstetricans*) takes its name from the behavior of the male. When the female lays its eggs, the male fertilizes them and then winds the string of eggs (which can be 3–4 ft. or 0.9–1.2 m long) around his thighs. The male, who is only 3 in. (7.6 cm) long, carries the eggs in this manner for up to four weeks. When the eggs are ready to hatch, the toad swims into suitable water for the tadpoles to be released.

Largest fish The largest fish is the rare plankton-feeding whale shark (*Rhincodon typus*), which is found in the warmer areas of the Atlantic, Pacific, and Indian Oceans. The largest scientifically recorded example of one of these creatures was 41 ft. 6 in. (12.65 m) long, 23 ft. (7 m) around the thickest part of the body and weighed an estimated 33,000–46,200 lb. (15–21 tons). It was captured off Baba Island, near Karachi, Pakistan, on November 11, 1949.

Largest predatory fish The largest predatory fish is the rare great white shark (*Carcharodon carcharias*). Adult specimens average 14–15 ft. (4.3–4.6 m) in length, and weigh between 1,150 lb. and 1,700 lb. (520–770 kg). There are many claims of huge specimens up to 33 ft. (10 m) in length and, although few have been authenticated, there is plenty of circumstantial evidence to suggest that great whites can grow to over 20 ft. (6 m) in length.

Largest freshwater fish The largest fish to spend their whole life in fresh or brackish water are the rare Mekong giant catfish (*Pangasius gigas*), principally of the Mekong River basin in Southeast Asia, and *Pangasius sanitwongsei,* principally of the Chao Phraya River basin, Thailand, both of which are reputed to attain a length of 10 ft. (3 m) and weigh 660 lb. (300 kg). However, *Arapaima giga* of South America is reported to attain a length of 14 ft. 9 in. (4.5 m), but weighs only 440 lb. (200 kg).

Heaviest bony fish The heaviest bony fish in the ocean is the sunfish (*Mola mola*), which has been recorded weighing 4,400 lb. (2 tons) and measuring 10 ft. (3 m) from fin tip to fin tip.

Deepest fish The fish that lives at the greatest recorded depth is a species of cusk-eel (family Ophidiidae) called *Abyssobrotula galatheae.* The 8-in. (20-cm-long) fish has been collected from the Puerto Rico Trench in the Atlantic Ocean at a depth of 27,460 ft. (8,370 m).

Longest fish migration Many fish species undertake long annual migrations between their feeding grounds. The longest straight line distance known to have been covered by a marine fish is 5,800 miles (9,335 km) for a bluefin tuna (*Thunnus thynnus*) that was dart tagged off Baja California, Mexico, in 1958 and caught 300 miles (483 km) south of Tokyo, Japan, in April 1963. During its journey, its weight increased from 35 lb. (16 kg) to 267 lb. (121 kg).

For freshwater fish, the European eel (*Anguilla anguilla*) holds the record.

MOST FEROCIOUS FRESHWATER FISH Attracted to blood and frantic splashing, a school of piranhas can completely strip an animal as large as a horse of its flesh within minutes, leaving only its skeleton. The most ferocious piranhas are those of the genera *Serrasalmus* and *Pygocentrus,* found in the large rivers of South America.

It spends between seven and 15 years in freshwater in Europe then suddenly changes into breeding condition and begins a marathon journey that may take it from landlocked waters to the Atlantic, where it heads for the species' spawning grounds in the Sargasso Sea. The entire journey—between 3,000 and 4,000 miles (4,800 and 6,400 km)—takes about six months.

Highest living fish The highest living fish is the Tibetan loach (Cobitidae), found at an altitude of 17,000 ft. (5,200 m) in the Himalayas.

Fastest fish The cosmopolitan sailfish (*Istiophorus platypterus*) is considered to be the fastest species of fish over short distances, although practical problems make it difficult to establish precise measurements of its speed. In a series of trials carried out at the Long Key Fishing Camp, Florida, U.S.A., one sailfish took out 300 ft. (91 m) of line in three seconds, which is equivalent to a velocity of 68 mph (109 km/h), compared with 60 mph (96 km/h) for the cheetah at high speed.

Lightest fish The lightest of all vertebrates is the dwarf goby (*Schindleria praematurus*), which weighs only 2 mg (equivalent to 14,184 to the ounce) and is 0.47–0.74 in. (12–19 mm) long. It is found throughout the Indo-Pacific.

Largest eye The Atlantic giant squid (*Architeuthis dux*) has the largest eye of any animal—living or extinct. It has been estimated that the record example from Thimble Tickle Bay, Newfoundland, Canada, found in 1878 had eyes measuring 15.75 in. (40 cm) in diameter—almost the width of an open hardcover edition of the *Guinness World Records* book.

SLOWEST FISH The swimming ability of sea horses (family Syngnathidae, pictured) is severely limited by a rigid body structure— only their pectoral and dorsal fins can move rapidly. Sea horses propel themselves along in an erect posture, never attaining speeds of more than 0.001 mph (0.016 km/h). Incapable of swimming against the current, they hang on to coral and marine plants with their prehensile tails to avoid being swept away.

Largest squid The largest intact specimen of a squid ever found was an immature female of the species *Mesonychoteuthis hamiltoni* that was caught in March 2003 in the Ross Sea, Antarctica. It had a total length of 16 ft. (5 m), a mantle length of 8 ft. (2.5 m), and weighed 330 lb. (150 kg). This species swims to a depth of 6,500 ft. (2,000 m) and is an aggressive killer, eating large prey like Patagonian toothfish, *Dissostichus eleginoides,* which can grow to more than 6 ft. (1.8 m) long. Mantle length (not total length) is the standard measure in cephalopods.

Animal with the most chromosomes The king crab has 208 pairs of chromosomes per cell. By comparison, humans have 23 pairs of chromosomes in each cell.

Most heat-tolerant water-based organism The most heat-resistant organism discovered to date is strain 121, a microbe belonging to the ancient group of bacteria-like organisms called archae. Strain 121 was discovered in superheated water from hydrothermal vents at the bottom of the Pacific Ocean. This organism can survive temperatures of 249.8°F (121°C).

Most dangerous sea urchin The most dangerous sea urchin is the flower sea urchin (*Toxopneustes pileolus*). Toxin from the spines and pedicellaria (small pincer-like organs) causes severe pain, respiratory problems, and paralysis in humans.

Deepest starfish The greatest depth from which a starfish has been recovered is 24,881 ft. (7,584 m) for a specimen of *Porcellanaster ivanovi* col-

MOST POISONOUS EDIBLE FISH The most poisonous fish are the puffer fish (*Tetraodon,* shown) of the Red Sea and Indo-Pacific region that deliver a fatal toxin called tetrodotoxin, one of the most powerful nonproteinous poisons. Less than 0.004 oz. (0.1 g) is enough to kill an adult person in as little as 20 minutes. In Japan, the puffer fish is served as a delicacy known as fugu-sashi. Improper preparation of this dish can cause fatal poisoning, so only specially licensed cooks are allowed to prepare it.

MOST VENOMOUS MOLLUSK The two closely related species of blue-ringed octopus *Hapalochlaena maculosa* and *H. lunulata* (pictured)—found around the coasts of Australia and parts of Southeast Asia—carry a neurotoxic venom so potent that their relatively painless bite can kill a human in a matter of minutes. It has been estimated that each individual, which measures just 4 in. (10 cm) in length, carries sufficient venom to cause the paralysis (or even death) of 10 adult people.

lected by the Soviet research ship *Vityaz* in the Marianas Trench in the Pacific Ocean ca. 1962.

Smallest starfish The asterinid sea star (*Patiriella parvivipara*) discovered on the west coast of Eyre Peninsula, South Australia, in 1975 has a maximum radius of only 0.18 in. (4.7 mm) and a diameter of less than 0.35 in. (9 mm).

Largest concentration of crustaceans The largest single concentration of crustaceans ever recorded was a swarm of krill (*Euphausia superba*), estimated to weigh 10 million tons, tracked by U.S. scientists off Antarctica in March 1981.

Largest crustacean The largest of all marine crustaceans is the giant spider crab (*Macrocheira kaempferi*). A specimen with a claw span of 12 ft. 1.5 in. (3.7 m) weighed 41 lb. (18.6 kg).

The largest freshwater crustacean is the crayfish or crawfish (*Astacopsis gouldi*), found in the streams of Tasmania, Australia. It has been measured up to 2 ft. (61 cm) in length and may weigh as much as 9 lb. (4.1 kg).

Largest oyster In 1999, a common oyster (*Ostrea edulis*) taken from Chesapeake Bay, Virginia, U.S.A., weighed in at 8 lb. (3.7 kg) and measured 12 in. (30.5 cm) long and 5 in. (14 cm) wide.

INSECTS & ARACHNIDS

Fastest wing beat of an insect The fastest wing beat of any insect under natural conditions is 62,760 per minute by a tiny midge of the genus *Forcipomyia*. The muscular contraction-expansion cycle of 0.00045 seconds, necessary for such rapid wing beats, moreover represents the fastest muscle movement ever measured.

Heaviest insect The heaviest insects are the goliath beetles (family Scarabaeidae) of equatorial Africa. *Goliathus regius, G. meleagris, G. goliathus* (=*G. giganteus*), and *G. druryi* are the largest. In measurements of one series of males (females are smaller), the lengths from the tips of the small frontal horns to the end of the abdomen were up to 4.3 in. (11 cm), with weights of 2.5–3.5 oz. (70–100 g).

FASTEST-FLYING INSECT Acceptable modern experiments have established that the highest maintainable airspeed of any insect, including the deer bot fly *(Cephenemyia pratti)*, hawk moths *(Sphingidae,* pictured), horseflies *(Tabanus bovinus),* and some tropical butterflies (Hesperiidae), is 24 mph (39 km/h), rising to a maximum of 36 mph (58 km/h) for the Australian dragonfly *(Austrophlebia costalis)* for short bursts.

LARGEST WASP NEST A wasp next found by Yoichiro Kawamura (Japan) on May 18, 1999 at Yonegaoka, Japan, had a circumference of 8 ft. (2.45 m) and weighed 17 lb. 8 oz. (8 kg).

Largest colony of ants The largest recorded colony of ants stretches 3,700 miles (6,000 km) from northern Italy, through France to the Atlantic coast of Spain, and is made up of a species of Argentine ant (*Linepithema humile*) introduced into Europe around 80 years ago. The ants have shown an amazing ability to recognize each other even though they may come from opposite ends of the colony.

Largest dragonfly *Megaloprepus caeruleata* of Central and South America has been measured up to 4.7 in. (120 mm) in length with a wing span up to 7.5 in. (190 mm).

Largest butterfly The huge and poisonous Queen Alexandra's birdwing (*Ornithoptera alexandrae*) of Papua New Guinea may have a wingspan that exceeds 11 in. (280 mm) and weigh over 0.9 oz. (25 g).

Largest millipede The largest millipede is a full-grown African giant black millipede (*Archispirostreptus gigas*) owned by Jim Klinger (U.S.A.). It measures 15.2 in. (38.7 cm) in length, 2.6 in. (6.7 cm) in circumference, and has 256 legs. The average length for this type of millipede is between 6.5 and 11 in. (16 and 28 cm).

Largest grasshopper An unidentified species of grasshopper from the border of Malaysia and Thailand measures 10 in. (25.4 cm) in length and is capable of leaping 15 ft. (4.6 m).

Highest jump by an insect The best jumping performance by an insect is the froghopper (spittlebug, *Philaenus spumarius*), which can reach heights of 28 in. (70 cm) or more than 115 times its body length.

Longest insect The longest known specimen of *Pharnacia kirbyi*, a stick insect from the rainforests of Borneo, is in the Natural History Museum in London, UK. It has a body length of 12.9 in. (328 mm) and a total length, including the legs, of 21.5 in. (546 mm). In the wild this species is often found with some legs missing because they are so long and easily trapped when the insect sheds its skin.

Largest scorpion One of the *Heterometrus swannerdami* species, found during World War II in the village of Krishnarajapuram, India, measured 11.5 in. (29.2 cm) in overall length from the tips of the pedipalps or "pincers" to the end of the sting.

Most venomous scorpion The Tunisian fat-tailed scorpion (*Androctonus australis*) is responsible for 80% of stings and 90% of deaths from scorpion stings in North Africa.

Heaviest scorpion The large, black West African species *Pandinus imperator* can weigh up to 2 oz. (60 g). It can also measure between 5 and 7 in. (13 and 18 cm) in length, the same average length as the hand of an adult human being.

Smallest spider The smallest known spider is *Patu marplesi* (family Symphytognathidae) of Western Samoa. A specimen (male) found in moss at an altitude of 2,000 ft. (600 m) in Madolelei, Upolu, in January 1965 measured 0.017 in. (0.43 mm) overall—about the size of a period on this page.

Largest spider The largest known spider is a male goliath bird-eating spider (*Theraphosa blondi*) collected by members of the Pablo San Martin Expedition at Rio Cavro, Venezuela, in April 1965. It had a record leg span of 11 in. (28 cm)—sufficient to cover a dinner plate. This species is found in

FASTEST-MOVING INSECT *Periplaneta americana,* a large tropical cockroach of the family Dictyoptera (pictured), clocked a record speed of 3.36 mph (5.4 km/h), or 50 body lengths per second, at the University of California at Berkeley, U.S.A., in 1991. There are about 4,000 species of cockroaches, known mainly from the tropics, as they prefer warm, humid climates.

OLDEST INSECT The longest-lived insects are the splendor beetles *(Buprestidae,* shown). On May 27, 1983, a specimen of *Buprestis aurulenta* appeared from the timber staircase in a house in Essex, UK, after at least 47 years as a larva.

the coastal rainforests of Surinam, Guyana, and French Guiana, but isolated specimens have also been reported from Venezuela and Brazil.

Heaviest spider Female bird-eating spiders (family Theraphosidae) are more heavily built than males, and in February 1985 Charles J. Seiderman (U.S.A.) captured a female example near Paramaribo, Surinam, that weighed a record 4.3 oz. (122.2 g) before its death from molting problems in January 1986. Other measurements included a maximum leg-span of 10.5 in. (267 mm), a total body length of 4 in. (102 mm), and 1-in. (25-mm-long) fangs.

Most venomous spider The Brazilian wandering spiders of the genus *Phoneutria,* and particularly the Brazilian huntsman (*P. fera*), has the most active neurotoxic venom of any living spider. Its venom is so potent that only 0.00000021 oz. (0.006 mg) is sufficient to kill a mouse. *Phoneutria* are usually dark in color and have a body-and-leg spread of approximately 6.75 in. (17 cm). These large and highly aggressive creatures often enter human dwellings and hide in clothing or shoes. When disturbed, they bite furiously several times, and hundreds of accidents involving these species are reported annually.

Strongest spider The strongest spider is the Californian trapdoor spider (*Bothriocyrtum californicum*), which is able to resist a force 38 times its own weight attempting to open its trapdoor: a silken structure covering the entrance to its underground burrow. If the average adult male human being weighs 180 lb. (82 kg), it would be similar to a man trying to hold a door closed while it was being pulled on the other side by the weight of a small jet.

Largest continuous area of spiderwebs The largest continuous areas of spiderwebs are created by members of the Indian genus *Stegodyphus*. They build huge three-dimensional interwoven and overlapping webs that have been known to cover vegetation in a continuous silken mass for several miles.

Simplest spiderweb The simplest web is that of the species of the genus *Miagrammopes,* found in Africa, Australia, and North America. They have reduced their web to a single strand averaging 3 ft. (1 m) long. This is woven between two small branches.

Strongest spider's web The American house spider (*Achaearenea tepidariorum*) spins an irregular cobweb strong enough to ensnare and hold small mice.

Oldest spider The oldest spider recorded lived for an estimated 26–28 years. It was a female of the tropical bird-eaters (family Theraphosidae) that was collected in Mexico in 1935.

REPTILES

Oldest living chelonian Harriet, one of three giant tortoises (*Geochelone nigra porteri*) collected by Charles Darwin (UK) from the Galapagos Islands in 1835, is thought to be the world's oldest resident at 173 years old. Born in November 1830, she currently resides at the Australia Zoo, near Brisbane, Queensland, Australia.

Deepest dive by a chelonian In May 1987, Dr. Scott Eckert (U.S.A.) reported that a leatherback turtle (*Dermochelys coriacea*) fitted with a pressure-sensitive recording device had reached a depth of 3,937 ft. (1,200 m) off the Virgin Islands in the West Indies.

Largest chelonian The leatherback turtle (*Dermochelys coriacea*) averages 6–7 ft. (1.8–2.1 m) from the tip of the beak to the end of the tail (with a carapace of 5–5 ft. 6 in. or 1.52–1.67 m). They measure about 7 ft. (2.1 m) across the front flippers and can weigh up to 1,000 lb. (450 kg).

Fastest chelonian The highest speed claimed for any reptile in water is 22 mph (35 km/h) by a frightened Pacific leatherback turtle (*Dermochelys coriacea*).

Largest tortoise The largest specimen was a Galapagos tortoise (*Chelonoidis nigra*) named Goliath, who resided at the Life Fellowship Bird Sanctuary in Seffner, Florida, U.S.A., from 1960 to 2002. He was 4 ft. 5 in. (135.8 cm) long, 3 ft. 4 in. (102 cm) wide and 2 ft. 3 in. (68.5 cm) high, and weighed 920 lb. (417 kg).

OLDEST CHELONIAN The greatest authenticated age recorded for a chelonian is at least 188 years, achieved by a Madagascar radiated tortoise (*Astrochelys radiata,* pictured) that was presented to the Tonga royal family by Captain Cook (UK) in either 1773 or 1777. The animal was called Tui Malila and remained in their care until its death in 1965.

Oldest crocodilian The greatest authenticated age for a crocodilian is 66 years—achieved by a female American alligator (*Alligator mississippiensis*) that arrived at Adelaide Zoo, South Australia, on June 5, 1914 when she was two years old. She died on September 26, 1978.

Most dangerous lizard With a length of up to 24 in. (60 cm), the Gila monster (*Heloderma suspectum*) is a large, heavily built, brightly colored lizard that lives in the arid parts of Mexico and southwestern U.S.A. They have eight well-developed venom glands in their lower jaws and carry enough venom to kill two adult humans. The venom is not injected but seeps into the wound inflicted when the Gila monster bites its victim with its sharp, fragile teeth. Because of this, a lizard may continue to hang on after it has bitten and actively chew for several minutes. In one study of 34 people bitten by these animals, there were eight fatalities. The lizard only attacks when provoked.

Largest lizard The largest lizard is the Komodo dragon (*Varanus komodoensis*), otherwise known as the Komodo monitor or ora, found on the Indonesian islands of Komodo, Rintja, Padar, and Flores. Males average 7 ft. 5 in. (2.25 m) in length and weigh about 130 lb. (59 kg). The largest accurately measured specimen was a male presented to an American zoologist in 1928 by the Sultan of Bima. For a short period in 1937 it was put on display in St. Louis Zoological Gardens, Missouri, U.S.A., by which time it was 10 ft. 2 in. (3.10 m) long and weighed 365 lb. (166 kg).

Longest lizard The slender Salvadori or Papuan monitor (*Varanus salvadorii*) of Papua New Guinea has been reliably measured at up to 15 ft. 7 in. (4.75 m) in length. Nearly 70% of its total length is taken up by the tail.

Fastest lizard The highest burst of speed recorded for any reptile on land is 21.7 mph (34.9 km/h), achieved by *Ctenosaura,* a spiny-tailed iguana from Central America.

Fastest land snake The fastest land snake is the aggressive black mamba (*Dendroaspis polylepis*) of southeastern, tropical Africa. The snake can reach speeds of 10–12 mph (16–19 km/h) in short bursts over level ground.

Heaviest living snake The heaviest living snake is a Burmese python (*Python molurus bivittatus*) that weighed 403 lb. (182.5 kg) on November

LARGEST CROCODILIAN The largest reptile in the world is the estuarine or saltwater crocodile *(Crocodylus porosus,* pictured), which ranges throughout the tropical regions of Asia and the Pacific. The Bhitarkanika Wildlife Sanctuary in Orissa State, India, houses four protected estuarine crocodiles measuring more than 20 ft. (6 m) in length, the largest being over 23 ft. (7 m) long. There are several unauthenticated reports of specimens up to 33 ft. (10 m) in length.

OLDEST SNAKE The greatest reliable age recorded for a snake is 40 years 3 months and 14 days for a male common boa (*Boa constrictor*, pictured) named Popeye, who died at Philadelphia Zoo, Pennsylvania, U.S.A., on April 15, 1977.

20, 1998. She is 25 years old, 27 ft. (8.22 m) long, and has a girth of 28 in. (71.1 cm). Known as "Baby," she lives at the Serpent Safari Park in Gurnee, Illinois, U.S.A., and is owned by Lou Daddano (U.S.A.). Snakes continue to grow throughout their lives, so Baby is still growing.

Longest snake The reticulated python (*Python reticulatus*) of Southeast Asia, Indonesia, and the Philippines regularly exceeds 20 ft. 6 in. (6.25 m), and the record length is 32 ft. 9.5 in. (10 m) for a specimen shot in Celebes, Indonesia, in 1912.

Longest venomous snake The longest venomous snake is the king cobra (*Ophiophagus hannah*), also called the hamadryad, which measures 12–15 ft. (3.65–4.5 m) in length and is found in Southeast Asia and India. The king cobra can stand tall enough to look an adult human in the eye and its head is as big as a man's hand. Its venom can stun the nervous system and cause asphyxiation while other toxins start digesting the paralyzed victim. The venom in a single bite from a king cobra is enough to kill an elephant or 20 people.

Most venomous land snake The small-scaled fierce snake or taipan (*Oxyuranus microlepidotus*) measures up to 5 ft. 7 in. (1.7 m) and is found mainly in the Diamantina River and Cooper Creek drainage basins in Queensland and western New South Wales, Australia. In a single strike, a taipan can inject 0.002 oz. (60 mg) of venom, sufficient to quickly paralyze a small marsupial, but also more than enough to kill several human adults. The average venom yield after milking is 0.00155 oz. (44 mg) but one male specimen yielded 0.00385 oz. (110 mg)—enough to kill 250,000 mice. Fortunately this species only lives in the arid deserts of central eastern Australia and no human death has been reported from its bite.

Heaviest venomous snake The heaviest venomous snake is probably the eastern diamondback rattlesnake (*Crotalus adamanteus*) of the south-eastern U.S.A., which weighs 12–15 lb. (5.5–6.8 kg) and is 5–6 ft. (1.52–1.83 m) in length. The heaviest on record weighed 33 lb. (15 kg) and was 7 ft. 9 in. (2.36 m) long.

PETS

Fastest car window opening by a dog The world record for the fastest time a dog has unwound a non-electric car window is 13 seconds and belongs to Striker, a border collie owned and trained by Francis Gadassi (Hungary). The record was set on August 14, 2003 in Québec City, Canada. Striker used his paw and nose to perform the record attempt.

Longest dog tongue Brandy, a boxer owned by John Scheid (U.S.A.), had a tongue that measured 17 in. (43 cm).

Smallest dog ever The smallest dog was a fist-sized dwarf Yorkshire terrier owned by Arthur Marples (UK). Fully grown, this tiny dog stood 2.8 in.

SMALLEST LIVING DOG The smallest living dog in terms of length is Tiny Pinocchio (pictured), who measured 8 in. (20.3 cm) long on May 23, 2003. Tiny Pinocchio is owned by Linda Skeels-Hopson (U.S.A.). The smallest dog in terms of height is Whitney, a Yorkshire terrier who measured 3 in. (7.6 cm) to the shoulder on November 26, 2002. Whitney is owned by Christopher and Patricia Sheridan (both UK).

TALLEST AND LONGEST DOG Harvey, a Great Dane owned by Charles Dodman (UK, both pictured), stands at 41.5 in. (105.41 cm) tall and measures 91 in. (231.14 cm) from nose to tip. Great Danes are one of the tallest dog breeds, with an average height from the ground to the top of the shoulder of around 29.5 in. (75 cm).

(7.11 cm) at the shoulder and measured 3.75 in. (9.5 cm) from its nose to the tip of its tail.

Highest jump by a dog The world record for the highest jump cleared by a dog is 66 in. (167.6 cm), achieved by Cinderella May A Holly Grey, a

TALLEST LIVING HORSE Goliath measured 19 hands 1 in. (195.58 cm or 77 in.) on July 24, 2003. Goliath is owned by Priefert Manufacturing, Inc. (U.S.A.) and is a male black Percheron draft horse, whose pedigree name is Prince Jordan of Lakeview. On average, he eats 50 lb. (22.6 kg) of hay and drinks 30 gallons (113.5 liters) of water per day.

greyhound owned by Kathleen Conroy and Kate Long (both U.S.A.), at the Purina Dog Chow Incredible Dog Challenge show, Gray Summit, Missouri, U.S.A., on October 3, 2003.

Largest dog litter Three dogs are on record as having given birth to 23 puppies. An American foxhound belonging to W. Ely (U.S.A.) is the first dog to have recorded this feat, on June 19, 1944. Between February 6 and 7, 1975 a St. Bernard belonging to R. and A. Rodden (U.S.A.) had 14 of its puppies survive. A Great Dane belonging to M. Harris (UK) had 16 of its litter survive in June 1987.

Longest ears on a dog The longest ears on a dog each measured 13 in. (33.2 cm) in length when they were measured on December 11, 2003. They belong to a basset hound named Jack vom Forster Wald, who lives with his owners, Claudia and Carsten Baus, in Fulda, Germany.

Most tennis balls held in the mouth by a dog Augie, a golden retriever owned by the Miller family (U.S.A.), successfully gathered and held five regulation-sized tennis balls in his mouth on July 6, 2003.

Oldest horse ever The greatest age reliably recorded for a horse is 62 years for Old Billy (foaled 1760), bred by Edward Robinson, Woolston, Lancashire, UK. Old Billy died on November 27, 1822.

Oldest donkey ever The donkey with the oldest documented age is Suzy, who reached the age of 54 in 2002. Suzy was owned by Beth Augusta Menczer (U.S.A.). The average life span of a donkey is 25–30 years.

Oldest pony ever The world's oldest pony was Sancho, a Welsh/Arab cross who reached the age of 54 years in 2003. Sancho was owned by Elizabeth Saunders (UK) and was discovered by the Veteran Horse Society, North Pembrokeshire, UK. The pony died in August 2003.

Oldest living rabbit The world's oldest living rabbit is Baby, a Holland Lop born in August 1990 and owned by Kayla and Sue Bulos (both U.S.A.). House rabbits usually live for around 7–10 years.

Oldest rabbit ever A wild rabbit named Flopsy was caught on August 6, 1964 and died 18 years and 10 months later at the home of L. B. Walker (Australia).

Longest rabbit ears The longest rabbit ears measured 31.1 in. (79 cm) in a complete span on November 1, 2003 at the American Rabbit Breeders Association National Show in Wichita, Kansas, U.S.A. The ears belong to an English Lop called Nipper's Geronimo, who is owned by Waymon and Margaret Nipper (U.S.A.).

Highest rabbit high jump The highest rabbit high jump is 18 in. (46 cm), achieved by Golden Flame, a castor satin rabbit belonging to Sam Lawrie (UK), on August 29, 2002.

LARGEST HORN CIRCUMFERENCE Lurch, an African watusi steer owned by Janice Wolf (U.S.A.), had a horn circumference of 37.5 in. (95.25 cm) when measured on May 6, 2003. Although they are not the longest horns on record, Lurch's horns are each approximately 7 ft. (2.1 m).

Largest mouse litter A mouse belonging to M. Ogilvie (UK) gave birth to a litter of 34 on February 12, 1982, 33 of which survived.

Smallest breed of domestic hamster The Roborovski hamster *(Phodopus roborovskii)* typically grows to a length of 1.5–2 in. (4–5 cm). These hamsters originate from Mongolia and northern China.

Largest hamster litter On February 28, 1974, a hamster belonging to the Miller family (U.S.A.) gave birth to a litter of 26. The average is eight babies per litter.

Largest cat litter On August 7, 1970 a Burmese/Siamese cross cat owned by V. Gane (UK) gave birth to 19 kittens, four of which were still-born.

Oldest kinkajou in captivity The oldest living kinkajou *(Potos flavus)* in captivity is Huggy Bear, who turned 27 years 6 months old in January 2004 and belongs to Sonja Pedersen (U.S.A.). A kinkajou is a member of the raccoon family.

Oldest goat ever The world's oldest goat was McGinty, who lived to the age of 22 years 5 months. Until her death in November 2003, she was owned by Doris C. Long (UK).

Oldest caged parrot The longest lived caged parrot was Prudle, owned by Iris Frost (UK). Prudle was captured in 1958 and lived to the age of 35. Before dying in 1994, Prudle had learned over 800 words and could even conduct polite conversation.

Cat with the most toes Jake, a male ginger tabby cat, has 28 toes, with seven on each paw, as counted by a veterinarian on September 24, 2002. Jake lives in Bonfield, Ontario, Canada, with his owners Michelle and Paul Contant (Canada).

UNUSUAL PLANTS

GWR TALKS TO Ron Hildebrant

Ron Hildebrant (U.S.A.) has spent much of his life tracking down the record-breakers of the tree world. He helped to measure the tallest living tree, the 396-ft. 4.8-in. (112.6-m) Stratosphere Giant (pictured on next page) in August 2000, and he's more than happy to share his enthusiasm for trees with *Guinness World Records* readers!

What exactly is a tree hunter? A tree hunter is someone who looks for the biggest, tallest, and oldest trees. Sometimes unusual ones are

LARGEST FLOWER The mottled orange-brown and white parasite *Rafflesia arnoldii* (pictured) has the largest of all blooms. These attach themselves to the cissus vines in the jungles of Southeast Asia. They measure up to 3 ft. (91 cm) across, weigh up to 24 lb. (11 kg) and their petals are 0.75 in. (1.9 cm) thick.

sought, such as rare specimens or those with unusually shaped trunks or strange branching, but most of the time tree hunters are searching for trees with measurable parameters—such as height, diameter, or age.

Redwoods are the tallest trees in the world. What is the most amazing one you have seen? I'd say the late great Dyerville Giant, which fell after a storm in March 1991. It was, until then, the world's tallest tree, being 113.4 m (372 feet) high, and indeed the tallest tree of modern times. It was 16.6 ft. (5.06 m) in diameter and perhaps up to 2,500 years old—I haven't yet determined its exact age—and had a trunk volume of 28,500 ft.³ (807 m³), making it one of the largest redwoods of modern times. After its fall I discovered it had at one time been even taller—390 to 400 ft. (119 to 122 m) high a couple of centuries ago.

You've seen the world's tallest tree. How old is it? Yes, I have; this is the well-named Stratosphere Giant, which towers very, very high, at 369 ft. 4.8 in. (112.6 m) as of 2002—and is still growing. I recently did an accurate age estimate of the tree after having greatly improved my methods for coast redwoods, and it's about 1,600 years old, plus or minus about a hundred years.

How do you measure a tree? In the pre-laser days it was a lot of grunt work—we'd lay out tape lines, plumbing treetops from three places and using a good surveyor's transit. It required taking slope angles into account, but the hardest part was adjusting for leaning or off-centered treetops. In the mid-1990s, the laser came out. These revolutionary devices have greatly reduced the time, labor, and effort involved, and are extremely accurate. With the laser, leaning tops are no longer an issue, for a direct measurement is determined by the laser itself. We can point and shoot at a tree and get a reading accurate to within a few feet in just seconds.

How do you become a tree hunter? If you're willing to invest in some good tools and you have some good math skills in algebra and trigonometry and keep yourself in good physical shape, that's a good start. It's helpful to know how a particular tree species behaves in certain environments, making it easier to find particular types of trees. A background in botany, geology, meteorology, soils, and ecology are all a big plus. Expect to do plenty of hiking: in some of my hikes I do 10 miles (16 km) or more in a day, or hike up to 11,000 ft. (3,350 m) or more in elevation. Finally, expect to fail in your quests now and then, but never give up!

Tallest living tree The world's tallest living tree is the Stratosphere Giant, which measured 369 ft. 4.8 in. (112.6 m) as of 2002. This coast redwood (*Sequoia sempervirens*) was discovered by Chris Atkins (U.S.A.) in August 2000 in the Rockefeller Forest of the Humboldt Redwoods State Park, California, U.S.A.

Fastest growing tree The fastest recorded rate of growth for any tree (discounting bamboo, which is classified as a woody grass) is 35 ft. 2.8 in. (10.74 m) in 13 months, or approximately 1.1 in. (2.8 cm) per day by an *Albizzia falcata* planted on June 17, 1974 in Sabah, Malaysia.

Earliest tree The earliest surviving species of tree is the maidenhair (*Ginkgo biloba*) of Zhejiang, China, which first appeared about 160 million years ago during the Jurassic era. It was rediscovered by Engelbert Kaempfer (Germany) in 1690. It has been grown in Japan since c. 1100, where it was known as ginkyou (silver apricot) and is now known as ichou.

Oldest tree ever documented The oldest age for a tree ever recorded is for a bristlecone pine (*Pinus longaeva*) known as Prometheus, which was cut down from Mt. Wheeler in Nevada, U.S.A., in 1963 and dated at approximately 5,200 years old. Although 4,867 rings were counted—the most ever—the tree was growing in a harsh environment which slowed its development, and so its actual age has been adjusted to approximately 5,200 years old.

Largest prey for carnivorous plants Of all the carnivorous plants or pitcher plants, the ones that digest the largest prey belong to the Nepenthaceae family (genus *Nepenthes*). Both the *Nepenthes rajah* and *N. rafflesiana* have been known to consume frogs, birds, and even rats, digesting their prey using enzymes. These

SMALLEST SEED Epiphytic orchids (orange epiphytic orchid, pictured) produce 28,130 million seeds per oz. (992.25 millions per gram). The largest seed is that of the giant fan palm or double coconut (*Lodoicea maldivica*).

The single-seeded fruit weighs up to 44 lb. (20 kg) and can take 10 years to develop.

OLDEST LIVING INDIVIDUAL TREE The oldest living individual tree is the ancient bristlecone pine (*Pinus longaeva*) called Methuselah (shown), which is 4,733 years old. It was found by Dr. Edmund Schulman (U.S.A.) in the White Mountains, California, U.S.A., and dated in 1957.

species are commonly found in the rainforests of Asia, notably Borneo and Indonesia.

Most dangerous stinger New Zealand's tree nettle (*Urtica ferox*) has been known to kill dogs and horses. Its stinging hairs inject potent toxins into the skin. The tree nettle can grow up to 10 ft. (3 m) in height. Fine white stinging hairs line its green leaves and contain many toxins, the main ones being histamine, 5-hydroxytryptamine, acetylcholine, and formic acid.

Smelliest flower Also known as the corpse flower, the *Amorphophallus titanum* is the smelliest flower on Earth. When it blooms, it releases an extremely foul odor—comparable to that of rotten flesh—that can be smelled half a mile away. This plant is native to the Sumatran rainforests and very few have flowered in Europe or the U.S.A. since first discovered in 1878.

Tallest wild cactus The tallest cacti ever recorded is a cardon (*Pachycereus pringlei*) found in the Sonoran Desert, Baja California, Mexico. It measures 63 ft. (19.2 m) and was discovered by Marc Salak and Jeff Brown (both U.S.A.) in April 1995. Its incredible height is about the same as the combined height of four giraffes.

HORTICULTURAL GIANTS

Longest zucchini A zucchini measuring 76 in. (1.93 m) on September 22, 2003 was grown by Sher Singh Kanwal (U.S.A.) in his garden in Niagara Falls, New York, U.S.A.

Longest beetroot A beetroot grown by Richard Hope (UK) measured 20 ft. 2 in. (6.146 m) on September 27, 2003 at the Llanharry Giant Vegetable Championships, Rhondda Cynon Taff, UK.

Most heads on one sunflower A sunflower plant with 837 heads was grown by Melvin Hemker (U.S.A.). The heads were counted on September 18, 2001.

Largest rosebush A specimen of the rosebush Lady Banks *(Rosa banksiae),* known as Banks at Tombstone, Arizona, U.S.A., has a trunk circumference of 13 ft. 5 in. (4.09 m), stands 9 ft. (2.75 m) high, and covers an area of 8,000 ft.^{2} (743 m^2). The bush is supported by 77 posts, and 250 people can sit under the arbor.

Largest homegrown lily bloom A lily bloom measuring 23.2 in. (59 cm) long on March 21, 2002 was grown by Natividad Rico Pérez (Spain) at her home in Monóvar, Alicante, Spain.

HEAVIEST LEMON The heaviest lemon (pictured) weighed 11 lb. 9.7 oz. (5.26 kg) on January 8, 2003 and was grown by Aharon Shemoel (Israel) on his farm in Kefar Zeitim, Israel. Its circumference was 29 in. (74 cm), it was 13.7 in. (35 cm) high, and it grew alongside another large lemon.

Largest gourd circumference Robert Weber (Australia) grew a gourd with a circumference of 69.6 in. (1.77 m) and presented it at the Australasian Giant Pumpkin and Vegetable Competition in Victoria, Australia, on April 7, 2001.

Largest tomato truss A record 185 tomatoes were counted on a tomato plant grown by Joe Hallam (UK) on August 19, 2003.

Tree with most different fruit The record for the most fruits produced from the same tree is five: apricot, cherry, nectarine, plum, and peach. The fruit species were grafted on to a prune tree in 2000 by Luis H. Carrasco (Chile).

★ HEAVIEST FRUIT AND VEGETABLES ★

FRUIT/VEGETABLE	WEIGHT	NAME & VENUE	DATE
Apple	3 lb. 11 oz. (1.67 kg)	Alan Smith (UK), Linton, Kent, UK	1997
Beetroot	51 lb. 9 oz. (23.4 kg)	Ian Neale (UK), Shepton Mallet, Somerset, UK	2001
Brussels sprout	18 lb. 3 oz. (8.3 kg)	Bernard Lavery (UK), Llanharry, Rhondda Cynon Taff, UK	1992
Cabbage	124 lb. (56.24 kg)	Bernard Lavery (UK), Llanharry, Rhondda Cynon Taff, UK	1989
Cantaloupe	63 lb. 8 oz. (28.8 kg)	Bill Rogerson (U.S.A.), Robersonville, North Carolina, U.S.A.	1997
Carrot	18 lb. 13 oz. (8.61 kg)	John Evans (U.S.A.), Palmer, Alaska, U.S.A.	1998
Cauliflower	54 lb. 3 oz. (24.6 kg)	Alan Hattersley (UK), Sheffield, UK	1999
Celery	63 lb. 4.8 oz. (28.7 kg)	Scott and Mardie Robb (both U.S.A.), Palmer, U.S.A.	2003
Cherry	0.76 oz. (21.69 g)	Gerado Maggipinto (Italy), Sammichele di Bari, Italy	2003
Courgette	64 lb. 8 oz. (29.25 kg)	Bernard Lavery (UK), Llanharry, Rhondda Cynon Taff, UK	1990
Cucumber	27 lb. 3 oz. (12.4 kg)	Alfred J. Cobb (UK), Shepton Mallet, Somerset, UK	2003
Garlic head	2 lb. 10 oz. (1.19 kg)	Robert Kirkpatrick (U.S.A.), Eureka, California, U.S.A.	1985
Gooseberry	2.15 oz. (61.04 g)	K. Archer (UK), Scholar Green, Cheshire, UK	1993
Gourd	94 lb. 5 oz. (42.8 kg)	Robert Weber (Australia), Victoria, Australia	2001
Grapefruit	6 lb. 12 oz. (3.065 kg)	Debbie Hazelton (Australia), Queensland, Australia	1995
Leek	17 lb. 13 oz. (8.1 kg)	Fred Charlton (UK), Somerset, UK	2002
Lemon	11 lb. 9.7 oz. (5.26 kg)	Aharon Shemoel (Israel), Kefar Zeitim, Israel	2003
Mango	4 lb. 4 oz. (1.94 kg)	John Painter (U.S.A.), Bokeelia, Florida, U.S.A.	1999

Marrow	135 lb. (61.23 kg)	John Handbury (UK), Temple Normanton, Chesterfield, UK	1998
Onion	15 lb. 15.5 oz. (7.24 kg)	Mel Ednie (UK), Anstruther, Fife, UK	1994
Parsnip	8 lb. 6 oz. (3.8 kg)	Norman Lee Craven (Canada), Toronto, Ontario, Canada	2003
Peach	25.6 oz. (725 g)	Paul Friday (U.S.A.), Coloma, Michigan, U.S.A.	2002
Pear	4 lb. 8 oz. (2.1 kg)	Warren Yeoman (Australia), Arding, New South Wales, Australia	1999
Pineapple	17 lb. 12 oz. (8.06 kg)	E. Kamuk (Papua New Guinea), Ais Village, West New Britain Province, Papau New Guinea	1994
Potato	7 lb. 11 oz. (3.5 kg)	K. Sloane (UK), Patrick, Isle of Man, UK	1994
Pumpkin	1,337 lb. 9 oz. (606.7 kg)	Charles Houghton (U.S.A.), Massachusetts, U.S.A.	2002
Quince	5 lb. 2 oz. (2.34 kg)	Edward Harold McKinney (U.S.A.), Citronelle, Alabama, U.S.A.	2002
Radish	68 lb. 9 oz. (31.1 kg)	Manubu Oono (Japan), Kagoshima, Japan	2003
Squash	962 lb. (436 kg)	Steve Hoult (Canada), Toronto, Ontario, Canada	1997
Strawberry	8.14 oz. (231 g)	G. Andersen (UK), Folkstone, Kent, UK	1983
Swede (rutabaga)	75 lb. 12 oz. (34.35 kg)	Scott Robb (U.S.A.), Palmer, Alaska, U.S.A.	1999
Sweet potato	49 lb. 9 oz. (22.5 kg)	Belinda Love (Australia), Gingin, Western Australia	1998
Tomato	7 lb. 12 oz. (3.51 kg)	G. Graham (U.S.A.), Edmond, Oklahoma, U.S.A.	1986

HEAVIEST CUCUMBER
Alfred J. Cobb (UK) grew a cucumber (held here by Mr. Atherton) weighing 27 lb. 5.3 oz. (12.4 kg). It was presented at the National Amateur Gardening Show's UK National Giant Vegetables Championship at Shepton Mallet, Somerset, UK, on September 5, 2003.

★ TALLEST PLANTS ★

PLANT	HEIGHT	NAME & VENUE	DATE
Bean	46 ft. 3 in. (14.1 m)	Staton Rorie (U.S.A.), Rienzi, Mississippi, U.S.A.	2003
Celery	9 ft. (2.74 m)	Joan Priednieks (UK), Westonzoyland, Somerset, UK	1998
Cactus (homegrown)	70 ft. (21.3 m)	Pandit S. Munji (India), Dharwad, Karnataka, India	2004
Chrysanthemum	14 ft. 3 in. (4.34 m)	Bernard Lavery (UK), Spalding, Lincolnshire, UK	1995
Dandelion	39.3 in. (100 cm)	Ragnar Gille and Marcus Hamring (both Sweden), Uppsala, Sweden	2003
Fuchsia	21 ft. 7 in. (6.58 m)	The Growing Place (UK), Spalding, Lincolnshire, UK	2003
Papaya tree	44 ft. (13.4 m)	Prasanta Mal (India), Arambagh, Hooghly, India	2003
Parsley	55 in. (1.39 m)	Danielle, Gabrielle, and Michelle Kassatly, (all U.S.A.), San Jose, California, U.S.A.	2003
Pepper	16 ft. (4.87 m)	Laura Liang (U.S.A.), Irvine, California, U.S.A.	1999
Periwinkle	7 ft. 2 in. (2.19 m)	Arvind, Rekha, Ashish, and Rashmi Nema (all India), Indrapuri, Bhopal, India	2003
Petunia	19 ft. 1 in. (5.8 m)	Bernard Lavery (UK), Llanharry, Rhondda Cynon Taff, UK	1994
Potato or brinjal	18 ft. 0.5 in. (5.5 m)	Abdul Masfoor (India), Karnataka State, India	1998
Rosebush	11 ft. 1 in. (3.38 m)	Kathleen Mielke-Villalobos (U.S.A.), San Diego, California, U.S.A.	2003
Sunflower	25 ft. 5.5 in. (7.76 m)	M. Heijms (Netherlands), Oirschot, Netherlands	1986
Tomato	65 ft. (19.8 m)	Nutriculture Ltd. (UK), Mawdesley, Lancashire, UK	2000

GWR TALKS TO Bernard Lavery

From monster corncobs to fantastic fuchsias, Bernard Lavery's (UK) records for giant fruit, vegetables, and plants are some of the best loved Guinness World Records. He currently holds 12 records, including the longest gourd, which grew to 41 ft. 4 in. (12.6 m) in 1992, and the longest corncob, which grew to a length of 36.25 in. (92 cm) in 1994.

How did you get involved in growing giants? I first caught the "growing" bug over 20 years ago while growing my first pumpkin (pictured). Although this didn't break any records, the pleasures I got from the experience were immense and soon multiplied when I directed my efforts to a whole range of different vegetable subjects. In 1985, I organized the first UK Giant Vegetable Championships in Cardiff.

How do you grow giant vegetables? The most important factor is to use the varieties of seeds that have the genetic capabilities to produce larger than average specimens. It's then advisable to obtain some advice from books or other giant growers. If these options are unavailable then you must just have a go yourself. You must remember that when you make a mistake another year will have to pass before you can try again. The second most important thing you must have is the presence of "Lady Luck." If she's sitting on your shoulder then you're halfway there.

What would you like to grow that you haven't tried? The aubergine (eggplant) would be my choice for a new challenge. I've grown some large ones already, but nowhere near a world record weight.

Can you eat these giants after they have been shown? Giant vegetables are much the same as ordinary size ones. When they're young and freshly harvested they are superb, but when they're grown on to well past their best, then like ordinary ones, they become tough and tasteless.

What is the record you are most proud of? I am most proud of the record I set in 1991 for the longest carrot that measured 16 ft. 10.5 in. (5.14 m).

What's your best advice for growing giant plants? Just try to enjoy it. It's a real challenge to stretch Mother Nature to her limits and beyond, but if at first you don't succeed then try, try again. It's magical when you succeed.

MODERN WORLD

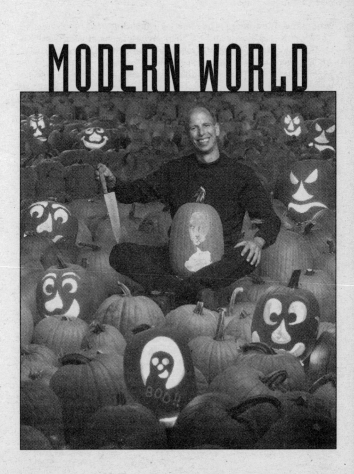

NATIONS

Largest country Russia's total area covers 11.5% of the world's total land area—6,592,848 miles² (17,075,400 km²). It is 70 times larger than the UK, with a population of 144,417,000 in 2001.

Most maritime boundaries The country with the largest number of maritime boundaries is Indonesia, with 19 (including boundaries with disputed territorial claims).

Most land boundaries The countries with the most land boundaries are China and Russia, both with 14. China's are: Mongolia, Russia, North Korea, Vietnam, Laos, Burma (Myanmar), India, Bhutan, Nepal, Pakistan, Afghanistan, Tajikistan, Kyrgyzstan, and Kazakhstan. These extend for 14,900 miles (24,000 km). Russia has boundaries with Norway, Finland, Estonia, Latvia, Lithuania, Poland, Belarus, Ukraine, Georgia, Azerbaijan, Kazakhstan, China, Mongolia, and North Korea. These boundaries extend for 12,365 miles (19,900 km).

Country of origin for most refugees The country from which most people seek asylum is Iraq. According to the 2002 figures from the United Nations High Commission for Refugees (UNHCR), 51,000 Iraqis applied for political asylum to one of 37 industrialized nations. The total number of applications made in 2002 was 587,400.

Country receiving most applications for political asylum According to figures from UNHCR, of the 587,400 applications for political asylum that were submitted in 2002, the country that received the highest number was the UK with 111,606 (19%).

Country with most administrative divisions The UK has a record 235 administrative divisions.

Country from which the most countries have gained independence A total of 62 countries have gained independence from the UK.

Country with the most official languages The Republic of South Africa has 11 official languages: English, Afrikaans, isiZulu, isiXhosa, Sesotho, Setswana, Sepedi, Xitsonga, siSwati, isiNdebele, and Tshivenda.

Highest and lowest inflation Zimbabwe has the highest inflation according to the Economist Intelligence Unit 2003 forecast, with consumer prices rising at over 300%. Hong Kong currently has the lowest inflation at -2.5%.

Highest and lowest cost of living According to the Economist Intelligence Unit's Worldwide Cost of Living Survey of January 2003 (for

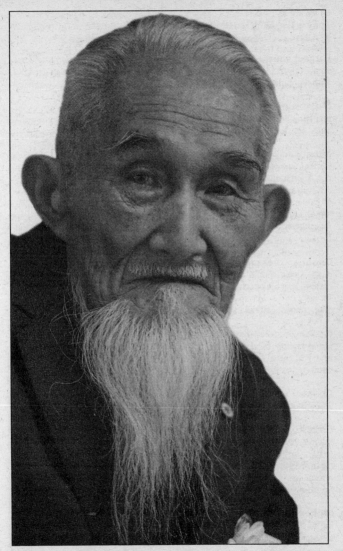

HIGHEST LIFE EXPECTANCY Japan had the highest life expectancy at birth in 2002 with a total population average of 81.1 years (77.5 years for men and 84.7 years for women).

December 2002 results), Japan's capital city, Tokyo, is the most expensive city in the world. Harare, the capital of Zimbabwe, is the world's cheapest.

Most and least taxed country In Denmark the highest rate of personal income tax is 62.9%, with the basic rate of income tax starting at 43.7% (June 2003). Bahrain and Qatar are the lowest taxed countries, where the rate, regardless of income, is zero. For both nations, oil provides over half of government revenues.

Highest and lowest GNI per capita According to the World Bank Atlas, the country with the highest Gross National Income (GNI) for 2002 was Bermuda, which overtook Luxembourg with $38,830 (£25,627). The Democratic Republic of Congo had the lowest GNI per capita with $90 (£59). GNI is the total value of goods and services produced by a country in one year, divided by its population. GNI per capita shows what part of a country's GNI each person would have if it was divided equally.

Country with the largest energy consumption The U.S.A. is the world's largest consumer of both fossil fuels (coal, oil, and natural gas) and commercial energy (fossil fuels plus nuclear and hydro power). In 1998, it consumed a total of 1,937 million tons of oil equivalent (Mtoe) of fossil fuels and 2,147 Mtoe of commercial energy. The total world energy consumption of fossil fuels was 7,624 Mtoe and the world total energy consumption of commercial fuel was 8,477 Mtoe.

Most densely populated country Monaco has a population density of 42,840 per mile^2 (16,476 per km^2) in 2003. Its population that year was

LOWEST LIFE EXPECTANCY According to 2001 data, life expectancy at birth in the Republic of Botswana in Africa is only 37.1 years (36.8 years for men and 37.5 years for women).

HIGHEST AND LOWEST GOVERNMENT REVENUES The country that produced the highest government revenues from taxation per km² of physical land is Vatican City (pictured) with $476,363,636 (£302,031,217) as of 2001. The lowest is the Democratic Republic of the Congo with only $115 (£72) per km² of land.

32,130 with a total area of 0.75 miles² (1.95 km²). This equates to each person having 652 ft.² (60.6 m²) of land.

Most sparsely populated country In 2001, Mongolia had a population of 2,435,000 in an area of 603,930 miles² (1,564,160 km²), giving a density of 4 people to every 1 mile² (1.6 people to every 1 km²).

Most populous country In 2003, China had an estimated population of 1,286,975,468—higher than that for the whole world 150 years ago, when the world population stood at 1,260,000,000. The UN's predicted population for China in 2025 is 1.48 billion.

Least populous country The Vatican City, or Holy See, had approximately 911 inhabitants in 2003. The Vatican is the world's smallest country.

Largest population of children In the Marshall Islands, in the north of the Pacific Ocean, 39.1% of the population were under the age of 15 in 2003. Out of an estimated total population of 56,429, approximately 22,063 individuals were aged between 0 and 14 years.

Most bombed country The most heavily bombed country has been Laos. It has been estimated that between May 1964 and February 26, 1973 some 5 billion lb. (2.26 million tons) of bombs were dropped along the North to South Ho Chi Minh Trail supply route to South Vietnam.

Country with highest military expenditure per capita Israel has the highest military expenditure per capita, with $1,487.68 (£819.07) spent per person as of 2003. Israel had a population of 6,258,000 in 2001.

Country with lowest military expenditure per capita From available figures, the country that spends the least money on military expenditure is Swaziland, with $17.80 (£9.80) per person as of 2003. Swaziland had a population of 1,104,000 in 2001.

POLITICS & GOVERNMENT

Longest lived prime minister The longest lived prime minister of any country was Antoine Pinay (France), who was born on December 30, 1891 and died on December 13, 1994 aged 102 years 348 days. He was his country's prime minister from March to December 1952.

Most reelected prime minister Lebanese prime minister Rashid Karami was first elected in 1955 and then officially reelected seven additional times between 1958 and 1976. His final term of office was in 1984, when most people hoped he would end the country's civil war, but he was assassinated in 1987 by a bomb thrown at his helicopter. Karami served in 1955–56; 1958–60; 1961–64; 1965–66; 1966–68; 1969–70; 1975–76; and 1984–87.

Longest ruling party The party with the longest uninterrupted spell in government is the PRI (Partido Revolucionario Institucional) of Mexico, which won every Mexican presidential election from 1929 to 2000, when it lost to the PAN (Partido de Accion Nacional).

Youngest president Jean-Claude Duvalier (Haiti, b. July 3, 1951) succeeded his father, François Duvalier, as Haitian president for life on April 22, 1971, becoming the world's youngest president at the age of 19 years 293 days. He served as president of Haiti until 1986.

Longest serving living president General Gnassingbe Eyadema (Togo) became president of the Togolese Republic on April 14, 1967 after leading a coup to oust President Nicolas Grunitzky.

Oldest president Joaquin Balaguer was president of the Dominican Republic in 1960–62, 1966–78, and 1986–96. He ultimately left office at the age of 89, having held the presidency for no fewer than 22 years.

Youngest UN ambassador Laura Sweeting (UK, b. June 1, 1984) became the United Nations' youngest Goodwill Ambassador on June 9, 2000. The 16-year-old schoolgirl's role in the Water4Life Appeal/Children Helping Children campaign raised awareness of the fact that over 5,000 people die each day because of the lack of clean water.

Youngest current head of state Yahya Jammeh (b. May 25, 1965) became president of the Provisional Council and Gambian head of state following a military coup on July 26, 1994. On September 27, 1996, he was elected president following a return to civilian government.

Longest serving mayor The longest recorded mayoralty was that of Edmond Mathis (France), who served as mayor of Ehuns, Haute-Sàne, France, for 75 years (1878–1953).

Youngest mayor The youngest mayor on record is Shane Mack (U.S.A.), born on November 15, 1969. Shane was elected Mayor of Castlewood, South Dakota, U.S.A., at the age of 18 years 169 days on May 3, 1988 and held office for eight years.

LONGEST REIGNING QUEEN The longest reigning queen is Victoria, Queen of Great Britain and, from 1876, Empress of India. She ruled for 63 years 216 days, from 1837 to 1901.

Wealthiest queen Owing to rising UK property values, the net worth of Queen Elizabeth II (UK) has increased nearly 60% in the last year. *Forbes World's Richest People 2004* estimates her wealth at £358.8 million ($660 million).

Largest political constituency The Kalgoorlie Australian federal parliamentary constituency in Western Australia covers more than 1,000,000

YOUNGEST REIGNING MONARCH Swaziland's King Mswati III was crowned on April 25, 1986 when aged 18 years 6 days. He was born Makhosetive, the 67th son of King Sobhuza II.

LARGEST PARLIAMENT The largest legislative assembly in the world is the National People's Congress (NPC, pictured) of the People's Republic of China. The 10th National People's Congress, elected at the beginning of 2003, is composed of 2,985 deputies legally elected by 35 electoral units nationwide. It is comprised of 31 provinces, autonomous regions, and municipalities, Hong Kong and Macao special administrative regions, and the Chinese People's Liberation Army. Every minority ethnic group has an appropriate number of representatives in the NPC.

miles^2 (2,600,000 km^2), an area greater than the whole of western Europe. The constituency measures 1,400 miles (2,250 km) from north to south and 1,000 miles (1,600 km) from east to west, and covers the whole state of Western Australia except for Perth in the southwest.

Most votes for a chimp in a political campaign In the 1988 mayoral elections campaign in Rio de Janeiro, Brazil, the antiestablishment "Brazilian Banana Party," presented a chimpanzee named Tião as their candidate. The chimp came third out of 12 candidates, taking just over 400,000 votes. Known for his moody temper, the chimp's campaign slogan was "Vote monkey—get monkey." Tião died in 1996 aged 33. Tião means "Big Uncle" in Portuguese.

Heaviest monarch In September 1976, King Taufa'ahau Tupou IV of Tonga recorded a weight of 462 lb. (209.5 kg). He is 6 ft. 3 in. (1.9 m) tall. By 1985, he was reported to have slimmed down to 307 lb. (139.7 kg); in early 1993, he was 279 lb. (127.0 kg); and by 1998 he had lost further weight as a result of a fitness program.

Oldest ruling house The Emperor of Japan, Akihito (b. December 23, 1933), is the 125th in line from the first Emperor, Jimmu Tenno, whose reign was traditionally from 660 BC to 581 BC but more probably dates from c. 40 BC to c. 10 BC.

Largest royal family There are more than 4,200 royal princes and more than 40,000 other relatives in the Saudi royal family.

Longest reigning living queen Born on April 21, 1926, Queen Elizabeth II (UK) is currently the longest reigning living queen. She succeeded to the throne on February 6, 1952 on the death of her father, King George VI. She is Queen of the United Kingdom and Head of the Commonwealth. The year 2002 saw the Queen's Golden Jubilee, marking 50 years since her accession.

Longest reigns ever Minhti, King of Arakan (now part of Burma [Myanmar]), is reputed to have reigned for 95 years between 1279 and 1374, but the longest well-documented reign of any monarch was that of Phiops II (also known as Pepi II), or Neferkare, a Sixth-Dynasty pharaoh of ancient Egypt. His reign began c. 2281 BC, when he was six years old, and is believed to have lasted around 94 years.

Musoma Kanijo, although not a monarch, was chief of the Nzega district of Tanganyika (now part of Tanzania) and reputedly reigned for more than 98 years from 1864, when he was eight years old, until his death on February 2, 1963.

THE ENVIRONMENT

Largest solar power facility In terms of nominal capacity, the largest solar electric power facility in the world is the Harper Lake Site (LSP VIII & IX) in the Mojave Desert, California, U.S.A., operated by UC Operating Services (U.S.A.). The two solar electric generating stations (SEGS) at Harper Lake have a nominal capacity of 160 MW (80 MW each). The site covers 1,280 acres (518 hectares) and houses 400,000 solar collectors—mirrors that concentrate solar energy—over a 1,000-acre (400-hectare) area.

Largest solar-slate roof In 1999, a former grain storage facility in Berne, Switzerland, was fitted with a 22,000-ft.^{2} (2,050-m^2) solar-slate roof comprising 16,650 photovoltaic cell-embedded slates known as Sunslates. The project was planned and engineered by Atlantis Energy Ltd., and generates 167,000 kWh (kilowatt-hours) of electrical energy, which is fed into the city's electricity grid. The total investment in the project was 2.6 million Swiss francs ($1.7 million or £1.1 million).

Most environmentally friendly country The country regarded as the most environmentally sustainable is Finland, which heads the Environmen-

HIGHEST SOLAR ENERGY USE PER CAPITA At 1.82 W per capita, Switzerland has the highest solar energy usage in the world. This picture shows a photovoltaic generating plant installed at a government office building in Berne, Switzerland.

tal Sustainability Index (ESI) compiled in 2002 by the World Economic Forum. Based on 20 core indicators covering five broad areas—environmental systems (e.g. air and water quality); reducing environmental stress (e.g. pollution levels); reducing human vulnerability to environmental degradation; social and institutional capacity to respond to environmental threats; and contribution to global stewardship—Finland scored 73.9 out of 100. The lowest was Kuwait with 23.9.

Largest producer of energy In 2001, the U.S.A. produced 75,295 petajoules of commercial energy, including solid, liquid, and gaseous fuels as well as primary electricity. A petajoule is 1,000,000,000,000,000 joules.

Fastest forest depletion Burundi, Central Africa, suffers the fastest decrease in forested area with an average loss of 9% every year between 1990 and 2000. If this rate was permanently sustained, Burundi's forested areas would be completely cleared in just over 11 years.

Largest deforestation The greatest deforestation rate is in Brazil where, between 1990 and 2000, an average of 8,596 miles² (22,264 km²) of forest was cleared every year. This is equivalent to a country the size of Wales.

Largest reforestation The greatest reforestation rate is in China where, between 1990 and 2000, enough trees were replanted every year to cover an average area of 6,974 miles² (18,063 km²). This is equivalent to a country the size of Kuwait.

Highest carbon dioxide emissions The U.S.A. has the highest emissions of CO_2, one of the key gases responsible for the "greenhouse effect." The U.S.A. emitted 11,578 billion lb. (5,789 million tons) of CO_2 in 2001, a 1.1% decrease on the previous year. The decrease in CO_2 emissions in 2001 was reportedly due to a reduction in U.S. economic growth from 3.8% in 2000 to 0.3% in 2001.

Highest carbon dioxide emissions per capita The United Arab Emirates (UAE) has the highest carbon dioxide (CO_2) emissions per capita. In 1999, the emissions level reached 68,750 lb. (31.25 tons) of CO_2 per capita. The total amount of CO_2 emissions for the UAE in 1999 was 190 billion lb. (88 million tons).

LARGEST OLIVE CULTIVATOR Spain is the world's leading cultivator of olives, producing 2.1 billion lb. (970,000 tons) of olives annually. The principal olive-producing regions are Catalonia and Andalusia. Spain and Italy together account for 54% of the total amount of olive oil produced worldwide.

LARGEST TURKEY FARM The world's largest turkey farm belongs to Bernard Matthews plc (UK). The farm is situated in North Pickenham, Norfolk, UK, and processes 1 million turkeys per year.

Greatest shrinkage of a lake The Aral Sea, on the border between Uzbekistan and Kazakhstan, has lost more than 60% of its area and approximately 80% of its volume since 1960. From 1960 to 1998, the lake decreased in area from 26,300 miles^2 (68,000 km^2) to 11,000 miles^2 (28,700 km^2) and in volume from approximately 250 miles^3 (1,040 km^3) to 43 miles^3 (180 km^3). The water level has dropped about 60 ft. (18 m) in the same time period. This dramatic shrinkage is almost entirely due to the large amounts of water being extracted from the major rivers that feed it. This water is diverted for irrigation purposes.

Greatest modern loss of agricultural land to aridity The greatest rate at which land has become arid in modern times has been experienced in Portugal where, since 1970, over 51% of agricultural land has become unable to support agriculture at former levels.

Highest glass recycling rate Switzerland leads the world in recycling glass. An estimated 91% of glass products sold in Switzerland are recycled.

Highest paper recycling rate Germany recycles between 70% and 80% of its consumption of paper and cardboard per year.

Waste generation The U.S.A. produces the most municipal waste per capita according to figures issued by the Organization for Economic Cooperation and Development in 2001. The estimated figure stands at 1,675 lb. (760 kg) per capita.

Highest proportion of organic farming In Austria, an estimated 10% of agricultural land is farmed organically. Austria has more than 20,000 organic farms. Although Italy is believed to have around 40,000 organic farms, they represent a lower proportion of the total land organically farmed.

Most polluted major city Mexico City is the world's most polluted major city and the most polluted capital city. The city is classified as having serious problems associated with sulfur dioxide, suspended particulate matter, carbon monoxide, and ozone (in all of which World Health Organization guidelines are exceeded by more than a factor of two), plus moderate to heavy pollution from lead and nitrogen dioxide. Factors contributing to the high pollution levels include the high altitude and geographical location, as high emissions from industry and vehicles are trapped by surrounding mountains.

Most acidic acid rain A pH reading of 1.87 was recorded at Inverpolly Forest in the Scottish Highlands, UK, in 1983, and a reading of 2.83 was recorded over the Great Lakes, U.S.A./Canada, in 1982. These are the lowest pH levels ever recorded in acid precipitation, making it the most acidic acid rain; pH values range from 0 to 14, with 7 being neutral.

Worst oil spill disaster The worst oil spill occurred as a result of a marine blowout beneath the drilling rig *Ixtoc I* in the Gulf of Campeche, Gulf of Mexico, on June 3, 1979. The oil slick had reached 400 miles (640 km) by August 5, 1979. The spill was capped on March 24, 1980, following a loss of up to 140 million gallons (500,000 tons or 636 million liters) of oil.

WAR & PEACE

Largest tank battle The largest tank battle ever is generally acknowledge to be the Battle of Kursk during World War II. On July 12, 1943, in the Prokhorovka region near the Russian town of Kursk, a total of 1,500 German and Russian tanks amassed for close-range fighting. By the end of the day both sides had lost over 300 tanks.

Costliest civil war The costliest civil war, in terms of the number of lives lost during combat and in events directly relating to the war, is the Russian Civil War of 1917–22. It is estimated that the former Soviet Union lost 939,755 soldiers, and over eight million civilians died following armed attacks, famine, and disease.

Longest continuous period of civil war The longest period of continuous civil warfare lasted for 254 years from 475 to 221 BC in China, and is

LARGEST ANTI-WAR RALLY On February 15, 2003, anti-war rallies took place across the globe—the largest occurring in Rome, Italy (pictured), where a crowd of three million gathered to protest the U.S.A.'s threat to invade Iraq. Police figures report that millions more demonstrated in nearly 600 cities worldwide.

known as the Warring States Period. Feudal lords in seven major state kingdoms sought dominance over each other in numerous intensive battles. King Ying Zheng of the Qin state was eventually victorious, becoming the first emperor (Qin Shihuang) of a unified China.

Most nationalities in one military force As of January 2004 the French Foreign Legion had 7,622 men serving in its ranks, with a diverse range of nationalities from 136 countries. Legionnaires serve in France and around the world.

Youngest modern conscripts In March 1976 President Francisco Macías Nguema of Equatorial Guinea (deposed in August 1979) decreed compulsory military service for all boys aged between seven and 14 years old. The edict stated that any parent that refused to hand over his or her son "will be imprisoned or shot."

Longest-serving military mule The unit mascot for the 853 AT Coy ASC (MA Mules) was a Spanish mule called Pedongi, who was on active service with the Indian Army from May 4, 1965 until her death on March 25, 1998 aged 37. Her name was derived from the first battle area she was sent to at Pedong, northeast India.

Largest contributors to peacekeeping Canada and Fiji have been part of almost all 55 United Nations (UN) peacekeeping operations.

Longest-running peacekeeping operation The UN Truce Supervision Organization (UNTSO) has been in place since June 1948. UNTSO is based in Jerusalem but maintains military posts throughout the Middle East.

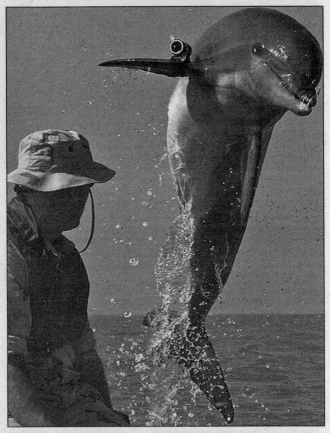

EARLIEST USE OF MARINE MAMMALS IN DEFENSE In 1970–71 during the Vietnam War, five U.S. Navy bottlenose dolphins *(Tursiops truncatus,* pictured) were sent to Cam Ranh Bay, Vietnam, to defend U.S. military boats from enemy swimmers. The most recent deployment of dolphins in active duty was during the Umm Qasr mission in the waters off Iraq in March 2003. Dolphins were trained by the U.S. to detect underwater mines in the Gulf, so that military boats and ships loaded with humanitarian aid could pass safely. The dolphins did not touch the mines, but released a balloon showing their location.

HIGHEST PERCENTAGE OF MILITARY PERSONNEL In North Korea in 1999, 5.05% of the total population of 21,386,000 (or one for every 19 people) was a member of the armed forces.

Largest current peacekeeping force The largest current peacekeeping force is the UN Mission in Liberia (UNMIL). On September 19, 2003 the UN Security Council agreed to the deployment of a 15,000-strong force on October 1, 2003 for a 12-month stay. Following the civil war, a cease-fire was signed in June 2003, but the UNMIL mandate is there to ensure that peace is maintained and that humanitarian relief is supplied, as well as to support the establishment of democratic elections.

Largest peacekeeping deployment ever The United Nations Protection Force (UNPROFOR), which was deployed in the former Yugoslavia from February 1992 to March 1995, reached a maximum strength of 39,922 military personnel in September 1994. Serious fighting in Croatia began in June 1991 when that Republic and its northern neighbour, Slovenia, declared themselves independent from Yugoslavia, and Serbs living in Croatia, supported by the Yugoslav People's Army, opposed this move.

Most expensive peacekeeping operation UNPROFOR cost $4.6 billion (£2.96 billion) from February 1992 to March 1995. This cost covers all missions deployed during this period, and equates to just under $3 million (£1.93 million) per day.

Bloodiest UN peacekeeping operation The conflict in the Balkans led to more fatalities than any other UN peacekeeping mission. The total number of fatalities for all missions in the region was 268, including 210 fatalities in UNPROFOR alone.

War & Peace

Peacekeeping mission with most contributing nations The United Nations Mission in Bosnia and Herzegovina (UNMIBH) drew troops from 44 different nations until the end of its mandate on December 31, 2002. UNMIBH was an umbrella organization overseeing the activities of the International Police Task Force (IPTF) that was set up in Bosnia and Herzegovina after the United Nations Protection Force (UNPROFOR) mission came to an end in 1995.

Largest humanitarian agency The UN World Food Program (WFP) is the largest humanitarian agency in the world. The organization was established in 1963 and to date has delivered a staggering 151 billion lb. (68.7 million tons) of food to over 1.2 billion people in 100 countries, with a total cost of $32 billion (£19.1 billion).

Largest single humanitarian operation The largest and most expensive humanitarian operation ever undertaken was feeding the 27.1 million people of Iraq following the 2003 war. The food-aid operation, organized by the WFP, began on April 1, 2003 and finished in October 2003 with 4.8 billion lb. (2.2 million tons) of food commodities being delivered under a budget of $1.5 billion (£927 million).

Largest and longest-running humanitarian airdrop The World Food Program has been in southern Sudan since 1992. Drought, civil war, flooding, and remote locations mean that an average of 2.5 million people suffer from food shortages annually. At its peak, the WFP operated 14 aircraft per day, each making three trips and delivering an average of 352,000 lb. (16 tons) of food per drop.

Most Nobel Peace Prizes The International Committee of the Red Cross, founded in Geneva, Switzerland, in 1893, has received three awards for Peace: 1917, 1944, and 1963. The latter award was shared with the League of the Red Cross Societies.

Largest demonstration A figure of 2.7 million demonstrators was reported from China for a demonstration against the USSR in Shanghai on March 3–4, 1969 following border clashes.

Largest landlocked navy Paraguay, a totally landlocked South American state, has a navy with 3,595 personnel (in 2000). The navy operates on the nation's major rivers, the Paraguay and Paraná. Military service in Paraguay is compulsory; for those opting for naval service the period in uniform is two years.

Oldest air force The earliest autonomous air force is the Royal Air Force (UK), the origins of which can be traced back to 1878, when the War Office commissioned the building of a military balloon. The Royal Air Force itself came into existence on April 1, 1918. The British were not the first to utilize balloons, however. The French used them for military observations at the Battle of Fleurus in June 1794 during the French Revolutionary War.

CRIME & PUNISHMENT

Highest murder rate per capita According to the seventh UN Survey of Crime Trends and Operations of Criminal Justice Systems, covering the period 1998–2000, Colombia has the most recorded intentional homicides per capita, with 65 murders per 100,000 people.

Most murders by a doctor Family doctor Harold Shipman (UK) murdered 215 of his patients between 1975 and 1998. Shipman killed his elderly victims, most of whom were women, with high doses of diamorphine injections. In January 2000, he was sentenced to a life term in prison for the 15 murders of which he was found guilty. Shipman hanged himself in his prison cell on January 13, 2004.

Greatest mass arrest The greatest mass arrest reported in a democratic country was that of 15,617 demonstrators rounded up on July 11, 1988 by South Korean police to ensure security in advance of the 1988 Olympic Games in Seoul.

Largest white-collar crime In February 1997, copper trader Yasuo Hamanaka (Japan) pleaded guilty to fraud and forgery in connection with illicit trading that cost the Japanese company Sumitomo an estimated $2.6 billion (£1.37 billion) accumulated over a 10-year period of unauthorized transactions.

Highest rate of gun ownership Among countries not at war or suffering civil unrest, the U.S.A. has the highest rate of

LARGEST HEROIN SEIZURE According to the Drug Enforcement Administration (DEA), the largest heroin seizure (pictured) took place in Bangkok, Thailand, on February 11, 1988 when 2,816 lb. (1,277 kg) was seized. It had an estimated street value of $75 million (£45.5 million).

civilian gun ownership. Surveys in 1999 found that around 40% of U.S. households have at least one firearm. The U.S.A. has over 200 million guns—more than the number of adults in the country.

Largest reward for counter-terrorism In July 2003, the U.S. government approved the payment of a $30-million (£16.4-million) reward to the informant who led U.S. forces to Saddam Hussein's (Iraq) two eldest sons, Uday and Qusay (both Iraq), in Mosul, Iraq. The $15 million (£8.2 million) for each is the largest ever paid by the U.S.A. under its Rewards for Justice program.

Fastest recorded speed on public roads Andrew Osborne (UK) was sentenced to 28 days in prison at Aylesbury Magistrates Court on July 16, 2003 after being clocked in March 2003 travelling at 252 km/h (158 mph) on his 1200-cc Kawasaki motorcycle at Tingewick bypass, Bucks, UK.

Longest serving judge The oldest recorded active judge was Judge Albert R. Alexander (U.S.A.). He was enrolled as a member of the Clinton County Bar, Missouri, U.S.A., in 1926 and was later the magistrate and probate judge of Clinton County until his retirement aged 105 years 8 months on July 9, 1965.

HIGHEST-RANKING CAMEL The world's highest-ranking law-enforcement camel is BERT (U.S.A., pictured), who was accepted as Reserve Deputy Sheriff for the Los Angeles County Sheriff's Department in San Dimas, California, U.S.A., on April 5, 2003 and who regularly goes on patrol with his handler Nance Fite (U.S.A.). Born on March 3, 1997, BERT, which stands for "Be Enthusiastic Responsible and True," is a dromedary (one hump). He weighed 1,770 lb. (802 kg) on May 27, 2003 and stands at a height of 82 in. (208 cm) to the top of his hump, although he will not be considered fully grown until he is eight years old.

EARLIEST SYSTEM OF FINGERPRINTING The first effective system of identification by fingerprints—the science of dactylography—was instituted in 1896 by Edward Henry (UK), an inspector general of police in British India, who eventually became Commissioner of Metropolitan Police in London.

Most viewed trial A daily average of 5.5 million Americans watched live coverage of the O.J. Simpson (U.S.A.) trial on three major cable television networks between January 24 and October 3, 1995. Simpson, an American football player and actor, was on trial for the June 12, 1994 murder of his ex-wife, Nicole, and a waiter, Ronald Goldman (both U.S.A.). He was acquitted of the charges when the jury reached a verdict of not guilty on October 3, 1995.

GWR TALKS TO Lois Gibson

Since 1982, over 150 criminals have been identified and brought to justice in Texas, U.S.A., thanks to the detailed composites drawn by forensic artist Lois Gibson (U.S.A.). This figure represents the record for most criminals positively identified from one artist's composites.

How did you become a forensic artist? I became a forensic artist because someone tried to kill me for fun when I was 21. My attacker got into my apartment and choked me for about half an hour straight. I couldn't bring myself to tell the authorities, but about six weeks later I got lost in Los Angeles and was driving by a house just as my attacker was being arrested. This changed my life. I want my witnesses to have that wonderful feeling when they know their attacker is caught.

What did you do next? After the attack, I got a Bachelor of Fine Arts with honors from the University of Texas in Austin, and went on to produce about 3,000 fine-art portraits for tourists. Then I moved to Houston, and was amazed to discover that they had had over 700 murders there that year. One day it just hit me: I could draw attackers' faces from witnesses' descriptions. I approached the Houston Police Department, who had no one doing that at the time. Every third sketch I did helped solve a crime, but it took them seven years to give me that job!

Four years later, I went to the FBI Academy in Quantico, Virginia, and completed the Forensic Art course there. Now I teach this profession at Northwestern University in Evanston, Illinois.

Do you work for different police forces across the U.S.A. or is it always the same one? I work at the Houston Police Department, but cities and counties near and far bring witnesses to me.

How long have you been doing it? Do you get better with practice? I've been a forensic artist for 21 years. One definitely gets better with practice, way better.

How long does it take to do each drawing? Now my drawings take one hour. In the beginning it took almost three hours. If I have a reclusive witness who definitely doesn't want to talk, I can do the sketch in 25 minutes. If the witness needs to talk a lot, it can take two hours.

Talk us through your procedure. I start at the top and go down. So, hair, forehead, eyebrows, eyes, nose, lips, chin, throw on the ears if they are seen, then neck and shoulders, in that order.

Do you do drawings digitally? No, I draw everything by hand. It is much faster to draw by hand than with a computer . . . and way more accurate.

What does it mean to you to have a Guinness World Record? It makes all that brutal, heart-wrenching work seem worthwhile. Since I deal with armed officers, I never say my sketch actually solved a case—indeed, the sketch can only help the officers make an arrest. But my fellow and future forensic artists need to know that forensic art can help solve cases.

Guinness World Records has given me a forum to spread compositry to other countries in the world besides the U.S.A. and Canada. All those countries need forensic artists too!

BUSINESS & WEALTH

Largest corporate bankruptcy In terms of assets, the largest corporate bankruptcy amounted to $103.9 billion (£65.8 billion) filed by the telecommunications company WorldCom, Inc. on July 21, 2002.

Largest corporation Based on revenues, the largest corporation as of 2003 was integrated oil company ExxonMobil (U.S.A.), which had revenues of $246.738 billion (£138.781 billion).

Highest share value On March 27, 2000 the share price of Yahoo! Japan stood at JPY120.4 million ($1.12 million). Yahoo! Japan is the nation's dominant information portal, and the scarcity of the stock contributed to the dramatic rise in price. Japanese company Softbank owns 41.93% of the

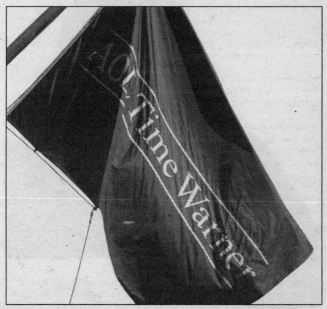

LARGEST COMPANY MERGER America Online (AOL), the largest Internet company, announced a $350 billion (£213 billion) merger with media corporate Time Warner on January 10, 2000. The completed merger created AOL Time Warner, the world's largest media company. The brands owned by the new company include AOL, Time, CNN, Warner Bros., Netscape, Sports Illustrated, TNT, and Cartoon Network.

company, with U.S.-based Yahoo! owning 33.49%. Yahoo! Japan's share price has increased 4,700% since December 1998.

Largest publishing company With 80,632 employees, the world's largest printing and publishing company is Bertelsmann AG (Germany). In 2002, the company had revenues of $19,192 million (£11,965 million) with profits of $972 million (£606 million).

Greatest annual profit In 2001, integrated oil company ExxonMobil (U.S.A.) announced profits of $15.320 billion (£10.932 billion), which represented a 13.5% growth in net income in 12 months. Exxon's refineries can handle over 6 million barrels daily.

LARGEST GLOBAL BRAND According to a study released by ACNielsen, the largest global brand in the world based on sales is Coca-Cola, which in 2002 had sales of $19 billion (£13 billion). The brand is present in over 200 countries.

LARGEST COMPANY BY ASSETS American multinational motor manufacturer Ford Motor Company (U.S.A., pictured) is the largest company in the world in terms of assets (excluding banks and financial institutions). At June 2003, its assets were worth a total of $311.791 billion (£189.113 billion).

Largest music company Universal Music Group (U.S.A.) is the largest music company with revenues of $6.276 billion (£3.455 billion) as of December 2002. Based in New York, U.S.A., the Universal Music Group has more than 12,000 employees, operates in 71 countries, and had an estimated worldwide market share in 2002 of 24.4%.

Largest retail company by number of outlets By the end of January 2003, Wal-Mart (U.S.A.) operated 4,688 retail stores worldwide.

Largest cell phone telecommunications company Vodafone Group plc (UK) is the world's largest cell phone telecommunications group, with revenues of $48.005 billion (£30.333 billion) in the fiscal year ending March 2003. The company reported more than 119.7 million subscribers worldwide as of March 2003. It operates in 28 countries on five continents.

Oldest stock exchange The Stock Exchange in Amsterdam, The Netherlands, was founded in 1602. It dealt in printed shares of the United East India Company of The Netherlands in the Oude Zijds Kapel.

Largest lottery By the end of January 2004, ticket sales for the UK's National Lottery (launched in November 1994) had reached £45 billion ($81 billion).

Richest woman Alice Walton (U.S.A.), daughter of Sam Walton, founder of the world's largest retailer Wal-Mart, and Helen, his widow, each have an estimated net worth of $20 billion (£11 billion) according to the *Forbes* 2004 Rich List.

GWR TALKS TO Bill Gates

Bill Gates (U.S.A.) is Chairman and Chief Software Architect of Microsoft Corporation. As well as being the world's richest living person, worth $46.6 billion (£25.4 billion) in March 2004 according to *Forbes* magazine, Bill and his wife Melinda hold the record for the largest single private charitable donation ($6 billion or £4.2 billion), which they made to their own Bill & Melinda Gates Foundation. The foundation itself holds the record for the largest single donation to AIDS research ($25 million or £15.08 million) and is also the world's largest charitable foundation. Its largest donation was $1 billion (£700 million) over 20 years for minority student scholarships, via the Gates Millennium Scholars Program.

How and when did you first become interested in technology and computers? When I was 13, my school installed a teletype machine that connected to a mainframe computer in downtown Seattle. From that point on, my friends and I spent most of our free time writing programs and figuring out how to make the computer do interesting things.

What are you working on for Microsoft now? My job is to figure out new ways to make computers more useful, and work with our software developers and product groups to set the technical direction for the company. Right now I'm working on a number of projects, including the next major release of our Windows operating system.

What do you think will be the interesting developments in tech-

nology in the near future? Everything from the TV to the refrigerator is taking on the intelligence and connectivity of the PC, and this opens up some amazing new possibilities. I think computers will change our lives more in the next ten years than they have in the past 20.

What personal achievement are you most proud of? Although it's great that I get to do the work I love and have been very successful at it, I'm proudest of my three children.

What does your charity do and what is the most satisfying part of running it? The Bill & Melinda Gates Foundation focuses most of its efforts on long-term global health issues. We have a tremendous opportunity to improve the quality of life for billions of people by treating and preventing disease, improving child and reproductive health, and slowing the spread of HIV and other global health threats. My wife and I are privileged to work with some of the world's smartest people to develop sustainable solutions to problems that affect a large percentage of the world's population.

What does it mean to have a Guinness World Record? It's a great honor, but I'm just happy that I've been able to use what I have to help improve people's lives.

What advice would you give to any young people who would like to follow in your footsteps? Most important of all is to choose work that you are truly passionate about. If you really love what you do, you'll barely notice how hard you work at it.

MODERN SOCIETY

Most and least hospital beds According to 2002 data, Switzerland has one bed per 155 people. Niger has only one hospital bed per 2,000 people.

Most and least physicians In Monaco, there is one physician for every 170 people. The country with the highest number of people per physician is Malawi with 49,118 people for every one doctor.

Most prevalent allergic disease Bronchial asthma affects up to 150 million people worldwide, with deaths from the condition reaching 180,000 each year. Globally, it is estimated that the economic costs associated with this disease exceed those of tuberculosis and HIV/AIDS combined.

Most common infectious disease The common cold is almost universal, afflicting everyone but those living in isolated communities or in Antarctica (no virus will survive the extreme cold). There are at least 40 cold viruses that are airborne or transmitted by direct contact.

Highest number of people with HIV/AIDS In the Republic of South Africa, one in nine people are affected by HIV/AIDS. In 2001, out of a total population of 43.5 million, 4.7 million people carried the virus.

Highest death rate from infectious disease The west African island-republic of São Tomé and Príncipe has 241 deaths from infectious diseases per 100,000 annually.

HIGHEST AND LOWEST HEALTH BUDGET The U.S.A. has the largest health expenditure at $3,724 (£2,359) per capita according to the World Health Organization's World Health Report 2000. Somalia has a health budget of only $11 (£6.80) per capita.

Leading cause of death In industrialized countries, diseases of the heart and of blood vessels (cardiovascular disease) account for more than 50% of deaths. The most common are heart attacks and strokes, generally due to atheroma (degeneration of the arterial walls) obstructing the flow of blood.

Largest school by pupils The largest school in terms of pupils is the City Montessori School in Lucknow, India, which had a record enrollment for the 2003/04 academic year of 27,911 pupils on September 24, 2003.

Oldest university The oldest existing and continually operating educational institution is the University of Karueein, founded in AD 859 in Fez, Morocco.

Longest lesson Murry Burrows (Australia) taught biology to his class of 26 students at Laidley State High School, Queensland, Australia, for 54 hours on April 15–17, 2003.

Most expensive course The Ivor Spencer International Finishing School for Young Ladies and Gentlemen, London, UK, began a one-month £77,500 ($126,000) "finishing" course in 1998. Students stayed at a top London hotel, went to the ballet and opera, and took lessons in protocol, etiquette, food, wine, cooking, and style.

Oldest doctorate On May 12, 2000, Elizabeth Eichelbaum (U.S.A.) received her doctorate in Education from the University of Tennessee, U.S.A., at the age of 90 years 58 days.

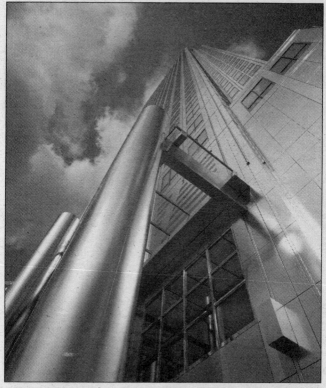

MOST AND LEAST EXPENSIVE OFFICE LOCATION Based on March 2003 prices, London (UK, pictured) has the most expensive office space in the world. Cost per m² including rent, taxes, and service charges is £1,014 ($1,596). Where country-comparable data is available, Sandton, in Johannesburg, South Africa, is the least expensive location for office space. Cost per m², allowing for similar expenses, is $125 (£79).

LOWEST AND HIGHEST SPENDING ON EDUCATION Somalia allocates just 0.4% of its Gross National Income (GNI) to primary, secondary, and tertiary education. The U.S.A. spent 5.4% of its GNI on education in 1997.

Longest time to complete a degree Robert F.P. Cronin (UK) began his biology degree on February 9, 1948 at Princeton University, New Jersey, U.S.A., and graduated on May 30, 2000, 52 years 111 days later at the age of 73 years 272 days. He is the world's oldest graduate.

Longest elapsed time before a class reunion The 1929 class of Miss Blanche Miller's kindergarten and continuation school, Bluefield, West Virginia, U.S.A., had their first reunion after 70 years. Ten members of the class had died but of the remaining group, 55% were in attendance.

Largest school reunion A total of 2,521 former pupils of Pestalozzi School, Guben, Germany, attended the school's 100th anniversary celebrations on June 29, 2002.

Longest annual class reunion The Cherokee County Community High School's class of 1929 held its 74th class reunion in Columbus, Kansas, U.S.A., on June 7, 2003. Of the original class of 110, 30 graduates remain, but only nine could make the reunion.

Largest employer Indian Railways had 1,583,614 regular employees when it was last assessed in March 1997. The Indian Railways' wage bill for the period 1996–97 worked out at a massive 105,145,000,000 rupees ($2.1 billion or £1.5 billion).

Longest working career The longest working life has been the 98 years worked by Shigechiyo Izumi (Japan), who began work goading draft animals at a sugar mill at Isen, Tokunoshima, Japan, in 1872. He retired as a sugarcane farmer in 1970 aged 105. He attributed his long life to "God, Buddha, and the Sun."

Highest and lowest rates of unemployment According to information available in 2002, the country with the highest rate of unemployment is Liberia with 70% of its labor force not in paid employment. Andorra and the South Pacific island of Nauru had the lowest rate of unemployment for any country with 0%.

Longest working career in a single company Thomas Stoddard (U.S.A.) started working at Speakman Company, Delaware, U.S.A., on February 16, 1928 as a 16-year-old mail boy. He remained an employee of the plumbing and pipe-fitting company until his retirement (as a member of the board of directors) 75 years later on February 16, 2003, when he was 91 years old.

MODERN LIFE

Highest bread consumption As of 2000, the country with the largest per capita consumption of bread was Turkey with 440 lb. (199.6 kg) per person. Turkish people eat more than three times their own body weight in bread annually.

Highest baked bean consumption The country with the largest annual consumption of baked beans per capita is the UK with 11 lb. 10 oz. (5.3 kg) per person according to surveys in 1999.

Highest chocolate consumption In Switzerland, the average person consumed 25 lb. 6 oz. of chocolate (11.5 kg) during 2000. This is equivalent to 230 1.76-oz. (50-g) bars a year.

Largest consumption of cigarettes The world's largest consumer of cigarettes, in terms of volume purchased, is China with 1.69 trillion sold in 2002. With a global consumption in 2000 of 5.5 trillion, this means that approximately one in every three cigarettes smoked today is smoked in China.

Highest wine consumption Luxembourg consumes an average of 111.3 pints (63.3 liters) of wine annually per person. The smallest measurable wine consumer is Egypt, where the average yearly wine consumption is about two tablespoons per person.

Highest alcohol consumption The alcohol consumption rate is highest

HIGHEST APPLE CONSUMPTION In 1998, China consumed the greatest amount of apples in the world overall with a total of 32.3 billion lb. (14.694 million tons) or 25 lb. 9 oz. (11.6 kg) per capita. Assuming an apple weighs 5.2 oz. (150 g), this is equivalent to 77 apples per person. Moldova consumes the most apples per person, with 156 lb. 4.9 oz. (70.9 kg) consumed per person in 1998. The country got through 682 million lb. (310,000 tons) of apples in that year—equivalent to 472 per person.

in Ireland where 21.6 pints (12.3 liters) of pure alcohol per person is consumed annually according to surveys done in 2000. This intake is based on the amount of pure alcohol consumed within wine, beer, and spirits.

Highest beer consumption The Czech Republic consumes 281 pints (160 liters) of beer annually per person as of 2000. The country that consumed the greatest volume of beer in the same year was the U.S.A. with 42.895 billion pints (24.376 billion liters). This is equivalent to a per capita consumption of 156 pints (89 liters).

Highest tea consumption In Ireland, the average annual consumption of tea is 5 lb. 14 oz. (2.69 kg) per capita, the equivalent of 1,184 cups per person each year.

Highest organic produce sales Denmark has annual organic retail sales of $349.2 million (£220 million) in a population of 5.3 million, averaging sales of $65.88 (£41.51) per capita.

Greatest fast-food expenditure In 2000, Americans spent over $110 billion (£166 billion) on fast-food—more than on higher education, personal computers, or new cars. On any one day, approximately 25% of adults in the U.S.A. visit a fast-food outlet. The typical American eats roughly three hamburgers and four orders of french fries a week. The U.S.A. has more than 300,000 fast food restaurants.

Most meat waste The country that wastes the most bovine meat (beef and veal) per year is Argentina, where 730 million lb. (332,000 tons) was thrown away in 1998.

Most and least telephones Monaco has the most telephones per 1,000 people with 1,000 receivers as of 1998. Nauru in the South Pacific has the least with 0.2 per 1,000 people in 1998.

Country with most cell phones There were 69,209,000 cell phones in the U.S.A. in 1998. By contrast, only 35 million people in the U.S.A. were cell phone subscribers in 1996.

Most Internet users As of the end of 2001, Sweden had 554.18 Internet users per 1,000 people.

Most TV sets The country with the most televisions is China, which had 400 million TV sets in 1997.

City to hold the most wedding ceremonies Las Vegas, Nevada, U.S.A., has

HIGHEST VODKA CONSUMPTION Russia is the leading vodka consumer with 25.5 pints (14.5 liters) per capita consumed in 1999. Considering that there is a proportion of Russians who do not drink, it is estimated that 80% of adult men consume, on average, 0.87 pints (220 half-liter) bottles of vodka per year.

over 100 chapels performing approximately 8,400 marriage ceremonies per month—that's about 280 per day or one wedding every 5 min. 17 sec.

Highest divorce rate As of September 2002, the country with the highest divorce rate was the Maldives, with 10.97 divorces per 1,000 inhabitants each year.

Longest marriage Wesley and Stella McGowen (both U.S.A.) have been married since February 6, 1920—over 84 years.

Biggest tourist spenders The biggest overseas travel spenders are U.S. citizens, who in 2002 spent $58 billion (£36.8 billion) while on holiday in foreign countries (excluding airfares) according to the World Tourism Organization.

Highest earnings from tourism Despite a fall of 7.4% in 2002, the U.S.A. remains the world leader in terms of earnings from international tourism, taking $66.5 billion (£44.3 billion) in that year. This is equivalent to a world market share of 14%.

Most popular tourist destination According to the WTO, in 2002 France attracted 77 million international visitors, singlehandedly accounting for 11% of all international travellers in that year.

FASTEST GROWING TOURISM REGION According to the World Tourism Organization (WTO), the region showing the greatest annual growth in the number of tourists in 2002 was the Middle East (Egypt's Sphinx shown here), where the 26.7 million international travelers reflected a 16.7% increase over the previous year. Saudi Arabia, the United Arab Emirates, Lebanon, Egypt, and Bahrain all showed double-digit growth during the year.

Most visited theme park An estimated 16.5 million people passed through the gates of Tokyo Disneyland in 2000. During the 1990s, the park had an estimated 179,112,000 visitors, making it the most visited park of the decade. This is well above the total population of the country (about 126 million).

Most popular form of international travel According to the WTO, 43.7% of tourists visiting foreign countries in 1998 arrived by air, compared with 41.4% who traveled by road.

Busiest airport for international passengers According to the Airports Council International, London's Heathrow Airport handled 53.79 million passengers arriving from, or departing to, destinations outside the UK during 2001.

Busiest airport by number of aircraft A total of 909,535 aircraft takeoffs and landings were made during 2001 at O'Hare International Airport, Chicago, Illinois, U.S.A. In terms of the number of passengers served, O'Hare is in second place behind Atlanta's Hartsfield-Jackson International.

Highest and lowest rate of car ownership The wealthy European state of Luxembourg has 576 cars per 1,000 people, or one for every 1.7 people. By contrast, Somalia and the former Soviet republic of Tajikistan jointly have the world's lowest rate of car ownership, with 0.1 cars per 1,000 people, or one car per 10,000 people.

Longest traffic jam The longest traffic jam ever stretched 109 miles (176 km) northward from Lyon towards Paris, France, on February 16, 1980. The biggest jam in terms of the number of cars was estimated to involve 18 million cars crawling bumper-to-bumper on the East-West German border on April 12, 1990.

Best-selling car The Ford Focus was the world's best-selling car in 2000 (the latest year for which statistics are available), with global sales of 941,938. This means that one in every 40 cars sold worldwide was a Focus.

RELIGION & BELIEFS

Largest religious structure The largest religious structure ever built is Angkor Wat (City Temple), enclosing 401 acres (162.6 hectares) in Cambodia. It was built to honor the Hindu god Vishnu by the Khmer King Suryavarman II in the period 1113–50. Its curtain wall measures 4,200 ft. (1,280 m), and its population, before it was abandoned in 1432, was 80,000. The whole complex of 72 major monuments, begun c. AD 900, extends over 15.4 miles (24.8 km).

HIGHEST PILGRIMAGE A route (pictured) on Mount Kailash (or Khang Rimpoche) in western Tibet, which measures 33 miles (53 km), reaches an altitude of 22,028 ft. (6,714 m). The mountain is sacred to followers of Buddhism, Jainism, Hinduism, and Bonpo, a pre-Buddhist religion.

Largest Buddhist temple The largest Buddhist temple in the world is Borobudur, near Yogyakarta, central Java, Indonesia, built between AD 750 and 842. The 2,118,880-ft.³ (60,000-m³) stone structure is 113 ft. (34.5 m) tall and its base measures 403 × 403 ft. (123 × 123 m).

Largest cathedral The world's largest cathedral is the Gothic church of the diocese of New York, U.S.A., St. John the Divine, which has a floor area of 120,986 ft.² (11,240 m²), equivalent to 43 tennis courts. The nave is the longest in the world at 601 ft. (183.2 m). (In comparison, Notre Dame de Paris is 427 ft. [130 m] long.) The vaulted roof reaches a height of 124 ft. (37.8 m), around 10 stories above floor level. The cornerstone was laid on December 27, 1892, but, incredibly, the building is only two-thirds complete.

Largest Hindu temple in use Srirangam Temple, at Tiruchirappalli, Tamil Nadu, India, is the world's largest Hindu temple. Dedicated to the Hindu god Vishnu, the temple complex covers an area of 156 acres (63.1 hectares) with a perimeter of 32,592 ft. (9,934 m).

Largest monolithic church The largest monolithic (or rock-hewn) church is Bet Medhane Alem in Lalibela, Ethiopia. The structure measures 110 ft. (33.5 m) long, 78 ft. (23.5 m) wide, and 36 ft. (11 m) high. It was carved from volcanic rock in the 12th or 13th century AD by King Lalibela.

Largest mosque The largest mosque is Shah Faisal Mosque, near Islamabad, Pakistan. The total area of the complex is 46.87 acres (18.97 hectares), with the covered area of the prayer hall being 51,666 ft.² (4,800 m²). The mosque can accommodate 100,000 worshipers in the prayer hall and the courtyard plus a further 200,000 people in the adjacent grounds.

Largest synagogue The largest synagogue in the world is Temple Emanu-El on Fifth Avenue at 65th Street, New York City, U.S.A., which has a total area of 37,922 ft.^{2} (3,523 m^2). The synagogue's main sanctuary is able to accommodate 2,500 people, while the adjoining Beth-El Chapel seats 350. When these and the temple's other three sanctuaries are in use, a combined total of 5,500 people can be accommodated.

Temple at highest altitude The Rongbuk temple, between Tingri and Shigatse in Tibet, China, is situated at an altitude of approximately 16,700 ft. (5,100 m). It is just 25 miles (40 km) from Mount Everest.

Most valuable sacred object The 15th-century gold Buddha in Wat Trimitr Temple in Bangkok, Thailand, has the highest intrinsic value of any sacred object. It is 10 ft. (3 m) tall and weighs an estimated 12,125 lb. (5.5 tons). As of January 2004's price of gold ($415 or £226 per fine ounce), it is now worth $78 million (£39.8 million). The gold under the plaster exterior was found only in 1954.

Largest statue of the Virgin Mary The largest statue of the Virgin Mary with Jesus measures 46 ft. (14 m) high and stands on a 55-ft. 9-in.

LARGEST CHURCH The largest church in the world is the Basilica of Our Lady of Peace (Notre Dame de la Paix, pictured) at Yamoussoukro, the legal and administrative capital of Ivory Coast/Côte d'Ivoire. It was completed in 1989 at a cost of $164 million (£100 million) and has a total area of 322,917 ft.^{2} (30,000 m^2) with seating for 7,000 people. Including its golden cross, it is 518 ft. (158 m) high.

(17-m) tall-base. It was unveiled on September 8, 2003, and stands over-looking the city of Haskovo, Bulgaria.

Largest single tomb The Mount Li tomb—the burial place of Qin Shi-huang, the first emperor of a unified China—was constructed during his reign, from 221 to 210 BC, and is situated 25 miles (40 km) east of Xian, China. The two walls around the grave measure 7,129 × 3,195 ft. (2,173 × 974 m) and 2,247 × 1,896 ft. (685 × 578 m).

Most Christian pilgrims The House of the Virgin Mary at Loretto, Italy, receives a total of 3.5 million pilgrims (as opposed to tourists) a year, over three times the number visiting the more famous shrine at Lourdes, France. The basilica of St. Antony at Padua, Italy, receives a similar number of pilgrims a year.

Largest religious crowd The greatest recorded number of people assembled with a common purpose was an estimated 20 million who gathered at the Hindu festival of Kumbh Mela, held at the confluence of the Jumna, the Ganges, and the mythical "Saraswati" rivers at Allahabad (Prayag), Uttar Pradesh, India, on January 30, 2001.

Tallest cemetery The permanently illuminated Memorial Necrópole Ecumônica, in Santos, near São Paulo, Brazil, is 10 stories high and occupies an area of 4.4 acres (1.8 hectares). Construction on the cemetery began in March 1983 and the first burial was on July 28, 1984.

MOST MUSLIM PILGRIMS The annual pilgrimage (Hajj) to Mecca, Saudi Arabia (shown), attracts greater numbers than any other Islamic mission—an average of two million people a year from 140 countries.

Longest papal reign The longest papal reign was that of Pius IX (Giovanni Maria Mastai-Ferretti, Italy), who was pope for 31 years 236 days between 1846 and 1878. St. Peter (c. AD 33–67), the first pope, is said to have been head of the Church for 34 years, although his papacy cannot be dated accurately.

Fastest growing religion Islam is the fastest growing religion in the world. In 1990, 935 million of the world's population were Muslims; however, the estimate for January 2004 is 1.4 billion, or 23% of the world's population. Although the religion originated in Arabia, in 2002 around 80% of all believers lived outside the Arab world.

Longest pole-sitting by an individual The monk St. Simeon the Stylite (c. AD 386–459) spent about 39 years on a stone pillar on the Hill of Wonders, near Aleppo, Syria—the longest time someone has remained on top of a pole. He did so as an act of self-persecution for people's sins, and in order to be nearer to God. The Church of St. Simeon or Qalaat Samaan was built in honor of the monk and houses the ruins of the column. St. Simeon's pole-sitting feat is the longest-standing record to be chronicled in the book of *Guinness World Records*.

Oldest Koran The Holy Koran Mushaf of Othman, owned by the Muslim Board of Uzbekistan, once belonged to Caliph Othman (c. AD 588–656), third successor to the Prophet Mohammed. Only about half of the original 706 pages survive. The parchment-made Mushaf Koran was compiled between AD 646 and 656.

FESTIVALS & TRADITIONS

Most participants in a ribbon-cutting ceremony There were 3,238 participants in the ribbon-cutting ceremony at the official launch of Raffles The Plaza and Swissotel The Stamford hotels in Singapore on January 6, 2002. The ribbon was 13,789 ft. (4,203 m) long.

Fastest youth team in a woolsack race In May 1997, the Raggy Dolls team from Sir William Romney School (UK) completed the World Woolsack Championship race in a record time of 3 min. 20.01 sec. The Annual Woolsack Champion Races, held in Tetbury, Gloucestershire, UK, involve relay teams of four that run up and down a steep hill while carrying a 60-lb. (27.2-kg) bag of wool on their shoulders.

Tallest erected maypole A maypole 127 ft. 7 in. (38.89 m) tall was erected in New Westminster, British Columbia, Canada, on May 20, 1995. A maypole dance was performed around it on May 27, 1995.

MOST PUMPKINS CARVED IN ONE HOUR School teacher and sports coach Steven Clarke (U.S.A.) set a new world record when he carved 42 pumpkins in one hour for the Halloween celebrations of CBS TV's *The Early Show* on October 31, 2002 in New York, U.S.A. He also holds the record for fastest pumpkin carver, having sculpted a single jack-o'-lantern in just 54.72 seconds.

Most participants in a ground-breaking ceremony On September 27, 2003, 2,453 people dug with shovels simultaneously to break the ground for the new Providence Newberg Medical Center in Newberg, Oregon, U.S.A.

Largest bonfire The largest bonfire measured 123 ft. (37.5 m) high, and had a base of 86 ft.² (8 m²) and an overall volume of 28,251 ft.³ (800 m³). The event was organized by Kure Commemorative Centennial Events Committee and lit on February 9, 2003 at Gohara-cho, Hiroshima, Japan, as part of a traditional ceremony to encourage good health and a generous harvest.

Thickest makeup The thickest three-dimensional makeup is Chutti, unique to the southwest Indian Kathakali dance-theater tradition. The villainous Redbeard characters have mask-like attachments that are built up using rice paste and paper and which extend 6 in. (15 cm) from the face. The makeup takes hours to apply and the colors used, together with the styles of the costumes, denote the different nature of each of the characters.

Largest annual gathering of women In February or March each year, over 1 million women gather at the Attukal Bhagavathy Temple, Thiruvananthapuram, Kerala, India, for the "Pongala" offering. The women, who come from all religions and communities in Kerala, gather with their cooking pots to perform a ritual for the health and prosperity of their families.

The highest ever attendance was 1.5 million women at the festival on February 23, 1997. The ceremony, which involves cooking rice as an offering to the deity, lasts six hours.

Largest gathering of giant papier-mâché models A total of 215 papier-mâché giants, made by 88 organizations, were gathered at Solsona, Catalonia, Spain, on July 6, 2003 to celebrate the third annual Colla Gegantera del Carnaval de Solsona. The origins of this tradition are unknown, although many European countries have adopted the practice of having these giants dance down the streets as part of their festival celebrations. In Catalonia, the earliest known records are from the 14th century when models of the biblical characters David and Goliath were created for the procession of the feast of Corpus Christi in Barcelona, Spain.

Longest fireworks waterfall The "Niagara Falls" measured 10,255 ft. 2.5 in. (3,125.79 m) when ignited on August 24, 2003 at the Ariake Seas Fireworks Festival, Fukuoka, Japan.

Largest jazz festival The Festival International de Jazz de Montreal in Québec, Canada, lasts 11 days over June and July each year and attracts more than 1.5 million people who watch around 400 concerts.

Largest beer festival Oktoberfest '99 (Munich, Germany), held September 18–October 5, was visited by 7 million people who consumed a

LARGEST ANNUAL FOOD FIGHT On the last Wednesday in August, the town of Buñol near Valencia, Spain, holds its annual tomato festival, the Tomatina (pictured). In 1999, 25,000 people spent one hour at this giant food fight throwing about 275,500 lb. (125 tons) of tomatoes at each other. From the backs of trucks, attendants dump the red fruit onto the streets for people to scoop up and throw. By the time the food fight is over, the streets and everyone in them is saturated with sloppy tomato paste. Rivers of tomato juice, as much as 12 in. (30 cm) deep, run through the town until area fire engines come in to hose down the streets and the people in them. The Tomatina was first held in 1944.

FASTEST SNAIL The annual World Snail Racing Championships held every July at Congham, Norfolk, UK, is conducted on a 13-in. (33-cm) circular course outside St. Andrews Church. The "runners" race from the center to the perimeter. Some race several times as they are divided into heats to cater for the 150 snail competitors who enter every year. The all-time record holder is a snail named Archie, trained by Carl Bramham (UK), who sprinted to the finish line in 2 min. 20 sec. in 1995.

record 1.53 million gal. (5.8 million liters) of beer in 11 beer tents covering an area as large as 50 football fields.

Largest maple syrup festival The 36th annual Elmira Maple Syrup Festival held in Elmira, Ontario, Canada, attracted 66,529 people on April 1, 2000.

Largest frogs' leg festival The Fellsmere Frogs' Leg Festival held in Fellsmere, Florida, U.S.A., annually attracts 75,000 visitors. Between January 18 and 21, 2001, more than 6,600 lb. (3,000 kg) of battered fried frogs' legs were served during the free four-day festival to 13,200 diners.

Largest garlic festival The three-day Gilroy Garlic Festival, held each summer in Gilroy, California, U.S.A., attracts 130,000 people, who can sample garlic-flavored food ranging from meat to ice cream. The event begins with the lighting of a 25-ft. (7.6-m)-high garlic bulb effigy.

Longest festival snake On August 27, 2000, 500 people were required to carry a monstrous 271-ft. 7-in. (82.8-m)-long, 4,400-lb. (2-ton) serpent made of bamboo and rice straw through the village of Sekikawa, Japan, in honor of the 12th annual Taishita Monja Festival.

Largest audience at a camel wrestling festival At the 1994 Camel Wrestling Festival in Selçuk, Turkey, 20,000 people gathered to watch 120 dromedaries wrestle in a 2,000-year-old stadium in Ephesus. There are around 1,200 specially bred wrestling camels in Turkey—known as tulu camels—and the sport extends over the Marmara, Aegean, and Mediterranean coasts of western Turkey.

Largest monkey buffet The Kala Temple (also known as Monkey Temple) in Lopburi province, north of Bangkok, Thailand, provides an annual spread of tropical fruit and vegetables weighing 6,600 lb. (3,000 kg) for the population of about 2,000 monkeys to enjoy.

Largest origami paper crane On January 20–21, 2001, an origami paper crane with a wingspan of 256 ft. 6 in. (78.19 m) was folded by 1,000 people at the Odate Jukai Dome in Odate City, Japan. The participants, mostly residents of Odate, spent eight hours on the first day sticking 80 pieces of paper together, creating a sheet of 861 ft.^{2} (80 m^2). It took another 8 hr. 40 min. to fold the crane.

MATERIAL WORLD

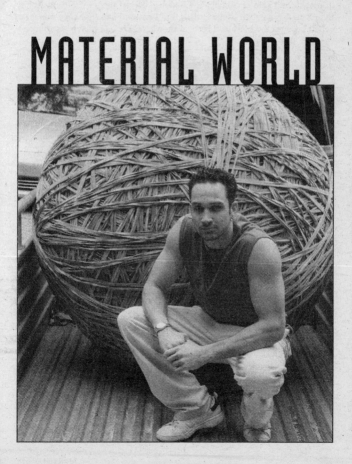

SPENDING POWER

Most valuable bicycle An 1891 diamond-frame safety bicycle was sold at Phillips, London, UK, in August 1999 for £105,000 ($170,310), breaking the previous record for a bicycle sold at auction by over 200%.

Most valuable glass A record £520,000 ($1,078,480) was paid at auction for a Roman glass cage-cup of ca. AD 300 known as the "Constable-Maxwell cage-cup." It measures 7 in. (17 cm) in diameter and 4 in. (10 cm) in height, and sold at Sotheby's, London, UK, on June 4, 1979, to Robin Symes (UK) on behalf of the British Rail Pension Fund. The cage-cup is so called because the body and base of the vessel are completely surrounded

MOST EXPENSIVE MASS-PRODUCED YO-YO Cold Fusion and Cold Fusion GT yo-yos, manufactured by Playmaxx, Inc. (U.S.A.) retail between $150 and $250. There is also a special version called Gold Fusion (pictured), which is plated with 24 karat gold and sells for between $200 and $300. In 1998, Playmaxx, Inc. generated approximately $96 million (£57.9 million) in retail sales and was given the Craze of the Year Award by the British Toy Association.

MOST VALUABLE GRASS On May 17, 2000, Ken Bates (UK), then chairman of Chelsea Football Club, paid £20,000 ($29,884) for a piece of turf from London's Wembley Stadium. The area of grass is fondly remembered by English soccer fans as the spot on the goal line where, during the 1966 World Cup final against Germany, the ball landed for the controversial goal scored by Geoff Hurst (right, with German goalkeeper Hans Tilkowski). At this rate, the entire field would have cost around £800 million ($1.2 billion).

by a delicate network or "cage" of glass. Cage-cups were owned by the very wealthiest of Roman society, and this is the only remaining example known to be in private hands.

Most valuable single-page music manuscript The greatest amount a single-page music manuscript has raised at auction is £1,326,650 ($1,932,398), paid for the earliest draft of Ludwig van Beethoven's (Germany) Ninth Symphony at Sotheby's, London, UK, on May 17, 2002. The buyer was an anonymous telephone bidder.

Most valuable music manuscripts The auction record for a musical manuscript is £2,585,000 ($4,340,215), paid by UK dealer James Kirkman at Sotheby's, London, UK, on May 22, 1987 for a 508-page, 8.5 × 6.5-in. (21.6 × 16.5-cm) bound volume of nine complete symphonies written in Wolfgang Amadeus Mozart's (Austria) hand.

Most valuable coin collection The highest price ever paid for a coin collection is $44.9 million (£31.8 million) for the Eliasberg Collection, which was sold over three auctions in 1982, 1996, and 1997 at Bowers and

Merena Galleries, New Hampshire, U.S.A. From the 1930s until 1950, Louis E. Eliasberg Sr. (U.S.A.), a leading Baltimore financier, attempted and accomplished what had never been tried before—to collect an example of every major U.S. coin variety from the 1793 half cent to the 1933 double eagle.

Most valuable clock The world record for a clock sold at auction is £1,926,500 ($3,001,294), paid for a Louis XVI ormulu-mounted ebony grande sonnerie astronomical perpetual calendar regulateur de parquet at Christie's, London, UK, on July 8, 1999.

Most valuable carpet A Louis XV Savonnerie carpet measuring 18 × 19 ft. (5.4 × 5.8 m), which was probably made for Louis XV's Château de la Mouette, ca. 1740–50, realized $4,406,000 (£2,993,512) at Christie's, New York, U.S.A., in November 2000.

Most valuable philatelic item A letter to wine merchants in Bordeaux, France, dated 1847 and franked with 1d (one penny) and 2d (two penny) first-issue stamps from Mauritius was bought anonymously in under a minute for CHF6,123,750 ($4,075,165) in a sale that was conducted by David Feldman (Ireland) at the Hotel International in Zürich, Switzerland, on November 3, 1993.

Most valuable kaleidoscope A fine English kaleidoscope in a mahogany case (ca. 1830) sold at Christie's, London, UK, in November 1999 for £45,500 ($74,934).

Most valuable comic The world's most valuable comic is the 1939 "Pay Copy" of *Marvel Comics* No. 1, which was sold to Jay Parrino's The Mint (U.S.A.) for $350,000 in November 2001. It is called the Pay Copy because some of its pages have notations relating to the payments to the creators of each piece.

Most valuable horse Cash Run, a six-year-old broodmare, was purchased on behalf of the Coolmore Stud for $7,100,000 by John Magnier (Ireland) in Lexington, Kentucky, U.S.A., on November 3, 2003.

Most valuable letter The highest price ever paid on the open market for a single signed letter was $748,000. This was paid on December 5, 1991 at Christie's, New York, U.S.A., for a letter written by Abraham Lincoln (U.S.A.) on January 8, 1863 defending the Emancipation Proclamation. It was sold to Profiles in History of Beverly Hills, California, U.S.A.

Most valuable jewel A "D" color internally flawless pear-shaped diamond weighing 100.1 carats was sold for CHF19,858,500 ($16,561,171) at Sotheby's, Geneva, Switzerland, on May 17, 1995. "D" is the highest grade that can be given to a diamond and indicates that the diamond is the finest white in color.

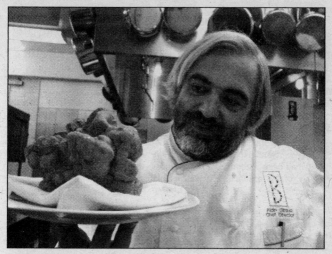

MOST VALUABLE EDIBLE FUNGUS A white truffle (*tuber magnatum pico*) weighing 2 lb. 3 oz. (1 kg) was sold in November 2002 for a record $35,000 at the annual charity truffle auction held simultaneously in Los Angeles, New York, U.S.A., and Alba in northern Italy, where the giant fungus was unearthed. It was bought by Joe Pytka (U.S.A.), owner of the Bastide restaurant in Los Angeles, California, U.S.A., and prepared by head chef Alain Giraud (France, pictured with the truffle).

Most valuable jewelry collection The world's largest jewelry collection, which included a Van Cleef and Arpels 1939 ruby and diamond necklace, belonged to Wallis Simpson, the Duchess of Windsor (U.S.A.). It realized £31,380,197 ($50,427,977) when sold at Sotheby's, Geneva, Switzerland, on April 3, 1987.

Most valuable telephone number The most valuable telephone number is 8888–8888. It was bought by a bidder representing Sichuan Airlines Co. Ltd. (China) on August 19, 2003 for 2.33 million yuan ($280,723) during an auction in Chengdu, China, of more than 100 telephone numbers. Eight is considered lucky in China as it is similar to the Cantonese word for "getting rich."

Most valuable Old Master painting *The Massacre of the Innocents* by Peter Paul Rubens (Netherlands) was sold at Sotheby's, London, UK, for a record £49.5 million ($76.7 million) on July 10, 2002 to David Thomson (Canada), chairman of the Thomson Newspapers empire.

Most valuable Old Master drawing The record for most valuable Old Master drawing is held jointly between *The Risen Christ* by Michelangelo

Buonarroti (Italy) sold in July 2000 and *Horse and Rider* by Leonardo da Vinci (Italy) sold in July 2001. Both raised £8,143,750 ($12,212,449 [2000] and $11,440,340 [2001]) at Christie's, London, UK.

Most valuable photograph *Athènes, 1842,* a photograph taken of the Athenian Temple of Olympian Zeus on the Acropolis in Athens, Greece, sold at Christie's, London, UK, for £565,250 ($922,488) on May 20, 2003. It was taken in 1842 by the 19th-century French artist and historian Joseph Philibert Girault de Prangey.

Most valuable illuminated manuscript *The Rothschild Prayerbook* (c. 1505), an illuminated manuscript, sold for £8,580,000 ($13,400,000) at Christie's, London, UK, on July 8, 1999. For the four-hour-long sale, 380 seats had been prebooked and 70 phones were in use. The entire sale made nearly three times its high presale estimate.

LARGER THAN LIFE

Largest beach towel A beach towel depicting the Walt Disney character Mickey Mouse measures 30 ft. 10 in. × 47 ft. 5 in. (9.4 × 14.46 m). It was manufactured by Maiden Sunshine (Spain) and displayed at the textile fair "Textile Hogar" held in Valencia, Spain, on January 25, 2000.

Largest condom A 72-ft.-tall (21.94-m) condom was fitted over the obelisk in the Place de la Concorde, Paris, France, on December 1, 1993, to mark World AIDS Day. The condom was funded by Italian clothes firm Benetton.

Largest beer bottle A beer bottle measuring 8 ft. 4 in. (2.54 m) tall and 7 ft. 1.5 in. (2.17 m) in circumference was unveiled at the Shepherd Neame Brewery in Faversham, Kent, UK, on January 27, 1993. It took 13 minutes to fill the bottle with 164.6 gal. (625.5 liters) of Kingfisher beer.

Largest continental broom On January 3, 2002, a continental (witch's) broom constructed by Comitato Festeggiamenti Campagnari (Italy) measured 72 ft. 9.5 in. (22.19 m). The handle alone measured 39 ft. 8.75 in. (12.11 m).

Largest boomerang A boomerang made from wood, plywood, and steel and measuring 5 ft. 11.25 in. (1.81 m) from tip to tip was successfully thrown by Heikki Niskanen (Finland) at Kuopio, Finland, on June 5, 2000. The boomerang traveled past the qualifying 65-ft. (20-m) mark and returned into the accuracy circle from where it was thrown.

Largest ceramic plate A plate created by the Inatsu Town Planning Association (Japan) on August 14, 1996 measured 9 ft. 2 in. (2.8 m) in diame-

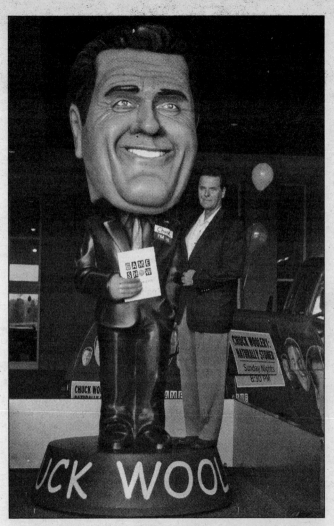

LARGEST BOBBLEHEAD Standing 11 ft. (3.35 m) tall and in the likeness of game show host Chuck Woolery (pictured), the world's largest bobblehead weighs 900 lb. (408 kg). It was created by the Game Show Network (U.S.A.) and displayed at McCormick Place, Chicago, Illinois, U.S.A., on June 8, 2003. The head on this oversized novelty item really bobbles.

ter. Made from 2,690 lb. (1,220 kg) of clay, it was left to dry out for five months before being painted and finally baked in a kiln for seven days.

Largest flag draped The American "Superflag" owned by "Ski" Demski (U.S.A.) measures 154 × 78 m (505 × 255 ft.) and weighs 3,000 lb. (1.36 tons). It was made by Humphrey's Flag Co. (U.S.A.), delivered to Demski on June 14, 1992, and unfurled in 1996 at Hoover Dam on the Colorado River, Arizona/Nevada, U.S.A., to mark the passing of the Olympic Torch.

Largest disco ball Derek Dyer (U.S.A.) has built a disco ball 10 ft. (3 m) in diameter that weighs 1,000 lb. (453.5 kg). It was unveiled at the Salt Palace in Salt Lake City, Utah, U.S.A., on December 31, 2002.

Largest drum A drum made from Japanese cedar and cowhide measuring 15 ft. 9 in. (4.80 m) in diameter, 16 ft. 3 in. (4.95 m) deep, and weighing 4,400 lb. (2,000 kg) was built by the Asano Taiko Company Ltd. (Japan). The final section of the drum was completed just a few hours before its first performance, on January 1, 2001.

Largest kettle A copper kettle that stood 3 ft. (0.9 m) high, with a 6-ft. (1.8-m) girth and a 23.6-gal. (90-liter) capacity, was built in Taunton, Somerset, UK, ca. 1800, for the hardware merchants Fisher and Son.

Largest flute The largest playable flute is 5 ft. (1.52 m) long and 3.5 in. (8.89 cm) in diameter and was made out of PVC by Dinesh Shandilya (India) in 1996.

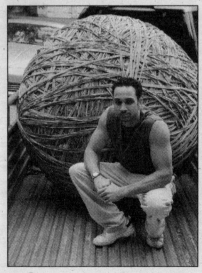

Largest fountain pen A pen made by Zbigniew Rozanek (Poland) in 1991 measured 2.22 m (7 ft.) long and 4 in. (11 cm) in diameter and had an 18-in. (48-cm) nib. The weight of the pen, including ink, was 20 lb. (9.5 kg). Without ink it weighed 7 lb. (3.3 kg).

LARGEST RUBBER BAND BALL John J. Bain (U.S.A.) constructed a rubber band ball with a circumference of 15 ft. 1 in. (4.59 m) that weighed 3,120 lb. (1,415.2 kg) when measured on October 22, 2003, at the Port Contractors in Wilmington, Delaware, U.S.A.

LARGEST DENTAL CAPS
Dental caps approximately 19 in. (50 cm) long, 5 in. (13 cm) in diameter, and weighing 28 lb. (13 kg) each were fixed onto a pair of cracked tusks belonging to Spike (pictured), a resident Asian elephant at the Calgary Zoo, Alberta, Canada, during a 3 hr. 30 min. operation on July 4, 2002. The stainless steel caps were designed and manufactured by the Southern Alberta Institute of Technology with metal donated by Corus Steel and adhesive by 3M (all Canada).

Largest jukebox A jukebox named "The Wall," which stood 41 ft. 4 in. (12.6 m) high and 63 ft. (19.2 m) wide, was built by Namco Ltd. (Japan) and unveiled in Sunshine Namjatown, Tokyo, Japan, in July 1996. Various features on the jukebox come to life when the music begins.

Largest hourglass The largest hourglass stands 42 in. (1.06 m) tall with a diameter of 15 in. (38 cm). Built by Bob Ciscell (U.S.A.), the hourglass contains 65 lb. (29.4 kg) of sand, which takes eight hours to run through.

Largest carpet of flowers A carpet of flowers measuring 21,958 ft.^{2} (2,040 m^2) was created by the Dubai Municipality at the Dubai Shopping Festival, Dubai, UAE, on February 12, 2003.

Largest set of wind chimes A 16-ft. 8-in.-tall (5.1-m) set of wind chimes built by Steve Kubler (U.S.A.) in May 2002 stands in front of the West Point Town Hall, Alabama, U.S.A.

Largest piggy bank A piggy bank called Pink Pig measured 10 ft. 9 in. tall, 16 ft. 8 in. long and 26 ft. 2 in. in circumference (3.28 m × 5 m × 7.9 m) on November 8, 2002. Pink Pig is owned by C. Michael Davenport (U.S.A.).

Largest wreath An Advent wreath measuring 164 ft. (50 m) in diameter was made from fir by Otter-Zentrum Hankensbüttel and Landfrauen Isenhagener (both Germany) on November 25, 2002.

LARGEST ACCORDION The largest playable accordion in the world (pictured) is 8 ft. 3.5 in. (2.53 m) tall, 6 ft. 2.75 in. (1.9 m) wide, 2 ft. 9.5 in. (85 cm) deep, and weighs approximately 440 lb. (200 kg). The instrument, built by Giancarlo Francenella (Italy), was begun in 2000 and finished in 2001. The giant accordion took over 1,000 hours to create and features 45 treble piano keys, 120 bass buttons, and 240 reeds. Built on a 5:1 ratio from the original, the instrument is made of wood (fir, cedar, mahogany, and walnut), metals (aluminum and steel), cardboard, cloth, and special varnishes.

Longest paper-clip chain made by an individual Between February 13 and 14, 2004, Dan Meyer (U.S.A.) created a paper-clip chain 5,340 ft. (1,627.6 m) long, consisting of 54,030 1.2-in.-long (3-cm) clips. The chain is nearly three times longer than the height of the CN Tower in Toronto, Canada.

Largest garland A 14,550-ft. (4,434-m) paper flower garland (or lei) was made by local citizens at the Hyatt Regency Waikiki, Honolulu, Hawaii, U.S.A., on December 19, 1992.

Largest ball of string From 1989 to 1992, J.C. Payne (U.S.A.) amassed enough string to create a ball 13 ft. 2.5 in. (4.03 m) in diameter and 41 ft. 6 in. (12.65 m) in circumference.

COLLECTIONS

Largest beer bottle collection The largest collection of beer bottles in the world is owned by Peter Broeker (Germany), who has amassed 12,548 bottles since 1980. The collection derives from 2,440 different breweries within 153 countries. Peter estimates that if all of his beer bottles were piled one on top of each other they would reach to a height of 9,983 ft. (3,043 m), which is almost eight times the height of the Empire State Building in New York, U.S.A.

Largest passport collection Guy Van Keer (Belgium) owns 7,637 passports and documents used in lieu of passports. They represent 130 countries and passport-issuing authorities, including many countries that no longer exist. The passports date from 1615 to the present day. The collection's most expensive item is a rare Chinese passport from 1898 valued at $52,830.

Largest collection of colored vinyl records Alessandro Benedetti (Italy) has collected 1,180 music records made of colored vinyl. His collec-

LARGEST AUTOGRAPHED DRUMSTICK COLLECTION Since 1980, Peter Lavinger (U.S.A.) has accumulated over 1,300 drumsticks, all of which have been played and handed to him by drummers from various popular bands, including Ringo Starr of The Beatles. He caught his first drumstick from the front row of a Good Rats concert in 1980.

tion includes 866 LPs (792 colored, 74 with pictures), 291 singles (277 colored, 14 with pictures), and 23 in unusual shapes.

Largest collection of photographs of professional sporting personalities Since 2000, Thomas Gill (UK) has built up a collection of 510 photographs taken of himself with professional soccer players. Thomas has photographs of himself with well-known British soccer players such as David Beckham, Sir Geoff Hurst, and Ryan Giggs. He also has a photo of himself with his all-time football hero Paul Merson.

Largest collection of uncut bank notes Leigh Follestad (Canada) has 123 sheets of uncut bank notes from 33 countries, representing 73 denominations, which he has been collecting since 1982.

Largest jet-fighter collection The world's biggest private collection of jet fighters numbers 110 and belongs to French winemaker Michel Pont. He started his collection in 1985, and it includes Russian MiGs, British Jaguars, and French Mirages. Michel buys the jets from governments, but is not permitted to fly the aircraft over French airspace. He also has a collection of 500 motorbikes, and 24 Fiat Abarth racing cars.

Largest collection of royal memorabilia Ronny Bragança (Portugal) has a collection of 2,950 pieces of memorabilia relating to Diana, Princess of Wales, which he has accumulated since 1991. He has items from many countries, including Japan, Mexico, and Australia. In 1999, he was fortunate enough to purchase a Christmas card signed by Charles and Diana in 1989.

Largest chamber pot collection Manfred Klauda (Germany) has amassed 9,400 chamber pots, the earliest dating from the 16th century. Currently his collection can be seen at the Zentrum für Aussergewöhnliche Museen, Munich, Germany.

LARGEST COLLECTION OF YO-YOS John "Lucky" Meisenheimer (U.S.A.) has a collection of 4,251 yo-yos, which he has amassed since 1971. His current collection is housed in 23 custom-made cases and is estimated to be worth around $100,000.

LARGEST BANANA COLLECTION Ken Bannister (U.S.A.), owner of the International Banana Club Museum in Altadena, California, U.S.A., has 17,000 different banana-related objects that he has amassed since 1972. All are on display in the museum.

Largest valid credit card collection Walter Cavanagh (U.S.A.) has accumulated 1,397 individual valid credit cards. The cost of acquisition to "Mr. Plastic Fantastic" was nothing, but they are worth more than $1.65 million in credit. They are kept in a 250-ft.-long (76.2-m) wallet—the world's longest.

Largest collection of soft drink cans from the same brand Christian Cavaletti (Italy) has a collection of 3,284 different Pepsi cans from 71 different countries. Christian, who has been collecting since 1989, belongs to the two largest soft drink can collectors' clubs: the National Pop Can Collectors (NPCC) and the Pepsi-Cola Collectors Club (PCCC).

Largest Popsicle stick collection Since 1988, Poul Lykke Jepsen (Denmark) has collected 449 different Popsicle sticks. Poul started collecting the sticks after he had eaten two Popsicles and noticed that they had different sticks. His collection grew after he got a job as a storage worker in 2001—his new employers manufactured Popsicle sticks.

COLLECTION	QUANTITY	HOLDER
airsickness bags	3,307 from 755 airlines	Niek Vermeulen (Netherlands)
airline tags	469 from 115 airlines	Raghav Somani (India)
badges	13,516	Daniel Hedges (UK)
ballpoint pens	285,150 from 148 countries	Angelika Unverhau (Germany)
Band-Aids (unused)	4,500	Brian Viner (UK)
Barbie dolls	1,125	Tony Mattia (UK)
beer cans	75,000 from 125 countries	William B. Christensen (U.S.A.)
bottle openers	20,884 from 136 countries	Dale Deckert (U.S.A.)
bottled water labels	5,115	Lorenzo Pescini (Italy)
bus tickets (used)	14,000	Yacov Yosipovv (Israel)
car bumper stickers	3,230	Bill Heermann (U.S.A.)
clothing tags	2,180	Angela Bettelli (Italy)
condoms	1,947	Amatore Bolzoni (Italy)
decorative pins	1,457	Gerhard Kühler (Germany)
five-leaf clovers	31,336	George Kaminski (U.S.A.)
fruit stickers	34,500	Antoine Secco (France)
hats	25,777	Tustumena Lodge (U.S.A.)
hotel baggage labels	2,016	Robert Henin (U.S.A.)
key chains	24,810	Kurt Meadows (U.S.A.)
mouse mats	1,947	Daniel Evans (UK)
mugs	4,567	Harold Swauger (U.S.A.)
pencils	6,885	Emilio Arenas (Uruguay)
pencil sharpeners	8,514	Demetra Koutsouridou (Greece)
phonecards	4,531 from 239 countries and territories	Harvinder Chohan (Canada)
piggy banks	5,750	Ove Nordström (Sweden)
rubber ducks	1,439	Charlotte Lee (U.S.A.)
rubber stamps	1,251	James Burton (UK)
shoehorns	1,594	Martien Tuithof (Netherlands)
shot glasses	8,411	Brad Rodgers (U.S.A.)
tea bag labels	8,661 from 88 countries	Felix Rotter (Germany)
thermometers	4,580	Richard T. Porter (U.S.A.)
traffic cones	137	David Morgan (UK)

TOYS

Largest stitched teddy bear The bear measuring 38 ft. 8.2 in. (11.79 m) in length was designed and made by Dana Warren (U.S.A.) over a period of six months.

Largest model railway engine A model of *Thomas the Tank Engine* character James, measuring 104 in. high, 59 in. wide, 256 in. long (264 ×

MOST VALUABLE TEDDY BEAR A Steiff bear named Teddy Girl (pictured) was sold for £110,000 ($171,600), more than 18 times the estimate and twice the previous world record, by Christie's, London, UK, on December 5, 1994. The buyer was Japanese businessman Yoshihiro Sekiguchi.

150 × 652 cm) and weighing nearly 3,351 lb. (1.52 tons) was built by BBC Visual Effects (UK) for a Thomas the Tank Engine tour in 2003. Models of Thomas, Percy, and Gordon were also part of the tour.

Largest kite flown The largest kite ever flown has a total lifting area of 7,319.4 ft.² (680 m²). When laid flat, it has a total area of 10,042.7 ft.² (933 m²). The "Megabite," designed by Peter Lynn (New Zealand), measured 210 ft. (64 m) long and 72 ft. (22 m) wide. The kite was officially measured on September 7, 1997.

Longest kite flown "The Cracken," created by Michel Trouillet (France), measures 3,394 ft. (1,034.45 m) in length, with a total mass of 233 lb. (106 kg). It was flown by Trouillet and his team on November 18, 1990, in Nîmes, France.

Largest spinning top A team of 25 workers from the Mizushima Plant of Kawasaki Steel Works in Okayama, Japan, created a spinning top measuring 6 ft. 6.75 in. (2 m) tall and 8 ft. 6.25 in. (2.6 m) in diameter and weighing 793 lb. (360 kg). They spun it for 1 hr. 21 min. 35 sec. on November 3, 1986.

Tallest LEGO structure A LEGO tower built in Tallinn, Estonia, on August 18–21, 1998, reached a height of 81 ft. 8.7 in. (24.91 m). It consisted of 391,478 plastic, eight-stud toy bricks. Over 6,000 children helped in the construction, which was organized by A.S. Rekato Ltd. (Estonia), to beat the previous record set in Moscow, Russia, in July 1998 by 9 in. (25 cm).

Longest LEGO structure A LEGO structure in the shape of a millipede measuring 3,451 ft. (1,052 m) and consisting of 2,477,140 bricks, was built by 20,000 children in Bangkok, Thailand, on April 27, 2003.

Largest hula hoop spun The largest hula hoop successfully rotated at least three times around a person's waist had a diameter of 13 ft. 4 in. (4.08 m). Nozomi Tsuju and Ai Kago (both Japan) rotated the hoop for 30 seconds each at the studios of Nippon Television Network, Tokyo, Japan, on January 1, 2004.

Longest Hot Wheels track The longest Hot Wheels track measured 1,650 ft. (502.92 m) and consisted of 2,100 pieces of track, held together by 2,150 connectors. The attempt was organized by Mattel Canada, Inc., for Big Brothers Big Sisters of Canada and was completed on July 7, 2002, at Thunder Alley, Toronto, Ontario, Canada.

Largest chess piece Mats Allanson (Sweden) has made a scaled-up king measuring 13 ft. (4 m) high and 4 ft. 6 in. (1.4 m) in diameter at the base.

Earliest chess pieces Chessmen found at Nashipur, modern-day Bangladesh, have been dated to ca. AD 900 and are the oldest known in existence.

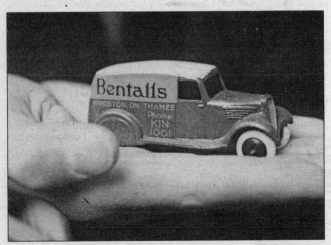

MOST VALUABLE MODEL CAR A very rare Dinky green 28 series 2nd Type Bentalls Department Store Promotional Delivery Van with yellow upper side panels and a white roof (pictured) was sold for £12,650 ($20,147) at Christie's, London, UK, on October 14, 1994. This example is believed to be one of only three known by Christie's experts to have survived.

MOST VALUABLE MICKEY MOUSE TOY A rare clockwork Mickey
Mouse motorcycle (ca. 1939, pictured) in its original box sold at
Christie's, London, UK, on June 16, 1997, for £51,000 ($83,466).

Largest commercially available board game Galaxion, manufactured by Cerebe Design International (Hong Kong), is played on a board
measuring 33 × 33 in. (83.8 × 83.8 cm).

Largest commercially available jigsaw puzzle The largest commercially available jigsaw puzzle is made by Ravensburger of Ravensburg, Germany, and measures 9 ft. 0.5 in. × 6 ft. 3.5 in. (2.76 × 1.92 m). It has 18,000
pieces—another record for a commercially available jigsaw.

Smallest commercially available jigsaw puzzle A 1,000-piece jigsaw puzzle manufactured by Educa Sallent (Spain) measures 18 × 12 in. (46
× 30 cm). The miniature puzzles made by Educa Sallent are all made from
recycled materials and depict a variety of images, ranging from European
landmarks to Disney and Sesame Street characters.

Largest jigsaw puzzle A puzzle devised by Great East Asia Surveyors
& Consultants Co. Ltd. measured 58,435.1 ft.² (5,428.8 m²) and consisted of

21,600 pieces in total. It was assembled by 777 people at the former Kai Tak Airport, Hong Kong, China, on November 3, 2002.

Largest set of Russian nesting dolls (matrioshka) A 51-piece set of nesting dolls was hand painted by Youlia Bereznitskaia (Russia). The largest doll is 1 ft. 9.25 in. (54 cm) in height, while the smallest measures 0.125 in. (0.31 cm) in height. The set was completed on April 25, 2003.

Largest ball bath The bath had a surface area of 2,722.2 ft.^{2} (252.9 m^2) with an average depth of 1 ft. 4 in. (0.4 m) and contained about 130,000 balls. It was made on December 30, 1999, in Plantagebaan, Wouwse Plantage, The Netherlands, by the Stichting Carnaval Wouwse Plantage as part of the festivities for a millennium carnival.

Largest yo-yo A yo-yo measuring 10 ft. 4 in. (3.17 m) in diameter and weighing 897 lb. (407 kg) was devised by J.N. Nichols (Vimto) Ltd. (UK) and constructed by engineering students at Stockport College. It was launched by crane from a height of 188 ft. 6 in. (57.5 m) at Wythenshawe, Greater Manchester, UK, on August 1, 1993, and subsequently yo-yoed about four times.

Largest permanent Monopoly board A Monopoly board made of granite and located in San Jose, California, U.S.A., measures 31 × 31 ft. (9.44 × 9.44 m). All the playing pieces are proportionally scaled up. The board was opened to the public on July 26, 2002.

GAMES & PASTIMES

Most darts bull's-eyes in 10 hours Perry Prine (U.S.A.) hit 1,432 bull's-eyes in 10 hours at the Lake Erie Classic Dart Tournament in Mentor, Ohio, U.S.A., on March 27, 1998.

Largest game of Poohsticks On July 22, 2000, the largest ever game of Poohsticks was played on the River Tweed from the Chain Bridge, Horncliffe, in the Scottish Borders, UK. A total of 2,313 Poohsticks were launched from the bridge to sail downriver to the finish line at Paxton House Boathouse. A stick stamped 8702 won. Poohsticks is a game invented by A.A. Milne (UK) of *Winnie the Pooh* fame—Christopher Robin and Pooh threw sticks in the water from one side of a bridge, then ran over to see which stick floated out first on the other side.

Farthest wink shot in tiddlywinks At the Queen's College Tournament, Cambridge, UK, Ben Soares (UK) of the St. Andrews Tiddlywinks Society made a wink shot measuring 31 ft. 3 in. (9.52 m), on January 14, 1995.

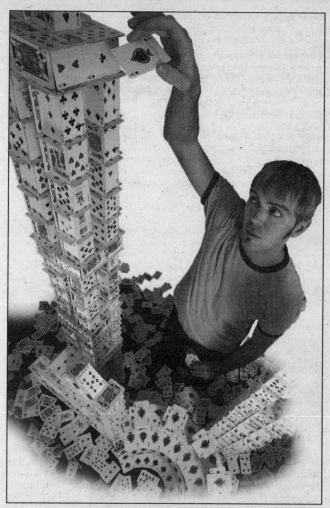

MOST STORIES IN A HOUSE OF CARDS The tallest freestanding house of cards was 131 stories high. The 25-ft. 3.48-in.-tall (7.71-m) structure was built by Bryan Berg (U.S.A.) on November 6, 1999. The house was created using 91,800 cards in the lobby of the casino at Potsdamer Platz, Berlin, Germany, and recorded for the *Guinness die Show der Rekord.* The total weight of the 1,765 packs of cards used was 242 lb. 8 oz. (110 kg).

Most opponents in consecutive chess games On February 27 and 28, 2001, Anna-Maria Botsari (Greece) played 1,102 consecutive games of chess against different opponents, with just seven draws and the rest wins, at Kalavryta, Greece.

Most simultaneous checkers opponents Ronald Suki King (Barbados) played 385 games of checkers simultaneously at the Houston International Festival, Texas, U.S.A., on April 26, 1998. King donned roller skates to move between the 385 games.

Largest game of pass the parcel On February 28, 1998, 3,918 students removed 2,200 wrappers from a parcel measuring 4 ft. 11 in. × 4 ft. 11 in. × 1 ft. 7 in. (1.5 × 1.5 × 0.5 m) in two and a half hours at Nanyang Technological University, Singapore. Owing to the numbers involved, the parcel went round on a cart and took an hour to complete one circuit.

Fastest Jenga tower built to 30 levels The fastest time to build a stable Jenga tower 30 levels high, within the rules of the game, is 11 min. 55 sec. by Sabrina Ibrahim, John Chua, and Alex Agboola (all UK) on the BBC's *Big Toe Radio Show,* London, UK, on January 28, 2003.

Most dominoes set up and toppled single-handedly Ma Li Hua (China) single-handedly set up and toppled 303,621 dominoes out of a total of 303,628 at Singapore Expo Hall, Singapore, on August 18, 2003. The event was organized by LG Electronics, Inc.

Most dominoes set up and toppled by a group The record for most dominoes toppled is 3,847,295 (from a possible 4 million). The attempt was organized by En-

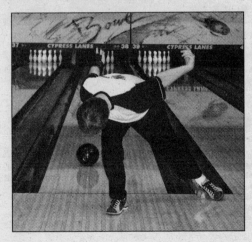

HIGHEST SINGLE GAME SCORE WHEN BOWLING BACKWARDS Del Lawson (U.S.A.) registered a score of 139 in a single game of backwards bowling at Cypress Lanes, Winter Haven, Florida, U.S.A., on April 21, 2002. He bowled a series of three games with a total score of 376.

LARGEST GAME OF PICK-UP STICKS Newmarket Recreation have made a game of pick-up sticks that was 36 times larger than the commercially available item (pictured). It consisted of 30 plastic sticks (7 gold, 7 red, 7 blue, 8 green, and 1 black), each measuring 19 ft. 10.5 in. (6.05 m) in length and 4.5 in. (11.4 cm) in width. A full game was played by four teams of 75 children at Newmarket, New Hampshire, U.S.A., on July 21, 2003.

demol Netherlands and took place at FEC EXPO, Leeuwarden, The Netherlands, on November 15, 2002. The 4 million dominoes were divided into 51 interconnected projects, all of which related to one central theme.

Most dominoes stacked on a single domino Matthias Aisch (Germany) stacked 726 dominoes on a single vertically standing supporting domino on December 28, 2003, in Radeburg, Germany. The stack remained standing for an hour.

Largest quiz A record 888 participants took part in a quiz at the Radisson SAS Hotel, Galway, Ireland, on October 14, 2003. Teams of four answered 10 rounds of 12 questions.

Fastest time to solve a Rubik's cube The fastest time to solve a Rubik's cube in an official championship is 16.53 sec. by Jess Bonde (Denmark) at the 2003 World Championships in Toronto, Ontario, Canada.

Fastest time to solve a Rubik's cube blindfolded The fastest time to solve a Rubik's cube in an official championship while blindfolded is 3 min. 56 sec. by Dror Vomberg (Israel) at the 2003 World Championships in Toronto, Ontario, Canada.

Highest overall Scrabble score Phil Appleby (UK) achieved a Scrabble score of 1,049 on June 25, 1989, at Wormley, Herts, UK. His opponent scored 253 and the margin of victory, 796 points, is also a record.

Largest sack race competition A total of 2,095 Dutch students—from Agnieton College and elementary schools in Zwolle, Wezep, and Hattem, The Netherlands, took part in a sack race on October 11, 2002, in Zwolle, The Netherlands.

Most participants in a wheelbarrow race The largest wheelbarrow race involved 318 people (159 pairs) and took place at Alexandra Park, London, UK, on August 31, 2002, in an attempt organized by Starwood Hotels & Resorts, London, UK.

Largest game of leapfrog A total of 849 people took part in a game of leapfrog at Brookfield Community School, Chesterfield, Derbyshire, UK, on September 26, 2003.

Highest altitude by a single kite Richard P. Synergy (Canada) flew a kite to an altitude of approximately 14,509 ft. (4,422 m) above the point of takeoff on August 12, 2000, near Kincardine, Ontario, Canada. The kite, a high-tech delta, had an area of 270 ft.^{2} (25 m^2) and was designed and built by Synergy himself. At its maximum altitude, the kite had 4.5 miles (7.31 km) of woven kevlar line connecting it to a winch on the ground. The record-breaking flight lasted 8 hr. 35 min.

Most powerful games console Microsoft's Xbox is powered by a 733-MHz Intel CPU, the fastest of any current games console. Its graphics processor, a custom-designed chip that runs at 250 MHz, is also the field leader. The Xbox's main rivals, the Sony Playstation 2 and Nintendo GameCube, have CPU clock speeds of 300 and 405 MHz respectively, and graphics chips running at 150 and 202.5 MHz respectively.

Best-selling Xbox game According to *Screen Digest,* the best-selling Xbox game is "Halo," which had sold 4 million units as of December 2003.

Best-selling Playstation 2 game According to *Screen Digest,* the best-selling Playstation 2 game is "Grand Theft Auto Vice City," which had sold 9 million units as of December 2003.

Best-selling GameCube game The best-selling GameCube game is "Mario Sunshine," which had sold 3.5 million units as of December 2003 according to *Screen Digest.*

FOOD & DRINK

Curly Wurly stretching Craig Glenday (UK) stretched a Curly Wurly chocolate bar a total distance of 3 ft. (0.91 m) in three minutes at the offices of Guinness World Records, London, UK, on June 27, 2003.

LARGEST POPCORN SCULPTURE The world's largest popcorn sculpture (pictured) is 13 ft. (4 m) tall and 8 ft. 9 in. (2.67 m) wide, and is made in the likeness of King Kong. The giant popcorn ape was displayed in front of Leicester Square's Odeon cinema, London, UK, on July 24, 2003, to celebrate the 70th anniversary of the original *King Kong* film (U.S.A., 1933).

Fastest sandwich made using only feet Using just his feet, Rob Williams (U.S.A.) made a bologna cheese and lettuce sandwich, complete with sliced tomatoes, mustard, mayonnaise, sliced pickles, and olives on cocktail sticks, in 1 min. 57 sec. on the set of *Guinness World Records: Primetime,* Los Angeles, California, U.S.A., on November 10, 2000.

Fastest time to husk a coconut using only teeth In 28.06 seconds, Sidaraju S. Raju (India) husked a coconut measuring 30.7 in. (78 cm) in circumference and weighing 10 lb. 6.4 oz. (4.74 kg) using only his teeth at the Ravindra Kalashetra, Bangalore, India, on March 30, 2003.

Fastest time to drink two pints of stout Scott Williams (Canada) drank two pints of Guinness in 6.3 seconds on May 23, 2003.

Most brussels sprouts eaten in one minute Dave Mynard (UK) consumed 43 cooked brussels sprouts in 1 minute on December 10, 2003.

Most ice cream eaten in 30 seconds Diego Siu (U.S.A.) ate 9.3 oz. (264 g) of ice cream in 30 seconds at the Central Florida Fair, Orlando, U.S.A., on March 2, 2003.

Fastest time to eat raw onion In only 2 min. 40 sec., Danny Healy (UK) ate a raw onion weighing 7.47 oz. (212 g) at the BBC Television Centre, London, UK, on November 15, 2003.

LARGEST GINGERBREAD MAN Chefs at the Hyatt Regency Hotel, Vancouver, Canada, made a gingerbread man that measured 13 ft. 11 in. (4.23 m) high, 5 ft. 8 in. (1.72 m) wide and 2 in. (5.08 cm) deep, on November 19, 2003. The gingerbread figure weighed 372 lb. 1.82 oz. (168.8 kg).

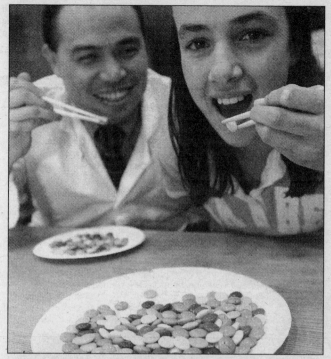

MOST SMARTIES EATEN IN THREE MINUTES The record for the most Smarties eaten in three minutes using chopsticks is held by Kathryn Ratcliffe (UK), who ate 138 Smarties at the Metro Centre, Gateshead, Tyne and Wear, UK, on October 25, 2003, breaking her own record of 112.

Greatest egg-dropping height The greatest height from which fresh eggs have been dropped to the ground and remained intact is 700 ft. (213 m) by David Donoghue (UK), who dropped a number of eggs from a helicopter onto a golf course in Blackpool, Lancs, UK, on August 22, 1994.

Most eggs crushed with wrist K.S. Raghavendra (India) crushed 13 eggs with the back of his wrist in 30 seconds at the Sree Rama Vidyalaya School, Bangalore, India, on September 9, 2003.

Farthest marshmallow nose-blow Scott Jeckel (U.S.A.) blew a marshmallow out of one nostril a distance of 16 ft. 3.5 in. (4.96 m), caught in the mouth of Ray Perisin (U.S.A.), on the set of *Guinness World Records: Primetime,* Los Angeles, California, U.S.A., on August 13, 1999.

Most baked beans eaten in five minutes Andy Szerbini (UK) ate a total of 226 baked beans in 5 minutes using a cocktail stick at London Zoo, UK, on November 18, 1996.

Most baked beans flicked The largest quantity of baked beans flicked from a bathtub into a bucket is 34.63 oz. (982 g) by Jamie Rickers (UK) on GMTV's program *Up On The Roof,* London, UK, on October 30, 2002.

Most expensive cocktail commercially available The Ritz Side Car, costing $496 (£400), features on the cocktail menu at Bar Hemingway, in the Hotel Ritz, Paris, France. The cocktail was invented by head bartender Frank Meier in 1923 and contains Ritz Fine Champagne, 1865 (pre-phylloxéral) cognac, Cointreau, and lemon juice. The cocktail could be bought for just $5 in 1923. (In terms of purchase power, the current-day equivalent of this is $67.)

Longest champagne-cork flight Heinrich Medicus (U.S.A.) ejected a cork from an untreated and unheated champagne bottle standing 4 ft. (1.22 m) from level ground to a distance of 177 ft. 9 in. (54.18 m) at the Woodbury Vineyards Winery, New York, U.S.A., on June 5, 1988.

Most grapes stuffed in the mouth Michael Levinson (Canada) stuffed 54 seedless grapes, weighing 4 oz. (113 g) into his mouth on the set of *Guinness World Records: Primetime,* Los Angeles, California, U.S.A., on September 27, 1999.

MOST EXPENSIVE BURGER The DB Burger Royale, created by chef Daniel Boulud (France), is available on the menu of DB Bistro Moderne, New York, U.S.A., for $59. The original DB burger was created to mark DB Bistro Moderne's opening in 2001, and the restaurant added the DB Royale burger to the menu in January 2003. It is served exclusively during the black truffle season.

Most candles on a cake The St. Ignatius Cub Scouts (U.S.A.) lit 12,432 candles on an iced cake measuring 75 × 25 in. (190.5 × 63.5 cm) as part of Ohio's bicentennial celebrations on May 9, 2003.

Most champagne bottles sabered in one minute Using a saber, Dean Opsal (U.S.A.) cut off the upper portion of the neck from each of 20 champagne bottles at the Coeur d'Alene Resort Hotel, Coeur d'Alene, Idaho, U.S.A., on October 31, 2001. He achieved this in one minute and without shattering the glass, leaving the contents safe to drink.

Most cherry stems knotted in three minutes Al Gliniecki (U.S.A.) tied 39 cherry stems into knots with his tongue in three minutes at the Guinness World of Records Experience, Orlando, Florida, U.S.A., on January 26, 1999.

Oldest restaurant Restaurante Botín in Calle de Cuchilleros, Madrid, Spain, was opened in 1725 by a French cook named Jean Botín and his Asturian wife. Today the restaurant is run by the third generation of the Gonzalez family, Antonio and José Gonzalez (all Spain). Located in the heart of Madrid near the Plaza Mayor, it now has four floors which retain the original 18th-century interiors as well as the original firewood oven.

Longest sesame twist The longest sesame twist measured 4 ft. 10.8 in. (1.5 m) and was made by chefs at Guifa Xiang, Tianjin, China, on December 1, 1999. A sesame twist is a traditional Chinese delicacy made from fried dough with a crispy stuffing.

Largest bag of cookies The largest bag of cookies was made by Loblaws Supermarkets Ltd. and was 10 ft. 8 in. (3.29 m) high, 7 ft. (2.13 m) deep and 45 in. (1.14 m) wide. It contained 3,852 trays, each with 26 cookies, making a total of 100,152. It went on display at Loblaws Wonderland Market, London, Ontario, Canada, on September 6 and 7, 2001.

Largest lollipop The largest lollipop weighed 4,759 lb. 1.6 oz. (2,158.7 kg) and was made by Franssons (Sweden) for a festival in Gränna, Sweden, on July 27, 2003. The lollipop was 6 ft. 6 in. (1.98 m) wide, 9 ft. 10 in. (3 m) long, and 9.5 in. (24 cm) thick and was peppermint-striped like traditional Gränna rock candy.

Largest marzipan confection The world's largest pistachio marzipan confection weighed 9,255 lb. (4.2 tons) and was made by 225 chefs in an event organized by Spacetel Syria at Hamadanya Stadium, Aleppo, Syria, on July 1, 2003.

Largest bowl of pasta The largest ever bowl of pasta weighed 3,265 lb. (1,480 kg), excluding the weight of the bowl. It was created by Nintendo of America, Inc., in conjunction with Buca Di Beppo restaurants (U.S.A.) on August 22, 2002, in Washington Square, San Francisco,

LARGEST PUMPKIN PIE The largest pumpkin pie weighed 418 lb. (189.6 kg). It was made by the Windsor Certified Farmers Market and the Windsor High School Culinary Arts Program (both U.S.A.) and served at the Farmers Market, Windsor, California, U.S.A., on October 26, 2003. The pie was 6 ft. 4 in. (1.936 m) in diameter and 3 in. (7.62 cm) deep.

U.S.A. The fiberglass bowl measured 3 ft. (0.91 m) high and 10 ft. (3.048 m) wide.

Longest salami A salami measuring 498 ft. 3.6 in. (151.89 m) was made by the Association of Friulian Butchers and the Udine Chamber of Commerce (both Italy) and was displayed at the Piazza San Giacomo, Udine, Italy, on October 13, 2002. The average circumference of the salami was 5.5 in. (14 cm) and the entire salami weighed 590.8 lb. (269 kg).

Largest serving of fish-and-chips The largest serving of fish-and-chips had a combined weight of 72 lb. (32.66 kg) and was made by Fedics Food Services, Port Elizabeth, Eastern Cape, South Africa, on November 22, 2003. Individually, the fish weighed 31 lb. 8 oz. (14.30 kg) and the french fries weighed 40 lb. 8 oz. (18.36 kg).

Largest pizza commercially available Paul Revere's Pizza (U.S.A.) will bake and deliver a pizza with a 4-ft. (1.21-m) diameter and an area of 12.59 ft.^{2} (1.17 m^2). The pizza, named the "Ultimate Party Pizza," is sold at $99.99. It is made up of 170 oz. (4.81 kg) of dough, 48 fl. oz. (1.36 liters) of sauce, various meats and vegetables, and about 5 lb. (2.25 kg) of cheese.

Largest box of chocolates Marshall Field's, Chicago, Illinois, U.S.A., created a box of Frango mint chocolates weighing 3,226 lb. (1,463 kg) on November 14, 2002.

Largest cup of coffee On January 29, 2002, Ettore Diana and Luca Braguti (both Italy) made a 394.7-gal. (1,500-liter) cappuccino at the Hotel Leon d'Oro, Verona, Italy.

Largest cocktail The world's largest cocktail was a 7,012-gal. (26,645-liter) margarita made on May 17, 2001, by staff at Jimmy Buffett's Margaritaville and Mott's, Inc., Universal City Walk, Orlando, Florida, U.S.A.

Largest milkshake The Comfort Diners, Parmalat U.S.A., and the American Dairy Association (all U.S.A.) made the world's largest milkshake, with a volume of 5,977 gal. (22,712.47 liters) in New York, U.S.A., on August 1, 2000.

Largest tea bag The world's largest tea bag was made by Lipton Yellow Label of Lever Brothers Pakistan Ltd. on June 22, 2002. The tea bag weighed 19 lb. 10 oz. (8.9 kg) and was displayed at the Avari Towers Hotel, Karachi, Pakistan. The giant tea bag measured 10 ft. (3.18 m) long and 7 ft. 3 in. (2.21 m) wide, and attached to the tea bag was a string measuring 14 ft. (4.26 m) long. The bag was made from original filter paper and contained

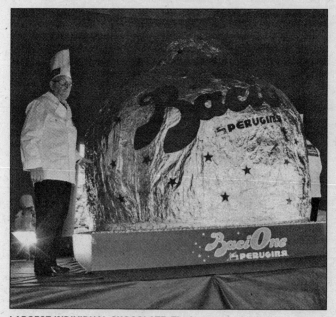

LARGEST INDIVIDUAL CHOCOLATE The largest single chocolate is a 13,183-lb. (5,980-kg) BaciOne. Made by Nestlé (Italy), it was displayed at the Perugina factory, San Sisto, Italy, on October 26, 2003.

LARGEST WEDDING CAKE The largest wedding cake ever weighed 6,818.40 kg (15,032 lb.) and was made by chefs at the Mohegan Sun Hotel and Casino, Uncasville, Connecticut, U.S.A., and displayed at their New England bridal showcase on February 8, 2004.

15 lb. 7 oz. (7 kg) of black tea. It is estimated that 3,500 cups of tea could be made from the tea bag.

Largest pizza On December 8, 1990, the largest pizza ever was baked at the Norwood Hypermarket, Johannesburg, South Africa. It was 122 ft. 8 in. (37.4 m) in diameter and took about 39 hours to prepare and cook.

Longest hot dog The world's longest hot dog measured 34 ft. 5.25 in. (10.5 m). It was made by students from the University of Pretoria and displayed at the Sonop Hostel, Pretoria, South Africa, on October 18, 2003.

Largest box of popcorn On September 11, 2003, BR Turbo (Brazil) filled a huge box with popcorn, 880 ft.^{3} (24.92 m^3) in volume, at the Mercado Público, Porto Alegre, Rio Grande do Sul, Brazil. It took them 5 hr. 59 min. to fill the box.

Largest candy cane Employees of Fabiano's Chocolates and Ice Cream (U.S.A.) made a candy cane measuring 36 ft. 7 in. (11.14 m) long and 4 in. (10.1 cm) in diameter at Lansing City Market, Michigan, U.S.A., on December 5, 1998.

Largest bubble-gum bubble blown from the mouth The greatest reported diameter for a bubble-gum bubble blown from the mouth under the strict rules of this highly competitive activity is 23 in. (58.4 cm), and was achieved by Susan Montgomery Williams (U.S.A.) at the ABC-TV studios in New York City, U.S.A., on July 19, 1994.

Largest bubble-gum bubble blown through the nose After pre-chewing for at least an hour, Joyce Samuels (U.S.A.) blew, from her nose, a bubblegum bubble with a diameter of 11 in. (28 cm) on *Guinness World Records: Primetime,* Los Angeles, U.S.A., on November 10, 2000.

Fastest jellybean sorting using a straw The fastest time in which 30 Jelly Belly jellybeans have been sorted into five flavors using a drinking straw is 1 min. 3.58 sec. by Euan Hamilton (UK) in a competition organized by the *Beano* comic (UK) in May 2004.

FEATS OF
ENGINEERING

BIG BUILDINGS

Largest ice village A village of 140 "igloos"—huts constructed solely of ice—was built near the famous Icehotel at Jukkasjärvi, Sweden, to accommodate 700 employees of Tetra Pak International during a conference at the hotel in December 2002. Each hut had a diameter of 14 ft. (4.3 m) and was 7 ft. (2.1 m) tall. The igloos slept up to five people each and were constructed of around 1,765 ft.³ (50 m³) of ice.

Largest wooden building Built in 1912, the Woolloomooloo Bay Wharf, Sydney, Australia, is 1,312 ft. (400 m) long, 206 ft. (63 m) wide, and stands on 3,600 piles. The building on the wharf is five stories high, 1,150 ft. (350.5 m) long, and 141 ft. (43 m) wide with a floor area of 688,890 ft.² (64,000 m²), and has been converted into a marina complex and hotel apartments.

Tallest residential-only building The tallest purely residential building in the world is the 21st Century Tower in Dubai, UAE, which has 54 floors

and tops out at 882 ft. (269 m). Its main roof is at 622 ft. (189.7 m). However, the roof of the 866-ft. (264-m) Tower Palace 3 Tower G, in Seoul, South Korea, is also its highest point, meaning that it

TALLEST MONUMENTAL COLUMN The tapering column on the bank of the San Jacinto River near Houston, Texas, U.S.A., is 570 ft. (173.7 m) tall, 47 ft. (14 m) square at the base and 30 ft. (9 m) square at the observation tower. Built between 1936 and 1939 to commemorate the Battle of San Jacinto (April 21, 1836), it is surmounted by a star weighing 440,000 lb. (200 tons).

LARGEST STADIUM ROOF The transparent acrylic glass "tent" roof over the Munich Olympic Stadium, Germany measures 915,000 ft.² (85,000 m²) in area. It rests on a steel net supported by masts.

can accommodate 69 floors of living space. Both towers were completed in 2003.

Tallest obelisk The world's tallest obelisk is the Washington Monument in Washington, D.C., U.S.A. It stands 555 ft. (169 m) tall and was completed in 1884 to honor George Washington. An obelisk is specifically classified as a tapered four-sided column, usually with a pointed top.

Tallest freestanding structure The tallest freestanding structure on Earth is the Petronius oil and gas drilling platform, which stands 1,870 ft. (570 m) above the ocean floor in the Gulf of Mexico. Operated by Texaco, the platform began commercial production on July 21, 2000. The highest point on the platform, the vent boom, stands in excess of 2,000 ft. (610 m) above the ocean floor. The tallest freestanding structure on land is the 1,815-ft. 5-in. (553.34-m) CN Tower in Toronto, Canada.

Largest airport roof The Hajj Terminal at the $5.3-billion King Abdul-Aziz Airport near Jeddah, Saudi Arabia, which was designed to cater for the annual influx of pilgrims, is the world's largest roofed structure, covering a total area of 370 acres (150 hectares).

Largest airport terminal The Hong Kong International Airport passenger terminal building is 0.8 miles (1.3 km) long and covers 5.92 million ft.² (550,000 m²). The baggage hall of this gargantuan structure is as big as the

Yankee Stadium in New York, U.S.A., and could hold five Boeing 747s parked wing tip to wing tip. The terminal is designed to accommodate 45 million passengers a year and handles 460 flights a day. It contains 3 km (1.8 miles) of moving walkways, 592,000 ft.^{2} (55,000 m^2) of glass cladding, and around 1.25 million ft.^{2} (117,000 m^2) of carpeting.

Largest soccer stadium The Maracanã Municipal Stadium in Rio de Janeiro, Brazil, has a standard capacity of 205,000 spectators, 155,000 of whom can be seated. It was built for the 1950 Football World Cup and housed a crowd of 199,854 for the final match of the tournament, Brazil v. Uruguay, on July 16, 1950—the greatest ever attendance for a sporting event. The oval stadium is 105 ft. (32 m) high and the distance between the middle of the field and the furthest spectator is 413 ft. (126 m).

Longest stadium roof span The longest roof span is 787 ft. 4 in. (240 m) for the major axis of the elliptical Texas Stadium, completed in 1971 at Irving, Texas, U.S.A.

Largest retractable roof The world's largest retractable roof covers the SkyDome, home of the Toronto Blue Jays baseball team, near the CN Tower in Toronto, Canada. Completed in June 1989, the roof covers 8 acres (3.2 hectares), spans 685 ft. (209 m) at its widest, and rises to 282 ft. (86 m). It weighs 24.6 million lb. (11,000 tons) and takes 20 minutes to open fully. When retracted, the entire field and 91% of the seats are uncovered. The stadium has a capacity of 67,000 for concerts, 55,000 for Canadian football, and 50,600 for baseball.

LARGEST PALACE The Imperial Palace in the center of Beijing, China, covers an area measuring 3,150 × 2,460 ft. (960 × 750 m) over an area of 178 acres (72 hectares). The outline survives from the construction of the third Ming emperor, Yongle (1402–24), but owing to constant reconstruction work, most of the intramural buildings (five halls and 17 palaces) are from the 18th century.

Largest stadium with air-supported roof The Pontiac Silverdome Stadium in Detroit, Michigan, U.S.A., has a capacity of 80,311. The 10-acre (4-hectare) translucent roof covering the 770 × 600-ft. (235 × 183-m) octagonal stadium is held up by pressurized air provided by 25 large fans. Made from flexible Teflon-coated fiberglass, the roof is 202 ft. (62 m) high. The air pressure in the stadium causes no discomfort and is within the limits of natural atmospheric pressure variations. The building is equipped with revolving doors to ensure that the air doesn't leak out as people enter.

Largest residential palace The Istana Nurul Iman—the palace of the Sultan of Brunei in the capital Bandar Seri Begawan—was completed in January 1984 at a reported cost of $422 million. It is the largest residence in the world, with a floor space of 2,152,780 ft.² (200,000 m²), 1,788 rooms, and 257 lavatories.

Largest pyramid The largest pyramid, and the largest monument ever built, is the Quetzalcóatl Pyramid at Cholula de Rivadavia, 63 miles (101 km) southeast of Mexico City. It is 177 ft. (54 m) tall, and its base covers nearly 45 acres (18.2 hectares). Its volume is estimated at 116.5 million ft.³ (3.3 million m³), compared with a volume of 84.8 million ft.³ (2.4 million m³) for the Pyramid of Khufu, or Cheops, at Giza.

Largest hotel The MGM Grand Hotel and Casino, Las Vegas, Nevada, U.S.A., consists of four 30-story towers on a 112-acre (45.3-hectare) site. The hotel has 5,005 rooms, with suites of up to 6,000 ft.² (560 m²), a 15,200-seat arena, and a 33-acre (13.3-hectare) theme park.

Tallest door Each of the four doors in the NASA Vehicle Assembly Building near Cape Canaveral, Florida, U.S.A., is 460 ft. (140 m) high, as tall as a 35-story building. They were originally designed to allow fully assembled Saturn and Apollo rockets to pass through them.

Highest clock The world's highest two-sided clock is 580 ft. (177 m) above street level on top of the Morton International building, Chicago, Illinois, U.S.A.

Largest shopping center West Edmonton Mall in Edmonton, Alberta, Canada, covers an area of 5.3 million ft.² (492,386 m²). The mall cost a staggering CAN$1.2 billion ($927 million) to build and features over 800 stores and services, as well as 11 major department stores.

Tallest air-traffic control tower The 425-ft. (130-m) tower at Kuala Lumpur International Airport, Malaysia, is the world's tallest air-traffic control tower. Its design imitates an Olympic torch.

TALLEST STRUCTURES

From earliest times, humans have aimed for the sky, originally to glorify a secular ruler or religious deity, but now mainly to gain international prestige.

Foundations Built as a tomb for a god-king, Egypt's Great Pyramid at Giza was probably the world's tallest building for 3,500 years, from 2500 BC until the construction of the great European cathedrals in the Middle Ages. The modern era of tall buildings was heralded by the completion in 1889 of the 1,023-ft.-high (312-m) Eiffel Tower in Paris, France. And from La Tour Eiffel onward, it has been big business, rather than religion, that has driven the construction of ever taller buildings. There is enormous prestige attached to being the home of the world's tallest structure—and some recent record holders are featured here (to scale).

The advent of skyscrapers During the early 20th century, the U.S.A. dominated the race to be the home of the world's tallest building. New York is still the most famous home of the "skyscraper," as these giants became known. New York's tallest ever buildings were the Twin Towers of the World Trade Center, dedicated in 1973 but destroyed in the terrorist atrocity of September 11, 2001. The north tower was the taller of the two and stood an amazing 1,368 ft. (417 m) high. The World Trade Center was the tallest building for a relatively short time, as in 1974, Chicago's Sears Tower was completed and took the title. Sears held on to that record for over 20 years.

Competition from Asia From the 1990s, the U.S.A. has had some stiff competition from Asia, and in 1996 the title of world's tallest building passed to the 88-story, 1,483-ft. (452-m) Petronas Twin Towers in Kuala Lumpur, Malaysia. The completion of the 1,667-ft. (508-m) Taipei 101 in Taipei, Taiwan, in 2004 means that the title remains in Asia for now, but several new proposed buildings, including the new Freedom Tower on the site of the World Trade Center in New York City, U.S.A., and the Burj Dubai in the United Arab Emirates—whose final height will not be made public until it is completed—means that the crown is likely to change hands several times in the near future.

1931 Empire State Building
New York City, New York, U.S.A.
Height to tip of antenna: **1,472 ft. (449 m)**
Height to roof: **1,250 ft. (381 m)**

1974 Sears Tower
Chicago, Illinois, U.S.A.
Height to tip of antenna: **1,728 ft. (527 m)**
Height to roof: **1,450 ft. (442 m)**

1996 Petronas Twin Towers
Kuala Lumpur, Malaysia
Height to tip of spire: **1,483 ft. (452 m)**
Height to roof: **1,242 ft. (378.6 m)**

2004 Taipei 101
Taipei, Taiwan
Height to tip of spire: **1,666 ft. (508 m)**
Height to roof: **1,470 ft. (448 m)**

Tallest freestanding structure But no building standing today is as tall as the world's tallest structure on land—the CN Tower in Toronto, Ontario, Canada. This communications tower is entirely freestanding and has no resi-

1975 CN Tower
Toronto, Ontario, Canada
Height to tip of spire/antenna: **1,815 ft. 5 in. (553.33 m)**

dential or office space. "Topped out" in April 1975, it measures a staggering 1,815 ft. 5 in. (553.33 m).

The future . . . Skyscraper buffs will continue to argue as to which of the world's architectural gems constitute the world's tallest building. There are plans being drawn up all over the world for new high-rise buildings so perhaps when Guinness World Records celebrates its centennial in 2055, there will be a building in existence that's twice the height of the current record holder!

GWR TALKS TO Ron Klemenic

Chairman, Council on Tall Buildings & Urban Habitat (CTBUH), the body that decides which building is the world's tallest.

Who makes the decision on the tallest building for the CTBUH? There's a committee of about a dozen people, and it's made up of architects and engineers from around the world.

How does the CTBUH define the height of a building? Our definition was put together by Fazlur Khan, the structural engineer on the Sears Tower in Chicago, who said that the height of the building should be measured from the elevation of the main entrance of the building to the top of the architecture. So you then have to interpret what the "top of the architecture" is. For the Sears Tower it's pretty clear—it's to the elevation of the main flat roof. Here, for instance, the antennae don't count, because if you remove them the fundamental appearance of the building doesn't change, it's still the same from an architectural point of view. Whereas if you removed the spire from the Chrysler building in New York it doesn't look like the Chrysler building any longer. That's really how the Petronas Towers captured the title, because if you were to remove the architectural spires, somehow the buildings wouldn't look the same.

Why is the CN Tower not considered to be the tallest building in the world? The CN Tower is the tallest free-standing structure in the world, but we don't consider it to be a building; it's a tower. The reason we look at it that way is because the lion's share of the tower is not occupiable space, it's simply a tower or a shaft.

Would you agree that since 9/11 the days of the skyscraper are numbered? It certainly doesn't appear to be the case. In North America, there aren't really any proposals for anything that would surpass the Sears Tower, aside from the proposed Freedom Tower in New York. It's mostly driven by economics—once buildings get above 80 stories or so, they start to lose their economic viability. However, when we look at Asia and the Middle East, there's still great interest in designing the tallest building in the world, and in Dubai there's a building being planned right now (the Burj Dubai) that would surpass everything that I'm aware of in terms of height.

So having the tallest building is all about prestige? For sure. For instance, the Petronas Towers remain only partially occupied, because the economy of Malaysia really can't support those buildings as economic entities. But they were symbolic for the Malaysian economy and people.

Is there a theoretical upper limit to tall buildings? From a structural point of view, there really is not; the limitations are primarily economic. I doubt that the new building in Dubai makes any sound financial sense. However, there's an individual behind that project who has the financial fortitude to fund it, despite the fact that it might never make him any money from leasing space. However, it may pay for itself in other ways, such as notoriety.

What are the biggest challenges facing anyone planning to build the tallest building in the world? Certainly if you want it to be a revenue-producing, profitable enterprise, one of the greatest challenges is moving people around. In other words, the amount of space the elevators consume as a ratio of the floor that's remaining to be leased. As you go taller and taller, you need more and more elevators to get the people up and down, and at some point—roughly around 80 stories—the floor area consumed by the elevators is so great that the area remaining to lease is too small to make the building economically viable. So one of the technical challenges is advances in elevator technology.

(At the time of going to press, the CTBUH had not yet officially confirmed Taipei 101 as the tallest building, because it had not yet been opened for business.)

CONSTRUCTIONS

Largest solar energy roof A huge solar energy roof was installed to cover the exposition hall at the Floriade 2002 flower festival, Haarlemmermeer, The Netherlands. The area of the roof is 281,045 ft.^{2} (26,110 m^2) and it has a generating capacity of 2.3 MW. It was created by Nuon Renewables. The festival opened on April 6, 2002 and ran until October 20, 2002.

Furthest distance to move a bridge London Bridge proved unable to handle increasing volumes of traffic in the 20th century. It was auctioned in 1962 to Robert McCulloch (U.S.A.) for $2,460,000 (then £876,068). The bridge was dismantled and moved brick by brick to Lake Havasu City, Arizona, U.S.A., where it was reassembled and opened in 1971. It had been moved a total of 5,300 miles (8,530 km). Legend has it that McCulloch had bought the wrong bridge—he had presumed he was buying the more decorative Tower Bridge.

Highest causeway In the mid-1990s, a causeway was constructed to replace a Bailey bridge that spanned Khardungla Pass, Ladakh, India. (A Bailey bridge is made out of prefabricated sections and is named after its inventor, Sir Donald Bailey.) At one time, this Bailey bridge had the highest altitude of any road bridge in the world: 18,380 ft. (5,602 m). However, because of constant damage from avalanches it was replaced by the causeway.

Longest cable suspension bridge The main span of the Akashi-Kaikyo road bridge, which links the Japanese islands of Honshu and Shikoku, is 1.24 miles (1,990.8 m) long. The overall suspended length, with side spans, is 2.43 miles (3,911.1 m). Two towers rise 974 ft. 5 in. (297 m) above water level and the two main supporting cables are 44 in. (1.12 m) in diameter, making both the tower height and the cable diameter world records. Work on the bridge began in 1988, and it was opened to traffic on April 5, 1998.

LONGEST WALL The Great Wall of China has a main-line length of 2,150 miles (3,460 km)—nearly three times the length of the UK—plus 2,195 miles (3,530 km) of branches and spurs. Construction of the wall began during the reign of Qin Shi Huangdi (221–210 BC). The height of the Great Wall varies from 15 to 39 ft. (4.5 to 12 m) and it is up to 32 ft. (9.8 m) thick. It stretches from Shanhaiguan, on the Gulf of Bohai, to Yumenguan and Yangguan.

Longest bridge-tunnel The Chesapeake Bay bridge-tunnel, which opened to traffic on April 15, 1964, extends 17.65 miles (28.4 km) from the Eastern Shore region of the Virginia Peninsula to Virginia Beach, U.S.A. The longest bridged section is Trestle C, at 4.56 miles (7.34 km), and the longest tunnel is the Thimble Shoal Channel Tunnel, at 1.09 miles (1.75 km).

Longest cantilever bridge The Québec Bridge (Pont de Québec) over the St. Lawrence River, Canada, has the longest cantilever truss span of any bridge in the world, measuring 1,800 ft. (549 m) between the piers and 3,239 ft. (987 m) overall. It carries a railroad track and two highways. Work started in 1899, and the bridge was finally opened to traffic on December 3, 1917, having cost a staggering CAN$22.5 million ($22.5 million) and, sadly, 87 lives.

Longest Tibetan bridge The longest Tibetan bridge (a bridge made entirely from rope) has a span of 1,187 ft. (362 m). It connects the islands of Procida and Vivara, Italy, and was constructed by the Sportchallengers (Italy) organization. The bridge was completed on July 15, 2001.

Highest bridge The world's highest bridge spans the Royal Gorge of the Arkansas River in Colorado, U.S.A., at 1,053 ft. (321 m) above the water. It is a suspension bridge with a main span of 880 ft. (268 m). The bridge took six months to construct and was completed on December 6, 1929.

Deepest road tunnel The Hitra Tunnel in Norway, linking the mainland to the island of Hitra, reaches a depth of 866 ft. (264 m).

LONGEST BRIDGE In 1969, the Second Lake Pontchartrain Causeway, which joins Mandeville and Metairie, Louisiana, U.S.A., and is 38.42 km (23.87 miles) long, was completed. It is shown here with the First Causeway, built in 1956.

LONGEST STEEL ARCH BRIDGE The Lupu Bridge (pictured), Shanghai, China, which stretches across the Huangpu River, has a span of 1,804 ft. (550 m). The bridge took three years to construct and opened on 28, June 2003. It is 104.9 ft. (32 m) longer than the previous record holder, the New River Gorge Bridge, near Fayetteville, West Virginia, U.S.A.

below sea level. It is 3.47 miles (5.6 km) long, with three lanes, and was opened in December 1994. The tunnel was built to provide an all-weather link to Hitra island across the turbulent waters of the Norwegian Sea.

Longest big-ship canal The Suez Canal links the Mediterranean Sea and the Red Sea. It took ten years to construct, employing a workforce of 1.5 million people—120,000 of whom perished during the construction—and finally opened on November 17, 1869. The canal runs from Port Said lighthouse to Suez Roads. It is 100.8 miles (162.2 km) long in total, with a minimum width of 984 ft. (300 m) and a maximum width of 1,198 ft. (365 m).

Longest bikeway bridge A bikeway bridge 779 ft. 6 in. (237.6 m) in length spans the 17 tracks at Cambridge Railway Station, UK.

Longest floating bridge The Second Lake Washington Bridge, Seattle, Washington State, U.S.A., has a total length of 2.39 miles (3.839 km), with a floating section measuring 1.42 miles (2.291 km). The bridge was built at a total cost of $15 million and was finally completed in August 1963.

Longest wooden bridge The Lake Pontchartrain Railroad Trestle, Louisiana, U.S.A., which connects the cities of New Orleans and Kenner, is 5.82 miles (9.369 km) long. Construction began on the bridge in February 1882 and was completed in September of that year. When it opened in 1883, the bridge originally stretched for 21.49 miles (34.6 km). It is made from re-inforced creosoted yellow-pine timber.

Longest plastic bridge The longest reinforced-plastic span bridge is at the Aberfeldy Golf Club at Aberfeldy, Perth and Kinross, UK. The main span is 206 ft. 8 in. (63 m) and the overall bridge is 370 ft. 9 in. (113 m) long.

Longest sewage tunnel When it is complete, the Chicago TARP (Tun-nels and Reservoir Plan) in Illinois, U.S.A., will involve 131 miles (211 km) of machine-bored sewer tunnels 9 to 33 ft. (2.7 to 10 m) in diameter. The system helps to control pollution and flooding and will service 3.9 million people in 52 communities over an area of 375 miles^2 (971 km^2).

Longest road- and rail-bridge system Japan's Seto Ohashi Bridge consists of six bridge sections stretching a distance of 5.8 miles (9.4 km). The bridge, which opened on April 10, 1988 (100 years after it was first pro-posed by the Japanese authorities), joins the city of Kurashiki on the island of Honshu with Sakaide City on the island of Shikoku.

Tallest structure The KVLY-TV tower, a stayed television transmitting mast between Fargo and Blanchard, North Dakota, U.S.A., is 2,063 ft. (629 m) tall. The tower and its anchors cover 160 acres (64 hectares), an area that is equivalent to 130 American football fields. The total weight of steel in the tower is 864,500 lb. (392 tons), and the total length of the guylines is 7.6 miles (12.2 km).

GARDENS

Largest garden In the late 17th century, André Le Nôtre (France) created a magnificent garden for King Louis XIV at Versailles, France. The gardens and parkland were created out of what had once been marshland. They cover more than 15,000 acres (6,070 hectares), of which the famous formal gar-den covers 247 acres (100 hectares).

Oldest botanical gardens The Orto Botanico in Padua, Italy, was cre-ated in 1545. The original design of a circular central plot (which symbol-izes the world) surrounded by a ring of water, remains, as does the gardens' original purpose—to serve as a place for scientific research.

Largest rose garden The Roseto di Cavriglia in Cavriglia, Italy, has more than 7,500 varieties of rose.

Largest scented garden The largest scented garden is at the Kirsten-bosch National Botanical Gardens on the slopes of Table Mountain, Cape

Town, South Africa. The Fragrance Garden includes a Braille Trail and many aromatic plants offering the opportunity for blind and visually impaired visitors to enjoy the plants.

Smallest park Circular in shape, Mill Ends Park, located on a safety island on SW Front Avenue, Portland, Oregon, U.S.A., measures a tiny 24 in. (60.96 cm) diameter and 452.16 in.^{2} (2,917.15 cm^2) in area. On March 17, 1948, it was designated as a city park, for snail races and as a colony for leprechauns, at the behest of the city journalist Dick Fagan (U.S.A.).

Largest saltwater garden park The largest gardens irrigated by saltwater are those that form the Zayed Project for Seawater Irrigation, on the coast of the Arabian Gulf in Abu Dhabi, United Arab Emirates. The gardens

MOST VISITED GARDEN WITH PAYING VISITORS The most visited garden for which an admission charge applies is the Royal Botanic Gardens, Kew, Surrey, UK, which has an average of one million paying visitors per year. The 326-acre (132-hectare) site has 40 historically important buildings and collections of more than 40,000 species of plants. Kew Gardens became a United Nations World Heritage site on July 3, 2003.

measure 215,278 ft.^{2} (20,000 m^2) and contain 22,000 specimens from 40 types of plants, all of which tolerate pure saltwater or a saltwater/freshwater mixture, either naturally or by genetic modification.

Largest permanent hedge maze and pathway The largest permanent hedge maze is the Peace Maze at Castlewellan Forest Park, County Down, Northern Ireland, UK, which has a total area of 2.77 acres (11,215 m^2) and a total path length of 2.18 miles (3.51 km). The maze opened on September 12, 2001 and was designed by Beverley Lear (UK) and created by the Forest Service, Northern Ireland, UK, assisted by members of the public. The 2.18-mile-long (3.51-km) pathway holds the record for the longest pathway in a permanent hedge maze.

Oldest cultivated decorative plant The oldest species of plant cultivated and used for decoration is the rose *(Rosa)*. Documents dating back to AD 50 suggest that ancient Romans grew the flowers in plantations and local hothouses to ensure a year-round supply of medicinal extracts, cooking ingredients, and ornamentation.

Largest plant conservatory The Eden Project, near St. Austell, Cornwall, UK, consists of two giant transparent domes, or "biomes." The largest of these, the humid tropics biome, stands 180 ft. (55 m) tall, covers 273,295 ft.^{2} (25,390 m^2), and has a total volume of 14.681 million ft.^{3} (415,730 m^3). The smaller warm temperate biome has 70,395 ft.^{2} (6,540 m^2) of floor space and a volume of 3.02 million ft.^{3} (85,620 m^3).

Largest seed collection The Millennium Seed Bank Project at Wakehurst Place Garden, West Sussex, UK, had 6,655 identified species preserved in its cold store as of July 4, 2003. In total, there are three million individual

LARGEST TEMPORARY CORN MAZE AND PATHWAY Stewarts GardenLands Maize Maze covered an area of 16.9 acres (68,271 m^2) when it opened on July 10, 2003 in Christchurch, Dorset, UK. The maze, which has a central lobster shape, was designed by Adrian Fisher (UK) and created by Martin and Susie Stewart (both UK). An 8.83-mile-long (14.22-km) pathway in the maze holds the record for the longest path in a temporary maze.

OLDEST TOPIARY GARDEN Topiary (pictured) is the art of clipping bushes and shrubs into ornamental shapes. The topiary garden at Levens Hall, Cumbria, UK, features designs that are more than 300 years old and were initially planted and trained during the 1690s. The topiary shapes in the garden include a judge's wig and umbrellas.

seeds preserved in the underground frozen vault. This amounts to 15,613 collections and represents approximately 2.8% of the world's flora.

Largest herbarium The largest herbarium contains 8,880,000 species of preserved plants and is in the Muséum National d'Histoire Naturelle, Paris, France.

Oldest vine Scientific measurement of the "Old Vine" in Maribor, Slovenia, carried out in 1972, established that it was then at least 350 years old and may have been up to 400 years old.

Largest vineyard A vineyard in the Languedoc region of France extends over the Mediterranean slopes between the Pyrénées and the Rhône in the départements Gard, Hérault, Aude, and Pyrénées-Orientales. It covers an area of 2,075,685 acres (840,000 hectare), 52.3% of which is "monoculture viticole," i.e. consisting only of wine crops.

Tallest and longest hedge The Meikleour beech hedge in Perthshire, UK, was planted in 1746 by Jean Mercer and Robert Murray Nairne (both UK) to define the eastern border of their land. The hedge is 1,771 ft. (540 m) long and averages 98 ft. (30 m) in height.

Largest permanent tree maze Designed by Erik and Karen Poulsen (both Denmark), the Samso Labyrinten on the Island of Samso in Denmark has an area of 645,835 ft.^{2} (60,000 m^2) and its path measures 16,830 ft. (5,130 m). It was created in September 1999 and opened to the public on May 6, 2000.

Oldest hedge maze The maze in the gardens of Hampton Court Palace, Surrey, UK, was built for King William III of England. Designed by royal gardeners George London and Henry Wise (both UK), it was planted between 1689 and 1695 using hornbeam *Carpinus*. The maze covers an area of 0.5 acres (0.2 hectares), with a total path length of 0.5 miles (800 m).

Longest running horticultural show The Shropshire Horticultural Society's "Shrewsbury Flower Show" celebrated its 116th event on August 15–16, 2003. The annual show has been held since 1875 at the Quarry Showground, Shrewsbury, UK, but stopped during the war years 1914–18 and 1940–45.

The earliest documented horticultural show, a "carnation and gooseberry" display held in July 1836, was organized by the Salop Horticultural Society in Shropshire, UK.

Largest horticultural library The Royal Horticultural Society's Lindley Library in London, UK, has more than 50,000 books. The library was established in 1861 and is named after the botanist John Lindley (UK).

THEME PARKS & RIDES

Oldest operating amusement park Bakken, located in Klampenborg, Denmark, opened in 1583. It features over 150 attractions, including a wooden roller coaster dating from 1932.

Greatest number of roller coasters in an amusement park In 2003, both Six Flags Magic Mountain in Valencia, California, U.S.A., and Cedar Point near Sandusky, Ohio, U.S.A., opened their 16th roller coaster to the public.

Largest amusement resort Walt Disney World in Orlando, Florida, U.S.A., is set in 30,000 acres (12,140 hectares)—twice the size of Manhattan. It opened on October 1, 1971 and cost $400 million.

Amusement park with the most rides Six Flags Great Adventure in Jackson, New Jersey, U.S.A., has a total of 71 different mechanical rides. The park, which now boasts 12 roller coasters, opened its doors on July 4, 1974 and covers a total area of 140 acres (56.6 hectares).

Largest indoor amusement park The world's largest shopping mall, West Edmonton Mall, Alberta, Canada, is home to Galaxyland, which covers 400,000 ft.^{2} (37,160 m^2). It holds 30 skill games and 27 rides and attractions, including "Mindbender"—a 14-story, triple-loop roller coaster—and "Drop of Doom," a 13-story free-fall ride.

Largest wave pool According to the World Waterpark Association, the largest wave pool covers around 4 acres (1.6 hectares) and can be found at Siam Park City, Bangkok, Thailand.

Longest full-circuit roller coaster "Steel Dragon," which opened on August 1, 2000 at Nagashima Spaland, Mie, Japan, is the longest full-circuit roller coaster at 8,133 ft. (2,479 m). It is a non-inversion steel-track giga-coaster that lifts riders a terrifying 311 ft. 8 in. (95 m) before dropping them 306 ft. 9 in. (93.5 m).

Tallest amusement park big wheel The "Dai-Kanransha" big wheel, at Pallet Town grounds, Tokyo, Japan, stands 377 ft. (115 m) from the base of its pedestal to the top of the wheel. It has a revolution velocity of 0.06 rpm, a wheel diameter of 328 ft. (100 m), and can carry up to 384 passengers.

Largest observation wheel The British Airways London Eye, designed by London architects David Marks and Julia Barfield (both UK), has a diameter of 443 ft. (135 m). Constructed on London's South Bank, it made its first "flight" on February 1, 2000, with regular service commencing the following month. The wheel continuously turns during normal operation. Each of the 32 fully enclosed capsules, carrying up to 25 passengers, completes a full 360° rotation every 30 minutes.

Greatest capacity observation wheel Walter Bassett (UK) constructed his first and largest observation wheel for the Oriental Exhibition at Earls Court, London, UK, in 1895. It had ten first-class and 30 second-class cars, each carrying 30 people. The wheel could carry a maximum of 1,200 passengers to a height of 276 ft. (84 m), before it was scrapped in 1906.

Longest walk-through horror house "Labyrinth of Terror" at Fujikyu Highland Amusement Park, Yamanashi Prefecture, Japan, is a hospital-

ROLLER COASTER WITH THE MOST INVERSIONS "Colossus," which opened in March 2002 at Thorpe Park, Surrey, UK, turns riders upside down ten times during each 2,789-ft. (850-m) run. It reaches a maximum height of 98 ft. (30 m) and a top speed of 40 mph (65 km/h).

themed house of horrors that opened on July 19, 2003. It has a 2,021-ft. (616-m) walk-through course, which takes visitors between 30 and 40 minutes to complete.

Tallest and fastest wooden roller coaster The first hill of "Son of Beast" at Paramount King's Island in Kings Mills, Ohio, U.S.A., is 218 ft. (66.4 m) high, making it the tallest wooden roller coaster in the world. The ride, which is roughly as high as a 16-story building, opened in April 2000. It was built by the Roller Coaster Corporation of America, and is also the world's fastest wooden coaster at 78.3 mph (126 km/h).

Steepest wooden roller coaster "Colossos" at Heide-Park near Soltau, Germany, has the steepest drop of any wooden roller coaster, with an angle of 61°. The 4,921-ft. (1,500-m) ride lasts for 2 min. 25 sec., during which it can reach speeds of up to 74.6 mph (120 km/h).

Oldest continually operating roller coaster "The Scenic Railway" at Luna Park, St. Kilda, Victoria, Australia, opened to the public on December 13, 1912 and has remained in operation ever since. This traditional wooden coaster was designed by La Marcus Adna Thompson (U.S.A.), who is regarded as the father of the modern roller coaster.

LARGEST INDOOR WATER PARK The Ocean Dome (pictured) at Sheraton Resort Phoenix Sengaia near Miyazaki, Japan, is 984 ft. (300 m) long, 328 ft. (100 m) wide, and 125 ft. (38 m) high, and contains a beach 459 ft. (140 m) long.

FASTEST FULL-CIRCUIT ROLLER COASTER The world's fastest and tallest roller coaster is "Top Thrill Dragster" (shown), a hydraulically launched "strata-coaster" at Cedar Point, near Sandusky, Ohio, U.S.A., which reaches its maximum speed of 120 mph (193 km/h) just four seconds after launch. The ride, which opened in May 2003, is 420 ft. (128 m) tall, 2,800 ft. (853 m) long, and cost $25 million to build.

Highest average age for a roller-coaster ride The highest average age of roller coaster passengers is 75.25 years, set by a group of 32 riders on the "Big Dipper" at Blackpool Pleasure Beach, Lancashire, UK, on September 24, 2003.

Longest roller-coaster marathon Richard Rodriguez (U.S.A.) rode the Expedition GeForce and Superwirbel roller coasters at Holiday Park, Hassloch, Germany, for 192 hours (8 days) nonstop, from August 20 to 28, 2003.

Most roller coasters ridden in 24 hours The greatest number of different roller coasters ridden in a 24-hour period is 74, a feat achieved by Philip A. Guarno, Adam Spivak, John R. Kirkwood, and Aaron Monroe Rye (all U.S.A.) on August 9, 2001. The four rode coasters in ten parks in four U.S. states, using helicopters to travel between each park.

Longest inner-tube water slide The 874-ft. 4-in.-long (266.5-m) "Triple Saurus" slide at Shibamasa World Water Amusement Park in Fukui, Japan, opened on July 7, 2001. The longest of three similar slides attached to the same tower, it stands 86 ft. 11 in. (26.5 m) high.

Tallest vertical-drop amusement ride The "Giant Drop" at Dreamworld, near Coomera, Queensland, Australia, drops from a height of 390 ft. (119 m), giving riders a terrifying five seconds of free-fall time before being brought to a halt by electromagnetic brakes.

Oldest operating merry-go-round The Vermolen Boden-Karussel at Efteling Theme Park in Kaatsheuvel, The Netherlands, was built in 1865. Originally powered by horses, it was converted to electric power during restoration.

TRAINS

Earliest railway As early as 1550, wagons running on wooden rails were used for mining at Leberthal, Alsace, France.

Earliest public electric railway On May 12, 1881, a public electric railway opened at Lichtervelde near Berlin, Germany. It was 1.5 miles (2.5 km) long, ran on 100 V current, and carried 26 passengers at up to 30 mph (48 km/h).

Longest train The longest freight train was 4.57 miles (7.35 km) long and consisted of 682 ore cars pushed by eight powerful diesel-electric locomotives. Assembled by BHP Iron Ore (Australia), it traveled 171 miles (275 km) from the company's Newman and Yandi mines to Port Hedland, Western Australia, on June 21, 2001.

Longest model train The longest model train was 230 ft. 3 in. (70.2 m) in length and consisted of 650 wagons hauled by four locomotives. It was run by the Arid Australia model railway group in Perth, Western Australia, on June 3, 1996. The train was built in the H0 scale of 1:87.1, meaning it was the equivalent length of a full-scale train measuring 3.8 miles (6.11 km).

Heaviest train pulled by single locomotive The heaviest train ever hauled by a single engine is believed to be one of 34.2 million lb. (15,545 tons) made up of 250 freight cars stretching 1.6 miles (2.5 km) and pulled by the *Matt H. Shay* (No. 5014), a steam engine that ran on the Erie Railroad in the U.S.A. from 1914 until 1929.

Largest steam locomotive The largest steam locomotives are generally considered to be the 4–8–8–4 "Big Boys," which were built by the American Locomotive Company from 1941 to 1944. They are 130 ft. 9 in. (39.85 m) long and weigh 1.12 million lb. (508.02 tons), including their tenders.

Largest railroad station by number of platforms In terms of the number of platforms, the world's largest railroad station is Grand Central Terminal, Park Avenue and 42nd Street, New York City, U.S.A. It was built from 1903 to 1913 and has 44 platforms situated on two underground levels, with 41 tracks on the upper level and 26 on the lower. The station covers 19

LONGEST SMALL-SCALE MODEL RAILWAY TRACK The Great American Railway (pictured) has a total track length of more than 50,000 ft. (15,250 m) of H0 scale (1:87.1) track and is the star exhibit at the Northlandz attraction in Flemington, New Jersey, U.S.A. The model railway and its miniature world covers an area of 50,000 ft.^{2} (4,645 m^2), including 4,000 buildings and over half a million lichen trees, and is the culmination of 25 years of single-handed work for Bruce Williams Zaccagnino (U.S.A., pictured here).

hectares (47 acres), and about 550 trains and 200,000 commuters use it daily.

Fastest speed on a national rail system *Atlantique,* a French SNCF high-speed TGV train, achieved a speed of 320.2 mph (515.3 km/h) between Courtalain and Tours, France, on May 18, 1990.

Highest sustained average train speed The highest average speed by a train over a distance in excess of 621 miles (1,000 km) is 190.37 mph (306.37 km/h) by a French Société Nationale des Chemins de fer Français (SNCF) Train à Grande Vitesse (TGV) traveling between Calais and Marseille on May 26, 2001. The unmodified train covered the 663 miles (1,067 km) between the cities in 3 hr. 29 min., reaching a top speed of 227 mph (366 km/h).

Fastest railed vehicle A four-stage rocket-sled system accelerated an 192-lb. (87-kg) payload to a speed of 9,468 ft./s (2,886 m/s) in 6.031 seconds at Holloman High Speed Test Track, Holloman.Air Force Base, New Mexico, U.S.A., on April 30, 2003. This is equivalent to a speed of 6,453 mph (10,385 km/h).

Fastest diesel train The former British Rail (UK) inaugurated its HST (High Speed Train) daily service between London, Bristol, and South Wales

FASTEST AVERAGE SPEED FOR A SCHEDULED TRAIN JOURNEY The West Japan Railway Company operates its 500-Series Nozomi bullet trains (pictured), or "shinkansen," at an average speed of 162.7 mph (261.8 km/h) on the 119-mile (192-km) line between Hiroshima and Kokura on the island of Honshu, Japan.

FASTEST STEAM LOCOMOTIVE The London North Eastern Railway "Class A4" (4–6–2) No. 4468 *Mallard* (shown here, later numbered 60022) recorded a speed of 125 mph (201 km/h) over a distance of 1,319 ft. (402 m) while hauling seven coaches weighing 535,722 lb. (243 tons) gross down Stoke Bank, near Essendine, (now) Rutland, UK, on July 3, 1938.

on October 4, 1976 using InterCity 125 trains. One of these holds the world speed record for diesel trains, at 148 mph (238 km/h), set on a test run between Darlington, York, and Durham, North Yorks, UK, on November 1, 1987.

Fastest train in regular public service The magnetically levitated (maglev) train linking China's Shanghai International Airport to the city's financial district reaches a top speed of 267.8 mph (431 km/h) on each 18-mile (30-km) run. The train, which was built by Transrapid International (Germany), had its maiden run on December 31, 2002.

Fastest maglev train The MLX01, a manned superconducting magnetically levitated (maglev) train operated by the Central Japan Railway Company and Railway Technical Research Institute, reached a speed of 361 mph (581 km/h) on the Yamanashi Maglev Test Line, Yamanashi Prefecture, Japan, on December 2, 2003.

Highest railroad line At La Cima, Peru, the standard-gauge (1,435-mm or 56.5-in.) track on the main line between Lima and La Oroya reaches 15,806 ft. (4,818 m) above sea level as it crosses the Andes. There are 67 tunnels and 59 bridges on the line. However, in 2001, China began building the Qinghai-Tibet railroad, which is planned to reach a height of 16,640 ft. (5,072 m).

Highest railway station Cóndor Station on the meter-gauge (39-in.) Río Mulatos-Potosí line in Bolivia lies at an altitude of 15,702 ft. (4,786 m).

Longest railroad platform The platform at Kharagpur Station, West Bengal, India, is 2,733 ft. (833 m) in length.

Least extensive subway The Carmelit underground system in Haifa, Israel, is just 5,905 ft. (1,800 m) long. The Carmelit, which opened in 1959, is a funicular railroad running at a gradient of 12 degrees and is the only subway in Israel. The line, which starts at Paris Square and finishes at Carmel Central, has six stations.

Longest monorail The Osaka Monorail in Osaka, Japan, has a total length of 13.8 miles (22.2 km). Fully operational since August 1997, the monorail runs between Osaka International Airport and Hankyu Railway Minami Ibaraki Station, with a second stage running between Hankyu and Keihan Railway Kadomashi Station.

CARS

Earliest full-scale automobile Nicolas-Joseph Cugnot (France) made a military steam tractor for the Paris Arsenal in October 1769 with a top speed of 2.5 mph (4 km/h). Cugnot's second, larger tractor, completed in May 1771, survives in the Conservatoire Nationale des Arts et Métiers in Paris, France.

Fastest production car On March 31, 1998, Andy Wallace (UK) drove a standard McLaren F1 production car at 240.14 mph (386.46 km/h) at the Volkswagen Proving Ground, Wolfsburg, Germany. Various de-tuned track cars have been licensed for road use but are not normal production models.

Fastest steam car On August 19, 1985, Robert E. Barber (U.S.A.) broke the 79-year-old speed record for a steam car when *Steamin' Demon,* built by Barber-Nichols Engineering Co. (U.S.A.), reached 145.607 mph (234.331 km/h) at Bonneville Salt Flats, Utah, U.S.A.

Fastest wheel-driven vehicle The highest speed achieved by a wheel-driven car is 409.986 mph (659.808 km/h), with a peak speed of 432.692 mph (696.331 km/h), by Al Teague (U.S.A.) in *Spirit of '76* at Bonneville Salt Flats, Utah, U.S.A., on August 21, 1991.

Fastest diesel-engined car Virgil W. Snyder (U.S.A.) drove a diesel-powered streamliner called *Thermo King-Wynns* at 235.756 mph (379.413 km/h) at Bonneville Salt Flats, Utah, U.S.A., on August 25, 1973.

Fastest open-road race The fastest road race in the world is the Silver State Classic on Route 318, Nevada, U.S.A., in which drivers maintain average speeds in excess of 190 mph (305 km/h) over the 90-mile (145-km) course. The highest ever average speed attained was 207.78 mph (334.38 km/h), set by Chuck Shafer and Gary Brockman (both U.S.A.) in May 2000.

Most valuable car The greatest confirmed price paid for a car is £8.45 million ($15 million) for the 1931 Bugatti Type 41 "Royale" Sports Coupé by Kellner. It was sold by Nicholas Harley (UK) to the Meitec Corporation of Japan on April 12, 1990.

Most expensive production car The Mercedes-Benz CLK/LM cost $1,547,620 when launched in 1997. It can travel from 0 to 62 mph (100 km/h) in 3.8 seconds and has a top speed of 200 mph (320 km/h).

Most valuable pop memorabilia John Lennon's 1965 Phantom V Rolls-Royce was bought for $2,229,000 by Jim Pattison, chairman of the Expo 86 World Fair in Vancouver, Canada, at Sotheby's, New York, U.S.A., on June 29, 1985.

Longest car Jay Ohrberg (U.S.A.) created a 100-ft.-long (30.5-m) 26-wheeled limousine. Its many features include a king-sized water bed and a swimming pool with diving board. It can be driven as a rigid vehicle or

FASTEST ELECTRIC CAR On October 22, 1999, the *White Lightning* electric streamliner (shown here), driven by Patrick Rummerfield (U.S.A.), achieved a speed of 245.951 mph (395.821 km/h) at the Bonneville Salt Flats, Utah, U.S.A. With its slender, aerodynamic carbon-fiber body, the 25-ft. (7.62-m) *White Lightning* looks more like a rocket than a car and can reach a speed of 100 mph (161 km/h) in eight seconds.

adapted to bend in the middle, and was designed for use in films and displays.

Largest production car The largest car produced for private use was the Bugatti Type 41 "Royale," known in the UK as the "Golden Bugatti," which was assembled at Molsheim, France, by the Italian Ettore Bugatti. First built in 1927, it measures over 22 ft. (6.7 m) in length with a hood more than 7 ft. (2.13 m) long.

Most powerful production car The 5,998-cc V12 engine of the Ferrari Enzo is claimed by its makers to generate 660 hp (492 kW) of power, making it the most powerful car ever to enter series production. Ferrari claims that the Enzo reaches 62 mph (100 km/h) in 3.65 seconds and has a top speed of 217 mph (349 km/h).

Best-selling two-seater sports car Mazda (Japan) has sold in excess of 677,000 units of its MX-5 Miata sports car. Production began in April 1989.

EARLIEST INTERNAL-COMBUSTION CAR The first successful gasoline-driven car, the Motorwagen (pictured), built by Karl Friedrich Benz (Germany), ran at Mannheim in late 1885. The three-wheeler weighed 560 lb. (254 kg) and could reach 8–10 mph (13–16 km/h). Its single-cylinder engine delivered 0.85 hp (0.63 kW) at 400 rpm. It was patented on January 29, 1886.

FASTEST PRODUCTION PICKUP TRUCK A standard 2004 Dodge Ram SRT-10 pickup truck (pictured), driven by National Association for Stock Car Auto Racing (NASCAR) driver Brendan Gaughan (U.S.A.), reached a speed of 248.783 km/h (154.587 mph) at the DaimlerChrysler Proving Grounds, Chelsea, Michigan, U.S.A., on February 2, 2004.

Highest car mileage A 1966 Volvo P-1800S owned by Irvin Gordon (U.S.A.) had covered in excess of 2,219,751 miles (3,572,342 km) by March 2004. The car is still driven on a daily basis and covers more than 100,000 miles (160,000 km) per year, thanks in part to being driven to numerous events in Europe and the U.S.A.

Longest journey by solar electric vehicle The *Radiance,* a sleek solar car built by the Queen's University Solar Vehicle Team (Canada), traveled 4,376 miles (7,043 km) across Canada from Halifax, Nova Scotia, to Vancouver, British Columbia, from July 1 to 29, 2000. *Radiance* was built for the annual World Solar Challenge between Darwin and Adelaide in Australia, and achieved second place in 1999.

Longest lawn mower ride Gary Hatter (U.S.A.) traveled 14,594 miles (23,487 km) in 260 consecutive days from May 31, 2000 to February 14, 2001 on his Kubota BX2200-60 mower. Starting in Portland, Maine, he passed through all contiguous U.S. states, as well as Canada and Mexico, ending his trip in Daytona Beach, Florida.

Longest-manufactured production car The Morgan 4/4 has been in production since December 1935. Produced by the Morgan Motor Car

Company (UK), all Morgans are hand built and take an average of 23 days to make. The company's total production for all four of its models is around 540 per year.

Longest single-model vehicle parade A total of 2,728 VW Beetles took part in a parade organized by the Volkswagen Aficionado Club of Brazil on a racetrack near São Paulo, Brazil, on May 1, 1995.

Most 360-degree spins ("doughnuts") in a production car in one minute Alistair Weaver (UK) performed 22 doughnuts in one minute in a 1.8-liter Caterham Superlight at Elvington Airfield, North Yorkshire, UK, on April 8, 2002.

Longest ramp jump by car The longest ramp jump, with the vehicle landing on its wheels and driving on, is 237 ft. (72.23 m) by Ray Baumann (Australia) in a Chrysler VH Valiant at Ravenswood International Raceway, Perth, Western Australia, on August 23, 1998.

Longest ramp jump in a limousine Michael Hughes (U.S.A.) jumped a distance of 103 ft. (31.4 m) in a 6,600-lb. (3-ton) Lincoln Town Car stretched limousine at Perris Auto Speedway, Perris, California, U.S.A., on September 28, 2002.

Largest parking lot West Edmonton Mall in Edmonton, Alberta, Canada, is the world's largest shopping and entertainment center and also houses the largest parking lot. The parking area can hold 20,000 vehicles, with overflow facilities on an adjoining lot for an additional 10,000 cars.

Largest automobile producer by country In 2002, the U.S.A. manufactured around 12.27 million vehicles, according to the Organization Internationale des Constructeurs d'Automobiles (OICA).

Largest car engine The production cars with the largest engines were the U.S. Pierce-Arrow 6–66 Raceabout of 1912–18, the U.S. Peerless 6–60 of 1912–14, and the Fageol of 1918. Each had an engine of 823.8 in.^{3} (13.5 liters).

LAND SPEED RECORD

Man has always been obsessed with speed. But it was the invention and refinement of the automobile that heralded a new century of land speed record breaking. Here are some highlights.

How it all began In the first edition of *Guinness World Records* (formerly *The Guinness Book of Records)* back in 1955, the land speed record was held by John Cobb (UK) and stood at 394.19 mph (634.39 km/h). But this was by no means the first record set. Land speed record attempts as we know them date back to **1898** when Count Gaston de Chasseloup-Laubat

1904
HENRY FORD: FORD ARROW
91.37 mph (147.04 km/h)

1935
MALCOLM CAMPBELL: BLUEBIRD
301.13 mph (484.62 km/h)

1947
JOHN COBB: RAILTON MOBIL
SPECIAL
394.19 mph (634.39 km/h)

1963
CRAIG BREEDLOVE: SPIRIT OF
AMERICA
407.45 mph (655.72 km/h)

1970
GARY GABELICH: BLUE FLAME
622.40 mph (1,001.66 km/h)

1983
RICHARD NOBLE: THRUST 2
633.47 mph (1,019.46 km/h)

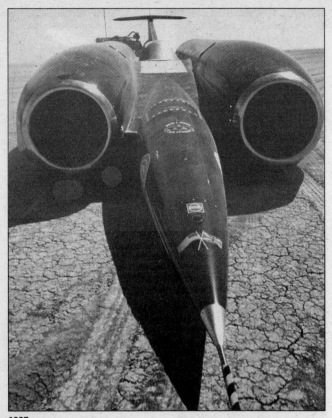

1997
ANDY GREEN: THRUST SSC
763.03 mph (1,227.98 km/h) or Mach 1.02

(France) did a single run through a measured kilometer, and registered an average speed of 39.24 mph (63.13 km/h). In **1904,** Henry Ford (U.S.A.) sought to prove the speed of his new automobiles and duly set a new record in the Ford *Arrow* on the frozen Lake St. Clair in Michigan, U.S.A. He reached an average speed of 91.37 mph (147.04 km/h), but said that it scared him so much he never wanted to race again.

Breaking the 100-mph barrier The 100-mph (161-km/h) barrier was broken later in **1904** when Louis Emile Rigolly (France) drove through the kilometer at 103.55 mph (166.64 km/h) and the land speed record went back to France. **1904** also marks the birth of the Fédération Internationale de l'Automobile (FIA), the governing body of motor sport worldwide, who officiate at every attempt on the land speed record. The rules have changed little over the years: the challenging car has to make two timed runs in opposite directions over a measured mile (or kilometer) within one hour.

Early triumphs Perhaps the most famous attempts on the record were by Malcolm Campbell and later his son Donald (both UK). On February 4, **1927** Campbell Sr. drove the Napier-Campbell *Bluebird* to 174.88 mph (281.45 km/h) on the beach at Pendine, Carmarthenshire, UK. Rivalry between Campbell Sr. and Major Henry Seagrave (UK) drove the record through the 300-mph (482.8-km/h) barrier on September 3, **1935** when Campbell achieved an average speed of 301.13 mph (484.62 km/h) on the Bonneville Salt Flats, Utah, U.S.A.

UK/U.S. rivalry John Cobb's (UK) record speed of 394.19 mph (634.39 km/h), set in his *Railton Mobil Special* in **1947,** stood for nearly 16 years. The 400-mph (643.7-km/h) barrier was eventually breached by Craig Breedlove (U.S.A.) in **1963,** driving the *Spirit of America.* Breedlove reached an average speed of 407.45 mph (655.72 km/h), although the record was disallowed at the time as the FIA did not recognize the use of jet power for land speed attempts.

Donald Campbell claimed the land speed record for Britain again on July 17, **1964** at Lake Eyre, Australia, in *Bluebird,* powered by a gas turbine engine. His 403.10-mph (648.73-km/h) record was the only one not set in the U.S.A. during that period of record attempts.

The second half of the **1960s** saw a battle for the record between two Americans: Art Arfons and Craig Breedlove. Arfons triumphed, achieving a speed of 576.55 mph (927.87 km/h) in *Green Monster* on the Bonneville Salt Flats on November 7, **1965.**

Through the sound barrier Advances in technology meant that breaking the sound barrier was becoming an increasingly real prospect. In **1970** Gary Gabelich (U.S.A.) drove through the 1,000-km/h (621.3-mph) barrier in *Blue Flame,* reaching a speed of 622.40 mph (1,001.66 km/h), and on October 4, **1983,** Richard Noble (UK) set a record of 633.47 mph (1,019.46 km/h) in *Thrust 2* in the Black Rock Desert, Nevada, U.S.A.

The next challenge was to build and drive a land speed vehicle that would break the sound barrier. This was achieved in October **1997,** when RAF fighter pilot Andy Green (UK), driving in the 10-ton, twin-jet-engine *Thrust SSC* (pictured on page 244), did the unimaginable by achieving a speed of 763.03 mph (1,227.98 km/h), or Mach 1.02. Green made the two runs through the measured mile, each time generating a shockwave in front of the car and a massive sonic boom. This record, which still stands, came almost 100 years after the first record was set in 1898.

GWR TALKS TO *Richard Noble OBE*

Richard Noble (UK, pictured) set a land speed record of 633.47 mph (1,019.46 km/h) in *Thrust 2* in 1983 and was Project Director for the successful *Thrust SSC* (supersonic car) land speed record attempt in 1997.

Did you have any high-speed experience before *Thrust 2*? From the driving point of view, no, I had no experience when I started off. As the *Thrust 2* project developed I learnt to fly, and the discipline of flying is much more akin to record breaking than driving a race car.

Why didn't you drive *Thrust SSC* yourself? I wanted to, but I realized that combining the jobs of driving the car and raising the money was absolutely hopeless. I decided that because I already held the land speed record I would raise the money and run the project.

Why go after the record again? We actually saw *Thrust SSC* as the third car in a range of three. *Thrust 1* was a very simple, elementary, jet-powered vehicle to introduce the project. *Thrust 2* was the record breaker, and *Thrust 3* we saw as being the supersonic car.

What was the biggest challenge? One was the culture challenge, because we were up against a mass of companies that said it couldn't be done. The second was that the funding was so difficult.

Are you planning to break the record again? We're very proud of what we've actually achieved, but nobody wants to go back again! The reality was that when we started going supersonic, I think it frightened a lot of us. I was watching this car coming up at supersonic speeds, and I realized what an enormous risk was being run by Andy (Green, the driver). Andy's comment was that he'd driven the car twice too often, so that was it really.

Is there a limit to this record? Yes, although it's a long way off. It's all about the human body's ability to withstand acceleration. If you think that 9 G is the upper limit of acceleration at which a human can usefully work, with acceleration of 9 G, speeds of twice or three times the speed of sound are possible. In terms of the car, the forces it experiences are absolutely enormous, so you need something that's as tough as a locomotive or a submarine. To give you an idea, the wheels on *SSC* were turning at 8,000 RPM, which means that you're running 35,000 radial G at the edge of the wheels. You're right at the limits of what materials will do.

Why is this record important? I think it's very, very important because it's a measure of a man's or a nation's ability to take on a challenge. It's very important because it inspires the next generation to do something similar.

★ LAND SPEED RECORDS SINCE 1947 ★

YEAR	DATE	CAR AND DRIVER	MPH	KM/H
1947	Sept. 16	*Railton Mobil Special* John Cobb	394.19	634.39
1963	Aug. 5	*Spirit of America:* Craig Breedlove	407.45	655.72
1964	July 17	*Bluebird:* Donald Campbell	403.10	648.73
1964	Oct. 2	*Wingfoot Express:* Tom Green	413.20	664.98
1964	Oct. 5	*Green Monster:* Art Arfons	434.02	698.49
1964	Oct. 13	*Spirit of America:* Craig Breedlove	468.72	754.33
1964	Oct. 15	*Spirit of America:* Craig Breedlove	526.28	846.97
1964	Oct. 27	*Green Monster:* Art Arfons	536.71	863.75
1965	Nov. 2	*Spirit of America:* Craig Breedlove—*Sonic I*	555.48	893.96
1965	Nov. 7	*Green Monster:* Art Arfons	576.55	927.87
1965	Nov. 15	*Spirit of America:* Craig Breedlove—*Sonic I*	600.60	966.57
1970	Oct. 23	*Blue Flame:* Gary Gabelich	622.40	1,001.66
1983	Oct. 4	*Thrust 2:* Richard Noble	633.47	1,019.46
1997	Sept. 25	*Thrust SSC:* Andy Green	714.10	1,149.29
1997	Oct. 15	*Thrust SSC:* Andy Green	763.03	1,227.98

BIKES & MOTORBIKES

Most stairs climbed on a bicycle On October 16, 2003, Javier Zapata (Colombia) climbed 1,318 steps on a bicycle in the Torre Major skyscraper, Mexico City, Mexico, without his feet touching the ground. The building is approximately 738 ft. (225 m) high and has 55 stories. The climb lasted 1 hr. 38 min.

Longest signposted bicycle route The North Sea Cycle Route is a signposted route that follows the coastline of the North Sea through The Netherlands, Germany, Denmark, Sweden, and Norway. It continues through Scotland and England, covering a distance of about 3,700 miles (6,000 km).

Furthest distance bicycled backward in one hour Markus Riese (Germany) bicycled 18 miles (29.1 km) backward in one hour at the Velocipedclubs Darmstadt 1899 eV bicycling club, Darmstadt, Germany, on May 24, 2003.

Longest snowmobile ramp jump on water Vance Irwin (Canada) performed a 48-ft. (14.6-m) ramp jump on water riding his unmodified Po-

HIGHEST SPEED ON A HUMAN POWERED VEHICLE (HPV) Sam Whittingham (Canada, pictured) reached a speed of 81 mph (130.36 km/h) on a flat road surface in his streamlined recumbent bicycle *Varna Diablo* (seen here) at the World Human Powered Speed Challenge near Battle Mountain, Nevada, U.S.A., on October 5, 2002.

laris 600 snowmobile at Fox Lake Municipal Park, Hanna, Alberta, Canada, on July 1, 2002.

Earliest motorcycle Gottlieb Daimler built the *Einspur,* a motorized bicycle with an internal combustion engine, in October and November 1885 at Bad Cannstatt, Germany. The wooden-framed machine was first ridden by Wilhelm Maybach. It had a top speed of 12 mph (19 km/h) and developed 0.5 hp (0.37 kW) from its single-cylinder 264-cc four-stroke engine at 700 rpm. It was lost in a fire in 1903.

Earliest mass-production motorcycle In 1894, Heinrich and Wilhelm Hildebrand and Alois Wolfmüller (all Germany) opened a motorcycle factory at Munich, Germany. In its first two years, this factory produced over 1,000 machines, each having a water-cooled 1,488-cc twin-cylinder four-stroke engine developing about 2.5 hp (1.9 kW) at 600 rpm.

Longest motorcycle ramp jump with passenger Jason Rennie (UK) jumped his Yamaha YZ250 motorcycle a distance of 96 ft. (29.2 m) with his girlfriend Sian Phillips on the back on November 12, 2000, at the Rednall airfield near Oswestry, Shropshire, UK.

Longest distance jumped on a trial motorcycle Joachim Hindren (Finland) jumped a distance of 13 ft. (4 m) on a trial motorcycle without the use of a ramp at Sipoo, Finland, on October 13, 2001.

TALLEST RIDABLE BICYCLE Brad Graham (Canada) successfully rode his SkyCycle, which measures 14 ft. 3 in. (4.34 m) to the handlebars, on July 1, 2003 at Thunder Bay, Ontario, Canada. The bicycle has only two wheels and no stabilizers of any kind.

Tallest ridable motorcycle *Bigtoe,* built by Tom Wiberg (Sweden), is 7 ft. 6 in. (2.3 m) tall at its highest point. The motorcycle has a top speed of 62 mph (100 km/h) and is powered by a Jaguar V12 engine.

Longest motorcycle Rick Dozer, Bill Decker, Rob Moore, and William Longest (all U.S.A.) built a ridable motorcycle measuring 29 ft. 3 in. (8.9 m) wheel to wheel. The chopper-style Harley-Davidson monster has forks 15 ft. (4.6 m) long and is 6 ft. (1.72 m) tall at its highest point. William Longest rode it on a public road near Georgetown, Kentucky, U.S.A., on June 15, 2003.

Fastest motorcycle speed Riding a 23-ft.-long (7-m) streamliner named *Easyriders,* powered by two 1,500-cc Ruxton Harley-Davidson en-

SMALLEST MOTORCYCLE Tom Wiberg (Sweden) built this motorcycle with a front wheel diameter of 0.62 in. (16 mm) and a rear wheel diameter of 0.86 in. (22 mm), and rode it for over 33 ft. (10 m) in Hökerum, Sweden, in 2003. The micro machine, called *Smalltoe,* has a seat height of 2.55 in. (65 mm), weighs 2.4 lb. (1.1 kg), and is powered to a top speed of 1.24 mph (2 km/h) by its 0.3-hp (0.22-kW) engine.

gines, Dave Campos (U.S.A.) set AMA and FIM absolute speed records with an average of 322.101 mph (518.522 km/h) over two 1-km runs in opposite directions at Bonneville Salt Flats, Utah, U.S.A., on July 14, 1990.

Fastest motorcycle and trailer On February 28, 2002, Kevin Smith (UK) reached 139.5 mph (224.5 km/h) on a Kawasaki ZZR1100 while towing a standard Squire D21 trailer at Millbrook Proving Ground, Bedfordshire, UK.

Fastest production motorcycle The Suzuki GSX-1300R Hayabusa is reported to reach speeds of 194 mph (312 km/h), making it the fastest production bike in the world.

Highest speed traveled seated backward on a motorcycle Szabolcs Borsay (Hungary) reached a speed of 124.725 mph (200.726 km/h) sitting backwards on his Suzuki GSX-R1000 at Balaton Airport, Sármellék, Hungary, on July 2, 2002.

Longest solo motorcycle ride by a woman Benka Pulko (Slovenia) traveled 111,856 miles (180,016 km) on a solo motorcycle journey that took

LARGEST ENGINE CAPACITY FOR A PRODUCTION MODEL MOTORCYCLE The Triumph Rocket III (shown here) is powered by a three-cylinder 2,294-cc engine, the largest ever fitted to a production motorcycle. The 705-lb. (320-kg) machine produces 140 hp (104 kW) of power and 147 lb/ft. (200 Nm) of torque, making it more powerful than most sedans.

her through 69 countries and seven continents. Her journey started in Ptuj, Slovenia, on June 19, 1997 and ended at the same location precisely 2,000 days later on December 10, 2002.

Longest continuous ride while standing on a motorcycle On December 13, 2002 in Beijing, China, Liu Jichun (China) rode 3.30 miles (5.32 km) while standing on the seat of a motorcycle and without touching the handlebars.

Longest motorcycle wheelie Yasuyuki Kudo (Japan) covered 205.7 miles (331 km) nonstop on the rear wheel of his Honda TLM220R motorcycle at the Japan Automobile Research Institute Proving Ground, at Tsukuba, near Tsuchiura, Japan, on May 5, 1991.

Fastest motorcycle wheelie over one kilometer Christopher McInnes (UK) reached a speed of 126.4 mph (203.4 km/h) while performing a motorcycle wheelie over a kilometer at Elvington airfield, North Yorkshire, UK, on November 18, 2001. He was riding a Suzuki GSX-R750.

Longest stoppie (front-wheel wheelie) on a motorcycle Craig Jones (UK) covered 873 ft. (266 m) on the front wheel of his Buell XB12R motorcycle at the Florida Evaluation Center, Naples, U.S.A., on August 15, 2003.

Largest motor scooter by engine capacity The Suzuki Burgman 650 motor scooter has a 638-cc four-stroke, two-cylinder engine, the largest available on any standard production model today. The 524-lb. (238-kg) Burgman went on sale in 2003, with a manufacturer's suggested retail price of $7,699.

Largest motorcycle manufacturer The Honda Motor Company of Japan is the world's largest manufacturer of motorcycles, having sold 8.08 million vehicles globally during the 2002/03 fiscal year. This figure includes quad motorcycles, or all-terrain vehicles (ATVs), and aquabikes, or personal watercraft (PWCs).

BOATS

Oldest active sailing ship The oldest square-rigged sailing vessel that is still seagoing is thought to be the 2.64 million-lb. (1,200-ton) iron bark *Star of India,* built at Ramsey, Isle of Man, UK, in 1863 as the full-rigged ship *Euterpe.* She has been restored and is now preserved as a museum ship in San Diego, California, U.S.A. The *Star of India* still makes occasional day trips under sail.

Highest speed on water Ken Warby (Australia) recorded a speed of 275.97 knots (317.58 mph or 511.11km/h) in the unlimited-class jet-powered hydroplane *Spirit of Australia* on Blowering Dam Lake, New South Wales, Australia, on October 8, 1978. A hydroplane is a lightweight flat-bottomed boat designed to "plane" (or skim) just above the surface with only its propellers and rudders in the water.

Fastest human powered speed on water Mark Drela (U.S.A.) pedaled the hydrofoil *Decavitator* at a speed of 18.5 knots (21.28 mph or 34.26 km/h) over a 328-ft. (100-m) course on the Charles River, Boston, Massachusetts, U.S.A., on October 27, 1991. Hydrofoils are light vessels, the hulls of which are lifted out of the water when in motion by winglike "foils" under them.

Fastest sailing vessel On October 26, 1993, the trifoiler *Yellow Pages Endeavour* reached a speed of 46.52 knots (53.53 mph or 86.15 km/h) while on a timed run of 1,640 ft. (500 m) at Sandy Point near Melbourne, Victoria, Australia.

Fastest propeller-driven boat Russ Wicks (U.S.A.) achieved a speed of 178.61 knots (205.54 mph or 330.79 km/h) in his hydroplane *Miss Freei* on June 15, 2000 at Lake Washington, Seattle, U.S.A. *Miss Freei* was powered by a Lycoming L-7C turbine engine from a Chinook helicopter that

LARGEST PROPELLER A six-bladed propeller (pictured) weighing 206,100 lb. (93.5 tons) and measuring 29 ft. 6 in. (9 m) in diameter was designed and manufactured by Stone Manganese Marine Ltd. (UK) for a PO NedLloyd container ship. The six-bladed propeller was cast on January 30, 1997 with 284,400 lb. (129 tons) of liquid metal.

EARLIEST HOVERCRAFT FLIGHT The first public flight by a full-sized hovercraft was made by the 8,800-lb. (4-ton) Saunders-Roe Nautical One (SR.N1, shown here) at Cowes, Isle of Wight, UK, on June 11, 1959. With a 1,500-lb.-thrust (680-kg) Viper turbojet engine, this craft reached 68 knots (78 mph or 126 km/h) in June 1961. The hovercraft was the brainchild of Sir Christopher Cockerell (UK).

generates 3,000 hp (2,237 kW) at 10,000 rpm. In contrast, most cars produce around 120 hp (90 kW) at no higher than 6,000 rpm.

Largest passenger liner The Cunard Line's *Queen Mary 2*, which made its maiden voyage in January 2004, is 1,132 ft. (345 m) long, has a beam (width) of 135 ft. (41 m), and space for 2,620 passengers and 1,253 crew. At approximately 150,000 gross registered tons (grt), the *Queen Mary 2* is nearly three times larger than *Titanic,* which had a tonnage of 46,000 grt.

Largest container ship The 1,059.61-ft.-long (322.97-m) Orient Overseas Container Line (OOCL) SX-class vessels have a registered capacity of 8,063 Twenty-foot Equivalent Units (TEU) of standard containers. The first, OOCL *Shenzhen,* was launched on April 30, 2003. It was built by Samsung Heavy Industries Co., Ltd. (South Korea), and is owned and operated by OOCL (China). Capable of carrying 253.5 million lb. (115,000 tons) of cargo, ships of this size will coast for 5 miles (8 km) when the engine is cut.

Largest sailing ship by weight The *France 2* was a steel-hulled, five-masted bark launched at Bordeaux, France, in 1911. Her hull measured 418 ft. (127.4 m) overall and she had a deadweight tonnage (cargo-carrying capacity) of 17.6 million lb. (8,000 tons). She was wrecked off New Caledonia on July 12, 1922.

Largest ship The world's largest ship of any kind is the oil tanker *Jahre Viking* (formerly the *Happy Giant* and *Seawise Giant*), which has a deadweight tonnage of 1.24 billion lb. (564,763 tons). The tanker is 1,504 ft. (458.45 m) long, has a beam of 226 ft. (68.8 m), and a draft of 80 ft. 9 in. (24.6 m).

Longest sailing ship The French-owned sister ships *Club Med I* and *Club Med II* are each 187 m (613 ft.) long. They have five aluminum masts and 30,100 ft.^{2} (2,800 m^2) of computer-controlled polyester sails. Each ship caters for around 400 passengers, with roughly half as many crew members. With their relatively small sail area and powerful engines, they are strictly motor-sailers.

Tallest sailing-ship mast The 246.7-ft.-long (75.2-m) luxury yacht *Mirabella V,* launched in November 2003, has a single carbon-fiber mast 295 ft. (90 m) tall. The largest ever single-masted yacht, *Mirabella V* was built by Vosper Thornycroft in Southampton, UK, and is available for rent at a rate of £200,000 ($250,000) per week.

Largest ship ever scrapped The 555,051-deadweight-ton (dwt) ultra-large crude carrier (ULCC) *Sea Giant* was bought by Wirana Shipping Corp. of Singapore in August 2003 for $17.6 million to be broken up for scrap metal. The second largest ship ever constructed, the giant tanker was 1,391 ft. (424 m) long and 206 ft. (63 m) wide.

Fastest hovercraft At the 1995 World Hovercraft Championships, Bob Windt (U.S.A.) recorded a speed of 85.38 mph (137.4 km/h) on the Rio

LARGEST STEAMBOAT The *American Queen* (pictured), a luxurious traditional steamboat (paddle-wheeled riverboat) launched in 1995, is 418 ft. (127.4 m) long and has a displacement of 10.78 million lb. (4,891 tons). Built at a cost of $65 million by the Delta Queen Steamboat Company (U.S.A.), it has six passenger decks and can accommodate around 450 people.

Douro River, Peso de Regua, Portugal. Windt was driving a streamlined 19-ft. (5.8-m) Universal UH19P hovercraft called *Jenny 2* that had a 110-hp (82-kW) V6 car engine driving its two fans (one at the rear to provide propulsion, and one underneath to provide lift). The speed of the craft was measured over a flying kilometer.

Largest car ferryboat Irish Ferries' *Ulysses,* launched on September 1, 2000, can carry 1,342 cars. The ship is 685 ft. (209 m) long and 104 ft. 6 in. (31 m) wide and has a capacity of 50,938 grt.

Deepest-diving submersible currently in service The Japanese research submarine *Shinkai 6500* is a three-person submersible 31 ft. (9.5 m) long, 8 ft. 10 in. (2.7 m) wide, and 10 ft. 6 in. (3.2 m) high. It reached a depth of 21,414 ft. (6,526 m) in the Japan Trench off Sanriku, Japan, on August 11, 1989.

Largest shipwreck On December 12, 1979, the 708 million-lb. (321,186-deadweight-ton) Very Large Crude Carrier (VLCC) *Energy Determination* blew up and broke in two in the Strait of Hormuz, in the Persian Gulf. Although the ship was not actually carrying any cargo at the time, the value of the hull alone was estimated at $58 million.

Greatest distance sailed in 24 hours On June 12 and 13, 2002, the 110-ft. (33.5-m) maxi catamaran *Maiden 2* covered 694.78 nautical miles (800.04 miles or 1,287.55 km) under sail in the North Atlantic. The average speed was 28.95 knots (33.31 mph or 53.61 km/h).

Fastest Atlantic crossing in a monohull yacht The monohull yacht *Mari-Cha IV,* captained by Robert Miller (UK), took 6 days 17 hr. 52 min. 39 sec. to cross the Atlantic. It set off from Ambrose Light Tower, New York, U.S.A., on October 2, 2003 and arrived at Lizard Point, Cornwall, UK, on October 9, 2003. A crew of 24 sailed the yacht.

AIRCRAFT

Earliest manned flight Frenchman François Pilâtre de Rozier is widely regarded as the first person to have flown. On October 15, 1783 he rose 84 ft. (26 m) into the air in a tethered hot-air balloon built by the inventors Joseph and Jacques-Etienne Montgolfier (France).

Earliest balloon flight A model hot-air balloon invented by Father Bartolomeu de Gusmão *(né* Lourenço) was flown indoors at the Casa da India, Terreiro do Paço, Portugal, on August 8, 1709.

Fastest circumnavigation by balloon Steve Fossett (U.S.A.) flew around the world alone in 13 days 8 hr. 33 min. in *Bud Light Spirit of Free-*

FIRST POWER-DRIVEN FLIGHT At 10:35 a.m. on December 17, 1903 near Kitty Hawk, North Carolina, U.S.A., Orville Wright (U.S.A.) flew the 12-hp (9-kW) chain-driven *Flyer I* (pictured) for 120 ft. (36.5 m). He traveled for 12 seconds at a speed of 6.8 mph (10.9 km/h) and an altitude of 8–12 ft. (2.5–3.5 m).

dom from June 19 to July 2, 2002. He took off from Northam, Western Australia, and landed at Eromanga, Queensland, Australia.

Highest altitude attained by a hot-air balloon Per Lindstrand (UK) achieved an altitude of 64,997 ft. (19,811 m) in a Colt 600 hot-air balloon over Laredo, Texas, U.S.A., on June 6, 1988.

Largest working airship The largest working airship is the WDL 1B, three of which have been built at Mulheim, Germany. Each WDL 1B is 197 ft. (60 m) in length and has a volume of 7,200 m³ (254,300 ft.³).

First jet-engined flight Flugkapitän Erich Warsitz (Germany) flew a Heinkel He 178 at Marienehe, Germany, on August 27, 1939. It was powered by a Heinkel He S3b turbojet engine weighing 834 lb. (378 kg) designed by Dr. Hans Pabst von Ohain (Germany).

Fastest biplane The Italian Fiat CR42B, which had a 1,010-hp (753-kW) Daimler-Benz DB601A engine, attained a speed of 323 mph (520 km/h) in 1941.

Fastest ever transatlantic flight Flying a Lockheed SR-71A "Blackbird" eastwards, Majors James V. Sullivan and Noel F. Widdifield (both U.S.A.) crossed the Atlantic in a time of 1 hr. 54 min. 56.4 sec. on September 1, 1974. The average speed for the New York-London stage of 3,461.53

miles (5,570.8 km) was 1,806.96 mph (2,908.02 km/h). This figure was reduced because of a period spent refuelling from a Boeing KC-135 tanker aircraft.

First circumnavigation by an aircraft without refueling Richard "Dick" Rutan and Jeana Yeager (both U.S.A.) circumnavigated the world in a westward direction from Edwards Air Force Base, California, U.S.A., from December 14 to 23, 1986. Their aircraft *Voyager* was specially designed by Dick's brother Burt.

Fastest air speed The fastest recorded speed in an aircraft capable of taking off and landing under its own power is 2,193.17 mph (3,529.56 km/h), by Captain Eldon W. Joersz and Major George T. Morgan, Jr. (both U.S.A.) in a Lockheed SR-71A "Blackbird" near Beale Air Force Base, California, U.S.A., on a 15.5-mile (25-km) course on July 28, 1976.

Fastest air-launched aircraft The experimental X-15A-2 aircraft flown by USAF test pilot Pete Knight (U.S.A.) reached a speed of 4,520 mph (7,274 km/h) over California, U.S.A., on October 3, 1967.

Fastest piston-engined aircraft On August 21, 1989, in Las Vegas, Nevada, U.S.A., the *Rare Bear,* a modified Grumman F8F "Bearcat" piloted

LARGEST AIRSHIP The world's largest airships were the 471,568-lb. (213.9-ton) German *Hindenburg* (LZ 129, pictured) and *Graf Zeppelin II* (LZ 130), each of which had a length of 804 ft. (245 m) and a hydrogen gas capacity of 7,062,000 ft.³ (200,000 m³). The *Hindenburg* first flew in 1936, exploding and crashing on May 6, 1937; the *Graf Zeppelin II* first flew in 1938, although it was decommissioned within a year, broken up for scrap and melted down to build fighter planes.

by Lyle Shelton (U.S.A.), set the world record of 528.31 mph (850.24 km/h) for a 1.8-mile (3-km) course, as officially approved by the Fédération Aéronautique Internationale (FAI).

Fastest propeller-driven aircraft The Russian Tupolev Tu-95/142 (NATO code-name "Bear") long-range bomber is the fastest propeller-driven aircraft in standard production form, with a maximum level speed of 575 mph (925 km/h). First produced in the 1950s, it is still in service with several air forces.

Fastest airliner The Tupolev Tu-144, first flown on December 31, 1968 in the former USSR, was reported to have reached approximately 1,600 mph (2,500 km/h). The aircraft was taken out of service in 1978. The BAC/Aerospatiale Concorde, first flown on March 2, 1969, cruised at up to 1,450 mph (2,330 km/h) and on January 21, 1976 became the first supersonic airliner to be used on passenger services. The Concorde was finally taken out of service by British Airways on October 24, 2003 because it was no longer profitable to run.

Largest amphibious aircraft currently in operation The Russian Beriev A-40 "Albatross" aircraft, which is capable of taking off and landing on both land and water, has a maximum take-off weight of 189,600 lb. (86 tons), a wingspan of 139 ft. (42.5 m) and is 150 ft. (45.7 m) long. The "Albatross" is powered by two turbojet engines with 33,000 lb. (15,000 kg) of thrust each. The multi-purpose aircraft can be used for search and rescue, cargo and passenger transport, maritime patrol, and military applications.

Largest wingspan The Hughes H4 Hercules flying boat, commonly known as the *Spruce Goose,* has a wingspan of 319 ft. 11 in. (97.51 m) and a length of 218 ft. 8 in. (66.65 m). The eight-engined 425,500-lb. (193-ton) aircraft was raised 70 ft. (21 m) into the air in a test run of 3,000 ft. (914 m), piloted by Howard Hughes (U.S.A.) off Long Beach Harbor, California, U.S.A., on November 2, 1947, but never flew again.

Largest wingspan of an aircraft currently flying A modified six-engine version of the Antonov An-124 "Ruslan," known as An-225 "Mriya" ("Dream"), which was built to carry the former Soviet Union space shuttle *Buran,* has a wingspan of 290 ft. (88.4 m).

Longest flight by an unmanned aircraft A USAF Northrop Grumman Global Hawk *Southern Cross II* completed a flight of 8,600 miles (13,840 km) on April 22, 2001. The *Southern Cross II,* a full-scale unmanned conventional aircraft, took off from Edwards Air Force Base, California, U.S.A., and landed at RAAF Base Edinburgh, South Australia, 23 hr. 23 min. later. Global Hawks can stay aloft for over 30 hours at altitudes of 65,000 ft. (20,000 m).

Highest altitude attained by a propeller-driven aircraft The unmanned, solar-powered *Helios* prototype flying wing achieved a height of

LARGEST FLYING BOATS IN PASSENGER SERVICE The Boeing Model 314 "Clipper" aircraft had a wingspan of 152 ft. (46.3 m), a length of 106 ft. (32.3 m) and a maximum take-off weight of 84,000 lb. (38.1 tons). Clippers were operated by Pan American Airlines during the "golden age" of flying boats in the late 1930s.

96,863 ft. (29,524 m) over the Hawaiian island of Kauai on August 13, 2001. Commissioned by NASA and developed by AeroVironment, Inc., of Monrovia, California, U.S.A., *Helios* is one of a new breed of slow-flying, high-altitude aircraft that its makers believe will present a viable alternative to communications satellites.

Greatest passenger load On May 24, 1991 an El Al Boeing 747 commercial airliner transported 1,088 passengers as part of Operation Solomon, which involved the evacuation of Ethiopian Jews from Addis Ababa, Ethiopia.

GWR TALKS TO Mike Bannister

For many people, a flight on Concorde was a once-in-a-lifetime taste of real luxury. The aircraft held several Guinness World Records, including those for the fastest transatlantic flight by a commercial aircraft and the fastest aerial circumnavigation. Mike Bannister (UK, page 261 right) piloted Concorde for a record 22 years, and though the aircraft was taken out of service in 2003, he cherishes very fond memories of it.

When did you first decide to become a pilot? When I was a little boy my family used to take holidays on the English south coast and the journey would take us five and a half hours by coach. One day I saw an airplane fly overhead while we were on the beach. I worked out the same journey would only take 20 minutes by air and immediately decided I wanted to learn to fly!

How long have you been flying? I went to pilot training school in 1967, and in 1969 I saw the first flight of Concorde and decided that was what I wanted to fly. I first flew Concorde on August 18, 1977 and worked as a copilot and instructor until 1989. I flew other aircraft for a few years and then, in 1995, I was offered the chance to go back to Concorde as Chief Pilot. I flew her 'til her retirement on November 25, 2003.

LARGEST OBJECTS TRANSPORTED BY AIR Though not the heaviest, the largest single objects to be transported by air are the 122.17-ft.-long (37.23-m) reusable NASA space shuttles, which are "piggy-backed" on top of modified Boeing 747 jets from various landing strips back to Florida's Cape Canaveral. The shuttles—*Discovery, Atlantis,* and *Endeavour* (pictured)—weigh around 220,500 lb. (100 tons) each when being transported.

Is flying Concorde different to flying other aircraft? Yes, it's a completely different experience. Concorde flew at both supersonic and subsonic speeds, and cruised at twice the altitude of normal aircraft. She was a delight to fly—you could control her using only your fingertips! Because she had a very tough fuselage, the cabin only needed to be pressurized at 5,000 feet; most aircraft are pressurized at 8,000 feet. Flying at the edge of space, you could see the Earth's curvature! Also, the aircraft traveled faster than the Earth rotates, so the sun was in effect going backward and your body clock would reset. This is why you'd feel less jetlagged flying by Concorde.

Did you have many memorable passengers? There was a subdued elegance about Concorde, and there were always a lot of business passengers on board. There were also always people taking the trip of a lifetime, and we had a number of celebrities too. After its retirement was announced, the atmosphere on board became more like a party!

What other aircraft have you flown? I've flown over 100 different types of aircraft over the years but most recently flew a Tiger Moth for the first time.

Finally, what tips would you give to any aspiring pilots? Whatever you dream of, live your dream—chase it! If you find something you want to do as a child and you do it in your adult life it's very satisfying and leads to a very happy life!

Fastest aerial circumnavigation The fastest flight under the Fédération Aéronautique Internationale (FAI) rules, which permit flights that exceed the length of the Tropic of Cancer or Capricorn (36,787.6 km or 22,858.8 miles), was one of 31 hr. 27 min. 49 sec. by an Air France Concorde (Capts. Michel Dupont and Claude Hetru, both France) from JFK airport in New York, U.S.A., eastbound via Toulouse, Dubai, Bangkok, Guam, Honolulu, and Acapulco on August 15 and 16, 1995. There were 80 passengers and 18 crew on board flight AF1995.

Fastest transatlantic flight by a commercial aircraft A British Airways Concorde took 2 hr. 52 min. 59 sec. to travel the 8,750 miles (6,035 km) between New York (JFK airport) and London (Luton) on February 7, 1996, breaking its own record set in April 1990 by one and a half minutes. The plane, piloted by Captain Leslie Scott (UK), averaged more than 1,250 mph (2,011 km/h).

Largest helicopter ever The Russian Mil Mi-12 was powered by four 6,500-hp (4,850-kw) turboshaft engines and had a rotor diameter of 219 ft. 10 in. (67 m). It was 121 ft. 5 in. (37 m) long and had a maximum take-off weight of 227,000 lb. (103 tons). Only one was ever produced.

Longest helicopter flight Robert Ferry (U.S.A.) piloted his Hughes YOH-6A helicopter 2,213.1 miles (3,561.6 km) from Culver City, California, U.S.A., to Ormond Beach, Florida, U.S.A., without landing. He completed his FAI-approved flight on April 6, 1966.

Fastest circumnavigation by helicopter John Williams and Ron Bower (both U.S.A.) flew around the world in a Bell 430 helicopter in 17 days 6 hr. 14 min. 25 sec. (average speed of 57.02 mph or 91.76 km/h). They left Fair Oaks, London, UK, on August 17, 1996 and flew west, against prevailing winds, arriving back at Fair Oaks on September 3, 1996.

Greatest altitude reached in an autogyro On April 17, 1998 William B. Clem III (U.S.A.) flew his home-built Dominator autogyro 24,462 ft. (7,456 m) above Wauchula, Florida, U.S.A. It was powered by an 115-hp (85-kW) Rotax 914 engine.

HEAVIEST PRODUCTION AIRCRAFT The Ukrainian Antonov An-124 "Ruslan" cargo aircraft (pictured) has a maximum take-off weight of 892,000 lb. (405 tons). It has a cargo hold with a usable volume of 35,800 ft.³ (1,014 m³).

Fastest speed in an autogyro On September 18, 1986, Wing Cdr. Kenneth H. Wallis (UK) flew his WA-116/F/S autogyro, with a 60-hp (45-kW) Franklin aero-engine, at 120.3 mph (193.6 km/h) over a 1.8-mile (3-km) straight course at Marham, Norfolk, UK.

Most powerful jet engine A General Electric GE90-115B turbofan engine achieved steady state thrust of 127,900 lb. (568,927 N) during final certification testing at Peebles, Ohio, U.S.A., in December 2002.

LARGEST HELICOPTER CURRENTLY IN PRODUCTION The five-person Russian Mil Mi-26 (shown here) has a maximum take-off weight of 123,500 lb. (56,000 kg). Unladen it weighs 62,200 lb. (28,200 kg) and its overall length is 131 ft. (40 m). The eight-bladed main rotor has a diameter of 105 ft. (32 m) and it is powered by two 11,400-hp (8,500-kW) turbine engines.

Largest ever airline In the last complete year of the former USSR's existence (1990), the official state airline Aeroflot employed 600,000 people—more than the top 18 U.S. airlines put together at that time. Aeroflot flew 139 million passengers annually with 20,000 pilots along 620,000 miles (1,000,000 km) of domestic routes across 11 time zones.

Longest duration flight in a human-powered vehicle Kanellos Kanellopoulos (Greece) kept his *Daedalus 88* aircraft aloft for 3 hr. 54 min. 59 sec. on April 23, 1988 while pedaling the 71.53 miles (115.11 km) between Heraklion, Crete, and the Greek island of Santorini. His flight ended prematurely when an offshore gust of wind broke off the plane's tail and it crashed into the sea a few meters from shore.

Largest parafoil The largest parafoil parachute has a span of 143 ft. (43.6 m) and a surface area of 7,500 ft.^{2} (700 m^2), nearly one and a half times the size of the wings of a Boeing 747. It was developed by NASA to bring its X-38 craft back to the Earth's surface after re-entering the atmosphere.

LARGE VEHICLES

Largest land vehicle The largest machine capable of moving under its own power is the 31.3 million-lb. (14,196-ton) RB293 bucket wheel excavator, an earthmoving machine manufactured by MAN TAKRAF of Leipzig, Germany. Employed in an opencast coal mine in the German state of North Rhine-Westphalia, it is 722 ft. (220 m) long, 310 ft. (94.5 m) tall at its highest point, and is capable of shifting 8.475 million ft.^{3} (240,000 m^3) of earth daily.

Longest vehicle The longest land vehicles ever made were the overland supply trains built by RG Le Tourneau, Inc. of Longview, Texas, U.S.A., for the U.S. Army. One example: the Arctic Snow Train, owned by the famous wire-walker Steve McPeak (U.S.A.), had 54 wheels, was 572 ft. (174.3 m) long, and had a gross weight of about 880,000 lb. (400 tons). The Snow Train had a top speed of 20 mph (32 km/h), and it was driven by a crew of six when used as an overland train for the military.

Longest road train A road train 4,052 ft. (1,235 m) long and comprising 87 trailers and a single prime mover was assembled near Mungindi, New South Wales, Australia, on March 29, 2003 at the Mighty Mungindi Truck and Trailer Pull.

Largest fork-lift truck In 1991, Kalmar LMV of Lidhult, Sweden, manufactured three counterbalanced fork-lift trucks capable of lifting loads up to 198,500 lb. (90 tons) at a load center of 7.87 ft. (2.4 m). They were built for a great man-made river project in Libya comprising two separate pipelines, one 620 miles (998 km) long, running from Sarir to the Gulf of Sirte, and the other 557 miles (897 km) long, running from Tazirbu to Benghazi.

Largest bulldozer The Komatsu D575A Super Dozer is the world's largest bulldozer, weighing in at 336,425 lb. (152.6 tons). Its 24.27 × 10.66-ft. (7.4 × 3.2-m) blade has a capacity of 2,437 ft.³ (69 m³). The 38-ft. 5-inch-long (11.72-m) pusher moves on tank-style tracks and is powered by a 1,150-hp (858-kW) turbocharged diesel engine.

Largest two-axle dump truck The T-282, manufactured by the Liebherr Mining Equipment Co. (U.S.A.), is the world's largest two-axle dump truck, with a payload capacity of about 720,900 lb. (327 tons). The diesel-electric-powered vehicle is 47 ft. 6 in. (14.47 m) long, 28 ft. 7 in. (8.7 m) wide, 24 ft. (7.3 m) high, and weighs around 443,100 lb. (201 tons).

Largest front-end loader The largest wheel-driven front-end loader is the LeTourneau L-2350, which weighs 578,000 lb. (262 tons) and can lift up to 160,000 lb. (72.5 tons) in its 1,430-ft.³-capacity (40.5-m³) bucket. This massive earth-mover is powered by a giant diesel engine that develops 2,300 hp (1,715 kW).

LARGEST LAND TRANSPORT VEHICLE The two 6 million-lb. (2,721-ton) crawler-transporters (pictured) that carry space shuttles to their launchpad at Kennedy Space Center, Florida, U.S.A., are the largest vehicles used for moving objects between two points (though they are not the largest mobile machines). Each one is 131 ft. (40 m) wide, 114 ft. (35 m) long, and runs on eight giant tank-style tracks.

Feats of Engineering

LARGEST MONSTER TRUCK *Bigfoot 5* (seen here) is 15 ft. 4 in. (4.7 m) tall with 10-ft.-tall (3-m) tires and weighs 38,000 lb. (17,200 kg). It was built in the summer of 1986 and is one of a fleet of 17 *Bigfoot* trucks created by Bob Chandler (U.S.A.). Now permanently parked in St. Louis, Missouri, U.S.A., it makes occasional exhibition appearances at local shows.

Largest dragline excavator *Big Muskie,* a walking earth-moving machine weighing 29.1 million lb. (13,200 tons), was the largest ever dragline excavator, weighing as much as nearly 10,000 sedans. It stood at the Central Ohio Coal Co.'s Muskingham opencast coal mine in Ohio, U.S.A., but was dismantled in 1999.

Largest operating dragline excavator The largest operating dragline excavator is the Bucyrus 2570WS, which is based at Peak Downs mine in Queensland, Australia, and weighs 16 million lb. (7,271 tons). It has a boom length of 360 ft. (109.7 m) to carry its giant 4,238-ft.³ (120-m³) bucket, which is in turn suspended from 5.62-in.-thick (14.3-cm) cables.

Largest shovel The largest mechanical shovel ever built was the Marion 6360 stripping shovel, which had an operating weight of around 28.6 million lb. (13,000 tons) and a bucket capacity of 4,860 ft.³ (137 m³). It had a 236-ft. (72-m) reach, a dumping height of 153 ft. (46.6 m), and was in service at an opencast coal mine near Percy, Illinois, U.S.A., until 1991, when it was taken out of service after a fire.

Largest operating shovel The largest mechanical shovel currently in use is the Bucyrus 1950B stripping shovel—known as "The Silver Spade"—which weighs in at approximately 14 million lb. (6,350 tons). It operates at an opencast coal mine near New Athens, Ohio, U.S.A.

Largest hydraulic shovel excavator The RH 400–2000 hydraulic shovel excavator manufactured by O&K Mining (Germany) is the largest of its kind in the world. The giant crawler, which is capable of filling the world's largest dump truck in just six passes, weighs 1,985,000 lb. (900 tons) and has a shovel capacity of 1,825.7 ft.³ (51.7 m³). The top of the driver's cab is 33 ft. 6 in. (10.2 m), or about three stories, above the ground, and the machine is powered by a 4,400-hp (3,280-kW) Cummins diesel engine, which is fed by a 4,210-gal. (16,000-liter) fuel tank.

Tallest mobile crane The Demag CC 12600, made by Mannesmann Dematic, is 650 ft. (198 m) high in its tallest configuration, which comprises a 394-ft. (120-m) "fixed jib" attached to a 374-ft. (114-m) near-vertical boom. It has a maximum lifting capacity of 3.5 million lb. (1,600 tons) at a 72-ft. (22-m) radius and is so large that it requires 100 trucks to transport all of its different parts to a site.

Largest tire Standing 13 ft. 1 in. (4 m) tall and weighing more than 8,800 lb. (4 tons), the world's largest tires are built by Michelin to fit onto the world's biggest dump trucks.

Longest ramp jump in a monster truck *Bigfoot 14,* driven by Dan Runte (U.S.A.), jumped 202 ft. (61.5 m) over a Boeing 727 passenger jet on September 11, 1999 at Smyrna Airport, Nashville, Tennessee, U.S.A. He was the first person to achieve this feat.

Fastest speed in a monster truck Dan Runte (U.S.A.) reached a speed of 69.3 mph (111.5 km/h) in *Bigfoot 14* on September 11, 1999, at Symrna Airport, Nashville, Tennessee, U.S.A., the highest speed ever recorded in a monster truck. The speed was recorded during the run-up to the longest ever monster truck jump of 202 ft. (61.5 m).

TALLEST LIMOUSINE The world's tallest limousine (pictured) measures 10 ft. 11 in. (3.33 m) from the ground to the roof. Built by Gary and Shirley Duval (both Australia), it has an eight-wheel independent suspension system and sits on eight monster-truck tires. It has two separate engines and took a little over 4,000 hours to build.

Longest bus The articulated DAF Super CityTrain buses of the Democratic Republic of Congo are 105 ft. (32.2 m) long and can carry 350 passengers comfortably. Each bus weighs 61,700 lb. (28 tons) unladen.

Largest bus fleet The Andhra Pradesh State Road Transport Corporation (India) operates around 18,900 buses on 8,678 routes, carrying an estimated 13 million passengers every day.

SCIENCE & TECHNOLOGY

SCIENCE ADVANCES

Most accurate kilogram The kilogram is the only Système International (SI) base unit of measurement whose definition is still based on a physical prototype. The world's most accurate kilogram is a cylinder of platinum and iridium that was made in 1889. It is maintained at the Bureau International des Poids et Mesures (BIPM) at Sèvres near Paris, France.

Smallest microchain drive The links on a microchain drive created by Sandia National Laboratories in Albuquerque, New Mexico, U.S.A., and announced in January 2002, are only 50 micrometers apart. The microchain is constructed of silicon and is designed to transmit power in microelectromechanical devices.

Darkest man-made substance A black coating composed of a nickel-phosphorus alloy, first developed by researchers in the U.S.A. and India in 1980, reflects just 0.16% of visible light, making it about 25 times less reflective than conventional black paint. In 1990, the Anritsu Corporation (Japan) refined this coating to produce the darkest version so far. In 2002, the National Physical Laboratory, UK, developed a new method for the commercial manufacturing of this coating.

LEAST DENSE SOLID Lawrence Livermore National Laboratory (U.S.A.) has produced an aerogel (pictured) with a density of just 0.47 grains/in³ (1.9 mg/cm³).

Aerogels are nanoporous, lightweight solids that physically resemble "solid smoke." Aerogels also have the lowest refractive index and the highest thermal insulation of any solid material.

MOST SENSITIVE GAMMA RAY DETECTOR Gammasphere (pictured) at the Argonne National Laboratory, Illinois, U.S.A., is a gamma ray "microscope" used in nuclear physics research. It is a cylinder measuring 10 ft. (3 m) high, pierced with 110 gamma ray detectors. These focus inward to a central target area that is bombarded with ions from a particle accelerator.

Lowest man-made temperature Scientists at the Massachusetts Institute of Technology, Cambridge, U.S.A., led by Aaron Leanhardt (U.S.A.), announced in September 2003 that they had achieved a temperature of 450 picokelvin above absolute zero (0.00000000045° above absolute zero).

Most powerful pulsed neutron spallation source ISIS, at the Rutherford Appleton Laboratory, Chilton, Oxfordshire, UK, is the world's most powerful pulsed neutron source. Covering the size of a soccer field, it produces 4×10^{16} fast neutrons per second. These are focused into beams in a neutron microscope, which allows scientists to study, at a microscopic scale, the atomic and molecular arrangements that give materials their unique properties.

Longest continuous observational science data Astronomers have access to a continuous set of observational data on the sunspot number (number of sunspots on the Sun) dating back to 1750.

Quietest place on Earth Ultrasensitive tests carried out on January 21, 2004 at the Anechoic Test Chamber, Orfield Laboratories, Minneapolis, Minnesota, U.S.A., gave a background noise reading of -9.4 decibels A-weighted (dBA).

Longest-running laboratory experiment The Pitch Drop Experiment has been running since 1930 at the University of Queensland, Australia. It consists of black pitch contained in a glass funnel, with the entire apparatus enclosed in a container. It demonstrates that pitch is actually an extremely viscous liquid. Once the stem of the funnel was cut, the pitch slowly began to drip. In late 2000, the eighth drop fell. From this experiment, it has been possible to show that the viscosity of pitch is about 100 billion times that of water. There is enough pitch left for this experiment to run for another hundred years.

Smallest abacus In November 1996, scientists at the IBM Research Division's Zurich laboratory built an abacus with individual molecules as beads, each with a diameter of less than one nanometer (one millionth of a millimeter). The IBM scientists succeeded in forming stable rows of 10 molecules along steps just one atom high on a copper surface. The steps acted as rails, similar to the earliest form of the abacus, which had grooves instead of rods to keep the beads in line.

Discoverer of greatest number of elements Albert Ghiorso (U.S.A.) has discovered or codiscovered 12 chemical elements since he began his scientific career in 1942. The first was element 95, americum, in 1944. Albert is still at the Lawrence Berkeley Laboratory, California, U.S.A., where he has worked since 1946.

Shortest flash of light In February 2004, a team of physicists led by Dr. Ferenc Krausz (Austria) of Vienna University of Technology, Vienna, Austria, announced that they had created pulses of ultraviolet laser light lasting just 250 attoseconds ($250 \times 10^{+16}$ seconds). Using these attosecond light pulses, they were able to observe electrons in neon atoms and distinguish between events just 100 attoseconds apart.

Largest telescope The twin Keck telescopes, on the summit of Hawaii's dormant Mauna Kea volcano, are the largest optical and infrared telescopes. Each of them is eight stories tall and weighs 661,000 lb. (300 tons). Both Kecks have a 32-ft. 9.6-in. (10-m) mirror composed of 36 hexagonal segments that act together to create a single reflective surface. Keck I began scientific observations in May 1993 and Keck II began in October 1996.

Largest robotic telescope The Liverpool Telescope, owned by the Astrophysics Research Institute (ARI) of Liverpool John Moores University, UK, has a main mirror with a diameter of 6.56 ft. (2 m). Located on La Palma, Canary Islands, Spain, it was designed for observing invisible and near-infrared wavelengths and achieved first light on July 27, 2003.

Highest-resolution optical image The highest-resolution image ever taken shows details smaller than 20 billionths of a meter across. Using a technique called "near-field Raman scattering," a team at the University of Rochester, New York, U.S.A., led by Professor Lukas Novotny (U.S.A.), was able to image individual carbon nanotubes with visible light. The research was announced in March 2003.

Most powerful X-ray generator The Z Machine at the Sandia National Laboratories in Albuquerque, New Mexico, U.S.A., can, very briefly, gener-

HIGHEST-INTENSITY FOCUSED LASER The Vulcan laser (seen here) at the Rutherford Appleton Laboratory, Chilton, Oxfordshire, UK, is the highest-intensity focused laser in the world. Following its upgrade, which was completed in 2002, it is now capable of producing a laser beam with an irradiance (focused intensity) of 10^{21} W/cm².

ate X rays with a power output roughly the equivalent to 80 times that of all the world's electrical generators.

Largest Van de Graaff generator In 1931 Dr. Robert J. Van de Graaff built the largest Van de Graaff generator at the Massachusetts Institute of Technology, U.S.A. It was originally used to help with research into high-energy X rays and atom smashing, and is now on permanent display at the Thomson Theater of Electricity at the Boston Museum of Science, U.S.A. It consists of two columns each with a 15-ft.-wide (4.57-m) hollow aluminum sphere at the top. Originally, the two spheres were oppositely charged, which resulted in lightning-like discharges of 5 million volts. Today, both spheres are joined together and discharge to props and grounded probes, rather than discharging to each other.

Greatest altitude achieved by a laser-powered craft On October 2, 2000, Lightcraft Technologies (U.S.A.) successfully flew a 4.8-in.-diameter (12.2-cm) craft to a height of 233 ft. (71 m), powered only by light. They used a U.S. Army 13.4-hp (10-kW) pulsed carbon dioxide laser on the ground, fired upward at the 1.8-oz. (51-g) craft, which reflects the light backward to a point just beneath it. The resulting expansion of the super-heated air provides the craft with thrust. These test flights took place at the White Sands Missile Range, New Mexico, U.S.A.

AMAZING SCIENCE

Heaviest and lightest quarks Of the six "flavors" of quarks (subatomic particles)—known as "up," "down," "top," "bottom," "strange," and "charmed"—the heaviest is the "top" quark, which has a mass of 170 gigaelectron-volts (GeV). It was discovered in February 1995 at Fermilab, Batavia, Illinois, U.S.A. The lightest are the "up" and "down" quarks, both at 0.15 GeV.

Fastest speed possible The speed of light is achieved only by light and other forms of electromagnetic radiation, e.g. radio waves, infrared radiation and X rays. The speed of light varies depending on what it is traveling through. Light travels fastest through a vacuum, where its velocity is 299,792,458 m/s (about 300,000 km/s or 186,000 miles per second). This means that when you look at the Moon, you see it as it was about 1.3 seconds ago, and the Sun as it was around 8.3 minutes ago.

Most common element Hydrogen (H) represents over 90% of all matter in the universe and 70.68% of all matter in the Solar System. Iron (Fe) is the most common element on Earth, making up 36% of its mass, and molecular nitrogen (N_2) is the most common element in the atmosphere at 75.52% by mass or 78.08% by volume.

Rarest element on Earth Only around 0.9 oz. (25 g) of the element astatine (At) occurs naturally in the Earth's crust. Astatine was discovered in 1931 by Fred Allison and E. J. Murphy (both U.S.A.).

Element with the highest melting and boiling point Of all the metals, tungsten (W) has the highest melting point at 6,177°F (3,414°C) and the highest boiling point at 10,557°F (5,847°C). The graphite form of carbon (C) sublimes directly to vapor at 6,699°F (3,704°C) and can be obtained as a liquid only from above a temperature of 8,546°F (4,730°C) and a pressure of 10 megapascals (100 atmospheres).

Most ductile element One gram of gold (Au) can be drawn to 1.5 miles (2.4 km), or 1 oz. to 43 miles (69 km).

Oldest biological molecules Biological molecules extracted from the rib of an iguanodon—a huge herbivorous dinosaur—found in a quarry in Surrey, UK, have been dated at about 125 million years old. The research was carried out by Liverpool University, the University of Wales, and the Natural History Museum (all UK), and the results were announced in September 2003.

Oldest living bacteria Bacteria trapped in suspended animation inside salt crystals for 250 million years have been revived and cultured by U.S. scientists. Designated *Bacillus 2-9-3,* this species is 10 times older than the previous oldest revived bacteria.

Most radiation-resistant microbe The bacterium *Deinococcus radiodurans* (formerly *Micrococcus radiodurans)* can withstand atomic radiation of 6.5 million roentgens, or 10,000 times the level that would be fatal to the average human.

HARDEST ELEMENT Carbon (C) has three different allotropes (different configurations of atoms), but the diamond allotrope, which has an extremely strong lattice structure, has the maximum value of 10 on Mohs' relative scale of hardness. Diamonds (pictured) are formed at least 93 miles (150 km) beneath the Earth's surface, where the pressures and temperatures are great enough to force the carbon atoms to adopt this structure.

Highest microbe In April 1967, NASA reported that bacteria had been discovered at an altitude of 25.56 miles (41.13 km).

Smelliest molecules Ethyl mercaptan (C_2H_5SH) and butyl seleno-mercaptan (C_4H_9SeH) have an odor reminiscent of a combination of rotting cabbage, garlic, onions, burnt toast, and sewer gas. Ethyl mercaptan is added to odorless gas to act as a warning agent.

Smelliest substances The smelliest substances are the man-made "Who-Me?" and "U.S. Government Standard Bathroom Malodor," which

WEAKEST FORCE Four fundamental forces in the universe account for all interactions between matter and energy. They are the strong nuclear, weak nuclear, electromagnetic, and gravitational forces. The weakest of these is gravity. A good example of how much weaker gravity is compared to, say, electromagnetism, is that it is easy for a toy magnet to pick up a handful of nails while the whole of Earth's gravity is trying to pull them back down. The strongest force is the strong nuclear.

ELEMENT WITH THE LOWEST MELTING AND BOILING POINT For metallic elements, mercury (Hg, pictured) has the lowest melting and boiling points at +37.892°F (+38.829°C) and 673.92°F (356.62°C) respectively. Helium (He) cannot be obtained as a solid at atmospheric pressure, the minimum pressure required being 2.532 megapascals (24.985 atmospheres) at a temperature of +458.275°F (+272.375°C). Helium also has the lowest boiling point at +452.070°F (+268.928°C).

have five and eight chemical ingredients respectively. "Who-Me?" was developed by the U.S. military during World War II and was intended to be sprayed on German troops, then occupying France, to humiliate them. Bathroom Malodor smells primarily of human feces and becomes incredibly repellent to people at just two parts per million. The substance was originally created to test the power of deodorizing products.

Lightest known particle Neutrinos are the lightest known particles in the universe, with a maximum mass of 0.00000000000000000000000000 0000000000018 kg. Neutrinos come in three varieties—electron, muon, and tau neutrinos. The mass is an average of the three types.

Oldest irrational number An irrational number is a number that cannot be expressed as a fraction or an integer. The first irrational number discovered was the square root of 2, by Hippasus of Metapontum (then part of Magna Graecia, southern Italy) in about 500 B.C.

Lowest temperature possible Temperature is a direct result of the vibrations of the atoms or molecules that make up matter. The coldest that any substance can be is when there is no vibration in its atoms or molecules. This is referred to as absolute zero, and is at 0 K (zero Kelvin) or –459.67°F (–273.15°C). Absolute zero has never been achieved in an Earth laboratory, and even in the coldest parts of deep space, the temperature is slightly above absolute zero. There is no upper limit to how hot something can be.

Largest known prime number A prime number is a number that is only divisible by 1 and itself. The largest known prime number is $2^{20,996,011}+1$, which contains 6,320,430 digits. It was discovered by Michael Shafer (U.S.A.), a chemical engineering student, on November 17, 2003. Shafer was running software on his computer as part of the Great Internet Mersenne Prime Search, or GIMPS.

Greatest time dilation The most time dilation experienced by an individual is around 1/50th of a second, for Russian cosmonaut Sergei Avdeyev. This is a consequence of the 747 days 14 hr. 22 min. he has spent in low Earth orbit, traveling at about 17,000 mph (27,000 km/h). Relative to people on Earth, Avdeyev has "time traveled" 1/50th of a second into the future, a phenomenon consistent with Albert Einstein's theory of relativity.

Longest time survived in space by bacteria From April 7, 1984 to January 11, 1990, *E. Coli* bacteria cells survived unshielded on board NASA's Long Duration Exposure Facility satellite in low Earth orbit. The satellite and its 57 experiments were retrieved by the space shuttle *Challenger.*

ARCHAEOLOGY

Largest prehistoric building Archaeological tests reveal that a 5,000-year-old structure, probably a temple, discovered at a sacred Stone Age site at Stanton Drew, Somerset, UK, had a diameter of 295 ft. (90 m) and was at least six times the size of Stonehenge. The building is estimated to have been 33 ft. (10 m) high, possibly with a thatched roof supported by more than 400 wooden columns, each approximately a meter in diameter, forming nine rings.

Earliest places of worship Many archaeologists are of the opinion that the decorated Upper Paleolithic caves of Europe (ca. 30,000–10,000 B.C.) were used as places of worship or religious ritual.

Earliest alphabet The earliest known example of alphabetic writing is that found on clay tablets showing the 32 cuneiform (wedge-shaped) letters of the Ugaritic alphabet, a now-extinct Semitic language of Syria. The tablets were found in 1929 at Ugarit (now Ras Shamra), Syria and were dated to around 1450 B.C.

Earliest castle The 20-story Gomdan or Gumdan Castle, in the old city of Sana'a, Yemen, dates from before A.D. 200 and is now a UNESCO World Heritage site.

LARGEST ANCIENT STONE CIRCLE The 28.4-acre (11.5-hectare) earthworks and stone circles of Avebury, Wiltshire, UK (seen here), which were "rediscovered" in 1646, represent the UK's largest prehistoric monument and largest henge (a circular area, often containing a circle of stones or wooden posts). The earliest calibrated date in the area of this Neolithic site is ca. 4200 B.C. The work is 1,200 ft. (365 m) in diameter with a ditch 40 ft. (12 m) wide around the perimeter.

Earliest parliament The earliest known legislative assembly, or *ukkim,* was a bicameral (two-chamber) gathering in Erech, Iraq, in ca. 2800 B.C.

The oldest recorded legislative body is the Icelandic *Althing* founded in A.D. 930.

The earliest known use of the term "parliament" came in an official royal document dating from December 19, 1241, in which the term referred to a summons to King Henry III's Council in England.

Oldest stained glass Pieces of stained glass dating back to before A.D. 850 (some possibly even back to the 7th century) were excavated by Rosemary Cramp (UK) at Monkwearmouth and Jarrow (both UK), set into a window of that date in St. Paul's Church, Jarrow, County Durham, UK.

Earliest canal Early in 1968, archaeologists found relics of canals dating back to ca. 4000 B.C. near Mandali, Iraq.

Earliest zoo The earliest known collection of animals was established at modern-day Puzurish, Iraq, by Shulgi, a 3rd-dynasty ruler of Ur from 2097 to 2094 B.C.

Earliest domestication of dogs Archaeologists believe that the Pale-olithic humans in east Asia domesticated dogs (*Canis familiaris*) approximately 15,000 years ago by successfully breeding aggression out of wolves (*C. lupus*).

Earliest domestication of horses Evidence from Ukraine indicates that the domestication of horses so that they could be ridden may have happened some time before 4000 B.C.

Oldest remains of modern humans The oldest remains of modern humans discovered so far date back 160,000 years. They consist of two complete crania, belonging to one adult and one child, and fragments from another adult skull. The remains were discovered in Ethiopia by a team of scientists led by Tim White of the University of California at Berkeley, U.S.A.

Oldest hominid footprints A hominid is any primate of the family Hominidae, which includes modern man (*Homo sapiens*) and his ancestors. The oldest known human-like footprints were discovered in Laetoli, northern Tanzania, in 1978. They belong to two or three hominids striding upright on the ashy plains of the area some 3.6 million years ago. The trackway consists of some 70 footprints in two parallel trails about 100 ft. (30 m) long.

LARGEST GEOGLYPHS The so-called Nazca lines are a group of gigantic figures (geoglyphs) engraved on the desert ground of Nazca, Peru, representing plants, animals (monkey, pictured), insects, and a variety of geometric shapes. Most can only be appreciated from the air. The designs occupy a 190-mile^2 (500-km^2) area of land and they average 600 ft. (180 m) in length, although one perfectly formed arrow exceeds 1,600 ft. (490 m).

OLDEST ICE BODY In September 1991, the preserved remains of a
Neolithic man were discovered, 5,300 years after he had died, by two
hikers on a melting glacier in the Tyrolean Alps on the Italian-Austrian
border. Analysis of "Ötzi" (seen here), as the mummy was named, and
his belongings have given a new insight into the technology and culture
of central Europe some 5,000 years ago.

Oldest mummy Mummification dates from 2600 B.C., or the 4th dynasty
of the Egyptian pharaohs. The oldest complete mummy is of Wati, a court
musician of ca. 2400 B.C. from the tomb of Nefer in Saqqâra, Egypt, found
in 1944.

Oldest coin The earliest coins recorded were made during the reign of
King Gyges of Lydia, Turkey, in ca. 630 B.C., and consisted of electrum, a
naturally occurring amalgam of gold and silver.

Earliest measures The *beqa* of the Amratian period of Egyptian civilization, ca. 3800 B.C., found at Naqada, Egypt, are cylindrical weights with
rounded ends. They weigh from 6.66 to 7.45 oz. (188.7 to 211.2 g).

Oldest industry Flint knapping, which involves the production of chop-
ping tools and hand axes, dates back 2.5 million years in Ethiopia. The earliest evidence of trading in exotic stone and amber dates from ca. 28,000
B.C. in Europe.

Oldest batteries Around a dozen clay jars, measuring about 5 in. (13 cm)
long and dating back about 2,000 years, are believed to be the world's oldest
electrical cells, or batteries. Some reports claim that they were discovered in
the basement of the Baghdad Museum, Iraq, by German archaeologist Wilhelm König in 1938. The jars contain a copper cylinder and an iron rod,

along with signs of acidic corrosion. Modern replicas of these objects have been shown to function as rudimentary electrical cells, and it is possible that they were used for electroplating.

Oldest Greek vessel excavated The "Kyrenia Ship" was built in the early 4th century B.C. and sank some 80 years later less than a mile off Kyrenia (northern Cyprus), carrying 400 amphorae (clay vessels) of Rhodian wine and volcanic grain from the island of Kos. The vessel, a 49-ft.-long (15-m) open boat, was found in 1967 by a Cypriot diver. It is considered to be the finest preserved ship of the late classical period of Greek civilization, the time of Alexander the Great.

Earliest use of the wheel The earliest documented use of the wheel for transport dates back 5,500 years to Mesopotamia (modern Iraq). Previous to this time, humans had moved heavy objects from one place to another by rolling them over logs.

Largest Bronze Age copper mine The Great Orme Mines, Llandudno, UK, contain at least 5 miles (8 km) of accessible tunnels. They were mined for copper from around 1800 B.C. until the end of the Bronze Age (ca. 750 B.C.). Mining occurred again from 1692 until 1881. The first chambers of the original mines were discovered in 1976.

INTERNET

First hypertext browser In October 1990, Tim Berners-Lee (UK) started work on a global hypertext browser. The result—the World Wide Web—was made available on the Internet in the summer of 1991. Berners-Lee had originally proposed a global hypertext project to let people combine their knowledge in a web of hypertext documents in 1989.

Largest Internet search engine Google, with around 4.28 billion pages, has the largest continually refreshed index of webpages out of all the world's search engines. The company was founded by Larry Page and Sergey Brin (both U.S.A.). Google handles 200 million search queries every day—2,000 a second during peak hours—and has an index of 3 trillion words.

Highest-capacity intercontinental Internet route In 2003, the Internet routes between Europe and the U.S.A./Canada had a bandwidth capacity of 386,221 megabits per second (Mbps). (This is the equivalent of between five and ten full-length DVD movies per second.) The lowest capacity was between Africa and U.S.A./Canada, with a bandwidth capacity of 1,351.5 Mbps.

Largest Internet joke vote Laughlab, an Internet experiment into humor, was conducted by psychologist Richard Wiseman, University of Hertfordshire, Hatfield, UK, and the British Association for the Advancement of Science. The experiment ran from September 2001 to October 2002, during which more than 40,000 jokes were submitted from the worldwide public, and around 2 million votes were cast on which one was the funniest.

If you'd like to find out what the winning joke was, and also see some of the runners-up, then visit our website: www.guinnessworldrecords.com/joke.

Most expensive Internet domain name The Internet domain name business.com was sold by entrepreneur Marc Ostrofsky (U.S.A.) on December 1, 1999 for $7.5 million.

Most searched-for plant and animal on the Internet According to Google, the most searched-for plant on the Internet is the rose.

The most searched-for animal is the domestic cat, according to the same search engine.

Largest single e-commerce transaction American Internet tycoon Mark Cuban (U.S.A.) bought a Gulfstream V business jet over the Internet in October 1999. The jet changed hands for $40 million.

Longest live event streamed over the Internet Beginning on October 21, 2001, the Canadian Musicians for Liberty Organization held the

FASTEST-GROWING INTERNET SERVICE PROVIDER Since its launch by NTT DoCoMo in February 1999, i-Mode has gained more than 40 million subscribers. i-Mode is a Japanese service specifically aimed at cell phone users.

longest live event ever streamed over the Internet. Around 1,000 musicians, comprising various bands and solo artists, took turns playing live music to a small local audience as well as directly to the Internet (in both video and sound). The concert continued for 181 hours, with breaks of only a few minutes while the acts swapped over. The event was held to raise money for the Canadian Red Cross U.S.A. Relief Fund and took place at Touchdowns Bar and Grill, Mississauga, Ontario, Canada.

Largest exclusive concert on the Internet A record 9,804 people logged on to a concert by Queen drummer Roger Taylor (UK) and five band members for 45 minutes, at the Cyberbarn, Thursley, Surrey, UK, on September 24, 1998. The concert was exclusive because it was held in Taylor's barn and the only audience was via the Internet.

Internet2 land speed record Internet2 is a consortium of 206 universities working to develop the next generation of the Internet. On April 14, 2004, an international team of scientists achieved a result of 69,073 terabit-meters per second, by transferring 838.86 gigabytes of data across 10,155 miles (16,343 kilometers) of network in 1588 seconds. This data rate was reached using Internet protocol version 4 (IPv4) and is roughly equivalent to 10,000 typical home broadband Internet connections. The start and end points were Luleå, Sweden, and San Jose, California, U.S.A.

Largest Internet café The cybercafé easyEverything in Times Square, New York, U.S.A., opened on November 28, 2000 with 760 computer terminals. It now has 648 terminals.

Country with the most Internet users According to the International Telecommunication Union, in 2002 the U.S.A. had over 159 million Internet users out of a world total of 623.48 million online users.

Most Internet users by continent According to the International Telecommunication Union, of

EARLIEST E-MAIL In 1971, Ray Tomlinson (U.S.A.) sent the first e-mail as an experiment to see if he could get two computers to exchange a message. It was Ray who decided to use the @ symbol to separate the recipient's name from their location. The first e-mail message was: "QWERTYUIOP," the letters on the top line of a keyboard.

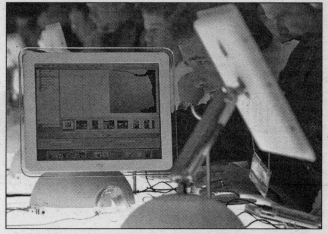

MOST GLOBALLY CONNECTED CITY ON THE INTERNET According to TeleGeography, London, UK, had an international Internet bandwidth of 550 gigabytes per second (Gbps) of Internet traffic in 2003. By contrast, New York City, U.S.A., had an Internet bandwidth of 339 Gbps in 2003.

the 623.48 million people online worldwide in 2002, 211.36 million were located in Asia.

Largest networked chess computer On January 30, 2004, Grand Master Peter Heine Nielsen (Denmark) played a game of chess against ChessBrain, the world's largest networked chess computer. ChessBrain consisted of 2,070 computers located in 56 countries, which simultaneously combined their processing power.

The match, which took place in Copenhagen, Denmark, ended in a draw after 34 moves.

Oldest electronic spam The oldest unsolicited mass e-mail was sent at 12:33 p.m. EDT on May 3, 1978 by Gary Thuerk (U.S.A.), who was working for Digital Equipment Corp. (U.S.A.). It was sent to 397 e-mail accounts on the Advanced Research Projects Agency Network (ARPAnet) of the U.S. Defense Dept., inviting account holders to a demonstration of the DEC-SYSTEM-2020, 2020T, 2060, and 2060T computers. ARPAnet is regarded as the predecessor to the Internet.

Oldest Internet bench On August 6, 2001, the world's first park bench with free access to the Internet was opened in Bury St. Edmunds, Suffolk, UK. The standard park bench was converted by msn.co.uk to allow four people to connect their laptops simultaneously, in an attempt to change the way people use the Internet.

Largest free web-based e-mail provider Microsoft's Hotmail had over 170 million active accounts as of February 2004. Every day Hotmail adds 100,000 new users. It is available in 230 countries and has 12 million unique log-ins per month.

Hotmail was launched in 1996 and its name is derived from the HTML programming language.

COMMUNICATIONS

Earliest telephone call The telephone was invented by Alexander Graham Bell (UK), who devised a way of converting human voices into electrical impulses, then back to voices. He filed his patent for the telephone on February 14, 1876 at the New York Patent office, New York, U.S.A. The first intelligible call occurred in March 1876 in Boston, Massachusetts, U.S.A., when Bell phoned his assistant in a nearby room and said, "Mr. Watson—come here—I want to see you."

First pole-to-pole telephone call On April 28, 1999, at 10:30 a.m. (GMT), the first phone call took place between people at the North and South Poles. It was carried out by NASA employees Mike Comberiate and Andre Fortin (both U.S.A.). It became a conference call coordinated from NASA's Marshall Space Flight Center, and lasted 45 minutes. Taking part in the call were George Morrow, Tom Carlson, Joel Michalski, Mike Comberiate, Claire Parkinson, Vince Hurley, and Ron Ruhlman (all U.S.A.).

LARGEST TELEVISION TELEPHONE VOTE The record for the largest TV phone vote belongs to *American Idol 2* (FOX, U.S.A.) on May 21, 2003, when 24 million viewers called in to the final of the show to vote for the winner of the pop contest (10 finalists pictured here) in Los Angeles, California, U.S.A.

LARGEST SWITCHBOARD The switchboard at the Pentagon,
Arlington, Virginia, U.S.A., has 34,500 lines handling nearly 1 million calls a
day through 100,000 miles (161,000 km) of telephone cable (Pentagon
switchboard of 1950 is pictured here). Its busiest ever day was June 6,
1994—the 50th anniversary of D-day—when there were 1,502,415 calls.

Most international telephone calls by country According to
TeleGeography, of the 155 billion minutes of international phone calls made
in 2002, 40.3 billion minutes were made from the U.S.A.

Busiest international telephone route According to TeleGeography,
the busiest international telephone route is between the U.S.A. and Canada.
In 2002, there were some 10.9 billion minutes of two-way traffic between
the two countries.

Largest fleet of ocean sensors ARGO is a global network of free-
floating ocean sensors designed to monitor global ocean-current patterns.
The sensors drift at depths of up to 6,560 ft. (2,000 m) then rise in order to
transmit data via satellites. By January 8, 2004, there were 996 active floats,
with a total of 3,000 planned by 2006.

Largest carrier of international phone calls According to TeleGeography, in 2002 the largest carrier of international telephone calls, in terms of
outgoing traffic, was AT&T Corp. (U.S.A.), with 12,796.5 million minutes
of communications.

Longest telephone cable The world's longest submarine telephone cable is FLAG (Fibre-optic Link Around the Globe), which runs for 16,800 miles (27,000 km) from Japan to the UK. It links three continents (Europe, Africa, and Asia) and 11 countries, and can support 600,000 simultaneous telephone calls.

Largest working telephone The world's largest operational telephone was exhibited on September 16, 1988 at a festival to celebrate the 80th birthday of Centraal Beheer, an insurance company based in Apeldoorn, The Netherlands. It was 8 ft. 1 in. (2.47 m) high and 19 ft. 11 in. (6.06 m) long, and weighed 7,700 lb. (3.5 tons). The handset, which was 23 ft. 5 in. (7.14 m) long, had to be lifted by crane for a call to be made.

Largest telephone conference call On September 29, 2003, U.S. Presidential Democrat candidate Howard Dean (U.S.A.) conducted a telephone conference call from Los Angeles, California, U.S.A., with his supporters. The greatest number of people simultaneously connected for at least 10 seconds was 3,466.

Most cell phones per capita According to statisticians Nation-Master.com, Taiwan had 106.45 cell phones per 100 people in 2002.

Fastest text message sent around the world On February 20, 2002, at the 3GSM World Congress in Cannes, France, Logica sent a text message around the world by forwarding it to cell phones in six countries in six continents, and finally back to the original phone in Cannes. The message was received back in France only 3 min. 17.53 sec. after the original sender began typing in the message.

Largest animal sound archive The world's largest animal sound archive, the British Library Sound Archive, London, UK,

EARLIEST CELLULAR TELEPHONE The idea for a portable phone was conceived at Lucent Technologies' Bell Labs, New Jersey, U.S.A., in 1947. The first actual portable phone handset was invented by Martin Cooper (U.S.A., pictured) of Motorola, who made the first call on April 3, 1973 to his rival, Joel Engel, research head at Bell Labs. The first commercial cell phone network was launched in Japan in 1979.

was established in 1969 and currently holds more than 130,000 wildlife recordings of sound-producing animals from all geographical areas. The sounds are used in numerous industries such as zoology, conservation, and television production—and some have even been sold as cell phone ringtones!

Fastest time to type a cell text message James Trusler (UK) typed a set text of 160 characters on his cell phone in a time of 1 min. 7 sec. on the live TV show *The Panel,* Ten Network, Sydney, NSW, Australia, on September 24, 2003.

Earliest instant telecommunication The telegraph system, invented by Samuel Morse (U.S.A.), was the first form of instant communication that was applied commercially. The first link, from Washington, D.C. to Baltimore, Maryland, U.S.A., was completed by May 1844. Morse sent the first message and soon the arrangements of dots and dashes was called Morse code.

Loudest signaling device The Chrysler air raid sirens are the loudest sirens ever, capable of producing 138 decibels at a distance of 100 ft. (30 m)—so loud that a normal person would be deafened within 200 ft. (60 m) of one during operation.

Largest live satellite radio broadcast On February 13, 2002, Ana Ann's (UK) debut single "Ride" was uplinked from the offices of Worldspace, London, UK, to Worldspace's AfriStar satellite and then beamed down to western Europe, the whole of Africa, and the Middle East.

Oldest commercial satellite station Goonhilly Satellite Earth Station on the Lizard Peninsula, Cornwall, UK, has 59 antennae of various sizes in operation. "Arthur" (Goonhilly One) began operation on July 11, 1962 and continues to carry telephone and data traffic around the world. It received the first live transatlantic television signals from the Telstar satellite.

Earliest communications satellite Echo 1 (sometimes called Echo 1A) was launched on July 10, 1962 from Cape Canaveral, Florida, U.S.A. It was a 98-ft.-diameter (30-m) balloon with a reflective aluminum coating, allowing radio and television signals to be passively reflected back to Earth. It ceased operations on May 24, 1968.

Largest civil communications satellite The Astra 1-K was built by Alcatel Space (France). It had a mass of 11,570 lb. (5,250 kg) and, fully deployed, would have been 121 ft. (37 m) in length and 21 ft. 7 in. (6.6 m) in height. Upon its launch on November 26, 2002, its Russian Proton booster failed, leaving the satellite stranded in low Earth orbit. It was safely deorbited on December 10, 2002 over the Pacific Ocean.

SPACE EXPLORATION

"There are things that are known and things that are unknown; in between is exploration."—**Anonymous**

The "space race" The first edition of *Guinness World Records* (formerly *The Guinness Book of Records*) was published six years before the first manned spaceflight by Yuri Gagarin (USSR) in 1961. In a special address to the U.S. Congress in the same year, President John F. Kennedy (U.S.A.) announced the ambitious goal of landing an American on the Moon and returning him safely to Earth before the end of the 1960s. This sparked the "space race" between the U.S.A. and the USSR that dominated the latter half of the 20th century, such that by the end of 2004—a mere 101 years since the first flight by Orville Wright (U.S.A.)—man has stood on the surface of the Moon and sent probes to other planets and there is now a permanent space station orbiting Earth.

Early landmarks The first man-made object to orbit the Earth was *Sputnik 1,* launched by the USSR on October 4, 1957. It remained in orbit until January 4, 1958. This was followed by *Sputnik 2* on November 3, 1957, which remained in orbit until April 13, 1958. *Sputnik 2* had a passenger—a dog named Laika. America's first foray into space was on January 31, 1958, when *Explorer 1,* the first U.S. satellite, lifted off from Cape Canaveral, Florida, U.S.A. The year 1958 was also the year of the founding of the National Aeronautics and Space Administration (NASA), which has controlled the American space program ever since.

Lunar success Since the 1950s, advances in science and technology have enabled man to continue to push back the boundaries of space exploration. Some eight years after Yuri Gagarin's (USSR) first spaceflight, Neil Armstrong (U.S.A.) took that "giant leap for mankind" in 1969 when he stepped onto the Moon.

More recently, the development of the reusable space shuttle has made possible the construction and development of the International Space Station (ISS) that is now orbiting Earth—a project that has brought together many spacefaring nations. This has allowed scientists to carry out important onboard scientific experiments that benefit mankind. The picture on page 293 shows John Herrington (U.S.A.) installing new equipment to the ISS's Canadarm2 on a scheduled space walk. China's first spaceflight, in October 2003, was another important landmark in the history of space exploration: China is only the third nation to send a human into orbit.

Next stop Mars? The exploration of our solar system is an ongoing project: in January 2004, following NASA's successful Mars Exploration Rover mission—which has brought the possibility of sending a human mission to Mars one step closer—President Bush (U.S.A.) called on NASA to "prepare for new journeys to the worlds beyond our own."

1961

First manned spaceflight The earliest manned space flight was by Cosmonaut Yuri Alekseyevich Gagarin (USSR) in *Vostok 1* on April 12, 1961. *Vostok 1* was launched from the Baikonur Cosmodrome, Kazakhstan, USSR, at 9:07 a.m. and landed near Smelovka, USSR, 115 minutes later. Gagarin ejected from *Vostok 1* 108 minutes into the flight as planned, and landed three minutes after his spacecraft by parachute. The maximum altitude during *Vostok 1*'s 25,394-mile (40,868-km) flight was listed at 203 miles (327 km), with a maximum speed of 17,560 mph (28,260 km/h).

1963

First woman in space Valentina Tereshkova (USSR) was launched into space in *Vostok 6* on June 19, 1963. At 26, she is the youngest woman ever to undertake such a mission.

1965

First space walk Alexei Arkhipovich Leonov (USSR) was the first person to engage in EVA, or extra-vehicular activity, commonly known as a "space walk," which he accomplished from *Voskhod 2* on March 18, 1965.

1968

First manned lunar mission On December 21, 1968, *Apollo 8* was launched into space. The crew—Frank Borman, Jim Lovell,

and Bill Anders (all U.S.A. pictured at left)—were the first men to orbit the Moon. They achieved 10 orbits during their six-day mission.

First men on the Moon Neil Armstrong (U.S.A.), commander of the *Apollo 11* mission, became the first man to set foot on the Moon, on the Sea of Tranquility, at 22:56:15 EDT on July 20, 1969. He was

- 12 men in total have walked on the Moon.
- 16 nations are participating in the construction of the International Space Station.
- The greatest distance from Earth achieved by humans was when the crew of *Apollo 13* (Jim Lovell, Fred Haise, and John Swigert, all U.S.A.) were 158 miles (254 km) from the lunar surface, on the far side of the Moon, and 248,655 miles (400,171 km) above the Earth's surface, at 8:21 EDT on April 15, 1970.

followed out of the lunar module *Eagle* by Edwin "Buzz" Aldrin, Jr. (U.S.A., pictured) while the command module *Columbia*, piloted by Michael Collins (U.S.A.), orbited above, before later re-docking.

1972
Longest manned Moon mission From December 7 to 19, 1972, the crew of

Apollo 17 stayed on the lunar surface for a record 74 hr. 59 min. 40 sec. During their stay Eugene Cernan and Harrison "Jack" Schmitt (who became the twelfth man on the Moon) collected a record 243 lb. 6 oz. (110.4 kg) of rock and soil during their three EVAs totaling 22 hr. 5 mins.

2002
Most spaceflights by an individual To date, two astronauts have

traveled into space a total of seven times: Jerry Ross (U.S.A., pictured at left) flew his seventh mission (STS 110) on board the space shuttle *Atlantis* from April 8 to 19, 2002. Franklin Chang-Dìaz (U.S.A.) flew his seventh mission on board the space shuttle *Endeavour* from June 5 to 19, 2002.

2003
Longest maiden flight Of the three nations to launch humans into space to date,

the longest maiden flight is by the Chinese. On October 15, 2003, Chinese "taikonaut" Yang Liwei (pictured) was sent into orbit on board the *Shenzou 5* spacecraft on a mission that lasted 21 hr. 23 min. from launch to touchdown.

INNOVATIONS FROM SPACE TECHNOLOGY

- Weather prediction
- Satellite navigation & communication
- TV satellite dishes
- Bar coding

- Pacemakers
- Heart monitors
- Ultrasound scanners
- Digital imaging

- Medical imaging
- CAT scans
- High-density batteries
- Flat screen TVs
- Joysticks
- Water purification systems
- Cordless tools

- Virtual reality programs
- Thermal clothing
- Radiation-blocking sunglasses
- Fire-fighting equipment
- Smoke detectors
- Shock-absorbing sneakers
- Invisible braces for teeth

SPACE TRAVEL

Most accurate measure of the age of the universe The Wilkinson Microwave Anisotropy Probe (WMAP) was designed to measure the cosmic microwave background of the universe—the heat echo of the Big Bang. The first results from WMAP, released on February 11, 2003, reveal minute temperature differences in the early universe. This has allowed scientists to estimate the age of the universe at 13.7 billion years old, with a margin of error of just 1%.

Most people in space at the same time The greatest number of people in space at any one time is 13. Seven Americans were aboard the space shuttle STS 67 *Endeavour,* three CIS cosmonauts were aboard the *Mir* space station, and two cosmonauts and a U.S. astronaut were aboard *Soyuz TM21* on March 14, 1995.

Most time spent in space Russian cosmonaut Sergei Avdeyev logged a total of 747 days 14 hr. 22 min. on three spaceflights to the *Mir* space station from July 1992 to July 1999.

Longest manned spaceflight Russian doctor Valeriy Poliyakov was launched to the *Mir* space station aboard *Soyuz TM18* on January 8, 1994 and landed back on Earth in *Soyuz TM20* on March 22, 1995, after a spaceflight lasting 437 days 17 hr. 58 min. 16 sec.

Longest spaceflight by a woman Shannon Lucid (U.S.A.) was launched to the *Mir* space station aboard the U.S. space shuttle STS 76 *Atlantis* on March 22, 1996, and landed aboard STS 79 *Atlantis* on September 26 that year. Her spaceflight, which lasted 188 days 4 hr. 14 sec., is the longest spaceflight by a woman. Her stay onboard the space station is also the longest by any U.S. astronaut. Upon returning to Earth, she was awarded the Congressional Space Medal of Honor by President Clinton (U.S.A.).

Furthest distance traveled on another world From January 16 to June 23, 1973, the unmanned Soviet *Lunokhod 2* rover traveled a distance of 23 miles (37 km) on the surface of the Moon, further than any other manned or unmanned lunar or planetary rover.

MOST REUSED SPACECRAFT NASA's space shuttle *Discovery* (pictured) was last launched on August 10, 2001 at 4:10 p.m. CDT. Its mission (STS-105) was to deliver the *Leonardo* cargo module to the International Space Station and to deliver a new crew to the station. This was the 30th mission for *Discovery,* which has been in operation since August 30, 1984.

Furthest distance traveled on Mars in one day On sol 70 (corresponding to April 5, 2004) of NASA's Mars Exploration rover mission, the robotic rover *Opportunity* traveled a total distance of 328 ft. (100 m) across Meridiani Planum on Mars. As a comparison, Mars Pathfinder's *Sojourner* rover traveled 334 ft. (102 m) during its entire mission in 1997.

Greatest spacecraft collision On June 25, 1997, an unmanned Russian *Progress* supply vehicle weighing 15,000 lb. (7 tons) collided with the Russian *Mir* space station. Cosmonauts Vasily Tsibliev and Alexander Lazutkin (both Russia) onboard *Mir* had to work quickly to seal a breach in the hull of *Mir's Spektr* module, while U.S. astronaut Michael Foale prepared *Mir's Soyuz* capsule for a possible evacuation. Although the loss of life was avoided, the station was left dangerously low on power and oxygen and temporarily tumbled out of control.

Longest space walk Astronauts Jim Voss and Susan Helms (both U.S.A.) spent 8 hr. 56 min. outside in space on March 11, 2001. Their job was to make room on the International Space Station for the Italian cargo module *Leonardo,* which was carried into space by the space shuttle *Discovery. Leonardo's* payload included around 11,000 lb. (5 tons) of supplies and equipment for the station.

Most durable space station *Mir,* the central core module of the *Mir* space station (USSR/Russia), was launched into orbit on February 20, 1986.

Over the following 10 years, five modules and a docking port for U.S. space shuttles were added to the complex. On March 23, 2001, the space station was de-orbited and destroyed in a controlled reentry over the Pacific Ocean. More than a hundred people visited the *Mir* space station in its 15-year operational history.

Longest orbital survey of an outer planet NASA's *Galileo* spacecraft was launched on October 18, 1989. It reached the planet Jupiter on December 7, 1995, where it slowed down and entered the orbit of the largest planet in the Solar System. *Galileo*'s survey of Jupiter and its moons represents the first time a man-made probe has orbited a world in the outer Solar System. With its onboard power and communications beginning to fail, *Galileo* burned up in the atmosphere of Jupiter on September 21, 2003. This was a deliberate destruction of the spacecraft, which ensured there was no chance of it inadvertently colliding with Europa (one of Jupiter's "moons") and contaminating it in the future.

Fastest atmospheric entry On December 7, 1995, a small probe released by the *Galileo* spacecraft began a fiery descent into the atmosphere of the giant planet Jupiter. During this, the most difficult atmospheric entry ever, the *Galileo* probe reached a speed of 106,000 mph (170,000 km/h).

Largest planetary rover Of the three robotic rovers sent to other planets, NASA's twin Mars Exploration rovers *Spirit* and *Opportunity* are the largest. Each has a mass of almost 396 lb. (180 kg) and stands 4 ft. 9 in. (1.44 m) high.

Clearest image of a comet On January 2, 2004, NASA's *Stardust* spacecraft encountered comet *Wild 2* in order to collect samples of cometary dust for return to Earth. From the closest approach distance of about 146 miles (236 km), the spacecraft was able to obtain images of the icy nucleus at a resolution of just 50 ft. (15 m) per pixel.

OLDEST ASTRONAUT
John Glenn, Jr. (U.S.A.) was 77 years 103 days old when he was launched into space as part of the crew of STS-95 *Discovery* on October 29, 1998. The mission lasted 11 days, landing on November 7, 1998.

HEAVIEST MAN-MADE OBJECT TO REENTER EARTH'S ATMOSPHERE The Russian space station *Mir* (seen here) was de-orbited during a successful controlled reentry of Earth's atmosphere on March 23, 2001. After 15 years in space, the 286,500-lb. (130-ton) outpost broke into incandescent pieces and splashed down in the ocean east of New Zealand.

Most powerful gamma-ray telescope Launched in 1991, the Compton Gamma-Ray Observatory is the most powerful gamma-ray telescope to date. After nine years of observations, it reentered the Earth's atmosphere and burned up on June 4, 2000.

Most distant image of Earth On February 4, 1990, NASA's *Voyager 1* spacecraft turned its camera back toward the Sun and the planets. After 12.5 years in space, traveling away from Earth, *Voyager 1*'s camera took a picture of our home planet from a distance of almost 4 billion miles (6.5 billion km).

Longest extraterrestrial balloon flight The twin Soviet spacecraft *Vega 1* and *Vega 2* were launched on December 15 and December 20, 1984 respectively. Both probes encountered Venus in June 1985, and dropped packages into the Venusian atmosphere. Each package split into a lander and a balloon. The *Vega 2* balloon sent data about the Venusian atmosphere for 46.5 hours, before contact was lost.

TECHNOLOGY

Most detailed human dissection The Visible Human Project is led by Dr. Victor Spitzer (U.S.A.) of the University of Colorado. The aim of the project is to create a virtual anatomy "textbook." Ultimately this digitized virtual body will be part of a medical simulator on which doctors and medical students will learn surgical techniques, in the manner of a pilot learning to fly by using an aeroplane simulator. To create these virtual humans, Dr. Spitzer and his team had to perform the most detailed human dissection.

The "Visible Man" is a real cadaver that was sliced into 1,878 sections. The thickness of each cut was 1 mm (1,000 microns). The "Visible Woman" cadaver was sliced into 5,189 slices, 0.33 mm (330 microns) thick. Each layer of the sliced cadaver was photographed with a digital camera and stored in a computer. Eventually, the recreation of the sliced images will form a minutely detailed 3-D virtual human body.

Furthest distance between patient and surgeon On September 7, 2001, Madeleine Schaal (France) had her gallbladder removed by a robot in an operating room at Strasbourg, France. Her surgeons, Jacques Marescaux and Michel Gagner (both France), remotely operated the ZEUS robotic surgical arms on a secure fiber-optic line from New York, U.S.A., a total distance of 3,866 miles (6,222 km) away.

Highest capacity multimedia jukebox The highest capacity multimedia jukebox available to date is the AV380, with 80 gigabytes of storage space on its internal hard drive. Created by Archos (France), the AV380 can store and play MP3 music tracks as well as MPEG4 video files. It was launched in August 2003.

Longest television display A screen measuring 230 ft. 10.8 in. (70.4 m) long by 26 ft. 2.4 in. (8 m) high was built by Mitsubishi Electric (HK) and Mitsubishi Corporation (Japan). Its installation at the Hong Kong Jockey Club, Shatin Horse Race Course, Hong Kong, China, was completed on May 25, 2003.

Smallest color television screen MicroEmissive Displays Ltd., Edinburgh, UK, has developed a tiny color television/video screen that measures just 0.15 × 0.11 in. (3.84 × 2.88 mm). The ME1602, which can be linked to video cameras, DVD players, and VCRs, has a resolution of 160 × 120 pixels. It works using organic light-emitting diode technology.

Largest computer touch screen Mega-mate, the largest computer touch screen in the world, was developed and built by Displaymate Touchscreens Ltd. (UK). Measuring 3.28 × 9.84 ft. (1 × 3 m), with an area of 32.29 ft.^{2} (3 m^2), it was specially commissioned by BRC Imagination Arts

HIGHEST RESOLUTION DIGITAL CAMERA The world's highest resolution digital camera is MegaCam, with a resolution of 320 million pixels. It is an astronomical camera used on the 11-ft. 9.6-in. (3.6-m) Canada-France-Hawaii telescope on the summit of Mauna Kea, Hawaii, U.S.A. (shown here). The camera was integrated with the telescope on June 28, 2002.

for Volkswagen's corporate identity center in Dresden, Germany, and delivered in November 2001.

Lightest document scanner The Docupen is the lightest A4 document scanner, weighing a mere 1.75 oz. (49.6 g). It was released by Planon System Solutions, Inc., Mississauga, Canada, in 2003.

Oldest computer mouse The computer mouse was invented in 1964 by Douglas Engelbart (U.S.A.), who was awarded a U.S. patent for it in 1970. It was described in the patent as an "X-Y position indicator for a display system" and was nicknamed a mouse because of the resemblance of the wire to a tail.

Highest-jumping robot Sandia National Laboratories (U.S.A.) has developed experimental "hopper" robots that use combustion-driven pistons to jump to heights of 30 ft. (9 m). The small robots have potential applications in planetary exploration, where several hoppers could be released by a lander to survey the surrounding landscape.

First business computer LEO I (Lyons Electronic Office) was the first ever business computer. It began operations in November 1951 at the Lyons headquarters, London, UK. The first of its many business applications was the valuation of the weekly output of bread and cakes from Lyons' bakeries. LEO I was supplemented by the more advanced LEO II in May 1957, but continued operations into the 1960s.

First stored-program computer The world's first stored-program computer was the Manchester University Mark I, which incorporated the Williams storage cathode ray tube (patented December 11, 1946). It ran its first program, written by Tom Kilburn (UK), for 52 minutes on June 21, 1948.

Earliest microprocessor The first microprocessor was the 4004 chip, designed and built by Intel (U.S.A.). The first one was completed in January

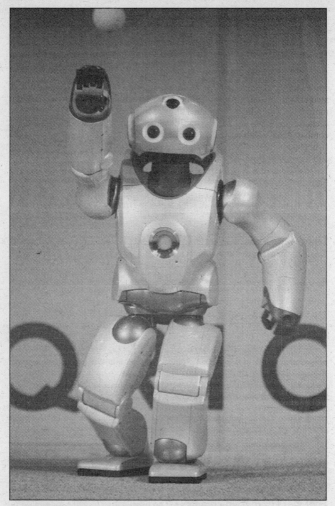

FASTEST RUNNING HUMANOID ROBOT QRIO, which stands for "Quest for Curiosity," is Sony Corporation's latest advanced humanoid autonomous robot (pictured). It is the world's first bipedal robot capable of running (i.e. capable of moving while both legs are off the ground at the same time). QRIO is capable of running at 9 in./sec. (23 cm/sec.). The robot measures 23 in. (58 cm) high and was revealed in September 2003.

1971. The size of a thumbnail, this first single-processor CPU had the same power as ENIAC (electronic numerical integrator and computer), the room-sized first electronic computer. The 4004 chip had 2,300 transistors and could perform around 100,000 instructions per second.

Most sophisticated battlefield simulator The most sophisticated battlefield computer simulator is the Combined Arms Tactical Trainer. Situated at Warminster, UK, and Sennelager, Germany, it is capable of training more than 850 military personnel at once in an integrated, realistic combat scenario involving vehicles, aircraft, soldiers, and commanders. Simulated combat arenas of more than 3,800 miles^2 (10,000 km^2) are used. It was constructed for the UK's Ministry of Defence by Lockheed Martin (U.S.A.), and became operational on September 1, 2002.

Fastest computer The NEC Earth Simulator at the Yokohama Institute for Earth Sciences, Japan, is capable of 35.6 trillion calculations per sec-

SMALLEST HARD DRIVE The disk of the smallest hard drive measures just 0.85 in. (2.16 cm) across (seen here). It was created by Toshiba (Japan) and announced at the International Consumer Electronics Show in Las Vegas, Nevada, U.S.A., in January 2004.
    The smallest commercially available hard drives contain a disk just 1 in. (2.5 cm) across. Of the models available in February 2004, the highest capacity is 2.2 gigabytes and is manufactured by GS Magicstor, Inc. (China).

ond—roughly five times the speed of the previous record holder. Built by HNSX Supercomputers, a division of NEC, the computer is designed to simulate Earth's complex climate in order to predict climate change and global warming, which will have severe consequences for Japan.

First computer virus The first computer program to replicate itself surreptitiously (i.e. a virus) was demonstrated by Fred Cohen, a student at the Massachusetts Institute of Technology, U.S.A., on November 11, 1983.

Most powerful quantum computer Whereas normal computers use a string of zeroes and ones (bits) to represent data, experimental quantum computers use qubits, which can be a zero, one, or simultaneously both. On December 20, 2001, IBM's Almaden Research Center, San Jose, California, U.S.A., announced that they had used a seven-qubit quantum computer to calculate the factors of the number 15.

The computer used a billion billion molecules that have seven nuclear spins for the calculation. Consisting of the nuclei of five atoms of fluorine and two of carbon, these molecules are able to interact with each other as qubits.

WEAPONS & ARMOR

Largest gun In the siege of Sevastopol, USSR (now Ukraine), in July 1942, the Germans used a gun with an 31.4-in. (80-cm) caliber and a 94-ft. 5-in.-long (28.87-m) barrel. Built by Krupp (Germany), its remains were discovered near Metzenhof, Germany, in August 1945. When fully assembled, the gun measured 141 ft. (42.9 m) in length and weighed 2,963,000 lb. (1,344 tons).

Largest cannonball The largest cannonball has a diameter of 36 in. (91 cm) and weighs over 2,204 lb. (1 ton) when filled with its charge of 400 lb. (180 kg) of gunpowder. It belongs to the Mallet mortar gun, which was designed by Robert Mallet (Ireland) and completed in March 1857. It is currently on display at the Royal Armouries, Fort Nelson, Hampshire, UK. Mallet's mortar required 35 kg (77 lb.) of powder to fire such a projectile to reach its range of 2.4 km (1.5 miles) and to bury the charge to a depth of 9.1 m (30 ft.) in soft earth, something that would cause the effect of a small earthquake and ultimately lead to the collapse of structures.

Tallest suit of armor The tallest suit of armor currently on display measures 6 ft. 8 in. (2.06 m) high. It was traditionally said to have been worn by England's John of Gaunt, Duke of Lancaster in the 14th century, but is actually German in origin and dated to around 1535. It is on display in The White Tower at the Tower of London, London, UK.

Earliest tank The No. 1 Lincoln built by William Foster & Co. Ltd. (UK), and modified to become Little Willie, first ran on September 6, 1915. Tanks first saw action with the Heavy Section, Machine Gun Corps (later the Tank Corps) at the Battle of Flers-Courcelette, France, on September 15, 1916. The Mark I "Male" tank, armed with a pair of 6-pounder guns and four machine guns, weighed 62,610 lb. (28.4 tons) and was powered by a 105-hp (78-kW) motor, giving a top road speed of 3–4 mph (4.8–6.4 km/h).

Fastest tank A production standard S 2000 Scorpion Peacekeeper tank (complete with appliqué hull armor, ballistic skirts, K10000 replaceable rubber pad track, and powered by an RS 2133 high-speed diesel engine) developed by Repaircraft plc (UK) achieved a speed of 51.10 mph (82.23 km/h) at the QinetiQ vehicle test track, Chertsey, UK, on March 26, 2002. The speed is an average of two consecutive runs in opposite directions.

Heaviest tank The heaviest tank ever was the German Panzerkampfwagen Maus II, which, at 423,280 lb. (192 tons), weighed as much as 130 modern sedans. By 1945, it had only reached the experimental stage and was

OLDEST DATED CANNON The Dardanelles Gun, cast in Turkey in 1464 for Sultan Mehmet II, is made from bronze, weighs 37,000 lb. (16.8 tons), and measures 17 ft. (5.2 m) long. It had a range of 5,250 ft. (1,600 m) when firing a 23.5-in.-diameter (600-mm), 670-lb. (304-kg) projectile. The date is engraved on the cannon, which is displayed at the Royal Armouries, Fort Nelson, Hampshire, UK.

abandoned. The heaviest operational tank used by any army was the 165,780-lb. (75.2-ton) 13-man French Char de Rupture 2C bis of 1922. It carried a 6.1-in. (15.5-cm) howitzer and was powered by two 250-hp (186-kW) engines giving a maximum speed of 7.5 mph (12 km/h).

Most heavily armed tank The Russian T-64, T-72, T-80, and T-90 tanks are all equipped with a 4.9-in. (12.5-cm) gun-missile system. The American Sheridan light tank mounts a 6-in. (15.2-cm) weapon that is a gun and a missile launcher combined, but this is not a long-barreled, high-velocity gun of the conventional type. The British Armoured Vehicle Royal Engineers (AVRE) Centurion had a 6.5-in. (16.5-cm) low-velocity demolition gun.

Most intelligent handgun The O'Dwyer Variable Lethality Law Enforcement (VLe) prototype pistol, made by Metal Storm Limited (Australia), has no moving parts: instead, projectiles are fired electronically by a built-in computer processor. The gun can only be fired by someone wearing an authorized transponder ring. The VLe has no magazine—the bullets are stacked behind one another in the barrel, and the handgrip—where the magazine would be on a conventional pistol—contains the electronic control systems. Capable of firing up to three shots in quick succession (within 1/500th of a second), the computer-controlled

LARGEST SUIT OF ANIMAL ARMOR A suit of armor designed for an adult Asian elephant (pictured) was made in the late 16th or early 17th century in northern India during the Mughul Empire. It weighs 260 lb. (118 kg) and, although part of the suit is missing, it is estimated that when complete with its original 8,439 individual metal plates, it would have weighed 350 lb. (159 kg). The suit is currently on display at the Royal Armouries Museum in Leeds, UK. It is thought to be the only one of its kind in existence.

MOST ACCURATE BOMB The U.S.-built Joint Direct Attack Munition (JDAM, pictured), in operation since 1997, is accurate to approximately 6 ft. 6 in. (2 m). JDAM is a steerable tail-kit attached to existing "dumb bombs." After release, the JDAM's location is continually checked by fixes from satellites.

firing also allows the pistol to fire at a rate equivalent to 60,000 rounds per minute.

Earliest use of infrared equipment in battle Infrared technology was first used in battle during World War II. Electric sniperscopes mounted on top of rifles converted the infrared light from enemy soldiers into visible light, enabling the shooter to fire accurately in darkness.

Earliest successful test of a high-powered microwave weapon A successful test for a high-powered microwave (HPM) weapon on electronic equipment occurred in April 1999 under the observation of the Joint Command and Control Warfare Center of San Antonio, Texas, U.S.A. HPMs are designed to bring maximum disruption to any military or civilian power system by discharging a powerful energy pulse that destroys any electronics within its 980-ft. (300-m) range.

Country with the most land mines or unexploded ordnance deployed The Egyptian Government has estimated that 19.7 million mines or unexploded ordnance (UXO) existed in Egypt as of November 2002. Most of the mines in Egypt were planted during World War II. According to the International Campaign to Ban Landmines there are between 85 and 125 million mines buried in countries around the world. In addition, over 200 million are stockpiled.

Most widely used firearm The most widely used firearm is the Automatic Kalashnikov 1947 (AK-47). During the Cold War, the former USSR supplied AK-47s to anti-Western insurgents, and the rifle therefore became a symbol of left-wing revolution. Between 50 and 80 million copies and variations of the AK-47 have been produced globally.

Earliest use of smallpox as a biological weapon During the French and Indian Wars of 1754–1767, British soldiers fighting in North America at that time distributed blankets contaminated with smallpox among the American Indians. Epidemics followed, killing more than 50% of the affected tribes.

Largest radar installation The largest of the three radar installations in the U.S. Ballistic Missile Early Warning System (BMEWS) is near Thule, Kalaallit Nunaat, Greenland, 931 miles (1,498 km) from the North Pole. Completed in 1960, it cost $500 million.

Earliest use of a graphite bomb A graphite bomb (G-bomb) was first used in 1991 when Allied forces used it to disable 85% of Iraq's power supplies during the Gulf War. G-bombs work by exploding a cloud of thousands of ultrafine carbon-fiber wires over electrical installations, short-circuiting electrical systems.

Largest non-nuclear conventional weapon in existence The Massive Ordnance Air Blast (MOAB), a precision-guided weapon, weighs 21,500 lb. (9,752 kg). It was first tested by the U.S. Air Force at the Eglin Air Force Armament Center, Florida, U.S.A., on March 11, 2003.

AIR & SEA WARFARE

Fastest warship The 78-ft. (23.7-m-long), 220,000-lb. (100-ton) U.S. Navy test surface-effect ship *SES-100B* attained a world record 91.9 knots (170 km/h or 105 mph) on January 25, 1980 at the Chesapeake Bay Test Range, Maryland, U.S.A. Similar to hovercraft, surface-effect ships travel on a cushion of air, but also have two sharp rigid hulls that remain in the water. Large fans under the ship create air pressure that is then trapped between the hulls, raising the ship.

Largest modern naval battle The largest purely naval battle of modern times was the World War I Battle of Jutland on May 31, 1916, in which 151 British Royal Navy warships faced 101 German warships. The Royal Navy lost 14 ships and 6,097 men, and the German fleet 11 ships and 2,545 men.

Largest amphibious ship The U.S. Navy's Wasp-class vessels have a full-load displacement of 80.5 million lb. (36,500 tons) and a length of 844 ft. (257 m). Capable of carrying aircraft, large numbers of troops, and various landing vessels, their primary role is to land troops on enemy shores. The ships also have 600-bed hospitals (the largest on any ship except for dedicated hospital ships). There are seven Wasp-class ships currently in service.

Largest warships The warships with the largest full-load displacement are the Nimitz-class U.S. Navy aircraft carriers USS *Nimitz, Dwight D. Eisenhower, Carl Vinson, Theodore Roosevelt, Abraham Lincoln, George Washington, John C. Stennis, Harry S. Truman,* and *Ronald Reagan,* the last five of which displace approximately 217 million lb. (98,550 tons). They are 1,092 ft. (333 m) long, have an 4.49-acre (1.82-hectare) flight deck, and are driven by four nuclear-powered 260,000-shp (194,000-kW) geared steam turbines. They can reach speeds in excess of 30 knots (56 km/h or 34.5 mph).

Largest stealth ship The largest ship incorporating stealth technology is the Swedish Visby-class corvette, which is approximately 236 ft. (72 m) long and has a displacement of 1.32 million lb. (600 tons). Developed by the Kockums shipyard (Sweden), the carbon-fiber vessel is lighter than a con-

LARGEST BATTLESHIPS IN ACTIVE SERVICE SINCE THE END OF WORLD WAR II The battleships USS *Iowa* (pictured), *New Jersey, Missouri,* and *Wisconsin* are each 887 ft. (270 m) long and have full-load displacements in excess of 90 million lb. (41,000 tons). All were commissioned during World War II and were in active service at various times until the early 1990s. Each ship is armed with nine 16-in. (40.64-cm) guns capable of firing 2,700-lb. (1,225-kg) projectiles a distance of 23 miles (39 km), and, when operational, had a crew complement of around 1,900.

ventional ship of its size, and features the large flat surfaces used in aircraft to provide low radar visibility. The Visby prototype made its maiden voyage in December 2001.

Longest military runway The runway at Edwards Air Force Base on the west side of Rogers dry lake-bed at Muroc, California, U.S.A., is 7.41 miles (11.92 km) in length.

Largest air force ever The United States Army Air Corps (now the U.S. Air Force) had 79,908 aircraft in July 1944 and 2,411,294 personnel in March 1944.

Fastest combat jet The fastest combat jet is the Russian Mikoyan MiG-25 fighter (NATO code name "Foxbat"). The "Foxbat-B" has been tracked by radar at about Mach 3.2 (3.2 times the speed of sound—3,395 km/h, or 2,110 mph). The MiG-25 was designed as a high-altitude interceptor and it can take off and climb to an altitude of 114,000 ft. (35,000 m) in a little over four minutes.

Most widely deployed military unmanned aircraft By early 2004, the "Predator" unmanned aerial vehicle (UAV) manufactured by General Atomics Aeronautical Systems (U.S.A.) had logged more than 65,000 flight hours, of which more than half were in combat areas such as Kosovo, Iraq,

EARLIEST STEALTH SHIP The U.S. Navy *Sea Shadow* (seen here) was completed in the mid-1980s but only revealed to the public in 1993.
  The bizarre looking twin-hulled ship is 164 ft. (49.98 m) long, 68 ft. (20.7 m) across, and has a full-load displacement of 1.25 million lb. (569 tons). Built by Lockheed Martin, it has a crew of 10 and a top speed of 41.5 mph (18.5 km/h).

and Afghanistan. The 100th example of the aircraft, which has a wingspan of 48.7 ft. (14.84 m) and a flight endurance time of over 40 hours, was delivered to the U.S. military in February 2004.

Longest range air attacks Seven B-52G "Stratofortress" bombers left Barksdale Air Force Base, Louisiana, U.S.A., on January 16, 1991 to deliver air-launched cruise missiles against targets in Iraq after the start of the first Gulf War. Each flew 14,000 miles (22,500 km), refueling four times in flight, with the round-trip mission lasting some 35 hours.

Heaviest bomber in service The Russian Tupolev Tu-160 "Blackjack" bomber has a maximum take-off weight of 606,270 lb. (275 tons) and a maximum speed of about Mach 2.05 (roughly 2,200 km/h or 1,350 mph). Although a Boeing 747 has a higher maximum take-off weight of 877,200 lb. (397 tons), the "Blackjack" is considerably smaller and, crucially, flies more than 2.5 times as fast.

Fastest operational bomber The U.S. variable-geometry or "swing-wing" General Dynamics FB-111A has a maximum speed of Mach 2.5. The Russian swing-wing Tupolev Tu-22M, which is known to NATO as "Backfire," has an estimated over-target speed of Mach 2 but could be as fast as Mach 2.5. Mach 2.5 is roughly equivalent to 1,650 mph (2,655 km/h).

Largest ever bomber wingspan The American 10-engined Convair B 36J "Peacemaker" had a 230-ft. (70.1-m) wingspan. The aircraft, which had a maximum take-off weight of 410,000 lb. (185 tons), was replaced in the 1950s by the Boeing B-52. The "Peacemaker" had a top speed of 435 mph (700 km/h).

Most produced fighter of World War II Over 36,000 Ilyushin Il-2 "Sturmovik" ground-attack aircraft are said to have been produced in Russia before, during, and immediately after World War II, making it the most produced aircraft of that conflict and one of the most numerous combat aircraft ever.

Fastest World War II propeller fighter The German Dornier DO-335 was unique in having a tractive (pulling) propeller in its nose and a propulsive (pushing) motor behind its cockpit. It had a maximum sustained speed of 413 mph (665 km/h), increasing to 477 mph (765 km/h) with emergency boost. Two models existed—A-1 and A-6—the latter a two-seater night fighter. Only 28 were completed before the end of World War II.

Top scoring air ace in World War II The highest officially attributed figure of aircraft shot down by any airman was 352 by Major Erich Hartmann (Germany). In one sortie on the Russian front on November 6, 1943 he shot down a record 13 planes in 17 minutes. His last mission was on

NAVY WITH THE MOST AIRCRAFT The U.S. Navy has over 4,000 aircraft in service. It operates about 20 different types of fixed-wing aircraft, including carrier-based F-14 Tomcat, and F/A-18 Hornet (pictured) fighters, and various reconnaissance, transport, anti-submarine, and airborne command-post aircraft. It also operates six different types of helicopters and the unique new V-22 "Osprey" tilt rotor aircraft.

May 8, 1945, when he shot down a YAK-7 fighter and later landed his plane to surrender to the British forces. He was handed over to the Russians who tried him for war crimes. He was sent to a work camp for 10 years.

ART & MEDIA

ART & INSTALLATIONS

Largest apple mosaic An apple mosaic unveiled on September 29, 2001 at Kivik, Österleden, Sweden, consisted of 25,000 apples. Entitled *Applecheek,* it measured 1,119 ft.² (104 m²) and was designed by Emma Karp Laggar and Jan Laggar (both Sweden). Each apple was nailed to a board by a team of eight people to form an abstract image of Earth. Approximately 5,000 lb. (2.26 tons) of 12 different apple varieties were used.

Largest photograph mosaic Unveiled in Novena Square, Singapore, on July 12, 2003, the world's largest photo mosaic, entitled *Smile Singapore!,* measured 20 ft. 6 in. × 50 ft. (6.24 × 15.24 m) and contained 16,800 individual photographs to create a giant map of Singapore. The mosaic was organized by the Heartware Network, and each photo represented a minimum $10 donation to charity.

Largest ball mosaic A mosaic containing 11,430 toy balls forming the image of a boy measured 37 × 15 ft. (11.2 × 4.5 m) and had a 100-ft. (30.48-m) circumference. It was created by Danny O'Connor (U.S.A.) and was installed from June 2001 to April 2002 in the Massachusetts Museum of Contemporary Art in North Adams, Massachusetts, U.S.A.

LARGEST CARDBOARD-BOX SCULPTURE A cardboard-box sculpture of a red Ford Gran Torino car (pictured) that measured 88.1 ft. (26.86 m) long, 23 ft. (7.02 m) high, and 7.4 ft. (2.26 m) wide was created to promote Empire Interactive's PS2 game of the 1970s TV show *Starsky & Hutch.* Completed on June 20, 2003, it was unveiled in Spitalfields Market, London, UK, by designers from Wreck Age Productions (UK). The sculpture was made by 34 people in just over four days using 4,855 boxes and 286 rolls of tape.

LARGEST NUDE PHOTO SHOOT On June 8, 2003, 7,000 volunteers (seen here) collectively posed in the nude on a street in Barcelona (Spain) for photographer Spencer Tunick (U.S.A.).

Largest balloon mosaic A mosaic depicting the Chicago skyline was made from 70,884 balloons and measured 58 × 86 ft. (17.6 × 26.21 m). It was created by delegates to the International Balloon Arts Convention on March 8, 1999 in the lobby of the Hyatt Regency O'Hare, Rosemont, Illinois, U.S.A.

Largest paper flower mosaic The largest mosaic made of paper flowers measured 2,496 ft.^{2} (231.8 m^2) and was assembled at East Point City, Tseung Kwan O, Hong Kong, China, on October 28, 2001.

Largest flower mural A flower mural that incorporated 770,000 fresh dahlias measured 20,117 ft.^{2} (1,868.94 m^2) when it was created on August 7, 2001. It was made by 1,250 people who represented 16 neighborhoods from the Dahlia Record Committee in Lemelerveld, The Netherlands. The flowers were glued on 900 individual panels, which were then all placed next to each other in a large square to make one continuous image.

Largest model made from canned food On December 24, 1998, an 8-ft. 6-in.-tall (2.58-m) Christmas tree made from 9,773 cans of food was displayed at the Hanford Mall, Hanford, California, U.S.A. The tree had an overall volume of 179.3 ft.^{3} (5.07 m^3).

Oldest paintings The world's oldest reliably dated paintings were found on the walls of the Chauvet cave in southern France in 1994. The paintings range from 23,000 to 32,000 years old.

LARGEST INFLATABLE SCULPTURE An inflatable sculpture entitled
Blockhead **is 114 ft. 9.6 in. (35 m) tall and was created by artist Paul**
McCarthy (U.S.A.) for display in front of the Tate Modern gallery,
London, UK, from May 19 until October 2003. *Blockhead* **is loosely**
based on the character Pinocchio.

Largest painting A painting of the sea that measured 92,419 ft.² (8,586 m²) was completed by I.D. Culture at The Arena, Amsterdam, The Netherlands, to mark the venue's opening on August 14, 1996. The size of the painting is equivalent to nearly four football fields.

Largest finger painting A finger painting measuring 5,100 ft.² (473.8 m²) was completed on July 22, 2003. Its creation was led by artists Jignesh Patel and Munir Rehman (both India) on behalf of the people of Surrey Central, British Columbia, Canada.

Largest handprint painting A 2,251.8-ft.² (209.2-m²) handprint painting was created on November 15, 2002 by 2,541 students organized by the Star Givers of Jeddah, Saudi Arabia. The image, created in honor of Queen Elizabeth II's Golden Jubilee, depicted the monarch's state coach pulled by horses and accompanied by yeoman wardens.

Longest painting The longest acrylic painting on one continuous canvas measured 6,600 ft. (2,011.68 m) on January 14, 2002 at Celestial Court, Toronto, Ontario, Canada, and was created by artist Danny Fong (Canada). The painting, entitled *Thousand Horses,* depicts more than 1,500 horses in different seasons, weather, and backgrounds.

Largest outdoor mural The Pueblo Levee Project in Pueblo, Colorado, U.S.A., has produced the largest mural in the world at 178,200 ft.² (16,554.8 m²). The connected murals are almost 2 miles (3.21 km) long and 58 ft. (17.67 m) tall.

Longest drawing A drawing that measured 9,251 ft. (2,820 m) was created by approximately 2,000 children in Batenburg Square, Sofia, Bulgaria, on June 1, 2003 as part of Children's Day. The theme of the artwork was "My World."

Largest painting by numbers The largest painting by numbers measures 4,068 ft.² (378 m²) and was created at the Island Festival, Dockyard Island, Budapest, Hungary, on July 28, 2003.

Artwork with the most artists The 48-ft.-long (14.63-m), 8-ft.-high (2.43-m) painting *A Little Dab of Texas,* designed by Jim Campbell (U.S.A.), was painted by 25,297 people. It was completed on June 14, 1998 after 3 years 7 months. The finished painting was unveiled on September 5, 1998 and exhibited in Washington, D.C., U.S.A., later that year.

Largest pencil drawing by one artist The largest pencil drawing by one artist, entitled *One World, One Song,* has an overall surface area of 2,002 ft.² (185.99 m²) and was completed by art teacher T. J. Johnson (U.S.A.) on August 2, 2002.

Largest photographic exhibition A total of 16,609 photographs were displayed by Kodak Greece in the grounds of their head office in Athens on

June 17, 2003. The photos had been sent in by Greeks around the world, who had been asked to submit a smiling photo to welcome the return of the Olympic Games in 2004.

Largest matchstick model Joseph Sciberras (Malta) constructed an exact scaled-down replica of St. Publius Parish Church, Floriana, Malta. It consisted of over three million matchsticks and measured 6 ft. 7 in. × 6 ft. 7 in. × 4 ft. 11 in. (2 × 2 × 1.5 m).

Largest single gallery space The Guggenheim Museum in Bilbao, Spain, which opened on October 18, 1997, has 450 ft. (137.16 m) of gallery space.

Most valuable piece of Art Nouveau A standard lamp in the form of three lotus blossoms by the Daum Brothers and Louis Majorelle (all France) sold for $1.78 million at Sotheby's, New York, U.S.A., on December 2, 1989.

FASHION & BEAUTY

Largest Hawaiian shirt In March 1999, Hilo Hattie (U.S.A.), a retailer of Hawaiian fashions from Honolulu, Hawaii, U.S.A., created an aloha shirt with a chest measurement of 14 ft. (4.26 m), a waist measurement of 11 ft. 6 in. (3.5 m), and a neck measurement of 5 ft. 0.5 in. (1.53 m).

Largest sweater An ecru-colored cable-stitch sweater made by the company Malhas Carjor of Palmeira, Portugal, on December 15, 1998 had a chest measurement of 7 ft. 2 in. (2.2 m), a body length of 7 ft. 11 in. (2.43 m), and a sleeve length of 6 ft. (1.85 m). Made from 70% acrylic and 30% wool, it was a scaled-up version of their Trintona design.

Largest pair of socks A pair of nylon socks measuring 45 in. (1.14 m) from top to toe and 10 in. (25 cm) wide was constructed by Michael Roy Layne (U.S.A.) in October 1986 and hung outside City Hall, Boston, U.S.A., to celebrate the Red Sox winning the American League Championship and playing in the World Series.

Longest scarf knitted by an individual Ray Ettinger (U.S.A.) knitted a continuous scarf that measured 3,523 ft. (1,073.8 m) long and 7 in. (17.7 cm) wide on May 8, 2001.

Longest zipper The world's longest zipper was laid around the center of Sneek, The Netherlands, on September 5, 1989. The brass zipper, made by Yoshida Ltd. (Netherlands), is 9,353 ft. 8 in. (2,851 m) long and consists of 2,565,900 metal teeth.

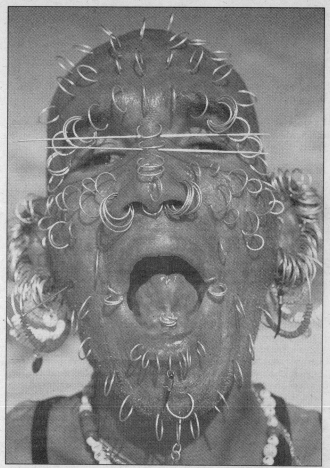

MOST PIERCED MAN Luis Antonio Agüero (Cuba, seen here) sports 230 piercings on his body and head. His face alone carries more than 175 rings. The most pierced woman is Elaine Davidson (UK). From January 1997 to May 2003 she had 1,500 piercings made over her body. Of these, 192 are on her ears, forehead, eyebrows, chin, nose, and tongue.

Largest underpants The world's largest pair of cotton underwear measured 31 ft. 4 in. (9.54 m) wide and 16 ft. (4.9 m) tall. It was created by the Exeter Council for Voluntary Service and unveiled on June 7, 2003 at the Exeter County Rugby Ground, Devon, UK.

MOST LEGS WAXED IN AN HOUR Beautician Laura Mitchell (UK) hot-waxed 22 pairs of legs (16 men, 6 women) in one hour at the Globe Inn pub, Aberdeen, UK, on May 2, 2002. The legs were fully stripped from the knee to the ankle, on the front, back, and sides.

Most scissors used for cutting hair Bruce Choy (U.S.A.) successfully styled a head of hair using eight pairs of scissors in one hand, controlling each pair independently. The record was set at his salon, Flyingshears, in San Francisco, California, U.S.A., on March 11, 2002.

Largest sandal The largest sandal in the world measures 12 ft. 10.8 in. (3.93 m) long, 4 ft. 9.6 in. (1.46 m) wide, and 6 ft. 3 in. (1.9 m) high, and was constructed by Pearl Shoes in front of the Milli Shoes showroom, Lahore, Pakistan, in April 2002.

Most valuable piece of jewelry The most valuable piece of jewelry is a pair of 58.6-karat and 61-karat diamond drop earrings bought and sold anonymously for $7.2 million at Sotheby's, Geneva, Switzerland, on November 14, 1980 as part of the Magnificent Jewels auction.

Most valuable jacket A jacket that once belonged to rock legend Jimi Hendrix (U.S.A.) sold to the Hard Rock Cafe chain for £35,000 ($49,185) at a sale organized by Sotheby's in the London branch of the Hard Rock Cafe (UK) on September 19, 2000.

Most body piercings by surgical needles Brent Moffat (Canada) inserted 700 18-gauge (0.47-in.-long or 1.2-cm) surgical needles into his body in 7 hr. 19 min. at Metamorphosis Custom Piercing and Tattoo, Winnipeg, Manitoba, Canada, on January 15, 2003.

Most body piercings in one session Kam Ma (UK) received a total of 600 new piercings to his body without the aid of an anesthetic. All piercings were executed by Charlie Wilson (UK) in one continuous session that lasted from 9:15 a.m. to 5:47 p.m. at Sunderland Body Art, Sunderland, Tyne and Wear, UK, on May 26, 2002.

Most rhinestones on body Body artist Maria Rosa Pons Abad (Spain) adorned a model's body with 30,361 rhinestones on the set of *El Show de los Récords,* Madrid, Spain, on November 22, 2001.

Most tattooed man Both Tom Leppard (UK) and Lucky Rich (UK) have approximately 99.9% of their bodies covered in tattoos. Tom, who resides on the Isle of Skye, Scotland, UK, has opted for a leopard print design, with all the skin between the dark spots tattooed saffron yellow. Lucky Rich has had his existing tattoos blacked over, with a white design tattooed on top.

LARGEST HANDBAG In April 2003, a handbag measuring 12 ft. 1 in. tall, 11 ft. 7 in. wide, and 5 ft. 3 in. deep (3.7 × 3.54 × 1.6 m) made by the leather accessories company Santa Marinella (Brazil) was unveiled in the Shopping Center, Iquatemi, Brazil. It is an exact replica of the original and made from synthetic leather (stamped lined PVC) with natural cow leather trim. The giant handbag (shown here) was used to store canned goods for charity.

Most tattooed woman The world's most decorated woman is strip artiste Krystyne Kolorful (Canada). Tattoos cover 95% of her body and took 10 years to complete.

Fastest "sheep to suit" The fastest time to manufacture a three-piece woolen suit, from shearing the sheep to sewing the finished article, is 1 hr. 2 min. 36 sec., achieved by members of FH Monchengladbach, Germany, on January 28, 1999. The record was broadcast on *Guinness—Die Show Der Rekorde* on January 30, 1999.

Largest traveling wardrobe For her 14-month debut on London's West End stage in *Mame,* Ginger Rogers (U.S.A.) arrived in England in 1969 with 118 pieces of luggage. Wisely, she came by ship.

Highest annual earnings by a supermodel According to *Forbes* magazine, Gisele Bundchen (Brazil) took in $12.8 million from June 2002 to June 2003, thanks to deals with Victoria's Secret, Christian Dior, and Dolce & Gabbana.

SMALLEST WAIST ON A LIVING PERSON Cathie Jung (U.S.A., pictured), who stands 5 ft. 8 in. (1.72 m) tall, has a tiny 15-in. (38.1-cm) waist. Cathie and husband Bob, an orthopedic surgeon, worked together to develop her tiny waist as part of their enthusiasm for Victorian dress. The 38-year-old mother of three started wearing a six-inch-wide training belt to gradually reduce her waist. Cathie does not eat a special diet or exercise to maintain her waist.

Longest distance covered on a catwalk by a male model From September 19 to 21, 1983, Eddie Warke walked a total distance of 83.1 miles (133.7 km) on a catwalk at Parkes Hotel, Dublin, Republic of Ireland.

Most designers represented at one fashion show A total of 89 different fashion designers from around the world were represented at Paris Fashion Week, France, in 1999. The event as a whole, which averaged 11 catwalk shows per day, outstrips all other international fashion showings and attracts the biggest following.

Highest hairstyle Ladies' hairstyles literally reached their high point in the 1770s. Queen Marie Antoinette's (France) hair was the tallest documented hairstyle. It stood at 36 in. (91.44 cm) high in 1775, and was decorated with a mass of ribbons and feathers that made it even higher.

Fastest haircut Trevor Mitchell (UK) cut a full head of hair in 1 min. 13 sec. on November 26, 1999 at the Southampton City Guildhall, UK, as part of BBC TV South's "Children in Need" appeal. The event was seen live on BBC TV.

Most valuable item of head wear The Alaskan State Museum bought a native North American Tlingit Kiksadi ceremonial frog helmet dating from ca. 1600 for $66,000 at an auction in New York City, U.S.A., in November 1981.

MOVIES

Fastest $100 million box office gross Two films have surpassed the $100-million mark in three days. The first was *Spider-Man* (U.S.A., 2002), which opened on May 3, 2002 at 3,615 theaters, followed by *The Matrix Reloaded* (U.S.A., 2003), which opened on May 5, 2003 at 3,603 theaters.

Fastest $200 million box office gross From its May 3, 2002 opening, *Spider-Man* (U.S.A., 2002) passed the $200-million mark in ten days, taking $223.04 million by May 12 and beating the previous record of 13 days set by *Star Wars: Episode 1—The Phantom Menace* (U.S.A., 1999).

Largest box office loss MGM's *Cutthroat Island* (U.S.A., 1995), starring Geena Davis and directed by her then-husband Renny Harlin (both U.S.A.), cost over $100 million to produce, promote, and distribute, and reportedly earned back just $11 million—11% of the cost.

Highest box office gross James Cameron's (U.S.A.) *Titanic* (U.S.A., 1997) was the first film to take $1 billion at the international box office, and had a total box office gross of $1.835 billion.

HIGHEST BOX OFFICE GROSS ON AN OPENING DAY *The Matrix Reloaded* (U.S.A., 2003) took a record $42.5 million on its opening day in the U.S.A. on May 15, 2003 from a total of 3,603 theaters. Keanu Reeves (U.S.A., pictured) stars as Neo in the *Matrix* trilogy.

Highest box office gross (inflation adjusted) Rising theater ticket prices mean the all-time top-grossing movies are nearly all recent releases. Although *Gone with the Wind* (U.S.A., 1939) took $393.4 million at the international box office, in an inflation-adjusted list it comes top with a total gross of $3,785 billion. In the U.S.A. alone, *Gone With The Wind* had 283.1 million admissions compared with 130.9 million for *Titanic*.

Most expensive film made Paramount's *Titanic* (U.S.A., 1997), which overran its budget during production, cost just over $200 million to make. Originally given a $125-million budget, it was due to have been released in July 1997, but postproduction problems set the date back to December 1997, a delay that added to the cost.

Largest pre-production budget for a film The war epic *Pearl Harbor* (U.S.A., 2001), which began shooting on April 3, 2000, had a pre-production budget of $145 million. The eventual total cost was $152.75 million.

Least expensive feature film made The total cost of production for the film *Die Alive* (Canada, 2000), produced and directed by Jean-François Leduc (Canada), was CAN$563.62 ($378.82). It premiered on July 26, 2001 at the Fantasi Film Festival, Montrèal, Canada.

Most prolific film producer Since 1963, D. Rama Naidu (India) has produced a total of 110 films during his career in Indian cinema.

Living actor with most screen credits Actor Christopher Lee (UK) has the most screen credits of any actor alive today, with 211. He has performed in English, French, Canadian, German, Russian, Norwegian, Swedish, Italian, Pakistani, Spanish, Japanese, American, Australian, and New Zealand productions, from *Corridor of Mirrors* (UK, 1947) to *Graduation Day* (U.S.A., 2003).

Actress with most leading film roles in a career Kinuyo Tanaka (Japan) made her debut role in *Genroku Onna* (Japan, 1924) and performed in a total of 241 films including her final role in *Daichi no Komoriuta* (Japan, 1974).

Actor with most leading film roles in a career John Wayne (U.S.A., born Marion Michael Morrison) appeared in 153 movies from *The Drop Kick* (U.S.A., 1927) to *The Shootist* (U.S.A., 1976). In all but 11 of these he played the lead.

Most film roles in a career Tom London (U.S.A.) made the first of his 2,000-plus screen performances in *The Great Train Robbery* (U.S.A., 1903) as the locomotive driver (his job in real life). By 1919, he had starring roles at Universal. His last role was in *The Lone Texan* (U.S.A., 1959).

Most Hollywood film performances in the same role William Boyd (U.S.A.) played the cowboy Hopalong

FAMILY WITH MOST STARS ON THE HOLLYWOOD WALK OF FAME When Drew Barrymore (U.S.A., pictured) received her star on the Hollywood Walk of Fame on February 4, 2004, she became the seventh member of her family to be so honored.

Stars had previously been awarded to her father John D. Barrymore, her great-uncle Lionel Barrymore, her great-aunt Ethel Barrymore, her grandparents John Barrymore and Dolores Costello, and her great-grandfather Maurice Costello.

FASTEST $1 BILLION BOX OFFICE GROSS *The Lord of the Rings: The Return of the King* (NZ/U.S.A. 2003), the final installment of the trilogy, took $1 billion at the international box office in just nine weeks four days from its release on December 17, 2003. It marks only the second film in history to break the billion-dollar barrier, the first being *Titanic* (U.S.A., 1997), which took the same amount in 11 weeks. The film, starring Orlando Bloom (UK, pictured) as Legolas, had accumulated a worldwide total of $1,005,380,412 in ticket sales by February 23, 2004.

Cassidy in Paramount's 66 *Hopalong* full-length features beginning with *Hopalong Cassidy* (U.S.A., 1935) and ending with *Strange Gamble* (U.S.A., 1948).

Most stars on the Hollywood Walk of Fame Gene Autry (U.S.A.), the actor, composer, and songwriter, has five stars on the Hollywood Walk of Fame strip—numbers 6,384, 6,520, 6,644, 6,667, and 7,000 Hollywood Boulevard—awarded for Recording, Motion Pictures, Television, Radio, and Theater.

Youngest No. 1 box office star Shirley Temple (U.S.A., b. April 23, 1928) was seven years old when she became No. 1 at the box office in 1935, holding the title until 1938.

Oldest No. 1 box office star Marie Dressler (Canada, 1868–1934) was 64 when she became the No. 1 box office star in 1933. Born Leila von Koerber in 1869, she began her film career in 1914 and won the Best Actress Oscar for playing the part of Min Divot in *Min and Bill* (U.S.A., 1930).

Highest annual earnings by an actor The world's top-earning actor is currently Will Smith (U.S.A.), who earned an estimated $60 million in 2002, according to the 2003 *Forbes* Celebrity 100 list.

Highest annual earnings by an actress The world's top-earning actress is currently Jennifer Aniston (U.S.A.), who earned an estimated $35 million in 2002, according to the 2003 *Forbes* Celebrity 100 list.

Actor in most films grossing over $100 million at the box office Harrison Ford (U.S.A.) has starred in a total of 15 movies that have grossed over $100 million at the international box office. The highest grossing was *Star Wars* (1997) with $798 million. Ford also holds the record for highest box office gross for an actor: his 27 films to date have grossed $3,369,662,963.

Actress in most films grossing over $100 million at the box office By February 2004, the actress Julia Roberts (U.S.A.) had starred in 11 movies that have grossed at least $100 million at the international box office. Her top-grossing film was *Pretty Woman* (U.S.A., 1990), which took a total of $463.4 million. Roberts' movies have grossed a record for an actress of $2,516,318,527.

Highest-paid actor per film Bruce Willis (U.S.A.) received a total of $100 million for playing the part of Dr. Malcolm Crowe in the $55-million film *The Sixth Sense* (U.S.A., 1999) through a combination of his salary and a percentage of the film's receipts.

Highest annual earnings by a film producer Producer-director Steven Spielberg (U.S.A.) topped the 2003 *Forbes* Celebrity 100 list, having earned an estimated $200 million during 2002.

AT THE MOVIES

Earliest public screening of a talkie The earliest public presentation of sound on film was *The Arsonist* (Germany/U.S.A., 1922), a short drama made using the Tri-Ergon process and shown at the Alhambra theater,

EARLIEST FEATURE-LENGTH TALKIE Alan Crossland's (U.S.A.) *The Jazz Singer* (U.S.A., 1927) premiered on Broadway on October 6, 1927. Warner Bros. intended the sound to be confined to music and songs, but Al Jolson (pictured with May McAvoy, both U.S.A.) ad-libbed some speech, which led to 354 words being spoken in all: 340 by Jolson; 13 by Eugenie Besserer (U.S.A.), who played his mother; and one ("Stop!") by Warner Oland (Sweden), who played his father.

Berlin, Germany, on September 17, 1922. It starred Erwin Baron (U.S.A.), who played seven of the nine parts.

Oldest theater chain The Wehrenberg Theatres chain first set up in 1906 with the opening of the Cherokee Theatre in St. Louis, Missouri, U.S.A., by former blacksmith Fred Wehrenberg (U.S.A.). Still run by the Wehrenberg family today, it currently operates 15 theaters in the states of Missouri and Illinois.

Largest theater chain Regal Entertainment Group, which includes Regal Cinemas, United Artists Theaters, and Edwards Theaters, operates 562 theaters with 6,119 screens (including two Imax screens) in 39 states of the U.S.A.

First circular theater The world's first circular theater is located in the European Park of the Moving Image at Futuroscope near Poitiers, France. It consists of nine projectors and nine screens covering a total surface area of 2,928 ft.^{2} (272 m^2). The process enables the projection of nine electronically synchronized films offering a 360° field of vision.

Largest drive-in theater by screens The Thunderbird Drive-in (also known as the Swap Shop Drive-in), Fort Lauderdale, Florida, U.S.A., which opened with a single screen on November 22, 1963, now has 13 screens of varying sizes, the largest (screen 9) being the original.

Largest drive-in theater screen ever The Algiers Drive-in, Detroit, Michigan, U.S.A., has a screen that measured 216 ft. (65.8 m) wide and covered 4,800 ft.^{2} (445.9 m^2). It first opened on August 15, 1956 to show the western *The Searchers* (U.S.A., 1956). The drive-in originally had a capacity of 1,200, which increased to 1,500 in 1977, but in 1985 the site was sold and is now a shopping center.

Smallest drive-in theater Both the Harmony Drive-in of Harmony, Pennsylvania, U.S.A., and the Highway 78 Drive-in of Bamberg, South Carolina, U.S.A., could hold no more than 50 cars.

Largest permanent theater screen The Panasonic IMAX Theatre at Darling Harbour, Sydney, Australia, holds the largest fixed projection screen in the world, measuring 117 × 97 ft. (35.72 × 29.57 m). It opened in September 1996 and can seat 540 people.

Smallest purpose-built theater in operation Cinema dei Piccoli was

built by Alfredo Annibali (Italy) in 1934 in the park of Villa Borghese, Rome, Italy, and today covers an area of 769.83 ft.^{2} (71.52 m^2). Originally called the Topolino Cinema (after the Italian name for Mickey Mouse), the theater used a Pathé-

LARGEST ANNUAL FILM OUTPUT India produces more feature-length films than any other country. A record 948 films were produced in 1990, and in 1994, 754 films were produced in a record 16 languages at India's three major centers of production—Mumbai (Bombay), Calcutta, and Madras.

Baby 9.5-mm projector and bed sheets for the screen, and played 78 rpm records for background music. Restored in 1991, the cinema has 63 seats, a 16-ft. 4.8-in. × 8-ft. 2.4-in. (5 × 2.5-m) screen, stereo sound, and air-conditioning.

Smallest theater by seat capacity Converted from an old workshop, the smallest theater in the world to operate as a regular commercial venture is The Screen Room on Broad Street, Nottingham, UK, which has 21 seats. The theater, owned by Steven Metcalf (UK), opened on September 27, 2002 with the film *Lost in La Mancha* (U.S.A./UK, 2002).

Largest audience to attend a film premiere A total of 23,930 people attended the premiere of *Brewster McCloud* (U.S.A., 1970) at the Houston Astrodome, Texas, U.S.A., on December 5, 1970. Paying from $2.50 to $50 per seat, the audience watched the film from a special 70-mm print made for the premiere at a cost of $12,000, which was projected onto a 156 × 60-ft. (47.54 × 18.28-m) screen.

Longest red carpet at a film premiere For the premiere of *Pirates of the Caribbean: Curse of the Black Pearl* (U.S.A., 2003), held at Disneyland, Anaheim, California, U.S.A., on June 28, 2003, a red carpet stretched 900 ft. (274 m) from Disneyland's entrance along Main Street U.S.A. to the Rivers of America in Frontierland.

Longest nonstop theater show A total of 136 feature films were shown consecutively during a 250-hour marathon at the 100 Years of Cinema Festival, Montreal, Canada, from June 11 to 22, 1992.

Movie watching marathon An audience of 11 people—Erik Acosta, Dina Agrapides, Eric Bailey, Kim Binal, Wayne Diana, Mark Huang, Cheryl Jones, Daniel Koenig, Ron Mathewson, Allan Press, and Nathan Snook—watched 34 films for 66 hr. 30 min. at an event organized by online DVD rental company Netflix.com at the Times Square Studios, New York City, U.S.A., from December 5 to 8, 2003.

Longest film documentary *Grandmother Martha* (1996), a documentary about the life of ex-actress and entertainer Martha Stelloo (Netherlands), runs for 24 hr. 12 min. The film was written, produced, and directed by Sydney Ling (Netherlands).

Widest theater screen A temporary screen was used at the 1937 Paris Exposition to show Henri Chrétien's (France) hypergonar films, which were the precursor of cinerama. The concave screen had a width of 297 ft. (90.5 m) and was 33 ft. (9.9 m) high.

Country with the most theaters per capita Belarus has more theaters per capita than any other country in the world, with one theater for every 2,734 inhabitants. In all, the country has 3,780 theaters for its population of 10,335,382.

WIDEST FILM RELEASE IN A SINGLE COUNTRY *X2* (U.S.A., 2003) was given the widest film release of any film in history when it opened in the U.S.A. at 3,741 theaters on May 2, 2003. Showing on 7,316 screens, it took $85.6 million during the opening weekend, an average of $22,871 per theater. Famke Jannsen (Netherlands) and Halle Berry (U.S.A., both seen here) were two of the movie's stars.

Highest annual theater attendance The largest theater audience ever in one year was 4.49 billion admissions, achieved in the U.S.A. in 1929.

Highest annual theater attendance per capita With a population of 279,384 and a total of 1,531,000 admissions at 46 theaters in 2003, Iceland has a greater theater attendance per capita than any other country. This figure translates as 5,480 visits per 1,000 people per year.

Lowest annual theater attendance per capita Malaysia has a population of 22,662,365 and had a total of 336,000 theater admissions in 2003. This figure translates as 14.83 visits per 1,000 people per year.

Longest first run of a film in one theater *Romance in Lushan* (China, 1980) first opened at the Jiangxi Movie Circulation and Screening Company, Lushan, China, on July 12, 1980 and has been shown four times a day since then. As of December 8, 2001, the film had been seen by 1,336,638 patrons.

OSCAR NIGHT

Longest Oscar-winning career Katharine Hepburn (U.S.A.) had the distinction of having the longest Oscar award-winning career, spanning 48 years 13 days from her first Oscar for *Morning Glory* (U.S.A., 1932) on March 16, 1934 to her last for *On Golden Pond* (U.S.A., 1981) on March 29, 1982.

Most Oscars for acting won by a film Both *A Streetcar Named Desire* (U.S.A., 1951) and *Network* (U.S.A., 1976) won three acting Oscars, in 1952 and 1977 respectively. No film has yet won all four acting Oscars.

Most Best Actor wins Seven actors have won Best Actor awards twice: Spencer Tracy (U.S.A.) for *Captains Courageous* (U.S.A., 1937) and *Boys Town* (U.S.A., 1938); Fredric March (U.S.A.) for *Dr. Jekyll and Mr. Hyde* (U.S.A., 1932) and *The Best Years of Our Lives* (U.S.A., 1946); Gary Cooper (U.S.A.) for *Sergeant York* (U.S.A., 1941) and *High Noon* (U.S.A., 1952); Marlon Brando (U.S.A.) for *On the Waterfront* (U.S.A., 1954) and *The Godfather* (U.S.A., 1972); Jack Nicholson (U.S.A.) for *One Flew Over the Cuckoo's Nest* (U.S.A., 1975) and *As Good As It Gets* (U.S.A., 1997);

MOST OSCARS WON BY A FILM At the 2004 American Academy Awards ceremony held on February 29, 2004, the third installment of the *The Lord of the Rings* trilogy, *The Return of the King* (NZ/U.S.A., 2003), won all 11 of its nominations. The film, directed by Peter Jackson, walked away with Best Picture, Best Director, Art Direction, Costume Design, Visual Effects, Sound, Editing, Makeup, Screenplay Based on Material Previously Produced or Published, Original Score, and Original Song. Pictured from left to right are Frances Walsh, Peter Jackson, and Philippa Boyens (all New Zealand) picking up their Oscars for Best Screenplay.

    The Return of the King shares this record of 11 Oscar wins with two other films. The first to achieve the record was *Ben-Hur* (U.S.A., 1959), which won 11 Oscars from 12 nominations on April 4, 1960, followed by *Titanic* (U.S.A., 1997) from 14 nominations on March 23, 1998.

Dustin Hoffman (U.S.A.) for *Kramer vs. Kramer* (U.S.A., 1979) and *Rain Man* (U.S.A., 1988); and Tom Hanks (U.S.A.) for *Philadelphia* (U.S.A., 1993) and *Forrest Gump* (U.S.A., 1994).

Most Best Actor nominations for the same film On March 5, 1936, Clark Gable (U.S.A.), Charles Laughton (UK), and Franchot Tone (U.S.A.) were all nominated for Best Actor for their performances in *Mutiny on the Bounty* (U.S.A., 1935). The winner was the fourth nominee, Victor McLaglen (UK), for *The Informer* (U.S.A., 1935).

Most Best Actress nominations in the same year At the 1929/30 Academy Awards held on November 5, 1930, of the five actresses nominated for Best Actress in a Leading Role, two were nominated twice: Greta Garbo (Sweden) for *Anna Christie* (U.S.A., 1930) and *Romance* (U.S.A., 1930) and Norma Shearer (Canada) for *Their Own Desire* (U.S.A., 1929) and *The Divorcee* (U.S.A., 1930).

Oldest Best Actor winner Henry Fonda (U.S.A., 1905–82) won the Best Actor Oscar on March 29, 1982 for his performance as Norman Thayer Jr. in *On Golden Pond* (U.S.A., 1981) aged 75 years 317 days.

Oldest Best Actress winner Jessica Tandy (UK, 1909–94) won the Best Actress Oscar for *Driving Miss Daisy* (U.S.A., 1989) on March 29, 1990 at the age of 80 years 295 days.

Oldest Best Supporting Actor winner The oldest recipient of the Best Supporting Actor award is George Burns (U.S.A., 1896–1996) for his role as Al Lewis in *The Sunshine Boys* (U.S.A., 1975) on March 29, 1976, when he was aged 80 years 68 days.

Most Best Director wins John Ford (U.S.A.) won an Oscar for Best Director on four occasions: for *The Informer* (U.S.A., 1936), *The Grapes of Wrath* (U.S.A., 1940), *How Green Was My Valley* (U.S.A., 1941), and *The Quiet Man* (U.S.A., 1952).

Oldest actress nominated for an Oscar Eva LeGallienne (UK, 1899–1991) was aged 82 years 80 days when she was nominated for the Best Supporting Actress Oscar for her role as Grandma Pearl in *Resurrection* (U.S.A., 1980) for the ceremony held on March 31, 1981.

Oldest actor nominated for an Oscar Richard Farnsworth (U.S.A., 1920–2000) was aged 79 years 207 days when the Academy nominated him Best Actor for his role as Alvin Straight in *The Straight Story* (U.S.A., 1999) at the ceremony held on March 26, 2000.

GWR TALKS TO
Keisha Castle-Hughes

Keisha Castle-Hughes (New Zealand) was 13 years 309 days old when she was nominated for Best Actress on January 27, 2004 for her role of Paikea "Pai" Apirana in *Whale Rider* (NZ/Germany, 2002). She is the youngest person to receive a Best Actress nomination.

How did you get into acting—was it something you always wanted to do? Yes. However, I didn't think it would happen quite so soon! I hadn't done anything prior to this, not even a school play! A casting director, Diana Rowan, came to my school and asked me to come to a series of workshops and auditions. It went from there.

What aspects of your acting experience have you enjoyed? We were about halfway through shooting when it suddenly dawned on me that I was really going to be in a film—that I was actually living my dream!

The director, Niki Caro, was great to work with. She helped me so much, especially to understand Pai.

I've also traveled extensively for publicity and promotion—to Canada, the U.S.A., Australia, the UK, and Japan, and I'll also visit Greece, Spain, and China.

What's your favorite movie to watch? Typically teen—I love *Bring it On.*

Who are your favorite movie stars? Julia Roberts and Johnny Depp.

What's it like being famous suddenly? I haven't let this experience change my life too much. I just like to do normal kid stuff. I hang out with my friends. We talk about fashion, boys, music, clothes, and just general "girl stuff." School is also very important to me. It's always good to get back into it, but I find I really need to be focused.

Do you get recognized when you are out? I do. I remember thinking about that before the film came out, wondering what it would be like with people staring at you. It's like I thought it would be—weird!

How does it feel to have a Guinness World Record? Incredible! Especially since this was my first acting job!

What advice would you give to anyone who wants to go into acting? If it's what you want to do, go for it! Be sure you have a clear goal in mind and be prepared to work hard. There's a lot of work involved right throughout the whole acting experience.

Oldest recipient of an Oscar by a performer Groucho Marx (U.S.A., 1890–1977) received an Honorary Award in recognition of his brilliant creativity and for the unequaled achievements of the Marx Brothers in the art of motion picture comedy, on April 2, 1974 aged 83 years 182 days.

Youngest Oscar winner The youngest Oscar winner is Tatum O'Neal (U.S.A., b. November 5, 1963), who was 10 years 148 days old when she received the Best Supporting Actress award for *Paper Moon* (U.S.A., 1973) on April 2, 1974.

Shirley Temple was awarded an Honorary Oscar at the age of 6 years 310 days for her achievements in 1934.

Most wins for acting and writing Emma Thompson (UK) won Best Actress in 1993 for her role in *Howards End* (UK/Japan, 1992) and was awarded Best Screenplay Based on Material from Another Medium for *Sense and Sensibility* (U.S.A./UK, 1995) in 1996, making her the first person ever to win Oscars for both acting and writing.

Most Oscar-winning generations The only family to contain three generations of Oscar winners are the Hustons (all U.S.A.). Walter Huston (1884–1950) won Best Supporting Actor for *The Treasure of the Sierra Madre* (U.S.A., 1948). His son John (1906–87) won Best Director for the same film and John's daughter Angelica (b. July 8, 1951) won Best Supporting Actress for *Prizzi's Honor* (U.S.A., 1985).

Most ceremonies presented Bob Hope (U.S.A.) served as master of ceremonies on Oscar night a total of 16 times (alone and in conjunction with others), participating in a record 27 Academy Awards presentations.

Longest speech After receiving the Best Actress award for her title role in *Mrs. Miniver* (U.S.A., 1942) at the 1942 Academy Awards held on March 4, 1943, Greer Garson (UK) made a speech that lasted 5 min. 30 sec.

Most people thanked by an Oscar winner On March 13, 1947, Olivia de Havilland (UK/U.S.A.; b. Japan) won Best Actress as Josephine Norris in *To Each His Own* (U.S.A., 1946). In her speech she thanked 27 people by name.

Longest ceremony The 71st Academy Awards ceremony, hosted by Whoopi Goldberg (U.S.A.) and broadcast by the ABC network, lasted 4 hr. 2 min. on March 21, 1999.

TITLE	NAME	NOMINATED	WON
Actor	Jack Nicholson (U.S.A.)	12	2
Actress	Meryl Streep (U.S.A.)	13	2
Director	William Wyler (U.S.A.)	12	3
Consecutively	Walt Disney (U.S.A.)	9	1
Ever	Walt Disney (U.S.A.)	64	26
Best Foreign Language Film	France	34	12
Foreign Language Film	*Crouching Tiger, Hidden Dragon* (Taipei, 2000)	10	4
Living person	John Williams (U.S.A.)	40	5
Before winning	Randy Newman (U.S.A.)	16	1
Without winning	Roland Anderson (U.S.A.)	15	0
Without winning (actor)	Richard Burton (UK)	7	0
	*Peter O'Toole (UK)	7	0
Without winning (film)	*The Turning Point* (U.S.A., 1977)	11	0
	The Color Purple (U.S.A., 1986)	11	0
One role	Barry Fitzgerald (Ireland)	2	1

*In 2003 he was finally acknowledged with an Honorary Award.

MOVIE PRODUCTION

GWR TALKS TO Vic Armstrong

In a career spanning five decades, Vic Armstrong (UK) has been a stuntman and stunt coordinator in more than 250 films, including the Indiana Jones trilogy. He has also doubled for every actor to have played the title role in the James Bond series. He currently holds the record for the most prolific movie stuntman.

How old were you when you started your career? I got into stunt work when I was 17 years old by lending a stuntman a horse for the movie *Arabesque* (U.S.A., 1966) with Gregory Peck (U.S.A.) and Sophia Loren (Italy). I was then asked to go and ride the horse as there was a big sequence involving lots of big jumps and from that day on all I did was stunt work.

Which film did you enjoy working on the most? My favorite would have to be *Raiders of the Lost Ark* (U.S.A., 1980)—I'm second from left here—but I also have a soft spot for all the James Bond films I've worked on.

What's the scariest stunt you've been involved with? All stunts are scary, but one of the scariest was a 100-ft. (30-m) fall I did on *The Final Conflict* (UK/U.S.A., 1981).

Have you ever been badly injured? I've had my share of injuries—it goes with the territory, as they say. I've broken a leg, shoulder, ribs, nose, arm, collarbone, etc., but even Michael Schumacher crashes his Formula One car occasionally and he is the best in the world at what he does.

What advice would you give? You need to achieve a skill that will make you better than the average person. Mine was riding horses, which came from my days as an amateur steeplechase rider. Then you have to stay cool, calm, and collected and analyze each situation to make sure it's safe and within your capabilities.

How do you feel about your Guinness World Record? I'm very proud: it's a great accolade for me and rates right alongside my Oscar and my BAFTA. I used to read the book when I was a lad: I *never* thought I'd get into it.

What's your favorite Guinness World Record? I'd go for Tony McCoy (UK), who rode the most steeplechase winners ever. As I started off in life dreaming of doing this, I can really relate to his amazing achievement.

Largest film studio The largest film studio complex is at Universal City, Los Angeles, California, U.S.A. The site, called the Back Lot, opened in 1915 and comprises 561 buildings and 34 soundstages totaling 420 acres (170 hectares). Recent films made there by Universal Pictures include *Hulk* (U.S.A., 2003) and *Thunderbirds* (U.S.A., 2004).

Largest indoor film set The UFO landing site built for the climax of Steven Spielberg's *Close Encounters of the Third Kind* (U.S.A., 1977) measured 90 × 450 × 250 ft. (27 × 137 × 76 m). Constructed in a 10 million-ft.^{3}

MOST EDITED SINGLE SEQUENCE IN A MOVIE For the chariot race scene in *Ben-Hur* (U.S.A., 1925, pictured), editor Lloyd Nosler (U.S.A.) had to compress 200,000 ft. (60,960 m) of film into a sparse 750 ft. (228.6 m). With a ratio of 267:1, it is the most edited scene in cinema history.

(283,000-m³) dirigible hangar at Mobile, Alabama, U.S.A., the building had six times the capacity of the largest soundstage in Hollywood.

Largest production crew for a feature film The largest number of craftspeople and technicians employed on a dramatic feature was 532 for the World War I flying story *Sky Bandits* (UK title *Gunbus;* UK, 1986), directed by Zoran Perisic (Yugoslavia) with a cast that included Nicholas Lyndhurst and Adrian Dunbar (both UK).

Largest annual film output by a Hollywood studio The highest output of any Hollywood studio was 101 features made by Paramount in 1921. The highest of the sound era was 68, jointly held by Paramount in 1936 and Warner Bros. in 1937.

Largest land-based prop The 60-ft.-long (18-m), 40-ft.-high (12-m) wooden horse of Troy used in Robert Wise's *Helen of Troy* (U.S.A./Italy, 1954) weighed 179,191 lb. (81,280 kg). It took 30 trees and over 1,000 lb. (453 kg) of nails to build it.

Most retakes for one scene with dialogue It was claimed that Stanley Kubrick (U.S.A.) demanded 127 retakes for a scene with Shelley Duval (U.S.A.) in *The Shining* (U.S.A., 1980).

Longest take in a commercially made film In *A Free Soul* (U.S.A., 1931), there is a 14-minute uninterrupted monologue by Lionel Barrymore (U.S.A.). Since a reel of camera film only lasts ten minutes, the take was achieved by using more than one camera.

Alfred Hitchcock's (UK) *Rope* (U.S.A., 1948) was shot in eight ten-minute takes (apart from one cut to the housekeeper in the first reel). The effect was of one continuous shot, since the action of the story occupied the same time period—80 minutes—as the length of film.

Longest film shot on a single camera *Russkij Kovcheg* (*Russian Ark;* Russia, 2002), directed by Aleksandr Sokurov (Russia), was the first uncompressed high-definition film. It was shot on a single camera for 90 minutes on December 23, 2001. The final film was shown without any cuts or edits on May 22, 2002 at the Cannes Film Festival, France, with a running time of 96 minutes (including title sequence and credits).

Longest monologue in a dramatic film In *L'Aigle à Deux Têtes (The Eagle has Two Heads,* France, 1948) written and directed by Jean Cocteau (France), a 20-minute speech was made by the character Natasha, played by Edwige Feuillère (France).

Most extensive screen test To find the actress to play Scarlett O'Hara in *Gone with the Wind* (U.S.A., 1939), MGM shot 149,000 ft. (45,415 m) of

LARGEST FRAME FORMAT USED IN FILM Imax (seen here) uses 70-mm film, three times larger than the standard 35-mm film usually used. With a dimension of 1.96 × 2.74 in. (5 × 7 cm), the film has 15 perforations per frame as opposed to the standard five.

black-and-white test film and another 13,000 ft. (3,962 m) of color with 60 actresses, none of whom got the part.

Most extensive digital character on film Created by WETA Digital, the computer-generated character Gollum in *The Lord of the Rings: The Two Towers* (NZ/U.S.A., 2002) had 250 facial expressions and 300 moving muscles. Gollum's body movements were based on those of actor Andy Serkis (UK), who filmed every scene in which Gollum appears wearing a unitard body stocking to facilitate the later addition of computer-generated images (CGIs).

Longest video documentary about an individual A documentary on Elvis Presley (U.S.A.) called *The Definitive Elvis Collection* produced by Passport International Productions (U.S.A.) is 13 hr. 52 min. long (including titles). It features over 200 interviews with Elvis's friends, family, fans, and co-stars. Production began in January 2000 and it was released on DVD/VHS on July 16, 2002.

Longest running film series Over 46 years, 103 features were made about the 19th-century martial arts hero Huang Fei-Hong, starting with *The True Story of Huang Fei-Hong* (Hong Kong, 1949) and continuing to the latest production, *Once Upon a Time in China 5* (Hong Kong, 1995).

Longest film ever made *The Cure for Insomnia* (U.S.A., 1987), directed by John Henry Timmis IV, is 85 hours long. It premiered in its entirety at the School of the Art Institute of Chicago, Illinois, U.S.A., from January 31 to February 3, 1987.

Most valuable film costume A blue and white gingham dress worn by Judy Garland (U.S.A.) as Dorothy in the MGM film *The Wizard of Oz* (U.S.A., 1939) was sold at Christie's, London, UK, on December 9, 1999 for £199,500 (then $324,068).

Shortest stuntman Measured on October 20, 2003, stuntman Kiran Shah (UK) stands 4 ft. 1.7 in. (1.263 m) tall. He has performed stunts in 31 movies including being perspective stunt-double for Elijah Wood (U.S.A.) in *The Lord of the Rings* trilogy (NZ/U.S.A., 2001–2003).

ANIMATION

Largest budget for an animation Walt Disney's *Tarzan* (U.S.A., 1999), first released on June 17, 1999, was made with a budget of $150 million. It was the first film to use the "deep canvas" technique, which allows 2-D hand-drawn characters to exist in a 3-D environment.

Most successful virtual band The most successful virtual band is the Gorillaz (UK), with global album sales of 3 million for their eponymous debut, including 1.3 million in the U.S.A. and certified sales of 600,000 in the UK. The release peaked at No. 3 on the UK album chart, went top 20 in the U.S.A., and was No. 1 on the Eurochart. The animated fourpiece were nominated for six BRIT awards and one Grammy in 2001.

Highest box office gross for an animation Walt Disney's *The Lion King* (U.S.A., 1994) took $777.9 million at the box office. The film starred the voices of Rowan Atkinson (UK) as Zazu the hornbill, Jeremy Irons (UK) as Simba's uncle Scar, and Whoopi Goldberg (U.S.A.) as Shenzi the hyena.

Highest box office gross for an animation (inflation adjusted) Walt Disney's first full-length feature film, *Snow White and the Seven*

LONGEST STOP-MOTION FEATURE FILM *Chicken Run* (UK, 2000), directed by Peter Lord and Nick Park (both UK), was released with a running time of 82 minutes and has 118,080 shots filmed using the "stop-motion" special-effects technique. (A normal live-action feature has between 500 and 1,000 shots.)

Chicken Run also holds the record for the most plasticine used in a feature film. Animators used 5,240 lb. (2,380 kg) of plasticine during filming.

Dwarfs (U.S.A., 1937), took $184.9 million at the box office worldwide—equivalent to $1,633,582,523 today.

Fastest $100 million box office gross for an animation *Finding Nemo* (U.S.A., 2003), the computer-animated film from Walt Disney and Pixar Animation Studios, cost $94 million to make and reached the $100 million mark at the U.S. box office in eight days from its release on May 30, 2003 at 3,374 theaters.

Most expensive computer-animated film *Monsters, Inc.* (U.S.A., 2001), from Walt Disney and Pixar Animation Studios, had a budget of $115 million.

Earliest animal cartoon Old Doc Yak, a tailcoated billy goat in striped pants, was brought to the screen by *Chicago Tribune* cartoonist Sidney Smith (U.S.A.) in a Selig Polyscope series started in July 1913. It was Smith's much-loved animal cartoon characters who gave animated films a distinct appeal of their own as suitable entertainment for children.

HIGHEST BOX OFFICE GROSS FOR AN ANIMATION ON AN OPENING WEEKEND *Finding Nemo* (U.S.A., 2003, seen here) directed by Andrew Stanton and Lee Unkrich (both U.S.A.) opened in the U.S.A. on May 30, 2003 to take $70,251,710 at the box office from 3,374 theaters. The tale of a father fish trying to find his son features the voices of Albert Brooks, Ellen DeGeneres, and Willem Dafoe (all U.S.A.).

First feature color cartoon The earliest full-length color cartoon talkie was Argentina's *Peludópolis,* made in 1931 by Quirino Cristiani (Argentina).

Earliest color cartoon series *The Red Head Comedies* (U.S.A., 1923), each a satire of an historical event by the Lee-Bradford Corporation, was the very first cartoon series.

First full-length cartoon The earliest full-length feature cartoon was *El Apóstol* (Argentina, 1917), written and directed by Federico Valle (Argentina), with a running time of 70 minutes. Compiled from 58,000 drawings, it took 12 months to finish.

Earliest cartoon talkie release Dave and Max Fleischer's (both Austria) *Come Take a Trip in my Airship* (U.S.A., 1924) opened with the animated figure of a woman in a white dress chattering as the lead-in to the song.

First all-talking cartoon On September 1, 1928, Paul Terry's (U.S.A.) *Dinner Time* (U.S.A., 1928) was premiered at the Mark Strand Theatre, New York, U.S.A.

Cartoon character most often portrayed on screen Zorro, created by Johnston McCulley (U.S.A.), has been portrayed in a record 69 films. He was also the first comic-strip character to be the subject of a major feature film, *The Mark of Zorro* (U.S.A., 1920).

Most valuable cartoon poster A film poster for a Walt Disney film short, *Alice's Day At Sea* (U.S.A., 1924), depicting Alice astride a fish above the waves, was sold at Christie's, London, UK, in April 1994 for £23,100 (then $34,072).

Earliest cartoon merchandise Pat Sullivan's (U.S.A.) Felix the Cat, who appeared in 1919 as the animal that "kept on walking," was not only the first cartoon character to attain the celebrity of a human star, but was, in 1924, also the first to be an image on packaging. Felix was then merchandized as a phenomenally successful cuddly toy two years later.

Most characters voiced by one artist in a TV cartoon series Kara Tritton (UK) voiced 198 cartoon characters for 75 episodes over six series of *Blues Clues* (Nick Jr., UK). Kara gave voices to furniture (Postbox, Paper Recycling Bin), food (Mr. Salt and Mrs. Pepper), animals (Owl, Hippo), ghosts, planets, and people.

Longest working career for a cartoon voice-over For the first few weeks, the original film series *Popeye* was voiced by William Costello (U.S.A.). Then in 1934, for the film *Let You and Him Fight,* Jack Mercer (U.S.A.) took over the role and voiced the character for the next 45 years and 294 productions, including the TV cartoons.

LONGEST CARTOON SERIES "TALKIE" From 1933 to 1957, Max Fleischer's (Austria) *Popeye the Sailor Man* (right) had 233 one-reelers and a single two-reeler *(Popeye the Sailor Meets Sinbad the Sailor;* U.S.A., 1936) in the cinema. The series was first aired on television in September 1956, making it the longest running syndicated cartoon series.

Most valuable color animation cell One of the 150,000 color cells (a clear plastic sheet onto which animation drawings are traced and then hand painted) from Walt Disney's *Snow White and the Seven Dwarfs* (U.S.A., 1937) was sold by art dealer Guthrie Courvoisier (U.S.A.) in 1991 for $222,525.

Most valuable black-and-white animation cell On May 16, 1989, a black-and-white drawing from Walt Disney's *The Orphan's Benefit* (U.S.A., 1934), depicting Donald Duck being punched by an orphan, raised $286,000 at Christie's, New York, U.S.A.

Fastest script-to-screen animation production KliK Animation in Montreal, Canada, produced and aired a topical one minute animation, entitled *Le JourNul de François Pérusse*, on the same day. It premiered on February 8, 1999 after the 6 P.M. news on the Canadian TVA network.

Longest full-length film made without a camera Frame by frame, artist José Antonio Sistiaga (Spain) painted his 75-minute animated one-man production, *Scope, Color, Muda* (Spain, 1970) directly on to the film stock. It took him 17 months from 1968 to 1970 to complete.

Most Emmy awards won for an animated TV series By September 2003, *The Simpsons* (FOX, U.S.A.) had won a total of 20 Emmy awards: eight for Outstanding Animated Program (one hour or less) in 1990, 1991, 1995, 1997, 1998, 2000, 2001, and 2003; 10 for Outstanding Voice-Over Performance in 1992 (six), 1993, 1998, 2001, and 2003; and two for Outstanding Music and Lyrics in 1997 and 1998.

MAGIC & ILLUSION

Highest viewing figures for a TV magic show Magician Doug Henning (Canada) attracted more than 50 million viewers for the first of his eight *World of Magic* one-hour television specials. The show, directed by Walter C. Miller (U.S.A.), was first transmitted live on NBC in the U.S.A. on December 26, 1975, guest starring Gene Kelly (U.S.A.). Henning performed spellbinding illusions including a re-creation of Harry Houdini's famous water torture cell, as well as close-up magic.

Longest running TV magic show Dick "Mr. Magic" Williams (U.S.A.) hosted 1,200 programs of WMC-TV's *Magicland*, a weekly half-hour magic show that was on air for 23 years from January 1966 to January 1989.

Largest illusion ever staged The largest illusion ever staged was presented by David Copperfield (U.S.A.), who created the illusion of vanishing

HIGHEST ANNUAL EARNINGS BY A MAGICIAN David Copperfield
(U.S.A., pictured) had the highest annual earnings of any magician in
2002 with $55 million according to the 2003 *Forbes* Celebrity 100 list.
The star of TV shows for both ABC and CBS, Copperfield has performed
illusions such as making a jet plane disappear and walking through the
Great Wall of China.

the Statue of Liberty in New York, U.S.A., on his fifth television special,
The Magic of David Copperfield, aired on CBS in 1983. The illusion was invented by Jim Steinmeyer and constructed by John Gaughan (both U.S.A.).

Most copied stage illusion Invented by Robert Harbin (South Africa)
in 1965, the Zig Zag Girl is the most popularly performed stage illusion in
the world. A girl, standing in an upright cabinet, is apparently cut into three
pieces and has the middle of her body pulled to one side. It was copied so
quickly that Harbin published a highly priced book in 1970 (limited to 500
copies) that allowed each purchaser to build one version of the prop. It is estimated that at least 15,000 Zig Zag illusions have been built to date, meaning that 14,500 are unauthorized copies.

Most escapes from handcuffs Nick Janson (UK) has escaped from handcuffs locked on him by more than 1,760 different police officers around the world since 1954.

Lowest Death Dive escape In 1997, Australian Robert Gallup was leg-manacled, handcuffed, chained, put into a secured mailbag, and then locked in a cage with a 8-ft.^{2} (0.74-m^2) floor area before being thrown out of a C-123 transport plane at 18,000 ft. (5,485 m) above the Mojave Desert, California, U.S.A. With less than a minute before impact and traveling at 150 mph (240 km/h), he escaped from the sack and cage to reach his parachute secured on the outside of the cage and deployed it with enough altitude to land safely.

Fastest transformation illusion Internationally renowned illusionists The Pendragons (both U.S.A.) present Houdini's metamorphosis illusion at

OLDEST MAGIC SOCIETY Houdini (Hungary/U.S.A., pictured) was one of the most famous illusionists in history. Nicknamed the King of Handcuffs, he was especially well known as an escape artist. Apart from inventing and performing illusions, he owned a share in the famous Martinka's magic shop in New York City, U.S.A., and he was president of the Society of American Magicians from 1917 until his death in 1926. This is the oldest magic society in the world and was founded in Martinka's on May 10, 1902 with only 24 members.

a speed that would have fooled its inventor. Jonathan Pendragon is locked in a trunk on top of which his wife Charlotte stands. She conceals herself behind a curtain which drops after just 0.25 seconds to reveal her transformation into her husband. She, of course, is now locked in the trunk.

Largest magic society Founded in 1968 in New York, U.S.A., The International Magicians' Society boasts 37,000 members worldwide, including, among others, David Copperfield (U.S.A.).

Earliest presentation of "sawing" a woman in half The first illusionist to seemingly saw a woman in half was its inventor Percy Selbit (UK, b. Percy Tibbles) on January 17, 1921 at the Finsbury Park Empire, London, UK.

Most living creatures produced during a magic performance Penn & Teller (U.S.A.) produced more than 80,000 bees during their television special *Don't Try This At Home* filmed in 1990. In their British TV version of the routine, the bees were replaced with a safer alternative—bluebottle flies.

Longest running theater of magic John Nevil Maskelyne and George Cooke (both UK) founded, produced, and starred in the Maskelyne & Cooke magic theater at the Egyptian Hall, Piccadilly, London, UK, from May 26, 1873 to December 10, 1904. Maskelyne and business partner David Devant (UK) moved the business to St. George's Hall, Langham Place, London, UK, on January 2, 1905 where the daily shows were regularly continued by three generations of the Maskelyne family until October 14, 1933—a span of more than 60 years.

Longest magic show Dr. A. Alexander (India) performed his magic show for 24 hours on February 27–28, 2004 at Renew 2000 Community Centre, St. Antony's Church Complex, Palakkarai, Tiruchirappalli, India, making it the longest by an individual before a paying audience.

Most magical effects in a stage play Directed and adapted by Ken Hill (UK), *The Invisible Man,* which opened in the West End at the Vaudeville Theatre, London, UK, on February 20, 1993, featured a total of 53 different magic effects and illusions.

Youngest magician The Yamagami Brothers (both Japan, Yoshinosuke b. August 11, 1994 and Akinoshin b. December 1, 1995) are the youngest professional illusion artists. Their debut appearance was on April 17, 2001 when they were aged 6 years 229 days and 5 years 128 days respectively.

Most non-magicians taught to present a trick in a single location Magician Luis de Matos (Portugal) taught 52,000 people a simple method to apparently vanish 52,001 silk handkerchiefs simultaneously at the Estádio do Dragão soccer stadium, Porto, Portugal. The effect (not the lesson) was shown live on RTP television on November 16, 2003.

MOST EXPENSIVE MAGIC SHOW EVER STAGED *Siegfried and Roy at the Mirage,* Las Vegas, Nevada, U.S.A., starring the German illusionists Siegfried Fischbacher (left) and Roy Horn (right), cost over $28 million to stage when it opened on February 1, 1990. The show, which featured dozens of wild animals, including an elephant and a giant fire-breathing mechanical dragon, and a cast of 60, closed after its 5,750th performance on October 3, 2003 after Roy was seriously injured by a white tiger called Montacore.

Oldest magic shop The world's oldest family-run magic business is Davenports, founded in 1898 by Lewis Davenport (UK) who opened his shop on London's Ryles Road in 1903 and another on Mile End Road in 1908. The business was inherited by his son George in 1926 and is now run by his granddaughter Betty, who took over in 1961. The shop moved to its current location in The Strand in 1984.

Largest magic convention The Blackpool Magicians' Club convention is held annually at the Opera House and Winter Gardens, Blackpool, Lancashire, UK, on the last weekend in February. First held in 1952, it attracts over 3,000 people from around the world.

Oldest weekly magic magazine *Abracadabra,* first edited by Goodliffe (UK), was first published on February 2, 1946 in Birmingham, UK. Currently edited by Donald Bevan (UK), issue 3,029 was published on February 19, 2004.

Highest selling magic magazine First published in September 1991, *MAGIC: The Magazine for Magicians* is published monthly by Stagewrite Publishing, Inc., Las Vegas, U.S.A., with an international circulation of 9,691.

LANGUAGE & LITERATURE

All-time best-selling book Excluding noncopyright works such as the Bible and the Koran, the world's all-time best-selling book is *Guinness World Records* (formerly *The Guinness Book of Records*). Since it was first published in October 1955, global sales in some 37 languages have exceeded 100 million (by October 2003).

Fastest selling fiction book Released on July 8, 2000, the 3.8 million initial print run of *Harry Potter and the Goblet of Fire,* J.K. Rowling's (UK) fourth Harry Potter book, is the fastest selling book in history. The book broke all sales records with an estimated 3 million copies sold after just 48 hours. (There are currently 27.6 million copies of the first three Harry Potter books in print.)

Longest running comic Since its first edition was published on December 4, 1937, *The Dandy* has been published continuously by DC Thomson & Co. of Dundee, UK. The weekly comic's best known character is Desperate Dan, an unshaven cowboy from a town called Cactusville, whose favorite food is cow pie.

Best-selling cookbook *Betty Crocker's Quick and Easy Cookbook* is the best-selling cookbook of all time with 50 million copies sold since 1950. Betty Crocker of General Mills is one of the most successful corporate trademarks of all time—the name appears on more than 130 General Mills products, sales of which amount to over $500 million a year.

Longest novel Published in 2003, *Knickers* by Simon Roberts (UK) contains a total of 14,156,074 characters (each letter counts as one character and spaces are also counted as one character each).

Longest poem ever published The lengthiest poem ever published is the Kirghiz folk epic *Manas,* which appeared in printed form in 1958 but which has never been translated into English. According to the *Dictionary of Oriental Literatures,* this three-part epic runs to about 500,000 lines. Translated excerpts appear in *The Elek Book of Oriental Verse.*

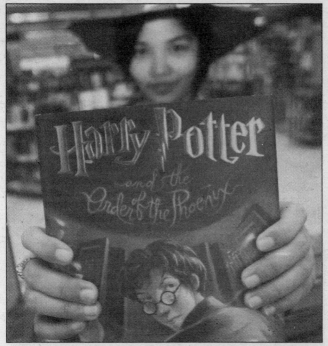

LARGEST FIRST-EDITION PRINT RUN The release of J.K. Rowling's (UK) *Harry Potter and the Order of the Phoenix* (pictured) on June 21, 2003 marked the largest first-edition print run in history, with 8.5 million copies.

Most widely read catalog The IKEA catalog of Swedish flat-packed furniture is the world's most widely read catalog, with 130 million copies printed every year. It is translated into 28 languages and distributed across 36 countries.

Longest kept diary Ernest Loftus (Zimbabwe) kept a daily diary for over 91 years. He began writing on May 4, 1896 at the age of 12 and continued until his death on July 7, 1987, aged 103 years 178 days.

Largest published crossword In July 1982, Robert Turcot (Canada) compiled a crossword comprising 82,951 squares. It contained 12,489 clues across and 13,125 down, and covered 38.21 ft.² (3.55 m²). The first ever crossword was created by journalist Arthur Wynne (UK) and published on December 21, 1913 in the Sunday newspaper *New York World* (U.S.A.). It had the shape of a diamond and contained no internal black squares.

Heaviest ever newspaper The most massive single issue of a newspaper was the Sunday *New York Times* of September 14, 1987, which weighed more than 12 lb. (5.4 kg) and contained 1,612 pages.

Earliest newspaper to achieve a circulation of a million The earliest newspaper to achieve a circulation of 1 million copies was *Le Petit Journal,* published in Paris, France. It reached this figure in 1886.

Biggest sign language mass participation A total of 1,920 children signed simultaneously to perform a song on "World Children's Day at McDonald's 2003." This event took place in Olympian City, Hong Kong, China, on October 5, 2003.

Longest reading-aloud marathon by an individual Adrian Hilton (UK) recited the complete works of Shakespeare in a "Bardathon" lasting 110 hr. 46 min. on the site of the Globe Theatre at the Shakespeare Festival, London, UK, and the Gold Hill Baptist Church, Chalfont St. Peter, Bucks, UK, on July 16–21, 1987.

GREATEST COMIC-READING NATION In Japan, manga comics (pictured) represent 40% of all printed material sold. Thirteen weekly magazines by the largest publishers, together with 10 biweeklies and about 20 monthlies, represent the core of this industry. Throughout the 1990s, yearly sales of manga reached an average of 600 billion yen ($5.5 billion), with roughly 60% spent on magazines and 40% on paperbacks. At any given time, at least 10 of these magazines reach sales of 1 million or more copies per issue. People of all ages read manga yet currently much of the market is targeted at adults.

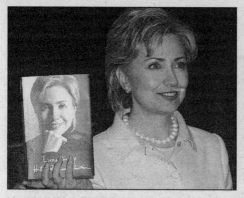

FASTEST SELLING NONFICTION BOOK *Living History,* former first lady Hillary Rodham Clinton's (U.S.A.) memoir of her life with U.S. President Bill Clinton (U.S.A.) and his relationship with the intern Monica Lewinsky (U.S.A.), is the fastest selling nonfiction book in history, shifting 200,000 copies on its first day of sales in the U.S.A. in June 2003.

Greatest living linguist The greatest living linguist is Gregg M. Cox (U.S.A.), who can read and write in 64 languages (speaking 14 fluently) and 11 different dialects.

Most common language The most common first language is Chinese, spoken by more than 1.1 billion people. The "common speech" (Pûtônghuà) is the standard form of Chinese, with a pronunciation based on that of Beijing.

The most widespread as well as the second most spoken language is English, with a conservative estimate of 800 million speakers. Of these, some 310 million are native speakers, mainly in the U.S.A. (about 270 million) and the UK (60 million). The third most spoken language is Spanish.

Longest place-name In its most scholarly transliteration, Krungthep Mahanakhon, the 167-letter official name for Bangkok, the capital of Thailand, has 175 letters. The official short version (without capital letters, which are not used in Thai) consists of 111 letters (6 words): *krungthephphramahanakhon bowonratanakosin mahintharayuthaya mahadilokphiphobnovpharad radchataniburirom udomsantisug.*

Most complex languages The Amele language of Papua New Guinea has the most verb forms, with over 69,000 finite forms and 860 infinitive forms of the verb. Haida, the North American Indian language, has the most prefixes (70), and Tabasaran, a language of southeast Dagestan, uses the most noun cases (48). The Eskimo language used by the Inuit has 63 forms of the present tense, and simple nouns have as many as 252 inflections.

Language with most consonants The language with the largest number of distinct consonantal sounds was that of the Ubykhs in the Caucasus,

LARGEST PUBLISHED BOOK The world's largest published book, entitled *Bhutan,* weighs 133 lb. (60.3 kg), contains 114 full-color pages, and measures 5 ft. high and 7 ft. wide (1.52 m × 2.13 m) when opened. It was devised by teams from MIT (Massachusetts Institute of Technology), Acme Bookbinding, and the Friendly Planet, and unveiled on December 15, 2003 in New York, U.S.A.

with 81. Ubykh speakers migrated from the Caucasus to Turkey in the 19th century, and the last fully competent speaker, Tevfik Esenc, died in Istanbul in October 1992.

Largest postcard In August 1994, two huge postcards measuring 310 ft.² (28.8 m²) were sent by the Canadian National Defence Headquarters to the Canadian headquarters of peacekeeping units, serving in Bosnia and Herzegovina and in Rwanda.

TV SHOWS & PEOPLE

Longest running TV variety show *Sábado Gigante* (Univision Television Network, U.S.A.) has been broadcast every Saturday evening since August 8, 1962. The Spanish-language show was created and has been continually hosted by Mario Kreutzberger (Chile), or "Don Francisco" as he is more popularly known. Each three-hour episode is filmed in front of a live audience.

Largest TV contract In May 2003, Oprah Winfrey (U.S.A.) signed a contract worth $279 million with the American TV station ABC to host *The*

HIGHEST PAID TV ACTRESS PER EPISODE As of April 2004, the highest paid TV actresses per episode were Jennifer Aniston (pictured), Lisa Kudrow, and Courteney Cox Arquette (all U.S.A.), who played the female leads in *Friends* (NBC, U.S.A.) since 1994 and earned approximately $1 million each per episode in the show's final season. Helen Hunt (U.S.A.) also reportedly earned $1 million per episode of *Mad About You* (NBC, U.S.A.) in the 1990s.

HIGHEST PAID TV ACTOR PER EPISODE
The world's highest paid TV actor per episode is Ray Romano (U.S.A., pictured), who earned $1.8 million per episode of *Everybody Loves Raymond* (CBS, U.S.A.) for the eighth season in 2004/05.

Oprah Winfrey Show for an extra two years until 2008. The show is among the highest rated daytime shows, with an average U.S. weekly audience of 26 million.

Longest working career as a TV chef
Eva Vicenta Uranga Roig Vda. de Zarate (Mexico), or "Mrs. Zarate" as she is better known, hosted her first cookery show, *Cocina Al Minuto* (Televisora Tapatia, Mexico), on December 1, 1960. She currently hosts the same show under the name of *Hasta La Cocina* for Televisa Guadalajara Co. in Guadalajara, Jalisco, Mexico. Mrs. Zarate has spent 6,610 hours cooking for TV shows. She was born on July 13, 1920, making her one of the oldest TV hosts in the world.

Longest running TV quiz show *It's Academic* (NBC, U.S.A.) has been on air weekly since October 7, 1961. The show, which features high-school teams competing against each other, was created by Sophie Altman (U.S.A.) and entered its 43rd season in fall 2003.

Longest TV quiz program The longest TV quiz programme began at 8:15 p.m. on August 29, 2003, finishing 52 hr. 45 min. later at 1 a.m. on September 1, 2003. The show was broadcast on 9Live (Germany) and co-hosted by Thomas Schürmann, Anna Heesch, Alida-Nadine Kurras, Robin Bade, and Jörg Draeger (all Germany) from the studio in Ismaning, Germany. Callers phoned in to answer a quiz question and hopefully win a cash prize, which increased with each wrong answer. On this occasion, 2,346 callers phoned in to try to win TK1 million ($1.2 million), answering approximately 1,500 questions.

Longest running TV show *Meet the Press* (NBC, U.S.A.) was first transmitted on November 6, 1947 and has been aired subsequently each week since September 12, 1948.

Longest time in the same role in a TV series Helen Wagner (U.S.A.) has played the character of Nancy Hughes McClosky in *As The World Turns* (CBS, U.S.A.) since it premiered on April 2, 1956. The 12,000th episode was broadcast on May 6, 2003.

Longest working career of a TV director on the same program The weekly sports show *Estadio Uno,* produced by SIFAR SA, Uruguay, and currently broadcast on Channel 5 of Sistema Nacional de Televisión, has been directed continuously by Julio Sánchez Padilla (Uruguay) since it was first aired on July 5, 1970.

Most expensive TV program The world's most expensive TV program, in terms of cost per episode, is *ER* (NBC, U.S.A.). At its peak, in January 1998, the makers, Warner Bros. (U.S.A.), agreed to a three-year deal with NBC for 22 one-hour episodes to be made at a cost of $13.1 million each.

Most prolific TV scriptwriter Since 1942, the output of Ted (later Lord) Willis is estimated to have been 20 million words. From 1949 until his death in 1992, he wrote 41 TV series, including the first seven years and 2.25 million words of *Dixon of Dock Green,* which ran on BBC Television, UK, from 1955 until 1976. He also wrote 37 stage plays and 39 feature films.

Most successful TV soap opera *Dallas* (CBS, U.S.A.) began in 1978 as a miniseries. By 1980, it had been watched by about 83 million people in

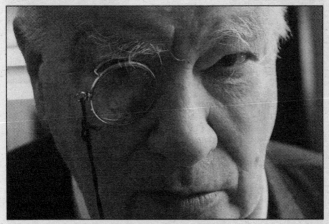

MOST DURABLE TV HOST Patrick Moore (UK, pictured) holds records for both the world's most durable TV host and the longest running TV show with the same host, for his monthly program *The Sky at Night* (BBC, UK), which he has hosted without a break since April 24, 1957. Episode number 614 was aired on February 2, 2004.

HIGHEST PAID TV DRAMA ACTOR PER EPISODE Noah Wyle (U.S.A., pictured) earned approximately $400,000 per episode of *ER* (NBC, U.S.A.) for the 2003/04 season. Wyle plays the character of the head doctor, Dr. John Carter.

the U.S.A., giving it a share of 76% of the television audience—a record at the time. It had also been seen in more than 90 countries, often in locally dubbed versions. After 11 years and 353 episodes, the last episode was broadcast in the U.S.A. on May 3, 1991.

Longest TV talk show marathon The record for the longest TV talk show marathon is 30 hours and is held by both Zoltán Kováry (Hungary) and Vador Lladó (Spain). Kováry continually interviewed guests and hosted from 4 p.m. on February 13, 2003 until 10 p.m. on February 14, 2003 at the Fix.tv studios, Budapest, Hungary; Lladó of Flaix TV did the same from May 3 to 4, 2002 in Barcelona, Spain.

Longest running sports TV program *Scotsport* (Scottish TV, UK) first aired on September 18, 1957 at 10:30 p.m. and is still running. The weekly show is hosted by Jim Delahunt (UK).

Highest fee per minute for an actor in a TV advertisement Nicole Kidman (Australia) reportedly earned $3.71 million for acting in a four-minute commercial for Chanel No. 5 in December 2003. This figure represents $928,800 per minute.

Most Emmy Awards for the same show ever *Sesame Street* (PBS, U.S.A.) has won 91 Emmy Awards. The program premiered on TV in 1969, and features puppet characters the Muppets, designed by Jim Henson (U.S.A.).

Most prolific TV, film, and theater stuntman Since 1968, Roy Alon (UK) has been credited for working on 893 TV, film, and theater productions as either a stunt coordinator, performer or 2nd Unit Director as of February 20, 2004. This total includes 11 theater productions, 36 commercials, 144 feature films (including all the Superman movies and most of the Bond series), and 701 TV shows.

Longest running children's magazine program *Blue Peter* (BBC, UK) was first transmitted from London's Lime Grove Studios on October 16, 1958, and celebrated 45 years on air in October 2003. So far it has had 29 hosts.

Longest running pop show The first edition of *Top of the Pops* (BBC, UK) was presented by DJ Jimmy Savile (UK) on January 1, 1964. The show celebrated its 2,000th edition on September 13, 2002 and its 40th year on air in January 2004.

Most TV variety shows hosted by same host The most live variety TV shows hosted by the same host is 5,000 as of April 5, 2002. Fuji Television Network, Inc.'s *Waratte litomo!* has been hosted by Kazuyoshi Morita (Japan), aka Tamori, since its first episode on October 4, 1982.

Most watched TV network The state-owned station China Central Television (CCTV) is transmitted to 90% of all viewers in China. It is estimated that more than 1.1 billion people have access to television in China.

Earliest television sponsor On June 19, 1946, Gillette sponsored the broadcast of a boxing match between Joe Louis and Billy Conn (both U.S.A.) in New York City, U.S.A.

Earliest color TV transmission On July 3, 1928, John Logie Baird (UK) showed television images of red and blue scarves, a UK policeman's helmet, a man poking his tongue out, the glowing end of a cigarette, and a bunch of roses during a demonstration at his studios in Covent Garden, London, UK.

Earliest underwater TV The first public demonstration of underwater TV occurred on August 26, 1952 at the 19th National Radio and Television

Exhibition, London, UK. Marconi Siebe Gorman showed model divers working on a sunken ship on monitor sets. The cameras used to film the divers weighed 1,984 lb. (900 kg), cost $6,400 (£3,500) and could transmit from depths of 1,492 ft. (455 m).

Deepest live-TV broadcast by a presenter Alastair Fothergill (UK) carried out an underwater broadcast at a depth of 1.5 miles (2.4 km) on *Abyss Live* (BBC, UK). The broadcast was televised on September 29, 2002 from inside a MIR submersible, along the Mid-Atlantic Ridge off the east coast of the U.S.A.

MOST VALUABLE TV COSTUME The Superman suit from the 1955 series *The Adventures of Superman* (seen here) sold for a record $129,800 (£81,307) at the Profiles in History auction, Los Angeles, California, U.S.A., on July 31, 2003. The suit was worn by George Reeves (U.S.A.) in the title role.

LARGEST TV AUDIENCE FOR A SPACE EVENT The first moonwalk
by the *Apollo 11* astronauts was watched on TV by an estimated
600 million people, a fifth of the world's population at the time.
The astronauts, Neil Armstrong, Edwin "Buzz" Aldrin, and
Michael Collins (all U.S.A., pictured), were the stars of a parade
through New York City, U.S.A., to celebrate their achievement on
August 14, 1969.

Earliest public TV commercial On June 27, 1941, the first open public
TV commercial ever was broadcast on NBC's WNBT station in New York,
U.S.A., for a Bulova watch.

Most awards won by a TV commercial The Levi "Drugstore" 501
jeans television commercial won 33 awards in 1995. These included a Lion
D'Or for director Michel Gondry (France) and a Grand Clio Award for the
commercial.

Longest running TV commercial The Discount Tire Company's
"Thank you" advert, produced by Swartwout Productions (U.S.A.), first
aired in 1975. The same commercial has been aired continuously every year
in parts of the U.S.A.

Longest running TV chat show *The Tonight Show* (NBC, U.S.A.) first
aired on September 27, 1954 hosted by Steve Allen (U.S.A.). *The Tonight
Show with Jay Leno* has been hosted by Jay Leno (U.S.A.) since 1992, when
he took over from Johnny Carson (U.S.A.). Carson began hosting the show
in 1962 and moved it to its present location in Hollywood, California,
U.S.A.

LARGEST MUSIC TV NETWORK MTV began broadcasting on August 1, 1981 and is currently transmitted to approximately 340 million households in 140 countries. This means it can be seen by one in three of the world's total TV audience. Britney Spears, Madonna, and Christina Aguilera (all U.S.A., pictured here left to right,) are shown here performing at the 20th Annual MTV Video Music Awards in August 2003.

Longest running TV drama Procter & Gamble Productions' *Guiding Light* (CBS, U.S.A.) was first aired on CBS on June 30, 1952, and is still shown each week day. It was originally broadcast as a radio serial on WLW Radio in 1937, then made the transition to TV in 1952.

Longest running TV forum *Question Time* (BBC, UK) was first broadcast on 25 September 1979 and still runs weekly in the UK. The program allows a TV studio audience and viewers at home to question a panel of top decision-makers about current policies and topics.

GWR TALKS TO Matt Groening

The Simpsons (FOX, U.S.A.), which is now watched in more than 70 countries, had its 326th episode on February 22, 2004. It is the longest running prime-time animated series and had won 20 Emmy Awards as of September 2003, a record for an animated TV series. GWR talks to the creator of this much-loved TV phenomenon, cartoonist Matt Groening (U.S.A.).

Congratulations! What's it like to be an official Guinness World Record holder? It really is an unexpected thrill. I don't care about awards, but to be in the *Guinness World Records* book is really great. It's something I'd never expected, you know, and I'm glad it's a record to be proud of. There are certain records you don't want to have . . . I'm glad I've not been sitting in baked beans!

The show also has a record for its many guest stars. Why are celebs so keen to appear? Firstly, it's the easiest gig in show-business! You can show up in curlers and barefoot, speak into the microphone and be on your merry way. You can literally phone it in—we've done phone hook-ups with some big stars. But it's more fun when we convince the stars to come in. When Mick Jagger was at the FOX studios, people on the show were very excited. That's why we do it—to entertain ourselves! We've had Michael Jackson as a 300-lb. white guy who thought he was Michael Jackson; we've had Elizabeth Taylor doing the voice of Maggie; Paul McCartney, George Harrison, and Ringo Starr.

But of all the people, I think *The Simpsons'* writing team was most excited to have Adam West, the original TV Batman!

What advice do you have for kids who want to work in TV?
My advice to kids who want to work in TV is don't spend all your time watching TV! One of the things about working in TV is that it's like a voracious beast . . . you need to keep filling it with content. So cram your brain full of culture, history, science, and politics, and you'll do very well in TV.

Do you have a favorite episode?
Ah; I like a lot of the very early episodes, particularly ones with Lisa. When Lisa first meets Bleeding Gums Murphy, her saxophone mentor, I was amazed that the show could actually be moving, given how garish the characters were drawn.

You'll need to last 30 years to beat the record for the longest running comedy show on TV. Do you think you can do it?
Aaah, I hope so! I don't see any end

in sight. It doesn't get easier to come up with new stories, but we continue to surprise ourselves. And that's basically our goal—to keep things surprising. It gets harder as the decades roll by. Everybody who likes the show compares the latest episode to their favorite, and it's hard to measure up to the past sometimes. But we're trying!

MUSIC &
ENTERTAINMENT

POP MUSIC

GWR TALKS TO Sir Paul McCartney

Sir Paul McCartney (UK) currently holds 22 Guinness World Records—more than any other person. He holds 16 records as a member of The Beatles (UK), the biggest selling group of all time. He also holds world records in his own right, including the earliest live debut performance of a classical work on the Internet (the 75-minute *Standing Stone* broadcast on November 19, 1997), and the record for the largest paying audience for a rock stadium concert, which he achieved on April 21, 1990 when more than 184,000 fans attended his concert at the Maracanã Stadium, Rio de Janeiro, Brazil.

Were you a fan of *Guinness World Records* as a child? Yes, as kids my friends and I were fans, we had many favorites—tallest, smallest, etc., and we used to dip into it for amazing facts. I never thought I'd get a world record myself!

How did you celebrate your first No. 1? That was "From Me to You," which hit the top of the UK chart back in 1963. It was a long time coming, so we partied a lot.

Did The Beatles expect to set so many records? We certainly didn't realize we were going to get into the record book, though we wanted to, like everyone else. It's an honor for a kid who sat in the pub and hoped to be the tiddlywinks champion of the world to get to our level of success.

Why do you think that sales of The Beatles' albums continue to rise? A lot of the sales are to young people, which is funny because we all

assumed it would be a lot of older people like ourselves on a nostalgia trip. Without being too immodest, I think that the writing was very good and it still holds up.

Are there any other world records that you'd like to have a go at? I'm working on tallest man! My main ambition is just to enjoy life.

What advice would you give to anyone wanting to go into the music industry? Work hard, be true to yourself and love what you do.

MOST WEEKS AT NO. 1 AND NO. 2 ON U.S. SINGLES CHART For eight weeks, from December 20, 2003 to February 7, 2004, hip-hop act OutKast (U.S.A., pictured) had singles at No. 1 and No. 2 on the U.S. singles chart with "Hey Ya!" and "The Way You Move" respectively.

Biggest selling single in the world since UK charts began The biggest selling single sales since UK charts began on November 14, 1952 is Elton John's (UK) "Candle In The Wind 1997"/"Something About The Way You Look Tonight," with worldwide sales of 33 million. By October 20, 1997, it had also reached No. 1 in 22 countries. All Elton John's artist royalties and PolyGram's profits were donated to the Diana, Princess of Wales Memorial Fund.

Biggest selling single by a group "Rock Around The Clock" sold an unaudited 25 million copies. Written by James E. Myers (U.S.A.), aka Jimmy DeKnight, and Max C. Freedman (U.S.A.), it was recorded on April 12, 1954 by Bill Haley and His Comets (U.S.A.).

Most UK singles to debut at No. 1 Westlife (Ireland) had 12 singles debut at No. 1 in the UK chart from May 1, 1999 to November 22, 2003.

Most consecutive No. 1 singles From July 28, 1997 to January 21, 2004, 19 consecutive singles by The KinKi Kids (Japan) debuted at No. 1 on the Japanese chart.

Biggest jump to No. 1 on UK singles chart Irish boy band Westlife's single "Unbreakable" made an unprecedented leap from No. 195 to No. 1 on the UK Top 200 in November 2002.

Biggest first UK chart week for a single Will Young's (UK) debut single "Anything Is Possible"/"Evergreen" sold 1,108,269 copies in its first "chart week"—i.e. its total sales from February 25 to March 2, 2002—including 385,000 on its first day of release. It went on to sell an unprecedented 2 million copies in the UK in 15 weeks.

Biggest selling UK single by a female group "Wannabe" by The Spice Girls (UK), released in July 1996, spent seven weeks at No. 1 in the UK, selling 1.2 million copies. The single hit No. 1 in a further 31 countries.

Most hit singles on UK chart As of April 2004, Elvis Presley (U.S.A.) had scored 135 hit singles on the UK chart.

Longest time spent on UK singles chart The longest time that a single has spent on the UK chart is 124 weeks for "My Way" by Frank Sinatra (U.S.A.), which entered and reentered the chart ten times from April 1969 to April 1994.

Biggest selling album ever *Thriller* by Michael Jackson (U.S.A.) has registered global sales of over 47 million copies to date since 1982.

BIGGEST JUMP TO NO. 1 ON U.S. SINGLES CHART Kelly Clarkson (U.S.A., pictured), winner of *American Idol*, broke a record set in 1964 by The Beatles (UK) when her first single, "A Moment Like This," jumped from No. 53 to No. 1 in October 2002. Its first-week sales of 236,000 were bigger than those for the rest of the Hot 100 combined.

BEST UK SOLO ALBUM CHART START Robbie Williams (UK, pictured) had five successive No. 1s on the UK album chart. The albums, released from September 1997 to November 2002, are: *Life Thru A Lens* (1997), *I've Been Expecting You* (1998), *Sing When You're Winning* (2000), *Swing When You're Winning* (2001), and *Escapology* (2002). From January 1, 2000 to December 31, 2003, he sold 5,608,000 albums in the UK—more than any other UK album act. Robbie has also won a record 14 British Record Industry Trust (BRIT) awards.

Biggest selling album on UK chart Over 4.5 million copies of The Beatles' (UK) *Sgt. Pepper's Lonely Hearts Club Band* are reported to have been sold in the UK since its release in June 1967.

Most albums on U.S. chart simultaneously Three bands—The Beatles (UK), The Monkees (U.S.A.), and U2 (Ireland)—have all had seven albums on the U.S. Top 200 simultaneously.

Best-selling debut album in the U.S.A. *Boston* by Boston (U.S.A.), released in 1976, has sold over 16 million copies.

Most No. 1 albums on U.S. chart by a group The Beatles had 19 U.S. No. 1 albums—more than double the number by Elvis Presley (U.S.A.) and The Rolling Stones (UK), both of whom have had nine No. 1 albums. In all, The Beatles' albums have spent 133 weeks at the top spot.

Biggest all-time sales by a group The all-times sales for The Beatles have been estimated by EMI at more than 1 billion discs and tapes.

Biggest selling teenage artist Before she turned 20 years old on December 2, 2001, Britney Spears (U.S.A.) had global sales of 37 million records.

Most vocal edits on a single recording Brian Transeau (U.S.A.) incorporated a total of 6,178 vocal edits in the production of his track "Simply Being Loved (Somnambulist)," which was released in August 2003. The single spent 11 weeks on the U.S. charts.

ROCK & COUNTRY

Largest paying rock band concert attendance The Molson Canadian Rocks for Toronto concert, which was held on July 30, 2003 at Downsview Park in Toronto, Ontario, Canada, attracted a paying audience of 489,176. The SARS benefit gig raised $7,590,507 from ticket sales.

Largest free rock concert attendance Rod Stewart's (UK) free concert at Copacabana Beach, Rio de Janeiro, Brazil, on New Year's Eve 1994, reportedly attracted an audience of 3.5 million.

Largest simultaneous charity rock concert Live Aid was organized by Bob Geldof (Ireland) and included two concerts, simultaneously held in London, UK, and Philadelphia, Pennsylvania, U.S.A., on July 13, 1985. More than 60 of rock music's biggest acts played for free to an estimated 1.5 billion TV viewers watching throughout the world, raising money for African famine relief. Geldof, then lead singer of the Boomtown Rats, was inspired to organize Live Aid after watching a BBC documentary on starvation in Ethiopia.

BIGGEST SELLING COUNTRY ALBUM BY A GROUP Since its release in 1998, *Wide Open Spaces* by the Dixie Chicks (U.S.A., pictured) has sold 10 million copies.

SHORTEST UK TOP 10 SINGLE The shortest single to chart on the UK Top 10 is Liam Lynch's (U.S.A., pictured) "United States of Whatever," which was 1 min. 26 sec. long and entered the chart on December 7, 2002, peaking at No. 10.

Largest rock star benefit concert A concert held at Wembley Stadium, London, UK, on April 20, 1992 in memory of rock star Freddie Mercury (UK), who died of AIDS, raised $35 million for AIDS charities. It was attended by about 75,000 people and is estimated to have been seen by almost 1 billion people in over 70 countries.

Most concerts performed in 50 days During a tour of the U.S.A., the rock band Jackyl (U.S.A.) played 101 concerts in 50 days, from September 12, to October 31, 1998. Jackyl appeared in a total of 59 cities in 26 states.

Biggest rock earnings from one venue The biggest gross from concerts played at a single venue is $38,684,050 by Bruce Springsteen (U.S.A.) from a series of 10 shows that he performed at Giants Stadium, New Jersey, U.S.A., from July 15 to August 21, 2003. The concerts were seen by a total of 566,560 people.

Highest grossing country music tour Garth Brooks' (U.S.A.) three-year "Sevens" tour, which commenced in March 1997, grossed a total of $105 million. He performed 350 shows in 100 cities with an average attendance of 55,000 people per show.

Most successful male country artist Garth Brooks (U.S.A.) is the most successful country recording artist of all time, with album sales of more than 100 million since 1989. He has also sold more albums than any other solo artist in the U.S.A.

Most successful female country artist Reba McEntire (U.S.A.) is the biggest selling female country vocalist in the U.S.A., with eight multiplatinum albums, 16 platinum albums, and 23 gold albums by February 2004, from a career spanning more than 25 years. She has sold 48 million albums in total.

Most successful country duo Six albums by Brooks & Dunn (Kix Brooks and Ronnie Dunn, both U.S.A.) have sold more than 1 million copies and 17 of their singles have got to No. 1 on the country chart, including "Boot Scootin' Boogie" (1992), "Little Miss Honky Tonk" (1995), and "Husbands and Wives" (1998).

Longest stay at No. 1 by U.S. rock single Canadian band Nickelback's single "Too Bad" held the top spot on the U.S. Mainstream Rock chart for a record-breaking 20 weeks from January to May 2002.

Most simultaneous album entries in a week on U.S. charts Seven different albums by U.S. rock group Pearl Jam entered the U.S. Top 200 chart on March 17, 2001. These were part of a series of 23 albums recorded live at different venues around the U.S.A. This feat broke the group's own record of five entries from a series of 25 simultaneously released live albums from concerts held during their successful European tour in 2000.

Biggest selling album in the U.S.A. by a female solo artist Since its release on November 4, 1997, Canadian country singer Shania Twain's album *Come On Over* has sold a total of 19 million copies in the U.S.A. and 30 million copies worldwide.

Most weeks on U.S. charts for an album by a female artist Patsy Cline's (U.S.A.) *12 Greatest Hits* was still on the U.S. Country catalog album chart in February 2001, 722 weeks after first entering it. The album spent 251 weeks (almost five years) at No. 1 in total.

Most weeks on U.S. Adult Contemporary chart Australian duo Savage Garden's single "I Knew I Loved You" had spent a record 124 weeks on the U.S. Adult Contemporary chart when it exited in February 2002, beating the record of 123 weeks set by another of their recordings, "Truly Madly Deeply."

YOUNGEST PLATINUM ALBUM ACT Billy Gilman (b. May 24, 1988, U.S.A., pictured) was 12 years 68 days old when his debut album *One Voice* was awarded a platinum certificate for achieving 1 million sales in the U.S.A. The album was released on June 20, 2000 and was certified platinum 12 weeks later in August 2000.

Most platinum RIAA albums by a country music artist

Since 1981, George Strait (U.S.A.) has earned 26 Recording Industry Association of America (RIAA) platinum album awards (for sales of over 1 million copies in the U.S.A.)—with 12 of these albums selling more than 2 million copies. His total sales are over 62 million.

Slowest climbing act on U.S. charts Rock group Creed's (U.S.A.) track "Higher" was on the U.S. Hot 100 for a record 36 weeks before it finally climbed into the Top 10 in July 2000.

Longest stay on the UK album chart Fleetwood Mac's (UK/U.S.A.) *Rumours* album, released on February 26, 1977, spent 477 weeks on the UK album chart. It included four singles chart entries, though none of them reached the Top 20.

Youngest female to top UK album charts Canadian singer/songwriter Avril Lavigne topped the UK album chart on January 11, 2003 aged 18 years 106 days. The album, *Let Go,* made No. 1 in its 18th week on the chart.

Longest gap between U.S. chart album hits There was a gap of 28 years between Santana's No. 1 U.S. album *Santana III* of November 1971 and their next No. 1 *Supernatural* of October 1999. The latter gave the group phenomenal worldwide success, selling 21 million copies.

Shortest music video In 1994, U.S. metal band Brutal Truth produced a video 2.18 seconds in length to accompany their track "Collateral Damage." The video features a sequence of flash frames depicting popular conservative American cultural icons of the late 20th century.

Loudest drummer A peak reading of 109.1 decibels was recorded during a show by The Jerome Experience (France) at the Celtic Warriors 10th

Birthday Bash at Woodgreen Animal Shelter, Cambridgeshire, UK, on April 12, 2003. The Jerome Experience is a one-man show featuring drummer Jéróme Dehèdin (France).

R&B & JAZZ

Best-selling rap/hip-hop album in the U.S.A. The best-selling rap/hip-hop album ever in the U.S.A. is *CrazySexyCool* by TLC (U.S.A.), which has achieved sales of 11 million, surpassing MC Hammer's (U.S.A.) *Please Hammer Don't Hurt 'Em* (which has sold 10 million units).

Rap artist with the most U.S. No. 1 albums When *The Black Album* topped the U.S. album charts in November 2003, Jay-Z (aka Shawn Carter, U.S.A.) became the only rap act to have scored six No. 1 albums.

MOST SIMULTANEOUS R&B HITS Rapper 50 Cent (aka Curtis Jackson, U.S.A., seen here) had nine simultaneous entries on the *Billboard* Top R&B/Hip-Hop Singles & Tracks chart on May 10, 2003.

Fastest selling female debut album Ashanti's (aka Ashanti S. Douglas, U.S.A.) eponymous debut album sold 503,000 copies in its first week on release in the U.S.A. in April 2002. In the same week, she became the first female performer to simultaneously hold the top two places on the Hot 100 singles chart with "Foolish" and "What's Luv?" (with Fat Joe).

Biggest UK first-week hip-hop album sales Eminem's (aka Marshall Mathers III, U.S.A.) album *The Eminem Show* sold 315,000 copies in its first week on sale in the UK in June 2002. This gave him his second UK No. 1 album, a feat that no other rap artist has achieved.

Most successful remix album In February 2002, Jennifer Lopez's (U.S.A.) album *J To Tha Lo!: The Remixes* became the first remix album to top the U.S. charts, with sales of over 1 million, including 156,000 in its first week.

Best chart start Rap artist DMX (aka Earl Simmons, U.S.A.) is the only artist whose first five albums have entered the U.S. chart at No. 1. The records are *It's Dark And Hell is Hot* (1998), *Flesh of My Flesh Blood of My Blood* (1999), *. . . And Then There Was X* (2000), *The Great Depression,* (2001) and *Grand Champ* (2003).

Most consecutive weeks at No. 1 on U.S. singles chart "One Sweet Day" by Mariah Carey and Boyz II Men (both U.S.A.) topped the U.S. chart for 16 consecutive weeks in 1995.

Oldest MOBO winner The oldest Music of Black Origin (MOBO) award winner is B. B. King (U.S.A.), who was 73 years old in 1998 when he picked up the Award for Lifetime Achievement.

Longest stay on U.S. Rap singles chart "Hot Boyz" by Missy "Misdemeanor" Elliott (aka Melissa Elliott), featuring Nas, Eve, and Q-Tip (all U.S.A.), spent a record 18 weeks at the top of the U.S. Rap chart in 1999–2000.

Longest U.S. singles chart span Louis Armstrong (U.S.A.) first appeared on a *Billboard* chart on April 6, 1946. His most recent entry to the listings came in 1988, 17 years after his death, with "What a Wonderful World" from the sound track to the film *Good Morning, Vietnam* (U.S.A., 1987). Armstrong also had over 50 hits before the "official" chart started in 1940, his first being "Muskrat Ramble" in 1926, thus taking his span of hits to more than 61 years.

Most consecutive weeks at No. 1 by the same producer Hip-hop producer Irv Gotti (U.S.A.) produced the No. 1 single on the U.S. Hot 100 pop chart for a record 19 successive weeks from February 23 to June 22, 2002. Chief executive officer of Murder Inc. Records, Gotti has worked with artists such as Ja Rule, Jay-Z, Ashanti, DMX, and Fat Joe.

LONGEST SPAN ON U.S. R&B CHART Ray Charles (U.S.A., pictured) has appeared on the U.S. R&B singles chart for seven decades. He first charted as leader of The Maxine Trio with "Confession Blues" in April 1949. His latest entry was in July 2002 with "Mother," a span of 53 years.

Youngest solo rap artist at No. 1 on U.S. Rap and R&B charts In July 2000, Lil' Bow Wow (aka Shad Lamar Moss, U.S.A.) went to No. 1 on the U.S. R&B and Rap charts with "Bounce With Me" (featuring Xscape), aged only 13 years 4 months.

Youngest solo artist at No. 1 on U.S. album chart Stevie Wonder (aka Steveland Morris, b. May 21, 1950, U.S.A.) was 13 years 3 months old when his album *Little Stevie Wonder—The 12 Year Old Genius* topped the U.S. charts in 1963.

Youngest R&B chart entrant Hailie Jade Mathers (b. December 25, 1995, U.S.A.) became the youngest performer, aged 6 years 210 days, to be credited with an R&B hit when "My Dad's Gone Crazy" charted in August 2002. She performed on the track with her father, Eminem (U.S.A.).

Biggest selling rap artist Rap legend 2Pac (aka Tupac Shakur, U.S.A.) has certified U.S. album sales of 36 million, and has now had more hits after his death (at the age of 25 in September 1996) than he did while he was alive. The posthumous hits include three U.S. No. 1 albums, *The Don Killuminati* (1997), *Until The End of Time* (2001), and *Better Dayz* (2002), and an additional 16 U.S. R&B chart singles.

Fastest rap MC Rebel XD (aka Seandale Price, U.S.A.) beat his own record and rapped 683 syllables in 54.501 seconds on the set of *Guinness*

World Records: Primetime in Los Angeles, California, U.S.A., on June 24, 1998.

Fastest selling rap artist Eminem's (U.S.A.) album *The Marshall Mathers LP* sold 1.76 million copies in its first week in the U.S.A. in May 2000.

Highest annual earnings by a rap act Eminem (U.S.A.) and rapper and producer Dr. Dre (aka Andre Young, U.S.A.) earned $35 million in 2002, according to the 2003 *Forbes* Celebrity 100 list.

Largest rap group With 124 members, hip-hop outfit Minority Militia (U.S.A.) is the world's largest rap group. Each member either raps, sings, plays an instrument, or produces on their 2001 album *The People's Army,* released on Low Town Records.

Longest working career by a recording artist Jazz singer Adelaide Hall (U.S.A.) is the most durable recording artist, having released material over eight consecutive decades. Her first record, "Creole Love Call," was recorded with Duke Ellington on October 26, 1927, and her last was made on June 16, 1991, at the Cole Porter Centennial Gala in London, UK.

Most Grammy awards won by a female artist Aretha Franklin (U.S.A.) has won 15 Grammys. She received her first in 1967 for Best Female R&B Vocal Performance with the song "Respect."

MOST WEEKS AT NO. 1 ON U.S. SINGLES CHART BY A GIRL BAND The single "Independent Woman," released by Destiny's Child (U.S.A., pictured) on November 20, 2000, subsequently spent a record 11 weeks at the top of the U.S. singles chart.

Most Grammy awards won by a solo performer Stevie Wonder (U.S.A.) has won 19 Grammy awards. Since 1973, he has won Best Male R&B Vocal Performance six times.

Hit act with the most grandchildren When soul singer Solomon Burke (U.S.A.) entered the U.S. album chart in August 2002 with the Grammy-nominated *Don't Give Up On Me,* he had 65 grandchildren and 10 great-grandchildren.

Earliest jazz record made The first jazz record included "Indiana" and "The Darktown Strutters' Ball" and was released on May 31, 1917. It was recorded for the Columbia label in New York City, U.S.A., in January 1917 by the Original Dixieland Jazz Band, led by Dominic "Nick" James La Rocca (U.S.A.).

CLASSICAL & WORLD MUSIC

Most prolific composer Georg Philipp Telemann (Germany) wrote 12 complete sets of services—one cantata every Sunday—for a year, 78 services for special occasions, 40 operas, 600 to 700 orchestral suites, 44 passions, plus concertos, and other chamber music.

Longest working operatic career Danshi Toyotake (Japan) sang Musume Gidayu (traditional Japanese narrative) for 91 years from the age of seven. Her professional career spanned 81 years.

Longest opera *Die Meistersinger von Nürnberg* by Richard Wagner (Germany) is the longest of commonly performed operas. A normal uncut version, as performed by the Sadler's Wells company (UK) from August 24 to September 19, 1968, entailed 5 hr. 15 min. of music.

Largest orchestra A total of 6,452 musicians from the Vancouver Symphony Orchestra and music students from all over British Columbia, Canada, played "Ten Minutes of Nine"—an arrangement by Frederick Schipizky of the "Ode to Joy" from Beethoven's Ninth Symphony—for 9 min. 44 sec. at B.C. Place Stadium, Vancouver, Canada, on May 5, 2000. It was conducted by Bramwell Tovey (UK).

Largest cello ensemble A total of 1,013 cellists played in the "Concert of 1,000 Cellists" held in Kobe, Japan, on November 29, 1998, conducted by Kazuaki Momiyama (Japan). Nine pieces of music were performed, the longest of which was Bach's Suite in D Major at 8 min. 26 sec.

Largest simultaneous percussion performance A percussive rhythm was played for over six minutes by 10,102 people at an event held at the Hong Kong Coliseum, Hong Kong, China, on July 2, 2002.

LARGEST ANIMAL ORCHESTRA The animal orchestra with the most members is the 12-piece Thai Elephant Orchestra (seen here), which gives concerts at the Thai Elephant Conservation Centre, Lampang, Thailand. The orchestra was founded by Richard Lair and David Soldier (both U.S.A.) in 2000, with the aim of conserving the Asiatic elephant species.

Largest full drum-kit ensemble The largest complete drum-kit ensemble consisted of 264 participants who gathered to play at Tacoma Narrows Airport, Gig Harbor, Washington, U.S.A., on March 29, 2003, under the direction of Gerard Schwarz (U.S.A.), conductor of the Seattle Symphony Orchestra.

Largest drum ensemble The largest drum ensemble consisted of 3,140 participants who gathered to play at the opening ceremony of the Hong Kong Drum Festival at Victoria Park, Hong Kong, China, on July 13, 2003.

Largest didgeridoo ensemble On April 19, 2003, 210 musicians assembled to play didgeridoos for 20 minutes at the Helitherme Bad Waltersdorf, Austria.

Largest harmonica ensemble Organized by CentrumKultury Zamek, 851 harmonica players gathered at the 10th Poznan Blues Festival, Poznan, Poland, to perform "When the Saints Go Marching In" on September 13, 2003.

Most durable living organist Stanley Hayes (UK) has been the organist at St. David's Church, Thelbridge, Devon, UK, since 1926, when he was 13. He continues in the post, providing a regular voluntary service for Sunday worship, weddings, funerals, and baptisms.

Longest working career of a conductor Torstein Grythe (Norway) has conducted the Silver Boys Choir of Oslo, Norway, for 63 years since 1940 and still continues to do so at the age of 85.

Longest concert by a group From September 21 to 23, 2002, the group John Jerome Sangamam (India) played for 40 hours at St. Montford Indoor Stadium, Mylapore, Chennai, India. The 20-strong band performed over 500 different numbers, all in Tamil.

Longest international career of a sitarist Indian classical sitarist Ravi Shankar's first sitar performance was in Allahabad, India, in 1939, and his first international sitar concert was in New York, U.S.A., in 1956. However, Shankar's first international stage appearances in Europe and the U.S.A. took place earlier, as a dancer and musical accompanist in his brother Uday Shankar's troupe in 1932, when he was aged 12. He continues to tour today, with dates in North America in 2004.

Best-selling Raï artist Algerian Raï singer Khaled has sold over three million albums worldwide, including *Khaled*, which featured his first international hit "Didi." Other albums include *N'ssi N'ssi*, *Sahra*, and *Kenza*. The live album *1, 2, 3 Soleils* sold one million copies worldwide. Khaled is also the best-selling artist singing in Arabic.

Biggest selling bhangra solo artist Malkit Singh (India) has sold an average of 260,000 copies of each of his albums, totaling sales of over 4.9

BEST-SELLING WORLD MUSIC ALBUM The 1998 Grammy award-winning album *Buena Vista Social Club* (1997) has sold over 4 million copies—1.5 million of which were sold in the U.S.A. The album brought together some of Cuba's best musicians, including Omara Portuondo and Teresita Garcia Caturla (seen here), Ibrahim Ferrer, and Compay Segundo, as well as inspiring Wim Wender's cinema documentary *Buena Vista Social Club* (Germany, 1999).

million records in his 20-year career. He also holds the record for the most recordings by a bhangra artist.

Longest running bhangra band Bhujhangy, a bhangra band based in Birmingham (UK), has been performing and recording bhangra albums since 1967. Balbir Singh (UK), who sings with his brother, Dalbir Singh (UK), is the only member of the band's original lineup.

Best-selling reggae album *Legend* (1984), by the late Bob Marley (Jamaica), is the biggest selling reggae album of all time. In the UK, where it topped the chart, it has had certified sales of 1.8 million, and although it did not reach the Top 40 in the U.S.A., it sold more than 10 million copies there.

Biggest selling album by a Latin artist Mexican-born Carlos Santana's *Supernatural* album, released in June 1999, has sold 14 million copies in the U.S.A. and 21 million worldwide.

Biggest selling female Latin artist Cuban-born singer Gloria Estefan has had total album sales estimated at over 35 million.

Most albums on Latin chart simultaneously Shortly after her death on July 16, 2003, the legendary "Queen of Salsa" Celia Cruz (Cuba) had eight albums in the Top 10 of *Billboard*'s Tropical Latin album chart.

Biggest selling male Latin artist Spanish vocalist Julio Iglesias is the most successful Latin music artist in the world, with reported global sales of more than 200 million albums.

Top selling album act in Japan Utada Hikaru (Japan) is the only Japanese act to sell over two million copies each of three consecutive albums. Her 1999 debut album *First Love* was the biggest ever seller in Japan, shifting over 10 million copies; her second, *Distance,* sold over 5.5 million; and her third, *Deep River* (2002), sold 1.6 million on its first day and 2.3 million in the first five days.

PERFORMANCE ARTS

Furthest building relocation The linked five-story Gem Theater (built 1927) and Century Club building (built 1903) in Detroit, Michigan, U.S.A., which weighed 5,500,000 lb. (2,495 tons), was moved a distance of 1,850 ft. (563 m) on 72 dollies, each with eight rubber tires, in 25 days from October 16, 1997.

Largest purpose-built theater The most capacious purpose-built theater is the Perth Entertainment Centre, Western Australia. It has 8,500 seats

HEAVIEST BUILDING RELOCATION ON WHEELS Built in 1910, the 5,816,000-lb. (2,638-ton) Shubert Theater in Minneapolis, Minnesota, U.S.A., was moved in one piece from Block E to a new site three blocks away on Hennepin Avenue over 12 days by Artspace Projects from February 9 to 21, 1999.

and a main stage area that measures 70 × 45 ft. (21.3 × 13.7 m). It was opened on December 26, 1974.

Largest theater stage The world's largest stage is at the Hilton Theater at the Reno Hilton, Reno, Nevada, U.S.A. It measures 175 × 241 ft. (53.3 × 73.4 m). The stage has three main lifts, each capable of raising 143,961 lb. (65.3 tons) and two turntables each with a circumference of 62 ft. 6 in. (19.1 m).

Most expensive stage prop For the musical stage version of *Chitty Chitty Bang Bang,* which opened at the London Palladium, London, UK, on April 16, 2002, the magical flying car of the title cost an estimated $1.07 million to make. The complete set, including the flying car, was designed by the award-winning set designer Anthony Ward (UK).

Most theatrical members of a family to appear on stage A total of 24 direct members of the Hurst family, headed by Mike and Marjorie (both UK), performed at the Kenton Theatre, Henley-on-Thames, Oxfordshire, UK, in a production of *Puss In Boots* on December 19 and 20, 2003. The performers, whose ages ranged from 1 to 63, included the Hursts' six children Timothy, Alexis, Muffin, Bryony, Jonas, and Adam, and their spouses Lynsey, Nathan, Ben, and Ruth, plus their grandchildren Ben, Ellie, Aisling, Cassian, Liberty, Flavia, Emerald, Tabitha, Antigone, Polyanna, Madeleine, and Amelie (all UK).

Longest working career of a theater director on the same production Enrique Pineda (Mexico) directed the monologue *La Virgen Loca* (*The Crazy Virgin),* performed by Hosmé Israel (Mexico), from its premiere on August 24, 1974, at the Teatro Rafael Solania, University of Veracruz, Mexico, until it closed on November 30, 2003, a total of 29 years 98 days.

Longest working career of a theater producer on the same production Mildred Ilse (U.S.A.), producer of *The Drunkard* (once the world's longest running play), was with the production for its entire run of 26 years 103 days from July 6, 1933, to October 17, 1959, a total of 9,477 performances, in Los Angeles, California, U.S.A.

Longest working career in the same role Terence Ranasinghe and his wife Malini (both Sri Lanka) have played the major roles in E.R. Sarachchandra's (Sri Lanka) *Sinhabahu* in over 5,000 theater performances from 1961 until 1991—a total of 30 years.

Most ardent theatergoer Howard Hughes, Prof. Emeritus of Texas Wesleyan College, Fort Worth, Texas, U.S.A., attended a record 6,136 theater shows in the period 1956–87.

First professional stage actress Margaret Hughes (UK, 1643–1719) appeared as Desdemona in Thomas Killigrew's version of *Othello, The*

Moor of Venice on December 3, 1660, at a converted tennis court called the Vere Street Theatre, London, UK.

Highest box office gross for a theater production Since first opening at Her Majesty's Theatre, London, UK, on October 9, 1986, Andrew Lloyd Webber's musical *The Phantom of the Opera* has played in 18 countries and taken over $3.2 billion at the box office.

Most scripted roles in different locations in one night On February 24, 2004, as part of Visit London's "One Amazing Week," Jerry Hall (U.S.A.) took on recognized scripted roles to appear at six different London West End theater productions during the course of a single night. Replacing a cast member each time, from her first appearance on stage at 7:30 p.m. to her last entrance at 10:09 p.m., she was Monsieur André in *The Phantom of the Opera* at Her Majesty's Theatre; one of four prostitutes in *Les Misérables* at the Palace Theatre; Mr. Myers in *Fame* at the Aldwych Theatre; Brenda in *Blood Brothers* at the Phoenix Theatre; one of the six "Swings" in *Anything Goes* at the Theatre Royal; and finally one of the 24 members of the ensemble in *Chitty Chitty Bang Bang* at the London Palladium.

Most costume changes demanded by a lead theatrical role Michael Jibson (UK) achieved 29 complete costume changes during each performance as Joe Casey in the West End musical *Our House,* directed by Matthew Warchus (UK) at the Cambridge Theatre, London, UK, from

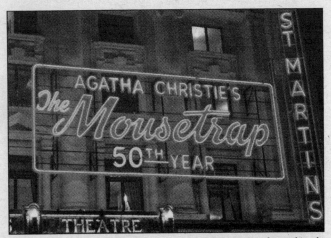

LONGEST THEATRICAL RUN The longest continuous run of any show in the world is *The Mousetrap* by Dame Agatha Christie (UK). By February 29, 2004, it had had 21,263 performances at St. Martin's Theatre, London, UK (pictured). The play celebrated its 50th anniversary in 2002.

LARGEST STAGE LIFT SYSTEM The stage of the Bellagio Theater, Las Vegas, Nevada, U.S.A., measures 3,650 ft.² (339 m²) and is divided into four sections, supported by four hydraulic lifting systems. Each system raises one of the four sections synchronously (or not) through a pool containing 1.5 million gallons (5.6 million liters) of water. The lift system was specially manufactured for Cirque du Soleil's (Canada) "O," performed in, above, and under water (two members pictured here).

October 28, 2002, to August 16, 2003. The quick-change costumes and illusion effects were designed by Paul Kieve (UK), allowing the fastest change to take just four seconds on stage. Assisted in the wings by principal dresser Murray Lane (UK), Warchus made additional partial changes during the 2-hr. 10-min. show.

Longest play *The Warp,* a ten-part play cycle by Neil Oram performed at the Institute of Contemporary Arts, London, UK, on January 18–20, 1979, and directed by Ken Campbell, lasted 18 hr. 5 min. Russell Denton (UK) was on stage for all but five minutes.

Longest running musical The off-Broadway musical *The Fantasticks* by Tom Jones and Harvey Schmidt (both U.S.A.) opened at the Sullivan Street Playhouse, New York, U.S.A., on May 3, 1960, and closed on January 13, 2002, after 17,162 performances.

Longest one-man show to run in London's West End *An Evening with Tommy Steele* opened at the Prince of Wales Theatre, London, UK, on October 11, 1979, and closed on November 29, 1980—a total of 414 days.

Largest amateur puppet show Working 463 puppets, a total of 402 puppeteers from Cockington Primary School (UK) performed the puppet show *Hurucan and the Feathered Snake* at the Riviera International Centre, Torquay, Devon, UK, on July 16, 2003.

Longest theatrical run for a revue The greatest number of performances of any theatrical presentation is 47,250 (to April 1986) for *The Golden Horseshoe Revue,* a variety show staged at Disneyland Park, Anaheim, California, U.S.A., from July 16, 1955, to October 12, 1986. It was seen by 16 million people.

Longest running annual theater revue The longest running annual revues were *The Ziegfeld Follies* (U.S.A., 1907–57), which went through 25 editions.

SPORT

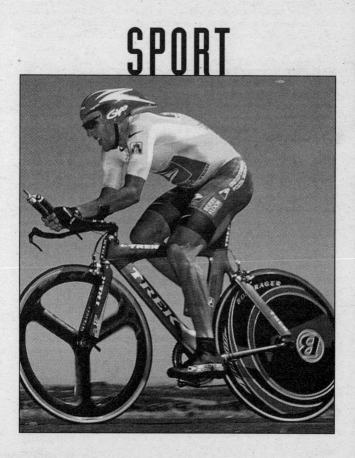

FOOTBALL

Most passes completed in a Super Bowl game Quarterback Tom Brady (U.S.A.) of the New England Patriots threw 32 completed passes in Super Bowl XXXVIII on February 1, 2004, in Houston, Texas, U.S.A.

Most passes received in a Super Bowl career Jerry Rice (U.S.A.) received 33 passes during his four Super Bowl appearances in 1989–90, 1995, and 2003, playing for the San Francisco 49ers and the Oakland Raiders.

Most field goals by an individual in a Super Bowl game The most field goals scored by an individual in a Super Bowl game is four, kicked by Don Chandler (Green Bay Packers) in 1968 and Ray Wersching (San Francisco 49ers) in 1982.

Most team interceptions in a Super Bowl In Super Bowl XXXVII, played in San Diego, California, U.S.A., on January 26, 2003, the Tampa Bay Buccaneers made a record five interceptions, returning them for 172 yards and three touchdowns.

Highest aggregate score in the Super Bowl The greatest aggregate score of 75 points was achieved in 1995 when the San Francisco 49ers beat the San Diego Chargers 49–26.

Coach with most wins The most games won as head coach is 347 by Don Shula (U.S.A.) of the Baltimore Colts (1963–69) and Miami Dolphins (1970–95).

Longest field goal The longest successful field goal in a National Football League (NFL) game is 63 yards by Tom Dempsey (U.S.A.) playing for the New Orleans Saints against the Detroit Lions on November 8, 1970; and by Jason Elam (U.S.A.) playing for the Denver Broncos against the Jacksonville Jaguars on October 25, 1998. Dempsey was born with no right hand, and no toes on his right foot (which was his kicking foot). He wore a modified shoe.

Most NFL titles The Green Bay Packers have won a record 12 NFL titles, in 1929–31, 1936, 1939, 1944, 1961–62, 1965–67, 1996.

Most points scored in a season The most points scored in a season is 176, by Paul Hornung (U.S.A.) for the Green Bay Packers in 1960.

Most NFL games played George Blanda (U.S.A.) played in a record 340 games in a record 26 seasons in the NFL (Chicago Bears 1949–58, Baltimore Colts 1950, Houston Oilers 1960–66, and Oakland Raiders 1967–75).

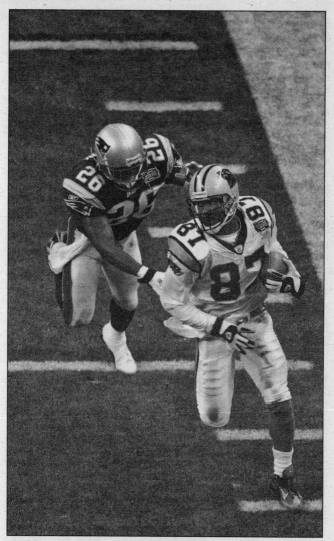

LONGEST TOUCHDOWN IN A SUPER BOWL The longest touchdown in
Super Bowl history is 85 yards, scored by Muhsin Muhammad (U.S.A.,
right), playing for the Carolina Panthers in Super Bowl XXXVIII, on
February 1, 2004.

Football

Highest score in an NFL regular season game The highest team score is 72 by the Washington Redskins against the New York Giants (41) at Washington on November 27, 1966. The aggregate score of 113 is also a record.

Most combined yards gained in an NFL season Lionel James (U.S.A.) gained 2,535 combined net yards in the 1985 NFL season playing for the San Diego Chargers.

Most combined yards gained in an NFL career The most combined net yards gained in an NFL career is 21,803 by Walter Payton (U.S.A.), playing for the Chicago Bears from 1975 to 1987.

Most touchdowns in an NFL game Ernie Nevers (U.S.A.) scored six touchdowns playing for the Chicago Cardinals against the Chicago Bears on November 28, 1929, equaled by William Jones (U.S.A.) playing for the Cleveland Browns against the Chicago Bears on November 25, 1951, and Gale Sayers (U.S.A.) playing for the Chicago Bears against the San Francisco 49ers on December 12, 1965.

Highest combined kick return yardage in an NFL season Michael Lewis (U.S.A.) of the New Orleans Saints set an NFL combined punt/kick-off return record with 2,432 yards in the 2002 season.

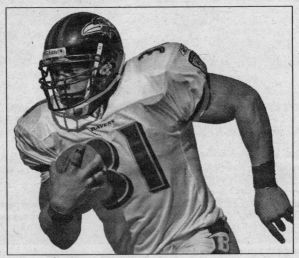

MOST YARDS GAINED RUSHING IN AN NFL GAME Jamal Lewis (U.S.A.) rushed for 295 yards playing for the Baltimore Ravens against the Cleveland Browns on September 14, 2003, scoring two touchdowns.

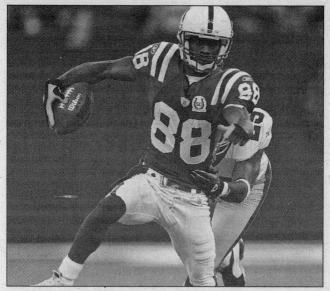

MOST PASSES RECEIVED IN AN NFL SEASON Marvin Harrison (U.S.A.) received a record 143 passes in the 2002 NFL season playing for the Indianapolis Colts.

Most passes received in an NFL career The most pass receptions in an NFL career is 1,519 by Jerry Rice (U.S.A.), playing for the San Francisco 49ers and the Oakland Raiders during 1985–2003.

Most passes received in an NFL game Tom Fears (U.S.A.) caught 18 passes in an NFL game against the Green Bay Packers on December 3, 1950, playing for the Los Angeles Rams.

Most passes completed in an NFL game Drew Bledsoe (U.S.A.), playing for the New England Patriots, completed 45 passes in an NFL game against the Minnesota Vikings on November 13, 1994.

Most passes completed in an NFL regular season The most passes completed in an NFL regular season is 418 by quarterback Rich Gannon (U.S.A.) for the Oakland Raiders in the 2002 season.

Most passes completed in an NFL career Dan Marino (U.S.A.) completed a total of 4,967 passes from 1983 until his retirement in 2000, playing for the Miami Dolphins. He holds many other records, including most yards gained passing in both a career (61,631) and a season (5,084 in 1984).

Most field goals by an individual in an NFL game Jim Bakken (U.S.A.) scored seven field goals in an NFL game against the Pittsburgh Steelers on September 24, 1967, playing for the St. Louis Cardinals.

Most field goals by an individual in an NFL season Olindo Mare (U.S.A.) kicked 39 field goals in the 1999 NFL season, playing for the Miami Dolphins.

Most field goals by an individual in an NFL career Gary Anderson (U.S.A.) kicked 465 field goals over his NFL career playing for the Pittsburgh Steelers (1982–94), Philadelphia Eagles (1995–96), San Francisco 49ers, (1997) and Minnesota Vikings (1999–2001).

Most yards gained passing in an NFL career Dan Marino (U.S.A.) gained 61,361 yards passing during his NFL career from 1983 to 1999, playing for the Miami Dolphins. In 1998, Marino received the Man of the Year award from the NFL in recognition of his support of various children's charities.

Most yards gained rushing in an NFL career Emmitt Smith (U.S.A.) of the Dallas Cowboys gained 17,418 yards rushing over his NFL career spanning 1990 to 2003.

Most sacks made in an NFL career Bruce Smith (U.S.A.) has made 199 sacks in the course of his NFL career, playing for the Buffalo Bills (1985–2000) and the Washington Redskins (2000–03).

Most NFL career interceptions Paul Krause (U.S.A.), a free safety from the University of Iowa, is the leading pass interceptor of all time with 81 steals during a 16-season career, playing for Washington Redskins (1964–67) and Minnesota Vikings (1968–79).

Most interceptions in an NFL season The most interceptions made in an NFL season is 14 by Dick "Night Train" Lane (U.S.A.) playing for the Los Angeles Rams in 1952, the first fully professional season. He returned them for 298 yards and two touchdowns.

Most games officiated Raymond Longden (U.S.A.) has officiated at well over 2,000 football games, more than any other referee. He has officiated in more than 50 games a season since 1947.

BASEBALL

Most games played Pete Rose (U.S.A.) played in a record 3,562 games with a record 14,053 at bats for the Cincinnati Reds (1963–78 and 1984–86), Philadelphia Phillies (1979–83), and Montreal Expos (1984).

Most consecutive games Calvin Edwin Ripken, Jr. (U.S.A.) played a record 2,632 consecutive games for the Baltimore Orioles from May 30, 1982, to September 19, 1998.

Most sacrifice bunts in a career The most sacrifice bunts made in professional baseball is 514 by Masahiro Kawai (Japan) during a career spanning 20 years from 1984 to 2003, playing for the Yomiuri Giants in Japan.

Longest major league game The Chicago White Sox and the Milwaukee Brewers played a game lasting 8 hr. 6 min. on May 9, 1984. The White Sox eventually won the game 7–6 in the 25th inning.

HIGHEST PAID PLAYER The richest contract, based on the average annual salary for the duration of the contract, is $25.2 million by Alex Rodriguez (U.S.A.) of the Texas Rangers ($252 million over 10 years), signed in December 2000. Rodriguez moved to the New York Yankees before the start of the 2004 season, in a complicated deal that sees the Rangers cover the player's wages, paying $67 million of the $179 million left on his contract, and with the Yankees paying him $112 million over the next seven years.

Most strikeouts in a major league career Nolan Ryan (U.S.A.) threw 5,714 strikeouts over his career from 1966 to 1993, playing for the New York Mets, the California Angels, the Houston Astros, and the Texas Rangers.

Most strikeouts in one major league game Roger Clemens (U.S.A.) threw 20 strikeouts in one game (9 innings) playing for the Boston Red Sox against the Seattle Mariners on April 29, 1986, and against the Detroit Tigers on September 18, 1996. The record was equaled by Kerry Wood (U.S.A.), playing for the Chicago Cubs against the Houston Astros on May 6, 1998.

Most runs in a major league career The most runs scored in a major league career is 2,295 by Rickey Henley Henderson (U.S.A.) up to 2003. Henderson began the first of his 25 seasons to date on June 24, 1979, with the Oakland Athletics, and then went on to play for nine franchises before finishing the 2003 season with the Los Angeles Dodgers.

Most doubles in a major league career Tris Speaker (U.S.A.) hit a record 792 doubles during his career, playing for the Boston Red Sox, the

MOST HOME RUNS IN A SEASON Barry Bonds (U.S.A.) of the San Francisco Giants hit 73 home runs in the 2001 season.

Cleveland Indians, the Washington Senators, and the Philadelphia Athletics from 1907 to 1928.

Most triples in a major league career The most triples hit in a major league career is 309 by Sam Crawford (U.S.A.), playing for Cincinnati Reds and the Detroit Tigers from 1899 to 1917.

Most no-hit games pitched in a major league career The most no-hitters pitched in a career is seven by Nolan Ryan (U.S.A.) from 1973 to 1991.

Most major league games pitched By the end of the 2003 season, Jesse Orosco (U.S.A.) had pitched a total of 1,251 games for the New York Mets, Los Angeles Dodgers, Cleveland Indians, Milwaukee Brewers, Baltimore Orioles, St. Louis Cardinals, Minnesota Twins, New York Yankees, and San Diego Padres.

Most stolen bases in a major league career Rickey Henley Henderson (U.S.A.) stole 1,406 bases during his career, from 1979 to 2003, playing for the Oakland Athletics, New York Yankees, Toronto Blue Jays, San Diego Padres, Anaheim Angels, Seattle Mariners, New York Mets, Boston Red Sox, and Los Angeles Dodgers.

Highest batting average in a major league career The highest career batting average is .367 by Tyrus Raymond "Ty" Cobb (U.S.A.), playing for the Detroit Tigers and Philadelphia Athletics from 1905 to 1928.

Most runs batted in in a major league career The most runs batted in in a career is 2,297 by Henry Hank Aaron (U.S.A.) from 1954 to 1976.

Most runs in a major league season William Robert Hamilton (U.S.A.) scored a record 196 runs playing for the Philadelphia Phillies in 1894.

Most consecutive major league games batted in safely Joseph Paul DiMaggio (U.S.A.), playing for the New York Yankees, safely batted in 56 consecutive games from May 15 to July 16, 1941.

Most consecutive hits in major league On June 19–21, 1938, Michael Franklin "Pinky" Higgins (U.S.A.) had 12 consecutive hits playing for the Boston Red Sox. Walter "Moose" Dropo (U.S.A.) equaled this on July 14–15, 1952, playing for the Detroit Tigers.

Highest percentage home runs in a career During his career (1914–35), George Herman "Babe" Ruth (U.S.A.) hit 714 homers from 8,399 times at bat, the highest home run percentage of 8.5% in major league history.

Most home runs in a single game The most home runs in a major league game is four, first achieved by Robert Lincoln "Bobby" Lowe

OLDEST MAJOR LEAGUE PLAYER Leroy Robert "Satchel" Paige (U.S.A.) began playing for the Cleveland Indians in 1948, aged 41. He pitched for the Kansas City Athletics at 59 years 80 days on September 25, 1965.

(U.S.A.) for the Boston Beaneaters against the Cincinnati Reds on May 30, 1894. The feat has been achieved many times since then.

Most Cy Young Award wins The Cy Young Award, given annually since 1956 to the most outstanding pitcher in the major leagues, has gone to Roger Clemens (U.S.A.) a record six times. During this time, he played for the Boston Red Sox (1986, 1987, 1991), Toronto Blue Jays (1997–98), and New York Yankees (2001).

Most wins of the Most Valuable World Series Player award The only men to have won the MVP twice are: Sanford "Sandy" Koufax (U.S.A.), playing for the Los Angeles Dodgers (1963, 1965); Robert "Bob" Gibson (U.S.A.), playing for the St. Louis Cardinals (1964, 1967); and Reginald Martinez "Reggie" Jackson (U.S.A.), playing for the Oakland Athletics (1973) and New York Yankees (1977).

Oldest World Series player Jack Quinn (U.S.A.) of the Philadelphia Athletics was 47 years 91 days old when he played on October 4, 1930.

Most durable announcer Ernest Harwell (U.S.A.) had a 55-year career that began in 1948 with the Brooklyn Dodgers, followed by the New York Giants (1951–53), Baltimore Orioles (1954–59), and Detroit Tigers (1960–2002). In the course of his career, Harwell announced more than 8,300 major league baseball games.

Largest replica bat The world's biggest ever replica baseball bat is 120 ft. (36.5 m) in length and weighs 68,000 lb. (30,844 kg) and was made by bat manufacturer Hillerich Bradsby (U.S.A.). The bat is modeled on the "R43" bat made for Babe Ruth in 1927 by the same manufacturer.

Fastest hit in Finnish baseball Sami Ahola (Finland) hit a ball at a speed of 108.1 mph (174 km/h) at the Lahti Indoor Arena, Finland, on February 20, 2002.

BASKETBALL

Highest aggregate score in an NBA game The highest aggregate score in an NBA game is 370, which occurred when the Detroit Pistons beat the Denver Nuggets 186–184 at Denver, Colorado, U.S.A., on December 13, 1983. The game went into overtime after a 145–145 tie.

Most consecutive NBA wins The Los Angeles Lakers won 33 games in succession from November 5, 1971, to January 7, 1972.

Most wins in an NBA season In the 1995/96 season, the Chicago Bulls won a total of 72 games.

Most losses in an NBA season The highest number of losses incurred in a season was by the Philadelphia 76ers, who were defeated 73 times and won just nine games during an 82-game season. This run of bad luck included a 20-game losing streak in the 1972/73 season.

Most points in an NBA season Wilt Chamberlain (U.S.A.) scored 4,029 points while playing for the Philadelphia Warriors in the 1961/62 season.

MOST BLOCKS IN AN NBA CAREER The greatest number of blocks in a National Basketball Association (NBA) career is 3,830 in 1,238 games by Hakeem Olajuwon (U.S.A., right), playing for the Houston Rockets (1984–2001) and the Toronto Raptors (2001–02).

During this season, Chamberlain also set the record for the highest scoring average in a season, with 50.4 points per game, and scored 1,597 field goals, the most in a season.

Most points scored by an individual in an NBA game Wilt Chamberlain (U.S.A.) scored 100 points for the Philadelphia 76ers against the New York Knicks on March 2, 1962.

Most three-point field goals in an NBA season Dennis Scott (U.S.A.) scored 267 three-point field goals for the Orlando Magic in 1996/97.

Most three-point field goals in an NBA career Reggie Miller (U.S.A.) scored 2,426 three-point field goals for the Indiana Pacers from 1987 to 2004.

Most consecutive NBA games played A.C. Green (U.S.A.) played 1,177 consecutive games for the Los Angeles Lakers, Phoenix Suns, Dallas Mavericks, and Miami Heat from November 19, 1986, to March 20, 2001.

Most games played in an NBA career Robert Parish (U.S.A.) played 1,611 regular-season games during his NBA career from 1976 to 1997. He achieved this record over 21 seasons playing for four teams: the Golden

State Warriors (1976–80), the Boston Celtics (1980–94), the Charlotte Hornets (1994–96), and the Chicago Bulls (1996–97).

Most free throws in an NBA career The greatest number of free throws made in a career is 9,715 in 1,458 games by Karl Malone (U.S.A.) playing for the Utah Jazz (1985–2003) and the Los Angeles Lakers (2003–04).

Most rebounds in an NBA career Wilt Chamberlain (U.S.A.) had 23,924 rebounds in 1,045 games. During his NBA career he played for the Philadelphia Warriors (1959–62), the San Francisco Warriors (1962–65), the Philadelphia 76ers (1964–68), and the Los Angeles Lakers (1968–73).

MOST NBA CHAMPIONSHIP TITLES The Boston Celtics have won a total of 16 NBA Championship titles, in 1957, 1959–66, 1968–69, 1974, 1976, 1981, 1984, and 1986. In their last three championship-winning years, their team included record-breaker Robert Parish (U.S.A., pictured).

Most points scored in an NBA career The greatest number of points scored in an NBA career is 38,387 (at an average of 24.6 points per game) by Kareem Abdul-Jabbar (b. Ferdinand Lewis Alcindor, U.S.A.) from 1969 to 1989. This total includes 15,837 field goals that were scored in regular season games and 5,762 points—including 2,356 field goals—that were scored in playoff games.

Most NBA playoff appearances in a career During his playing career, Kareem Abdul-Jabbar (U.S.A.) took part in 237 playoff games. He played for the Milwaukee Bucks from 1969 to 1975 and the Los Angeles Lakers from 1975 to 1989.

Most fouls in an NBA career Kareem Abdul-Jabbar committed a total of 4,657 fouls in 1,560 games during a playing career that lasted from 1969 to 1989.

Most steals and assists in an NBA career John Stockton (U.S.A.) made 3,265 steals in 1,504 games, playing for the Utah Jazz from 1984 to 2003.

Stockton made a total of 15,806 assists in 1,504 games playing for the Utah Jazz from 1984 to 2003, another world record.

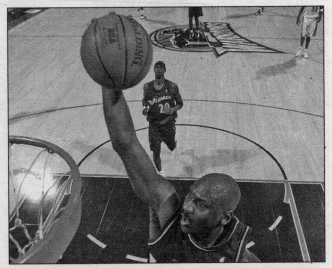

HIGHEST POINT-SCORING AVERAGE IN AN NBA CAREER The highest point-scoring average for players who have exceeded 10,000 points is 30.1 by Michael Jordan (U.S.A., above), who scored a total of 32,292 points in 1,072 games playing for the Chicago Bulls (1984–98) and the Washington Wizards (2001–03).

Tallest player Suleiman Ali Nashnush (Libya) was reputed to be 8 ft. 0.25 in. (2.45 m) when he played for his national team in 1962.

Longest time to spin a basketball on one finger Zhao Guang (China) spun a regulation basketball on one finger while maintaining the spin for 3 hr. 59 min. on January 29, 2003, in Shenyang, China.

Longest basketball marathon A match lasting 26 hr. 42 min. was played at Warwick Academy, at the Bermuda College Gym, Paget, Bermuda, on March 15–16, 2003. The Blue and White teams played a total of 27 games against each other.

Most basketballs dribbled simultaneously by one person Joseph Odhiambo (U.S.A.) dribbled six basketballs simultaneously on August 15, 2000, at his home in Mesa, Arizona, U.S.A. This beat his previous record of dribbling five basketballs at once.

Most consecutive shots with head Eyal Horn (Israel) made a total of 19 consecutive layups, controlling and shooting the ball using only his head, on the set of *Guinness Rekord TV,* Stockholm, Sweden, on November 29, 2001.

Most consecutive free throws Ted St. Martin (U.S.A.) made 5,221 consecutive free throws at Jacksonville, Florida, U.S.A., on April 28, 1996.

Most free throws in one minute David Bergström (Sweden) made 48 free throws in one minute at Fyrishov, Uppsala, Sweden, on October 2, 2001. The attempt was filmed by *Guinness Rekord TV,* Sweden.

Most three-pointers in one minute Lea Hakala (Finland) made 19 successful three-point shots in a minute on the set of *Guinness World Records,* Helsinki, Finland, on October 22, 2001.

Greatest distance to dribble a basketball in 24 hours Suresh Joachim (Australia) dribbled a basketball a distance of 97.37 miles (156.71 km) at Vulkanhallen, Oslo, Norway, on March 30–31, 2001.

Longest goal thrown in an exhibition match Iain McKinney (UK) scored a basketball goal from a distance of 90 ft. 6 in. (27.6 m) playing for the Sheffield Sharks at Ponds Forge, Sheffield, South Yorkshire, UK, on April 8, 1996.

ICE HOCKEY

Most wins in a National Hockey League (NHL) season The Detroit Red Wings achieved 62 wins during the 1995/96 NHL season.

Longest NHL winning streak The longest run of winning games—both at home and away—in NHL history is 17 by the Pittsburgh Penguins from March 9 to April 10, 1993.

Fewest defeats in an NHL season In the 1976/77 season, the Montreal Canadiens lost just eight games, the fewest ever in a season of 70 or more games, from 80 played (60 wins, 12 ties, and a record 132 points).

Most losses in an NHL season The San Jose Sharks had 71 losses during the 1992/93 season, including a record 32 games lost at home.

Most points scored in an NHL career Wayne Gretzky (Canada) scored 2,857 points for the Edmonton Oilers, Los Angeles Kings, St. Louis Blues, and New York Rangers from 1979 to 1999. The points total includes 894 goals and 1,963 assists, achieved in 1,487 games.

Most goals scored in an NHL season Wayne Gretzky (Canada) scored 92 goals for the Edmonton Oilers during the 1981/82 season.

Most goals scored by a team in an NHL season The Edmonton Oilers scored 446 goals in the 1983/84 season.

MOST NHL CAREER WINS BY A GOALTENDER Having begun his career with the Montreal Canadiens in 1985, goalie Patrick Roy (Canada, pictured) of the Colorado Avalanche had 516 wins up to the end of the 2002 regular season. With 22 shutouts, Roy also holds the record for the most shutouts by a goaltender in NHL playoff history.

Most goals scored by an individual in an NHL game Joe Malone (Canada) scored seven goals for the Québec Bulldogs in their game against the Toronto St. Patricks in Québec City, Québec, Canada, on January 31, 1920.

Longest NHL suspension for an infraction during a game Marty McSorley (U.S.A.) of the Boston Bruins incurred a 23-game suspension in February 2000 for hitting Vancouver Canucks' Donald Brashear (Canada) on the head with his stick in a game in Vancouver, British Columbia, Canada, on February 21, 2000.

Most penalty minutes in an NHL career In the 17 seasons from 1971 to 1988, Dave "Tiger" Williams (Canada) had 3,966 penalty minutes—the most in NHL history—playing for the Toronto Maple Leafs, Vancouver Canucks, Detroit Red Wings, Los Angeles Kings, and the now-defunct Hartford Whalers.

Most penalties against an individual in an NHL game Chris Nilan (U.S.A.) had a record 10 penalties called against him when playing for the Boston Bruins against the Hartford Whalers on March 31, 1991.

Most penalties in an NHL game The most penalties awarded in any NHL game is 85, when the Edmonton Oilers played the Los Angeles Kings in Los Angeles, California, U.S.A., on February 28, 1990.

Most NHL goaltending appearances The most NHL goaltending appearances is 971 by Terry Sawchuk (Canada) for the Detroit Red Wings, Boston Bruins, Toronto Maple Leafs, Los Angeles Kings, and New York Rangers from 1949 to 1970.

Most goaltending shutouts in an NHL career The most goaltending shutouts in an NHL career is 103 by Terry Sawchuk (Canada) for the Detroit Red Wings, Boston Bruins, Toronto Maple Leafs, Los Angeles Kings, and New York Rangers from 1949–70.

Most NHL All-Star selections Gordie Howe (Canada) was selected 21 times for the NHL All-Star game while playing for the Detroit Red Wings from 1946 to 1979. He played in the first team 12 times and in the second team nine times.

Quickest goal scored in an NHL match The quickest goals in an NHL match were scored five seconds after the opening whistle. This record is held by Doug Smail (Canada) for the Winnipeg Jets against the St. Louis Blues in Winnipeg, Manitoba, Canada, on December 20, 1981; by Bryan John Trottier (Canada) for the New York Islanders against the Boston Bruins in Boston, U.S.A., on March 22, 1984; and by Alexander Mogilny (Russia) for the Buffalo Sabers against the Toronto Maple Leafs in Toronto, Ontario, Canada, on December 21, 1991.

Most ties in an NHL season The Philadelphia Flyers played 24 tied games over a 76-game season in 1969/70.

Most men's ice hockey Olympic wins Ice hockey was first contested at the Winter Olympics in 1920. The most wins is eight by the USSR—in 1956, 1964, 1968, 1972, 1976, 1984, 1988, and in 1992—as the CIS, when all players were Russian.

Most points scored by an individual in a professional ice hockey game A record 10 points in a game has been scored twice by two professional players: Jim Harrison (Canada) with three goals and seven assists for the Alberta (later Edmonton) Oilers in a World Hockey Association (WHA) match in Edmonton, Canada, on January 30, 1973; and Darryl Sittler (Canada) with six goals and four assists for the Toronto Maple Leafs against the Boston Bruins in an NHL match in Toronto, Ontario, Canada, on February 7, 1976.

Most Stanley Cup wins by a team The Montreal Canadiens have won the Stanley Cup 24 times (1916, 1924, 1930–31, 1944, 1946, 1953, 1956–60, 1965–66, 1968–69, 1971, 1973, 1976–79, 1986, and 1993) from a record 32 finals.

MOST WOMEN'S ICE HOCKEY OLYMPIC WINS Women's ice hockey has been contested twice at the Winter Olympics, in 1998 and 2002. The U.S.A. beat Canada in the final in 1998, and Canada (pictured) got revenge by beating the U.S.A. in the 2002 final.

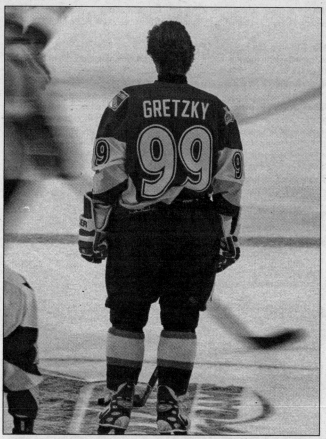

MOST HAT TRICKS IN AN NHL CAREER The most hat tricks scored in an NHL career is 50 by Wayne Gretzky (Canada), for the Edmonton Oilers, Los Angeles Kings, St. Louis Blues, and New York Rangers from 1979 to 1999.

Most individual Stanley Cup wins Henri Richard (Canada) had 11 individual Stanley Cup wins for the Montreal Canadiens from 1956 to 1975.

Most points scored in a Stanley Cup series Wayne Gretzky (Canada) scored a record 47 points for the Edmonton Oilers in the 1985 Stanley Cup. The points scored included 17 goals and 30 assists, which are in themselves records.

Most games played in a professional ice hockey career Gordon Howe (Canada) played 2,421 games in his professional ice hockey career from 1946 to 1979.

Largest ice hockey stick An ice hockey stick made by the Millwork Home Centre in Oshawa, Ontario, Canada, measured 44 ft. 3.6 in. (13.5 m) from the heel of the blade to the top of the shaft on October 25, 2003.

Most durable ice hockey player The most durable ice hockey player is James Bernard Hawkins (U.S.A.), who began playing in organized hockey leagues in 1932 and played for a total of 71 years.

Ice hockey marathon The longest duration for a game of ice hockey is 130 hr. 7 min., played at the Moosomin Communiplex, Moosomin, Saskatchewan, Canada, on October 13–18, 2003.

SOCCER

Fastest World Cup red card Ion Vladoiu (Romania) was sent off after only three minutes in a World Cup finals match against Switzerland on June 22, 1994, at the Pontiac Silverdome, Detroit, Michigan, U.S.A.

Most World Cup finals goals Gerd Müller scored 14 goals in World Cup finals tournaments for West Germany. This total includes 10 goals in 1970 in Mexico and four in West Germany in 1974, when the host nation went on to lift the trophy.

Most goals in a single World Cup finals The most goals scored by an individual player in a World Cup finals tournament is 13 by Just Fontaine (France) in 1958 in Sweden.

Most women's World Cup wins A women's World Cup competition was initiated in 1991 and is held quadrennially. The tournament has been held on four occasions so far. The U.S.A. won two of these (1991 and 1999), while the winners in 1995 were Norway, with Germany winning in 2003.

Most World Cup clean sheets Goalkeeper Peter Shilton (UK) played in 10 World Cup finals matches for England without conceding a single goal over three tournaments and a total of 17 games between 1982 and 1990.

Most countries in FIFA World Cup qualifiers A total of 198 federations registered to play in the FIFA qualifiers for the 2002 World Cup, which were held jointly in South Korea and Japan. The soccer federations of Afghanistan, Burundi, New Guinea, Niger, and North Korea were the exceptions.

FASTEST GOAL IN A WORLD CUP SOCCER MATCH The quickest goal in a World Cup finals match, as recognized by the Fédération Internationale de Football Association (FIFA), was timed at 11 seconds. It was scored by Hakan Sukur of Turkey (far right) against the Republic of Korea at Daegu, Korea, on June 29, 2002.

Most World Cup wins FIFA instituted the first World Cup on July 13, 1930, in Montevideo, Uruguay. The tournament is held every four years and has been won five times by Brazil, in 1958, 1962, 1970, 1994, and 2002.

Highest score in an international match Australia defeated American Samoa 31–0 in a World Cup qualifying match at Coffs Harbour, New South Wales, Australia, on April 11, 2001.

Youngest scorer in a World Cup finals Edson Arantes do Nascimento, better known as Pelé, was aged 17 years 239 days when he scored for Brazil against Wales, in Gothenburg, Sweden, on June 19, 1958.

Youngest player in a World Cup finals The youngest person ever to play in a finals match is Norman Whiteside (UK), who played for Northern

Ireland against Yugoslavia aged 17 years 41 days in Zaragoza, Spain, on June 17, 1982.

Oldest player in World Cup finals Albert Roger Milla (b. May 20, 1952) played for Cameroon against Russia at Stanford, Palo Alto, California, U.S.A., on June 28, 1994, at the age of 42 years 39 days.

During the course of this match, Milla also scored, making him the oldest person ever to score in the World Cup finals.

Most goals scored by a goalkeeper in one game Paraguayan goal-keeper José Luis Chilavert scored a hat trick of penalties for Vélez Sarsfield in their 6–1 defeat of Ferro Carril Oeste on November 28, 1999, in the Argentine professional league.

Chilavert specializes in penalties and free kicks. He is the only keeper to have scored in a World Cup qualifying game (against Argentina in Buenos Aires, 1997) and the only one to have taken a direct free kick in a World Cup (France, 1998).

He also holds the record for the most goals scored by a goalkeeper, with a total of 56 official league and international goals from July 1992 to October 2001. Chilavert currently plays for his country and for the French club Strasbourg.

MOST AFRICA CUP OF NATIONS WINS The record for the most wins of the Africa Cup of Nations is four, jointly held by Ghana, who won in 1963, 1965, 1978, and 1982; Egypt, who won in 1957, 1959, 1986, and 1998; and Cameroon (pictured), who won in 1984, 1988, 2000, and 2002.

FASTEST INTERNATIONAL HAT TRICK Japanese international Masashi "Gon" Nakayama (pictured) scored a hat trick in 3 min. 15 sec. against Brunei during an Asian Cup qualifying match on February 16, 2000. Nakayama netted on 1 minute, 2 minutes, and 3 min. 15 sec., bettering the 62-year-old record set by George William Hall (UK), who scored three in 3 min. 30 sec. for England against Ireland at Old Trafford, Manchester, UK, on November 16, 1938.

Most goals scored in an international by an individual During the record-breaking 31–0 defeat by Australia of American Samoa, Archie Thompson (Australia) scored an international record 13 goals.

Oldest regular player Enrique Alcocer (Mexico, b. August 28, 1924) is currently the world's oldest regular soccer player. He plays for the Reforma Athletic Club in Mexico City, Mexico. Alcocer began playing regularly in 1936 for the Grosso Junior and High School in Mexico City, and subsequently played professionally for the Marte Football Club in 1944 in Mexico's first division before joining his current club in 1952.

Largest tournament by players The Chappies Little League Cup competition was held in South Africa from March to September 2003, and was contested by 6,023 teams which included a total of 138,529 players. The tournament is the South African national schools' under-12 competition.

Most durable referee Jozsef Magyar (Hungary) regularly refereed competitive soccer for 50 years. He gained his refereeing qualification in 1953 and officiated his last match on March 9, 2003, in Sitke, Hungary, aged 80.

Most women's international caps The greatest number of international appearances by a woman for a national team is 270 by Kristine Lilly (U.S.A.), who represented the U.S.A. from 1987 to 2004.

Most men's international caps The most international appearances for a national team is 171 by Claudio Suarez for Mexico from 1992 to 2003.

Most South American Championships Argentina won the South American Championship (known as the Copa América since 1975) a record 15 times from 1910 to 1993.

Most expensive goalkeeper In July 2001, Gianluigi Buffon (Italy) transferred between Italian Serie A clubs Parma and Juventus for a record fee of $46.8 million.

Highest score in a women's international The record score line of 21–0 has been achieved on four separate occasions: by Japan against Guam at Guangzhou, China, on December 5, 1997; by Canada against Puerto Rico at Centennial Park, Toronto, Canada, on August 28, 1998; and by Australia against American Samoa and by New Zealand against Samoa—both of these matches taking place at Mt. Smart Stadium, Auckland, New Zealand, on October 9, 1998.

Largest attendance The greatest recorded crowd at any soccer match was 199,854 for the Brazil against Uruguay World Cup match in the Maracanã Municipal Stadium, Rio de Janeiro, Brazil, on July 16, 1950.

Largest soccer complex The National Sports Center at Blaines, Minnesota, U.S.A., has 57 playing fields, 55 of which are playable at any one time.

Furthest distance traveled between competitors in the same league The furthest distance traveled between two clubs in the top division of a professional national league is 2,979 miles (4,794 km) between the home stadiums of the U.S. Major League Soccer teams Los Angeles Galaxy and New England Revolution.

Most goals in a Champions League season The most goals scored in a UEFA Champions League season is 12 by Ruud van Nistelrooy (Netherlands) for Manchester United in the 2002/03 season.

Fastest Champions League goal The fastest goal in a Champions League match was scored by Gilberto Silva (Brazil) in 20.07 seconds playing for Arsenal against PSV Eindhoven in Eindhoven, The Netherlands, on September 25, 2002. Arsenal went on to win the game 4–0.

MOST ENGLISH LEAGUE CUP WINS Liverpool (team members Michael Owen, left, and Steven Gerrard, right; both UK) has won the English League Cup seven times, in 1981–84, 1995, 2001, and 2003.

MOST EXPENSIVE SOCCER PLAYER The highest transfer fee for a player is 13 billion Spanish pesetas ($66 million) for Zinédine Zidane (France) for his transfer from Juventus to Real Madrid on July 9, 2001.

Most Champions League goals The most goals in UEFA Champions League matches is 44 by Raúl González Blanco (Spain) playing for Real Madrid from 1992 until present.

Highest score in a national cup final In 1935, Lausanne-Sports beat Nordstern Basel 10–0 in the Swiss Cup final. Two years later, they suffered defeat by the same score at the hands of Grasshopper Club (Zurich) in the 1937 Swiss Cup final.

Most consecutive Champions League match victories The longest winning streak in the UEFA Champions League is 11 games by FC Barcelona in the 2002/03 season.

Most Cup Winners' Cups The Cup Winners' Cup, contested until 1999 by the winners of the national cups in Europe, was won a record four times by FC Barcelona (1979, 1982, 1989, and 1997).

Most assists in a Major League Soccer season Carlos Valderrama (Colombia) made 26 assists in a Major League Soccer season, playing for the Tampa Bay Mutiny in 2000.

Longest clean sheet in goalkeeping Abel Resino (Spain) of Atlético de Madrid succeeded in preventing goals being scored past him in top-class competition for 1,275 min. (just over 14 matches) during the 1990/91 La Liga season. The record in international matches is 1,142 min. (nearly 13 matches) by Dino Zoff (Italy) from September 1972 to June 1974.

Most domestic league titles The most domestic league titles won by a soccer club is 50, by Rangers FC (UK) in the Scottish Division 1 and Premier Division Championships, from 1891 to 2003.

Fastest time to score a hat trick Tommy Ross (UK) scored three goals in 90 seconds for Ross County against Nairn County at Dingwall, Ross-shire, UK, on November 28, 1964.

Most Futsal World Cup titles Since it was first held in 1989, the most wins at the Futsal (indoor soccer) World Cup is three by Brazil (1989, 1992, and 1996). The fourth tournament, held in 2000 in Guatemala, was won by Spain, who beat Brazil 4–3 in the final.

Unbeaten premiership season In the premiership season of 2003/04, Arsenal FC were unbeaten in 38 games, winning 26, drawing 12, and losing none. In the process they scored 73 goals and conceded 26, failing to score on only four occasions.

Most premiership goals Alan Shearer (UK) scored 243 goals in the English Premiership. Shearer began his career with Southampton, before moving to Blackburn Rovers and finally to Newcastle United in July 1996 for a record fee of £15.6 million ($22.4 million).

Longest penalty shoot-out In the Derby Community League (UK) under-10s cup match between Mickleover Lightning Blue Sox and Chellaston

Boys "B" on January 17, 1998, a total of 66 penalties were taken to decide the match, which had finished 1–1. The Blue Sox eventually won the marathon shoot-out 2–1, with 35 penalties being saved, the rest going wide of the target.

Most consecutive passes The most consecutive soccer passes is 557 and was set by members of the McDonald's Youth Football Scheme, Tsing Yi, Hong Kong, China, on May 4, 2002.

Most goals scored direct from corners The most goals scored in a match by an individual direct from corners is three by Steve Cromey (UK) for Ashgreen United against Dunlop FC on February 24, 2002, at Bedworth, Warwickshire, UK, and by Daniel White (UK) for Street and Glastonbury under-11s against Westfield Boys on April 7, 2002.

Fastest ball control marathon distance Jan Skorkovsky (Czechoslovakia) kept a soccer ball up while running a distance of 26.219 miles (42.195 km) in the Prague City Marathon in 7 hr. 18 min. 55 sec. on July 8, 1990.

MOST CAREER GOALS Edson Arantes do Nascimento (Brazil, pictured), better known as Pelé, scored a total of 1,279 goals from September 7, 1956, to October 1, 1977, in 1,363 games. Pelé's best year was 1959, in which he scored 126 goals. The milésimo (1,000th) came from a penalty for his club Santos at the Maracanã Stadium, Rio de Janeiro, Brazil, on November 19, 1969, in his 909th first-class match. He later added two more goals in special appearances.

Most touches of a soccer ball in 30 seconds The most touches of a soccer ball in 30 seconds, while keeping the ball in the air, is 141 by Ferdie Adoboe (U.S.A.) in New York, U.S.A., on August 27, 2003.

The women's record is 137 touches by Tasha-Nicole Terani (U.S.A.) in New York, U.S.A., on August 27, 2003.

Longest ball control with feet, legs, and head Martinho Eduardo Orige (Brazil) juggled a regulation-size soccer ball for 19 hr. 30 min. non-stop with feet, legs, and head without the ball ever touching the ground at Padre Ezio Julli Gym in Araranguá, Brazil, on August 2–3, 2003.

Longest ball control while lying down Tomas Lundman (Sweden) managed to keep a regulation-size soccer ball up in the air using his feet while lying on his back for 7 min. 36 sec. at Angebo Svågagården Hudiksvall, Sweden, on September 20, 2003.

Most soccer management rejection letters The most rejection letters received for soccer management jobs is 29 by Richard Dixon (UK). Dixon applies only for jobs that are available and has received official letters from clubs such as Tottenham Hotspur, Manchester United, Atlético de Madrid, and the English and Cypriot national teams. The hobby began in 2000 when physical education teacher Dixon contracted infectious mononucleosis and applied for the Millwall job.

RUGBY

Most points by an individual player in a Rugby Union international In the World Cup qualifying match between Hong Kong and Singapore at Kuala Lumpur, Malaysia, on October 27, 1994, Hong Kong's Ashley Billington scored 50 points (10 tries).

Most penalties by an individual player in a Rugby Union international The record is shared by two players: Keiji Hirose kicked nine successful penalties for Japan against Tonga (44–17) in Tokyo, Japan, on May 9, 1999; and Andrew Mehrtens also kicked nine for New Zealand against Australia (34–15) at Auckland, New Zealand, on July 24, 1999.

Most points in a Rugby Union international career Neil Jenkins (UK) scored 1,049 points in 87 matches (1,008 points in 83 matches for Wales, 41 points in four matches for the British Lions) from 1991 to March 2001.

Fastest Rugby Union World Cup try Elton Flatley (Australia) scored a try just 18 seconds after kick-off when playing for Australia against

MOST SUPER LEAGUE TITLES The most Super League titles won by a team is four by St. Helens (pictured) in 1996, 1999, 2000, and 2002. The Super League is the UK's premier Rugby League competition, instituted in 1996.

Romania on October 18, 2003, at the Suncorp Stadium, Brisbane, Queensland, Australia.

Largest rugby tour From April 11 to 14, 2003, 264 players and coaches from Ealing Rugby Club (UK) played matches on tour in Ireland.

Most women's Rugby Union World Cup titles The women's World Cup has been contested four times (1991, 1994, 1998, and 2002). New Zealand has won the title twice, in 1998 and 2002, while the U.S.A. and England have one win apiece.

Most wins in the Hong Kong Sevens First held in 1976, this is the world's most prestigious international tournament for seven-a-side Rugby Union. Fiji has won a record nine times, in 1977–78, 1980, 1984, 1990–92, and 1998–99. For 1997 the contest was replaced by the World Cup Sevens, which Fiji also won.

Highest attendance at a Rugby Union match The largest paying attendance for a Rugby Union international is 109,874 for New Zealand's 39–35 victory over Australia at Stadium Australia, Sydney, Australia, on July 15, 2000.

Highest attendance at a Rugby League match A total of 104,583 spectators saw a Rugby League doubleheader at Stadium Australia, Sydney, Australia, on March 7, 1999. The Newcastle Knights beat the Manly Sea Eagles 41–18, and the Parramatta Eels beat the St. George Illawarra Dragons 20–10.

Most Rugby League World Cup wins The Rugby League World Cup competition was first held in 1954. Australia has most wins, with eight, in 1957, 1968, 1970, 1977, 1988, 1992, 1995, and 2000, as well as a win in the International Championship of 1975.

Most Rugby League Challenge Cup wins The Rugby League Challenge Cup (inaugurated in the 1896/97 season) has been won a record 17 times by Wigan (in 1924, 1929, 1948, 1951, 1958–59, 1965, 1985, 1988–95, and 2002).

Most National Rugby League (NRL) titles The Brisbane Broncos have won two NRL titles, in 1998 and 2000. The NRL is Australia's premier Rugby League competition. Instituted in 1998, it replaced the Australian Rugby League (1995–97), which in turn replaced the New South Wales Rugby League (1908–94).

Most tries scored in an amateur Rugby League season Richard Lopag (UK) scored 169 tries for the Deighton Juniors Under-13 side, West Yorkshire, UK, in the 2001/02 season.

Most hat tricks in a Rugby League season Richard Lopag (UK) of Deighton Juniors Under-13s, Huddersfield, West Yorkshire, UK, scored 43 hat tricks during the 2001/02 season.

Fastest Rugby League hat trick Chris Thorman (UK) scored a hat trick of tries within 6 min. 54 sec. of the start of a match, for Huddersfield Giants against Doncaster Dragons in the semifinal of the Buddies National

League Cup at Doncaster, South Yorkshire, UK, on May 19, 2002.

Most rugby tackles in one hour Cranleigh RFC Under-11s

MOST RUGBY UNION WORLD CUP WINS The William Webb Ellis Trophy (shown here) is awarded to the winners of the Rugby Union World Cup (instituted in 1987). The most wins is two by Australia, in 1991 and 1999.

BIGGEST RUGBY UNION WORLD CUP MATCH WIN The largest winning margin recorded in Rugby Union World Cup matches is 142 points, when host nation Australia beat Namibia 142–0 in Adelaide, Australia, on October 25, 2003. Matt Giteau (Australia) is pictured here scoring one of his tries.

made 1,644 rugby tackles in one hour on April 21, 2002, at Cranleigh Rugby Club, Surrey, UK.

GWR TALKS TO Jason Leonard OBE

Jason Leonard (UK, pictured on page 417 with his international Rugby Players Association Asprey Special Merit Award, presented in 2002) played in 114 international Rugby Union matches for England from 1990 to 2004. The England prop became the most capped player of all time when he came on for Phil Vickery (UK) in the fourth minute of England's World Cup semi-final victory over France at the Telstra Stadium, Sydney, Australia, on November 16, 2003. England won the match 24–7 with Leonard having been on the pitch for one minute.

Who inspires you? Muhammad Ali, the Greatest.

Did you always want to be a rugby player? At school, I wanted to be a soccer player—I was a pretty good defender—but then I discovered rugby, and that was that!

If you hadn't pursued a career in rugby what do you think you would have done? When I left school, I worked in the building trade, so I'd probably have carried on with that.

Did you think your international career would go on this long? When I started playing for England, back in 1990, 30 caps was considered a great career, so I'm amazed I managed to carry on playing for 14 years! I've recently decided to bow out of competitive rugby, but I've enjoyed every minute and achieved more than I could have ever dreamed of when I started, so I've no regrets.

What is your greatest achievement in rugby? Winning the World Cup with England in Australia in 2003.

What advice would you give to young sportsmen and -women? Enjoy it, and always give 100%.

Which is your favorite Guinness World Record? Mine!

CRICKET

Highest test team score Sri Lanka scored 952 for 6 against India at Colombo, Sri Lanka, on August 4–6, 1997.

Most runs in test cricket Allan Border (Australia) scored a total of 11,174 runs in 156 tests (an average of 50.56) from 1978 to 1994.

Highest test batting average Don Bradman (Australia) retired with a batting average of 99.94 after playing for Australia in a total of 52 tests. He scored 6,996 runs in 80 innings from 1928 to 1948.

Highest partnership in a test match The highest partnership is 576 for the second wicket by Sanath Jayasuriya at 340 and Roshan Mahanama (both Sri Lanka) at 225 for Sri Lanka against India at Colombo, Sri Lanka, on August 4–6, 1997.

Most test match wickets Muttiah Muralitharan (Sri Lanka) is the leading test match wicket-taker with 521 (average 22.76 runs per wicket) in 89 matches, from August 1992 to May 2004.

MOST TEST MATCH APPEARANCES Steve Waugh (Australia) played in 168 test matches from 1984 to 2004. He scored 10,927 runs and took 92 wickets and 112 catches.

Most catches by a wicket keeper in test cricket Ian Healy (Australia) made a total of 366 catches (in 119 tests) playing for Australia from 1988 to 1999.

Most catches by a fielder in test cricket Mark Waugh (Australia) made 181 catches in 128 tests for Australia from 1990 to 2003.

Most "ducks" in test cricket The player who has the dubious honor of registering the most "ducks" (a score of nothing) in test cricket is Courtney Walsh (Jamaica) with 43 in 185 innings for the West Indies from November 1984 to April 2001.

HIGHEST TEST INNINGS Brian Lara (Trinidad) scored 400 not out for West Indies v. England at Antigua Recreation Ground, St. John's, Antigua, on April 10–12, 2004. The innings included four sixes and 43 fours, in a team total of 751–5. Lara became the only player to have set this record twice, having previously scored 375 against the same opposition on the same ground in April 1994.

Most sixes in a test match innings Wasim Akram (Pakistan) hit 12 sixes in his 257 not out for Pakistan against Zimbabwe at Sheikhupura, Pakistan, on October 18–20, 1996.

Most extras conceded in a test match The West Indies conceded 71 extras in Pakistan's first innings at Georgetown, Guyana, on April 3–4, 1988. The figure consisted of 21 byes, eight leg byes, four wides, and 38 no-balls.

Most test centuries Sunil Gavaskar (India) scored a total of 34 centuries (in 214 innings) playing for India from 1971 to 1987.

Longest test match The longest-lasting recorded cricket match was the "timeless" test between England and South Africa at Durban, South Africa, from March 3 to 14, 1939. Neither side was able to secure victory and the match was abandoned after 10 days (the eighth day was rained out) because the ship taking the England team home was due to leave. The total playing time was 43 hr. 16 min. and a record test match aggregate of 1,981 runs was scored.

Most consecutive test wins Australia recorded a run of 16 successive test victories when they beat India by 10 wickets at Mumbai (Bombay), India, in March 2001.

Youngest test player The youngest test player ever is Hasan Raza (Pakistan, b. March 11, 1982), who made his debut aged 14 years 227 days against Zimbabwe at Faisalabad, Pakistan, on October 24, 1996.

Most catches by a fielder in a World Cup match The greatest number of catches in a cricket World Cup match is four by Mohammad Kaif (India) against Sri Lanka in Johannesburg, South Africa, on March 10, 2003.

Most catches by a fielder in a World Cup career Ricky Ponting (Australia) made 18 catches in 28 matches from 1996 to 2003.

Most catches by a fielder in a cricket World Cup tournament Ricky Ponting (Australia) took 11 catches in the World Cup tournament in South Africa in 2003.

Highest team score in World Cup cricket The highest team score in a World Cup match is 398 for 5 by Sri Lanka against Kenya at Kandy, Sri Lanka, on March 6, 1996.

The lowest team score is 36 by Canada against Sri Lanka at Boland Park, Paarl, South Africa, on February 19, 2003.

Most centuries in first-class cricket Jack Hobbs (UK) scored 197 centuries out of a total of 1,315 innings while playing for Surrey and England from 1905 to 1934.

Highest individual innings score Brian Charles Lara (Trinidad) scored 501 not out in 7 hr. 54 min. playing for Warwickshire against Durham at Edgbaston, UK, from June 3 to 6, 1994.

During his innings he also broke two other cricketing records: the most runs in a day (390 on June 6) and the most runs from strokes worth four or more (308, comprising 62 fours and 10 sixes).

Highest individual score in one-day internationals Saeed Anwar (Pakistan) scored 194 while playing for Pakistan against India at Madras (Chennai), India, on May 21, 1997.

Most runs off a ball Garry Chapman (Australia), partnered by Chris Veal (Australia), scored 17 (all run, with no overthrows) off a single delivery while playing for Banyule against Macleod at Windsor Reserve, Victoria, Australia, on October 13, 1990. Chapman had pulled the ball to mid-wicket, where it disappeared into 10-in.-high (25-cm) grass.

Most runs off one over The first batsman ever to score 36 runs off a six-ball over was Garfield St. Aubrun Sobers (Barbados) off Malcolm Andrew

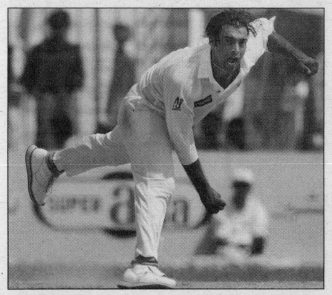

FASTEST BOWLING The highest electronically measured speed for a ball bowled by any bowler is 100.23 mph (161.3 km/h) by Shoaib Akhtar (Pakistan) against England on February 22, 2003, in a World Cup match at Newlands, Cape Town, South Africa.

Nash (UK) for Nottinghamshire against Glamorgan at Swansea on August 31, 1968.

Ravishankar Jayadritha Shastri (India) achieved the same feat for Bombay against Baroda in Mumbai (Bombay), India, on January 10, 1985, off the bowling of Tilak Raj Sharma (India).

Longest cricket marathon Cricket Club des Ormes (France) played a cricket marathon of 26 hr. 13 min. at Dol de Bretagne, France, on June 21–22, 2003. Two teams of 12 played six matches in all, with the Young Guns team winning five matches to the Veterans' one.

Oldest umpire After playing professionally for Staffordshire, UK, as a younger man, Joe Filliston (UK) applied to become an umpire at the age of 82. The Marylebone Cricket Club invited him to umpire for the Lord's Taverners on many occasions and he was still umpiring at the age of 100.

Youngest cricketer to hit six sixes in an over The youngest cricketer to hit six consecutive sixes in the same over is Anthony McMahon (UK), who achieved the feat at the age of 13 years 261 days, on May 24, 2003, while playing for Chester-le-Street against Eppleton at Eppleton Cricket Club, Durham, UK.

BALL SPORTS

Most men's volleyball World Championships The USSR has won six titles (in 1949, 1952, 1960, 1962, 1978, and 1982).

Most women's volleyball World Championships World Championships were instituted in 1952 for women, and the USSR has won a record five titles (in 1952, 1956, 1960, 1970, and 1990).

Most beach volleyball titles (AVP tour) Karch Kiraly (U.S.A.) has won a record 143 AVP tour titles through the end of the 2003 season.

Most Olympic medals for men's volleyball The record for men is three, held jointly by Yuriy Mikhailovich Poyarkov (USSR), who won gold medals in 1964 and 1968 and a bronze in 1972; Katsutoshi Nekoda (Japan), who won gold in 1972, silver in 1968, and bronze in 1964; and Steve Timmons (U.S.A.), who won gold in 1984 and 1988, and bronze in 1992.

Longest volleyball marathon The longest game of volleyball played was one of 24 hr. 10 min. at the Vocational School Center, Torgau, Germany, on September 30–October 1, 2002.

Handball target shooting Jonas Källman (Sweden) hit eight handball targets in 30 seconds on the set of *Guinness Rekord TV,* Stockholm, Sweden, on November 27, 2001.

Most women's World Championships handball titles won Three women's titles (all indoor unless stated) have been won by Romania in 1956, 1960, (both outdoor) and 1962; the GDR in 1971, 1975, and 1978; and the USSR in 1982, 1986, and 1990.

Highest score in an international handball match In August 1981, the USSR beat Afghanistan 86–2 in the "Friendly Army Tournament" at Miskolc, Hungary.

Longest handball marathon The longest game of handball was 70 hours, set by 12 players from the HV Mighty/Stevo team in Geesteren, Tubbergen, The Netherlands, on August 30–September 2, 2001.

Most women's lacrosse World Championships The first World Cup was held in 1982, replacing the World Championships, which had been held three times since 1969. The U.S.A. has won a record six times (in 1974, 1982, 1989, 1993, 1997, and 2001).

HIGHEST BEACH VOLLEYBALL CAREER EARNINGS (AVP TOUR) Karch Kiraly (U.S.A.) has won a record $2,929,158 in official Association of Volleyball Professionals (AVP) Tour earnings through to the end of the 2002 season.

MOST MEN'S HANDBALL WORLD CHAMPIONSHIPS WON Two countries have won the men's world title four times. Sweden (1999 team members seen here) won in 1954, 1958, 1990, and 1999, and Romania in 1961, 1964, 1970, and 1974.

Most men's lacrosse World Championships The U.S.A. has won eight of the nine World Championships (in 1967, 1974, 1982, 1986, 1990, 1994, 1998, and 2002). Canada won the other world title in 1978, beating the U.S.A. 17–16 after extra time—in what was the first drawn international match.

Highest score in men's lacrosse The highest score in a World Cup match is Scotland's 34–3 win over Germany in Manchester, UK, on July 25, 1994. In the World Cup premier division, the record score is the U.S.A.'s 33–2 win over Japan in Manchester on July 21, 1994.

Highest score in women's lacrosse The highest score by an international team was by Great Britain and Ireland with their 40–0 defeat of Long Island during their 1967 tour of the U.S.A.

Longest lacrosse throw The longest recorded lacrosse throw is 488 ft. 6 in. (148.91 m), by Barnet Quinn (Canada) on September 10, 1892.

Most korfball World Championships The Netherlands has won the World Championships (instituted 1978) a record six times, in 1978, 1984, 1987, 1995, 1999, and 2003.

Highest score in a korfball World Championship final The highest team score in the final of the World Championships is 23 by The Netherlands against Belgium (11) in 1999.

Longest korfball marathon Members of the korfball club de Vinken in Vinkeveen, The Netherlands, played a game of korfball lasting 26 hr. 2 min. on May 23–24, 2001.

Biggest winning margin in a korfball World Championship final In the final of the Centennial Championship, held in Rotterdam, The Netherlands, on November 9, 2003, there was a winning margin of 13 points, between The Netherlands (22) and Belgium (9).

Most World Games titles won for korfball Korfball was first held as part of the World Games in 1985 and the most titles won is five (every occasion the event has been held) by The Netherlands, in 1985, 1989, 1993, 1997, and 2001. In winning these five titles, The Netherlands has never lost a match.

Highest score in international women's hockey The England women's hockey team beat France 23–0 in Merton, Greater London, UK, on February 3, 1923.

Highest score in international men's hockey The highest international score was when India defeated the U.S.A. 24–1 in Los Angeles, California, U.S.A., in the 1932 Olympic Games.

MOST CHAMPIONS' TROPHIES IN WOMEN'S HOCKEY The women's Champions' trophy, first held in 1987, has been won a record six times by Australia. They won in 1991, 1993, 1995, 1997, 1999, and 2003. Pictured are Wendy Alcorn (right), playing for Australia against China (Zhaoxa Chen, left).

Most women's hockey World Cups won The Fédération Internationale de Hockey (FIH) World Cup for women was first held in 1974. The most wins is five by The Netherlands (in 1974, 1978, 1983, 1986, and 1990).

Most men's hockey World Cup titles The FIH World Cup for men was first held in 1971. The most wins is four by Pakistan (in 1971, 1978, 1982, and 1994).

Most Champions' trophies in men's hockey This competition was first held in 1978 and has been contested annually since 1980 by the top six men's teams in the world. The most wins is eight by Germany (1986–88 as West Germany, 1991–92, 1995, 1997, and 2001).

Most goals scored in an international hockey career David Ashman (UK) has scored a record 2,326 goals having played for Hampshire, Southampton, Southampton Kestrals, and Hamble Old Boys (for whom he has scored 2,165 goals, a record for one club), in 1958–99.

Most goals scored in an international hockey career The greatest number of goals scored in international hockey is 267 by Paul Litjens (Netherlands) in 177 games.

Highest attendance for a hockey match The match between England and the U.S.A. at Wembley, London, UK, on March 11, 1978, was attended by 65,165 people.

Most hockey Olympics umpired Graham Dennis Nash (UK) umpired in five successive Olympics (1976–92) and retired after the Barcelona Games, having officiated in a record 144 international matches.

Largest hockey stick A hockey stick made by the Jubilee Committee of AMHC Upward, Arnhem, The Netherlands, measured 39 ft. 7 in. (12.07 m) long and weighed 1,278 lb. (580 kg) on September 11, 1999.

BALL SPORTS 2

Most AFL Premiership titles Two clubs have won the AFL Premiership 16 times: Carlton, from 1906 to 1995, and Essendon, from 1897 to 2000.

Highest AFL team score The AFL record for one team is 239 (37–17) by Geelong against Brisbane on May 3, 1992.

Highest aggregate score in an AFL match The highest aggregate record score is 345 points when St. Kilda beat Melbourne 204–141 on May 6, 1978.

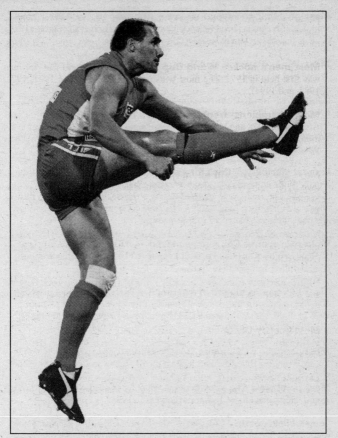

MOST GOALS IN AN AUSTRALIAN FOOTBALL CAREER Tony Lockett (Australia) scored 1,357 goals during his Australian Football League (AFL) career playing for St. Kilda and the Sydney Swans from 1983 to 1999.

Most goals kicked in an AFL Grand Final Two players have kicked nine goals in an AFL Grand Final: Gordon Coventry (Australia) for Collingwood against Richmond in the 1928 AFL Grand Final and Gary Ablett (Australia) for Geelong against Hawthorn in the 1989 AFL Grand Final.

Most goals scored in a debut The greatest number of goals scored in an Australian Rules football debut is 12, by John Coleman (Australia) playing for Essendon against Hawthorn in Round One of the 1949 season.

Most goals by an individual in an AFL season The AFL season's record is 150 and has been reached by two players: Bob Pratt (South Melbourne) in 1934 and Peter Hudson (Hawthorn) in 1971.

Most games played in an AFL career Michael Tuck (Australia) played 426 AFL games in his career from 1972 to 1991.

Longest winning streak Geelong won 23 consecutive games in the AFL Premiership in the 1952/53 season.

Longest losing streak University lost 51 consecutive games in the AFL Premiership from 1912 to 1914.

Largest disciplinary fines for a single AFL match The highest disciplinary fines imposed as a result of a single AFL match is AUS$67,500 ($49,773). The fines were incurred during a match between Western Bulldogs and St. Kilda on May 4, 2003. Nine players from each team were fined and one player was banned for three matches.

Most consecutive CFL games played Bob Cameron (Canada) played 353 consecutive Canadian Football League (CFL) games for the Winnipeg Blue Bombers from 1980 to 2000.

Most CFL games played in a career Lui Passaglia (Canada) played in 408 CFL games for the British Columbia Lions (aka the BC Lions) from 1976 to 2000. He also scored a CFL career record 3,991 points for the BC Lions from 1976 to 2000.

Most points in a CFL game Bob McNamara (Canada) scored 36 points for the Winnipeg Blue Bombers against the BC Lions on October 13, 1956.

Most points in a CFL season Lance Chomyc (Canada) scored a season record 236 points for the Toronto Argonauts in 1991.

Longest field goal in a CFL game The longest field goal in a regular game was 62 yards. It was kicked by Paul McCallum (Canada) for the Saskatchewan Roughriders against the Edmonton Eskimos on October 27, 2001.

Most Grey Cup wins The Toronto Argonauts have won the Grey Cup a record 14 times from 1914 to 1997.

Most receptions in a CFL season Derrell Mitchell (Canada) made a record 160 pass receptions for the Toronto Argonauts in 1998.

Most pass receptions in a CFL career The greatest number of passes caught over the course of a CFL career is 972, by Darren Flutie (Canada) playing for the BC Lions, Edmonton Eskimos, and Hamilton Tiger-Cats from 1991 to 2002.

MOST YARDS PASSING IN A CANADIAN FOOTBALL CAREER Damon Allen (Canada) threw for a record 61,802 yards during his CFL career for Edmonton Eskimos, Ottawa Roughriders, Hamilton Tiger-Cats, Memphis Mad Dogs, British Columbia Lions, and Toronto Argonauts from 1985 to 2003.

Longest rush in a CFL game Two players have gained 109 yards running from the line of scrimmage: George Dixon (Canada) for the Montreal Alouettes against the Ottawa Roughriders on September 2, 1963; and Willie Fleming (U.S.A.) for the BC Lions against the Edmonton Eskimos on October 17, 1964.

Longest punt in a CFL game Zenon Andrusyshun (Canada) kicked a punt a distance of 108 yards for the Toronto Argonauts against the Edmonton Eskimos on October 23, 1977.

Most punt return touchdowns in a CFL career Henry Williams (Canada) returned a total of 26 punts for touchdowns during his CFL career for the Edmonton Eskimos from 1986 to 1999.

Most touchdowns scored in a CFL season Milt Stegall (Canada) scored a record 23 touchdowns for the Winnipeg Blue Bombers in 2002.

Most touchdowns scored in a CFL career George Reed (Canada) scored a total of 137 touchdowns for the Saskatchewan Roughriders during his CFL career from 1963 to 1975.

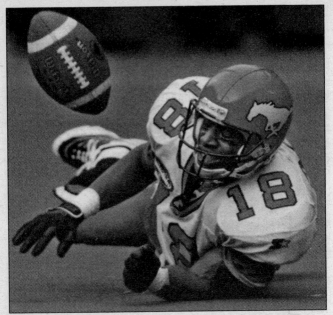

MOST YARDS RECEIVING IN A CFL CAREER Allen Pitts (Canada) gained a total of 14,891 yards receiving for the Calgary Stampeders during his CFL career from 1990 to 2000.

Most yards rushing in a CFL career George Reed (Canada) rushed for a career-record 16,116 yards for the Saskatchewan Roughriders from 1963 to 1975.

Most kicks blocked in a CFL career The greatest number of kicks blocked over the course of a CFL career is 10 by Gerald Vaughn (Canada) while playing for three teams—the Calgary Stampeders, the Winnipeg Blue Bombers, and the Hamilton Tiger-Cats—from 1993 to 2002.

Longest pass completion in Canadian football The longest pass completion in the CFL covered a distance of 109 yards and has been achieved by three different sets of players: Sam Etcheverry to Hal Patterson (both Canada) for the Montreal Alouettes against the Hamilton Tiger-Cats on September 22, 1956; Jerry Keeling to Terry Evanshen (both Canada) for the Calgary Stampeders against the Winnipeg Blue Bombers on September 27, 1966; and Damon Allen to Albert Jackson (both Canada) for the BC Lions against the Montreal Alouettes on August 21, 2002.

Most Shinty Challenge Cup team wins From 1907 to 1986, Newtonmore won the Camanachd Association Challenge Cup (instituted in 1896 and also known as the Scottish Cup) 28 times. Shinty is a game similar to Ireland's hurling and is played almost exclusively in Scotland.

Most Shinty Challenge Cup winners' medals won by an individual David Ritchie and Hugh Chisholm (both UK) of Newtonmore have won 12 Challenge Cup winners' medals each.

Highest score in a Shinty cup final Kingussie beat Newtonmore 12–1 at Fort William, Highland, UK, in 1997.

Highest individual score in a Shinty cup final John Macmillan Mactaggart (UK) scored 10 hails, or goals, for Mid-Argyll in a Camanachd Cup match in 1938.

TENNIS

Fastest serve by a woman Venus Williams (U.S.A.) served at 127.4 mph (205 km/h) during the European Indoor Championships in Zurich, Switzerland, on October 16, 1998.

Youngest female world No. 1 Martina Hingis (Switzerland, b. September 30, 1980, in the former Czechoslovakia) was 16 years 182 days when she became world No. 1 on March 31, 1997. She is also the youngest female Wimbledon champion: she was 15 years 282 days when she won the ladies doubles in 1996 with partner Helena Sukova (Czechoslovakia).

Youngest male world No. 1 Marat Mikhailovich Safin (Russia, b. January 27, 1980) was 20 years 234 days when he achieved the world No. 1 ranking by winning the President's Cup tournament in Tashkent, Uzbekistan, on September 17, 2000.

Youngest Davis Cup player The youngest player to compete in the Davis Cup is Kenny Banzer (Liechtenstein) at the age of 14 years 5 days on February 16, 2000, against Algeria.

Most consecutive Davis Cup wins The U.S.A. won a record seven consecutive Davis Cup tournaments in 1920–26. Their reign was brought to an end by France in 1927, who went on to keep the title for six years, the second longest winning streak, before losing to Great Britain in 1933.

Most Davis Cup wins The most wins in the Davis Cup, the men's international team championship, has been 31 by the U.S.A. from 1900 to 1995.

FASTEST TENNIS SERVE The fastest tennis service by a man (measured with modern equipment) is 150 mph (241.4 km/h) by Andy Roddick (U.S.A.) during a Davis Cup match against Stefan Koubek (Austria) at the Mohegan Sun Arena, Uncasville, Connecticut, U.S.A., on February 6, 2004.

Oldest Davis Cup player The oldest player to compete in the Davis Cup is Yaka-Garonfin Koptigan (Togo, b. December 23, 1941) aged 59 years 147 days on May 27, 2001.

Most Wimbledon men's singles titles Pete Sampras (U.S.A.) won seven Wimbledon men's singles tennis titles in 1993–95 and 1997–2000.

Most Wimbledon singles titles won by a woman The most Wimbledon singles tennis titles won by a woman is nine by Martina Navratilova (U.S.A.) in 1978–79, 1982–87, and 1990.

Best wild card performance at Wimbledon The best ever performance by a wild card entrant at the Wimbledon Championships was that of Goran Ivanisevic (Croatia) in 2001. Invited to play in the competition by the All England Club, Ivanisevic, ranked 125th in the world, won the men's singles title by beating Pat Rafter (Australia) 6–3, 3–6, 6–3, 2–6, 9–7 in the final. The Croatian's popular win came in his fourth final appearance, and he also served a record 213 aces throughout the tournament, including 27 in the final.

Longest Wimbledon career The longest Wimbledon tennis career is 55 years and is held by Jean Borotra (France), who competed in the men's singles competition 35 times from 1922 to 1964. He then went on to compete in the men's veteran doubles and the mixed doubles events from 1965 to 1977, retiring when he was 78.

Oldest U.S. Open champion Margaret du Pont (U.S.A., b. March 4, 1918) won the mixed doubles at the age of 42 years 166 days in 1960.

Youngest U.S. Open champion Vincent Richards (U.S.A., b. March 20, 1903) was 15 years 139 days when he won the men's doubles with Bill Tilden (U.S.A.) in 1918.

Youngest female to win the U.S. Open singles championship Tracey Austin (U.S.A., b. December 12, 1962) was 16 years 271 days when she won the women's singles in 1979.

Youngest male to win the U.S. Open singles championship Pete Sampras (U.S.A., b. August 12, 1971) was 19 years 28 days when he won the U.S. Open on September 9, 1990.

Most U.S. Open singles titles won by a woman Molla Mallory (née Bjurstedt, Norway) won eight U.S. Open singles tennis titles in 1915–18, 1920–22, and 1926.

Most U.S. Open singles titles won by a man The most U.S. Open singles tennis titles won by a man is seven and is shared by Bill Tilden (U.S.A.) in 1920–25 and 1929, Richard Sears (U.S.A.) in 1881–87, and William Larned (U.S.A.) in 1901, 1902, and 1907–11.

Most French Open singles titles won by a woman Chris Evert (U.S.A.) won seven French Open singles tennis titles in 1974, 1975, 1979, 1980, 1983, 1985, and 1986.

MOST FRENCH OPEN SINGLES TENNIS TITLES WON BY A MAN Björn Borg (Sweden) won six French Open singles titles in 1974–75 and 1978–81.

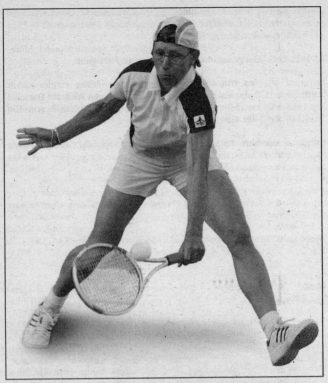

OLDEST WIMBLEDON CHAMPION The oldest main draw Wimbledon tennis champion is Martina Navratilova (U.S.A.). She was 46 years 261 days when she won the mixed doubles with Leander Paes (India) on July 6, 2003.

Most Australian Open singles titles won by a man Roy Emerson (Australia) won a record six Australian Open singles tennis titles in 1961 and 1963–67.

Most men's wheelchair tennis World Team Cups The World Team Cup for wheelchair tennis has been contested annually since 1985. The U.S.A. has won the men's competition a record nine times (1985–91, 1995, and 1997).

Most Grand Slam tournament singles titles won Margaret Court (Australia) won 24 Grand Slam tournament singles from 1960 to 1973.

Oldest tennis player The oldest tennis player is José Guadalupe Leal Lemus (Mexico, b. December 13, 1902), who began playing tennis in 1925 and has been playing regularly ever since, a total of 79 years. Now aged 101, he currently plays every Wednesday at the Club Campestre Morelia, Morelia, Mexico, with a group of doctors 20–25 years his junior.

Longest singles marathon The longest competitive singles match lasted 25 hr. 25 min. and was played between Christian Albrecht Barschel and Hauke Daene (both Germany) on September 12–13, 2003, at Mölln Tennis Club, Mölln, Germany.

Longest doubles marathon The longest competitive doubles tennis match lasted 48 hr. 6 min. and was played between Jaroslaw Kadzielewski and Rafal Siupka, and Mateusz Zatorski and Kamil Milian (all Poland) on August 30 to September 1, 2002, at Giliwice Sports Hall, Poland.

Longest doubles marathon by one pair The longest competitive doubles tennis match, by one pair playing against all comers, lasted 26 hours and was played by Mike Geraghty and Francis Power (both Ireland) on June 20–21, 2003, at Galway Lawn Tennis Club, Galway, Ireland.

RACKET SPORTS

Most badminton World Championships titles A record five titles have been won by Park Joo-bong (South Korea), for the men's doubles in 1985 and 1991 and mixed doubles in 1985, 1989, and 1991.

Most mixed team badminton World Championship wins The most wins at the mixed team badminton World Championships for the Sudirman Cup (instituted in 1989) is four by China, in 1995, 1997, 1999, 2001.

Most badminton World Cup women's singles wins Susi Susanti (Indonesia) won five World Cup women's singles tournaments in 1989, 1993–94, and 1996–97.

Most badminton Thomas Cup wins The most wins at the men's world team badminton championships for the Thomas Cup (instituted in 1948) is 13 by Indonesia (1958, 1961, 1964, 1970, 1973, 1976, 1979, 1984, 1994, 1996, 1998, 2000, and 2002).

Most badminton World Championship singles titles Four Chinese players have each won two individual world titles. Yang Yang won the men's singles in 1987 and 1989, and the women's singles have been won by Li Lingwei in 1983 and 1989; by Han Aiping in 1985 and 1987; and by Ye Zhaoying in 1995 and 1997.

Longest badminton match in competition In the final of the men's singles at the 1997 World Championships at Glasgow, UK, on June 1, Peter Rasmussen (Denmark) beat Sun Jun (China) 16–17, 18–13, 15–10 in a match that lasted 2 hr. 4 min.

Shortest badminton match Ra Kyung-min (South Korea) beat Julia Mann (England) 11–2, 11–1 in 6 minutes during the Uber Cup in Hong Kong on May 19, 1996.

Oldest badminton player Henry Paynter (Canada, b. February 24, 1907) is an active member of the Kelowna Badminton Club, British Columbia, Canada, and was still playing regularly in March 2004, aged 97.

Highest speed of a shuttlecock off a badminton racket In tests at Warwickshire Racquets and Health Club, UK, on November 5, 1996, Simon Archer (UK) hit a shuttlecock at a measured speed of 162 mph (260 km/h).

Longest table tennis singles marathon The longest marathon singles match was 132 hr. 31 min. by Danny Price and Randy Nunes (both U.S.A.) at Cherry Hill, New Jersey, U.S.A., on August 20–26, 1978.

Longest table tennis doubles marathon On April 9–13, 1979, Lance, Phil, and Mark Warren and Bill Weir (all U.S.A.) played doubles table tennis for 101 hr. 1 min. 11 sec. in Sacramento, California, U.S.A.,

Most women's table tennis World Championships
Angelica Rozeanu (Romania) won a record six

MOST UBER CUP WINS China holds the record for the most wins at the women's team badminton World Championships for the Uber Cup, instituted in 1956. They won eight times: in 1984, 1986, 1988, 1990, 1992, 1998, 2000, and 2002. Zhou Mi (China, pictured) played in the 2002 competition.

MOST MEN'S TABLE TENNIS WORLD CHAMPIONSHIP WINS Viktor Barna (Hungary) won a record five men's singles table tennis World Championships (1930, 1932–35).

consecutive women's singles table tennis World Championship titles from 1950 to 1955.

Longest table tennis rally John Duffy and Kevin Schick (both New Zealand) achieved a table tennis rally lasting 5 hr. 2 min. 18.5 sec. at Whangarei, New Zealand, on November 5, 1977.

Most combined team wins at the racquetball World Championships The World Championships were instituted in 1981, have been held biennially since 1984, and are based on the U.S. version of the game. The U.S.A. has won a record ten combined team titles, in 1981, 1984, 1986 (tie with Canada), 1988, 1990, 1992, 1994, 1996, 1998, and 2002.

Most women's racquetball World Championship wins The most women's racquetball World Championships won by an individual is three by Michelle Gould (U.S.A.) in 1992, 1994, and 1996.

Most women's team wins at the racquetball World Championships The U.S.A. has won nine women's team titles, in 1986, 1988, 1990, 1992, 1994, 1996, 1998, 2000, and 2002.

Most wheelchair racquetball World Championships Chip Parmelly (U.S.A.) won a record three wheelchair racquetball World Championships, in 1990, 1992, and 1994.

Most men's Real Tennis World Championships The first recorded Real Tennis world champion was Clerg (France) in ca. 1740. Jacques Edmond Barre (France) held the title for a record 33 years from 1829 to 1962. Pierre Etchebaster (France) holds the record for the greatest number of successful defenses of the title with eight during his career (1928–52).

Most women's Real Tennis World Championships Instituted in 1985, the women's World Championships has been won six times by Penny Lumley (née Fellows, UK) in 1989, 1991, 1995, 1997, 1999, and 2003.

Oldest Real Tennis court The oldest of the surviving active Real Tennis courts in Great Britain is that at Falkland Palace, Fife, built by King James V of Scotland in 1539.

Most squash World Open Championship titles Jansher Khan (Pakistan) won a record eight World Open titles, in 1987, 1989, 1990, and 1992–96.

Most squash club championships The most club championships won by an individual at the same club is 21 (including a record 17 consecutively) by Carole Cameron (UK) at the Thurso and District Squash Club, Thurso, Caithness, UK, in 1982–85 and 1987–2003.

Most squash World Championships Jahangir Khan (Pakistan) won six World Open titles, in 1981–85 and 1988. He has also won the International Squash Rackets Federation world individual title three times, in 1979, 1983, and 1985.

MOST MEN'S WORLD TEAM SQUASH TITLES Australia has won eight men's world team titles, in 1967, 1969, 1971, 1973, 1989, 1991, 2001, and 2003. David Palmer (Australia, pictured) was one of the players in the 2001 World Championship team.

Most women's squash World Championship wins The women's title has been won seven times by Australia, in 1981, 1983, 1992, 1994, 1996, 1998, and 2002.

Most women's world team titles for squash Sarah Fitzgerald (Australia) has won five women's World Open titles, in 1996–98 and 2001–02.

Longest squash match The longest recorded competitive match was one of 2 hr. 45 min. when Jahangir Khan (Pakistan) beat Gamal Awad (Egypt) 9–10, 9–5, 9–7, 9–2, the first game lasting a record 1 hr. 11 min., in the final of the Patrick International Festival in Chichester, West Sussex, UK, on March 30, 1983.

Highest speed of a squash ball In tests at Wimbledon Squash and Badminton Club in January 1988, Roy Buckland hit a squash ball by an overhead service at a measured speed of 144.6 mph (232.7 km/h) over the distance to the front wall. This is equivalent to an initial speed at the racket of 150.8 mph (242.6 km/h).

ATHLETICS

★ MEN'S INDOOR WORLD RECORDS ★

EVENT	MIN:SEC	NAME AND COUNTRY	VENUE	DATE
TRACK				
50 m	5.56	Donovan Bailey (Canada)	Reno, U.S.A.	February 9, 1996
		Maurice Greene (U.S.A.)	Los Angeles, U.S.A.	February 3, 1999
60 m	6.39	Maurice Greene (U.S.A.)	Madrid, Spain	February 3, 1998
		Maurice Greene (U.S.A.)	Atlanta, U.S.A.	March 3, 2001
200 m	19.92	Frank Fredericks (Namibia)	Liévin, France	February 18, 1996
400 m	44.63	Michael Johnson (U.S.A.)	Atlanta, U.S.A.	March 4, 1995
800 m	1:42.67	Wilson Kipketer (Denmark)	Paris, France	March 9, 1997
1,000 m	2:14.36	Wilson Kipketer (Denmark)	Birmingham, UK	February 20, 2000
1,500 m	3:31.18	Hicham El Guerrouj (Morocco)	Stuttgart, Germany	February 2, 1997
1 mile	3:48.45	Hicham El Guerrouj (Morocco)	Ghent, Belgium	February 12, 1997
3,000 m	7:24.90	Daniel Komen (Kenya)	Budapest, Hungary	February 6, 1998

EVENT	MIN:SEC	NAME AND COUNTRY	VENUE	DATE
TRACK				
5,000 m	12:49.60*	Kenenisa Bekele (Ethiopia)	Birmingham, UK	February 20, 2004
50-m hurdles	6.25	Mark McCoy (Canada)	Kobe, Japan	March 5, 1986
60-m hurdles	7.30	Colin Jackson (GB)	Sindelfingen, Germany	March 6, 1994
4 × 200-m relay	1:22.11	Great Britain (Linford Christie, Darren Braithwaite, Ade Mafe, John Regis)	Glasgow, UK	March 3, 1991
4 × 400-m relay	3:02.83	U.S.A. (Andre Morris, Dameon Johnson, Deon Minor, Milton Campbell)	Maebashi, Japan	March 7, 1999
5,000-m walk	18:07.08	Mikhail Shchennikov (Russia)	Moscow, Russia	February 14, 1995
FIELD				
High jump	7 ft. 11.6 in. (2.43 m)	Javier Sotomayor (Cuba)	Budapest, Hungary	March 4, 1989
Pole vault	20 ft. 2 in. (6.15 m)	Sergei Bubka (Ukraine)	Donetsk, Ukraine	February 21, 1993
Long jump	28 ft. 9.96 in. (8.79 m)	Carl Lewis (U.S.A.)	New York City, U.S.A.	January 27, 1984
Triple jump	58 ft. 5 in. (17.83 m)	Aliecer Urrutia (Cuba)	Sindelfingen, Germany	March 1, 1997
Shot put	74 ft. 4 in. (22.66 m)	Randy Barnes (U.S.A.)	Los Angeles, U.S.A.	January 20, 1989
Heptathlon	6,476 points	Dan O'Brien (U.S.A.)	Toronto, Canada	March 13–14, 1993

Events: 60-m 6.67 sec. long jump 25 ft. 6.2 in. (7.84 m); shot put 52 ft. 6.6 in. (16.02 m); high jump 6 ft. 11.76 in. (2.13 m); 60 m hurdles 7.85 sec.; pole vault 17 ft. 0.7 in. (5.20 m); 1,000 m 2:57.96

*From January 1, 1987, the International Athletics Association Federation (IAAF) recognized world indoor records. Prior to that the best performances had been noted as world bests. After this date, performances needed to better the world best performances to be officially accepted by the IAAF as records.

Most women's gold medals in the athletics World Championships Gail Devers (U.S.A.) won five World Championship gold medals: for the 100 m in 1993, the 100-m hurdles in 1993, 1995, and 1999, and for the 4 × 100-m in 1997.

Most men's successive World Championship athletics wins in a single event Sergei Bubka (Ukraine) won six athletics World Championships in the pole vault event from 1983 to 1997.

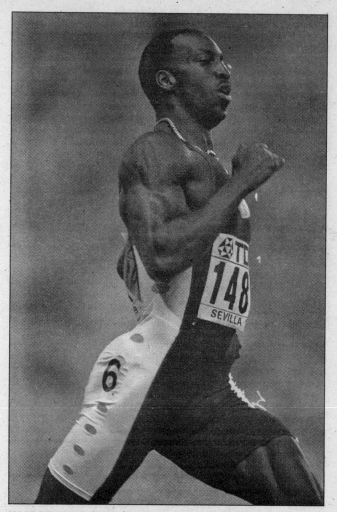

MOST MEN'S GOLD MEDALS IN THE ATHLETICS WORLD CHAMPIONSHIPS The World Championships were inaugurated in 1983, when they were held in Helsinki, Finland. The greatest number of World Championship men's gold medals won by an individual is nine, by Michael Johnson (U.S.A., pictured), who won the 200 m in 1991 and 1995, the 400 m in 1993, 1995, 1997, and 1999, and the 4 × 400-m relay in 1993, 1995, and 1999.

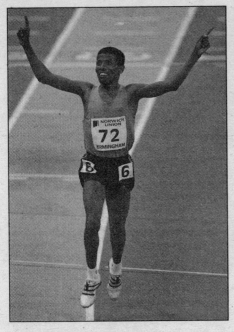

FASTEST 10,000 M
Haile Gebrselassie (Ethiopia) ran 26:22.75 for the men's 10,000-m event at Hengelo, The Netherlands, on June 1, 1998. He also holds the record for the fastest 5,000 m (12:39.36).

Most women's athletics World Championship medals Merlene Ottey (Jamaica) won 14 athletics World Championship medals from 1983 to 1997: gold for 200 m in 1993 and 1995 and 4 × 100-m in 1991; silver for 100 m in 1993 and 1995, 200 m in 1983, and 4 × 100-m in 1991; and bronze for 100 m in 1987 and 1991, 200 m in 1987, 1991, and 1997, and 4 × 100-m in 1983 and 1993.

★ MEN'S OUTDOOR WORLD RECORDS ★

EVENT	MIN:SEC	NAME AND COUNTRY	VENUE	DATE
TRACK				
100 m	9.78	Tim Montgomery (U.S.A.)	Paris, France	September 14, 2002
200 m	19.32	Michael Johnson (U.S.A.)	Atlanta, U.S.A.	August 1, 1996
400 m	43.18	Michael Johnson (U.S.A.)	Seville, Spain	August 26, 1999
800 m	1:41.11	Wilson Kipketer (Denmark)	Cologne, Germany	August 24, 1997
1,000 m	2:11.96	Noah Ngeny (Kenya)	Rieti, Italy	September 5, 1999
1,500 m	3:26.00	Hicham El Guerrouj (Morocco)	Rome, Italy	July 14, 1998
1 mile	3:43.13	Hicham El Guerrouj (Morocco)	Rome, Italy	July 7, 1999

EVENT	MIN:SEC	NAME AND COUNTRY	VENUE	DATE
TRACK				
2,000 m	4:44.79	Hicham El Guerrouj (Morocco)	Berlin, Germany	September 7, 1999
3,000 m	7:20.67	Daniel Komen (Kenya)	Rieti, Italy	September 1, 1996
5,000 m	12:39.36	Haile Gebrselassie (Ethiopia)	Helsinki, Finland	June 13, 1998
10,000 m	26:22.75	Haile Gebrselassie (Ethiopia)	Hengelo, The Netherlands	June 1, 1998
20,000 m	56:55.60	Arturo Barrios (Mexico, now U.S.A.)	La Fièche, France	March 30, 1991
25,000 m	1:13:55.80	Toshihiko Seko (Japan)	Christchurch, New Zealand	March 22, 1981
30,000 m	1:29:18.80	Toshihiko Seko (Japan)	Christchurch, New Zealand	March 22, 1981
1 hour	21,101 m	Arturo Barrios (Mexico, now U.S.A.)	La Fièche, France	March 30, 1991
110-m hurdles	12.91	Colin Jackson (GB)	Stuttgart, Germany	August 20, 1993
400-m hurdles	46.78	Kevin Young (U.S.A.)	Barcelona, Spain	August 6, 1992
3,000-m steeplechase	7:55.28	Brahim Boulami (Morocco)	Brussels, Belgium	August 24, 2001
4 × 100-m relay	37.40	U.S.A. (Michael Marsh, Leroy Burrell, Dennis Mitchell, Carl Lewis)	Barcelona, Spain	August 8, 1992
		U.S.A. (John Drummond, Andre Cason, Dennis Mitchell, Leroy Burrell)	Stuttgart, Germany	August 21, 1993
4 × 200-m relay	1:18.68	U.S.A. (Michael Marsh, Leroy Burrell, Floyd Heard, Carl Lewis)	Santa Monica Track Club Walnut, U.S.A.	April 17, 1994
4 × 400-m relay	2:54.20	U.S.A. (Jerome Young, Antonio Pettigrew, Tyree Washington, Michael Johnson)	New York City, U.S.A.	July 23, 1998
4 × 800-m relay	7:03.89	Great Britain (Peter Elliott, Garry Cook, Steve Cram, Sebastian Coe)	London, UK	August 30, 1982
4 × 1,500-m relay	14:38.80	West Germany (Thomas Wessinghage,	Cologne, Germany	August 17, 1977

EVENT	MIN:SEC	NAME AND COUNTRY	VENUE	DATE
TRACK				
		Harald Hudak, Michael Lederer, Karl Fleschen)		
FIELD				
High jump	8 ft. 0.25 in. (2.45 m)	Javier Sotomayor (Cuba)	Salamanca, Spain	July 27, 1993
Pole vault	20 ft. 1.68 in. (6.14 m)	Sergei Bubka (Ukraine)	Sestriere, Italy	July 31, 1994
Long jump	29 ft. 4.32 in. (8.95 m)	Mike Powell (U.S.A.)	Tokyo, Japan	August 30, 1991
Triple jump	60 ft. (18.29 m)	Jonathan Edwards (GB)	Gothenburg, Sweden	August 7, 1995
Shot put	75 ft. 10.2 in. (23.12 m)	Randy Barnes (U.S.A.)	Los Angeles, U.S.A.	May 20, 1990
Discus	243 ft. (74.08 m)	Jurgen Schult (GDR)	Neubrandenburg, Germany	June 6, 1986
Hammer	284 ft. 7 in. (86.74 m)	Yuriy Sedykh (USSR)	Stuttgart, Germany	August 30, 1986
Javelin	323 ft. 1 in. (98.48 m)	Jan Zelezny (Czech Republic)	Jena, Germany	May 25, 1996
Decathlon	9,026 points	Roman Sebrie (Czech Republic)	Gützis, Austria	May 26–27, 2001
Day 1:		Events: 100 m 10.64 sec.; long jump 26 ft. 7.25 in. (8.11 m); shot put 15.33 m (50 ft. 3.7 in.); high jump 6 ft. 11.4 in. (2.12 m)		
Day 2:		110-m hurdles 13.92 sec.; discus 157 ft. 2.5 in. (47.92 m); pole vault 15 ft. 9 in. (4.80 m); javelin 230 ft. 2 in. (70.16 m); 1,500 m 4:21.98		

Most men's athletics World Championship medals Carl Lewis (U.S.A.) won a total of 10 World Championship medals. He won eight gold medals—for the 100 m, long jump, and 4 × 100-m relay in 1983; the 100 m, long jump, and 4 × 100-m relay in 1987; and the 100 m and 4 × 100-m relay in 1991—as well as silver for the long jump in 1991 and bronze for the 200 m in 1993.

Most men's athletics Olympic gold medals Raymond Clarence Ewry (U.S.A.) won 10 Olympic gold medals, in the standing high, long, and triple jumps in 1900, 1904, 1906, and 1908.

Most women's athletics Olympic gold medals The most gold medals won by a woman is four, shared by: Francina "Fanny" Elsje Blankers-Koen (Netherlands) for the 100 m, 200 m, 80-m hurdles, and the 4 × 100-m relay, in 1948; Elizabeth "Betty" Cuthbert (Australia) for the 100 m, 200 m, and 4 × 100-m relay in 1956 and the 400 m in 1964; Bärbel Wöckel (GDR) in the 200 m and 4 × 100-m relay in 1976 and 1980; and

MOST MEN'S ATHLETICS OLYMPIC MEDALS Paavo Nurrni (Finland, right) won 12 Olympic medals (nine gold and three silver) in the Games of 1920, 1924, and 1928.

Evelyn Ashford (U.S.A.) in the 100 m in 1984 and the 4 × 100-m relay in 1984, 1988, and 1992.

Most athletics Olympic gold medals in one Games Paavo Nurmi (Finland) won five gold medals in 1924: in the men's 1,500 m, 5,000 m, 10,000-m cross-country, and the 3,000-m team and cross-country team events.

The most medals won in individual events is four by Alvin Christian Kraenzlein (U.S.A.), who won the men's 60 m, 110-m hurdles, 200-m hurdles, and long jump in 1900.

Most women's athletics Olympic medals Three women athletes share this record: Shirley Barbara de la Hunty (Australia) won seven medals—three gold, one silver, and three bronze—in the 1948, 1952, and 1956 Games. A reread of the photo finish indicates that she finished third, not fourth, in the 1948 200-m event, thus unofficially increasing her medal haul to eight. Irena Szewinska (Poland) won a total of seven medals—three gold, two silver, and two bronze—in 1964, 1968, 1972, and 1976, and is the only woman athlete to win a medal in four successive Games. Merlene Ottey (Jamaica) has also won seven medals—two silver and five bronze—in 1980, 1984, 1992, and 1996.

FASTEST MAN

The men's 100 m is a classic record that holds a unique place in sport, with the record holder arguably able to claim the title of world's fastest man. The history of this event encompasses many of the greatest names in athletics.

10.2 seconds In the first edition of *Guinness World Records* (formerly *The Guinness Book of Records*) in 1955, the record for the men's 100 m was 10.2 seconds and was jointly held by six athletes: Jesse Owens (U.S.A., who ran this time in 1936), Harold Davis (U.S.A., 1941), Lloyd LaBeach (U.S.A., 1948), Norwood "Barney" Ewell (U.S.A., 1948), McDonald Bailey (Trinidad, 1951), and Heinz Fütterer (West Germany, 1954).

1936
Jesse Owens 10.2 seconds

1960
Armin Hary 10 seconds

1968
Jim Hines 9.95 seconds

1983
Calvin Smith 9.93 seconds

1991
Carl Lewis 9.86 seconds

1996
Donovan Bailey 9.84 seconds

1999
Maurice Greene 9.79 seconds

Unlike today, many records set before January 1977 were hand-timed using stopwatches that were accurate to the nearest tenth of a second. This meant that an athlete needed to break the record by a clear tenth of a second to set a new record, increasing the odds of joint record holders. Today, automatic electronic timers accurately register up to one hundredth of a second, meaning that it is possible to ratify records with smaller margins than ever before.

In 1956, two further names were added to the 10.2-second record: Americans Bobby Morrow and Ira Murchison both ran times of 10.2 seconds that year. The 10.2-second barrier was finally breached in August 1956 by Willie Williams (U.S.A.), and his time of 10.1 seconds was equaled by four other athletes before the 10-second time was eventually set by Armin Hary (West Germany) in 1960.

Under 10 seconds Electronic timing was introduced at the Mexico Olympics in 1968. The first athlete to have his electronically timed run recognized by the International Amateur Athletics Federation (IAFF) as a record was Jim Hines (U.S.A.), who ran 9.95 seconds for Olympic gold. The IAAF recognized Hines' 9.95 time, but continued to recognize the other 11 athletes who shared or equaled the existing record of 9.9 seconds, until Carl Lewis (U.S.A.) ran the 100 m in an amazing time of 9.86 seconds in 1991.

A record-breaking decade The 1980s saw extraordinary 100-m runs. Calvin Smith (U.S.A.) ran 9.93 seconds in 1983 and Carl Lewis equaled this time in 1987 before running a new time of 9.92 at the Seoul Olympics in 1988. Lewis actually finished in the silver medal position behind Ben Johnson (Canada) in the Olympic final, but Johnson failed the mandatory drug test, and his 9.79 time was disqualified, allowing Lewis to take gold. During the race, Lewis looked over at Johnson three times, which cost him a precious hundredth of a second.

Rivalry The next six years marked a great rivalry between Carl Lewis and Leroy Burrell (U.S.A.), and further hundredths of a second were shaved off the record. Burrell set a new time for the 100 m on June 14, 1991 in New York with 9.90 seconds, but Lewis snatched it back later that year with a new record of 9.86. This race at the World Championships in Tokyo was rated as one of the greatest 100 m of all time, with six athletes beating 10 seconds, and the top two (Lewis and Burrell) beating the listed world record. Burrell broke the record again in 1994 running a time of 9.85, but lost it to Donovan Bailey (Canada) in July 1996 with a time of 9.84. Bailey won this race with an incredible final burst of speed; he was only in fifth place at 50 m, but had moved up to first place by the 90-m mark.

Maurice Greene (U.S.A.) dominated the 100 m for the following three years, culminating with his 9.79-second run in June 1999.

Fastest man on Earth Maurice Green's record was finally broken by Tim Montgomery (U.S.A.) on September 14, 2002 in Paris at the IAAF Grand Prix final. Montgomery flew out of the starting blocks, winning in 9.78 seconds (0.42 seconds faster than the record set by Jesse Owens in 1936), and running at an average speed of 22.9 mph (36.8 km/h).

★ MEN'S 100-M RECORD BREAKERS ★

TIME	ATHLETE	DATE	VENUE
10.2	Jesse Owens (U.S.A.)	June 20, 1936	Chicago
10.1	Willie Williams (U.S.A.)	August 3, 1956	Berlin
10.0	Armin Hary (West Germany)	June 21, 1960	Zurich
9.9	Jim Hines (U.S.A.)	June 20, 1968	Sacramento
9.95	Jim Hines (U.S.A.)	October 14, 1968	Mexico City
9.93	Calvin Smith (U.S.A.)	July 3, 1983	Colorado
9.92	Carl Lewis (U.S.A.)	September 24, 1988	Seoul
9.90	Leroy Burrell (U.S.A.)	June 14, 1991	New York
9.86	Carl Lewis (U.S.A.)	August 25, 1991	Tokyo
9.85	Leroy Burrell (U.S.A.)	July 6, 1994	Lausanne
9.84	Donovan Bailey (Canada)	July 27, 1996	Atlanta
9.79	Maurice Greene (U.S.A.)	June 16, 1999	Athens
9.78	Tim Montgomery (U.S.A.)	September 14, 2002	Paris

GWR TALKS TO Tim Montgomery

When did you realize that you wanted to pursue a career in athletics? As a very young child, I knew that I was athletic and pretty fast, but I didn't look at it as the profession for me until later on in my life. I remember when I had to cut the grass and I would run around our huge yard and overexert myself until I would just pass out! I guess I was about 14 when people began to recognize that I had great potential to be a top-class athlete.

Who encouraged you? My mother was always a great source of motivation and support. She encouraged me to dream big and reach for anything I desired. I also received encouragement from coaches, teachers, and many other people.

What's your typical training day? Very strenuous. We practice six days a week for several hours a day. Every day varies. One day we may be doing intervals and blocks/starts and the next day we have running drills followed by weight training.

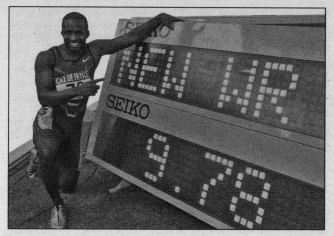

2002
Tim Montgomery 9.78 seconds

Do you have to follow a special diet? Not really. I train really hard so I don't have to diet. But you have to be sensible and eat healthily or else it could jeopardize your training. I will say, however, that I'm a big fan of pizza!

What do you consider to be your greatest achievement? The world record is very important to me. I can't describe what it feels like to know that you've beaten everyone in the world and that you can be considered the best on the entire planet! Another favorite moment was when I set the world junior record in 1994.

Is it true that you once competed in borrowed shoes and still won? Yes! My luggage got lost and I had to borrow Marion Jones's shoes. That definitely has to be the most hilarious and odd thing that has ever happened to me.

What does being a record holder mean to you? To know that you hold one of the most coveted titles in the sport makes you feel like you can touch the sky. It has been a confirmation that if you work hard and be persistent and keep the faith you can overcome even the greatest obstacles.

Who was your idol when you were growing up? Muhammad Ali. I loved everything about him: his gracefulness in the ring, his attitude, his athletic ability . . . everything!

What are your future goals? I'd love to break my own record! On a personal level, I'd like to start up and run the Tim Montgomery Foundation to help young people reach their goals and overcome adversity and other challenges in life.

What advice would you give to youngsters who want to pursue a career in athletics? If you believe in yourself, what other people think won't matter. If you want to play a sport or break a record, there is nothing stopping you except you.

What gives you your drive? God, my family, and myself. With those three things, I can and will reach all my goals.

★ WOMEN'S OUTDOOR WORLD RECORDS ★

EVENT	MIN:SEC	NAME AND COUNTRY	VENUE	DATE
TRACK				
100 m	10.49	Florence Griffith-Joyner (U.S.A.)	Indianapolis, U.S.A.	July 16, 1998
200 m	21.34	Florence Griffith-Joyner	Seoul, South Korea	September 29, 1988
400 m	47.60	Marita Koch (GDR)	Canberra, Australia	October 6, 1985
800 m	1:53.28	Jarmila Kratochvilova (Czechoslovakia)	Munich, Germany	July 26, 1983
1,000 m	2:28.98	Svetlana Masterkova (Russia)	Brussels, Belgium	August 23, 1996
1,500 m	3:50.46	Qu Yunxia (China)	Beijing, China	September 11, 1993
1 mile	4:12.56	Svetlana Masterkova (Russia)	Zurich, Switzerland	August 14, 1996
2,000 m	5:25.36	Sonia O'Sullivan (Ireland)	Edinburgh, UK	July 8, 1994
3,000 m	8:06.11	Wang Junxia (China)	Beijing, China	September 13, 1993
5,000 m	14:28.09	Jiang Bo (China)	Beijing, China	October 23, 1997
10,000 m	29:31.78	Wang Junxia (China)	Beijing, China	September 8, 1993
20,000 m	1:05:26.60	Tegla Loroupe (Kenya)	Borgholzhausen, Germany	September 3, 2000
25,000 m	1:27:05.90	Tegla Loroupe (Kenya)	Megerkirchen, Germany	September 21, 2002
30,000 m	1:45:50.00	Tegla Loroupe (Kenya)	Warstein, Germany	June 6, 2003
1 hour	18,340 m	Tegla Loroupe (Kenya)	Borgholzhausen, Germany	August 7, 1998
100-m hurdles	12.21	Yordanka Donkova (Bulgaria)	Stara Zagora, Bulgaria	August 20, 1988
400-m hurdles	52.34	Yuliya Pechonkina (Russia)	Tula, Russia	August 8, 2003

EVENT	MIN:SEC	NAME AND COUNTRY	VENUE	DATE
3,000-m steeplechase	9:08.33	Gulnara Samitova (Russia)	Tula, Russia	August 10, 2003
4 × 100-m relay	41.37	GDR (Silke Gladisch, Sabine Rieger, Ingrid Auerswald, Marlies Göhr)	Canberra, Australia	October 6, 1985
4 × 200-m relay	1:27.46	U.S.A. "Blue" (LaTasha Jenkins, Latasha Colander Richardson, Nanceen Perry, Marion Jones)	Philadelphia, U.S.A.	April 29, 2000
4 × 400-m relay	3:15.17	USSR, (Tatyana Ledovskaya, Olga Nazarova, Maria Pinigina, Olga Bryzgina)	Seoul, South Korea	October 1, 1988
4 × 800-m relay	7:50.17	USSR, (Nadezhda Olizarenko, Lyubov Gurina, Lyudmila Borisova, Irina Podyalovskaya)	Moscow, Russia	August 5, 1984
FIELD				
High jump	6 ft. 10.25 in. (2.09 m)	Stefka Kostadinova (Bulgaria)	Rome, Italy	August 30, 1987
Pole vault	15 ft. 9.75 in. (4.82 m)	Yelena Isinbayeva (Russia)	Gateshead, UK	July 13, 2003
Long jump	24 ft. 8.25 in. (7.52 m)	Galina Chistyakova (USSR)	St. Petersburg, Russia	June 1, 1988
Triple jump	50 ft. 10.25 in. (15.50 m)	Inessa Kravets (Ukraine)	Gothenburg, Sweden	August 10, 1995
Shot put	74 ft. 3 in. (22.63 m)	Natalya Lisovskaya (USSR)	Moscow, Russia	June 7, 1987
Discus	252 ft. (76.80 m)	Gabriele Reinsch (GDR)	Neubrandenburg, Germany	July 9, 1988
Javelin	234 ft. 8 in. (71.54 m)	Osteidys Menédez (Cuba)	Réthymno, Greece	July 1, 2001
Heptathlon	7,291 points	Jacqueline Joyner-Kersee (U.S.A.)	Seoul, South Korea	September 23–24, 1988

Events: 100-m hurdles 12.69 sec.; high jump 6 ft. 1.25 in. (1.86 m); shot put 51 ft. 10 in. (15.80 m); 200 m 22.56 sec.; long jump 23 ft. 10.25 in. (7.27 m); javelin 149 ft. 10 in. (45.66 m); 800 m 2:8.51

Longest winning sequence in a track event Ed Moses (U.S.A.) dominated the men's 400-m hurdling event for almost 10 years. His record of 122 consecutive wins began on September 2, 1977 and ended when he was beaten by Danny Harris (U.S.A.) in Madrid, Spain, on June 4, 1987.

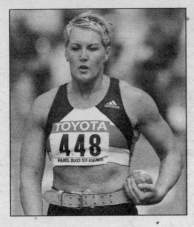

MOST SUCCESSIVE WINS BY A WOMAN IN THE ATHLETICS WORLD CHAMPIONSHIPS Astrid Kumbernuss (Germany) won three successive shot put events from 1995 to 1999.

Longest winning sequence in a field event Iolanda Balas (Romania) won 150 consecutive competitions in the high jump from 1956 to 1967.

Greatest standing long jump The farthest long jump from a standing position is 12 ft. 2 in. (3.71 m) by Arne Tvervaag (Norway) in 1968.

The women's best is 9 ft. 7 in. (2.92 m) by Annelin Mannes (Norway) at Flisa, Norway, on March 7, 1981.

Greatest standing high jump The greatest high jump from a standing position is 6 ft. 2.75 in. (1.90 m) by Rune Almen (Sweden) at Karlstad, Sweden, on May 3, 1980.

The women's best is 4 ft. 11.75 in. (1.52 m) achieved by Grete Bjordalsbakka (Norway) in 1984.

Fastest 1,000-mile relay by a team of 10 Willie Mtolo, Graham Meyer, Jan van Rooyen, Dimitri Grishine, Daniel Radebe, Pio Mpolokeng, Oliver Kandiero, Frans Moyo, Simon Mele, and Philip Molefi (all South Africa) ran a 1,000-mile (1,600-km) relay from Cape Town to Johannesburg, South Africa, in 99 hr. 3 min. 27 sec. from August 14 to 18, 2002.

Fastest men's 100 × 1,000-m relay A team from the Centro Universitario Sportivo, Bari, Italy, completed a 100 × 1,000-m relay in 5 hr. 13 min. 21.9 sec. on March 14, 1999.

Most participants in a relay race A total of 7,175 runners (287 teams of 25) participated in the Batavierenrace from Nijmegen to Enschede, The Netherlands, on April 24, 1999.

Fastest 100 × 1-mile relay The record for 100 miles (160 km) by 100 runners is 7 hr. 35 min. 55.4 sec. by the Canadian Milers Athletic Club at York University, Toronto, Ontario, Canada, on December 20, 1998.

The equivalent women's record was set by the Canadian Women's Milers Club who completed a 100 × 1-mile relay in a time of 9 hr. 23 min. 39 sec. on December 27, 1999.

Most athletics world records set on one day Jesse Owens (U.S.A.) set six world records in 45 minutes at Ann Arbor, Michigan, U.S.A., on May 25, 1935 with a 9.4-sec. 100 yd. at 3:15 p.m., a 26-ft. 8.25-in.-long (8.13-m) jump at 3:25 p.m., a 20.3-sec. 220 yd. (and 200 m) at 3:45 p.m., and a 22.6-sec. 220-yd. low hurdles at 4 p.m. (which also included a record for the 200-m hurdles).

★ WOMEN'S INDOOR WORLD RECORDS ★

EVENT	MIN:SEC	NAME AND COUNTRY	VENUE	DATE
TRACK				
50 m	5.96	Irina Privalova (Russia)	Madrid, Spain	February 9, 1995
60 m	6.92	Irina Privalova (Russia)	Madrid, Spain	February 11, 1993 February 9, 1995
200 m	21.87	Merlene Ottey (Jamaica)	Liévin, France	February 13, 1993
400 m	49.59	Jarmila Kratochvílová (Czechoslovakia)	Milan, Italy	March 7, 1982
800 m	1:55.82	Jolanda Ceplak (Slovenia)	Vienna, Austria	March 3, 2002
1,000 m	2:30.94	Maria Mutola (Mozambique)	Stockholm, Sweden	February 25, 1999
1,500 m	3:59.98	Regina Jacobs (U.S.A.)	Boston, U.S.A.	February 2, 2003
1 mile	4:17.14	Doina Melinte (Romania)	East Rutherford, U.S.A.	February 9, 1990
3,000 m	8:29.15	Berhane Adere (Ethiopia)	Stuttgart,	February 3, 2002
5,000 m	14:39.29	Berhane Adere (Ethiopia)	Stuttgart, Germany	January 31, 2004
50-m hurdles	6.58	Cornelia Oschkenat (GDR)	Berlin, Germany	February 20, 1988
60-m hurdles	7.69	Lyudmila Engquist (Russia)	Chelyabinsk, Russia	February 4, 1993
4 × 200-m relay	1:32.55	SC Eintracht Hamm (Helga Arendt, Silke-Beate Knoll, Mechthild Kluth, Gisela Kinzel, all West Germany)	Dortmund, Germany	February 19, 1988
		LG Olympia Dortmund Karlsrune (Esther Möller, Gabi Rockmeier, Birgit Rockmeier, Andrea Philipp, all Germany)	Germany	February 21, 1999
4 × 400-m relay	3:24.25	Russia (Tatyana Chebykina,	Maebashi, Japan	March 7, 1999

EVENT	MIN:SEC	NAME AND COUNTRY	VENUE	DATE
TRACK				
		Svetlana Goncharenko, Olga Kotlyarova, Natalya Nazarova)		
3,000-m walk	11:40.33	Claudia Iovan (Romania)	Bucharest, Romania	January 30, 1999
FIELD				
High jump	6 ft. 9.5 in. (2.07 m)	Heike Henkel (Germany)	Karlsruhe, Germany	February 9, 1992
Pole vault	15 ft. 11 in. (4.85 m)	Svetlana Feplanova (Russia)	Athens, Greece	February 22, 2004
Long jump	24 ft. 2.25 in. (7.37 m)	Heike Drechsler (GDR)	Vienna, Austria	February 13, 1988
Triple jump	49 ft. 9 in. (15.16 m)	Ashia Hansen (GB)	Valencia, Spain	February 28, 1998
Shot put	73 ft. 10 in. (22.50 m)	Helena Fibingerová (Czechoslovakia)	Jablonec, Czechoslovakia	February 19, 1977
Pentathlon	4,991 points	Irina Belova (Russia)	Berlin, Germany	February 14–15, 1992

Events: 60-m hurdles 8.22 sec.; high jump 6 ft. 4 in. (1.93 m); shot put 43 ft. 5.75 in. (13.25 m); long jump 21 ft. 10.75 in. (6.67 m); 800 m 2:10.26

Most athletics Indoor World Championship medals Merlene Ottey (Jamaica) won six Indoor World Championship medals in individual events: three gold (60 m in 1995 and 200 m in 1989 and 1991), two silver (60 m in 1991 and 200 m in 1987), and one bronze (60 m in 1989).

The men's record is five medals and is held jointly by Ivan Pedroso (Cuba), for the long jump (gold in 1993, 1995, 1997, 1999, and 2001) and Javier Sotomayor (Cuba) for the high jump (gold in 1989, 1993, 1995, and 1999 and bronze in 1991).

Greatest average mileage run daily During the year from August 1, 1996 to July 31, 1997, Tirtha Kumar Phani (India) ran every day, running 14,021.7 miles (22,565.76 km) in total. This equates to an average of 38.41 miles (61.824 km) per day.

Most individual medals won at half marathon World Championships The most individual medals won at the IAAF Half Marathon World Championships is eight by Lidia Simon-Slavuteanu (Romania). From 1996 to 2000, she won three team gold, one team silver, one individual silver, and three individual bronze. The men's record is five medals by Hendrick Ramaala (South Africa)—two team gold, one team silver, and two individual silver from 1997 to 1999.

FASTEST WOMEN'S INDOOR 800 M Jolanda Ceplak (Slovenia) set a new record for the women's indoor 800-m event on March 3, 2002 in Vienna, Austria, with a time of 1 min. 55.82 sec.

Most team wins in the half marathon World Championships The most team wins at the IAAF Half Marathon World Championships is seven for men by Kenya (1992–95, 1997, 2000, 2002), and six for women by Romania (1993–97, 2000).

Largest half marathon The world's largest half marathon is The BUPA Great North Run between Newcastle-upon-Tyne and South Shields, Tyne and Wear, UK. For the 2000 event held on October 22, there were 36,822 finishers out of 50,173 entries.

Fastest half marathon speed march William MacLennan (UK) completed a half marathon wearing full military combat gear and carrying a 40-lb. (18-kg) backpack, in 1 hr. 43 min. 42 sec. at the Redcar Half Marathon, North Yorkshire, UK, on March 25, 2001.

Most marathons run in a calendar year The most marathons completed in one year is 100 by Angela Gargano (Italy). Starting with the Dubai Marathon on January 11, 2002, she went on to run 99 more, the last of which was the Maratona di San Silvestro, Italy, on December 31, 2002.

Fastest aggregate time to run a marathon on each continent From February 13 to May 23, 1999, Tim Rogers (UK) ran a marathon on each of the seven continents in an aggregate time of 34 hr. 23 min. 8 sec.

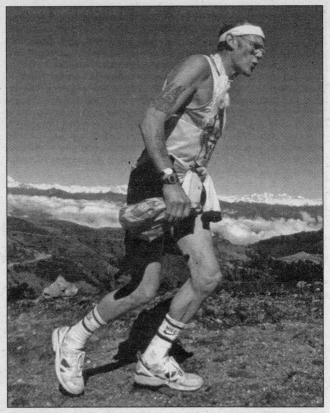

HIGHEST ALTITUDE MARATHON The biennial Everest marathon, which was first run on November 27, 1987, begins at Gorak Shep at an altitude of 17,100 ft. (5,212 m), and ends at Namche Bazar at 11,300 ft. (3,444 m). The men's record is 3 hr. 56 min. 10 sec. by Hari Roka (Nepal), set in 1999, and the women's record is 5 hr. 16 min. 3 sec., set by Anne Stentiford (UK) in 1997.

The attempt took 99 days to complete, which is also a record for the shortest duration.

The women's world record is 37 hr. 20 sec. by Kimi Puntillo (U.S.A.), who ran them all from November 3, 1996 to October 4, 1998. The attempt took 700 days to complete—a record in itself.

★ MEN'S ULTRA-LONG DISTANCE WORLD RECORDS ★

EVENT	RECORD	NAME, NATIONALITY & VENUE	DATE
100 km	6:10:20	Don Ritchie (GB), London, UK	October 28, 1978
100 miles	11:30:51	Don Ritchie (GB), London, UK	October 15, 1977
1,000 km	5 days 16:17:00	Yiannis Kouros (Greece), Cotac, Australia	November 26–December 1, 1984
1,000 miles	11 days 13:54:58	Piotr Silikin (Lithuania), Nanango, Australia	March 11–23, 1998
24 hours	188.589 miles (303.506 km)	Yiannis Kouros (Australia), Adelaide, Australia	October 4–5, 1997
6 days	635.083 miles (1,022.068 km)	Yiannis Kouros (Greece), New York, U.S.A.	July 2–8, 1984

★ WOMEN'S ULTRA-LONG DISTANCE WORLD RECORDS ★

EVENT	RECORD	NAME, NATIONALITY & VENUE	DATE
100 km	7:23:28	Valentina Liakhova (Russia), Nantes, France	September 28, 1996
100 miles	14:29:44	Ann Trason (U.S.A.), Santa Rosa, U.S.A.	March 18–19, 1989
1,000 km	8 days 00:27:06	Eleanor Robinson (GB), Nanango, Australia	March 11–18, 1998
1,000 miles	13 days 01:54:02	Eleanor Robinson (GB), Nanango, Australia	March 11–24, 1998
24 hours	149.234 miles (240.169 km)	Eleanor Adams (GB), Melbourne, Australia	August 19–20, 1989

Fastest time to complete three marathons in three days The fastest combined time for three marathons in three days is 8 hr. 22 min. 31 sec. by Raymond Hubbard (UK). The races were held from April 16 to 18, 1988: Belfast 2 hr. 45 min. 55 sec.; London 2 hr. 48 min. 45 sec.; and Boston 2 hr. 47 min. 51 sec.

Fastest speed march marathon by an individual Chris Chandler (UK) set an individual record in the RAF Swinderby Marathon at Swinderby, Lincolnshire, UK, on September 25, 1992, when he completed the marathon carrying a pack weighing 40 lb. (18 kg). His time was 3 hr. 56 min. 10 sec.

FASTEST 25-KM AND 30-KM ROAD RACES Naoko Takahashi (Japan) ran the 25-km women's road race in Berlin, Germany, in 1 hr. 22 min. 31 sec. on September 30, 2001. At the same event, she also set the record for the 30-km race, finishing in a time of 1 hr. 39 min. 2 sec.

★ MEN'S ROAD RACE ★

EVENT	RECORD	NAME, NATIONALITY & VENUE	DATE
10 km	27:02	Haile Gebrselassie (Ethiopia), Doha, Qatar	December 11, 2002
15 km	41:29	Felix Limo (Kenya), Nijmegen, The Netherlands	November 11, 2001
20 km	56:18	Paul Tergat (Kenya), Milan, Italy	April 4, 1998
Half marathon	59:17	Paul Tergat (Kenya), Milan, Italy	April 4, 1998
25 km	1:13:14	Rodgers Rop (Kenya), Berlin, Germany	May 6, 2001
30 km	1:28:36	Takayuki Matsumiya (Japan), Kumamoto, Japan	February 16, 2003
Marathon (26 miles 385 yards)	*2:04:55	Paul Tergat (Kenya), Berlin, Germany	September 28, 2003
100 km	6:13:33	Takahiro Sunanda (Japan), Yubetsu, Japan	June 21, 1998

*The marathon record printed in the first edition of *Guinness World Records* in 1955 was 2:17:39.4

★ WOMEN'S ROAD RACE ★

EVENT	RECORD	NAME, NATIONALITY & VENUE	DATE
10 km	30:21	Paula Radcliffe (GB), San Juan, Puerto Rico	February 23, 2003
15 km	46:57	Elana Meyer (RSA), Cape Town, South Africa	November 2, 1991
20 km	1:03:26	Paula Radcliffe (GB), Bristol, UK	October 6, 2001
Half marathon	1:06:44	Elana Meyer (RSA), Tokyo, Japan	January 15, 1999
25 km	1:22:31	Naoko Takahashi (Japan), Berlin, Germany	September 30, 2001
30 km	1:39:02	Naoko Takahashi (Japan), Berlin, Germany	September 30, 2001
Marathon	2:15:25	Paula Radcliffe (UK), London, UK	April 13, 2003
100 km	6:33:11	Tomoe Abe (Japan), Yufutsu, Japan	June 25, 2000

Fastest marathon speed march without rifles The fastest time for a team of eight to 10 to complete a marathon while carrying 40-lb. (18-kg) backpacks is 4 hr. 19 min. 7 sec. by eight members of 29 Commando Regiment Royal Artillery at the Luton Marathon, Bedfordshire, UK, on November 29, 1998.

Fastest marathon speed march team with rifles A team of nine representing II Squadron RAF Regiment from RAF Hullavington, Wiltshire, UK, completed the London Marathon in 4 hr. 33 min. 58 sec. on April 21, 1991. Each carried a pack weighing at least 40 lb. (18 kg), including a rifle.

Longest running race ever The longest running race ever staged was the 1929 transcontinental race from New York City, to Los Angeles, California, U.S.A., a distance of 3,635 miles (5,850 km). Johnny Salo (Finland) won in 79 days, running from March 31 to June 17. His elapsed time of 525 hr. 57 min. 20 sec. at an average speed of 6.91 mph (11.12 km/h) left him only 2 min. 47 sec. ahead of Englishman Pietro "Peter" Gavuzzi.

MOST INDIVIDUAL CROSS-COUNTRY WINS The greatest number of men's individual cross-country victories in the World Championships is five by Paul Tergat (pictured) in 1995–99 and John Ngugi (both Kenya) in 1986–89 and 1992.

FASTEST MEN'S 20-KM ROAD WALK Jefferson Pérez, (Ecuador) set a new record of 1 hr. 17 min. 21 sec. for the men's 20-km road walk in Paris St.-Denis, France, on August 23, 2003.

Oldest marathon The Boston Marathon was first held on April 19, 1897, when it was run over 24 miles 1,232 yd. (39 km). John A. Kelley (U.S.A.) finished the Boston Marathon 61 times from 1928 to 1992, winning in 1935 and 1945.

Most marathons completed Horst Preisler (Germany) ran 949 races of 26 miles 385 yd. or longer from 1974 to March 25, 2000.

Most consecutive weekends of marathon running Richard Worley (U.S.A.) ran either a marathon or an ultramarathon (a race longer than marathon distance) for 159 consecutive weekends. The first was the Walt Disney World Marathon in Orlando, Florida, U.S.A., on January 5, 1997, and the last was the Houston Methodist Marathon in Houston, Texas, U.S.A., on January 16, 2000. In the course of the records, Richard ran a marathon in all 50 U.S. states in one year, for three consecutive years.

★ MEN'S WALKING WORLD RECORDS ★

EVENT	RECORD	NAME & NATIONALITY	VENUE	DATE
TRACK				
20 km	1:17:25.6	Bernardo Segura (Mexico)	Fana, Norway	May 7, 1994
30 km	2:01:44.1	Maurizio Damilano (Italy)	Cuneo, Italy	October 4, 1992
50 km	3:40:57.9	Thierry Toutain (France)	Héricourt, France	September 29, 1997
2 hrs.	29,572 m	Maurizio Damilano (Italy)	Cuneo, Italy	October 4, 1992
ROAD				
20 km	1:17:21.0	Jefferson Pérez (Ecuador)	Paris St.-Denis, France	August 23, 2003
50 km	3:36:03.0	Robert Korzeniowski (Poland)	Paris St.-Denis, France	August 27, 2003

★ WOMEN'S WALKING WORLD RECORDS ★

EVENT	RECORD	NAME & NATIONALITY	VENUE	DATE
TRACK				
10 km	41:56.23	Nadezhda Ryashkina (USSR)	Seattle, U.S.A.	July 24, 1990
20 km	1:26:52.30	Olimpiada Ivanova (Russia)	Brisbane, Australia	September 6, 2001
ROAD				
20 km	1:26:22.0	Yang Wang (China)	Guangzhou, China	November 19, 2001
	equal	Yelena Nikolayeva (Russia)	Cheboksary, Russia	May 18, 2003

OLDEST FEMALE MARATHON FINISHER Jenny Wood-Allen (UK, pictured, b. 1911) ran the London Marathon on April 14, 2002 aged 90 years 145 days, in 11 hr. 34 min.

Fastest baby-carriage-pushing half marathon Martin de Scally (South Africa) completed the Vaal Half Marathon in Vereeniging, South Africa, in a time of 1 hr. 21 min. 1 sec. on March 2, 2003 while pushing a baby carriage.

The women's equivalent record is 1 hr. 30 min. 51 sec. by Nancy Schubring (U.S.A.) at the Mike May Races Half Marathon, Vassar, Michigan, U.S.A., on September 15, 2001.

Fastest baby-carriage-pushing marathon The fastest time to run a marathon while pushing a baby carriage is 3 hr. 54 min. 36 sec., by Han Frenken (Netherlands) at the Leidsche Rijn Marathon, Utrecht, The Netherlands, on April 21, 2003.

Fastest skipping marathon The fastest time to complete a marathon while skipping rather than running is 5 hr. 55 min. 13 sec. by Ashrita Furman (U.S.A.) at the Comox Valley Roads Marathon, Vancouver Island, British Columbia, Canada, on August 31, 2003.

Fastest half marathon in a two-person pantomime costume On October 6, 2002, Paul Donaghy and Steve Langley (both UK) completed the Great North Run, Newcastle, Tyne and Wear, UK, in a time of 2 hr. 9 min. 13 sec. wearing a pantomime camel costume.

Fastest 10-km road race in a two-person pantomime costume Wearing a pantomime camel costume, Simon Wiles and Les Morton (both UK) set a time of 44 min. 2 sec. for the Percy Pud 10-km race in Loxley, Sheffield, South Yorkshire, UK, on December 2, 2001.

Fastest three-legged marathon Identical twins Nick and Alastair Benbow (both UK) set a three-legged running record in the London Marathon with a time of 3 hr. 40 min. 16 sec. on April 26, 1998. They were tied together at the wrist and shared a pair of three-legged running trousers. They also hold the equivalent half-marathon record: they ran the London Half Marathon in 1 hr. 37 min. 53 sec. on March 2, 2003.

Most siblings to complete a marathon The eight Hughes brothers—Richard, Harry, Declan, Owen, Seamus, Patrick, Cathal, and Vincent (all Ireland)—competed in and completed the Dublin Marathon on October 29, 1984.

Oldest male marathon finisher On October 10, 1976, 98-year-old Dimitrion Yordanidis (Greece) ran a marathon in 7 hr. 33 min. in Athens, Greece.

Fastest 24-hour running relay by a team of 10 The greatest distance covered in 24 hours by a team of 10 is 302.281 miles (487.343 km) by Puma Tyneside RC at Monkton Stadium, Jarrow, Tyne and Wear, UK, from September 10 to 11, 1994.

Fastest 100-mile relay by a team of 10 Ten cadets from the 2331 (St. Ives) Squadron Air Training Corps completed 100 miles in relay in 10 hr. 21 min. 35 sec. at the St. Ives Outdoor Centre, St. Ives, Cambridgeshire, UK, on September 21, 2003. The team members were Sgt. M. Trace, CWO C. Trace, Sgt. D. Dew, Cpl. L. McGregor, CWO J. Martin, Sgt. B. Blewett, Comm. T. Philpot, Cpl. J. Young, CWO A. Owen, and Cpl. R. Jepp.

Fastest backward run from Los Angeles to New York Arvind Pandya (India) ran backward across the U.S.A. from Los Angeles, California, to New York City in 107 days from August 18 to December 3, 1984. Arvind runs backward in marathons and races all over the world to raise funds for various public causes. He has raised money for good causes in Africa, India, and Europe.

★ TREADMILL WORLD RECORDS ★

EVENT	RECORD	NAME & NATIONALITY	VENUE	DATE
TEAM				
1,000,000 m (Team of 12)	82 hr. 46 sec.	HMP Downview UK	Sutton, UK	August 14–17, 2000
12 hours (women)	161.3 km (100.2 miles)	Australia	Prahran, Australia	September 5, 2003
12 hours (men)	178.6 km (110.9 miles)	Australia	Prahran, Australia	September 5, 2003
INDIVIDUAL				
24 hours (female)	151.48 km (94.12 miles)	Georginia McConnell (Australia)	Wests Illawerra, Unanderra, Australia	November 25, 2003
24 hours (male)	222.41 km (138.2 miles)	Tony Mangan (Ireland)	Dublin, Ireland	October 25, 2003
48 hours	372.08 km (231.2 miles)	Tony Mangan (Ireland)	Dublin, Ireland	October 26, 2003
1 week	283.2 miles (455.83 km)	David Taylor (Australia)	Wests Illawerra, Unanderra, Australia	November 30, 2003
100 km	9 hr. 5 min. 37 sec.	Richard Donovan (Ireland)	Galway, Ireland	July 31, 2003
100 miles	16 hr. 23 min. 16 sec.	Andrew Rivett (UK)	Alverthorpe, UK	April 6, 2003

★ WALKING BACKWARDS WORLD RECORDS ★

EVENT	RECORD	NAME & NATIONALITY	VENUE	DATE
100 m	13.60	Ferdie Ato Adoboe (Ghana)	Northampton, U.S.A.	July 25, 1991
200 m	32.78	Timothy Bud Badyna (U.S.A.)	Santa Clarita, U.S.A.	January 17, 2001
1 km	3:36.07	Thomas Dold (Germany)	Messkirch, Germany	July 13, 2003
1 mile	6:00:2.35	D. Joseph James (India)	Columbatore, India	August 10, 2002
10 km	45:00:31.0	Vangal A. Mathiyazhagan (India)	Columbatore, India	May 30, 1999
Marathon	3:53:17.0	Timothy Bud Badyna (U.S.A.)	Toledo, U.S.A.	April 24, 1994
24 hours	95.40 miles (153.52 km)	Anthony Thornton (U.S.A.)	Minneapolis, U.S.A.	December 31, 1988– January 1, 1989

COMBAT

Most undefeated boxing matches Edward Henry Greb (U.S.A.) was unbeaten in a sequence of 178 bouts in 1916–23 (including 117 "no decisions," of which five were unofficial losses). Of boxers with complete records, Packey McFarland (U.S.A.) had 97 fights (five draws) in 1905–15 without a defeat. Pedro Carrasco (Spain) won 83 consecutive fights from April 22, 1964 to September 3, 1970, drew once, and had a further nine

MOST HEAVYWEIGHT BOXING WORLD TITLE RECAPTURES Three boxers have regained the heavyweight championship of the world twice. Muhammad Ali (U.S.A., right) first won the title on February 25, 1964, defeating Sonny Liston (U.S.A.). Having been stripped of the title by the world boxing authorities on April 28, 1967, he beat George Foreman (U.S.A.) on October 30, 1974. He then won the WBA title from Leon Spinks (U.S.A.) on September 15, 1978 after losing to him on February 15, 1978.

Evander Holyfield (U.S.A.) won the title in October 1990 by defeating James Douglas (U.S.A.). He regained the WBA and IBF versions when he beat Riddick Bowe (U.S.A.) in November 1993 and regained the WBA version again, on November 9, 1996, when he defeated Mike Tyson.

Lennox Lewis (UK) was awarded the WBC title in January 1993 after the then champion Riddick Bowe (U.S.A.) refused to fight him. He then won the WBC title on February 7, 1995, beating Oliver McCall (U.S.A.), and regained the WBC, IBF, and IBO titles when he defeated Hasim Rahman (U.S.A.) on November 17, 2001.

wins before his loss to Armando Ramos (U.S.A.) in a World Boxing Council (WBC) lightweight contest on February 18, 1972.

Longest reign as world heavyweight boxing champion Joe Louis (U.S.A.) was champion for 11 years 252 days, from June 22, 1937—when he knocked out James Joseph Braddock (U.S.A.) in the eighth round in Chicago, Illinois, U.S.A.—until announcing his retirement on March 1, 1949. During his reign, Louis made a record 25 defenses of his title.

Shortest reign as world boxing champion Tony Canzoneri (U.S.A.) was world light-welterweight champion for 33 days, from May 21 to June 23, 1933, the shortest period for a boxer to have won and lost a world title in the ring.

Most heavyweight titles won by a former middleweight This remarkable feat has been achieved only twice in 106 years. The first time was by Robert James "Bob" Fitzsimmons (UK) when he knocked out James J. Corbett (U.S.A.) in Carson City, Nevada, U.S.A., on March 17, 1897. Roy Jones, Jr. (U.S.A.) matched this when he beat John Ruiz (U.S.A.) for the World Boxing Association (WBA) title by unanimous decision on March 2, 2003 in Las Vegas, Nevada, U.S.A.

Heaviest heavyweight boxing world champion Primo Carnera (Italy), the "Ambling Alp" who won the title from Jack Sharkey (U.S.A.) in New York City, U.S.A., on June 29, 1933, scaled 260 lb. (118 kg) for this fight but his peak weight was 269 lb. (122 kg).

Longest boxing fight The world title fight (under Queensbury rules) between the lightweights Joe Gans (U.S.A.) and Oscar Matthew "Battling"

MOST WORLD CHAMPIONSHIP WRESTLING TITLES Aleksandr Karelin (Russia, left) won a record 12 world titles in the Greco-Roman under-130-kg class from 1988 to 1999.

LARGEST SUMO YOKOZUNA WRESTLER Hawaiian-born Chad Rowan, alias Akebono became the first foreign rikishi to be promoted to the top rank of yokozuna in January 1993. At 6 ft. 8 in. (2.04 m) and 501 lb. (227 kg), he is the tallest and the heaviest yokozuna in sumo history.

Nelson (Denmark), the "Durable Dane," in Goldfield, Nevada, U.S.A., on September 3, 1906 was terminated in the 42nd round when Gans was declared the winner on a foul.

Youngest national heavyweight champion Bill Sutherley (UK) won the Scottish Amateur Boxing Association (ABA) heavyweight title on February 23, 1961, at the age of only 18 years and 11 days.

Youngest boxing world champion Wilfred Benitez (Puerto Rico) was 17 years 176 days when he won the WBA light-welterweight title in San Juan, Puerto Rico, on March 6, 1976.

Youngest world heavyweight boxing champion Mike Tyson (U.S.A.) was 20 years 144 days when he beat Trevor Berbick (U.S.A.) to win the WBC belt in Las Vegas, Nevada, U.S.A., on November 22, 1986. He added the WBA version when he beat James "Bonecrusher" Smith on March 7, 1987 at the age of 20 years 249 days. He became undisputed champion on August 2, 1987 when he beat Tony Tucker (U.S.A.) for the International Boxing Federation (IBF) title.

Most knockouts in a boxing career The greatest number of finishes classed as "knockouts" in a career is 145 (129 in professional bouts) by Archie Moore (U.S.A., b. Archibald Lee Wright).

Undefeated heavyweight boxing world champion Rocky Marciano (U.S.A., b. Rocco Francis Marchegiano) is the only world champion at any weight to have won every fight of his entire completed professional career, from March 17, 1947 to September 21, 1955 (he announced his retirement on April 27, 1956); 43 of his 49 fights were by knockouts or stoppages.

Longest boxing career Bob Fitzsimmons (UK) had a career lasting more than 31 years (1883–1914). On December 20, 1905, aged 42 years 208 days, he had his last world title bout. Jack Johnson (U.S.A.) also had a career of over 31 years, 1897–1928.

Most jiujitsu team World Championships The World Council of Jiu-Jitsu Organizations has staged World Championships biennially since 1984. Canada has won the team competition on five occasions (1984, 1986, 1988, 1992, and 1994).

Most team kata titles at a karate World Championship A kata team event was introduced at the 1986 karate World Championships. Of the nine championships held biennially since, in both the men's and women's disciplines, Japan has failed to win on only four occasions out of 16 competitions in both classes.

Most countries represented at a karate World Championship At the 16th staging of the biennial karate World Championships, held in 2002 in Madrid, Spain, 84 countries were represented.

Most competitors at a karate World Championship In 1988, a total of 1,157 competitors took part in the karate World Championships at the ninth staging of the biennial tournament in Cairo, Egypt.

Fastest 100-man kumite ("sparring") karate On March 22, 1995,

Francisco Alves Filho (Brazil) defeated 100 consecutive opponents in full-contact knockdown fighting in 3 hr. 8 min. He won 26 fights by Ippon (full points), 50 by decision, and drew 24. He did not lose a single fight.

Most judo throws in one hour The most judo throws completed in one hour by a pair is 3,786 by Dale Moore and Nigel Townsend (both UK) at Esporta Health Club, Chiswick Park, Greater London, UK, on February 23, 2002.

Most judo throws in 10 hours Csaba Mezei and Zoltán Farkas (both Hungary) of the Szany judo sport team completed 57,603 judo throws in a 10-hour period at the Szany Sports Hall, Szany, Hungary, on May 1, 2003.

Most bout successes in annual sumo tournaments Yokozuna Mitsugu Akimoto, aka Chiyonofuji (Japan), set a record for domination of one of the six annual tournaments by winning the Kyushu Basho for eight successive years (1981–88). He also holds the record for the most career wins (1,045) and Makunouchi (top division) wins (807).

STAMINA & STRENGTH

Most Olympic weight lifting medals Norbert Schemansky (U.S.A.) won four Olympic weight lifting medals from 1948 to 1964.

Youngest weight lifting record breaker Naim Suleymanoglü (Turkey, b. January 23, 1967) was 16 years 62 days old when he set the world records for clean and jerk, at 160 kg, and combined total, at 285 kg, at Allentown, New Jersey, U.S.A., on March 26, 1983.

WOMEN'S +75-KG TOTAL Ding Meiyuan (China) achieved a record total lift of 300 kg in Sydney, Australia, on September 22, 2000. She also set the +75-kg snatch record with a lift of 137.5 kg in Vancouver, Canada, on November 21, 2003.

BODY WEIGHT	EVENT	WEIGHT, NAME, & NATIONALITY		VENUE	DATE
	Clean & jerk	168 kg	Halil Mutlu (Turkey)	Trencin, Siovakia	April 24, 2001
56 kg	Snatch	138.5 kg	Halil Mutlu (Turkey)	Antalya, Turkey	November 4, 2001
	Total	305.0 kg	Halil Mutlu (Turkey)	Sydney, Australia	September 16, 2000
	Clean & jerk	182.5 kg	Maosheng Le (China)	Busan, Korea	October 2, 2002
62 kg	Snatch	153 kg	Zhiyong Shi (China)	Izmir, Turkey	June 28, 2002
	Total	325 kg	World Standard		
	Clean & jerk	197.5 kg	Guozheng Zhang (China)	Qinhuangdad, China	September 11, 2003
69 kg	Snatch	165 kg	Georgi Markov (Bulgaria)	Sydney, Australia	September 20, 2000
	Total	357.5 kg	Galabin Boevski (Bulgaria)	Athens, Greece	November 24, 1999
	Clean & jerk	210 kg	Oleg Perepetchenov (Russia)	Trencin, Slovakia	April 27, 2001
77 kg	Snatch	173 kg	Sergey Filimonov (Kazakhstan)	Busan, Korea	October 4, 2002
	Total	377.5 kg	Plamen Zhelyazkov (Bulgaria)	Doha, Qatar	March 27, 2002
	Clean & jerk	218 kg	Zhang Yong (China)	Tel Aviv, Israel	April 25, 1998
85 kg	Snatch	182.5 kg	Andrei Ribakov (Bulgaria)	Havirov, Czech Republic	June 2, 2002
	Total	395 kg	World Standard		
	Clean & jerk	232.5 kg	Szymon Kolecki (Poland)	Sofia, Bulgaria	April 29, 2000
94 kg	Snatch	188 kg	Akakios Kakiashvilis (Greece)	Athens, Greece	November 27, 1999
	Total	417.5 kg	World Standard		
	Clean & jerk	242.5 kg	World Standard		
105 kg	Snatch	198.5 kg	Marcin Dolega (Poland)	Havirov, Czech Republic	June 4, 2002
	Total	440 kg	World Standard		
	Clean & jerk	263 kg	Hossein Rezazadeh (Iran)	Warsaw, Poland	November 26, 2002
+105 kg	Snatch	213.0 kg	Hossein Rezazadeh (Iran)	Qinhuangdad, China	September 14, 2003
	Total	472.5 kg	Hossein Rezazadeh (Iran)	Sydney, Australia	September 26, 2000

From January 1, 1998, the International Weightlifting Federation (IWF) introduced modified body weight categories, thereby making the then world records redundant. This is the new listing with the world standards for the new body weight categories. Results achieved at IWF-approved competitions exceeding the world standards by 0.5 kg for snatch or clean and jerk, or by 2.5 kg for the total, will be recognized as world records.

MOST OLYMPIC WEIGHT LIFTING GOLD MEDALS Three competitors have won a record total of three Olympic weight lifting gold medals: Naim Suleymanoğlü (Turkey) at the Olympic Games in 1988, 1992, and 1996; Pyrros Dimas (Greece, pictured) in 1992, 1996, and 2000; and Akakios Kakiasvili (Greece) in 1992, 1996, and 2000.

In 1992, Kakiasvili was known as Kakhi Kakhiachbili and he represented the EUN/CIS, also known as the United Team of the former Soviet Republics.

Most accumulative weight bench-pressed in one hour
Eamonn Keane (Ireland) lifted a total weight of 305,300 lb. (138,480 kg) in one hour at World Gym, Marina del Ray, California, U.S.A., on July 22, 2003.

Greatest multiple of body weight lifted by a man
Lamar Gant (U.S.A.) was the first man to deadlift nearly five times his own body weight. He lifted 661 lb. (299.5 kg), when he weighed 131 lb. (59.5 kg), in 1985.

Greatest multiple of body weight lifted by a woman using one arm
Cammie Lynn Lusko (U.S.A.) became the first woman to lift more than her body weight with one arm. She lifted a total weight of 131 lb. (59.5

MEN'S 56-KG CLEAN AND JERK Halil Mutlu (Turkey) lifted a record 168 kg at Trencin, Slovakia, on April 24, 2001. He also set the record for men's snatch, with a lift of 138.5 kg in Antalya, Turkey, on November 4, 2001, and for the total, with a lift of 305 kg in Sydney, New South Wales, Australia, on September 16, 2000.

kg) when she had a bodyweight of 128 lb. 7 oz. (58.3 kg), at Milwaukee, Wisconsin, U.S.A., on May 21, 1983.

Most push-ups in one minute Jack Zatorski (U.S.A.) performed 133 push-ups in one minute at Fort Lauderdale, Florida, U.S.A., on March 1, 2003.

Most push-ups in one minute using the back of the hands Steve Bugdale (UK) completed 89 push-ups in one minute at Plymstock Health and Fitness Club, Plymouth, Devon, UK, on May 12, 2003.

Most push-ups in one hour using the back of the hand of one arm Bruce Swatton (UK) completed 441 one-arm push-ups in one hour at Plymstock Health and Fitness Club, Plymouth, Devon, UK, on May 12, 2003.

Most sit-ups in one minute using an abdominal frame B.M. Gopikrishnan (India) carried out 138 sit-ups in one minute using an abdominal frame at Somers Town Community Sports Centre, London, UK, on December 9, 2003.

Gopikrishnan also holds the record for most sit-ups in one hour using an abdominal frame. He completed 8,367 sit-ups at Gundeldinger Hall, Basel, Switzerland, on December 20, 2003.

BODY WEIGHT	EVENT	WEIGHT, NAME, & NATIONALITY	VENUE	DATE
	Clean & jerk	116.5 kg Zhuo Li (China)	Qinhuangdao, China	September 10, 2003
48 kg	Snatch	93.5 kg Zhuo Li (China)	Qinhuangdao, China	September 10, 2003
	Total	207.5 kg Mingjuan Wang (China)	Warsaw, Poland	November 19, 2002
	Clean & jerk	127.5 kg Xueju Li (China)	Busan, South Korea	November 20, 2002
53 kg	Snatch	102.5 kg Ri Song Hui (North Korea)	Warsaw, Poland	October 1, 2002
	Total	225 kg Yang Xia (China)	Syndney, Australia	September 18, 2000
	Clean & jerk	133 kg Caiyan Sun (China)	Izmir, Turkey	June 28, 2002
58 kg	Snatch	110 kg Li Wang (China)	Bali, Indonesia	August 10, 2003
	Total	240 kg Li Wang (China)	Bali, Indonesia	August 10, 2003
	Clean & jerk	138 kg Natalia Skakun (Ukraine)	Vancouver, Canada	November 18, 2003
63 kg	Snatch	113.5 kg Anna Batsiushka (Belarus)	Vancouver, Canada	November 18, 2003
	Total	247.5 kg Xia Liu (China)	Qinhuangdao, China	September 12, 2003
	Clean & jerk	150 kg Chunhong Liu (China)	Vancouver, Canada	November 19, 2003
69 kg	Snatch	120 kg Chunhong Liu (China)	Vancouver, Canada	November 19, 2003
	Total	270 kg Chunhong Liu (China)	Vancouver, Canada	November 19, 2003
	Clean & jerk	152.5 kg Ruiping Sun (China)	Busan, South Korea	October 7, 2002
75 kg	Snatch	118.5 kg Ruiping Sun (China)	Busan, South Korea	October 7, 2002
	Total	270 kg Ruiping Sun (China)	Busan, South Korea	October 7, 2002
	Clean & jerk	168.5 kg Dan Sun (China)	Hyderabad, India	October 31, 2003
+75 kg	Snatch	137.5 kg Ding Meiyuan (China)	Vancouver, Canada	November 21, 2003
	Total	300 kg Ding Meiyuan (China)	Syndney, Australia	September 22, 2000

Greatest height attained on a climbing machine in one hour Paddy Doyle (UK) climbed to a height of 3,144 ft. (958.29 m) on a "VersaClimber" machine in one hour, while carrying a 40-lb. (18.1-kg) pack, on the TV show *This Morning,* Carlton TV Studios, London, UK, on October 17, 2002.

Fastest time to climb the height of Everest on a machine Kelvin Turner (UK) climbed the equivalent of the height of Mount Everest (29,035 ft. or 8,850 m) in a time of 2 hr. 57 min. 56.5 sec. on February 19, 2003 at the LivingWell Health Club, Redland, Bristol, UK.

Most skips by an individual in 24 hours Jim Payne (Ireland) skipped 141,221 jumps of a rope in 24 hours at City Square Shopping Centre, Waterford, Ireland, on March 26–27, 2004. The attempt was carried out to raise funds for Our Lady's Hospital for Sick Children in Crumlin, Ireland.

WINTER SPORTS

Highest speed in an Olympic downhill race On February 13, 1998, Jean-Luc Crétier (France) attained an average speed of 66.81 mph (107.53 km/h) in the Olympic downhill race at Nagano, Japan.

Fastest World Cup downhill speed Armin Assinger (Austria) reached a speed of 69.8 mph (112.4 km/h) at Sierra Nevada, Spain, on March 15, 1993.

Most World Cup downhill wins Franz Klammer (Austria) won 25 downhill races from 1974 to 1984.

Longest downhill ski run The Weissfluhjoch-Küblis Parsenn course, near Davos, Switzerland, measures 7.6 miles (12.23 km).

Most men's Alpine skiing Olympic gold medals The most Alpine skiing Olympic gold medals won by a male is three. The record is shared by Anton "Toni" Sailer (Austria) for downhill, slalom, and giant slalom in 1956; Jean-Claude

MOST MEN'S ALPINE SKIING OLYMPIC MEDALS The most Olympic Games medals won by a man is seven by Kjetil André Aamodt (Norway) who, in addition to his record three gold medals, has won two silver (for the downhill and combined events in 1994), and two bronze (for the giant slalom in 1992 and the supergiant slalom in 1994).

MOST WOMEN'S ALPINE SKIING OLYMPIC GOLD MEDALS Four women have won three Olympic gold medals: Vreni Schneider (Switzerland, pictured) (giant slalom in 1988, slalom in 1988 and 1994); Katja Seizinger (Germany) (downhill in 1994 and 1998, combined in 1998); Deborah Compagnoni (Italy) (supergiant slalom in 1992, giant slalom in 1994 and 1998); and Janica Kostelic (Croatia) (combined, giant slalom, and slalom in 2002).

Killy (France) for downhill, slalom, and giant slalom in 1968; Alberto Tomba (Italy) for slalom and giant slalom in 1988 and giant slalom in 1992; and Kjetil André Aamodt (Norway), for supergiant slalom in 1992 and 2002 and the combined event in 2002.

Most women's Alpine skiing Olympic medals Two women have won five skiing medals in the Olympic Games. In addition to her record three gold medals, Vreni Schneider (Switzerland) won silver in the combined event and bronze in the giant slalom in 1994. Katja Seizinger (Germany) won bronze in the 1992 and 1998 supergiant slalom in addition to her three gold successes.

Most men's Alpine skiing World Championship titles The Alpine skiing World Championships debuted at Murren, Switzerland, in 1931. Anton "Toni" Sailer (Austria) has won a record seven titles: all four titles in 1956 (giant slalom, slalom, downhill, and non-Olympic Alpine combination) and the downhill, giant slalom, and combined in 1958.

Most women's Alpine skiing World Championship titles Christl Cranz (Germany) has won the most Alpine skiing World Championship titles, with seven individual—four slalom (in 1934 and from 1937 to 1939) and three downhill (in 1935, 1937, and 1939)—and five combined (in 1934 and 1935, and 1937 to 1939). She also won the gold medal for the combined in the 1936 Olympic Games.

Highest speed by a skier Philippe Goitschel (France) reached a speed of 155.77 mph (250.7 km/h) at Les Arcs, France, on April 23, 2002.

Highest speed by a female skier Karine Dubouchet (France) reached a speed of 150.53 mph (242.26 km/h) at Les Arcs, France, in May 1999.

Most World Cup race wins The most individual event wins is 86 (46 giant slalom, 40 slalom, from a total of 287 races) by Ingemar Stenmark (Sweden) from 1974 to 1989, including a men's record 13 in one season in 1978/79, of which 10 were part of a record 14 successive giant slalom wins from March 18, 1978 (Ingemar's 22nd birthday) to January 21, 1980.

Most women's World Cup race wins Annemarie Moser (née Proll, Austria) won 62 individual event wins from 1970 to 1979, including a record 11 consecutive downhill wins from December 1972 to January 1974. She has also claimed the World Cup Overall Champion title (downhill and slalom events combined) a record six times since the tour began in 1967.

Most men's freestyle World Cup titles Eric Laboureix (France) won five men's freestyle World Cup titles, from 1986 to 1988 and in 1990 and 1991.

Most women's freestyle World Cup titles Connie Kissling (Switzerland) won 10 World Cup freestyle titles from 1983 to 1992.

Most freestyle skiing World Championship titles The first World Championships were held at Tignes, France, in 1986, when titles were awarded in ballet, moguls, aerials, and combined events. Edgar Grospiron (France) has won a record three World Championship titles: moguls in 1989 and 1991, and aerials in 1995. He also won an Olympic title in 1992.

The greatest number of world titles won by a woman is also three by Candice Gilg (France), who won the moguls in 1993, 1995, and 1997.

Most somersaults and twists in a freestyle aerial jump The greatest number of twists and somersaults achieved in a freestyle jump was set by Matt Chojnacki (U.S.A.), who completed a quadruple-twisting quadruple back flip at Winter Park Resort, Colorado, U.S.A., on April 4, 2001.

Most Nations Cup wins The Nations Cup is awarded according to the combined results of individual performances by men and women in the World Cup. The Cup has been won 22 times by Austria, in 1969, 1973–80, 1982, and 1990–2001.

Farthest vertical distance skied in 12 hours The greatest vertical distance skied in a 12-hour period by an individual, skiing both the downhill and the uphill sections, is 33,070 ft. (10,080 m) by Manfred Tod (Austria) at Mariazeller Burgeralpe, Austria, on February 24, 2003.

Most "vertical feet" skied by a woman in 24 hours Jennifer Hughes (U.S.A.) skied 305,525 vertical feet (93,124 m) at Atlin, British Columbia, Canada, on April 20, 1998. She was accompanied by snowboarder Tammy

McMinn (U.S.A.) during her record attempt and the two women were lifted from the bottom of the run to the top by helicopter.

Longest competitive ski jump by a man Andreas Goldberger (Austria) made a ski jump of 738 ft. (225 m) at Planica, Slovenia, on March 18, 2000.

Longest ski jump by a woman Eva Ganster (Austria) achieved a distance of 367 ft. (112 m) in the ski jump at Bischofshofen, Austria, on January 7, 1994.

Most ski flips in 10 minutes Tommy Waltner (U.S.A.) completed 23 front inverted aerial jumps within 10 minutes on April 25, 2000. The event

MOST "VERTICAL FEET" SKIED BY A MAN IN 24 HOURS On April 29, 1998, Chris Kent, Edi Podivinsky (pictured), Luke Sauder (all Canada), and Dominique Perret (Switzerland) skied 353,600 ft. (107,777 m) in 14 hr. 30 min. on a slope at Blue River, British Columbia, Canada. They completed the run 73 times and were lifted back to the summit each time by helicopter. Podivinsky is shown here in action at the World Cup in Wengen, Switzerland, in 2000.

took place on Aspen Mountain, Colorado, U.S.A., in order to raise money for Waltner's "Loops for Lupus" campaign.

Largest flare run The largest flare run ever consisted of 1,321 skiers and snowboarders who followed a course of 4.3 miles (7 km) between Piz Martegnas and Savognin, Switzerland, on January 1, 2000 while carrying flares.

Longest ski lift The Grindelwald-Männlichen gondola ski lift in Switzerland is 3.88 miles (6,239 m) long.

Most men's medals in Olympic biathlon Ricco Gross (Germany) won seven Olympic biathlon medals: three golds (4 × 7.5 km in 1992, 1994, and 1998), three silvers (10 km in 1992 and 1994, and 4 × 7.5 km in 2002), and a bronze (for the pursuit in 2002).

Most women's medals in Olympic biathlon Uschi Disl (Germany)

MOST MEN'S SNOWBOARDING WORLD CUP TITLES Mathieu Bozzetto (France) has won six titles: the overall in 1999 and 2000 and the slalom/parallel slalom in 1999–2002.

won a total of eight Olympic biathlon medals: two golds (4 × 7.5 km in 1998 and 2002), four silvers (3 × 7.5 km in 1992, 4 × 7.5 km in 1994, and 7.5 km in 1998 and 2002), and two bronzes (15 km in 1994 and 1998).

Highest snowboarding speed Darren Powell (Australia) reached a speed of 125.459 mph (201.907 km/h) at Les Arcs, France, on May 2, 1999.

Fastest snowboard on a bobsled run Reto Lamm (Switzerland) surfed down a bobsled run on his snowboard at 49.7 mph (80 km/h) at Königssee, Germany, in November 1998 for *Guinness—Die Show der Rekorde*.

Most snowboarding World Cup titles The greatest number of titles won is 16 by Karine Ruby (France). She won overall titles in 1996–98 and 2001–02; the slalom/parallel slalom in 1996–98 and 2002; the giant slalom in 1995–98 and 2001; and the snowboard cross in 1997 and 2001.

The first snowboarding World Cup series began in 1995, with World Championships inaugurated the following year.

Most snowboarding championship titles The greatest number of snowboarding titles won (including Olympic titles) is three, by Karine Ruby. She won the giant slalom in 1996, the Olympic title in 1998 (the first year that snowboarding became an Olympic sport), and the snowboard cross in 1997.

Most X-Games snowboarding medals Shaun Palmer (U.S.A.) has won a record three gold medals at the Winter ESPN X-Games for the Boarder X discipline (1997–99) since the inaugural X-Games in 1997. Across all the disciplines, he has won a total of six gold medals at the X-Games.

The most X-Games snowboarding medals won by a woman is six, by Barrett Christy (U.S.A.).

Oldest sled dog racing trail The oldest established sled dog trail is the 1,049-mile (1,688-km) Iditarod Trail, which runs from Anchorage to Nome, Alaska, U.S.A. The trail has existed since 1910 and has been the course of an annual race since 1967.

Longest trail in dogsled racing The longest race is run on the 1,243-mile (2,000-km) Berengia Trail from Esso to Markovo, Russia, which started as a 155-mile (250-km) route in April 1990. Now established as an annual event, the fastest time to complete the trail was achieved in 1991 by Pavel Lazarev (USSR) in 10 days 18 hr. 17 min. 56 sec. His time was equivalent to an average speed of 5 mph (8 km/h).

Most ski orienteering World Championship team wins Sweden has won the men's relay title six times, in 1977, 1980, 1982, 1984, 1990, and 1996.

HIGHEST AVERAGE SPEED IN MAJOR 50-KM NORDIC SKIING The record time for a 50-km race in a major championship is 1 hr. 54 min. 46 sec. by Aleksey Prokurorov (Russia) at Thunder Bay, Canada, on March 19, 1994, at an average speed of 16.24 mph (26.14 km/h).

Finland has won the women's relay eight times, in 1975, 1977, 1980, 1988, 1990, 1998, 2000, and 2004.

Vidar Benjaminsen (Norway) has won a record 15 medals, including four gold, two individual, and two relay.

Most individual ski orienteering World Championships Ragnhild Bratberg (Norway) has won four individual titles: the classic in 1986 and 1990 and the sprint in 1988 and 1990.

The men's record is also four by Nicolo Corradini (Italy), who won the classic in 1994 and 1996 and the sprint in 1994 and 2000.

Most Nordic skiing Olympic gold medals Bjørn Dæhlie (Norway) won eight Olympic gold medals for Nordic skiing (on the flat), for the 15 km, 50 km, and 4 × 10 km in 1992; the 10 km and 15 km in 1994; and the 10 km, 50 km, and 4 × 10 km in 1998.

The most Olympic gold medals won by a woman is six by Lyubov Yegorova (Russia), for the 10 km, 15 km, and 4 × 5 km in 1992, and the 5 km, 10 km, and 4 × 5 km in 1994.

Most World Nordic Championship title wins The first World Nordic Championships were those of the 1924 Winter Olympics in Chamonix, France. The most titles won by a woman is 17 by Yelena Välbe (Russia). Her total consists of 10 individual and seven relay wins from 1989 to 1998. With an additional seven medals, her total of 24 is also a record.

The most titles (including those for the Olympics) won by a man is 17 by Bjørn Dæhlie (Norway)—12 individual and five relay from 1991 to 1998. Dæhlie won a record 29 medals from 1991 to 1999.

Most Olympic Nordic skiing medals The greatest number of medals won by a man in Nordic skiing is 12 by Bjørn Dæhlie (Norway), who in addition to his record eight gold medals, also won four silver from 1992 to 1998.

The record for women is 10 by Raisa Smetanina (USSR/CIS), who won four gold (the 5 km in 1980, the 10 km in 1976, and the 4 × 5 km in 1976 and 1992), five silver (the 10 km in 1984 and 1988, the 5 km in 1976, the 20 km in 1984, and the 4 × 5 km in 1980), and one bronze (the 20 km in 1988).

★ SNOWSHOE RACE ★

EVENT	TIME	NAME & NATIONALITY	VENUE	DATE
Men				
100 m	13.23	Keith Sendziak (U.S.A.)	Gabriels, New York, U.S.A.	February 27, 1999
200 m	28.73	Birger Ohisson (Sweden)	Gabriels, New York, U.S.A.	February 27, 1999
400 m	1:03.24	Birger Ohisson (Sweden)	Gabriels, New York, U.S.A.	February 27, 1999
1,500-m run	5:20.47	Matthew Dougherty (U.S.A.)	Saranac Lake, New York, U.S.A.	February 23, 2002
1,500-m walk	8:37.00	Michel Lavoie (Canada)	St. Luc, Québec, Canada	February 17, 1996
Women				
100 m	14.98	Mary Shanly (U.S.A.)	St. Luc, Québec, Canada	February 17, 1996
200 m	34.31	Mary Shanly (U.S.A.)	St. Luc, Québec, Canada	February 17, 1996
400 m	1:24.43	Ann Herbowy (U.S.A.)	Gabriels, New York, U.S.A.	February 27, 1999
1,500-m run	6:51.67	Rebecca Harman (U.S.A.)	Saranac Lake, New York, U.S.A.	February 23, 2002
1,500-m walk	10:46.00	Lynn Dextradeur (Canada)	Hull, Québec, Canada	Unknown 1989

Greatest Nordic skiing distance in 24 hours Seppo-Juhani Savolainen (Finland) covered 258.2 miles (415.5 km) at Saariselk, Finland, on April 8–9, 1988.

Kamila Horakova (Czech Republic) achieved a women's record distance of 206.91 miles (333 km) in the event from April 12 to 13, 2000 at the Canmore Nordic Centre, Alberta, Canada.

Most Nordic ski-jumping World Championships Birger Ruud (Norway) won five ski-jumping titles in 1931–32 and 1935–37.

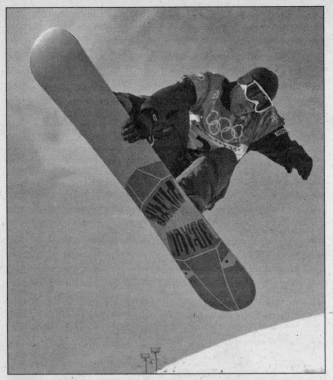

MOST SNOWBOARDING OLYMPIC MEDALS Since the introduction of snowboarding to the Winter Olympics in 1998, the most medals won is two by Ross Powers, (U.S.A., pictured), who won gold for the half pipe in 2002 and bronze for the same event in 1998; and Karine Ruby (France), who won gold for parallel giant slalom in 1998 and silver for the same event in 2002.

Ruud is the only person to have won Olympic events in each of the dissimilar Alpine and Nordic disciplines. In 1936, he won the ski-jumping and the Alpine downhill (which was not then a separate event, but only a segment of the combined event).

Most Nordic combined skiing Olympic gold medals The most gold medals won at the Olympic Games is three by Ulrich Wehling (GDR), for the individual in 1972, 1976, and 1980; and Sampaa Lajunen (Finland), for the individual, sprint, and relay in 2002. Lajunen also won silver at individual and relay in 1998, for a record total of five medals.

Fastest game of curling Eight curlers from the Burlington Golf and Country Club curled an eight-end game in 47 min. 24 sec., with time penalties of 5 min. 30 sec., at Burlington, Ontario, Canada, on April 4, 1986. The time is taken from when the first rock crosses the near hog-line until the last rock comes to a stop.

Longest curling stone throw Eddie Kulbacki (Canada) threw a curling stone a distance of 576 ft. 4 in. (175.66 m) at Park Lake, Neepawa, Manitoba, Canada, on January 29, 1989. The attempt took place on a specially prepared sheet of curling ice on frozen Park Lake a record 1,200 ft. (365.76 m) long.

Most World Championship and Olympic Games luge wins by a man The most single-seater World Championship and Olympic titles (instituted in 1953) won is six by Georg Hackl (GDR/Germany) in 1989, 1990, 1992, 1994, 1997, and 1998. Jan Behrendt and Stefan Krausse (both GDR/Germany) have won a record six two-seater titles, in 1989, 1991–93, 1995, and 1998.

Most Olympic gold luge medals by a woman Steffi Walter (née Martin, GDR) won two gold medals for lugeing, with victories at the women's single-seater luge event in 1984 and 1988.

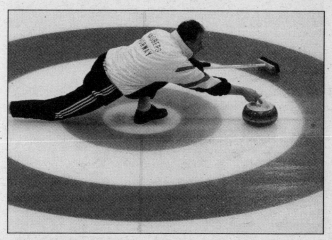

MOST OLYMPIC GAMES CURLING WINS Curling became an Olympic sport in 1998. It has only been part of the Olympics twice altogether and to date four countries have won one title each. In 1998, Switzerland won the men's title and Canada won the women's. In the 2002 Games, Norway's men's team (Lars Vaagberg, pictured) and Great Britain's women's team were the winners.

Most luge World Championship titles by a woman Margit Schumann (GDR) won four luge World Championships, in 1973–75 and 1977.

Youngest Olympic bobsled champion William Guy Fiske (U.S.A.) was 16 years 260 days old when he won the gold medal with the five-man bobsled team during the 1928 Winter Olympics held at St. Moritz, Switzerland.

Oldest Olympic bobsled champion Jay O'Brien (U.S.A.) was 47 years 357 days old when he won the gold medal with the four-man bobsled team during the 1932 Winter Olympics held at Lake Placid, New York, U.S.A.

Most individual Olympic bobsled medals Bogdan Musiol (GDR) won a record seven individual Olympic bobsled medals (one gold, five silver, one bronze) from 1980 to 1992.

Most Olympic gold bobsled medals won by an individual Meinhard Nehmer and Bernhard Germeshausen (both GDR) have each won three gold bobsled medals, in the 1976 two-man and the 1976 and 1980 four-man events.

FASTEST LUGEING SPEED Tony Benshoof (U.S.A.) reached a speed of 86.6 mph (139.39 km/h) on the track built for the 2002 Olympics at Park City, Utah, U.S.A., on October 16, 2001. The speed was reached during training for the 2001 Luge World Cup Series.

MOST WINS IN THE FOUR-MAN BOBSLED The world four-man bobsled title (instituted in 1924) has been won 20 times by Switzerland (pictured), in 1924, 1936, 1939, 1947, 1954–57, 1971–73, 1975, 1982–83, 1986–90, and 1993. This total includes a record five Olympic victories, in 1924, 1936, 1956, 1972, and 1988.

Most individual World Championship bobsled titles
The greatest number of bobsled World Championship titles won by an individual is 11 by Eugenio Monti (Italy) from 1957 to 1968. He accomplished this feat by winning eight two-man titles and three four-man titles.

Most bobsled World Championship by a women's team
A women's bobsled World Championships was introduced in 2000 and the sport made its debut at the 2002 Winter Olympic Games. Since 2000, Germany has won the title a record three times, in 2000, 2003, and 2004.

Most medals won at the women's bobsled World Championships
Since the introduction of the bobsled to the World Championships in 2000, the greatest number of medals won by an individual is four by Susi-Lisa Erdmann (Germany). She won gold in 2004 (with Kristina Bader) and in 2003 (with Annegret Dietrich), and bronze in 2001 (with Tanja Hees) and in 2002 (with Nicole Hershmann).

Most wins in the two-man bobsled World Championships and Olympic Games
Switzerland has won the two-man bobsled title 17 times, in 1935, 1947–50, 1953, 1955, 1977–80, 1982–83, 1987, 1990, 1992, and 1994. It has also had a record four Olympic wins, in 1948, 1980, 1992, and 1994.

Fastest Cresta Run completion time
The Cresta Run, which dates from 1884, is 3,977 ft. (1,212 m) long and has a drop of 514 ft. (157 m). On February 13, 1999, James Sunley (UK) made the run in 50.09 seconds at an average speed of 54.13 mph (87.11 km/h).

Most Cresta Run wins The greatest number of wins in the Cresta Run Curzon Cup competition (instituted in 1910) is eight by 1948 Olympic champion Nino Bibbia (Italy) in 1950, 1957–58, 1960, 1962–64, and 1969; and by Franco Gansser (Switzerland) in 1981, 1983–86, 1988–89, and 1991.

Fastest Cresta Run time from Junction On January 17, 1999, Johannes Badrutt (Switzerland) made a time of 41.02 seconds and covered a distance of 2,921 ft. (890 m) on the Cresta Run starting at Junction, the second point of the run from which competitors can officially start.

Most Olympic gold figure skating medals by a man Gillis Grafstrom (Sweden) won three gold medals in 1920, 1924, and 1928, and a silver in 1932.

Most Olympic gold figure skating medals by a woman Sonja Henie (Norway) won three gold medals at the 1928, 1932, and 1936 Winter Olympics.

Most Olympic gold figure skating medals as a pair Irina Rodnina (USSR) won three pairs figure skating Olympic gold medals, with two different partners. In 1972, she won the gold with Alexei Ulanov, and in 1976 and 1980 she won the gold with Alexandr Zaitsev (both USSR).

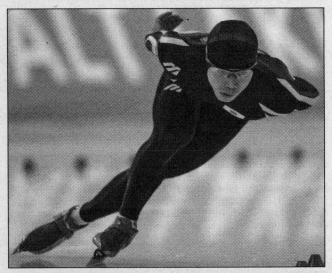

FASTEST 500 M SPEED SKATING Hiroyasu Shimizu (Japan) achieved a record time of 34.32 seconds in the men's 500 m speed skating competition in Salt Lake City, Utah, U.S.A., on March 10, 2001.

Most figure skating Grand Slams by a man The most figure skating Grand Slams—which consist of the European, World, and Olympic titles— won by a man is two by Karl Schäfer (Austria) in 1932 and 1936.

Most figure skating Grand Slams by a woman Two women have won two figure skating Grand Slams: Sonja Henie (Norway) in 1932 and 1936, and Katarina Witt (West Germany) in 1984 and 1988.

Most figure skating pairs World Championship titles Irina Rodnina won 10 World Championship pairs titles (instituted in 1908)—four with Aleksey Nikolayevich Ulanov in 1969–72 and six with her husband Aleksandr Gennadyevich Zaitsev (all USSR) in 1973–78.

The most ice dance titles (instituted in 1952) won is six by Lyudmila Alekseyevna Pakhomova and her husband Aleksandr Georgiyevich Gorshkov (both USSR) in 1970–74 and 1976. The pair also won the first ever Olympic ice dance title in 1976.

★ MEN'S SPEED SKATING WORLD RECORDS ★

EVENT	TIME	NAME & NATIONALITY	VENUE	DATE
500 m	34.32	Hiroyasu Shimizu (Japan)	Salt Lake City, U.S.A.	March 10, 2001
1,000 m	1:07.18	Gerard van Veide (Netherlands)	Salt Lake City, U.S.A.	February 16, 2002
1,500 m	1:43.95	Derek Parra (U.S.A.)	Salt Lake City, U.S.A.	February 19, 2002
3,000 m	3:42.75	Gianni Romme (Netherlands)	Calgary, Canada	August 11, 2000
5,000 m	6:14.66	Jochem Uytdehaage (Netherlands)	Salt Lake City, U.S.A.	February 9, 2002
10,000 m	12:58.92	Jochem Uytdehaage (Netherlands)	Salt Lake City, U.S.A.	February 22, 2002
Short track				
500 m	41.184*	Jean-Francois Monette (Canada)	Calgary, Canada	October 18, 2003
1,000 m	1:24.674*	Jiajun Li (China)	Bormio, Italy	February 2, 2004
1,500 m	2:10.639*	Hyun-Soo Ahn (Korea)	Marquette, U.S.A.	October 24, 2003
3,000 m	4:32.646*	Hyun-Soo Ahn (Korea)	Beijing, China	December 7, 2003
5,000-m relay	6:43.730	Canada (Eric Bédard, Marc Gagnon, Jean-Francois Monette, Matthieu Turcotte)	Calgary, Canada	October 14, 2001

*Subject to ratification by the International Skating Union (ISU) Council

Most continuous upright spins by an ice-skater The most continuous upright spins on ice skates on one foot is 115 by Lucinda Ruh (Switzerland) at Chelsea Piers Sky Rink, New York City, U.S.A., on April 3, 2003.

Longest jump flip by a figure skater Robin John Cousins (UK) achieved 19 ft. 1 in. (5.81 m) in an axel jump and 18 ft. (5.48 m) with a back flip at Richmond Ice Rink, Surrey, UK, on November 16, 1983.

Greatest ice-skating distance in 24 hours Martinus Kuiper (Netherlands) skated a total distance of 339.67 miles (546.65 km) in Alkmaar, The Netherlands, on December 12–13, 1988.

Most speed skating sprint World Championship wins Igor Zhelezovskiy (USSR/Belarus) has won a record total of six men's sprint titles. His victories came in 1985–86, 1989, and 1991–93.

Most men's speed skating Olympic gold medals The greatest number of Olympic gold medals won by a man is five. The record is shared by two speed skaters: Clas Thunberg (Finland) in 1924 and 1928 (including one tied); and Eric Arthur Heiden (U.S.A.) who, uniquely, won all his gold medals at one Games at Lake Placid, New York, U.S.A., in 1980. In the process, he broke a world speed record.

Most women's speed skating Olympic gold medals The most Olympic speed skating gold medals won by a woman is six by Lidiya Pavlovna Skoblikova (USSR), who won two golds in 1960 and four in 1964.

Most men's World Championship speed skating titles The most World Championship speed skating titles won by a man is five. The record

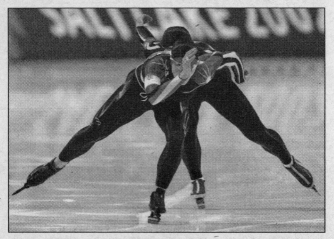

FASTEST WOMEN'S 1,500 M SPEED SKATING Anni Friesinger (Germany, pictured in foreground) achieved a time of 1 min. 54.02 sec. in Salt Lake City, Utah, U.S.A., on February 20, 2002.

LONGEST ICE-SKATING RACE The *Elfstedentocht* ("Tour of the 11 Towns," seen here), which started in the 17th century, covers 124.27 miles (200 km). It was held in The Netherlands in 1909–63, 1985–86, and 1997. As the weather does not permit an annual race in The Netherlands, *Elfstedentochts* also take place at alternative venues. The record men's time is 5 hr. 40 min. 37 sec. by Dries van Wijhe (Netherlands); the women's record is 5 hr. 48 min. 8 sec. by Alida Pasveer (Netherlands), both at Lake Weissensee, Austria, on February 11, 1989.

is shared between two speed skaters. Oscar Mathisen (Norway) won titles in 1908–9 and 1912–14, while Clas Thunberg (Finland) won in 1923, 1925, 1928–29, and 1931.

Most women's speed skating World Championship titles
The most titles won by a woman is eight by Gunda Niemann-Stirnemann (Germany) in 1991–93 and 1995–99.

Most speed skating Single Distance World Championship titles
The Single Distance World Championships were instituted in 1996. Since that time, Gunda Niemann-Stirnemann (Germany) has won 11 titles: the 1,500 m in 1997, the 3,000 m in 1996–99 and 2001, and the 5,000 m in 1997–2001.

The greatest number of titles won by a man is seven by Gianni Romme (Netherlands). He won the 5,000 m in 1998–2000 and the 10,000 m in 1996–98 and 2000.

Lowest men's speed skating World Championship score The lowest, and therefore best, score achieved for the men's World Championship speed skating title is 152.651 points by Rintje Ritsma (Netherlands) in Hamar, Norway, on February 6–7, 1999.

Lowest women's speed skating World Championship score The lowest score for a woman is 161.479 points, achieved by Gunda Niemann-Stirnemann (Germany) in Hamar, Norway, on February 6–7, 1999.

Most men's short-track speed skating Olympic medals Marc Gagnon (Canada) has won a total of five Olympic medals for short-track speed skating. His record tally includes three gold medals (for the 500 m in 2002 and the relay in 1998 and 2002) and two bronze medals (for the 1,000 m in 1994 and the 1,500 m in 2002).

Most women's short-track speed skating Olympic medals Two women have won five medals. Chun Lee-kyung (South Korea) won four gold medals (the 1,000 m in 1994 and 1998, and the relay in 1994 and 1998) and one bronze (the 500 m in 1998). Yang Yang (China) won four silver medals (the 500 m in 1998, the 1,000 m in 1998, and the relay in 1998 and 2002) and one bronze (the 1,000 m in 2002).

★ WOMEN'S SPEED SKATING WORLD RECORDS ★

EVENT	TIME	NAME & NATIONALITY	VENUE	DATE
500 m	37.22	Catriona LeMay Doan (Canada)	Calgary, Canada	December 9, 2001
1,000 m	1:13.83	Christine Witty (U.S.A.)	Salt Lake City, U.S.A.	February 17, 2002
1,500 m	1:54.02	Anni Friesinger (Germany)	Salt Lake City, U.S.A.	February 20, 2002
3,000 m	3:57.70	Claudia Pechstein (Germany)	Salt Lake City, U.S.A.	February 10, 2002
5,000 m	6:46.91	Claudia Pechstein (Germany)	Salt Lake City, U.S.A.	February 23, 2002
Short track				
500 m	43.671	Evgenia Radanova (Bulgaria)	Calgary, Canada	October 19, 2001
1,000 m	1:30.483	Chun-Sa Byun (Korea)	Budapest, Hungary	February 3, 2002
1,500 m	2:18.861*	Eun-Ju Jung (Korea)	Beijing, China	January 11, 2004
3,000 m	5:01.976	Chai Eun-kyung (South Korea)	Calgary, Canada	October 22, 2000
3,000-m relay	4:12.793	South Korea (Park Hye-won, Joo Min-jin, Choi Min-kyung, Chai Eun-kyung)	Salt Lake City, U.S.A.	February 20, 2002

*Subject to ratification by the ISU Council

Most wins in men's short-track speed skating World Championships The most successful skater in these championships, which were instituted in 1978, has been Marc Gagnon (Canada). He was men's overall champion in 1993–94, 1996, and 1998.

Most wins in women's short-track speed skating World Championships In the women's competition, the most successful skaters have been Sylvie Daigle (Canada), with victories in 1983 and 1988–90, and Yang Yang (China), who was champion in 1998–2001.

GOLF

Most British Open titles Harry Vardon (UK) won six British Open titles, in 1896, 1898, 1899, 1903, 1911, and 1914.

Most U.S. Open titles Four golfers have won the U.S. Open four times: Willie Anderson (UK) in 1901 and 1903–05; Bobby Jones, Jr. (U.S.A.) in 1923, 1926, 1929, and 1930; Ben Hogan (U.S.A.) in 1948, 1950, 1951, and 1953; and Jack Nicklaus (U.S.A.) in 1962, 1967, 1972, and 1980.

Most Solheim Cup wins The Solheim Cup, the women's equivalent of the Ryder Cup, was first held in 1990 and is contested biennially between the top professional players of Europe and the U.S.A. The U.S.A. has won five times: 1990, 1994, 1996, 1998, and 2002. Europe won three times, in 1992, 2000, and 2003.

Most successful Ryder Cup captain The most successful Ryder Cup captain is Walter Hagen (U.S.A.) with four wins. Hagen captained the U.S. team to victory in 1927, 1931, 1935, and 1937. He was one of the most colorful sports personalities of his time, and is credited with doing more than any other golfer to influence the perception of his profession.

Lowest score over 18 holes by a woman The lowest recorded score on an 18-hole course over 5,600 yd. (5,120 m) for a woman is 59 by Annika Sorenstam (Sweden) in the 2001 Standard Register PING tournament at Moon Valley Country Club, Phoenix, Arizona, U.S.A., on March 16, 2001.

Biggest margin of victory in a golf tournament The biggest margin of victory in a major golf tournament was achieved by Tiger Woods (U.S.A.), who won the 2000 U.S. Open by 15 shots. He finished with a round of 67 to add to rounds of 65, 69, and 71 for a 12-under-par total of 272.

Lowest individual score at the World Cup The lowest individual total score for the four rounds of the World Cup is 263 by Tiger Woods (U.S.A.) at Kuala Lumpur, Malaysia, from November 18 to 21, 1999.

HIGHEST CAREER EARNINGS ON THE U.S. LPGA TOUR Annika
Sorenstam (Sweden) earned $13,199,874 on the U.S. Ladies
Professional Golf Association (LPGA) Tour from 1993 to the end of 2003.
She also holds the record for the highest season's earnings on the U.S.
LPGA Tour, earning $2,863,904.

Most U.S. PGA Driving Distance titles Driving distance is the average number of yards per measured drive and is measured on two holes per
round. Care is taken to select two holes that face in opposite directions to
counteract the effects of wind, and drives are measured to the point at which
they come to rest, regardless of whether they are on the fairway or not. John
Daly (U.S.A.) won 11 U.S. PGA Driving Distance titles from 1991 to 1993
and from 1995 to 2002. His longest average drive was 306.8 yd. (280.44 m)
in 2002.

Most consecutive holes-in-one There are at least 20 cases of holes-in-
one (or "aces") being achieved in two consecutive holes, of which the greatest

was Norman L. Manley's (U.S.A.) unique "double albatross" on the par-4 330-yd. (301-m) seventh hole and par-4 290-yd. (265-m) eighth hole on the Del Valle Country Club course, Saugus, California, U.S.A., on September 2, 1964.

An albatross occurs when a player completes a hole three under par, and is therefore a hole-in-one only when hit on a par-4 hole.

Most holes-in-one by husband and wife at same hole John and Jenny Dixon (both UK) scored consecutive holes-in-one during a four-ball competition on the third hole at Knaresborough Golf Club, Knaresborough, North Yorkshire, UK, on August 22, 1996. This was equaled by Elmer and Marilyn James (both U.S.A.) on the 16th at Halifax Plantation Golf Club, Ormond, Florida, U.S.A., on April 19, 1998.

Most holes played in 24 hours Ian Colston [Australia] played 22 rounds and five holes (401 holes) at Bendigo Golf Club, Victoria, Australia, (par 73—6,061 yd. or 5,542 m) on November 27–28, 1971.

Most holes played in 24 hours using a golf cart On August 6–7, 1990, David Cavalier (U.S.A.) played 846 holes at Arrowhead Country Club, North Canton, Ohio, U.S.A., on a nine-hole course 3,013 yd. (2,755 m) in length.

Most holes played in a year Leo Fritz (U.S.A.) played a record 10,550 holes in 1998.

YOUNGEST GOLFER TO PLAY IN THE RYDER CUP Sergio Garcia (Spain) competed for Europe in the Ryder Cup in 1999 aged 19 years 8 months and 15 days.

Most walking golfers on a single course in 24 hours The greatest number of walking golfers to complete a full round on the same course on the same day is 491 on the Torrance course at St. Andrews Bay Golf Resort and Spa, St. Andrews, Fife, UK, on June 8, 2003.

Largest bunker The world's biggest bunker (or "trap") is Hell's Half Acre on the 585-yd. (535-m) seventh hole of the Pine Valley course, Clementon, New Jersey, U.S.A., built in 1912 and generally regarded as the world's most testing course. The hazard starts 280 yd. (265 m) from the tee and extends another 150 yd. (137 m) to the next section of fairway.

Longest tournament putt The longest recorded holed putt in a major tournament is 110 ft. (33.5 m) by Jack Nicklaus (U.S.A.) in the 1964 Tournament of Champions, and Nick Price (Zimbabwe) in the 1992 U.S. PGA.

Bob Cook (U.S.A.) sank a putt measured at 140 ft. 2.75 in. (42.74 m) on the 18th hole at St. Andrews in the International Fourball Pro Am Tournament on October 1, 1976.

Longest nontournament putt On November 6, 2001, Fergus Muir (UK) sank a putt measuring 375 ft. (114.3 m) on the Eden Course at St. Andrews Links, Fife, UK.

Longest golf carry with one hand Petri Takkunen (Finland) drove a golf ball 236.22 yd. (216 m) using only one hand at Ruukkigolf, Pohja, Finland, on June 16, 2003.

HIGHEST CAREER EARNINGS ON THE U.S. PGA CIRCUIT Tiger Woods (U.S.A.) won $41,508,265 from August 1996 to March 2004 on the U.S. Professional Golfers' Association (PGA) circuit. He also holds the record for the highest season's earnings on the U.S. PGA Tour, earning $9,188,321.

Greatest distance between two rounds of golf played on the same day The greatest distance between two rounds of golf played on the same day is 7,496 miles (12,063 km) by Larry Olmsted (U.S.A.), who played two full 18-hole rounds at New South Wales Golf Club, Sydney, Australia, and then Pelican Hill Golf Club, Newport Beach, California, U.S.A., on February 18, 2004.

Fastest round of golf by an individual With great variations in the lengths of golf courses, speed records are of little comparative value, even for rounds under par. The fastest round played when the golf ball comes to rest before each new stroke is 27 min. 9 sec. by James Carvill (UK) at Warrenpoint Golf Course, County Down, UK, who completed 18 holes over 6,154 yd. (5,628 m) on June 18, 1987.

Fastest round of golf by a team The WBAP News/Talk 820 (U.S.A.) team of golfers completed 18 holes in 8 min. 47 sec. at Bridlewood Golf Club, Flower Mound, Texas, U.S.A., on August 12, 2003. A total of 95 golfers took part on an 18-hole course measuring 6,021 yd. (5,505 m) in length.

WATER SPORTS

Most water polo Olympic medals Five players share the record of three gold medals: George Wilkinson in 1900, 1908, and 1912; Paulo "Paul" Radmilovic and Charles Sidney Smith in 1908, 1912, and 1920 (all GB); and Desz Gyarmati and György Kárpáti (both Hungary) in 1952, 1956, and 1964.

Paul Radmilovic also won a gold for the 4 × 200-m freestyle relay swimming in 1908.

Most water polo goals in an international game The greatest number of goals scored by an individual in a water polo international is 13 by Debbie Handley for Australia (16) against Canada (10) at the World Championship in Guayaquil, Ecuador, in 1982.

Longest water polo marathon A match lasting 24 hours was played by Rapido 82 Haarlem at the De Planeet pool, Haarlem, The Netherlands, from April 30 to May 1, 1999.

Longest water-skiing marathon Ralph Hildebrand and Dave Phillips (both Canada) water-skied simultaneously for 56 hr. 35 min. 3 sec. around Indian Arm, Rocky Point, British Columbia, Canada. They completed their feat on June 12, 1994 after covering a distance of 1,337.46 miles (2,152.3 km) at an average speed of 30 mph (48 km/h). While skiing at night, they used infrared binoculars and spotlights.

Most barefoot water-skiing World Championships The record is held jointly by Kim Lampard (Australia), for wins in 1980, 1982, 1985, and 1986, and Jennifer Calleri (U.S.A.), who won in 1990, 1992, 1994, and 1996.

The most titles won by a man is three by Brett Wing (Australia), in 1978, 1980, and 1982, and Ron Scarpa (U.S.A.), in 1992, 1996, and 1998.

The team title has been won six times by the U.S.A., in 1988, 1990, 1992, 1994, 1996, and 1998.

Largest wave surfed (unlimited) The largest wave successfully surfed had a face 70 ft. (21.3 m) in height. It was ridden by Pete Cabrinha (U.S.A.) at a break known as Jaws (Peahi) on the North Shore of Maui, Hawaii, U.S.A., on January 10, 2004. He was towed into the wave using a wave runner.

Most amateur surfing World Championships Surfing's World Amateur Championships were inaugurated in May 1964 in Sydney, Australia. The greatest number of titles won is three by Michael Novakov (Australia), who won the knee-board event in 1982, 1984, and 1986.

Longest surfboard ride on a river bore The longest recorded rides on a river bore have been set on the Severn bore, UK. The Official British Surfing Association distance record for riding a surfboard is 5.7 miles (9.1 km) by David Lawson (UK) from Windmill Hill to Maisemore Weir (both Gloucestershire, UK) on August 29, 1996.

MOST WATER POLO WORLD CHAMPIONSHIPS Water polo was first held at the World Swimming Championships in 1973. The most wins is two by Italy (1978 and 1994; shown here, back), the USSR (1975 and 1982), Yugoslavia (1986 and 1991), and Spain (1998 and 2001).

LARGEST "PADDLE-IN" WAVE SURFED A wave measuring 50 ft. (15.2 m) in height from trough to crest was ridden by Taylor Knox (U.S.A.) at a break known as Killers at Todos Santos Island off Ensenada, Mexico, on February 22, 1998. Knox caught the wave by using an arm-powered paddle-in rather than being towed.

Longest continuous journey by a kite surfer Fabrice Collard, Kent Marincovik, and Neil Hutchinson (all U.S.A.) traveled a distance of 88 nautical miles (101.3 miles or 163 km) between Key West, Florida, U.S.A., and Varadero, Cuba, on boards pulled by kites on December 21, 2001.

Their journey, during which they were not permitted to touch any other vessel, lasted 8 hr. 38 min. at an average speed of 12 knots (14 mph or 22 km/h).

Most windsurfing World Championships From 1979 to 1983, Stephan van den Berg (Netherlands) won five windsurfing world titles.

Longest windsurfing marathon Sergiy Naidych (Ukraine) windsurfed for 71 hr. 30 min. at Radyschev Lake, Simerferopol, Crimea, Ukraine, from June 6 to 9, 2003.

Longest windsurfing journey Steve Fisher (U.S.A.) crossed the Pacific from California to Hawaii on *Da Slipper II,* a highly modified 17-ft. 8-in.-long (5.4-m) Windsurfer. The 2,269-nautical mile (2,612-mile or 4,203-km) journey took a total of 47 days and Steve arrived on a beach on Maui, Hawaii, on September 3, 1997.

Fastest time to windsurf across the Atlantic Sergio Ferrero (Italy) windsurfed across the Atlantic from the Canary Islands to Barbados, a distance of approximately 2,600 nautical miles (3,100 miles or 5,000 km) in 24 days from June 6 to 30, 1982.

★ WATER-SKIING—MEN'S WORLD RECORDS ★

EVENT	SCORE	NAME & NATIONALITY	VENUE	DATE
Slalom	1 buoy/ 9.75-m line	Jeff Rogers (U.S.A.)	Charleston, South Carolina, U.S.A.	August 31, 1997
		Andy Mapple (GB)	Miami, Florida, U.S.A.	October 4, 1998
		Jamie Beauchesne (U.S.A.)	Charleston, South Carolina, U.S.A.	July 6, 2003
Tricks	12,320 points	Nicolas Le Forestier (France)	Chaugey, France	July 13, 2003
Ski fly	298 ft. 10 in. (91.1 m)	Jaret Llewellyn (Canada)	Orlando, Florida, U.S.A.	May 4, 2000
Jump	235 ft. 9.6 in. (71.9 m)	Jimmy Siemers (U.S.A.)	Lago Santa Fe, Texas, U.S.A.	August 10, 2003
Overall	2,818.8 points	Jaret Llewellyn (Canada)	Seffner, Florida, U.S.A.	September 29, 2002

★ WATER-SKIING—WOMEN'S WORLD RECORDS ★

EVENT	SCORE	NAME & NATIONALITY	VENUE	DATE
Slalom	1 buoy/ 10.25-m line	Kristi Overton Johnson (U.S.A.)	West Palm Beach, Florida, U.S.A.	September 14, 1996
Tricks	8,630 points	Tawn Larsen Hahn (U.S.A.)	Wilmington, Illinois, U.S.A.	July 11, 1999
Ski fly	227 ft. 7 in. (69.4 m)	Elena Milakova (Russia)	Pine Mountain, Georgia, U.S.A.	May 26, 2002
Jump	186 ft. (56.6 m)	Elena Milakova (Russia)	Rio Linda, California, U.S.A.	July 27, 2002
Overall	2,854.01 points	Elena Milakova (Russia)	Hazelwood Ski World, Lincolnshire, UK	July 29, 2001

★ BAREFOOT WATER-SKIING—MEN'S WORLD RECORDS ★

EVENT	SCORE	NAME & NATIONALITY	VENUE	DATE
Jump	89 ft. 9.6 in. (27.4 m)	David Small (GB)	Mulwala Water Ski Park, New South Wales, Australia	February 8, 2004
Slalom	20.5 crossings of the wake in 15 sec.	Brian Fuchs (U.S.A.)	Liverpool, New South Wales, Australia	April 1994
Tricks	9,550 points	David Small (GB)	Mulwala Water Ski Park, New South Wales, Australia	February 5, 2004

EVENT	SCORE	NAME & NATIONALITY	VENUE	DATE
Jump	67 ft. 6.9 in. (20.6 m)	Nadine de Villiers (RSA)	Roodeplaat Dam, South Africa	March 4, 2000
Slalom	17.0 crossings of the wake in 15 sec.	Nadine de Villiers (RSA)	Wolwekrans, South Africa	January 5, 2001
Tricks	4,400 points	Nadine de Villiers (RSA)	Wolwekrans, South Africa	January 5, 2001

Most consecutive days spent surfing Dale Webster (U.S.A.) has surfed every day since September 2, 1975, passing his 10,407th consecutive day of surfing on February 29, 2004. He set himself the condition that a "surf" should consist of catching at least three waves to shore.

MOST MEN'S PROFESSIONAL SURFING WORLD CHAMPIONSHIPS The most Association of Surfing Professionals (ASP) Tour World Championship titles won by a man is six by Kelly Slater (U.S.A., pictured), in 1992 and 1994–98.

The equivalent women's title has been won six times by Layne Beachley (Australia) from 1998 to 2003.

★ ESHIMO ROLLS ★

EVENT	SCORE	NAME & NATIONALITY	VENUE	DATE
Fastest 1,000 (no paddle)	31 min. 55 sec.	Colin Hill (UK)	Durham, UK	March 12, 1987
Fastest 1,000 (paddle)	34 min. 43 sec.	Ray Hudspith (UK)	Newcastle Upon Tyne, UK	March 20, 1987
Fastest 100 (no paddle)	2 min. 39 sec.	Colin Hill (UK)	London, UK	February 22, 1987
Fastest 100 (paddle)	3 min. 7 sec.	Ray Hudspith (UK)	Tyne and Wear, UK	March 3, 1991
Fastest 100 (female, paddle)	3 min. 42 sec.	Helen Barnes (UK)	London, UK	August 2, 2000
Most consecutive	1,796	Randy Fine (U.S.A.)	Florida, U.S.A.	June 8, 1991
Tandem (paddle) (one minute)	23	Emmanuel Baclet & Yann Hascoet (France)	Benodet, France	July 29, 2003

★ ROWING WORLD RECORDS ★

EVENT	SCORE	NAME & NATIONALITY	VENUE	DATE
Men				
Single sculls	6:36.33	Marcel Hacker (Germany)	Seville, Spain	2002
Double sculls	6:04.37	Luka Spix, Iztok Cop (Slovenia)	St. Catherines, Canada	1999
Quadruple sculls	5:37.68	Italy	Indianapolis, U.S.A.	1994
Coxless pairs	6:14.27	Matthew Pinsent, James Cracknett (GB)	Seville, Spain	2002
Coxless fours	5:41.35	Germany	Seville, Spain	2002
*Coxed pairs	6:42.16	Igor Boraska, Tihomir Frankovic, Milan Razov (Croatia)	Indianapolis, U.S.A.	1994
*Coxed fours	5:58.96	Germany	Vienna, Austria	1991
Coxed eights	5:22.80	The Netherlands	St. Catharines, Canada	1999
Women				
Single sculls	7:07.71	Roumiana Neykova (Bulgaria)	Seville, Spain	2002
Double sculls	6:38.78	Georgina Evers-Swindell, Caroline Evers-Swindell (New Zealand)	Seville, Spain	2002
Quadruple sculls	6:10.80	Germany	Duisburg, Germany	1996
Coxless pairs	6:53.80	Georgeta Andrunache, Viorica Susanu (Romania)	Seville, Spain	2002
*Coxless fours	6:25.47	Canada	Vienna, Austria	1991
Coxed eights	5:57.02	Romania	Lucerne, Switzerland	1999
Men's lightweight				
*Single sculls	6:47.97	Karsten Nielsen (Denmark)	St. Catharines, Canada	1999
Double sculls	6:10.80	Elia Luini, Leonardo Pettinari (Italy)	Seville, Spain	2002
*Quadruple sculls	5:45.18	Italy	Montreal, Canada	1992
*Coxless pairs	6:29.97	Christian Yantani Garces, Miguel Cerda Silva (Chile)	Seville, Spain	2002
Coxless fours	5:45.60	Denmark	Lucerne, Switzerland	1999
*Coxed eights	5:30.24	Germany	Montreal, Canada	1992

EVENT	SCORE	NAME & NATIONALITY	VENUE	DATE
Women's lightweight				
*Single sculls	7:15.88	Marit van Eupen (Netherlands)	Lucerne, Switzerland	1999
Double sculls	6:50.63	Berit Christoffersen, Lene Andersson (Denmark)	Copenhagen, Denmark	1995
*Quadruple sculls	6:29.55	Australia	Seville, Spain	2002
*Coxless pairs	7:18.32	Eliza Blair, Justine Joyce (Australia)	Aiguebelette, France	1997

*denotes non-Olympic boat classes

FASTEST SINGLE SCULLS Roumiana Neykova (Bulgaria) set a record of 7 min. 7.71 sec. for the single sculls in Seville, Spain, in 2002.

	DEPTH	NAME & NATIONALITY	VENUE	DATE
Constant weight				
Men	311 ft. (95 m)	Herbert Nitsch (Austria)	Deitach, Millstatter See, Austria	September 4, 2003
Women	229 ft. (70 m)	Tanya Streeter (UK)	Guadeloupe, France	May 11, 2001
Constant weight without fins				
Men	200 ft. (61 m)	Stig Avall Severinsen (Denmark)	Puerto de la Cruz, Venezuela	September 28, 2003
Women	141 ft. (43 m)	Mandy Rae Cruickshank (Canada)	Vancouver, Canada	September 1, 2003
Variable weight				
Men	393 ft. (120 m)	Patrick Musimu (Belgium)	Playa del Carmen, Mexico	November 12, 2002
Women	400 ft. (122 m)	Tanya Streeter (UK)	Turks and Caicos	July 21, 2003
No limits				
Men	531 ft. (162 m)	Loic Leferme (France)	Nice, France	October 20, 2002
Women	525 ft. (160 m)	Tanya Streeter (U.S.A.)	Turks and Caicos	August 17, 2002
Free immersion				
Men	331 ft. (101 m)	Carlos Coste (Venezuela)	Puerto de la Cruz, Venezuela	October 4, 2003
Women	232 ft. (71 m)	Annabel Briseno (U.S.A.)	Kana, Hawaii, U.S.A.	November 15, 2003
Dynamic apnea with fins				
Men	656 ft. (200 m)	Peter Pedersen (Denmark)	Randers, Denmark	July 18, 2003
Women	492 ft. (150 m) (25 m pool)	Nathalie Desreac (France)	Réunion Island, France	November 14, 1998
	492 ft. (150 m) 50 m pool)	Natalia Molchanova (Russia)	Limassol, Cyprus	May 26, 2003
Dynamic apnea without fins				
Men	544 ft. (166 m)	Stig Avall Severinsen (Denmark)	Aarhus, Denmark	July 19, 2003
Women	328 ft. (100 m)	Renate De Bruyn (Netherlands)	Eindhoven, The Netherlands	October 10, 2003
Static apnea				
Men	8 min. 24 sec.	Stephane Mitsud (France)	Rouen, France	November 8, 2003
Women	6 min. 21 sec.	Annabel Briseno (U.S.A.)	Kana, Hawaii, U.S.A.	November 13, 2003

Greatest distance by canoe in 24 hours Ian Adamson (U.S.A.) paddled 203.3 miles (327.1 km) in a canoe on the Colorado River from Gore Canyon, Colorado, to Potash, Utah, U.S.A., from June 7 to 8, 1997.

The record for the same time canoeing on the ocean is held by Randy Fine (U.S.A.), who paddled 120.6 miles (194.1 km) along the Florida coast on June 26–27, 1986.

Fastest 75-ft. descent by canoe Shaun Baker (UK) descended a vertical height of 75 ft. (22.86 m) in 19.9 seconds in a canoe on a river in Snowdonia, UK, on August 26, 2000.

Most women's Olympic & World canoeing titles Birgit Fischer (GDR/Germany) won seven Olympic gold medals from 1980 to 2000. She also won three silver medals for a record total of 10 medals. In addition, she won 29 world titles from 1979 to 1998, for a record 34 titles overall.

Most men's World & Olympic canoeing titles The men's record is 13 by Gert Fredriksson (Sweden), 1948–60, Rüdiger Helm (GDR), 1976–83, and Ivan Patzaichin (Romania), 1968–84.

Most canoeing gold medals won at a single Olympic Games The most gold medals at one Games is three by Vladimir Parfenovich (USSR) in 1980 and Ian Ferguson (New Zealand) in 1984.

Most consecutive kayak cartwheels Koya Morita (Japan) set a record of 264 consecutive cartwheels in a kayak on the Tama River, Ome-shi, Japan, on August 17, 2003. One kayak cartwheel is a full 360° rotation—vertically rather than horizontally.

GWR TALKS TO Tanya Streeter

Free diver Tanya Streeter (UK, pictured on next page) currently holds three free-diving world records: the no-limits free dive (525 ft. or 160 m), free diving with a constant weight (229 ft. or 70 m), and the variable weight free-diving record of 400 ft. (122 m), which she set on the Atlantic islands of Turks and Caicos on July 21, 2003. Free diving involves staying underwater for as long as possible on just one breath. Some free-diving records require diving to incredible depths.

How and when did you first become interested in free diving? I grew up on a Caribbean island and I was a good snorkeler. Technically, snorkeling is free diving; any time you take a breath and go underwater you're free diving. I started free diving when I was 25. I was inspired by people around me who knew more about the sport than I did.

What's your training regime? A huge part of this sport is about fitness and being in peak physical condition. Much of my training is endurance based: I do a lot of spinning (static bicycling), and lots of aerobic training to get my cardiovascular system working efficiently. Then there's the conditioning work, getting my body used to not breathing, and operating without breathing during the course of the dive; this work is often pool based. Finally, free diving is largely dependent on mental strength, so I need to train myself mentally, which is probably the hardest part.

Is it fair to say that free diving is an extreme sport? No, absolutely not. People think that because we can hold our breaths for so long, or dive so deep, we must in some way be superhuman, or are attempting to do very extreme things, when really what we're attempting to do is on the extreme edge of human potential. Most people will have tried to swim as far as they

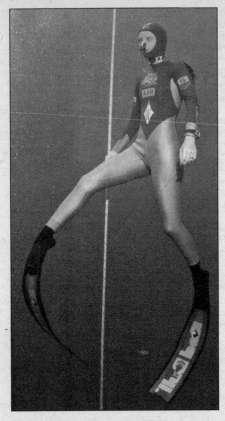

can underwater on one breath: when you compare their 40 seconds with our six minutes, what free divers do seems impossible.

Free diving is also a very controlled environment isn't it? It is. We have to consider every element of the dive. People breathe instinctively; once you take away that option, it makes you think about absolutely everything you're going to need to do to be able to breathe again. It's highly, highly controlled.

What do you consider your greatest achievement so far? I don't think that my achievement in my sport has actually been at the forefront for me; it's the fact that I have the opportunity to inspire people. I get lots of e-mails from people who have read about me and were inspired, and I get much more emotional satisfaction from that than I ever have done from a world record. I train very hard and I face every human fear that everyone else faces when embracing challenges. But it's the personal experience and the journey to those goals that stay with you. Never giving up on a goal has taught me the most.

What advice would you give someone wanting to free dive? Safety. You must never do any breath-hold activity alone, even if it's just holding your breath in a pool. You must get some instruction, because it's more complicated than it seems. Many free divers like myself are happy to give advice, but this sport should only be done with at least one companion, never alone.

SWIMMING

★ WOMEN'S SWIMMING [SHORT COURSE] ★

EVENT	SCORE	NAME & NATIONALITY	VENUE	DATE
50-m freestyle	23.59	Therese Alshammar (Sweden)	Athens, Greece	March 18, 2000
100-m freestyle	52.17	Therese Alshammar (Sweden)	Athens, Greece	March 17, 2000
200-m freestyle	1:54.04	Lindsay Benko (U.S.A.)	Moscow, Russia	April 7, 2002
400-m freestyle	3:59.53	Lindsay Benko (U.S.A.)	Berlin, Germany	January 26, 2003
800-m freestyle	8:13.35	Sachiko Yamada (Japan)	Nishinomya-shi, Japan	January 24, 2004
1,500-m freestyle	15:43.31	Petra Schneider (GDR)	Gainesville, U.S.A.	January 10, 1982
4 × 50-m freestyle	1:37.52	The Netherlands (Hinkelien Schreuder, Annabel Kosten, Chantal Groot, Marleen Veldhuis)	Dublin, Ireland	December 12, 2003
4 × 100-m freestyle	3:34.55	China (Le Jingyl, Na Chao, Shan Ying, Nian Yin)	Gothenburg, Sweden	April 19, 1997
4 × 200-m freestyle	7:46.30	China (Xu Yanvei, Zhu Yingven, Tang Jingzhi, Yang Yu)	Moscow, Russia	April 3, 2002
50-m butterfly	25.36	Anna-Karin Kammerling (Sweden)	Stockholm, Sweden	January 25, 2001
100-m butterfly	0:56.34	Natalie Coughlin (U.S.A.)	New York, U.S.A.	November 22, 2002
200-m butterfly	2:04.04	Yu Yang (China)	Berlin, Germany	January 18, 2004
50-m backstroke	26.83	Hui Li (China)	Shanghai, China	December 2, 2001
100-m backstroke	0:56.71	Natalie Coughlin (U.S.A.)	New York, U.S.A.	November 23, 2002
200-m backstroke	2:03.62	Natalie Coughlin (U.S.A.)	New York, U.S.A.	November 27, 2001
50-m breaststroke	29.96	Emma Igelström (Sweden)	Moscow, Russia	April 4, 2002
100-m breaststroke	1:05.09	Leisel Jones (Australia)	Melbourne, Australia	November 28, 2003
200-m breaststroke	2:17.75	Leisel Jones (Australia)	Melbourne, Australia	November 29, 2003
100-m medley	58.80	Natalie Coughlin (U.S.A.)	New York, U.S.A.	November 23, 2003
200-m medley	2:07.79	Allison Wagner (U.S.A.)	Palma de Mallorca, Spain	December 5, 1993
400-m medley	4:27.83	Yana Klochkova (Ukraine)	Paris, France	January 19, 2002
4 × 50-m medley	1:48.31	Sweden (Therese Alshammar, Emma	Valencia, Spain	December 16, 2000

EVENT	SCORE	NAME & NATIONALITY	VENUE	DATE
4 × 100-m medley	3:55.78	Sweden (Therese Alshammar, Emma Igelström, Anna-Karin Kammerling, Johanna Sjöberg)	Moscow, Russia	April 5, 2002

★ MEN'S SWIMMING [SHORT COURSE] ★

EVENT	SCORE	NAME & NATIONALITY	VENUE	DATE
50-m freestyle	21.13	Mark Foster (GB)	Paris, France	January 28, 2001
100-m freestyle	46.74	Aleksandr Popov (Russia)	Gelsenkirchen, Germany	March 19, 1994
200-m freestyle	1:41.10	Ian Thorpe (Australia)	Berlin, Germany	February 6, 2000
400-m freestyle	3:34.58	Grant Hackett (Australia)	Sydney, Australia	July 18, 2002
800-m freestyle	7:25.28	Grant Hackett (Australia)	Perth, Australia	August 3, 2001
1,500-m freestyle	14:10.10	Grant Hackett (Australia)	Perth, Australia	August 7, 2001
4 × 50-m freestyle	1:25.55	The Netherlands (Mark Veens, Johan Kenkhuis, Gijs Damen, Pieter van de Hoogenband)	Dublin, Ireland	December 14, 2003
4 × 100-m freestyle	3:09.57	Sweden (Johan Nystr-öm, Lars Frolander, Mattias Ohlin, Stefan Nystrand)	Athens, Greece	March 16, 2000
4 × 200-m freestyle	6:56.41	Australia (William Kirby, Ian Thorpe, Michael Klim, Grant Hackett)	Perth, Australia	August 7, 2001
50-m butterfly	22.74	Geoff Huegill (Australia)	Berlin, Germany	
100-m butterfly	50.02	Cavic Milorad (Serbia and Montenegro)	Dublin, Ireland	December 12, 2003
200-m butterfly	1:50.73	Frank Esposito (France)	Antibes, France	December 8, 2002
50-m backstroke	23.31	Matthew Welsh (Australia)	Melbourne, Australia	September 2, 2002
100-m backstroke	50.58	Thomas Rupprath (Germany)	Melbourne, Australia	December 8, 2002
200-m backstroke	1:51.17	Aaron Peirsol (U.S.A.)	Moscow, Russia	April 7, 2002

EVENT	SCORE	NAME & NATIONALITY	VENUE	DATE
50-m breaststroke	26.20	Oleg Lissogor (Ukraine)	Berlin, Germany	January 26, 2002
100-m breaststroke	57.47	Ed Moses (U.S.A.)	Stockholm, Sweden	January 23, 2002
200-m breaststroke	2:02.92	Ed Moses (U.S.A.)	Berlin, Germany	January 17, 2004
100-m medley	52.63	Peter Mankoc (Slovenia)	Antwerp, Belgium	December 15, 2001
200-m medley	1:54.65	Jani Sievinen (Finland)	Kuopio, Finland	April 21, 1994
400-m medley	4:02.72	Brian Johns (Canada)	Victoria, Canada	February 21, 2003
4 × 50-m medley	1:34.46	Germany (Thomas Rupprath, Mark Warnecke, Fabian Friedrich, Carstein Dehmlow)	Dublin, Ireland	December 11, 2003
4 × 100-m medley	3:28.12	Australia (Matthew Welsh, Jim Pipes, Geoff Huegill, Ashley Callus)	Melbourne, Australia	September 4, 2002

★ WOMEN'S SWIMMING [LONG COURSE] ★

EVENT	SCORE	NAME & NATIONALITY	VENUE	DATE
50-m freestyle	24.13	Inge de Bruijn (Netherlands)	Sydney, Australia	September 22, 2000
100-m freestyle	53.77	Inge de Bruijn (Netherlands)	Sydney, Australia	September 20, 2000
200-m freestyle	1:56.64	Franziska van Almsick (Germany)	Berlin, Germany	August 3, 2002
400-m freestyle	4:03.85	Janet Evans (U.S.A.)	Seoul, South Korea	September 22, 1988
800-m freestyle	8:16.22	Janet Evans (U.S.A.)	Tokyo, Japan	August 20, 1989
1,500-m freestyle	15:52.10	Janet Evans (U.S.A.)	Orlando, U.S.A.	March 26, 1988
4 × 100-m freestyle relay	3:36.60	Germany (Franziska van Almsick, Petra Dallmann, Sandra Volker, Kathrin Meibner)	Berlin, Germany	July 29, 2002
4 × 200-m freestyle relay	7:55.47	GDR (Manuela Stellmach, Astrid Strauss, Anke Mohring, Heike Friedrich)	Strasbourg, France	August 18, 1987
50-m butterfly	25.57	Anna-Karin Kammerling (Sweden)	Berlin, Germany	July 31, 2000
100-m butterfly	56.61	Inge de Bruijn (Netherlands)	Sydney, Australia	September 17, 2000
200-m butterfly	2:05.78	Otylia Jedrejczak (Poland)	Berlin, Germany	August 2, 2002

★ WOMEN'S SWIMMING (LONG COURSE) CONT'D ★

EVENT	SCORE	NAME & NATIONALITY	VENUE	DATE
50-m backstroke	28.25	Sandra Voelker (Germany)	Berlin, Germany	June 17, 2000
100-m backstroke	59.58	Natalie Coughlin (U.S.A.)	Fort Lauderdale, U.S.A.	August 13, 2002
200-m backstroke	2:06.62	Krisztina Egerszegi (Hungary)	Athens, Greece	August 25, 1991
50-m breaststroke	30.57	Zoe Baker (UK)	Manchester, UK	July 30, 2002
100-m breaststroke	1:06.52	Penny Heyns (South Africa)	Sydney, Australia	August 23, 1999
200-m breaststroke	2:22.99	Hui Qi (China)	Hangzhou, China	April 13, 2001
200-m medley	2:09.72	Wu Yanyan (China)	Shanghai, China	October 17, 1997
400-m medley	4:33.59	Yana Klochkova (Ukraine)	Sydney, Australia	September 16, 2000
4 × 100-m medley relay	3:58.30	U.S.A. (Megan Quann, Jenny Thompson, B.J. Bedford, Dara Torres)	Sydney, Australia	September 23, 2000

★ MEN'S SWIMMING (LONG COURSE) ★

EVENT	SCORE	NAME & NATIONALITY	VENUE	DATE
50-m freestyle	21.64	Alexander Popov (Russia)	Moscow, Russia	June 16, 2000
100-m freestyle	47.84	Pieter van den Hoogenband (Netherlands)	Sydney, Australia	September 19, 2000
200-m freestyle	1:44.06	Ian Thorpe (Australia)	Fukuoka, Japan	July 25, 2001
400-m freestyle	3:40.17	Ian Thorpe (Australia)	Fukuoka, Japan	July 22, 2001
800-m freestyle	7:39.16	Ian Thorpe (Australia)	Fukuoka, Japan	July 24, 2001
1,500-m freestyle	14:34.56	Grant Hackett (Australia)	Fukuoka, Japan	July 29, 2001
4 × 100-m freestyle relay	3:13.67	Australia (Michael Klim, Chris Fydler, Ashley Callus, Ian Thorpe)	Sydney, Australia	September 16, 2000
4 × 200-m freestyle relay	7:04.66	Australia (Grant Hackett, Michael Klim, William Kirby, Ian Thorpe)	Fukuoka, Japan	July 27, 2001
50-m butterfly	23.44	Geoff Huegill (Australia)	Fukuoka, Japan	July 27, 2001
100-m butterfly	51.81	Michael Klim (Australia)	Canberra, Australia	December 12, 1999

EVENT	SCORE	NAME & NATIONALITY	VENUE	DATE
200-m butterfly	1:54.58	Michael Phelps (U.S.A.)	Fukuoka, Japan	July 24, 2001
50-m backstroke	24.99	Lenny Krayzelburg (U.S.A.)	Sydney, Australia	August 28, 1999
100-m backstroke	53.60	Lenny Krayzelburg (U.S.A.)	Sydney, Australia	August 24, 1999
200-m backstroke	1:55.15	Aaron Peirsol (U.S.A.)	Minneapolis, U.S.A.	March 20, 2002
50-m breaststroke	27.18	Oleg Lisogor (Ukraine)	Berlin, Germany	August 2, 2002
100-m breaststroke	59.94	Roman Sloudnov (Russia)	Fukuoka, Japan	July 23, 2001
200-m breaststroke	2:10.16	Mike Barrowman (U.S.A.)	Barcelona, Spain	July 29, 1992
200-m medley	1:55.94	Michael Phelps (U.S.A.)	Maryland, U.S.A.	August 9, 2003
400-m medley	4:09.09	Michael Phelps (U.S.A.)	Barcelona, Spain	July 27, 2003
4 × 100-m medley relay	3:33.48	U.S.A. (Aaron Peirsol, Brendon Hanson, Michael Phelps, Jason Lezak)	Yokohama, Japan	August 29, 2002

Most Olympic diving medals

The most medals won by a diver is five. Klaus Dibiasi (Italy) won three gold and two silver (1964–76), and Greg Louganis (U.S.A.) won four golds and one silver (1976, 1984, and 1988). Dibiasi is the only diver to win the same event (high board) at three successive Games (1968–76). Two divers have won high board and springboard

doubles at two Games: Patricia Joan McCormick (née Keller, U.S.A.) in 1952 and 1956, and Louganis in 1984 and 1988.

MOST WOMEN'S OLYMPIC MEDALS Three women have won eight medals. Dawn Fraser (Australia, pictured right) won four golds and four silvers (1956–64); Kornelia Ender (GDR) won four golds and four silvers (1972–76); and Shirley Babashoff (U.S.A.) won two golds and six silvers (1972–76).

Most diving World Championships Greg Louganis (U.S.A.) won five world titles—high board in 1978, and high board and springboard in 1982 and 1986—and four Olympic gold medals in 1984 and 1988. Philip George Boggs (U.S.A.) also won three golds in one event, for springboard in 1973, 1975, and 1978.

Most men's Olympic swimming medals Mark Spitz (U.S.A.) won nine gold medals: the 100-m and 200-m freestyle (1972), the 100-m and 200-m butterfly (1972), 4 × 100-m freestyle (1968 and 1972), the 4 × 200-m freestyle (1968 and 1972), and the 4 × 100-m medley (1972). All but one of these (the 4 × 200-m freestyle of 1968) were also new world records. He also won a silver (100-m butterfly) and a bronze (100-m freestyle) in 1968, giving him a record 11 medals in all.

Most individual Olympic swimming gold medals

Krisztina Egerszegi (Hungary) won five gold medals: 100-m backstroke (1992), 200-m backstroke (1988, 1992, and 1996) and 400-m medley (1992).

Five men have four Olympic golds: Charles Meldrum Daniels (U.S.A.) for the 100-m freestyle (1906 and 1908), 220-yd.

MEN'S 200-M SHORT COURSE BACKSTROKE
Aaron Peirsol (U.S.A.) completed the men's 200-m short course backstroke in a record time of 1 min. 51.17 sec. in Moscow, Russia, on April 7, 2002. He also holds the record for the long course race over the same distance, with a time of 1 min. 55.15 sec., recorded in Minneapolis, U.S.A., on March 20, 2002.

freestyle (1904), and 440-yd. freestyle (1904); Roland Matthes (GDR) for the 100-m and 200-m backstroke (1968 and 1972); Mark Spitz (U.S.A.) for the 100-m and 200-m freestyle, and the 100-m and 200-m butterfly (1972); Tamás Daryni (Hungary) for the 200-m and 400-m medley (1988 and 1992); and Aleksandr Popov (Russia) for the 50-m and 100-m freestyle (1992 and 1996).

Farthest distance swum Martin Strel (Slovenia) swam the Mississippi River, U.S.A., from its source in northern Minnesota to the Gulf of Mexico, from July 4 to September 9, 2002. He swam a total of 2,360 miles (3,797 km) in 68 days.

SADDLE SPORTS

Most men's show jumping World Championships The most show jumping World Championships won by a man is two, by Hans Günter Winkler (Germany) in 1954 and 1955 and Raimondo d'Inzeo (Italy) in 1956 and 1960.

Most women's show jumping World Championships Janou Tissot (France) won two World Championship titles on Rocket in 1970 and 1974.

Most show jumping World Championship team titles The most show jumping team World Championship titles is two and the record is shared by France in 1982 and 1990, Germany in 1994 and 1998, and the U.S.A. in 1986 and 2002.

Most Badminton wins The Badminton Three-Day Event (instituted 1949) has been won six times by Lucinda Green (UK) in 1973 (on Be Fair), 1976 (Wide Awake), 1977 (George), 1979 (Killaire), 1983 (Regal Realm), and 1984 (Beagle Bay).

Jockey with most St. Leger wins From 1821 to 1846, jockey Bill Scott (UK) won the St. Leger (instituted 1776), the world's oldest classic race, nine times.

Fastest time to run the St. Leger In 1926, Coronach ran the St. Leger in a time of 3 min. 1.6 sec. This was equaled by Windsor Lad in 1934.

Fastest time to run the Epsom Derby In 1995, Lammtarra ran the Epsom Derby in 2 min. 32.3 sec.

Fastest time to run the Kentucky Derby Secretariat, ridden by Ron Turcotte (Canada), ran a record time of 1 min. 59.4 sec. on May 5, 1973 at Churchill Downs, Kentucky, U.S.A.

Greatest total prize money for a day's racing The Dubai World Cup race meeting at Nad Al Sheba, Dubai, United Arab Emirates, held annually in March, has total prize money of $15.25 million. Since 2002, the seven-race meeting has included the world's richest race, the Dubai World Cup.

MOST SHOW JUMPING WORLD CUP WINS The show jumping World Cup (instituted 1979) has been won three times by Hugo Simon (Austria) in 1979, 1996, and 1997; and Rodrigo Pessoa (Brazil, pictured) in 1998–2000. Pessoa's wins were all on the same horse, Gandini Baloubet du Rouet (pictured).

MOST HORSE RACING CAREER WINS BY A JOCKEY Laffit Pincay, Jr. (U.S.A., pictured far right) rode a total of 9,531 winners from May 16, 1964 to March 1, 2003. Pincay announced his retirement aged 56 at the end of April 2003, nearly two months after breaking his neck in a fall at Santa Anita, California, U.S.A.

Highest amount won in a single race The highest amount won in one horse race is $3.6 million for the Dubai World Cup by: Dubai Millennium, 2000; Captain Steve, 2001; Street Cry, 2002; Moon Ballard, 2003; and Pleasantly Perfect, 2004.

Oldest horse to win a race Al Jabal, a purebred Arabian horse, ridden by Brian Boulton and owned by Andrea Boulton (both UK), was aged 19 years when he won the Three Horseshoes Handicap Stakes on June 9, 2002 at Barbury Castle, Wiltshire, UK.

Most polo World Championships Argentina has won three polo World Championships: in 1987 in Argentina, 1992 in Chile, and 1998 in the U.S.A.

Most goals in polo World Championships Argentina has scored 35 goals during final matches of the polo World Championships.

Highest rodeo earnings Ty Murray (U.S.A.) holds three records for rodeo earnings: he has record career earnings of $2,931,227 won from 1989 to 2002; he won the most prize money in a single season with $377,358 earned in 1998; and he won the most money at a single rodeo with a win of $124,821 at the National Finals Rodeo in Las Vegas, Nevada, U.S.A., in 1993.

Highest bull riding score Wade Leslie (U.S.A.) scored 100 points out of a possible 100 on Wolfman Skoal at Central Point, Oregon, U.S.A., in 1991.

HIGHEST SADDLE BRONC SCORE The highest scored saddle bronc ride is 95 out of a possible 100 by Glen O'Neill (Australia, pictured) on Franklin's Airwolf at Innisfail, Alberta, Canada, in 1996; and also by Doug Vold (U.S.A.) on Transport at Meadow Lake, Saskatchewan, Canada, in 1979.

Highest bareback riding score Wes Stevenson (U.S.A.) scored 94 out of a possible 100 on Kesler Rodeo's Cover Girl in Dallas, Texas, U.S.A., in 2002.

GWR TALKS TO Tony McCoy

Jockey Tony McCoy (UK) holds the record for the most steeplechase wins in a career, with 2,078 winners ridden from 1992 to May 2004. He has also won more steeplechase races in a season than any other jockey, with 289 in 2001/2002.

What first got you interested in horses and how old were you when you started riding? My dad had horses and I thought that I'd like to ride them—I was fortunate enough to have my own ponies. I also liked watching it on TV. I first sat on a horse when I was about seven or eight but I started racing at the age of 16— the age you have to be to compete legally.

What do you do to keep fit for your sport? With riding every day I don't really have to do anything to keep fit. If you do a certain activity a lot, that keeps you fit for that activity. If I was having time off I'd use my gym.

What's your favorite memory from your career so far? That would be a few years ago when I broke Sir Gordon Richards' 55-year record for the most wins in a season—he was champion flat jockey 26 times.

Is your record for steeplechase wins in a career as special? Yes, it's a different type of record. Every record you hold is special, but with this one, so many great jockeys before me set it, like John Francome, Peter Scudamore, Richard Dunwoody; and being able to say that I've brought home more winners than them means a lot as they were the people I looked up to when I was younger.

So are they also your idols? They are definitely, very much so, and I'm very lucky now as they're my friends as well, even though when I was young and growing up I looked up to them a lot.

What's your favorite racecourse? For me personally, Cheltenham because it's just got a brilliant atmosphere. Liverpool's not too bad either.

What's the most races you've ridden in one day? The most in one day is 11. The most wins in one day is five.

What keeps you going? What's your motivation? I love doing it and the day I don't enjoy doing it I won't do it. Anyone that's lucky enough to earn their living from their sport would tell you how lucky they are.

If you had to name one major goal that you haven't achieved so far, what would it be? I have to win the Grand National. It's not really happening at the moment. It's one of the biggest courses and one of the biggest sporting events in the world.

You're an inspiration to those wishing to get involved in the sport. Is that important to you? If you can help young children or get them involved in any sport it's great, and if they have as much luck as I have had, then they're going to be very lucky people.

AIR SPORTS

Longest free-fall parachute jump Eugene Andreev (USSR) holds the official Fédération Aéronautique Internationale (FAI) record for the longest free-fall parachute jump after falling for 80,380 ft. (24,500 m) from an altitude of 83,523 ft. (25,458 m) near the city of Saratov, Russia, on November 1, 1962.

Largest FAI-approved free-fall parachute formation A free-fall formation consisting of 357 sky divers from more than 40 countries was formed over Takhli, Thailand, on February 6, 2004. The event was organized by World Team '04 and formed part of the Thailand Royal Sky Celebration, which was supported by the Royal Thai Air Force and took place in honor of the Thai royal family.

Most parachute descents On July 13, 2003, Don Kellner (U.S.A.) made his 34,000th free-fall sky dive in accordance with the U.S. Parachute Association basic safety requirements. He made his first jump on June 14, 1961.

Cheryl Stearns (U.S.A.) holds the corresponding women's record, with a total of 15,560 descents as of August 2003.

Most people to tandem parachute in 24 hours The greatest number of tandem parachute jumps performed from the same airfield in a 24-hour period is 41, achieved at The Big Jump 2001 event at Hinton Airfield, Banbury, Oxfordshire, UK, on September 16, 2001.

Largest canopy formation The largest canopy formation consisted of 70 parachutes and was formed by an American-led international team over Lake Wales, Florida, U.S.A., on November 29, 2003. The formation involved 15 "layers" of parachutes stacked on

GREATEST PARAGLIDING ALTITUDE GAIN Robbie Whittal (UK, pictured) achieved a record height gain of 14,849 ft. (4,526 m) at Brandvlei, South Africa, on January 6, 1993. As a comparison, Boeing 747s normally cruise at 32,808 ft. (10,000 m).

The greatest height gained with a paraglider by a female is 14,189 ft. (4,325 m) by Kat Thurston (UK) over Kuruman, South Africa, on January 1, 1996.

MOST PARACHUTISTS TO JUMP FROM A BALLOON Thirty members of Paraclub Flevo (pictured), Lelystad, The Netherlands, jumped from a balloon over Markelo, The Netherlands, on May 10, 2003.

top of one another, with each parachutist in contact with the canopy of the person below them.

Highest static-line parachute jump with a round canopy Graham Spicer and Martin Cruickshank (both UK) completed a static-line parachute jump using round canopies from an altitude of 30,300 ft. (9,235 m) over Yolo County, California, U.S.A., on September 19, 2002. Both men are members of the Association of British Military Parachutists.

Longest flight by powered parachute (absolute) The official FAI record for the longest distance flown in a single hop by powered parachute is 400 miles (644 km), by Juan Ramon Morillas Salmeron (Spain), from Almonte, Huelva, Spain, to Minuesa, Teruel, Spain, on June 21, 1998.

Fastest speed in a paraglider over a 25-km triangular course The fastest speed achieved over a 15.53-mile (25-km) triangular course for an official FAI world record is 17.55 mph (28.26 km/h) by Patrick Berod (France) at Albertville, France, on June 27, 1995.

The fastest speed achieved by a woman is 14.13 mph (22.75 km/h) by Fiona Macaskill (UK) at Plaine Joux, France, on April 24, 2003.

Greatest distance in a paraglider On June 21, 2002, William Gadd (Canada) traveled a distance of 423.4 km (263.08 miles) by paraglider, from Zapata, Texas, to south of Ozona, Texas, U.S.A.

The greatest distance flown by a woman in a paraglider is 177.1 miles

(285 km) by Kat Thurston (UK) from Kuruman, South Africa, on December 25, 1995.

Greatest distance in a tandem paraglider Richard Westgate and Jim Coutts (both UK) flew a tandem paraglider for a total distance of 136.95 miles (220.4 km) without landing from Quixada, Brazil, to Bom Principio, Brazil, on November 30, 2000.

Greatest height gain in a tandem paraglider The height gain record for a tandem paraglider is 14,370 ft. (4,380 m), achieved by Richard and Guy Westgate (both UK) at Kuruman, South Africa, on January 1, 1996.

Most men's hang gliding World Championships World championships for hang gliding were first held in 1976. The most individual wins is three by Tomas Suchanek (Czech Republic) in 1991, 1993, and 1995, and Manfred Ruhmer (Austria) in 1999, 2001, and 2003.

The women's hang gliding World Championships were first held in 1987. The most individual wins is three by Kari Castle (U.S.A.) in 1996, 2000, and 2002.

Greatest distance flown in a hang glider The greatest distance flown when setting an official FAI hang gliding record is 435.33 miles (700.6 km) by Manfred Ruhmer (Austria) from Zapata, Texas, to Lamesa, Texas, U.S.A., on July 17, 2001.

Greatest straight distance in a hang glider by a woman The FAI straight-line distance record by a woman in a hang glider is 250.7 miles (403.5 km), achieved by Kari Castle (U.S.A.) at Zapata, Texas, U.S.A., on July 28, 2001.

Greatest return distance in a hang glider Rohan Holtkamp (Australia) achieved a record out-and-return distance of 205.4 miles (330.6 km) at Eucla, Australia, on February 12, 1998.

The farthest out-and-return distance traveled by a woman with a hang glider is 89.38 miles (143.85 km), achieved by Tascha McLellan (New Zealand) at Forbes, Australia, on January 3, 1999.

Greatest distance in triangular hang gliding Tomas Suchanek (Czech Republic) achieved a record triangular-course distance of 221.9 miles (357.12 km) at Riverside, New South Wales, Australia, on December 16, 2000.

The equivalent women's record is 103.9 miles (167.2 km), achieved by Nichola Hamilton (UK) on January 2, 1997 at Croydon Hay, New South Wales, Australia.

Greatest height gain in a hang glider Larry Tudor (U.S.A.) achieved a height of 14,250 ft. (4,343 m) over Owens Valley, California, U.S.A., on August 4, 1985.

GREATEST ABSOLUTE ALTITUDE IN A GLIDER Robert Harris (U.S.A.) achieved a height of 49,009 ft. (14,938 m) in a glider over California City, U.S.A., on February 17, 1986.

The women's single-seater glider world record for absolute altitude was set by Sabrina Jackintell (U.S.A.), who achieved a height of 41,460 ft. (12,637 m) over Black Forest Gliderport, Colorado Springs, U.S.A., on February 14, 1979.

Judy Leden (UK) achieved the equivalent women's record with a height of 13,025 ft. (3,970 m) on December 1, 1992 at Kuruman, South Africa.

Most consecutive loops in a hang glider Chad Elchin performed 95 consecutive loops at the Highland Aerosports flight park at Ridgely, Maryland, U.S.A., on July 16, 2001. Elchin was towed to 15,900 ft. (4,846 m) and looped his Aeros Stealth Combat nonstop down to 700 ft. (213 m), at speeds ranging from 17 to 80 mph (28–128 km/h).

Fastest speed in a glider The highest average speed reached in a glider when setting an official FAI world record is 153.78 mph (247.49 km/h) by James and Thomas Payne (both U.S.A.) when setting the out-and-return course of 500 km (310 miles) speed record at California City, U.S.A., on March 3, 1999.

Greatest altitude gain in a glider The greatest height gain in a glider is 42,303 ft. (12,894 m) by Paul F. Bikle (U.S.A.) over Lancaster, California, U.S.A., on February 25, 1961.

The equivalent record for women is a height of 33,504 ft. (10,212 m), achieved by Yvonne Loader (New Zealand) at Omarama, New Zealand, on January 12, 1988.

TARGET SPORTS

Highest archery score in 24 hours The highest point score in 24 hours shooting FITA 18 rounds is 26,064 by Michael Howson and Stephen Howard (both UK) at Oakbank Sports College, Keighley, West Yorkshire, UK, on November 11–12, 2000.

Longest rifle shooting marathon Five members of the St. Sebastianus Schützenbruderchaft Ettringen 1901 eV shooting club shot for 26 hours at Ettringen, Germany, on September 20–21, 2003. The five members were: Karl Westhoften, Rainer Lanz, Dieter Franken, Christian Lanz, and Manfred Savelsberg (all Germany), who shot from three positions—prone, standing, and kneeling—and followed all International Shooting Sport Federation (ISSF) regulations.

Highest skeet shooting score by a woman Svetlana Demina (Russia) set a world record on June 1, 1999 with her score of 99 (75 + 24) in the women's skeet-shooting event held in Kumamoto City, Japan.

Highest men's trapshooting score Marcello Tittarelli (Italy) shot an incredible 150 out of 150 (125 + 25) in the men's trapshooting 125 targets

HIGHEST WOMEN'S TEAM FITA OUTDOOR RECURVE SCORE In 1992, the South Korea women's team (Kim Soo-nyung [pictured], Cho Younjeong, and Lee Eun-kyung) scored 4,094 points out of a possible 4,320 in the single FITA round, women's team category in Barcelona, Spain. The international governing body of archery, the Fédération Internationale de Tir à L'Arc (FITA), was founded in 1931. FITA regulates archery around the world through more than 125 member associations.

on June 11, 1996 at the World Cup in Suhl, Germany. In the trap events, named after the device that launches clay targets into the air, a bank of three traps is set at varying heights and angles within a trench in front of each shooter. The shooter does not know which of the three traps will release next. As each target is released, the shooter is allowed two shots.

★ ARCHERY INDOOR RECORDS ★

EVENT	PTS	NAME & NATIONALITY	VENUE	DATE
18 m				
Men	597	Michele Frangilli (Italy)	Nimes, France	January 2001
Women	591	Lina Herasymenko (Ukraine)	Istanbul, Turkey	March 1997
25 m				
Men	598	Michele Frangilli (Italy)	Galtarate, Italy	November 2001
Women	592	Petra Ericsson (Sweden)	Oulu, Finland	March 1991

★ ARCHERY MEN [SINGLE FITA ROUNDS] ★

EVENT	PTS	NAME & NATIONALITY	VENUE	DATE
FITA	1,379	Oh Kyo-moon (South Korea)	Wonju, South Korea	Nov. 2000
90 m	337	Jang Yong-ho (South Korea)	New York, U.S.A.	July 2003
70 m	347	Choi Young-kwang (South Korea)	Hongseong, South Korea	Aug. 2002
50 m	351	Kim Kyung-ho (South Korea)	Wonju, South Korea	Sept. 1997
30 m	360/17	Kye Dong-hyun (South Korea)	Cheongju, South Korea	Sept. 2002
Team	4,074	South Korea (Jang Yong-ho, Choi Young-kwang, Im Bong-hyun)	New York, U.S.A.	July 2003

★ ARCHERY WOMEN [SINGLE FITA ROUNDS] ★

EVENT	PTS	NAME & NATIONALITY	VENUE	DATE
FITA	1,388	Park Seong-hyun (South Korea)	Yechoen, South Korea	March 2003
70 m	348	Lee Hee-jeong (South Korea)	Cheongju, South Korea	Oct. 2001
60 m	350	Kim Jo-soon (South Korea)	Wanju, South Korea	Sept. 1998
50 m	350	Park Seong-hyun (South Korea)	Yechoen, South Korea	March 2003
30 m	360/14	Lee Hyun-jeong (South Korea)	Cheongju, South Korea	Oct. 2001
Team	4,094	South Korea (Kim Soo-myung, Lee Eun-kyung, Cho Yuon-jeong)	Barcelona, Spain	Aug. 1992

Highest men's rifle shooting score (50 m, three positions) With an overall score of 1,287.9, Rajmond Debevec (Slovenia) set a world record for the men's rifle 50 m (3 × 40 shots) in Munich, Germany, on August 29, 1992.

Most croquet World Championship wins by an individual The first croquet World Championships were held at the Hurlingham Club, London, UK, in 1989 and have been held annually since. The most wins is four by Robert Fulford (UK) in 1990, 1992, 1994, and 1997.

Most national croquet titles won by an individual Bob Jackson (New Zealand) won the New Zealand croquet Open Championship Singles title 14 times—1975, 1978, 1982–84, 1989, 1991–92, 1995, 1997–99, and 2002–03.

Longest indoor "bowls" marathon Six members of Arnos Bowling Club, Southgate, UK, played indoor bowls for a record 36 hours on April 20–21, 2002.

Highest bowling pin-fall in one lane over 24 hours The highest pin-fall achieved bowling on one lane in 24 hours is 36,781 by 12 bowlers at Go Bowling, Dunstable, Bedfordshire, UK, from August 21 to 22, 2003.

Longest bowling marathon The longest bowling marathon is 52 hr. 15 min. by Fred Miller (UK) at the AMF Bowling Centre in Wigan, Lancashire, UK, from February 28 to March 2, 2003.

Most darts World Championship titles The most darts World Championship titles won is 11 by Phil Taylor (GB). He won the World Darts Or-

MOST MacROBERTSON SHIELD WINS The MacRobertson Shield (instituted 1925) has been won a record 12 times by the Great Britain croquet team (GB team member David Foulser): 1925, 1937, 1956, 1963, 1969, 1974, 1982, 1990, 1993, 1996, 2000, and 2003.

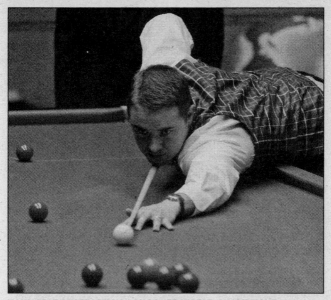

YOUNGEST PROFESSIONAL SNOOKER WORLD CHAMPION Stephen Hendry (pictured, UK, b. January 13, 1969) became the youngest professional snooker World Champion at 21 years 106 days on April 29, 1990.

ganization (WDO) championship in 1990 and 1992, and the Professional Darts Corporation (PDC) championship in 1995–2002 and 2004.

Fastest snooker 147 break The fastest snooker 147 break in a professional tournament is 5 min. 20 sec. by Ronnie O'Sullivan (UK) during the 1997 World Championships held at Sheffield, South Yorkshire, UK, on April 21, 1997. The only way to get a 147 clearance is to "pot" the black ball after every red, then clear the colored balls in order: yellow, green, brown, blue, pink, and black.

Highest break in snooker Wally West (UK) recorded a break of 151 in a snooker match at the Hounslow Lucania, London, UK, in October 1976. The break involved a free ball, which created an "extra" red, when all 15 reds were still on the table. In these very exceptional circumstances, the maximum break is 155.

Longest billiards marathon Pierre De Coster (Belgium) played billiards against all corners for 181 hr. 8 min. at SK Kampenhout clubhouse,

Kampenhout, Belgium, from June 3 to 10, 2003. De Coster played a total of 820 games, winning 518.

Longest pool marathon by a team A four-man team played pool for 120 hours at the Heritage Inn, Brooks, Alberta, Canada, from January 15 to 20, 2003. The team members were Jack Nemeth, Doug Webster, Harlan Ivarson, and Doug Prenevost (all Canada).

Longest pool marathon by an individual Raf Goossens (Belgium) played pool against all corers for 75 hr. 19 min. 17 sec. at Café St.-Jozef, Kampenhout, Belgium, from February 19 to 22, 2003.

MOTOR SPORTS

Most wins in a NASCAR season Richard Petty (U.S.A.) won 27 races in 1967. During the same season, Petty also set the mark for the most consecutive wins, with 10.

Petty holds a number of other NASCAR records. He won a record 200 races during his NASCAR career, which lasted from 1958 to 1992, and achieved an unrivaled 126 pole positions during this time, winning 61 races from the front of the grid.

Petty also started 1,184 races during his career, more than any other NASCAR driver.

Most NASCAR titles Since the NASCAR Championship was first held in 1949, two drivers have won it a total of seven times: Richard Petty (U.S.A.) in 1964, 1967, 1971–72, 1974–75, and 1979; and Dale Earnhardt (U.S.A.) in 1980, 1986–87, 1990–91, and 1993–94.

Most consecutive NASCAR Championships Eight drivers have won back-to-back NASCAR Championships, but only one, Cale Yarborough (U.S.A.), has won three Championships consecutively, from 1976 to 1978.

Most Formula One Grand Prix wins by a driver Michael Schumacher (Germany) won a total of 70 Formula One Grand Prix races from 1991 to 2003.

Schumacher holds the record for the most points scored in a Formula One career, with 1,038 points from 1991 to 2003.

He also holds the record for the greatest number of points scored by a driver in a Formula One season, after scoring 144 points in 2002.

During the same season, Schumacher also won an unrivaled 11 Formula One Grand Prix.

Most consecutive wins of the same Grand Prix Ayrton Senna (Brazil) took first place in the Monaco Grand Prix a total of five times in a row from 1989 to 1993.

LARGEST NASCAR SPEEDWAY Talladega Superspeedway (pictured) in Alabama, U.S.A., is the largest National Association for Stock Car Auto Racing (NASCAR) Speedway. The tri-oval-shaped track is 2.66 miles (4.28 km) long, has a banking angle of 33°, and can accommodate more than 143,000 seated guests and thousands more in the 215-acre (87-hectare) infield.

The track was known as Alabama International Motor Speedway when it opened in 1969 and was built at a cost of more than $4 million.

Senna's exceptional career was tragically cut short when he was killed on May 1, 1994 while competing in the San Marino Grand Prix.

Most consecutive Formula One pole positions Alain Prost (France) had seven consecutive Formula One pole positions in the 1993 season driving for the Williams-Renault team. Prost was also world champion that year.

Most Formula One pole positions in season The greatest number of Formula One pole positions in a season by one driver is 14 by Nigel Mansell (UK). Driving for the Williams-Renault team in 1992, Mansell won the World Championship before switching over to Indy cars the following year, winning the 1993 Indy car series at his first attempt.

Most Formula One pole positions in a career The greatest number of Formula One pole positions is 65 by Ayrton Senna (Brazil) from 161 races (including 41 wins), from 1985 to 1994, for the Toleman, Lotus, McLaren, and Williams teams.

Most Formula One fastest laps in a season The greatest number of fastest laps recorded by one driver in a Formula One season is nine by Mika Hakkinen (Finland) in 2000 while driving for the McLaren-Mercedes team.

Hakkinen finished the World Drivers' Championship second that year with 89 points. Michael Schumacher (Germany) won the Championship with a total of 108 points.

Oldest Grand Prix driver The oldest ever Grand Prix driver was Louis Alexandre Chiron (Monaco, 1899–1979), who finished sixth in the Monaco Grand Prix on May 22, 1955 at the age of 55 years 292 days.

Youngest Grand Prix driver The youngest driver ever to qualify for a Grand Prix was Michael Christopher Thackwell (New Zealand, b. March 30, 1961). He took part in the Canadian Grand Prix on September 28, 1980 at the age of 19 years 182 days.

Oldest Formula One world champion Juan Manuel Fangio (Argentina, b. June 24, 1911) won his last World Championship on August 4, 1957 at the age of 46 years 41 days.

Youngest Formula One world champion The youngest ever Formula One world champion was Emerson Fittipaldi (Brazil, b. December 12, 1946), who won his first World Championship on September 10, 1972 aged 25 years 273 days.

Youngest driver to claim a Formula One World Championship point When he finished in sixth place in the Brazilian Grand Prix on March 26, 2000, Jenson Button (UK, b. January 19, 1980) was only 20 years 67 days old.

Button originally finished in seventh position, out of the points, but after McLaren driver David Coulthard (UK) was disqualified from his second-place finish, Button was promoted to a points-scoring position.

Most Formula One Grand Prix retirements The greatest number of race retirements in Formula One is 135 by Andrea de Cesaris (Italy), during a career that spanned 14 years from 1980 to 1994.

De Cesaris also has the dubious honor of holding the record for most Grand Prix races (208) without a victory.

MOST WINS BY AN INDIVIDUAL AT THE LE MANS 24-HOUR RACE Jacky Ickx (Belgium, left) won the Le Mans 24-hour race six times, in 1969, 1975–77, and 1981–82.

MOST WORLD DRIVERS' CHAMPIONSHIP WINS Inaugurated in 1950, the World Drivers' Championship has been won a record six times by Michael Schumacher (Germany, pictured) in 1994–95 and 2000–03.

Most Grand Prix wins by a constructor As of the end of the 2003 season, Ferrari (Italy) had won 166 Formula One Grand Prix races.

Most Formula One Constructors' World Championship titles Ferrari has won 13 Formula One Constructors' World Championship titles, in 1961, 1964, 1975–77, 1979, 1982–83, and 1999–2003.

Most points by a constructor in a Formula One season In the 2002 Formula One season, the Ferrari team amassed 221 World Championship points. The team's drivers that year were Michael Schumacher (Germany) and Reubens Barichello (Brazil).

The Ferrari team won 15 races out of 17 and wrapped up both the drivers' and the constructors' titles in record time.

Most wins by a constructor in a Formula One season The greatest number of wins by a constructor in a Formula One season is 15. This feat has been achieved by two teams: McLaren in 1988 and Ferrari in 2002.

Most team wins at the Le Mans 24-hour race Porsche has won the Le Mans 24-hour race on 16 occasions, in 1970–71, 1976–77, 1979, 1981–87, 1993, and 1996–98.

Longest motorcycle race circuit The "Mountain" circuit on the Isle of Man, over which the principal TT (Tourist Trophy) races have been run since 1911 (with minor amendments in 1920), has 264 curves and corners and measures 37.73 miles (60.72 km).

Most superbikes World Championship race wins by a manufacturer Ducati (Italy) won 219 superbikes World Championship races from 1988 to 2004.

Most superbikes World Championship titles won by a manufacturer Ducati (Italy) has won 12 superbikes World Championships manufacturers' titles, in 1991–96 and 1998–2003.

Most superbikes World Championship pole positions by a manufacturer In the superbikes World Championships from 1988 to 2004, Ducati (Italy) achieved a record 118 pole positions.

Most superbikes World Championship titles Carl Fogarty (UK) won four superbikes World Championship titles, in 1994, 1995, 1998, and 1999.

Most superbikes World Championship race wins Carl Fogarty (UK) won a record 59 races in superbikes World Championships from 1992 to 1999.

Most sidecar World Championship titles The most sidecar World Championship titles won by the same pair is five, by Klaus Enders and

MOST MOTORCYCLE WORLD CHAMPIONSHIP 250-CC TITLES Two riders have won the 250-cc World Championship four times: Max Biaggi (Italy, leading here) from 1994 to 1997 and Phil Read (UK) in 1964, 1965, 1968, and 1971.

MOST SUPERBIKE WORLD CHAMPIONSHIP POLE POSITIONS Troy Corser (Australia) achieved 28 pole positions in the superbike World Championships from 1995 to 2001.

Ralph Engelhardt (both Germany) riding a BMW machine in 1967, 1969, and 1972–74.

Most 500-cc motocross World Championship titles Two riders have both won five 500-cc motocross World Championships: Roger de Coster (Belgium) in 1971–73 and 1975–76, and Joel Smets (Belgium) in 1995, 1997–98, 2000, and 2003.

Most 250-cc motocross World Championship titles Joël Robert (Belgium) won six 250-cc motocross World Championships, in 1964 and 1968–72. From April 25, 1964 to June 18, 1972, he won a record 50 250-cc Grand Prix.

Most 125-cc motocross World Championship titles The 125-cc class of the motocross World Championship has been won three times by three riders: Gaston Rahier (Belgium) in 1975–77, Harry Everts (Belgium) in 1979–81, and Alessio Chiodi (Italy) in 1997–99.

Most motorcycle World Championship 500-cc titles The most motorcycling World Championship 500-cc titles won is eight by Giacomo Agostini (Italy) from 1966 to 1972 and in 1975.

Most motorcycle World Championship 350-cc titles Giacomo Agostini (Italy) won seven motorcycling World Championship 350-cc titles from 1968 to 1974.

Most motorcycle World Championship 125-cc titles Angel Roldán Nieto (Spain) won seven motorcycling World Championship 125-cc titles, in 1971, 1972, 1979, and 1981–84.

Most motorcycle World Championship 80-cc titles Jorge Martinez (Spain) won three motorcycling World Championship 80-cc titles from 1986 to 1988. This class ran for only six years from 1984 to 1989.

Most motorcycle World Championship 50-cc titles Angel Roldán Nieto (Spain) won six motorcycling World Championship 50-cc titles in 1969, 1970, 1972, and 1975–77.

Lowest elapsed time for a National Hot Rod Association (NHRA) drag racing Pro Stock motorbike Angelle Savoie (U.S.A.) covered 440 yd. in 7.049 seconds on her Suzuki Pro Stock motorbike in Matthews, Louisiana, U.S.A., in May 2002.

Fastest speed for an NHRA Pro Stock motorbike Matt Hines (U.S.A.) achieved 194.10 mph (312.37 km/h) on a Suzuki in Englishtown, New Jersey, U.S.A., in May 2001—the highest terminal velocity for a gasoline-driven piston-engined motorcycle (Pro Stock).

Lowest elapsed time for an NHRA Pro Stock car Greg Anderson (U.S.A.) covered 440 yd. in 6.670 seconds driving a Pontiac Grand Am in Concord, North Carolina, U.S.A., on May 18, 2003.

Fastest speed in an NHRA Pro Stock car Set by Greg Anderson (U.S.A.) in Concord, North Carolina, U.S.A., on May 18, 2003, the highest terminal velocity for a Pro Stock car is 207.18 mph (333.42 km/h).

Lowest elapsed time for an NHRA Top Fuel drag racer Anthony Schumacher (U.S.A.) covered 440 yd. in 4.441 seconds in a McKinney dragster at Long Grove, Illinois, U.S.A., on October 4, 2003. Top Fuel cars run on 90% nitromethane and 10% methanol, also known as racing alcohol. As a result, the engine is about 2.4 times as powerful as a similar displacement engine running gasoline and produces at least 8,000 horsepower.

Fastest speed for an NHRA Top Fuel drag racer The highest terminal velocity at the end of a 440-yd. run is 333.25 mph (536.31 km/h) by

MOST RALLY WORLD CHAMPIONSHIP RACE WINS Two drivers have each won 25 World Championship races: Colin McRae (UK) in 1993–2002 and Carlos Sainz (Spain, driving here) in 1990–2003.

Douglas Kalitta (U.S.A.) at Ypsilanti, Michigan, U.S.A., on November 9, 2003 in a McKinney dragster.

Lowest elapsed time in an NHRA funny car John Force (U.S.A.) covered 440 yd. in 4.721 seconds in a Ford Mustang in Yorba Linda, California, U.S.A., on June 1, 2003. Funny cars are rear-wheel-driven dragsters with a massive front-mounted engine and huge, distinctive rear wheels.

Fastest speed in an NHRA funny car Gary Scelzi (U.S.A.) reached 329.18 mph (529.76 km/h) from a standing start over 440 yd. in a Dodge Stratus in Fresno, California, U.S.A., on September 28, 2003.

Most rally World Championship race wins in a season Didier Auriol (France) won a record six rally World Championship races in 1992.

Youngest rally World Championship driver The youngest driver to compete in a Fédération Internationale de l'Automobile (FIA) World Championship rally is Jari-Matti Latvala (Finland), who was 18 years 61 days when he drove in the 50th Acropolis Rally, Athens, Greece, on June 6–8, 2003.

Most rally World Championship race wins by a manufacturer Lancia (Italy) won 73 rally World Championship races from 1972 to 2004.

Most rally World Championship wins by a manufacturer Lancia (Italy) won 11 rally World Championship titles from 1972 to 1992.

Most Dakar Rally wins Ari Vatanen (Finland) has won the Dakar Rally a record four times, first in 1987 and then on three more occasions from 1989 to 1991.

Most Dakar Rally bike category wins Stéphane Peterhansel (France) had a record six wins in the bike category of the Dakar Rally in 1991–93, 1995, and 1997–98.

BICYCLING

Fastest women's 200 m, unpaced, flying start The fastest unpaced 200 m bicycled from a flying start is 10.831 seconds by Olga Slyusareva (Russia) in Moscow, Russia, on April 25, 1993.

Fastest men's 200 m, unpaced, flying start Curtis Harnett (Canada) bicycled a distance of 200 m in 9.865 seconds from an unpaced flying start in Bogota, Colombia, on September 28, 1995.

Fastest women's 500 m, unpaced, flying start The fastest unpaced 500 m bicycled from a flying start is 29.655 seconds, by Erika Salumäe (USSR, now Estonia), in Moscow, USSR, on August 6, 1987.

Fastest men's 500 m, unpaced, flying start Arnaud Duble (France) finished the men's 500 m unpaced in 25.850 seconds from a flying start in La Paz, Bolivia, on October 10, 2001.

Fastest women's 500 m, unpaced, standing start The fastest unpaced 500 m bicycled from a standing start is 34.000 seconds, by Yong Hua Jiang (China), in Kunming, China, on August 10, 2002.

Fastest men's 1 km, unpaced, standing start The world record time for the 1-km bike race is 58.875 seconds by Arnaud Tournant (France) in La Paz, Bolivia, on October 10, 2001.

Fastest women's 3 km, unpaced, standing start The world record for the 3-km Women's Individual Cycling Pursuit race is 3 min. 30.816 sec., set by Leontien Zijlaard-van Moorsel (Netherlands) at the 2000 Olympic Games held in Sydney, Australia, on September 17, 2000.

Fastest men's team 4 km, unpaced, standing start The Australian team consisting of Peter Dawson, Graham Brown, Mark Renshaw, and Luke Roberts bicycled 4 km in 3 min. 59.583 sec. The time was set at the Commonwealth Games in Manchester, UK, on August 1, 2002.

MOST TOUR DE FRANCE WINS Lance Armstrong (U.S.A., pictured) has won the Tour de France a record six times from 1999 to 2004. He is the only man ever to accomplish this in the history of the Tour. Jacques Anquetil (France) in 1957, 1961–64; Eddy Merckx (Belgium) in 1969–72 and 1974; Bernard Hinault (France) in 1978–79, 1981–82, and 1985; and Miguel Indurain (Spain) in 1991–95, have all won the Tour five times, the previous record-breaking total.

Fastest men's 4 km, unpaced, standing start Chris Boardman (UK) bicycled a distance of 4 km in 4 min. 11.114 sec. in Manchester, UK, on August 29, 1996.

Greatest distance bicycled in 24 hours The 24-hour record behind pace is 1,216.8 miles (1,958.196 km) by Michael Secrest (U.S.A.) at Phoenix International Raceway, Arizona, U.S.A., on April 26–27, 1990. Solo and unpaced, Secrest achieved a distance of 532.74 miles (857.36 km) over the same time at the Olympic Velodrome, California State University, Carson, U.S.A., on October 23–24, 1997.

Farthest bicycling in an hour, unpaced, standing start The official Union Cycliste Internationale (UCI) one-hour record of 30.72 miles (49.441 km) was set in Manchester, UK, on October 27, 2000 by Chris Boardman (UK).

Greatest distance bicycled in one hour by a woman, unpaced, standing start The official UCI one-hour record by a woman is 28.02 miles (45.094 km) by Jeanie Longo (France) in Mexico City, Mexico, on December 7, 2000.

Longest one-day bicycle race The longest one-day "massed start" road race is the Bordeaux-Paris event in France, which is 342–385 miles (551–620 km) long, depending on the route.

Fastest bicycling end-to-end Andy Wilkinson (UK) bicycled from Land's End, Cornwall, to John O'Groats, Highland, UK, in 1 day 21 hr. 2 min. 18 sec. from September 29 to October 1, 1990.

The holder of the women's record is Pauline Strong (UK). She finished the distance in 2 days 6 hr. 49 min. 45 sec. from July 28 to 30, 1990.

Fastest trans-Europe two-person relay cycle Kevin Moreland and Guy Lawton (both UK), supported by the Twisting Compass Team, bicycled in relay from Tarifa, Spain, to North Cape, Norway, in a time of 9 days 20 hr. 43 min. from July 6 to 16, 2002.

Youngest Tour de France winner Henri Cornet (France) was aged 19 years 350 days when he won the Tour de France in 1904. Cornet actually finished the race in fifth position, but was awarded the victory after the first four riders were all disqualified.

Oldest Tour de France winner Firmin Lambot (Belgium) was 36 years 4 months when he won the Tour de France in 1922.

BIGGEST WINNING MARGIN IN A TOUR DE FRANCE The greatest time gap between the winner and the runner-up at the finish of a Tour de France is 28 min. 27 sec., between Fausto Coppi (Italy, left) and Stan Ockers (Belgium) in 1952.

MOST DOWNHILL MOUNTAIN-BIKING WORLD CHAMPIONSHIPS WON BY A WOMAN Anne-Caroline Chausson (France, pictured) has won 10 downhill World Championships—three in the junior championship from 1993 to 1995 and seven in the senior class from 1996 to 2002.

Closest Tour de France race The closest Tour de France race ever was in 1989 when, after 2,030 miles (3,267 km) over 23 days (July 1–23), Greg LeMond (U.S.A.) completed the Tour in 87 hr. 38 min. 35 sec., beating Laurent Fignon (France) to the finish in Paris by 8 seconds.

Most Tour de France stage wins Eddie Merckx (Belgium) has 34 Tour de France stage wins.

Fastest average speed in the Tour de France During the 1999 Tour, Lance Armstrong (U.S.A.) cycled at an average speed of 25.026 mph (40.276 km/h).

Most Tour of Spain wins The most wins in the Tour of Spain bicycling race is three by Tony Rominger (Switzerland) from 1992 to 1994.

Most Tour of Italy wins The most Tour of Italy wins is five and is shared by Alfredo Binda (Italy) in 1925, 1927–29, and 1933; Fausto Coppi (Italy) in 1940, 1947, 1949, and 1952–53; and Eddy Merckx (Belgium) in 1968, 1970, and 1972–74.

Fastest trans-Australia bicycling Tomio Uranyu (Japan) bicycled from Perth, Western Australia, to Sydney, New South Wales, in 9 days 23 hr. 25 min. from March 28 to April 7, 1992.

The women's record is held by Helen Shelley (Australia), who bicycled the distance in 13 days 2 hr. 55 min. from April 24 to May 7, 1999.

Fastest bicyclist on snow The fastest ever speed attained bicycling downhill on snow or ice is 132 mph (212.139 km/h), by downhill mountain bike racer Christian Taillefer (France) on a Peugeot bicycle at the speed ski slope in Vars, France, in March, 1998.

Most downhill mountain-biking World Championship wins Nicolas Vouilloz (France) had a record 10 World Championship wins— three in the junior championships from 1992 to 1994 and seven in the senior class in 1995–99 and 2001–02.

Most downhill mountain-biking World Cup event wins Nicolas Vouilloz (France) won 16 World Cups from 1992 to 2001.

WHEEL SKILLS

Longest skateboard journey The longest recorded journeys by skateboard were completed by Jack Smith (U.S.A.) in July 1976 and again in July 1984, when he covered just under 3,000 miles (4,830 km) between Lebanon, Oregon, and Williamsburg, Virginia, U.S.A.

Highest skateboarding ollie On February 6, 2000, Danny Wainwright (UK) popped the highest ollie at 44.5 in. (113 cm) off flat ground to win the Reese Forbes Ollie Challenge at the ASR Show, Long Beach, California, U.S.A.

Highest skateboard drop into a quarter pipe Adil Dyani (Norway) dropped into a 18-ft.-high (5.5-m) quarter-pipe ramp from a height of 30 ft. (9.15 m) on a skateboard in Oslo, Norway, on October 4, 2003. The drop was effectively made from 12 ft. (3.65 m) above the ramp lip.

Highest skateboarding jump Trevor Baxter (UK) cleared a bar set at 5 ft. 5 in. (1.65 m) by jumping off a moving skateboard and landing on it after it had passed under the bar, in Grenoble, France, on September 14, 1982.

HIGHEST AIR ON A SKATEBOARD PROFESSIONAL SKATEBOARDER
Danny Way (U.S.A.) performed an 18-ft. 3-in. (5.56-m) method air off the
top of a 20-ft. (6-m) quarter pipe at Point X Camp near Aguanga,
California, U.S.A., on April 17, 2002. The height was measured from the
top of the ramp.

Fastest speed on a skateboard Gary Hardwick (U.S.A.) reached
62.55 mph (100.66 km/h) in a standing position in Fountain Hills, Arizona,
U.S.A., on September 26, 1998.

Fastest speed on a street luge The highest speed set for riding a skateboard in a prone position is 78.37 mph (126.12 km/h) by Roger Hickey
(U.S.A.) on a course near Los Angeles, California, U.S.A., on March 15, 1990.

Longest 50-50 rail grind on a skateboard The longest skateboard rail
grind is 33 ft. 10 in. (10.31 m) by Chad Fernandez (U.S.A.) on the *Today*
show in New York City, U.S.A., on August 25, 2003.

Most continuous skateboard revolutions Richard Carrasco (U.S.A.)
completed a total of 142 continuous 360° revolutions on a skateboard on
August 11, 2000 in Santa Ana, California, U.S.A.

Longest ramp jump on a skateboard Danny Way (U.S.A.) performed
a 65-ft. (19.8-m) skateboard jump between two ramps at Point X Camp near
Aguanga, California, U.S.A., on April 16, 2002.

Highest BMX vertical air Mat Hoffman (U.S.A.) achieved a 26-ft. 6-in.
(8.07-m) air from a 24-ft.-tall (7.3-m) quarter-pipe ramp on March 20,
2001, in Oklahoma City, U.S.A. Hoffman was towed by a motorcycle in the
run-up to the jump to reach the required speed.

Highest bunny hop Bruno Arnold (France) achieved the highest ever bunny hop on a mountain bike, clearing a 3-ft. 10.2-in.-high (1.17-m) horizontal bar without using a ramp on the set of *L'Été de Tous les Records,* Le Touquet, France, on July 24, 2003.

Highest vertical drop on a bicycle Walter Belli (Italy) and David Cachón Labrador (Spain) both rode their BMX bicycles off a 13-ft. 1-in.-high (4-m) platform and continued to bicycle upon landing without their feet touching the ground on the set of *El Show de los Récords,* Madrid, Spain, on December 5, 2001. In accordance with the record rules, they were not allowed a run-up before dropping off the platform.

Highest ramp jump on a BMX bike Timo Pritzel (Germany) and Jesús Fuentes (Spain) cleared a bar 16 ft. 9.5 in. (5.12 m) above floor level using BMX bicycles on the set of *El Show de los Récords,* Madrid, Spain, on September 21, 2001.

Longest power-assisted ramp jump by bicycle Professional stunt rider Colin Winkelmann (U.S.A.) jumped his BMX bicycle 116 ft. 11 in. (35.63 m) after being towed to a speed of approximately 60 mph (100 km/h) behind a motorcycle at Agoura Hills,

LONGEST BMX BACK FLIP On February 9, 2002, Allan Cooke (U.S.A.) performed a 54-ft. (16.45-m) back flip on his BMX between two specially constructed ramps at Point X Camp near Aguanga, California, U.S.A.

HIGHEST MOTO X STEP UP JUMP The greatest height achieved in the XGames Moto Cross Step Up event is 35 ft. (10.67 m) by Tommy Clowers (U.S.A.) on August 18, 2000. The feat is a motorcycle high-jump, in which riders must try to clear a bar placed at the top of a steep take-off ramp. This record is the equivalent of jumping onto the roof of a two-story building. In the photo above, Clowers is performing a trick called a mulisha air.

California, U.S.A., on December 20, 2000 for the *Guinness World Records: Primetime* TV show.

Longest standing jump on a mountain bike Marc Caisso (France) achieved a standing-bike-jump distance of 9 ft. 6 in. (2.9 m) on his mountain bike at the studios of *L'Émission des Records,* Paris, France, on October 26, 2000.

Longest wheelie with feet off the pedals Martti Kuoppa (Finland) was able to maintain a wheelie on the front wheel of his BMX for 23.25 seconds, while covering a distance of 328 ft. (100 m) and without his feet touching the bike's pedals, on June 26, 2001 in Helsinki, Finland.

Most BMX gyrator spins in one minute The record for the greatest number of gyrator spins in one minute is 29 by Sam Foakes (UK) for BBC1's *Blue Peter* in London, UK, on March 11, 2002.

Farthest distance on a unicycle in one hour Dieter Dölling (Germany) covered 6.617 miles (10.65 km) in one hour around an indoor track on July 11, 1998.

Fastest 100 m on a unicycle Peter Rosendahl (U.S.A.) covered 328 ft. (100 m) in 12.11 seconds, at a speed of 18.47 mph (29.72 km/h), from a standing start in Las Vegas, Nevada, U.S.A., on March 25, 1994.

Most skipping revolutions in one minute on a unicycle Amy Shields (U.S.A.) performed 209 skips (or rope revolutions) on a unicycle in one minute in St. Paul, Minnesota, U.S.A., on February 23, 2002.

Highest in-line skate ramp jump José Félix Hormaetxe Henry (Spain) cleared a bar set at 14 ft. 9 in. (4.5 m) on in-line skates at the studios of *El Show de los Récords,* Madrid, Spain, on December 14, 2001.

Farthest distance on in-line skates in one hour Massimilliano Sorrentino (Italy) covered 23.254 miles (37.425 km) on in-line skates in one hour in Rieti, Italy, on July 27, 2003.

Longest and fastest journey on in-line skates Russell "Rusty" Moncrief (U.S.A.) crossed the U.S.A. on in-line skates in 69 days 8 hr. 45 min. from January 5 to March 15, 2002. He started out from Crescent Beach, near Jacksonville, Florida, and completed his journey at Soltana Beach, near San Diego, California, after covering 2,595 miles (4,175 km).

Greatest distance on in-line skates in 24 hours Kimberly Ames (U.S.A.) covered 283.07 miles (455.55 km) in 24 hours on in-line skates in Portland, Oregon, U.S.A., on October 2, 1994.

UNUSUAL SPORTS

Most entrants at a bog snorkeling World Championships Entrants in the bog snorkeling World Championships have to complete two lengths of a 60-yd. (54.8-m) trench cut through a peat bog as quickly as possible, wearing snorkels and flippers. On August 25, 2003, 96 people entered the competition at Waen Rhydd peat bog, Llanwrtyd Wells, Powys, UK. Fifteen-year-old Philip John (UK) won in a record time of 1 min. 35 sec.

Farthest distance to throw a rolling pin Lori La Deane Adams (U.S.A.) threw a rolling pin weighing 2 lb. (970 g) a distance of

175 ft. 5 in. (53.47 m) at the Iowa State Fair, Iowa, U.S.A., on August 21, 1979.

Farthest haggis hurl Alan Pettigrew (UK) threw a haggis (of minimum weight 1 lb. 8 oz. or 680 g) a distance of 180 ft. 10 in. (55.11 m) at Inchmurrin, Argyll, UK, on May 24, 1984.

Fastest 40-m walk on water The fastest time to walk 131 ft. (40 m) on water using self-propelled buoyancy shoes was 1 min. 10.8 sec. It was achieved by the team Gemini Dawn on April 11, 2003 at the Royal Commonwealth Pool, Edinburgh, UK. The event was part of the 2003 Edinburgh Science Festival.

Most sheep shorn manually in eight hours The record for the most sheep shorn manually with scissors and hand blade in eight hours is 50. János Marton (Hungary) achieved the feat, without any breaks, on April 26, 2003 at Hódmezővásárhely Animal Husbandry Show, Hódmezővásárhely, Hungary.

Farthest dyno climbing by a man In dyno climbing, participants launch themselves from one set of handholds to a higher set with no intermediate holds. Matt Heason (UK) achieved a distance of 8.53 ft. (2.6 m) in the Bendcrete Dyno Competition held at the Edge Climbing Centre, Sheffield, South Yorkshire, UK, on April 20, 2002.

MOST CONSECUTIVE BOG SNORKELING WORLD CHAMPIONSHIPS
Steve Griffiths (UK) is the only person to have won the bog snorkeling World Championships three times, consecutively, from 1985 to 1987. This annual event takes place in the dense Waen Rhydd peat bog on the southern outskirts of Llanwrtyd Wells, Powys, UK.

Farthest dyno climbing by a woman The farthest distance achieved by a woman is 6.233 ft. (1.9 m) by Katherine Schirrmacher (UK) at the Bendcrete Dyno Competition held at the Edge Climbing Centre, Sheffield, South Yorkshire, UK, on April 20, 2002.

Longest soccer field The annual Shrovetide Football Match has been played for more than 300 years. It is a game short on rules and long on physical contact between the two teams from Ashbourne, Derbyshire, UK: the Up'ards (those born north of the River Henmore) and the Down'ards (those born south of the river). The goals are the waterwheels at Clifton (target for the Down'ards) and Stursdton (target for the Up'ards) 3 miles (4.8 km) apart. The most goals in modern times was three in a day, but one a day is average.

Greatest competitive distance flown in a career by a pigeon Brazilian Beauty, a blue check hen owned by Robert Koch (South Africa), flew 25,507 miles (41,050 km) during a competitive career that lasted from 1990 to 1997.

Longest shaft achieved by a man in kiiking The aim of kiiking, a sport native to Scandinavian and Baltic countries, is to complete a 360° revolution on a swing. Success is measured by the length of the shafts of the

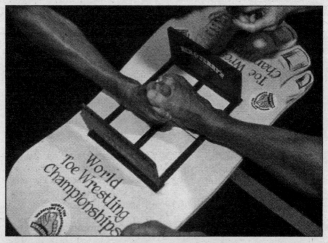

MOST TOE WRESTLING WORLD CHAMPIONSHIPS Alan Nash (UK) has won five toe wrestling World Championships, in 1994, 1996–97, 2000, and 2002. The women's category has been won four times by Karen Davies (UK) from 1999 to 2002. The Championships are held annually on the first Saturday in June at Ye Olde Royal Oak, Wetton, Staffordshire, UK. Contestants must push an opponent's foot to the other side of a specially constructed ring called a "toerack" using only their toes.

swing—the longer the shafts the better. The longest shaft used to success-fully complete a rotation is 23 ft. (7.01 m) by Andrus Aasamäe (Estonia) at Rakveres, Estonia, on July 16, 2000.

Longest shaft achieved by a woman in kiiking The longest shaft used to successfully complete a rotation in kiiking by a woman is 19 ft. 2.7 in. (5.86 m) by Kätlin Kink (Estonia) at Pärnus, Estonia, on September 2, 2001.

Most pea-shooting World Championships Mike Fordham (UK) won a total of seven pea-shooting World Championships, in 1977–78, 1981, 1983–85, and 1992.

Most coal-bag carrying titles by a man Terry Lyons (UK) holds the record for the most titles at the annual Coal Carrying Championship race at Gawthorpe, West Yorkshire, UK, held on Easter Monday every year. Lyons carried a 110-lb. (50-kg) bag of coal over the 3,322-ft. (1,012.5-m) course and won the race every year from 1977 to 1985 inclusively, with the sole exception of 1980, when the race was won by Colin Claypole (UK).

Fastest individual coal-bag carrying by a man On April 1, 1991, David Jones (UK) carried a 110-lb. (50-kg) bag over the course of the annual Coal Carrying Championship race at Gawthorpe, West Yorkshire, UK, in 4 min. 6 sec.

Fastest individual coal-bag carrying by a woman Ruth Clegg (UK) holds the women's record for the annual Coal Carrying Championship race at Gawthorpe, West Yorkshire, UK, carrying a 44-lb. (20-kg) bag over the course in 5 min. 4 sec. on April 6, 2002.

Most horseshoe pitching World Championship wins by a man Ted Allen (U.S.A.) won a total of 10 horseshoe pitching World Championships from 1933 to 1959. Since their inception, the Championships have been played at irregular intervals, but have been held every year since 1946.

Most horseshoe pitching World Championships wins by a woman Vicki Chappelle Winston (U.S.A.) won an unrivaled 10 horseshoe pitching World Championships in the women's category. She won the first of her titles in 1956, and the last in 1981. Her other championship wins were in 1958–59, 1961, 1963, 1966–67, 1969, and 1975.

Most ringers in a horseshoe pitching World Championship game The term "ringer" describes a horseshoe that comes to rest encircling the stake. The most ringers scored by an individual in a horseshoe pitching World Championship games is 175 by Glen Henton (U.S.A.) in 1965.

Longest horseshoe pitching winning streak The longest winning streak in the horseshoe pitching World Championships is 69 games by Fernando Isais (U.S.A.) from 1950 to 1952.

WORLD CHAMPIONSHIPS WITH THE HEAVIEST PARTICIPANTS The World Elephant Polo Association (WEPA) was founded in 1982 and has hosted a championship tournament (pictured) every year since. Elephant polo is played by riders on elephants, four to a team. The invitational tournament is held every December on a grass airfield in Megauly, on the edge of the Royal Chitwan National Park in Nepal.

Largest Wellington boot race The most participants to take part in and finish a race while wearing Wellington boots is 981. The race was held at Waimea College, Nelson, New Zealand, on September 3, 2003.

Most extreme ironing World Championships On September 20–21, 2002, the inaugural extreme ironing World Championships, organized by the German Extreme Ironing Section (GEIS), was held in Munich, Germany. It was won by Inga Kosak (Germany) with a score of 522. Participants are scored on style and textile, and against the clock, over five disciplines: Forest, Water, Rocky, Urban, and Freestyle.

Index

This index concentrates on the subjects of the records (e.g. kissing, chocolates, tortoises) rather than the type of record (e.g. highest, longest, widest). Personal names of record holders are not included. Page numbers in **bold type** indicate the main entry on a topic. Page numbers in *italic type* indicate an interview with or feature on the person named.

balloons (toys) (cont'd)
balloon sculptures, 29
helium-filled, altitude reached, 54
mosaics, 313
water balloon fights, 39
balls
ball bath, 198
ball mosaics, 312
ball sports *see* specific sports (e.g. baseball)
basketballs spinning, 399
cannonballs, 302
disco balls, 188
golf ball carry, 494
hairballs, 15
rubber band balls, 188
soccer ball control skills, 53, 412–13
speed of delivery *see* ball speed
string balls, 190
tennis ball holding, 30, 125
zorbs, 29
Baluchitherium, 96
banana items collections, 193
bandwidth, 282, 284, 285
banjo playing, 49
bank notes & coins, 29, 183–84, 192, 281
bankruptcies, 159
banks, seed banks, 228–29
Bannister, Mike, *259–61*
barbers, 33
bareback riding (rodeo), 514
barefoot waterskiing, 34, 496, 498–99
bartenders, 33
BASE jumping, 34
baseball, **391–95**
basketball, **395–99**
basketballs spinning, 30
slam dunks from trampolines, 29
baths, ball baths, 198
bats, baseball, 395
batteries, 281–82
batting averages
baseball, 393
cricket, 417
battlefield simulators, 301
battles *see* wars, battles & peacekeeping
battleships, 307
beach towels, 186
beach volleyball & volleyball, **422, 423**
beaks, birds, 101, 102
beans, 134
baked beans, 167, 206
beards
train pulling with, 45
weight lifting with, 48
bears, teddy bears, 194, 195
beavers, 99–100
beds
bed pushes, 41

beds of nails, 47, 51
hospital beds, 163
beer & stout, 168, 177–78, 204
beer bottles, 186, 191
bees, 346
beetles, 114, 117
beetroot, 131, 132
beliefs & religion, **171–75**
bell ringing, 35
benches, Internet benches, 285
bending iron bars into suitcases, 49
bestsellers (books), 348, 349, 351
bhangra, 378–79
biathlon, 478–79
bicycling & bicycles, 182, 247, 248, 249, **532–40**
bikeway bridges & routes, 225, 247
Pan-American Highway, 65
spinning, 53
Big Bang, 71, 294
big wheels & observation wheels, 231
Bigfoot trucks, 265, 266
Bigtoe (motorcycle), 249
bikes & bicycles *see* bicycling & bicycles; motorcycling & motorcycles
billiards, 35, 523–24
billionaires & wealth, 25, 144, 159–63
bills, birds, 101, 102
biological molecules, 274–75
biological weapons, 306
biomes, 228
biplanes, 256
bird-eating spiders, 116–17
birds, **101–5**
caged, 127
eaten by plants, 129–30
headless chickens, 62
origami, 179
prehistoric, 96
racing pigeons, 542
turkey farming, 149
births & babies
animals *see* litters & offspring
humans, 19–22
life expectancy at birth, 139
biscuits (cookies), 207
bites, Gila monsters, 119
black coatings, 270
black holes, 68–69
black mamba, 120
Blackbird (aircraft), 256–57
bladder stones, 12
blind & blindfolded driving, 56, 57
Blockhead (inflatable sculpture), 314
blocks, concrete blocks strength events, 47, 48
blocks & blocking (sport)
basketball, 396
Canadian football, 430

infrared telescopes & sniperscopes, 272, 305
in-line skating, 540
inner-tube water slides, 234
innings scores, cricket, 421
innovations, space technology, 293–94
insects, **114–17**, 346
  prehistoric, 96
interceptions, American football, 386, 390
internal combustion engine, 240
international appearances & caps
  rugby union, 416–17
  soccer, 408
International Space Station (ISS), 290, 292, 295
Internet, 159, 169, **282–86**, 364
invertebrates *see* specific groups of
  invertebrates (e.g. insects)
iron-bar bending, 49
ironing, 51, 544
irrational numbers, 277
irrigation, saltwater garden parks, 227–28
Islam, 174, 175
islands, 92, 93
Isle of Man TT circuit, 527
ISPs (Internet service providers), 283
ISS (International Space Station), 290, 292, 295

J

jackets, 318
javelin (athletics), 444, 451
jaw, sperm whale, 106–7
jazz, 177, 375, 376
JDAM (Joint Direct Attack Munition), 305
jellybeans, 211
Jenga towers, 200
jet aircraft
  collections, 192
  engine power, 262
  first flight, 256
  Internet purchase, 283
  speed, 257, 258, 308, 309
jewelry, 184–85, 318
jigsaw puzzles, 197–98
jockeys, horseracing, 511, 513, 514–15
Joint Direct Attack Munition (JDAM), 305
joints, human, 11, 12, 14
jokes
  Internet joke votes, 282–83
  joke-telling marathons, 50
journeys & expeditions, 25–26, **62–66**
  see also specific journeys (e.g.
    transatlantic crossings)
judges (legal cases), 156
judo, 469
juggling on unicycles, 30
jujitsu, 468

jukeboxes, 189, 298
jumping jacks, 32
jumps
  air bag landings, 56
  BMX, 537, 538
  bungee jumping, 55, 56
  cars, 242
  dogs, 123, 125
  dolphins, 107
  high jump (athletics), 440, 444, 451, 452, 454
  in-line skating, 540
  insects, 115
  jump flips (figure skating), 488
  jumping jacks, 32
  limousines, 242
  long jump (athletics), 440, 444, 451, 452, 454
  monster trucks, 266
  motorcycling, 248, 539
  mountain biking, 538, 539
  pole vault (athletics), 440, 444, 451, 454
  power-assisted bicycles, 538–39
  rabbits, 125
  robots, 299
  show jumping, 511, 512
  skateboarding, 536–37
  ski flips, 477–78
  ski-jumping, 476, 477, 481–82
  snowmobiles, 247–48
  standing jumps (athletics), 452
  triple jump (athletics), 440, 444, 451, 454
  see also parachutes & parachuting
Jupiter (planet), 69, 72, 75, 76, 292

K

kaleidoscopes, 184
karaoke marathons, 50
karate, 468–69
kayaking & canoeing, **500, 502–3**
Kentucky Derby (horse race), 511
kettles, 188
Kew Gardens, 227
keying in text messages, 289
kickoff returns, American football, 388
kidney transplants & disorders, 18
kiiking, 542–43
killer whales, 106
kilogram measurements, accuracy, 270
king cobra, 121
kings, 144, 145, 146
kinkajous, 126
kissing, 40, 53
kites, 195, 202
  kite surfing, 497
Klemenic, Ron, 221–22
knee cap (patella), 11

movies (cont'd)
  budgets, costs & stars' earnings, 322,
    325, 338, 340
  directors & producers, 28, 322, 325,
    330, 331
  documentaries, 328, 338, 378
  early movies, 325–26, 340, 341
  Indian theater, 327
  marathon events, 328, 338
  memorabilia, 338, 341, 343
  Oscars, **329–34**
  series, 323–24, 338, 341, 342
  takes, editing & production, 336, 337
  theater chains, screens & drive-ins,
    326–27, 328
  see also specific topics (e.g. screen tests)
mules, 151
multimedia jukeboxes, 298
multiple births, 19, 22
mummies (human remains), 281
murals, 313, 315
murders, 155
muscles
  human, 10–11
  insects (wing-beat speed), 114
museums, gallery space, 316
music
  astronomical sounds, 68–69
  awards, 373, 375–76, 378
  circus bandmasters, 34
  classical, 183, 364, 376, 378, 379
  companies & corporations, 161
  jazz, 177, 375, 376
  jukeboxes, 189, 298
  manuscripts, 183
  marathon events, 49–50, 51, 283–84, 378
  R&B, 372, 374
  rap & hip-hop, 372, 373–75
  salsa, 36, 379
  yodeling, 38
  see also dance; pop, rock & country
    music
musical chairs, 38
musical instruments
  accordions, 190
  drums, drumsticks & drumming, 49,
    188, 371–72, 377
  flutes, 188
  orchestras & ensembles, 376, 377
  playing marathons, 49–50
musicals, 382–84
MVP (Most Valuable Player) awards,
  baseball, 395

N

nails (human body), fingernail length, 4,
  5–6
nails (metal objects), beds of nails, 47, 51

names
  domain names, 283
  mammals with multiple names, 100
  place names, 351
nanotechnology, 272
nasal ejections
  candy & confectionery, 205, 211
  sneezes, 18
NASCAR (National Association for
  Stock Car Auto Racing) motor
  racing, 524, 525
national flags, 37, 188
National Hockey League (NHL) ice
  hockey, 400–4
National Hot Rod Association (NHRA)
  racing, 530–31
National Rugby League (NRL), 415
Nations Cup (skiing), 476
natural arches, 81
navies & naval battles, 152, 154, 306–8, 310
Nazca lines, 280
NBA basketball, **395–98**
nebulae, 68
Nepenthes (carnivorous plants), 129–30
Neptune (planet), 72, 75
nerve cells, 13
nesting dolls (matrioshka), 198
nests
  birds, 102–3
  gorillas, 98
  wasps, 115
nettles, 130
networks *see* television
neurons, motor, 13
neutrinos, 277
neutron sources & microscopes, 271
newspapers, 350
newts, 108
NFL American football, 386–90
  stadiums visited, 65
NHL (National Hockey League) ice
  hockey, 400–4
NHRA (National Hot Road Association)
  racing, 530–31
Nile (river), 91
Nintendo GameCube, 202
nipples, weight lifting with, 47
no-hitters, baseball, 393
Nobel Peace Prize, 154
Noble, Richard, *246–47*
noise
  background noise levels, 271
  see also sound
nominations, Oscars (Academy Awards),
  330, 331–33, 334
nonfiction *see* books
Nordic skiing, **480–82**
North & South poles
  pole-to-pole circumnavigations, 62–63

singles & albums charts hits, **364–79**, 378–80
sirens (signaling devices), 289
sit-ups, abdominal frame, 472
sitar playing, 378
sitting
   mass-participation events, 39
   pole-sitting, 175
sixes, cricket, 419, 420, 422
skateboarding, **536–37**
skating
   figure skating, 26–27, 486–88
   in-line skating, 540
   speed skating, **486–91**
skeet-shooting, 520
skeletons
   prehistoric life, 17, 93–97
   whale jaws, 106–7
skiing
   Alpine skiing, **474–79**
   flare runs, 478
   freestyle skiing, 476
   marathon events, 53
   Nordic skiing, **480–82**
   ski flips, 477–78
   ski-jumping, 476, 477, 481–82
   ski lifts, 478
   ski orienteering, 479–80
   waterskiing, 34, 495–96, 498–99
skipping
   body skips, 28
   ducks & drakes, 30
   marathon events, 463, 474
   mass-participation events, 39
   Texas skips, 52
   tightrope skill, 29–30
   unicycling, 540
skulls
   dinosaurs, 93, 95
   human remains, 17, 280
   objects removed from, 61
   plate insertion, 15
SkyCycle, 249
skydiving & freefall, 57–58, 515–17
skyscrapers, 55, 214–15, 217, **218–22**
slam dunks from trampolines, 29
slates, solar, 146
sled dog racing, 479
sleepovers, 40–41
slides, water slides, 44, 234
sliming, 40
smallpox, 306
Smalltoe (motorcycle), 249
Smart cars, people in, 42
Smarties eaten with chopsticks, 205
smells, 130, 276–77
snail racing, 178
snakes (effigies), 178
snakes (reptiles), 31, 96, 120–22

snatch (weight lifting), 469, 470, 472, 473
sneezing, 18
sniperscopes, 305
snooker, 523
snow
   downhill bicycling, 536
   sheep survival in snowdrift, 62
   snow depth, 78
   snowball fights, 39
   snowboarding, 479, 482
   snowfall, 79
   snowmobiles, 247–48
   snowshoe racing, 481
   see also skiing
soap operas, 355–56, 360
soccer, 27, **404–13**
   ball control skills, 53, 412–13
   indoor soccer, 411
   memorabilia, 183
   stadiums & grounds, 216, 408–9
societies & clubs, magicians, 345, 346, 347
socks, 316
Sojourner (planetary rover), 295
solar energy/solar power
   aircraft (flying wing), 258–59
   cars, 241
   generation & use, 146, 147, 222
solar phenomena
   solar flares, 73
   solar haloes, 80
   solar wind, 78
   sunspot data, 271
Solar System, **72–76**
   see also space travel & exploration
soldiers *see* military forces
Solheim Cup (golf), 491
solids, density, 270
somersaults, freestyle skiing, 476
Son of Beast (roller coaster), 232
sound
   air raid sirens, 289
   astronomical sounds, 68–69
   background noise levels, 271
   drumming, 376–77
   human voice, intelligible range, 16
   sound archives, 288–89
   talkies (movies), 325–26, 341, 342
South American Championships (soccer), 408
South pole *see* North & South poles
southern & northern lights, 78
Southern Cross II (aircraft), 258
Southern Magnetic Anomaly, 84
sovereign countries visited, 64
Soyuz spacecraft, 294, 295
space shuttles, 292, 294, 295, 296
   transporters, 260, 264
space stations, 290, 292, 294, 295–96, 297

Acknowledgments

Special thanks go to the following people for their work during the production of this year's edition:

Jim Booth, Nicky Boxall, James Bradley, Caroline Butler, Scott Christie, Ann Collins, Chris Darley, Sam Fay, Marco Frigatti, Lisa Gibbs, Sophie Gimber, Simon Gold, James Herbert, Mary Hill, Laura Hughes, Caius Julyan, Peter Laker, Joyce Lee, Scott Lindsay, Anthony Liu, Andi Mercer, Shazia Mirza, Rob Molloy, Alistair Richards, David Roberts, Nicola Savage, Malcolm Smith, Ryan Tunstall, Kate White, Sophie Whiting.

The team also wishes to thank the following individuals and organizations:

Academy of Motion Picture Arts and Sciences, Ernest Adams, AIDA (Association Internationale pour le Développement del'Apnée), Dr. Leslie Aiello, Airports Council International, Amnesty International, Dr. Martyn Amos, Jorgen Vaaben Andersen, Anritsu, Antietam Recreation Centre, Vic Armstrong, Gee Armytage, Sir David Attenborough, Australia Zoo, Ron Baalke, Capt. Mike Baker, Bank of England, Ken Bannister, Mike Bannister, Dr. Peter Barham, Peter Baroody, Brenda Barton (World Food Program), BBC, Guenter Bechly, Bryan Berg, Gabe Bevilacqua, Jackie Bibby, Aase Bjerner, Richard Boatfield, Ian Bottomley (Royal Armouries, Leeds), Dr. Richard Bourgerie, BP, Britannica Book of the Year, British Academy of Film & Television Arts, British Airways, British Antarctic Survey, British Board of Film Classification, British Flydog Association, British Geological Survey, British Llamaand Alpaca Association, British Museum, British National Space Centre, Prof. John Brown, BT, Dr. Robert Angus Buchanan, Prof. Michael Burrows, CAIDA, Caltech, Cambridge University, Cancer Research UK, Dr. Robert Carney, Casella CEL inc., John Cassidy, Keisha Castle-Hughes, CERN, Dr. Franklin Chang-Diaz, Dr. Hubert Chanson, Prof. Phil Charles, Janina Chilcot, Chinese Embassy (London), Christie's, CIA World Factbook, Admiral Roy Clare, Isabelle Clark, Richard Clark, Stephen Clarke, Bridget Clifford (Royal Armouries Library, Tower of London), CMR/TNS Media Intelligence, Competitive Media Reporting/TNS Media Intelligence, ConocoPhillips, Dr. Mike Coughlan, Dr. Paul Craddock, Sarah Crane (Bernard Matthews plc), Dr. Phillip Cribb, Crufts, Prof. Mike Cruise, Cushman, Wakefield Healey & Baker, Dr. Pam Dalton, Danmarks Kaninavlerforening (DK), Prof. Kris Davidson, Dr. Ashley Davies, Jim DeBosh, Deutschland GmbH for RTL, Dr. David Dilcher, Discovery News, Martin Dodge, Gary Duval, Edinburgh Science Festival, EETimes, Dr. Farouk El-Baz, Dr. Cynan Ellis-Evans, Mark Elmore, Elysium, Dr. John Emsley, Encyclopaedia Britannica, Louis Epstein, ESA, eTForecasts, Exeter University, FAI (Fédération Aeronautique Internationale), Dr. Xiaohui Fan, David Feldman, FIA (Fédération Internationale de l'Automobile), Sir Ranulph Fiennes, FIM (Fédération Internationale de Motocyclisme), FINA

(Fédération Internationale de Natation Amateur), Max Finberg, Sarah Finney, Firefly Encyclopedia of Birds, FIRS (Fédération Internationale de Roller Skating), FIS (Fédération Internationale de Ski), FISA (Fédération Internationale des Sociétés d'Aviron), FITA (Fédération Internationale de Tir a l'Arc), Forbes, Brian Ford, Ford Press Office, Foreign & Commonwealth Office, Freemont Street Experience, Jono Friedman, Keith Friedman, Arran Frood, Ashrita Furman, Tim Furniss, Drew Gardner, Bill Gates, Martin Gedny, Geological Society of London, Dr. Richard Ghail, Lois Gibson, Andy Gillard (Scootering magazine), Globastat, Carlos Gómez, Antonio González, Kim Goodman, Stephanie Gordon, Steve Gould, Visual Impact, Chris Gravett, Woburn Abbey, GRF, Matt Groening, Cornelius Growweblaar, Prof. John Guest, Guinness World Records: Die Grössten Weltrekorde—Endemol, Guinness World Records: Fifty Years, Fifty Records—Granada for ITV, Dr. Jim Gunson, Stuart Haggard, Nicholas Hall (Royal Armouries, Fort Nelson), Mary Hanson, Andy Harris, Ziggy Harrison-Tikisci, Colin Hart, Harvard-Smithsonian Center for Astrophysics, Roger Hawkins, Peter Haynes, Ron Hildebrant, Peter Hillary, Sir Edmund Hillary, Dr. Paul Hillyard, Neil Holloway, Adam Honeywill, Hoovers, Dr. David Horne, Graham Hudson, Paul Hughes, IAAF (International Association of Athletics Federation), IHPVA (International Human Powered Vehicle Association), IMDB, Imperial College London, Institute of Nanotechnology, Intel, International Energy Agency, International Tea Committee, Ltd., ISAF (International Sailing Federation), IWF (International Weightlifting Federation), IWSF (International Water Ski Federation), Jetstream Servers, Prof. Steve Jones, Cathie Jung, Sandra & Myles Kannemeyer, Emily Kao, Robin Karpan (Alton Museum of History of Art), Dr. Nichol Keith, Keo Films, Michael Kettman, Paul Kieve, Prof. Joseph Kirschvink, Naomi Kitchener, Ron Klemenic, Jay Koch, Sir John Kreb, Arthur M. Kyengo, L'Été De Tous Les Records—R et G Productions for France 3, Lancaster University, Steve Landis, Dr. Rolf Landua, Dr. Roger Launius, Bernard Lavery, Peter Lavinger, Andy Lee, Alain Leger, Jason Leonard, Dr. Melinda Lewis, Martin Lindsey, Martin Lockheed, Los Alamos National Laboratories, Dr. Robert Loss, Louisiana State University, Dané Ludik, Dr. Karl Lyons, The Magnificent Seven, Simone Mangaroo, Prof. Giles Marion, Brian Marsden, Dr. Jim Marshall, Jenny Marshall, Jessie Masson, Dave McAleer, Sir Paul McCartney, Tony McCoy, Grant McLachlan, Dr. Alan McNaught, Medlowlands Stadium, The Met Office, Mi2g, Microsoft Corporation, Lucy Millington, Alice Mills, Chris Mills, Rosie Mills, Dr. Edgar Mitchell, Hia Mofmann, Monell Chemical Senses Center, Tim Montgomery, Dr. Sir Patrick Moore, Prof. Jon Morse, Mosaique crew, Pam & Gary Mount, Munich Re, Sal Murillo, Munt Martin, NASA, National Academy of Sciences, National Federation of Master Window & General Cleaners, National Geographic, National Hamster Council, National Maritime Museum, National Physical Laboratory, National Science Foundation, Natural History Museum, Randy Nelson, NetNames, FFG Neustrashimy, Dr. Ted Nield, A. C. Nielsen, NOAA, Richard Noble, Henry Northcroft, Barry Norman (WKVL Amusement Research Library), Andrew Nottage, Oracle, Oxford University, PADI (Professional Association of Diving Instructors), PAF, Morag & Stephen Paskins, John Payne, Jack Pearce, Giles Porter (Visual Impact), PPARC, Carla Prashad (Ascent Media Group), Productschap voor Gedistilleerde Dranken, Publishers Weekly, Salvador Pujol Miralles, Qinetiq, Lee Redmond, John Reed (WSSRC—sailing governing body), Prof. Sir Martin Rees, William, Benjamin & Jeremy Rees, Victoria Reeves, Regional Planetary Image Facility (University College London), Iain Reid, Ian Ridpath, Graeme Rimer (Royal Armouries), Dan Roddick, Dr. Mervyn Rose, Ros Rossington, Andrew Rotz, Mary Rotz, Royal Astronomical Society, Royal Botanical Gardens, Kew, Royal Horticultural Society, The Royal Institution, Royal Philips Electronics, Royal Society of Chemistry, Russia Monitor, Rutherford Appleton Laboratory, Ryan Sampson, Jeff Saward (Caerdroia—The Journal of Mazes and Labyrinths), Science Museum (London), Search Engine Watch, Istvan Sebestyen, Dr. Paul Selden, Prof. Dick Selley, SETI Institute, Bill Sharp, Dr. Craig Sharp, Brunel University, Dr. Seth Shostak, Dr. Martin Siegert, Siemens, Frank Simon, The Smithsonian Institution, Peter Smithurst (Royal Armouries, Fort Nelson), Sotheby's, Lara Speicher, Graham Spicer, SpinaHering Marcelo (World Food Program), Statistics Iceland, Tanya Streeter, Peter Strongwater, Strongwater Studios, Danny Sullivan, Greg Swift, The Tate Modern, Debbie Tawse, Charlie Taylor, Heather Tinsley, Turhune Orchards, UIM (Union Internationale Motonautique), UK Planetary Forum, Prof. Martin Uman, UN Factbook, United Nations Centre for International Crime Prevention, University of Bath, University of Birmingham, University of Boston, University of Colorado, University of Dundee, University of Florida, University of Greenwich, University of Hertfordshire, University of Oklahoma, University of Southampton, U.S. Drug Enforcement Agency, Melga van der Herwe, Juhani Virola, Geoff Wald, Dr. David Wark, Prof. Kevin Warwick, Dr. David Webb, Mark Wells (Controller, Entertainment, Granada), Kelly Wessell (WFDF—World Flying Disc Federation), Wildlife Campus (South Africa), Prof. Andrew Willmott, Punch Wilson, Richard Winter, Prof. Richard Wiseman, Greg Wood, The World Bank Group, World Footbag Association, World Health Organization, World Meteorological Organization, World Sailing Speed Record Council, World Tourism Organization, World Wildlife Fund, Malaysia, Prof. Joshua Wurman, www.EverestNews.com, www.globastat.com, www.landspeed.com, www.nationmaster.com, www.nua.com, Dr. David Wynn-Williams, Robert Young.

Additionally to the many (too many to list individually) websites, periodicals and newspapers around the world for their help.

Picture Credits

368	Rex Features	452	Getty Images
369	Getty Images	455	Getty Images
371	Getty Images	456	Getty Images
372	Rex Features	457	Associated Press
374	Getty Images	459	Getty Images
375	Rex Features	460	Getty Images
377	Rex Features	462	P A Photos
378	Rex Features	465	Getty Images
379	London Features International	466	Getty Images
380	c/o Artspace Projects, Inc.	467	Rex Features
382	Rex Features	469	Getty Images
383	Rex Features	471	Corbis
387	Getty Images	472	Getty Images
388	Getty Images	474	Getty Images
389	Getty Images	475	Corbis
391	Getty Images	477	Getty Images
392	Getty Images	478	Getty Images
394	Getty Images	480	Getty Images
396	Getty Images	482	Getty Images
396	Getty Images	483	Getty Images
398	Getty Images	484	Getty Images
400	Getty Images	485	Getty Images
402	Getty Images	486	Corbis
403	Getty Images	488	Reuters
405	Getty Images	489	Reuters
406	Getty Images	492	Getty Images
407	Getty Images	493	Getty Images
409	Getty Images	494	Getty Images
410	Getty Images	496	Getty Images
412	Getty Images	497	Getty Images
414	Getty Images	499	Getty Images
415	Getty Images	501	Getty Images
416	Getty Images	504	Associated Press
417	Getty Images	509	Getty Images
418	Getty Images	510	Getty Images
419	Getty Images	512	Reuters
421	Getty Images	513	Corbis
423	Getty Images	514	Reuters
424	Associated Press	514	Getty Images
425	Getty Images	516	Airsport Photo Library
427	NewsPix	517	c/o Paraclub Flevo
429	Associated Press	519	Airsport Photo Library
430	Reuters	520	Empics
432	Getty Images	522	Leo Nikora
433	Getty Images	523	Getty Images
434	Getty Images	525	Getty Images
436	Getty Images	526	Getty Images
437	Getty Images/Hulton Archive	527	Getty Images
438	NewsPix	528	Getty Images
441	Getty Images	529	Getty Images
442	Getty Images	531	Getty Images
445	Getty Images	533	Corbis
446	Getty Images	534	Corbis
446	Getty Images	535	Getty Images
446	Associated Press	537	Getty Images
446	Getty Images	538	Corbis
446	Corbis	539	Buzz Pictures
446	Getty Images	541	Rex Features
447	Getty Images	542	Rex Features
449	Getty Images	544	Getty Images

BE A RECORD BREAKER

IF YOU THINK YOU'VE GOT WHAT IT TAKES TO BE A WORLD RECORD HOLDER WE WANT TO HEAR FROM YOU!

COULD YOU BE A RECORD BREAKER?

DECIDE WHICH RECORD YOU WANT TO BREAK

Guinness World Records features many people who have accomplished extraordinary feats. If you think you have what it takes to join this exclusive record-breaking club then read on. There are thousands of records to choose from. You could gather a large group of people to break a mass participation record, or perhaps you have an unusual collection that we would be interested in. You might even suggest something new, as we are always on the lookout for innovative and exciting categories.

What we are looking for in a new category is a challenge that is inspiring, interesting, requires skill and is likely to attract subsequent challenges from people all around the world.

MAKE AN APPLICATION

You need to contact us BEFORE you make your attempt. Every Guinness World Record is governed by a unique set of rules that MUST be followed. You need to apply for these rules before you can make an attempt. If you have a new record idea, you need to find out if we have accepted your proposal before you attempt the record. If we like your idea, we will draw up rules specifically for your attempt in order to set a standard for all subsequent challenges.

The easiest and fastest way to make an application is via our website. Click on the link that says "Make a Record Attempt"; this will take you to an online application form. You'll be asked to choose a password which we will send you with a membership number to allow you access to our new tracking feature. Through this you can monitor the progress of your claim and ask any questions that you have about your record attempt.

If you don't have Internet access, you can contact us by post. Ensure that you have provided adequate contact details. Please be advised that proposals received this way take much longer to process than those received via the website.

Our website:
www.guinnessworldrecords.com

Write to us:
GUINNESS WORLD RECORDS
338 EUSTON ROAD
LONDON NW1 3BD
UK

Call us: +44 (0) 870 241 6632
Fax us: +44 (0) 207 891 4501

WAIT UNTIL YOU HEAR FROM US

Once your application has been processed, your proposal will be passed on to one of our specialist researchers who will look into your claim. If the application is successful, we will write to you with the corresponding rules and regulations which must be strictly adhered to for the attempt to be considered. We'll also send you some general guidelines that explain the evidence you need to provide to have your record attempt verified. If we reject your proposal we will explain why and, if appropriate, suggest an alternative.

ORGANIZING THE RECORD ATTEMPT

We can provide you with advice and guidance regarding record-related queries. As long as there is no violation of the guidelines, your record attempt can be organized in any way you choose. Guinness World Record adjudicators are able to attend events but will charge a fee to do so. Please remember that all record attempts are undertaken at the sole risk of the competitor and Guinness World Records cannot be held responsible for any liability arising out of any attempt.

HAVE YOUR ATTEMPT VERIFIED

Once you've completed your attempt, you must send *one* package containing all the verification documents that have been requested by us (i.e., videos, photographs, witness statements, and, where required, other more specialized items that will depend on your specific record attempt).

All evidence must be sent to our mailing address clearly marked with your membership number and claim identification number, which will have been provided in prior correspondence. If your claim passes all inspections, including a final scrutiny from the Keeper of the Records, you will be declared a Guinness World Record holder!

RECOGNITION OF YOUR ATTEMPT

All Guinness World Record holders receive a complimentary certificate to commemorate their achievement, recognizing that they have become members of the exclusive Guinness World Records hall of fame. We can't guarantee that any specific record will appear in our book, as the record selection changes annually. But as long as you hold on to your current world record, there is always the chance that your record could appear in a future edition.

Good luck!